# CRITICAL COMPANION TO

# Eugene O'Neill

VOLUME I

# Eugene O'Neill

## A Literary Reference to His Life and Work

### VOLUME I

## ROBERT M. DOWLING

Facts On File

*An imprint of Infobase Publishing*

Critical Companion to Eugene O'Neill:
A Literary Reference to His Life and Work

Facts On File, Inc.
An imprint of Infobase Publishing
132 West 31st Street
New York NY 10001

**Library of Congress Cataloging-in-Publication Data**
Dowling, Robert M., 1970–
Critical companion to Eugene O'Neill : a literary reference to his life and work /
Robert M. Dowling.
2 v. cm.
Includes bibliographical references and index.
ISBN-13: 978-0-8160-6675-9 (acid-free paper)
ISBN-10: 0-8160-6675-2 (acid-free paper) 1. O'Neill, Eugene, 1888–1953—
Criticism and interpretation—Handbooks, manuals, etc. I. Title.
PS3529.N5Z627266 2009
812'.52—dc22    2008024135

Text design by Erika K. Arroyo

Printed in the United States of America

VB Hermitage 10 9 8 7 6 5 4 3 2 1

This book is printed on acid-free paper and
contains 30 percent postconsumer recycled content.

*This project is dedicated to my mother,*
*Janet B. Kellock*

# CONTENTS

# ACKNOWLEDGMENTS

I would first like to thank my mother, Janet B. Kellock, to whom I warmly dedicate this volume. It was she who first introduced me to the plays of Eugene O'Neill, and without her indefatigable assistance in editing and advising, this companion could never have been completed. She is the first person ever to have read both volumes all the way through, myself included. I owe a great debt to Jeff Soloway, the executive editor of this series, for his sustained patience and supportive comments throughout this project, one that turned out to be far more expansive than he or I originally bargained for. I would especially like to commend the remarkable work of Elin Woodger, my principal copy editor, whose line-by-line mind defies the restricted abilities of us humans.

I would next like to express my gratitude to the leadership of Central Connecticut State University, including my chair, Gil Gigliotti; the Dean of the College of Arts and Sciences, Susan Pease; Ellen Benson of the CSU-AAUP; Provost Carl Lovitt; and President Jack Miller. All of them have shown remarkable interest in my work and generously provided critical time and resources for this project's completion with a series of course releases, CCSU faculty development grants, and AAUP university research grants. I would also like to thank the administrators in the back room—the English Department's Darlene Gable and Min Fang, Kathy Knopf at the Grants Administration Office, and Mimi Kaplan of the Office of Sponsored Programs—for their invaluable aid throughout this process.

Special thanks to Zander Brietzke, Jackson R. Bryer, Eileen Herrmann, Sally Pavetti, Robert Richter, and Brian Rogers, important mentors during my first serious forays into the world of O'Neill studies. I would like to thank the contributors to Part III of this volume for their remarkable efforts to meet tough deadlines, take on new essay topics under constant duress from yours truly, and continually demonstrate exceptional patience and collegial support: Judith Barlow, Karen Blansfield, Per Brask, Zander Brietzke, Tom Cerasulo, Patrick Chura, John Curry, Laurie Deredita, Thierry Dubost, Richard Eaton, Drew Eisenhauer, James Fisher, Brian Folker (significantly, and justifiably, my sole contributor for Part II with his essay on *The Ancient Mariner,* O'Neill's dramatization of Samuel Coleridge's poem), Sheila Garvey, John Hagan, Jane Harris, Linda Herr, Eileen Herrmann, Jeff Kennedy, William Davies King, Shawna Lesseur-Blas, Rupendra Majumdar, Mary Mallett, Cynthia McCown, Brenda Murphy, Jennifer Palladino, Robert Richter, Nelson Ritschel, Alex Roe, Brian Rogers, Erika Rundle, Richard Sater, J. Shantz, Troy Sheffield, Madeline Smith, David White, and Beth Wynstra. It was a true pleasure working with you all, and I look forward to future collaborations.

Next is the staff at Connecticut College's Sheaffer-O'Neill collection, particularly Laurie M. Deredita, Director of Special Collections and Archives at Connecticut College's Charles E. Shain Library, who offered invaluable assistance in negotiating their extensive and beautifully organized collection. Other important help came from my graduate research assistants Katie Kollar and Sheryl Anne Springer and librarians Deborah A. Herman and Sarah Lawson (some of my greatest saviors) of Central Connecticut State University's Elihu Burritt Library, each of whom did a remarkable job helping with contributors, compiling the O'Neill chronology, handling permissions and images, and accepting, always with a smile and a joke, a variety of other tasks.

I would also like to thank the Wooster Group actors—Willem Dafoe, Roy Faudree, Paul Lazar, Dave Shelley, and Kate Valk—for granting permission to publish their likenesses; archivist George C. Riser and associate director Edward Gaynor of the University of Virginia's Special Collections Library; the staffs at the Houghton Library of Harvard University and the Library of Congress; Louise Bernard, Patricia Willis, and Nancy Kuhl of Yale University's Collection of American Literature at the Beinecke Rare Book and Manuscript Library; Harley Hammerman, the engine behind eoneill.com, an invaluable online resource for O'Neill studies; Alex Roe, the artistic director of the Metropolitan Playhouse, New York City; Derren Wood, the executive artistic director, and Michael Langlois, associate artist, of Flock Theatre, New London, Connecticut; Clay Hapaz of the Wooster Group, New York City; and computer maven Sandy Selders for her much-needed assistance throughout this project.

Finally and affectionately, my undying gratitude goes to close friends and family members—especially my daughter Mairéad Dowling—for their sustained support, understanding, and patience throughout this lengthy, rather all-consuming process.

# INTRODUCTION

**Per aspera ad astra—Through difficulties to the stars**

Eugene Gladstone O'Neill is the United States' greatest playwright and the founding father of modern American drama. To date the only American dramatist awarded the Nobel Prize in literature, O'Neill also received four Pulitzer Prizes over the course of his remarkable career, the last posthumously awarded for his autobiographical tragedy *Long Day's Journey into Night*. *Critical Companion to Eugene O'Neill* explores the personal, historical, and artistic influences that combined to form such American masterpieces as *Long Day's Journey* (arguably the finest play ever written by an American), *The Emperor Jones, Desire Under the Elms, Strange Interlude, Mourning Becomes Electra, The Iceman Cometh, A Touch of the Poet*, and *A Moon for the Misbegotten*, along with lesser-known theatrical experiments such as *All God's Chillun Got Wings, Lazarus Laughed, Marco Millions*, and *More Stately Mansions*. The first of its kind in 25 years, this volume is designed to reach a broad audience and strengthen national and international interest in O'Neill's dramatic art for the general public. Most important, it aims to stimulate new avenues for discussion of O'Neill's work, a prodigious body of writing that single-handedly gave rise to an American dramatic style that still resonates in the dramas of virtually every working playwright in our own time.

*Critical Companion to Eugene O'Neill* is deliberately structured to reproduce the life and drama of the playwright in a sustained dialogue with nearly five generations of O'Neill critics, scholars, fellow dramatists, friends, and family members. Each essay contains original commentary but also attempts to capture the critical mood surrounding his work over time. Various luminaries of O'Neill criticism and biography, including Doris Alexander, Stephen A. Black, Travis Bogard, Virginia Floyd, Arthur and Barbara Gelb, Margaret Loftus Ranald, and Louis Sheaffer, among others, rightfully have much to say in this volume. O'Neill himself conducted a series of critical dialogues on his own artistry that we find in letters, journal entries, interviews, and published articles, all of which are exhaustively mined for their remarkable artistic and social insights.

America's most closely studied dramatist, Eugene O'Neill is often characterized as a solitary poet howling in the wilderness, a mystical individualist who envisions ancient universal themes—the tension between surface illusion and the reality of inner pain, the eternal struggle between Dionysian ecstasy and Apollonian pragmatism, the simultaneous adulation and terror of the overwhelming power of the sea, and the desperate search for a god figure in an apparently godless universe. These preoccupations have been well mapped over the decades and are treated here comprehensively and accessibly. O'Neill, however, also revolutionized the theater world by deeply probing his cultural and historical period with issues that remain social flashpoints today. Abortion, incest, parricide, interracial marriage, immigration, prostitution, alcoholism, drug addiction, Western materialism and imperialism, suicide, anarchism, and socialism all appear in various plays by O'Neill. Rather than exclusively evaluating O'Neill's work within the framework of dramaturgy and formal literary analysis, *Critical Companion to Eugene O'Neill* emphasizes the playwright's complex worldview, an approach to O'Neill that has just begun receiving its deserved attention in the interdisciplinary realm of 21st-century humanities.

This project's aim is to present accessibly and instructively such influences as O'Neill's Irish connection, his time in the United States Merchant Marine, his exposure to the urban black experience, his bohemian roots and belief in "philosophical anarchism," his deep sympathy for prostitutes, and his open attack on puritanical Victorian morality and melodramatic theatrical convention. O'Neill reaches broadly across the American social matrix—sailors, prostitutes, pimps, gamblers, anarchists, hotel clerks, down-and-outers, black gangsters, tenant farmers, bohemian artists, safecrackers, bartenders, and Broadway "rounders"—covering virtually every type from America's disenfranchised and "misbegotten" cultural topography. Once uncovered, such historical, cultural, sociological, and philosophical underpinnings will allow the reader to grapple with the "ironic fates" suffered by so many of his tragic characters.

Scholars and O'Neill enthusiasts often avoid, or dismiss outright, another vital truth about this playwright: He was not a natural-born artist. After his 1913 decision to pursue a vocation as a professional dramatist while convalescing at a tuberculosis sanatorium (an experience foreshadowed in *Long Day's Journey into Night* and fully dramatized in *The Straw*), O'Neill's subsequent career consisted of a mostly triumphant, but often painfully flawed, progression through which he ultimately achieved his current stature as an international literary giant. "No major dramatist, with the possible exception of Shaw," theater critic Robert Brustein once candidly admitted, "has written so many second-rate plays" (321). Indeed, Eugene O'Neill has probably received more bad reviews than any major American writer, and it is not enough to ignore missteps and tout genius. Every word O'Neill wrote, from his early days as an amateur poet to his achievements as a master of his craft, are all part of one story— each vital to his development as a playwright—and his decades of grueling labor produced some of the

finest plays ever written. The invaluable lesson to would-be artists, one that comes from witnessing the hard-won achievement of so potent an artistic voice, is this: The successes of a writer of O'Neill's stature, including four Pulitzer Prizes and a Nobel Prize, are due less to any natural "genius" than to discipline, grueling labor, and perseverance. Criticism can be healthy, but omission is deceptive; and so each work—including early efforts such as *A Wife for a Life* and *Bread and Butter,* his first one-act and full-length plays, respectively, and late critical disasters such as *Dynamo* and *Days Without End*—are discussed in this volume in nearly as much detail as his finest work.

At age 26, O'Neill vowed to his famed Harvard playwriting instructor George Pierce Baker that he was determined to be "an artist or nothing" (Bogard & Bayer *Selected Letters* 26). He then proceeded on a heroic trajectory through difficulties—a drug-addicted mother, an absentee father, severe alcoholism, scores of dreadful reviews, two divorces, a tumultuous third marriage, the suicide of his first (and favorite) son, and the heroin addiction of his second son—to the stars. Paradoxically embracing human suffering as an avenue toward exaltation, O'Neill did not consider his worldview pessimistic but life-affirming. The "tragic tension" and "ironic fate" one finds in his plays might be considered the most revolutionary, perhaps even the most un-American, aspect of his art. In the words of one recent historian, this playwright "elevated pain into a noble emotion, no small feat in a country dedicated to pleasure and the pursuit of happiness" (Diggins 75). Along the way, he experimented with seemingly incompatible literary forms—naturalism, expressionism, Greek tragedy, and melodrama—frequently confounding friends and reviewers alike. To O'Neill's consternation, theater critics erratically labeled him, in his own words, "'a sordid realist' one day, a 'grim pessimistic Naturalist' the next, a 'lying Moral Romanticist' the next, etc. . . . I've tried to make myself a melting pot for all these methods," he explained, "seeing some virtues for my ends in each of them, and, thereby, if there is enough real fire in me, boil down to my own technique" (quoted in Törnqvist 28).

O'Neill's 1934 debacle *Days Without End* proved to be a dreadfully simplistic, perversely overwritten "God play," in which his individualist protagonist John Loving regresses with almost childlike devotion back to the Roman Catholicism of his (and O'Neill's) youth. So began the 12-year period critics refer to as "the silence." Another O'Neill play would not appear on the world stage until *The Iceman Cometh* opened in New York in 1946, a mistimed, mediocre production that bored most audiences and collected lackluster reviews. Following his untimely death by pneumonia and neurological problems in a hotel room in Boston, however, audiences were astonished to discover that O'Neill, who had all but vanished from the public eye after winning the Nobel Prize in 1936, was hard at work through the 1930s and 1940s. Over this period, he had sequestered himself at Tao House, his California ranch home, writing distractedly though resolutely in his serene cloister as most of the planet stormed and crashed around him in a horrifying second world war. Posthumous premieres of *Long Day's Journey into Night*, *Hughie*, and *A Touch of the Poet* appeared through the late 1950s, along with revivals of *The Iceman Cometh* and *A Moon for the Misbegotten,* and the nation's "master of the misbegotten" once more redefined American theater history. "He fell silent," wrote an incredulous Tony Kushner in 2004, "isolated himself, withered and died. And rose again, almost immediately!" (253). Thus O'Neill was resurrected from the grave in what became known as the Eugene O'Neill Renaissance to accompany his younger counterparts and set the stage for the next gifted generation of American dramatists—Tennessee Williams, Arthur Miller, Lorraine Hansberry, Edward Albee, August Wilson, David Mamet, Sam Shepard, Tony Kushner, et al.—each of whom in their own distinctive fashion continued the staged exploration of what O'Neill once called "the Force behind" (Letter to Arthur Hobson Quinn 125).

Over the turn of our own century, O'Neill's plays have enjoyed another remarkable rebirth, with highly successful Broadway revivals of *"Anna Christie"* (1993, starring Liam Neeson and Natasha Richardson); *Ah, Wilderness!* (1998, starring Debra Monk and Craig T. Nelson); *The Iceman Cometh* (1999, starring Kevin Spacey); *Long Day's Journey into Night* (2003, starring Brian Dennehy, Vanessa Redgrave, Philip Seymour Hoffman, and Robert Sean Leonard); *A Touch of the Poet* (2005, starring Gabriel Byrne); and *A Moon for the Misbegotten* (2000, starring Gabriel Byrne, and 2006, Kevin Spacey); as well as Off-Broadway productions of *The Hairy Ape* (The Wooster Group, 1995, starring Willem Dafoe and Kate Valk), *The Emperor Jones* (The Wooster Group, 1993, starring Kate Valk and Willem Dafoe, with a return engagement in 2005), *Hughie* (1996, starring Al Pacino, and 2004 and 2008, Brian Dennehy), *Marco Millions* (Waterwell, 2006); and even such early one-acters as *The Web*, *The Movie Man*, *Before Breakfast*, and *Ile* (Metropolitan Playhouse, 2007). American and international audiences alike have demonstrated a voracious, unrelenting hunger for O'Neill and his plays over half a century after his death, and there appears to be no end in sight for this singular playwright's power to speak to contemporary audiences as he once spoke to theatergoers of his own era.

## BIBLIOGRAPHY

Brustein, Robert. *The Theatre of Revolt.* Boston: Little, Brown, 1964.

Diggins, John Patrick. *Eugene O'Neill's America: Desire Under Democracy.* Chicago: The University of Chicago Press, 2007.

Floyd, Virginia, ed. *Eugene O'Neill at Work: Newly Released Ideas for his Plays.* New York: Ungar, 1981.

Kushner, Tony. "The Genius of O'Neill." *The Eugene O'Neill Review* 26 (2004): 248–256.

O'Neill, Eugene. Letter to George Pierce Baker. July 16, 1914. In *O'Neill and His Plays: Four Decades of Criticism,* edited by Oscar N. Cargill, Bryllion Fagin, and William J. Fisher, 19–20. New York: New York University Press, 1961.

———. Letter to Arthur Hobson Quinn. In *O'Neill and His Plays: Four Decades of Criticism,* edited by Oscar N. Cargill, Bryllion Fagin, and William J. Fisher, 125–126. New York: New York University Press, 1961.

Törnqvist, Egil. *A Drama of Souls: Studies in O'Neill's Super-Naturalistic Technique.* New Haven, Conn.: Yale University Press, 1969.

## How to Use This Book

Part I of this volume contains a biographical essay that connects O'Neill's personal experiences to his development as a writer and has been designed to act as a chronological and topical road map for the rest of the book. Part II consists of synopses, commentaries, and character analyses for all 50 of O'Neill's published plays and three works of fiction. Part III includes original essays on a broad variety of people, places, and topics related to O'Neill, American history, world literature, and the global environment of the first half of the 20th century. For convenient cross-referencing among the essays, entry titles are printed in SMALL CAPITAL LETTERS at first mention in each essay. Characters are cited under the title of the work in which they figure; they are not cross-referenced individually. The appendices in Part IV include a concise chronology of O'Neill's life, a bibliography of his writings, and a bibliography of secondary sources referenced in this volume. All page references in discussions of O'Neill's plays are from the three-volume *Eugene O'Neill: Complete Plays*, edited by Travis Bogard (Library of America, 1988).

# PART I

# *Biography*

# Eugene Gladstone O'Neill
## (1888–1953)

Eugene O'Neill is best known as American theater's "master of the misbegotten." Plumbing the psychological and social depths of men and women who hit rock bottom and keep on digging, O'Neill was a fearless innovator in the face of CENSORSHIP laws, puritanical morality, and patriotic fervor. One of the most autobiographical of our major American writers, O'Neill's philosophies, obsessions, ambitions, and addictions come through more emphatically in his plays than in the most diligent efforts by BIOGRAPHERS. Audiences, readers, and aspiring writers also gain a great deal by considering the trajectory of his artistic maturity over time. "Our deepest interest in these plays," wrote an early observer of O'Neill's career, "is aroused not so much by their theatrical vigor as by the opportunity they afford of watching a dramatist at work—a man in the process of growth and development" (in Miller 28–29). Four plays by O'Neill have won PULITZER PRIZES, and he remains the only American dramatist awarded the NOBEL PRIZE IN LITERATURE. A cursory glance over some of his most famous titles can evoke, with startling clarity, the breadth of this playwright's creative vision: "ANNA CHRISTIE," The EMPEROR JONES, The HAIRY APE, DESIRE UNDER THE ELMS, STRANGE INTERLUDE, MOURNING BECOMES ELECTRA, AH, WILDERNESS!, A TOUCH OF THE POET, The ICEMAN COMETH, LONG DAY'S JOURNEY INTO NIGHT, and A MOON FOR THE MISBEGOTTEN, all of which have enjoyed successful revivals on and off Broadway into the 21st century.

Eugene Gladstone O'Neill was born on October 16, 1888, in a hotel room at the BARRETT HOUSE in New York City. (A family hotel located on the northeast corner of Broadway and 43rd Street, the Barrett House, now defunct, stood at an intersection that not long after O'Neill's birth became the theatrical center of the United States.) Two days later, O'Neill joined his family on the first of many tours with his father, the matinee idol JAMES O'NEILL. One of the most celebrated actors of his day and early on considered a natural successor to the great Shakespearean actor Edwin Booth,

Eugene O'Neill *(Courtesy of the Yale Collection of American Literature, Beinecke Rare Book and Manuscript Library)*

James O'Neill was the son of EDWARD AND MARY O'NEILL, first-generation Irish immigrants (see IRISH AMERICANS) of the peasant CLASS. In 1850, the O'Neills transplanted to the United States with their eight children to escape the devastation of the Irish potato famine, a journey so harrowing James rarely spoke of it in his adult years. Edward O'Neill abandoned the family soon after, dying in Ireland under suspicious circumstances and leaving the remaining O'Neills to fend for themselves.

After working as a menial laborer from the age of 10, James discovered a talent for acting that propelled him into national stardom. In early winter 1883, he accepted a role that would notoriously limit his career while at the same time bring him fame and wealth: Edmond Dantès in the stage adaptation of Alexander Dumas's novel *The Count of Monte Cristo*, a role he played over 6,000 times for the next 25 years.

O'Neill's mother, MARY ELLEN "ELLA" O'NEILL, was also born into a first-generation Irish family. Her parents, THOMAS JOSEPH QUINLAN AND BRIDGET LUNDIGAN QUINLAN, were famine refugees as well, but they thrived as tobacco and liquor merchants in Cleveland, Ohio. Ella met James, by then a sought-after heartthrob, in 1872 through her father, whom James had befriended on tour. James and Ella were married in a private ceremony at St. Ann's Roman Catholic Church in New York on June 14, 1877, and they had three sons: JAMES O'NEILL, Jr. (Jamie); EDMUND BURKE O'NEILL; and Eugene. In March 1885, Edmund died tragically at only a year and a half. The O'Neills had left their sons under the care of Bridget Quinlan when James was performing in Colorado. Jamie contracted measles in their absence, and the six-year-old most likely disobeyed his grandmother's strict orders not to come in contact with his younger brother, who was infected and succumbed to the disease in only a few days' time. Eugene O'Neill believed that Ella could never forgive his older brother for infecting Edmund, and the playwright apparently experienced a level of survivor's guilt himself, as he named his autobiographical character in *Long Day's Journey into Night* "Edmund" and the dead baby "Eugene." To make matters worse, when Eugene was born, a doctor prescribed morphine for Ella's pain, thereby launching an addiction that would come to haunt her and the O'Neill men for more than a quarter of a century. The debacle planted a deep-seated distrust of DOCTORS in the family,

along with James's predilection for crying penury and choosing the cheapest "quacks." "I know what doctors are," protests Mary Tyrone, Ella's character in *Long Day's Journey into Night*, "They're all alike. Anything, they don't care what, to keep you coming to them" (3: 728).

Eugene toured with his family for the first seven years of his life under the immediate care of his nanny, Sarah Sandy; they spent their summers at NEW LONDON, CONNECTICUT, first in a small cottage called the Pink House and then at a larger, Victorian-style house on the property next door at 325 Pequot Avenue, MONTE CRISTO COTTAGE, which James O'Neill built by combining the existing structures of a schoolhouse and a store. At age seven, Eugene entered St. Aloysius Academy at Mt. St. Vincent in the Bronx, New York, which he would always consider an early act of abandonment and betrayal by his parents. In 1898, the family made New London their permanent residence. Given James O'Neill's hectic nine-month performance schedule, there was no place like home for the O'Neills, but Monte Cristo Cottage, which they bought in 1900, was as close as they would come.

In 1900, O'Neill entered De La Salle Institute in Manhattan and boarded at his family's hotel apartment nearby. Two years later, he transferred to Betts Academy, a now-defunct preparatory school in Stamford, Connecticut. On a fogbound night the following summer, 1903, Ella O'Neill, with all three O'Neill men as horror-stricken witnesses, ran out of morphine and attempted suicide by running headlong into the icy waters of New London's Thames River across the road from the cottage. Both Jamie and James had been aware of the addiction for years, but up to that point it had been kept secret from Eugene. This traumatic incident caused O'Neill to renounce CATHOLICISM and initiate his own addiction, ALCOHOLISM, reinforced by the influence of his ne'er-do-well brother, Jamie. Drink was a psychic painkiller for O'Neill; he drank heavily for 23 years, until 1926, when he sought help from the psychiatrist Dr. Gilbert V. Hamilton and separated from his second wife, AGNES RUBY BOULTON. He also frequented New London's Bradley Street brothels and New York's seamy Tenderloin

Eugene O'Neill with notebook on a rock in New London. Signed to Carlotta Monterey O'Neill *(Courtesy of the Nickolas Muray Photo Archives, LLC)*

Eugene O'Neill (far left) with James O'Neill, Jr., and James O'Neill (at right) on the porch of Monte Cristo Cottage (New London, Connecticut), 1898 *(Courtesy of the Yale Collection of American Literature, Beinecke Rare Book and Manuscript Library)*

district throughout his teenage years. This early knowledge of PROSTITUTION, again instigated by his brother, informed O'Neill's plays, from early efforts such as *The WEB*, through the 1920s in *The GREAT GOD BROWN* and *WELDED*, to his late masterpieces *The Iceman Cometh* and *Long Day's Journey into Night*.

In 1906, O'Neill graduated from Betts Academy and entered Princeton University, a short train ride from New York City. During his brief stint at Princeton, he befriended a young rebel named Louis Holladay, whose sister Polly ran a famous café for radical intellectuals off Washington Square in GREENWICH VILLAGE. Holladay introduced the 18-year-old O'Neill to BENJAMIN R. TUCKER, a radical publisher, translator, editor of the anarchist journal *Liberty*, and bookstore proprietor of the Unique Book Shop at 502 Sixth Avenue near 30th Street. Tucker dedicated his life to promoting intellectual freedom, and he espoused nonviolent social and political protest, in contrast to the communist ANARCHISM of the EMMA GOLDMAN variety. It was Tucker who first introduced the young O'Neill to PHILOSOPHICAL ANARCHISM, also known as individualist anarchism. This worldview, along with a varied group representing what Tucker called "advanced literature"—philosophers, playwrights, and writers such as FRIEDRICH NIETZSCHE, Max Stirner, GEORGE BERNARD SHAW, HENRIK

IBSEN, Maxim Gorky, and others from outside the mainstream—would combine to form an intellectual foundation from which O'Neill would draw for a career's worth of ideas and inspiration.

In spring 1907, the play *Hedda Gabler,* by the brilliant and controversial Norwegian dramatist Henrik Ibsen, opened in New York. O'Neill rode up to the city from Princeton to attend this celebrated production no less than 10 times. Ibsen's revolt against genteel convention coupled with his frank exploration of human failings spoke to O'Neill more than any play he had seen up to that point, particularly those he had attended while touring with his father. His views on James O'Neill's generation of AMERICAN THEATER, which eschewed the REALISM of European dramatists like Ibsen in favor of MELODRAMA, are echoed years later in a speech by the guileless character Marco Polo in O'Neill's historical play *MARCO MILLIONS*. In this play, Polo uses the lackluster word *good* no less than six times to emphasize the bourgeois taste for mediocrity O'Neill equated with his father's generation of American theater: "There's nothing better than to sit down in a good seat at a good play after a good day's work in which you know you've accomplished something, and after you've had a good dinner, and just take it easy and enjoy a good wholesome thrill or a good laugh and get your mind off serious things until it's time to go to bed" (2:431). Similarly, in O'Neill's early satire *NOW I ASK YOU* (1916), his character Lucy Ashleigh, a pretentious adorer of Ibsen's tragic heroine Hedda Gabler, argues against attending vaudeville shows because "those productions were concocted with an eye for the comfort of the tired businessman" (1:451).

In June 1907, O'Neill was expelled from Princeton for "poor scholastic standing," as college life proved too stultifying for his rebellious temperament (quoted in Black 94). That summer, his father landed him a job in Manhattan working as a clerk for the New York–Chicago Supply Company. He and Holladay continued combing the bars and brothels of the Tenderloin, listening to ragtime and JAZZ, forms of MUSIC O'Neill would always collect and admire, and writing dilettantish POETRY. In the fall, O'Neill befriended JAMES FINDLATER BYTH, a former Boer War correspondent who had been hired that September as James O'Neill's press agent. Sharing the O'Neills' predilection for drink but little of their ambition, Byth became the model for James "Jimmy" Anderson in O'Neill's short story "TOMORROW," the drunken roommate Jimmy in his 1919 one-act play EXORCISM, and James "Jimmy Tomorrow" Cameron in *The Iceman Cometh*.

Having quit his job and scraping by on an allowance of seven dollars a week from his father, O'Neill shared a studio in the Lincoln Arcade Building at 65th Street and Broadway with a New London friend, Ed Keefe, along with the painters George Bellows and Ed Ireland. Bellows, who later became a contributor to the socialist magazine the *Masses*, was teaching at the progressive Ferrer Center, also called Modern School, in Harlem with fellow "Ashcan" painter Robert Henri, a staunch philosophical anarchist who appears as the character Eugene Grammont in O'Neill's earliest full-length play, BREAD AND BUTTER. At this time, O'Neill met an adventurous young woman from a respectable family named KATHLEEN JENKINS. After a summerlong affair instigated by Bellows, who believed O'Neill required a "nice girl" for stability, Jenkins became pregnant with O'Neill's first son, EUGENE O'NEILL, JR., and the two married in New Jersey on October 2, 1909. But after only a week, with encouragement from his parents, who disapproved of his marrying a Protestant, O'Neill fled to Honduras with a gold-prospecting associate of James O'Neill's. On October 16, he celebrated his 21st birthday on a banana boat off the western coast of Mexico. Miserable in the tropical jungles of Central America for five long months, O'Neill contracted malaria, and no gold was found.

Upon O'Neill's inglorious return to New York, Eugene O'Neill, Jr., was born on May 4, 1910. Within the month, O'Neill once again fled the country, this time with the MERCHANT MARINE as a passenger on the Norwegian bark CHARLES RACINE, sailing from Boston to BUENOS AIRES, ARGENTINA. After a two-month voyage, he arrived in Buenos Aires, and for more than nine months he worked odd jobs and lived hand-to-mouth, touring the city's brothels and low waterfront dives of the city's "sailortown" and the notorious pornographic theaters of the Barracas suburb. Dead broke and fed

up with the lifestyle of a destitute beachcomber, O'Neill returned to New York in March 1911 as a seaman on the British steamship SS IKALA.

On April 15, 1911, he left the *Ikala* in New York and spent several months as a boarder at JIMMY "THE PRIEST'S," a now defunct waterfront flophouse and bar located at 252 Fulton Street. Jimmy's catered to sailors, longshoremen, prostitutes, clerks, and small-time show-business types, and provided the settings of his short story "Tomorrow" and the plays such as *Exorcism*, CHRIS CHRISTOPHERSEN, "*Anna Christie*," and (in part) *The Iceman Cometh*. On July 22, he signed on as a crewman on the SS NEW YORK. Arriving in Southampton, England, he found himself in the middle of the Great General Strike of 1911. O'Neill's early full-length drama *the* PERSONAL EQUATION fictionalizes the anarchist movement's involvement in the dock laborer and transport worker strike, which was supported by the American anarchist labor syndicate known as the INDUSTRIAL WORKERS OF THE WORLD. On August 26, he arrived back in New York on the SS PHILADELPHIA, having earned the rank of able-bodied seaman (now called able seaman), an achievement that, almost beyond his accomplishments as a playwright, would fill him with pride for the remainder of his life.

Back in New York, O'Neill returned to Jimmy "the Priest's" where he roomed with his shipmate DRISCOLL from the *Philadelphia*. Driscoll, who later committed suicide by leaping to his death during an Atlantic crossing, would appear as both the character Driscoll in O'Neill's SS GLENCAIRN series of one-act SEA plays and as Robert "Yank" Smith in *The Hairy Ape* (the mystery behind Driscoll's suicide provided the inspiration for this play). O'Neill met with Jenkins once, and possibly Eugene, Jr.; but he would not see his son for over a decade and Jenkins never again.

That fall of 1911, O'Neill arranged a liaison with a prostitute, as adultery was New York's only legal pretext for divorce. Byth and O'Neill shared a room at Jimmy "the Priest's" from late 1911 to 1912, paying three dollars a month in rent. One night, Byth and another fellow boarder at Jimmy's named Major Adams found O'Neill half-dead in his room on either New Year's Eve 1911 or some night over the following two weeks (Alexander 2005, 23). O'Neill had attempted suicide by overdosing on the barbiturate Veronal, presumably humiliated over the means by which he had attained his divorce. He recounted this harrowing experience in *Exorcism*, an intensely personal play that was produced in 1920 but soon after destroyed by the playwright (an act of retroactive privacy that foreshadows his later unwillingness to publish or produce *Long Day's Journey into Night*). During this time, he and Byth attended every play of Ireland's famed Abbey Players of Dublin's ABBEY THEATRE during the company's six-week engagement in New York, a historic revue that included plays by JOHN MILLINGTON SYNGE, William Butler Yeats, Lady Gregory, and T. C. Murray; it proved extremely influential for O'Neill.

In early winter 1912, soon after his suicide attempt, O'Neill joined his family in a vaudeville tour out west, where he played minor characters in a truncated version of *Monte Cristo*, then returned to New York in March. He moved to Monte Cristo Cottage in April 1912, and his divorce from Jenkins became official that July. Jenkins requested no alimony or child support and was granted sole custody of Eugene, Jr. Much later, O'Neill pointedly observed to his third wife, CARLOTTA MONTEREY O'NEILL, with whom he had a tempestuous relationship, "The woman I gave the most trouble to has given me the least" (quoted in Gelb 337). In August, he took a job as a staff writer for the *New London Telegraph*. This is the summer portrayed in *Long Day's Journey into Night*. Ella O'Neill's addiction deteriorated badly, and O'Neill was diagnosed with tuberculosis in November. He blamed his time at Jimmy "the Priest's" for contracting the disease, having roomed on the same floor with a sailor nicknamed "the Lunger" (slang for a victim of tuberculosis).

After two days at a state sanatorium in early December, on Christmas Eve 1912, O'Neill checked into GAYLORD FARM SANATORIUM in Wallingford, Connecticut. To his surprise, he discovered some relief from the chaos of life in New York and New London in the nurturing, structured atmosphere of a tuberculosis sanatorium. At Gaylord Farm, he befriended several patients and nurses and found a

kind of father figure in his attending physician, Dr. David Russell Lyman. Tuberculosis was a devastating and lethal disease before the arrival of antibiotics, and a similar disease, pleurisy, kills O'Neill's autobiographical avatar Robert Mayo in the final scene of BEYOND THE HORIZON. O'Neill based his full-length play *The STRAW* on his experience with Gaylord Farm's patients and staff and a fleeting romance with a working-class fellow patient named Catherine "Kitty" Mackay.

It turned out that O'Neill had a mild case of the disease (some questions have been raised about whether he had been correctly diagnosed), and in the spiritual and psychological haven of Gaylord Farm, he read the plays of AUGUST STRINDBERG, John Millington Synge, and Gerhart Hauptmann, among others. It was there that O'Neill made the conscious decision to pursue a career as a playwright, comprehending that his experiences growing up with his father would prove invaluable for such a profession. James O'Neill, Sr., once said of playwriting, "Now and then, a genius may write a play without any degree of technical knowledge. . . . The average writer for the stage, however, has to serve a dramatic apprenticeship of some sort before he is qualified to write a play of any practical value" (quoted in Gelb 443). Eugene O'Neill was no average writer, but over the years, regardless of their differing views on the theater, he certainly received a prodigious dramatic apprenticeship under James O'Neill.

In early June 1913, the *New York Times* reported that James Byth had died of head injuries after falling out of his third-floor window at Jimmy's. O'Neill probably heard of his friend's death soon after his June 3 release from Gaylord Farm, and he was convinced Byth had committed suicide (Doris Alexander persuasively argues that Byth's death was more likely the result of a drunken accident [Alexander 2005, 22]). That summer, now determined to "become an artist or nothing" (O'Neill *Selected Letters* 1988, 26), O'Neill wrote at a breakneck pace, completing drafts of *A WIFE FOR A LIFE*, *The Web*, THIRST, RECKLESSNESS, and WARNINGS in New London.

O'Neill wrote his first full-length plays *Bread and Butter* and SERVITUDE in the spring and summer of 1914, along with the one-act plays *Fog*, BOUND EAST FOR CARDIFF (first titled *Children of the Sea*), *The* MOVIE MAN, and ABORTION. In August, his father paid for Gorham Press to publish his son's first book, THIRST AND OTHER ONE-ACT PLAYS, which includes *Thirst*, *The Web*, *Recklessness*, *Fog*, and *Warnings*. Also that summer, O'Neill became involved with his first true love, a New London girl named BEATRICE FRANCES ASHE, to whom he would write love letters and poetry until she ended the relationship two years later, a time when his prospects for future professional success appeared slim. O'Neill reacted badly to the breakup, drinking irresponsibly, visiting prostitutes, and associating with promiscuous women and dangerous men.

Then in autumn 1914, O'Neill joined the famous playwriting workshop run by Professor GEORGE PIERCE BAKER at Harvard University. In his first semester, he wrote the one-act play *Dear Doctor* and the full-length *Belshazzar* (both destroyed by O'Neill), and in spring 1915, he completed *The* SNIPER and *The Personal Equation*. In quantity if not quality, this 12-month period was quite possibly the most productive of O'Neill's career. Much of this early work remained unpublished and unproduced in his lifetime. Fortunately for O'Neill studies, the playwright copyrighted nearly everything he wrote at the Library of Congress, which became the source for the later publication of his so-called lost plays.

Baker believed O'Neill showed great promise but reflected that the young playwright's skills to "manage the longer forms" still required fine-tuning. He understood, however, that at the time "his means . . . made this impossible" (quoted in Clark 39). In fact, James O'Neill refused to pay the tuition for his son to continue at Harvard for a third semester, ostensibly because of financial trouble. O'Neill reluctantly moved back to New York and took a room at the Garden Hotel at Madison Avenue and 27th Street.

During fall 1915, O'Neill helped distribute the anarchist weekly *Revolt* and spent a good deal of time with Robert Henri and George Bellows at the Ferrer Center (Alexander 2005, 30). He also discovered the Golden Swan at Sixth Avenue and Fourth Street, a dive bar in Greenwich Village that patrons referred to as the HELL HOLE. In his years as

a Hell Hole regular, until Prohibition shut the place down in 1920, O'Neill socialized with a West Side Irish gang called the Hudson Dusters (a truly violent mob of ruffians, but so devoted to O'Neill they once offered to steal a coat for him when he was cold); he also met various members of Greenwich Village's radical LIBERAL CLUB, the social activist DOROTHY DAY, his close friend and future editor SAXE COMMINS, the radical HIPPOLYTE HAVEL (the editor of *Revolt* and the model for Hugo Kalmar in *The Iceman Cometh*), and the "philosophical anarchist" TERRY CARLIN (the model for the character Larry Slade in *The Iceman Cometh*). A vagabond alcoholic, much older than O'Neill but also of Irish descent, Carlin fatefully convinced O'Neill to join him on a lark to visit friends in Provincetown, Massachusetts, in June 1916.

Up to that point, O'Neill's life had amounted to virtually nothing of consequence. Filled up with whiskey, the loquacious middle-aged Irish ne'er-do-well Carlin and his young drinking partner arrived drunk, exhausted, and broke at the remote fishing village located on the outermost point of Cape Cod. Carlin suggested they "put the bite" on his friend, the author and radical journalist Hutchins Hapgood, for 10 dollars (years before, Hapgood had written a book about Carlin and his onetime girlfriend entitled *An Anarchist Woman* [1909]). Hapgood lent them the money, though by 1939, after three Pulitzer Prizes and a Nobel, O'Neill still owed him the ten-spot (Hapgood 396).

A more legendary story, though probably untrue, concerns the time the playwright SUSAN GLASPELL ran into Carlin on the street in Provincetown and asked him if he had any plays to share for an experimental theater group who summered there, calling themselves the PROVINCETOWN PLAYERS. "No, I don't write," Carlin reportedly told her, but said his pal Gene "has got a whole trunk full of plays" (quoted in Gelb 556). Actually, O'Neill stored them in a wooden box with the words *Magic Yeast* stamped across it (Black 189). The Provincetown Players were an august cohort of bohemian artists and writers that included Hapgood; Glaspell; director GEORGE CRAM "JIG" COOK (Glaspell's husband); author Neith Boyce (Hapgood's wife); journalists JOHN SILAS REED, LOUISE BRYANT (Reed's bride-to-be), and Mary Heaton Vorse; poet Harry Kemp; fiction writer Wilbur Daniel Steele; and O'Neill's future set designer ROBERT EDMOND JONES, among others. O'Neill and Louise Bryant conducted a tumultuous affair during that summer—since dramatized for the big screen in the film *Reds* (1981) with Jack Nicholson as O'Neill, Warren Beatty as Reed, and Diane Keaton as Bryant. The torrid romance, which continued even after Bryant's marriage to Reed in November 1916, only fully ended when O'Neill met Agnes Boulton at the Hell Hole the following spring.

Whatever the actual events of O'Neill's initiation into the Provincetown Players, Harry Kemp credibly recalled in an April 1930 *Theater Magazine* reminiscence that on the first night O'Neill pitched an idea to the group, he read "a play that was frightfully bad, trite and full of the most preposterous hokum. It was, as I remember, something about an American movie man who financed a Mexican revolution for the sake of filming its battles" (96). This would have been *The Movie Man*, but a new draft of it that he transposed into a short story, "The SCREENEWS OF WAR," a few months later. His choice was probably an attempt to impress John Reed, who had worked as a correspondent during the Mexican Revolution in 1913 and published a widely circulated series of articles on the war in *Metropolitan Magazine*.

The Provincetown Players rejected *The Movie Man* outright, but O'Neill then read them a play critics still consider one of his finest early works, *Bound East for Cardiff*. This one-act sea play contains a deceptively simple dialogue between two veteran sailors, Driscoll and Yank, who reminisce about their dreams, regrets, and mutual experiences in sailor towns around the world as Yank lies in his bunk, dying from an on-the-job injury. O'Neill's reading took place at Mary Heaton Vorse's house in front of all the Players, and though accounts of the evening differ, O'Neill later confirmed that he read the script to the group, and Kemp recalled that he "delivered [the play] in his low, deep, slightly monotonous but compelling voice." After the final lines had been read, everyone in the room understood that "here was a genuine playwright" (quoted in Gelb

556), and Vorse later remembered that "there was no one there during that reading who did not recognize the quality of this play" (quoted in Richter 106). A strong case can be made that this single summer evening permanently altered the course of American theater history.

O'Neill enjoyed his triumphant premiere as a playwright with *Bound East for Cardiff* on July 28, 1916, at Provincetown's WHARF THEATRE, a crude performance space in a fish house at the end of a dilapidated wharf adjoining Vorse's property, and the Players produced *Thirst* in August. In a *Boston Sunday Globe* article entitled "Many Literary Lights Among the Provincetown Players," the *Globe* reported, "It begins to look as if the American drama may be richer for the fun and the work of the Provincetown Players this summer. They have put on two plays by Eugene O'Neil [sic], a young dramatist whose work was heretofore unproduced and who, they are confident, is going to be heard from in places less remote than Provincetown" (quoted in Gelb 573). Regardless of the victory, the intensity of O'Neill's output never wavered. That summer he also wrote the one-act plays BEFORE BREAKFAST and *The G.A.N.* (or G.A.M., destroyed by O'Neill); the full-length play *Now I Ask You*; and "Tomorrow," the only short story he published in his lifetime. On his return trip to New York in late September or early October, O'Neill visited his family in New London, where he probably finished "The Screenews of War," a lengthy and poorly written work of fiction that he attempted to get into print, but it remained unpublished until 2007 (O'Neill 2007).

On November 3 in New York, the Provincetown Players held their debut at the Playwrights' Theatre (named this on O'Neill's suggestion) at 139 Mac-Dougal Street in Greenwich Village. Their first bill included *Bound East for Cardiff*, and they produced *Before Breakfast* later that season, on December 1. In early March the following year, O'Neill moved into rented rooms above John Francis's grocery in Provincetown and lived there through the summer of 1917 to write his sea plays *The* LONG VOYAGE HOME, *The* MOON OF THE CARRIBEES, IN THE ZONE, and *ILE*—four of his finest one-act plays. Each work takes its cue from literary NATURALISM, and draws from his experience in the merchant marine, representing the sea as a ruthlessly deterministic, near-supernatural force in sailors' lives.

In late spring 1917, O'Neill and his friend HAROLD DEPOLO, a pulp-fiction writer and proficient drinking partner, were arrested on charges of espionage at the still-operating Atlantic House bar in Provincetown. Secret Service agents were summoned from Boston, as the United States had just entered the First World War and there was a general scare of German spies on American soil. The bohemian vagabonds looked highly suspicious to local Provincetowners—particularly O'Neill, who was carrying a black satchel that appeared as if it might contain surveillance equipment but was most likely his typewriter case. (This episode strangely corresponds to the plot of *In the Zone*, though O'Neill and DePolo insisted the play had already been written at the time of their arrest.) After a night in the local jail, O'Neill's identity as the great James O'Neill's son was verified, and the shaken young men were promptly set free.

The prominent literary journal *The Seven Arts* published "Tomorrow" in June and then *The Long Voyage Home* in October; O'Neill moved back to New York in autumn. Over the course of 1917, a triumphant year for O'Neill, the Provincetown Players produced *Fog* on January 5, *The Sniper* on February 16, *The Long Voyage Home* on November 2, and *Ile* on November 30, and the WASHINGTON SQUARE PLAYERS produced *In the Zone* on October 31. That fall, he met the popular fiction writer Agnes Boulton at the Hell Hole, and he courted her persistently over the following months, during which time he also wrote SHELL SHOCK.

O'Neill and Boulton moved to Provincetown in early spring 1918, joined for a time by his older brother Jamie, and they married on April 12. While there, he completed *The* ROPE, produced by the Provincetown Players on April 26; *The* DREAMY KID; WHERE THE CROSS IS MADE (inspired by a short story idea by Boulton called "The Captain's Walk"); *Beyond the Horizon*, which would eventually win him his first Pulitzer Prize in 1920; and his final short story, based closely on *Warnings*, entitled "S.O.S." Broadway producer J. D. Williams optioned *Beyond the Horizon* with encouragement from GEORGE JEAN NATHAN, the celebrated "father of American drama

criticism" and before long one of O'Neill's closest friends. In the fall, O'Neill and Boulton moved to West Point Pleasant, New Jersey. Boulton recounts this early period of their relationship in her 1958 memoir *Part of a Long Story: Eugene O'Neill as a Young Man in Love*. On November 22, 1918, O'Neill's one-act *Where the Cross Is Made* was produced by the Provincetown Players, who had relocated their theater to 133 MacDougal, now called the Provincetown Playhouse, and *The Moon of the Caribbees* was produced on December 20. In May 1919, O'Neill and Boulton moved to PEAKED HILL BARS in Provincetown, a former life-saving station that James O'Neill bought them as a wedding present.

PUBLISHERS Boni & Liveright brought out *The Moon of the Caribbees and Six Other Plays of the Sea* in 1919 as well; and at Peaked Hill Bars, O'Neill completed *The Straw* and *Chris Christophersen* (optioned by producer George C. Tyler). He wrote the one-act plays *Exorcism*, based on his 1912 attempted suicide at Jimmy "the Priest's"; *Honor Among the Bradleys*; and *The Trumpet*, each of which he later destroyed (the last two were never produced). When Boulton became too pregnant to live in the barren isolation of Peaked Hill Bars, the couple rented a house in downtown Provincetown. O'Neill's second child, SHANE RUDRAIGHE O'NEILL, was born there on October 30, 1919.

*The Dreamy Kid*, historically the first American play by a white production company with a cast made up exclusively of AFRICAN AMERICANS, was produced on October 31. The inspiration for this play about a southern black man turned gangster after migrating north with his family came from one of O'Neill's Hell Hole associates named Joe Smith, a black man whom Boulton described as "the boss of the Negro underworld near the Village [whose] tales were startling." Smith had regaled O'Neill with the story of a black New York gangster with the street name Dreamy. "I remember Gene speaking that name almost lovingly and then laughing," Boulton wrote, a "Negro gangster named Dreamy—so Joe had spoken of him. *Why Dreamy?*" (quoted in Floyd 154).

On February 3, 1920, after nearly two years of anguished impatience on the part of its author, *Beyond the Horizon* was finally produced at the

Morosco Theater on Broadway. Often criticized for its melodramatic dialogue (with lines paradoxically similar to those he satirizes in *Now I Ask You*), *Beyond the Horizon* is a tragic account of two loving brothers with opposing temperaments—one a poet who dreams of exploring the world "beyond the horizon," the other a salt-of-the-earth New England farmer, who, as a result of desiring the same woman, fatefully pursue each other's true path. Not one of his best plays and rarely revived today, *Beyond the Horizon* won O'Neill the Pulitzer Prize in June 1920. (Ironically, O'Neill had never heard of the newly endowed award, but he was delighted over the 1,000 dollars that came with it.) In spite of its flaws, the play is O'Neill's first mature full-length effort. Meanwhile, that March in Provincetown, he completed GOLD, a four-act version of *Where the Cross Is Made*. *Chris Christophersen* opened in Atlantic City on March 8, receiving extremely bad reviews, and *Exorcism* enjoyed a moderately successful run at the Provincetown Playhouse beginning on March 26.

James O'Neill, Sr., died of intestinal cancer on August 10, 1920, in New London. Eugene O'Neill wrote to Boulton that in spite of their differences, his father was always "a good man, in the best sense of the word—and about the only one I have ever known" (quoted in Alexander 2005, 147). James O'Neill's last words to his son expressed a profound pessimism that he generally kept buried deep beneath the surface: "Eugene—I'm going to a better sort of life. This sort of life—here—all froth—no good—rottenness!" (quoted in Diggins 33). After James's death, his son Jamie successfully quit drinking and joined his mother to manage the family estate. Ella O'Neill had overcome her own addiction in June 1914, possibly with a short relapse in 1917, by cloistering herself in a Brooklyn convent and renewing her Catholic faith.

O'Neill returned to Provincetown that fall and, working through his loss, completed *"Anna Christie," The Emperor Jones,* and DIFF'RENT. *The Emperor Jones,* O'Neill's initial foray into the grotesque contrasts of European EXPRESSIONISM, premiered at the Provincetown Playhouse on November 1, 1920. Another historic milestone, *The Emperor Jones* was the first real work of expressionism by an American and the first American production to cast a black man for the leading role of a white theater company, with CHARLES S. GILPIN as Brutus Jones. Gilpin acted brilliantly (one of the few performances of any of his characters O'Neill heartily approved of, though he was furious when Gilpin toned down the racial epithets in the dialogue), and the production soon moved uptown to Broadway. *Diff'rent,* a strangely compelling domestic version of *Gold,* opened on December 27 to mixed reviews.

In March 1921, O'Neill completed *The* FIRST MAN, which opened one year later on March 4, 1922. A critical failure that attacks women for thwarting men's professional dreams, *The First Man* still contains interesting evocations of the evolutionary theory of DARWINISM that significantly influenced the literary naturalism found in much of O'Neill's work. Few plays in the canon, save perhaps the unproduced *Bread and Butter* and *Servitude,* more openly expresses the playwright's often sour view of the opposite GENDER.

In June 1921, *Gold* was produced on Broadway but closed after only 13 poorly reviewed performances. *"Anna Christie"* opened on November 2, 1921, to great critical acclaim and won O'Neill a second Pulitzer Prize. On November 10, *The Straw* appeared and was dismissed by most critics as merely depressing, though O'Neill himself would always think very highly of it.

*"Anna Christie"* is a substantial revision of *Chris Christophersen* that treats the story of Anna Christopherson, a young prostitute who reunites with her seafaring father, Chris Christopherson, then sails with him on his barge from New York to Boston. Trapped in a fog bank off the Provincetown coast, they rescue a shipwrecked Irish sailor named Matt Burke, and he and Anna fall in love. Most audiences believed the ending redeemed the prostitute and domesticated the sailor, and they applauded O'Neill's diversion from his usually morbid tone. O'Neill claimed they had missed the point, however, insisting that the ending once again represents the sea's pitiless grip on its victims. In the final scene, both men sign on for a deep-sea voyage, with Chris cursing "dat ole davil, sea," thus leaving Anna behind to long for their safe return (1:1,027). Few critics got this, with the exception of one of O'Neill's most ardent early supporters, ALEXANDER

WOOLLCOTT: "O'Neill seems to be suggesting to the departing playgoers," he observed, "that they can regard this as a happy ending if they are short-sighted enough to believe it and weak-minded enough to crave it" (Alexander Woollcott quoted in Houchin 29–30). O'Neill later renounced the play, not for the failures of interpretation but for its naturalism, since by the early 1920s he was entering the most experimental phase of his career. "Naturalism is too easy," O'Neill said, "It would, for instance, be a perfect cinch to go on writing *Anna Christies* all my life. I could always be sure to pay the rent then . . . shoving a lot of human beings on a stage and letting them say the identical things in a theatre they would say in a drawing room or a saloon does not necessarily make for naturalness. It's what those men and women do not say that usually is most interesting" (quoted in Kantor 48).

In December 1921, O'Neill completed *The Hairy Ape*, a masterwork of American expressionism that builds on the structural technique of *The Emperor Jones*. It consists of eight scenes over the course of which the protagonist is systematically stripped of his delusional self-aggrandizement. *The Hairy Ape* strenuously voices O'Neill's views on the conditions of his time—class relations, materialism, alienation, dehumanization, and the disillusionment resulting from the modern industrialization of society and its attendant consumer culture. Along with *The Emperor Jones, The Hairy Ape* signals O'Neill's transformation from a naturalistic writer to a fully formed avant-garde modernist of the 1920s.

After numerous years as an absentee parent, O'Neill met his son Eugene, Jr., in New York in fall 1921. Up to that point, Eugene, Jr., believed his name to be Richard Pitt-Smith and that he was the son of his mother's second husband, George Pitt-Smith. It was a promising meeting for both sides, however, as Eugene, Jr., took his father's name back, O'Neill agreed to finance his son's education, and the two remained close over the following decades—closer, in fact, than he would ever be with Shane.

O'Neill's gain of a son was followed by an equally great loss: On February 28, 1922, Ella O'Neill died of a brain tumor in Los Angeles, California. Her body arrived in New York on March 9, the same day *The Hairy Ape* premiered. O'Neill's brother Jamie, who had been with their mother in California, accompanied her remains. Jamie's alcoholism had recurred badly, and his mother may have witnessed him drunk before she died. The scene of Ella O'Neill's death is recounted by Jamie's biographical character James Tyrone in *A Moon for the Misbegotten* (3:930), though the accuracy of the tragic scene cannot be verified. Whatever happened in California, Jamie had, verifiably, drunk and whored his way across the continent and arrived stumbling drunk at New York's Grand Central Station. He also missed Ella's funeral on March 10, 1922, which outraged O'Neill. The two brothers fell out over the affair, and Jamie, who lived for a time with Harold DePolo (at whose house O'Neill would see his brother for the last time), continued to drink with abandon. Stephen A. Black points out, however, that in *A Moon for the Misbegotten*, "many sordid details are omitted, including the attempt to exclude Eugene from inheriting [property the family owned in New York City], and the nomination of Jamie's woman friend as Ella's executrix" (467).

After being awarded his second Pulitzer Prize for *"Anna Christie"* on May 21, 1922, O'Neill completed *The FOUNTAIN*, a historical play that charts the Spanish conquistador Ponce de Leon's expedition to the New World and his subsequent obsession to discover the fountain of youth. It would be O'Neill's last summer in Provincetown, as he then relocated his family to an estate called BROOK FARM in Ridgefield, Connecticut, a location closer to New York for commuting to rehearsals and pre-production meetings.

In 1923, O'Neill agreed to team up with KENNETH MACGOWAN and Robert Edmond Jones as a production company the media impressively referred to as "The Triumvirate." The trio replaced the now-defunct Provincetown Players with a new title, the EXPERIMENTAL THEATRE, INC., but retained their theater space and the name of the Provincetown Playhouse. Also that year, O'Neill received a gold medal from the National Institute of Arts and Letters and completed *Welded*, a groping exploration of his relationship to Boulton. In the late summer and fall, he wrote ALL GOD'S CHILLUN GOT WINGS, a spectacularly expressionistic play that, with occasional lapses into racial stereotyping, soberly treats the complications of mixed-race marriage in the 20th century.

Meanwhile, Jamie's alcoholism became so acute that he was institutionalized, reportedly arriving in a straitjacket at the Riverlong sanatorium in Paterson, New Jersey, in June 1923. Jamie's hair had turned white from the shock of his mother's death, and due to the poor quality of liquor during Prohibition, he had lost much of his eyesight as well. His body was so dependent on alcohol by this time that part of his treatment was taking 10 drinks of whiskey a day (Floyd 581n). Jamie O'Neill died of alcoholism at Riverlong on November 8, 1923, a year and a half after Ella O'Neill's death and one month before the action of *A Moon for the Misbegotten*.

The Experimental Theatre, Inc. produced three full-length O'Neill plays in spring 1924: *Welded* on March 17, his dramatic adaptation of Samuel Coleridge's poem THE ANCIENT MARINER on April 6, and *All God's Chillun Got Wings* on May 15. During the months leading up to the premiere of *All God's Chillun*, a firestorm erupted over the Provincetown Playhouse's controversial production. The Playhouse received poison-pen letters, bomb threats, and warnings of race riots. The Long Island Ku Klux Klan threatened to bomb the theater on opening night. "If you open this play," they warned, "the theater will be bombed, and you will be responsible for all the people killed." A worse threat came to O'Neill from the Georgia KKK's "Grand Kleagle": "You have a son [Shane]. If your play goes on, don't expect to see him again." According to a friend, without a second's hesitation O'Neill scrawled "Go fuck yourself!" in bold letters across the same letter and sent it back to Georgia (quoted in Sheaffer 1973, 140). The cause of the uproar? A *New York Herald* reporter had discovered that in the new O'Neill production, the white actress Mary Blair was to kiss the hand of her black costar, PAUL ROBESON (Sheaffer 1973, 135).

On November 11, 1924, *Desire under the Elms*—another brilliant hybrid of naturalism and expressionism, but this time about New England Yankee culture—opened to strong reviews at the Greenwich Village Theater. His third child, OONA

O'NEILL, was born on May 14, 1925, in Bermuda. He moved his family to Nantucket in July and then, in October, back to Brook Farm. Earlier in the year, he had completed a shortened version of *Marco Millions* and *The Great God Brown*. In the winter of 1924, O'Neill relocated his family to Bermuda. *The Fountain* was produced on December 10. O'Neill's alcoholism had worsened over the course of the year, and when it reached a head, he was persuaded by Kenneth Macgowan to consult the psychoanalyst Dr. Gilbert V. Hamilton.

*The Great God Brown*, an experimental mask play, was produced on January 23, 1926. One of O'Neill's most philosophically complicated works, *The Great God Brown* applies Friedrich Nietzsche's theory of tragedy to the lives of two tortured men from America's capitalist classes, and it received somewhat perplexed but generally appreciative reviews. In February, the O'Neills traveled back to Bermuda, where O'Neill bought a grand oceanside residence called SPITHEAD. He continued therapy with Dr. Hamilton and after several setbacks finally quit drinking. It remains unclear the extent to which psychoanalysis helped him overcome his addiction to alcohol; but he did so, and with only a couple of relapses, he remained sober for the rest of his life.

On June 23, 1926, Yale University awarded O'Neill an honorary doctorate. That summer he rented a cottage at Belgrade Lakes, Maine. By October, his marriage to Boulton was in shambles, and he began a love affair in New York with the strikingly beautiful actress Carlotta Monterey, whom he knew from her work playing Mildred Douglas in *The Hairy Ape*. Upon his return to Bermuda in November, he wrote his only FILM TREATMENTS, one for *The Hairy Ape* and one for *Desire Under the Elms*. They remain unproduced, but throughout the 20th century, Hollywood generated many important, if often bowdlerized, FILM ADAPTATIONS of his work, including *The Emperor Jones* (1933), starring Paul Robeson, and one of his SS *Glencairn* series entitled *The Long Voyage Home*, starring John Wayne and directed by John Ford (1940; O'Neill's personal favorite).

Though O'Neill's marriage with Boulton was swiftly deteriorating, and he longed for Monterey in New York, he completed LAZARUS LAUGHED and *Strange Interlude* over the next two years.

The THEATRE GUILD, New York's preeminent production company, accepted *Marco Millions* as a sweetener for optioning the superior *Strange Interlude*. In August, O'Neill arranged a liaison with Carlotta in New York; he returned to Bermuda in October, then went back to New York in November. *Marco Millions,* another historical drama like *The Fountain* but now about notorious exploits of the Italian explorer and trailblazing global capitalist Marco Polo, was produced on January 9, 1928, and *Strange Interlude* on January 30. *Lazarus Laughed,* a four-act curiosity that speculates on the biblical Lazarus as a figure of Roman worship after Jesus Christ miraculously raises him from the dead, premiered on April 9 at the unlikely venue of the Pasadena Community Playhouse in California.

In 1928, O'Neill was awarded his third Pulitzer Prize, this time for *Strange Interlude,* a lengthy psychological drama that stunned audiences with its "thought asides," an innovative technique in which actors on the stage freeze while one soliloquizes his or her conscious thoughts. The playwright George Lewys, the pen name of Gladys Lewis, brought PLAGIARISM charges against O'Neill for the idea, but notes from his WORK DIARY were submitted as exonerating evidence at a trial on March 13, 1931. *Strange Interlude* is O'Neill's self-described "woman play," whose character Nina Leeds succeeds in capturing the hearts of three men who together satisfy her need for a father, a husband, and a lover. The father-figure character, Charles Marsden, exhibits the only evident tendencies of HOMOSEXUALITY in any O'Neill play, and his name evokes the combined names of the homosexual artists Charles Demuth and Marsden Hartley, whom O'Neill knew from his Provincetown days. *Strange Interlude* is one of O'Neill's most striking psychological dramas and his most popular play before World War II.

With O'Neill's marriage to Boulton essentially over, he and Carlotta traveled to Europe on February 10, 1928, in an attempt to avoid the scandal-mongering that would surely follow the breakup. In March, they rented a villa in Guéthary, FRANCE, where O'Neill completed DYNAMO. He initiated divorce negotiations with Boulton, then visited China with Monterey in October, absorbing much about EAST ASIAN THOUGHT; he went to Manila on his own in December. During his travels, O'Neill contracted influenza and suffered a severe relapse in his drinking. He and Monterey separated on January 1, 1929, in Ceylon, but they reunited in Egypt on January 15.

*Dynamo,* a strangely conceived, melodramatic "god play" in which a New England preacher's son substitutes science for the Judeo-Christian God as the ruling force of the cosmos, was produced by the Theatre Guild on February 11. It was universally panned by the critics, and O'Neill blamed his absence at rehearsals for its poor reception. *Dynamo* is still considered an artistic gaffe, however, and it is rarely, if ever, revived today. In June 1929, O'Neill and Monterey moved to Chateau du Plessis in the Loire Valley. He and Boulton, whom he had grown to hate, finalized their divorce on July 2, and Monterey became Carlotta Monterey O'Neill in Paris on July 22.

In October 1930, O'Neill resumed his solitary wanderings, this time through Spain and Morocco; but he returned a month later to write several drafts of his trilogy *Mourning Becomes Electra,* corresponding throughout with the Pulitzer Prize-winning theater critic BROOKS ATKINSON, who gave him advice and support.

In 1931, O'Neill completed *Mourning Becomes Electra,* one of his finest plays. He visited Las Palmas in the Canary Islands in March and on May 17 returned to New York to oversee rehearsals for the Theatre Guild's production of the play. A trilogy that borrows from GREEK TRAGEDY, specifically Aeschylus's *Oresteia, Mourning Becomes Electra* charts the tragic decline of a prominent New England family just after the Civil War (the Trojan War in Aeschylus). It opened on October 26, 1931, to enormous critical acclaim, and it was undoubtedly this play that won O'Neill his Nobel Prize five years later. Though it was five years old by the time he was awarded the prize, *Mourning Becomes Electra* had played triumphantly in theaters across Europe throughout the 1930s and into the next decade.

In November 1931, O'Neill and Carlotta visited SEA ISLAND, GEORGIA, and decided to build a house there together. Struggling through many drafts of his next "god play" DAYS WITHOUT END, he and Carlotta then settled into Casa Genotta ("Gene" + "Carlotta") on Sea Island. On the morning of September 1, 1932, he awoke at Casa Genotta with the setting (Monte Cristo Cottage), plot, characters, themes, and even title—*Ah, Wilderness!*—of a full-length play that, according to O'Neill, he envisioned from a dream "fully formed and ready to write" (quoted in Alexander 1992, 172). O'Neill's only mature comedy, *Ah, Wilderness!* was finished within three weeks and opened on Broadway on October 2, 1933. Another Theatre Guild production, the play is an acknowledged anomaly in the O'Neill canon—a sentimental portrait of a happy, middle-class, New England family based on O'Neill's boyhood friend Art McGinley's family, the kind O'Neill longed to have been a part of as a child but had earlier derided as complacent and soul-destroying in his plays *Bread and Butter* and *The First Man. Ah, Wilderness!* had terrific popular appeal for audiences desperate for respite from the terrible realities of the Great Depression.

In late 1933, O'Neill completed *Days Without End*, on which he had labored more than any other work in his career (seven drafts and many title changes from late 1931 to early 1934), then took a vacation that summer at Wolf Lake in New York. *Days Without End* opened on January 8, 1934, and received disastrous reviews. O'Neill intended the play to be a thematic sequel to *Dynamo* and the second of a planned trilogy entitled "Myth Plays for the God-Forsaken" or "God Is Dead! Long Live— What?" According to O'Neill, each play would explore "the spiritual futility of the substitute-God search" (quoted in Floyd 406). Both were critical failures, and he never bothered to complete the third planned installment, *It Cannot Be Mad*, in which he had envisioned the "substitute-God" as the almighty dollar. In the histrionic final scene of *Days Without End*, O'Neill depicts a former Nietzschean individualist named John Loving praying to God and Christ, the idols of his youth (and O'Neill's), for redemption in a Catholic church; John stretches his arms apart, Christ-like, and

Eugene O'Neill in New York City, 1934 *(Courtesy of the Sheaffer-O'Neill Collection, Charles E. Shain Library of Connecticut College)*

shouts, "Loves lives forever. . . . Life laughs with God's love again! Life laughs with love!" (3:180).

O'Neill fumed at accusations that *Days Without End* marked his return to Catholicism. At one point, the Catholic Writers Guild, who otherwise appreciated the plot, demanded some alterations if he wanted their preproduction endorsement. "*It is not Catholic propaganda!*" he wrote his publisher Bennett Cerf over the misunderstanding, "If, after it comes out, the Church wants to set the seal of its approval on it, well, that's up to them. But I don't give a damn whether they do or not—and I certainly will not make the slightest move to win that approval in advance!" (quoted in Alexander 1992, 206). One of O'Neill's close friends, the radical author Benjamin De Casseres, even wrote a lampoon of the play entitled "Drivel without End," a cruel prank that instantly destroyed their friendship (De Casseres). Nearly suffering a nervous breakdown, O'Neill returned to Wolf Lake for two months in August and September. This was the first step toward a 12-year period critics refer to as "the silence." The next O'Neill production would not appear until *The Iceman Cometh* in 1946.

Dividing his time between New York and Sea Island, O'Neill suffered from gastritis, prostate problems, and chronic hand tremors. In spite of his ailments, he worked hard on scenarios and drafts for a planned American history cycle, A TALE OF POSSESSORS SELF-DISPOSSESSED, including a complete draft of A *Touch of the Poet*. On November 12, 1936, he became the first and only American dramatist awarded the Nobel Prize in literature. Due to health complications, O'Neill did not attend the ceremony, but he sent a brief statement acknowledging the great influence of the Swedish playwright August Strindberg on modern drama. That same month he rented a house in Seattle, Washington, and in December he had his appendix removed in Oakland, California. He and Carlotta then moved to San Francisco, where he nearly died of an infection, though he continued serious work on his historical cycle.

In April and June 1937, O'Neill and Carlotta rented houses in Berkeley and Lafayette, respectively, before moving in December into TAO HOUSE in Danville, California, where they resided from 1937 to 1944, and where he wrote the finest plays of his career. During these years, his worsening hand tremor and as-yet-undiagnosed neurological problems compelled O'Neill to shelve his historical cycle, including drafts of A *Touch of the Poet* and MORE STATELY MANSIONS—the planned sixth play of the cycle that takes place four years after A *Touch of the Poet*—in favor of writing *The Iceman Cometh*, and he completed a near-final draft in December 1939. This was just months after Adolf Hitler ignited World War II by invading Poland, and in a series of letters to family and friends, O'Neill expressed severe agitation over the onset of the war. "The war news," O'Neill wrote to Oona just after completing *Iceman*, "has affected my ability to concentrate on my job. With so much tragic drama happening in the world, it is hard to take theatre seriously. But I am beginning to snap out of this demoralization" (O'Neill *Letters* 1988, 508). Two weeks later, he wrote to producer Lawrence

Langner: "I'm working again on something . . . after a lapse of several months spent with an ear glued to the radio for war news. You can't keep a hop head off his dope for long!" (O'Neill *Letters* 1988, 510). O'Neill coyly refers here to his tragic masterpiece *Long Day's Journey into Night*.

*The Iceman Cometh* features a band of down-and-out regulars at Harry Hope's bar, a rundown Raines Law Hotel modeled after Jimmy "the Priest's," the taproom at the Garden Hotel, and the Hell Hole. All of the characters closely resemble figures from O'Neill's drinking days in the 1910s, including James Byth, Terry Carlin, and Joe Smith. The one exception, though arguable, is the jovial salesman Theodore "Hickey" Hickman. Near the end of the first act, Hickey arrives to celebrate Harry Hope's birthday, but with a messianic agenda to strip his friends of their life-sustaining "pipe dreams." By doing so, he believes he can offer them salvation from their misbegotten lives. *The Iceman Cometh* is

Eugene O'Neill at Tao House writing *The Iceman Cometh*, 1939 *(Courtesy of the Sheaffer-O'Neill Collection, Charles E. Shain Library of Connecticut College)*

O'Neill's deepest exploration into one of his major themes, "the horror that comes to those who deny their dreams" (Bogard 147).

O'Neill well understood that this play contained some of his very best material, but he deliberately delayed production until after the war's conclusion, feeling that the postwar American public would experience a hangover of disillusionment on a national scale. Only then, he argued to his friend Dudley Nichols, would audiences comprehend the play's thesis: that humankind requires pipe dreams to endure the devastating realities of modern life.

In late 1940, the O'Neills' beloved pet SIL-VERDENE (Emblem "Blemie") O'NEILL, a Dalmatian the couple had bought in France over a decade before, died at Tao House. O'Neill memorialized the dog with "The Last Will and Testament of Silverdene Emblem O'Neill," a reflective statement on the inner world of animals and man. A few months later, despite the death of Blemie and his declining health, worsening hand tremors, and despair over the war, he completed *Long Day's Journey into Night*, a tragic account of his family in the summer of 1912. In the published dedication to Carlotta (signed, July 22, 1941), O'Neill wrote that he composed the play "in tears and blood," in order to "face my dead at last and . . . write it with deep pity and understanding and forgiveness for *all* the four haunted Tyrones" (3:714). Set at Monte Cristo Cottage over the course of one day, the tragedy candidly lays bare revelations about his mother's addiction, his Irish-born father's inadequacies, his brother's demoralizing influence, and his own diagnosis with tuberculosis (though never mentioning his marriage and divorce from Jenkins or their child). O'Neill understood that *Long Day's Journey* was his greatest achievement, and most critics, scholars, and serious theatergoers consider it the finest play ever written by an American.

In 1942, O'Neill began work on *A Moon for the Misbegotten*, a sequel to *Long Day's Journey* meant to exorcise the ghost, once and for all, of his older brother Jamie. He also completed the last draft of *A Touch of the Poet*—a maudlin but brilliant portrait of the portentous son of an Irish shebeen (illegal bar) keeper who immigrates to the United States

and embraces the pompous manners of a British aristocrat during the radically democratic presidential race of Andrew Jackson. *A Touch of the Poet* remains the only finished play of O'Neill's historical cycle. Also in 1942, he completed HUGHIE, his only one-act play since *Exorcism* 23 years earlier. He had begun the play in 1941, and it remains the sole surviving installment of a planned series of one-acters entitled *By Way of Obit*, in which each single act is meant to be read as a short story more than performed on the stage. *Hughie*, about a washed-up gambler and a desk clerk at a flea-bitten Broadway hotel, was never produced in O'Neill's lifetime, but the short piece contains some of his most soul-searching insights in both its dialogue and STAGE DIRECTIONS.

On June 16, 1943, O'Neill's daughter Oona, at 18 years old, married the 54-year-old British-born actor and filmmaker Charlie Chaplin. Infuriated by the union, O'Neill shut his daughter from his life permanently. Oona and Chaplin raised eight children together, none of whom O'Neill ever met, and the couple enjoyed a contented family life in Switzerland. (It is widely believed that Carlotta O'Neill exacerbated the break between O'Neill and his daughter by intercepting dozens of Oona's letters apprising him of his grandchildren's development.)

O'Neill completed his last play, *A Moon for the Misbegotten*, in 1943, and the following year he was diagnosed with cortical cerebellar atrophy. Because of Danville's lack of local conveniences during the war, he and Carlotta sold Tao House in February 1944 and moved to a hotel in San Francisco. In October 1945, O'Neill returned to New York, and on November 29, he sent the script of *Long Day's Journey into Night* to Bennett Cerf, his publisher at Random House. In the accompanying letter, he insisted the manuscript be locked in their safe, remain unpublished until 25 years after his death, and never be produced for the stage.

O'Neill and Carlotta moved into a New York penthouse on East 84th Street in spring 1946. That year, the aging playwright bitterly denounced the progression of American history in a *New Yorker* magazine interview, in which he summed up the sins of the nation with one biblical question (the "sentence" referred to below): "For what shall it profit a man, if he shall gain the whole world and lose his own soul?" (Matthew 16:26).

> Some day this country is going to get it—really get it. We had everything to start with—everything—but there's bound to be a retribution. We've followed the same selfish, greedy path as every other country in the world. We talk about the American Dream and want to tell the world about the American Dream, but what is that dream, in most cases, but the dream of material things? I sometimes think that the United States, for this reason, is the greatest failure the world has ever seen. We've been able to get a very good price for our souls in this country—the greatest price perhaps that has ever been paid—but you'd think that after all these years, and all that man has been through, we'd have sense enough—all of us—to understand the whole secret of human happiness is summed up in that same sentence (from the Bible) which also appears in the teachings of Buddha, Lao-tse, and even Mohammed. (quoted in Bowen 313)

On October 9, 1946, the Theatre Guild produced *The Iceman Cometh* on Broadway. The four-and-a-half-hour production received lackluster reviews, but after its successful revival at Circle in the Square in 1956, it is now considered one of American drama's highest achievements. *A Moon for the Misbegotten* opened in Columbus, Ohio, on February 20, 1947. Neither the public nor O'Neill himself thought much of *Moon* by the time of its opening, and it was banned in many venues for its sexual content. Today, however, it is considered one of O'Neill's most compassionate tragedies. *Moon* is an amalgamation of the tragic story of his brother Jamie's squandered opportunities with Irish humor—including a hilarious verbal joust between his father's old tenant JOHN "DIRTY" DOLAN (Phil Hogan in the play) and EDWARD S. HARKNESS (T. Stedman Harder)—and it has since enjoyed many successful revivals.

O'Neill's son Shane, who attempted suicide multiple times and had become a chronic drug and alcohol abuser, was arrested in August 1948 for heroin possession and received a two-year suspended sentence. Doris Alexander suggests that it was Shane, even more than Jamie O'Neill, who fueled the character of James Tyrone and the theme of squandered gifts in both *Long Day's Journey* and *Moon*. O'Neill continually accused Shane, as James Tyrone does Jamie in *Long Day's Journey*, of being a "loafer" who was "never willing to start at the bottom" (quoted in Alexander 2005, 87). O'Neill refused to help him through the legalities or provide money for expenses and fines. (A kind and charming man in his way but never freed of his addictions, Shane committed suicide in 1977 by jumping to his death from a fourth-floor apartment window in Manhattan.)

In fall 1948, O'Neill and Carlotta moved to a cottage in MARBLEHEAD, MASSACHUSETTS, at a time when O'Neill's tremor had grown so severe that he was incapable of writing. On September 25, 1950, his oldest son, Eugene, Jr.—a successful classics professor at Yale University who also became an alcoholic and disillusioned with success—committed suicide at a friend's house in Woodstock, New York. O'Neill was hospitalized with a broken leg the following February at Salem Hospital. Soon after, Carlotta was hospitalized as a psychiatric patient; her unstable mental condition was diagnosed as having been caused by bromide poisoning. Encouraged by friends, O'Neill signed a statement that Carlotta was, in fact, mentally deranged.

Nonetheless, O'Neill and Carlotta were reconciled on May 17, 1951, and they sold their cottage in Massachusetts and moved into the Shelton Hotel in Boston. That same year, O'Neill bequeathed his papers and manuscripts to Yale University, the largest repository of several existing O'Neill COLLECTIONS, and designated Carlotta as the executrix of his literary and financial estate. Before sending his papers to Yale, he destroyed many drafts of unfinished plays but apparently overlooked *More Stately Mansions*, and the manuscript has since been published.

On November 27, 1953, Eugene Gladstone O'Neill died from pneumonia in a hotel room at age 65. His final words were no more optimistic than his father's to him: "Born in a hotel room, and, god dammit, died in a hotel room" (quoted in Diggins 29). He was buried on December 2 at Forest Hills Cemetery in Boston, Massachusetts.

Eugene O'Neill. Photo by Carl Van Vechten *(Courtesy of the Van Vechten Trust)*

Carlotta O'Neill soon after disregarded her husband's wishes and approved the publication and production of *Long Day's Journey into Night*. In 1956, Yale University Press published the manuscript, and on February 10, 1956, it premiered at the Royal Dramatic Theatre in Sweden, then opened in the United States on November 7, 1956, at the Helen Hayes Theatre in New York. Audiences were as awed by the play's craftsmanship as they were shocked by the revelations it contained about O'Neill's family. This remarkable tragedy gave O'Neill a fourth, posthumous Pulitzer Prize.

Close behind the American premiere of *Long Day's Journey*, *The Iceman Cometh* was revived at the Circle in the Square Theatre. The now-mythic productions of *Long Day's Journey* and revival of *The Iceman Cometh*, both directed by JOSÉ QUIN-

TERO and starring JASON ROBARDS as Jamie Tyrone and Hickey, respectively, followed by *A Moon for the Misbegotten* starring Robards and COLLEEN DEWHURST, ignited a full-scale EUGENE O'NEILL RENAISSANCE. The subsequent demand for O'Neill plays also whetted the appetite of theatergoers internationally for new plays and revivals of younger American dramatists such as TENNESSEE WILLIAMS, Thornton Wilder, Loraine Hansberry, Arthur Miller, Edward Albee, August Wilson, David Mamet, and Tony Kushner. Several academic and educational journals, societies, Web sites, and theaters have since been formed to honor the great playwright, notably the *EUGENE O'NEILL REVIEW*, the EUGENE O'NEILL SOCIETY, the Web sites eoneill.com and eugeneoneillsociety.org, and the EUGENE O'NEILL THEATER CENTER near New London, all of which actively distribute new work in O'Neill studies and uphold his reputation as America's greatest dramatist.

## BIBLIOGRAPHY

Alexander, Doris. *Eugene O'Neill's Creative Struggle: The Decisive Decade, 1924–1933*. University Park: Pennsylvania State University Press, 1992.

———. *Eugene O'Neill's Last Plays: Separating Art from Autobiography*. Athens: University of Georgia Press, 2005.

———. *The Tempering of Eugene O'Neill*. New York: Harcourt, Brace, and World, Inc., 1962.

Berlin, Normand. *Eugene O'Neill*. New York: Grove Press, 1982.

Black, Stephen A. *Eugene O'Neill: Beyond Mourning and Tragedy*. New Haven, Conn.: Yale University Press, 1999.

Bogard, Travis. *Contour in Time: The Plays of Eugene O'Neill*. Rev. ed. New York: Oxford University Press, 1988.

Bowen, Croswell. *The Curse of the Misbegotten: A Tale of the House of O'Neill*. New York: McGraw-Hill, 1959.

Boulton, Agnes. *Part of a Long Story: Eugene O'Neill as a Young Man in Love*. Garden City, N.Y.: Doubleday & Company, 1958.

Bowen, Croswell. *The Curse of the Misbegotten: A Tale of the House of O'Neill*. New York: McGraw-Hill, 1959.

Brietzke, Zander. "The Gift of Ric Burns." *Eugene O'Neill Review* 28 (2006): 113–130.

Clark, Barrett H. *Eugene O'Neill: The Man and His Plays.* Rev. ed. New York: Dover, 1947.

De Casseres, Benjamin. "'Denial without End': Benjamin De Casseres' Parody of Eugene O'Neill's 'God Play' *Days Without End*." Edited by Robert M. Dowling. *Eugene O'Neill Review* 30 (Fall 2008): 145–159.

Diggins, John Patrick. *Eugene O'Neill's America: Desire under Democracy.* Chicago: University of Chicago Press, 2007.

Dowling, Robert M. "On Eugene O'Neill's 'Philosophical Anarchism.'" *Eugene O'Neill Review* 29 (Spring 2007): 50–72.

Flanagan, Thomas. "Master of the Misbegotten." *New York Review of Books* (October 5, 200). Reprinted in *There You Are: Writings on Irish and American Literature and History,* by Thomas Flanagan, edited by Christopher Cahill, 41–61. New York: New York Review Books, 2004.

Floyd, Virginia. *The Plays of Eugene O'Neill: A New Assessment.* New York: Ungar, 1985.

Gelb, Arthur, and Barbara Gelb. *O'Neill: Life with Monte Cristo.* New York: Applause Books, 2000.

Hapgood, Hutchins. *A Victorian in the Modern World.* New York: Harcourt, Brace and Company, 1939.

Kantor, Louis. "O'Neill Defends His Play of the Negro." In *Conversations with Eugene O'Neill,* edited by Mark W. Estrin, 44–49. Jackson: University of Mississippi Press, 1990.

Kemp, Harry. "Out of Provincetown: A Memoir of Eugene O'Neill." In *Conversations with Eugene O'Neill,* edited by Mark W. Estrin, 95–102. Jackson: University Press of Mississippi, 1990.

Kushner, Tony. "The Genius of O'Neill." *Eugene O'Neill Review* 26 (2004): 248–256.

Miller, Jordan Y. *Playwright's Progress: O'Neill and the Critics.* Chicago: Scott, Foresman and Company, 1965.

O'Neill, Eugene. *Complete Plays.* 3 vols. Edited by Travis Bogard. New York: Library of America, 1988.

———. "'The Screenews of War': A Previously Unpublished Short Story by Eugene O'Neill." Edited with an Introduction by Robert M. Dowling. *Resources for American Literary Study* 31. (Fall 2007): 169–198.

———. *Selected Letters of Eugene O'Neill.* Edited by Travis Bogard and Jackson R. Bryer. New Haven, Conn.: Yale University Press, 1988.

Quintero, José. *If You Don't Dance They Beat You.* Boston: Little, Brown, 1974.

Richter, Robert A. *Eugene O'Neill and Dat Ole Davil Sea: Maritime Influences in the Life and Works of Eugene O'Neill.* Mystic, Conn.: Mystic Seaport, 2004.

Shaughnessy, Edward L. *Down the Nights and Down the Days: Eugene O'Neill's Catholic Sensibility.* Notre Dame, Ind.: University of Notre Dame Press, 2000.

Sheaffer, Louis. *O'Neill: Son and Playwright.* Boston: Little, Brown, 1968.

———. *O'Neill: Son and Artist.* Boston: Little, Brown, 1973.

# PART II

## Works A–R

# Abortion: A Play in One Act
## (completed, 1914; first produced, 1959)

Eugene O'Neill wrote *Abortion* at MONTE CRISTO COTTAGE, the O'Neill homestead in NEW LONDON, CONNECTICUT, in spring 1914. The play was one of nine one-act plays and two full-length plays he composed before his apprenticeships with GEORGE PIERCE BAKER in Baker's playwriting workshop at Harvard University and his work with the PROV-INCETOWN PLAYERS. Though it was probably one of two plays O'Neill sent Baker to gain entry into the seminar, the other most likely being *BOUND EAST FOR CARDIFF* (then titled *Children of the Sea*), the play was never produced in his lifetime. It was first produced, along with *The MOVIE MAN* and *The SNIPER*, at the Key Theater in New York City on October 27, 1959. Barrett H. Clark, O'Neill's contemporary and a tireless chronicler of the playwright's career, mistakenly wrote that *Abortion*, along with O'Neill's first full-length play, *BREAD AND BUTTER*, were destroyed before the possibility of a production. But O'Neill actually copyrighted the piece on May 19, 1914, and it appeared in the 1950 collection *The Lost Plays of Eugene O'Neill*. In fact, O'Neill's matinee idol father, JAMES O'NEILL, agreed to perform in the play if they could find a producer, which they never did; GEORGE CRAM "JIG" COOK, the director of the Playwrights' Theater, rejected it as unworthy of either O'Neill (whose *Bound East for Cardiff* astounded him as an experimental revelation) or his theater in 1916 (Gelb 591).

Probably set at Princeton University, where O'Neill spent only one year of study, *Abortion* reveals the enormity of O'Neill's feelings of guilt for abandoning his first wife, KATHLEEN JENKINS, and their son, EUGENE O'NEILL, JR., along with his father's moral and financial support through that period. The story of a young college man who inadvertently impregnates a working-class girl and pays for her abortion but then commits suicide after discovering she has died of postprocedural complications, *Abortion* comprises O'Neill's first serious attempt at self-analysis. More important than the autobiographical elements, however, the play contains many vital themes that infiltrate much of O'Neill's later work, particularly in the way he depicts how, as Paul D. Voelker argues, "the veneer of social conscience, which is obviously present in the play, becomes simply a device for obscuring the deeper psychological motives truly at work."

## SYNOPSIS

The scene is a comfortable study in a ground-level dormitory suite at a privileged university in the eastern United States (Princeton University). A wide, bowed window in back center looks out onto the campus. Doors to the right lead to the dormitory hallway and the bedroom. The walls are adorned with typical college paraphernalia—*"flags, banners, framed photographs of baseball and football teams, college posters, etc."* A table in the center is strewn with ashtrays, pipes, books, and magazines. The room is suffused in the *"dim glow of the dying twilight but as the action progresses this slowly disappears."* Voices are heard from the hallway, and Mrs. Townsend, Lucy Townsend, and Donald "Bull" Herron enter. There is some fumbling for the light, and Herron, having bumped his shins in the process, stifles his instinct to swear and lets out a guarded "Oh darn!" (1:203). The lights come on, and the characters are now visible. Lucy is a 19-year-old beauty; as it is commencement week, she is carrying a flag and has a bouquet of flowers attached to her waist. Mrs. Townsend is a soft-featured, matronly woman in her early 50s. Herron is a massive, athletic type with a thick neck and powerful six-foot frame. Lucy good-naturedly teases Herron, as a well-educated young woman might, for resembling the god Pluto (though not as "fat . . . nor as clumsy") and for being, no matter his bulk, a "delicate fragile butterfly" when it comes to playful criticism (1:204). The good-natured banter is brought to an end with the appearance of Joe Murray at the hall door. Murray is a sickly, emaciated youth wearing a threadbare suit, who asks to see Jack Townsend. Herron informs him Jack will arrive shortly but advises Murray to leave a message instead of waiting. Murray refuses, so Herron contemptuously instructs him to wait in the hallway outside, which he grudgingly does. Herron muses that Murray is most likely a "townie," a town resident as opposed to a student, who undoubtedly wants to hit up his overly compassionate roommate for money. (This may explain O'Neill's choice of the name *Townsend,* as Jack's presence leads to at least two townies' ends, if one includes an unborn child's.) We learn that Jack is the star baseball pitcher at the university, and the action of the play follows a championship game at which Jack has played brilliantly.

Jack and his fiancée, Evelyn Sands, enter the study. She is wearing, like so many O'Neillian women, a simple white dress. Jack is a typical all-star—confident, handsome, and good-natured—whom O'Neill describes as someone who *"is accustomed to the deference of those around him"* (1:206). His father, John Townsend, is in the hallway talking with a Professor Simmons, who was an instructor there when Townsend himself was a student. Herron tells Jack about the "townie," which makes his roommate *"visibly uneasy"* (1:207). Everyone but Jack heads off to a postgame carnival. Before Evelyn leaves, however, she describes to her fiancé the sensation of selfish rapture she experienced while watching Jack pitch the game: "It was a horrid sort of selfish pride. . . . I couldn't help saying to myself from time to time: he loves me, *me!* He belongs to *me;* and I thought of how jealous all the girls around me who were singing his praises would be if they knew" (1:208). This speech disconcerts Jack terribly, and he responds that she makes him feel "mean—and contemptible" when she flatters him like that. To make matters worse, Evelyn associates his sportsmanship with the way she envisions his role in "the game of life"—"fairly, squarely, strengthening those around you, refusing to weaken at critical moments, advancing others by sacrifices, fighting the good fight for the cause, the team, and always, whether vanquished or victor, reserving a hearty, honest cheer for the other side." "I won't listen any longer," Jack says with a *"strong note of pain in his voice,"* "I positively refuse." Evelyn believes he is just being humble, but Jack continues in earnest, "I shall try—with all my strength—in the future, Evelyn,—to live as you have said and become worthy of you" (1:209).

John Townsend enters. He is a *"well-preserved, energetic"* man of around 60, who is smartly, but *"soberly"* dressed. Evelyn departs to watch the parade, which is, significantly, scheduled to pass by the room's window. Townsend, an alumnus of the university, lights a cigar and makes some nostalgic remarks about the college when he attended it. The conversation quickly shifts to a lingering problem Jack and his father know they must resolve during their moment alone. Jack has conducted a relationship with a young woman from town, and she became pregnant; the previous Monday, she had had an abortion. There is some question as to how her recovery went, as Jack did not answer her letter calling for him. Townsend admonishes his son for this but remains supportive as he had similar experience in his college days; he writes off the affair, which is torturing Jack's conscience, as a result of evolutionary biology: "We've retained a large portion of the original mud in our make-up. That's the only answer I can think of." Jack agrees, insisting that it was not Evelyn's fiancé who impregnated the girl but "the male beast who ran gibbering through the forest after its female thousands of years ago" (1:212).

Townsend's line of tolerance is drawn with this, however—Jack alone is responsible for his lack of "restraint," he insists, and he must assume responsibility for his poor judgment. Jack disagrees, arguing that not only are biological urges responsible, but the pathological behavior that results from society's hypocritical moral laws compel men and women into such "evasions" (1:213). Nellie Murray, the victim in question, is working-class, a stenographer whose father is dead and who, along with her brother, supports the reminder of her family. Jack admits he has "played the scoundrel all the way through" (1:213) but vows to make amends as a good husband and citizen after he and Evelyn marry. The abortion cost $200, an expense Townsend was more than happy to shoulder in order to avoid a scandal.

As Townsend and Jack head to the doorway into the hall, Joe Murray enters. He blocks their exit and demands to speak to Jack. Jack complies and sullenly invites him in, while Townsend, unsettled by Murray's appearance, leaves the two to work it out. At first Jack plays the condescending well-to-do social superior, and Joe can barely contain his fury. But after Joe informs him that his sister, Jack's lover Nellie Murray, died that morning due to complications caused by the "faker of a doctor" Jack had hired to perform the surgery, Jack's superior facade slips away. Jack feebly denies the verity of this. Joe keeps on, calling him a murderer for seducing his sister, demanding she have an abortion, and then hiring an incompetent doctor.

During their exchange, the sound of cheers and band music fills the air as the commencement parade moves toward Jack's dormitory. Joe declares that he interrogated his sister's doctor at gunpoint, which is how he discovered Jack's identity. The doctor paid him the $200 Jack had given him in "blood money" to keep quiet (1:218). He threatens to expose the truth while Jack pleads for him to save both of their families, "innocents" in the torrid affair, from the mutual humiliation they would suffer if the scandal went public. Jack also offers to bribe him to stay silent, which enrages Joe, who draws his revolver and points it at Jack threateningly. After a short struggle, Jack disarms the weaker youth, who then cautiously backs away toward the door. But Jack's remorse is extreme, and he hands the gun back, telling Joe that he deserves whatever punishment he receives. Joe considers death too merciful and heads off to inform the police.

The sound of the parade grows louder, and Jack, overcome with despair, shuts the window and pulls down the shades. The parade arrives outside the window, and students are heard wondering over Jack's whereabouts. They strike up a chorus of "For He's a Jolly Good Fellow," which drives Jack insane with guilt: He rushes to the revolver, puts the barrel to his temple, and pulls the trigger. The gunshot is barely heard above the din outside. Evelyn enters cheerfully to coax him outside, again mistaking guilt for humility, but seeing his dead frame sprawled over the table, she faints and drops in a heap to the floor. The scene ends with the crowd of students continuing on their way, ironically singing the last line of the play, "For he's a jolly good fellow, which nobody can deny" (1:220).

## COMMENTARY

*Abortion,* if artistically unremarkable, has great value for O'Neill studies, as it provides an early window into O'Neill's later thematic obsessions. First and foremost is the figure of the philandering scoundrel, in this case Jack Townsend, whom O'Neill generally treats sympathetically as a victim of both humans' natural, biological sex drive and the unnatural social result of puritanical morality. Virginia Floyd and Travis Bogard both agree that Jack's rejection of Nellie Murray must have arisen from O'Neill's pain at rejecting his first wife, Kathleen Jenkins, and their child, Eugene O'Neill, Jr., in 1909 (Floyd 71; Bogard 23). In a perverse way, these men are often victimized by women who adore them. Jack's response to Evelyn's praise—the resentment of a dissolute, guilt-ridden man or husband who feels undeserving of the attentions of a loving, dedicated woman or wife—is an early suggestion of what would become one of the most important themes in O'Neill's plays.

Jack's argument to his father that not only are biological urges responsible, but the behavior that results from society's hypocritical moral laws compel men and women into such "evasions" (1:213) are drawn in the vein of NATURALISM—a movement that included Stephen Crane, Jack London, Frank Norris, and Theodore Dreiser among its practitioners in the United States, all of whom wrote similar, though generally far more sophisticated, tales of this kind. O'Neill stops short, however, of making the kind of far-reaching statements of CLASS conflict of Crane, London, Norris, and Dreiser. "He does not approach social protest," writes Travis Bogard, "nor does he suggest any remedy for the iniquities of class. In the end, withdrawing from any large view of the social opposition he has sketched, O'Neill makes Jack's suicide a matter of merely private expiation" (24).

The theme of self-loathing in the face of virtuous love is most powerfully treated in O'Neill's late masterpieces *The ICEMAN COMETH* and *A TOUCH OF THE POET.* Both Theodore "Hickey" Hickman from *Iceman* and Cornelius "Con" Melody from *A Touch of the Poet,* like Jack, are driven to self-destruction by the love of a faithful, trusting woman—in Jack's case his fiancée Evelyn, in Hickey's case his wife (also called Evelyn), and in Con Melody's his wife Nora. Similarly, the trope of the devastating struggles that ensue when a working-class girl desires a wealthy boy appears in early plays, notably BEFORE BREAKFAST and *The STRAW*, and is treated in powerful ways in such later masterpieces as *A Touch of the Poet*, its sequel, MORE STATELY MANSIONS, and *A MOON FOR THE MISBEGOTTEN*.

Of course, abortion was criminalized in the mid-19th century, partly due to pressure from religious groups to preserve, in their view, the sanctity of life; partly to the needs for an increased population following the Industrial Revolution; and partly to maintain women's "proper" roles as wives and mothers. In 1914, whomever Jack employed to perform the operation would have been committing a criminal act, and his willingness to do so might suggest a pernicious correspondence with his abilities as a physician. O'Neill's treatment of physicians here also resembles that of the "quack" DOCTORS O'Neill's character Mary Tyrone (based on his mother, MARY ELLEN "ELLA" O'NEILL) would later revile in LONG DAY'S JOURNEY INTO NIGHT.

Lesser details reappear in O'Neill's late plays as well. The chandelier that hangs above the table in *Abortion*, like the one in both AH, WILDERNESS! and *Long Day's Journey*, among many others, dangles an electric wire to a reading lamp on the table below. As with the tom-toms in *The EMPEROR JONES*, the sound of cheers and marching-band music grows ever louder as the action progresses. Evelyn's simple white dress is worn again and again by O'Neill's female characters. In later plays, the white dress will symbolize destructive potential of women such as Mildred Douglas in *The HAIRY APE*, Ruth Atkins in BEYOND THE HORIZON, and Deborah Harford in *A Touch of the Poet*. Additionally, as with *Beyond the Horizon* and, most significantly, *Long Day's Journey into Night*, a cycle of tragedy is set off by a penurious, miserly, or uncaring character hiring a cheap doctor, as James O'Neill had done when his wife, Ella, was pregnant with Eugene (causing her to become addicted to morphine) and also when Eugene was diagnosed with tuberculosis. Both of these are dramatized in *Long Day's Journey*. Finally, though by no means exhaustively, dusk settles into night over the course of the play, symbolizing Jack's journey down into the depths of shame, just

as O'Neill's greatest tragedy follows the course of the sun's descent, leading us deeper and deeper into the Tyrone family's self-loathing and tragic revelations.

## CHARACTERS

**Herron, Donald "Bull"** Jack Townsend's college roommate. Herron is a good-natured, athletic type whom Jack's sister, Lucy Townsend, flirtatiously teases in the opening scene. O'Neill describes Herron as the kind of stereotypical hail-fellow-well-met "jock"—something like Sam Evans in STRANGE INTERLUDE—he generally contrasted with more sympathetic "deep" philosophical characters; he is *"a huge, swarthy six-footer with a bull neck and an omnipresent grin, slow to anger and understanding but—an All-American tackle"* (1:204).

**Murray, Joe** The brother of Jack Townsend's working-class lover. Joe is a machinist in the town where Jack's university resides, and upon learning that his sister died from complications after an abortion, seeks revenge on Jack. O'Neill describes Joe in ways that starkly contrast with Jack's athletic good looks: *"He is a slight, stoop-shouldered, narrow-chested young fellow of eighteen, with large, feverish, black eyes, thin lips, pasty complexion, and the sunken cheeks of a tuberculosis victim"* (1:205). Joe has a strong desire to murder Jack but decides instead to report him to the authorities, as killing him would be a less exacting revenge than exposing the scandal to the community.

**Townsend, Jack** An all-star baseball pitcher and popular man-on-campus, Jack has an affair with a working-class girl named Nellie Murray, who dies after aborting his child. Jack is overwhelmed with guilt when her brother, Joe Murray, visits him in his dormitory study seeking revenge. Jack resigns himself to be murdered, but Joe thinks better of it and decides to notify the police instead, which would make the scandal public. Joe leaves his revolver in Jack's room, and Jack uses it against himself in the final scene. Jack is first introduced in the STAGE DIRECTIONS as a *"well-built handsome young fellow of about twenty-two years old, with blond* hair brushed straight back from his forehead, intelligent blue eyes, a good-natured, self-indulgent mouth, and ruddy, tanned complexion. He has the easy, confident air of one who has, through his prowess in athletics, become a figure of note in college circles and is accustomed to the deference of those around him" (1:206). The depth of the guilt Jack feels, however, causes his "easy, confident air" to be gradually stripped away. Though some critics allude to Jack as an autobiographical avatar like Richard Miller in Ah, Wilderness! or Edmund Tyrone in Long Day's Journey into Night, the resemblance is mainly philosophical, as Jack believes that his situation was brought on by the beast within him (evolutionary biology) and society's puritanical aversion to allowing those inner desires some free reign. In addition, Jack's scandal resembles O'Neill's experience of two years before the play's composition, when he abandoned his first wife, Kathleen Jenkins, after she became pregnant with his son, Eugene O'Neill, Jr.

**Townsend, John**  Jack Townsend's father. O'Neill describes him as "a tall, kindly old man of sixty or so with a quantity of white hair. He is erect, well-preserved, energetic, dressed immaculately but soberly" (1:209). Townsend offers his son paternal support during their conversation about the causes and possible outcomes of the abortion Jack set in motion after his affair with a working-class girl. Townsend himself, according to Jack's professor, had conducted similar affairs when he, an alumnus of Jack's university, attended the school. James O'Neill had conducted an affair that resulted in his possible child (though he was relieved of obligation in court) by Nettie Walsh—whose name strikes a close resemblance to Nellie Murray, the fatally jilted woman in Abortion. As with James Tyrone in Long Day's Journey into Night, Townsend censures his son for his political views: "Save your radical arguments for the younger generation" (1:213). He is also like O'Neill's father, upon whom Tyrone is closely based; James O'Neill also was supportive of his son during the scandal with the playwright's first wife, Kathleen Jenkins, and even arranged for his escape to Honduras after she became pregnant with O'Neill's son.

**Townsend, Lucy**  Jack Townsend's sister. Lucy is a "small, vivacious blond nineteen years old, gushing with enthusiasm over everything and everybody" (1:204). In the opening scene, Lucy flirts with Jack's roommate, Donald "Bull" Herron, and genuinely relishes the excitement of campus life.

**Townsend, Mrs.**  Jack Townsend's mother. Mrs. Townsend is an innocuous "sweet-faced, soft-spoken, gray-haired lady in her early fifties" (1:204) who serves little purpose in the plot, other than as a guileless counterpoint to her husband, John Townsend, who happily pays for Jack's mistress to have an abortion. Like Mrs. Brown in Bread and Butter, she is a rather unfortunate symbol of moral and intellectual female simplicity.

**Sands, Evelyn**  Jack Townsend's fiancée. O'Neill describes Evelyn as "a tall, dark-haired, beautiful girl about twenty years old. Her eyes are large and brown; her mouth full-lipped, resolute; her figure lithe and graceful" (1:206). Evelyn represents the class of woman Jack could marry, but more than this, she is a catalyst for escalating the tremendous guilt he harbors. She is notable for having the same first name as Theodore "Hickey" Hickman's wife in The Iceman Cometh. Like Hickey, Jack is driven to impossible depths of shame by her ill-placed trust and admiration.

## BIBLIOGRAPHY

Bogard, Travis. Contour in Time: The Plays of Eugene O'Neill. Rev. ed. New York: Oxford University Press, 1988.
Floyd, Virginia. The Plays of Eugene O'Neill: A New Assessment. New York: Ungar, 1985.
Gelb, Arthur, and Barbara Gelb. O'Neill: Life with Monte Cristo. New York: Applause Books, 2000.
Voelker, Paul D. "Politics, but Literature: The Example of Eugene O'Neill's Apprenticeship." The Eugene O'Neill Newsletter 8, no. 2 (Summer–Fall) 1984. Originally a paper presented at the Twelfth Annual Twentieth-Century Literature Conference: Politics of Literature, held at the University of Louisville in February 1984. Available online. URL: http://eoneill.com/library/newsletter/viii_2/viii-2b.htm. Accessed December 15, 2006.

# *Ah, Wilderness!* (completed, 1932; first produced, 1933)

On July 1, 1932, Eugene O'Neill visited his boyhood home, MONTE CRISTO COTTAGE in NEW LONDON, CONNECTICUT. It looked smaller than he remembered and poorly maintained. He wished he had never gone. Two months later, however, on the morning of September 1, 1932, he awoke at his home Casa Genotta on SEA ISLAND, GEORGIA, with the setting (Monte Cristo), plot, characters, themes, and even title of a full-length play that, according to O'Neill, he envisioned from a dream "fully formed and ready to write" (quoted in Alexander 172). Three weeks later, on September 27, O'Neill completed the first draft of his only mature comedy, *Ah, Wilderness!* "Wrote the whole damned thing in the month of September," O'Neill boasted to his friend, the editor SAXE COMMINS (quoted in Gelb 190). (This remarkable burst of creative energy recalls the dream that inspired *DESIRE UNDER THE ELMS* on New Years Eve 1923.) After a tryout of the play in Pittsburgh, followed by several substantial cuts, the THEATRE GUILD's immensely popular production of *Ah, Wilderness!* opened in New York City on October 3, 1933, and received very fine reviews. But the play, often referred to as O'Neill's "digression," confused as much as beguiled audiences unused to America's "master of the misbegotten" working outside the tragic vein.

*Ah, Wilderness!* takes place during New London's Fourth of July celebration in the year 1906. The Miller family of the play, though similar in many respects, should not be mistaken for O'Neill's own family, which he immortalized later in his autobiographical masterpiece *LONG DAY'S JOURNEY INTO NIGHT*. Rather, the Millers are a wish-fulfillment fantasy, a sentimental portrait of the happy, middle-class New England family O'Neill longed to have been born into. Nevertheless, the adolescent poet/child Richard Miller shares many traits with his creator, and beneath the veneer of the Millers' nostalgic innocence lies more than a touch of cynical reality. O'Neill dedicated *Ah, Wilderness!* to his producer GEORGE JEAN NATHAN, "who also," he wrote, "once upon a time, in peg-top trousers went

*Ah, Wilderness!* (Courtesy of the Yale Collection of American Literature, Beinecke Rare Book and Manuscript Library)

the pace that kills along the road to ruin" (quoted in Alexander 181).

*Ah, Wilderness!* continues to draw large audiences around the globe. Since its 1933 premiere, two FILM ADAPTATIONS have been made, one a musical entitled *Summer Holiday* (1948); it has also been adapted as a Broadway musical, *Take Me Along* (1959) and a made-for-television miniseries.

## SYNOPSIS

### Act 1

The Miller family sitting room in "*a large small-town in Connecticut*" (New London) at around 7:30 in the morning on July 4, 1906. The room is decorated in the "*scrupulous medium-priced tastelessness of the period.*" Two bookcases line the walls packed with "*cheap sets*" of literature, young adult fiction, and "*the best-selling novels of many past years*" (3:5). Sunlight streams in from the windows. A set of sliding doors opens to an unlit parlor in the back, and another to a well-lit parlor and the front door; a screen door leads to the outside porch, and a table sits at center with five chairs positioned around it. The Millers have just finished breakfast. Essie Miller's voice commands her son, Tommy, to return to the table and finish his milk. Tommy, a blond-haired, chubby 11-year-old, appears at the doorway to the back parlor, impatient to begin the Fourth of July festivities. His father, Nat Miller's, voice can be heard in the dining room offstage. Essie grants Tommy permission to go outside, and he rushes out the screen door. Nat shouts not to set off firecrackers too close to the house.

Mildred Miller, a tall, slightly mannish, but attractively vivacious 15-year-old girl, and her brother Arthur, a 19-year-old with a heavyset build and collegiate attire, enter from the back parlor. Mildred and Arthur tease each other about their plans for the day and who they expect to spend it with. Essie, a woman of about 50 with a *"bustling, mother-of-the-family manner,"* carps at Tommy's having thoughtlessly left the porch door open. Lily Miller, her 42-year-old sister-in-law, who looks like the *"conventional type of old-maid school teacher,"* defends the boy's excitement over the holiday. Nat, a tall, thin man in his late 50s with *"fine, shrewd, humorous gray eyes,"* and his brother-in-law Sid Davis, a squat 45-year old *"with the Puckish face of a Peck's Bad Boy who has never grown up,"* follow close behind (3:7).

Nat, the owner of a local paper called the *Evening Globe*, and Sid chat amiably about Sid's new job as a reporter in Waterbury, Connecticut, as a series of firecrackers explodes loudly outside. Essie goes out the screen door and orders Tommy away from the house. Throughout the scene, Tommy's firecrackers continue to explode, *"not nearly so loud as the first . . . but sufficiently emphatic to form a disturbing punctuation to the conversation"* (3:8). Nat and Sid discuss the Sachem picnic they will attend, and Essie quips that those picnics are simply an excuse to drink. Lily assures her that Sid, an alcoholic, has reformed, though from his joking response he has not—"They're running me for president of the W.C.T.U." (the Women's Christian Temperance Movement) (3:9). Nat defends Sid's right to celebrate on the Fourth of July. They

all report their plans for the day: Arthur will go to a picnic with his girlfriend Elsie Rand and another couple; Mildred to a beach party; and Essie and Lily, who had not yet made plans, decide on a drive in the family Buick. Sid offers to escort Lily to the fireworks; she accepts on the condition that he not get intoxicated at the picnic. They all discuss the missing Richard, Nat and Essie's son. Mildred remarks that he must be writing a poem for his paramour, Muriel McComber, and the rest discuss his obsession with books and poetry, particularly the kind associated with political radicalism, which Essie has found hidden in his room.

They call for Richard, and, book in hand, he appears from the doorway of the back parlor. Richard, almost 17 and dressed in preppy clothes, closely resembles both parents, though with *"something of extreme sensitiveness added—a restless, apprehensive, defiant, shy, dreamy, self-conscious intelligence about him"* (3:12); his character waffles between being *"a plain simple boy and a posey actor solemnly playing a role"* (3:12). Distracted by his reading, Richard gets tripped by Mildred as he enters the room; he responds by pushing her onto the couch and tickling her with his free hand. They ask what his plans are—the beach party? a date with Muriel? playing with Tommy and the firecrackers?—but he rejects them all, considering the Fourth of July a "stupid farce." "I'll celebrate the day the people bring out the guillotine again and I see Pierpont Morgan being driven by in a tumbrel!" he shouts. Everyone stifles laughter but Arthur, who is offended by his brother's lack of patriotism. "Son," Nat responds with tolerant good-humor, "if I didn't know it was you talking, I'd think we had EMMA GOLDMAN with us" (3:13). Richard has been reading Thomas Carlyle's history of the French Revolution and is astonished to find that his father has read it too. He defends his other favorite authors, the ones he hides from his mother—Oscar Wilde, GEORGE BERNARD SHAW, and Algernon Charles Swinburne, along with *The Rubáiyát of Omar Khayyám*. This last sparks admissions of appreciation and short recitations from both Sid and Lily, then Richard himself, all of which shocks Essie.

Arthur spots Muriel's father, David McComber, a dry-goods merchant who advertises in Nat's newspaper, approaching the house. Arthur and Mildred head off to catch the trolley downtown, and the rest flee from McComber's disagreeable company. "I only wish I didn't have to be pleasant with the old buzzard," Nat quips, "but he's about the most valuable advertiser I've got" (3:18). Nat invites McComber into the sitting room. After some brief pleasantries on the part of Nat, McComber announces he has come regarding Richard's "dissolute and blasphemous" behavior "deliberately attempting to corrupt the morals" of his daughter (3:19). Nat adamantly defends his son's integrity, chalking up his rebelliousness to that of a typical adolescent. McComber shows Nat poems that Richard had given Muriel and demands he punish the boy. Their argument becomes heated, and McComber threatens to remove his advertisement from Nat's newspaper. Nat responds by refusing his advertisement from ever being run again and vows to help an outside dry goods company take over McComber's business. Leaving Nat with the poems and a letter from Muriel to Richard, McComber departs, disturbed by the threat but retaining a superior look of indignation.

Sid reenters, impressed with Nat's ability to deal with McComber. But Nat believes his son did, in fact, cross the line of decency by sending one particularly "warm" poem to young Muriel—Swinburne's sexually-charged "Anactoria." Richard appears, and Nat scolds him for having exposed a young girl to the material. He demands to know if Richard has sexual designs on Muriel, and Richard indignantly responds that they are engaged, and he would never sully her reputation. He insists he gave her the poems to "give her the spunk to lead her own life, and not be—always thinking of being afraid" (3:25). Nat hands him the letter. Richard reads it silently; his face grows "wounded and tragic," then "flushed with humiliation and wronged anger." "The little coward!," he shouts, "I hate her! She can't treat me like that! I'll show her!" (3:25). Hearing his mother and Lily's voices coming from the back parlor, he shoves the letter in his pocket and claims he is too sick to join the family in any of their activities. When pressed, he again curses the Fourth of July, and the family reluctantly leave him in the sitting room, as the curtain falls.

## Act 2

The Millers' dining room just after six o'clock that evening. A dark rug covers the floor in a room too small for the "medium-priced, formidable dining-room set." A chandelier hangs from the center above; in front of two windows stands a "heavy, ugly sideboard with three pieces of silver on its top." The wallpaper is "a somber brown and dark-red design," and a doorway leads to the side porch with a china closet to its right. Essie and the family's "second girl," Norah—"a clumsy, heavy-handed, heavy-footed, long-jawed, beamingly good-natured young Irish girl—a 'greenhorn'" (3:27)—attempt with comic difficulty to set the table and turn on the chandelier's lights. Essie voices her exasperation over Norah's clumsiness and dismisses the girl. Her sister-in-law Lily, wearing a new dress, steps in from the back parlor to help. Essie insists she relax after a year of "teaching a pack of wild Indians of kids" (3:28). She regrets that such a fine woman should be without a husband and children. Noticing her new dress, Essie warns her not to expect Sid to be sober after spending the day celebrating with his friends from town; however, she adds that Lily might reconsider Sid as a husband, now that he makes enough money to settle down: "I know darned well you love him. And he loves you and always has" (3:29). Lily refuses to consider marrying him while he continues to drink but reassures her that teaching and life with the Millers makes her feel less like a "useless old maid" (3:30). Essie praises her stalwartness, then tells her about a shared family joke on Nat. He has always claimed to be allergic to bluefish, but she has served him bluefish for years, lying to him that it is weakfish.

Essie heads out to warn Tommy not to give away her secret, and Richard enters from the back parlor. Since receiving Muriel's letter, Richard, "after his first outburst of grief and humiliation, has begun to take a masochistic satisfaction in his great sorrow, especially in the concern which it arouses in the family circle" (3:31). Lily's face shows some worry, but Richard announces that he has never taken Muriel seriously. When he pushes this line too far, his aunt grows offended by his cynicism. Essie returns and asks if Richard is hungry; he shrugs off the thought of food with theatrical disdain. She tells him that

Production photo of Eugene O'Neill's *Ah, Wilderness!*, Westminster Theatre (London, England), 1936 *(Courtesy of the Yale Collection of American Literature, Beinecke Rare Book and Manuscript Library)*

he deserves to lose Muriel after exposing "a nice girl like her things out of those indecent books!" (3:32). Richard storms out reciting, "Out, then, into the night with me!" (3:33). Essie and Lily go into the sitting room. Richard reappears and, contrary to his prior scorn for food, is caught by Norah pilfering some olives. She scolds him, then heads back into the kitchen. Wint Selby, a classmate of Arthur's, appears at the side door, beckoning to Richard in hushed tones. He has set up a date for that night with two "swift babies from New Haven," Belle and Edith, and is disappointed to hear Arthur has left for the night. Richard has 11 dollars (money he meant to spend on a gift for Muriel) and convinces Wint he has much experience with drinking and older women. He says he can lie his way out of family festivities. They agree to meet at the Pleasant Beach Hotel at 9:30 that night. Richard will entertain Belle while Wint

goes off with Edith. Richard considers this a perfect revenge for Muriel's deception.

Wint heads off into the night. Tommy enters, hungry for dinner. Essie reenters, saying they will have lobster and bluefish and reminding Tommy not to blow the secret they share about Nat. Lily follows close behind her. From a distance, Sid can be heard singing drunkenly as he and Nat approach the house. Mildred runs into the room, stifling a fit of laughter, and Essie sternly orders everyone to sit. Nat enters in a jovial mood, only slightly intoxicated. He slaps Essie playfully on the behind, and everyone bursts into laughter. Scandalized by her husband's behavior, Essie shouts for Norah, also laughing, to bring the soup to the table. She then orders the children to behave. Nat warns everyone that Sid has had too much to drink but hopes no one will hold it against him on a holiday. Sid enters, drunk but trying hard, at first, to conceal it.

He acts out a comedy routine that amuses every-one but Lily. Nonetheless, his sense of humor while drunk—drinking soup without a spoon, accusing Nat of being shamefully intoxicated, and wooing Norah playfully—even wins over Lily for a time.

Nat inquires whether the dinner is bluefish, and Tommy explodes into laughter. Essie informs her husband that he has eaten bluefish for years with no allergic reaction. Nat stubbornly refuses to eat the fish and changes the subject. Talk of swim-ming provokes him to retell a story about saving his friend's life 45 years before, a story they have heard hundreds of times. They laugh again at his expense, but Essie jumps to his defense. Sid continues joking brazenly and begins eating lobster, shell and all. When he refers to Lily as a tragic alcoholic, Essie sends him off to bed. He departs singing a Salva-tion Army marching song. Everyone laughs, and Lily accuses them all, including herself, of enabling Sid's ALCOHOLISM, then excuses herself.

Nat tells the remaining family members that Sid lost his job at the Waterbury newspaper. He will, of course, offer him a position at his own newspa-per as long as he stops "his damn nonsense." He orders the children outside. Richard remains, how-ever, and blames Lily for Sid's condition—"like all women love to ruin men's lives! I don't blame him for drinking himself to death! What does he care if he dies, after the way she's treated him!" (3:49). Nat orders him never to speak like that again and storms out. Essie scolds Richard, then follows her husband out. Feeling *"bitter, humiliated, wronged,"* he then smiles rebelliously and says, "Aw, what the hell do I care? I'll show them!" (3:50). He charges out the screen door as the curtain falls.

### Act 3, Scene 1

Around 10 o'clock that night in the back room of the Pleasant Beach Hotel. Four tables with chairs fill the room, which is dimly lit by *"two fly-specked globes in a fly-specked gilt chandelier"* hanging from the ceiling; a stairway to rooms upstairs and the "Family Entrance" are at the rear wall right; at left, front, a swinging door to the bar. A nickel-in-the-slot player piano plays "Bedelia." Cigarette and cigar butts are strewn on the floor, and each table has a cuspidor. A 20-year-old woman named

Belle, attractive but cheap-looking, is discovered sitting with Richard, who nurses a flat beer and looks *"horribly timid, embarrassed and guilty, but at the same time thrilled and proud of at last mingling with the pace that kills"* (3:51). The bartender, a tough-looking Irishman with a *"foxily cunning, stupid face and a cynically wise grin,"* looks on at them with amusement from the doorway to the bar. Richard is spending generously, which keeps Belle in good spirits, but she does not fully understand his inten-tions. *Her* intentions are clear enough—to per-suade Richard to go upstairs with her and pay her for sex. She convinces him to "have a man's drink," and he orders a sloe-gin fizz, ordering like someone "in the know"; she winks at the bartender to get him "something that'll warm him up" (3:53). The bartender returns with the drink, and Richard gives him a dollar—far too much—and the bartender thanks him now respectfully. He encourages Belle to keep at him and exits.

Belle offers Richard a smoke, though she must conceal hers—women can only smoke upstairs. She taunts Richard into downing the powerful drink in one gulp, which he does; she then takes a seat on his lap. *"He looks desperately uncomfortable, but the gin is rising to his head and he feels proud of himself and devilish, too."* She kisses him full on the lips, making him extremely anxious, and offers to take him upstairs for only five dollars. According to her, that's half price because she has become "just crazy" about him (3:55). Richard makes for the door, overcome with *"timidity, disgust at the money element, shocked modesty, and the guilty thought of Muriel"*; but he reconsiders, now seeing the "tart" as a *"romantic, evil vampire"* (3:56). He still refuses to take her upstairs, however, which makes her furious, and he gives her the five dollars for noth-ing. Belle calls for another round, promising to pay for his drink, and asks why he does not want to get his money's worth. He admits to swearing an oath of fidelity to a girl, then preaches reform to her. This infuriates Belle, and she taunts him that Muriel is probably unfaithful to him. They fall into an angry silence. A salesman enters, and he and Belle regard each other knowingly.

Richard commences a melodramatic POETRY recitation. Belle abandons Richard's lap and sits with the salesman, who happily eggs Richard on. "This gal of yours don't appreciate poetry," he says. "She's a lowbrow. But I'm the kid that eats it up" (3:60). Richard recites lines from HENRIK IBSEN's play *Hedda Gabbler*, and then, comprehending the salesman's motives with Belle, abruptly swears to protect her from disrepute. Belle and the salesman laugh at him. The salesman advises the bartender to turn the young man out for being underage, and the bartender roughly kicks Richard out onto the street. When the salesman asks Belle who her young escort was, he recognizes the name, deduces Richard is Nat Miller's son, and, out of respect for Nat, goes out to make sure Richard safely catches the trolley home. This revelation terrifies the bartender, as Miller is a respected man in the community. He lambastes Belle for failing to inform him of Richard's identity. When she defiantly yells back at him, he orders her out, threatening to call the police. Belle exits and vows revenge, slamming the door behind her. "Them lousy tramps is always getting this dump in Dutch!," he remarks with a sigh, and the curtain falls (3:62).

## Act 3, Scene 2

The Miller family's sitting room at around 11 o'clock that night. Essie, Nat, Lily, Mildred, and Tommy are discovered. The adults are in a terrible state of worry over Richard's whereabouts. Mildred is practicing her signature, and Tommy can barely keep his eyes open. Nat is reading a newspaper, Essie is sewing a doily, and Lily is reading a novel, but these distractions fail to alleviate their anxiety. Essie is the most evidently upset. Mildred passes around her new signature, and the adults absent-mindedly praise her work. Everyone offers Essie a rational explanation for Richard's tardiness—he has missed the trolley, is spending time with Muriel, is staying out to watch the fireworks. None of these explanations work, and Essie sends Tommy off to bed. They hear someone come through the front door, but it is Arthur, whistling "Waltz Me Around Again, Willie" and appearing *"complacently pleased with himself"* (3:66). Once apprised of the situation, Arthur assures his mother that Richard must have gone to the fireworks but did not ask to go because of his radical pose. "Didn't you hear him

this morning showing off bawling out the Fourth like an anarchist? He wouldn't want to reneg on that to you—" (3:67). Nat heartily agrees.

Arthur has been with Elsie Rand, and Mildred teases him and voices her dislike of Elsie, "the stuck-up thing!" (3:67). Nat persuades Arthur to sing, accompanied by Mildred on the piano, to ease their mother's anxiety. Sid enters from the front parlor terribly hungover and visibly contrite—*"nervous, sick, a prey to gloomy remorse and bitter feelings of self-loathing and self-pity"* (3:69). He begins to apologize, but Nat silences him so they can hear Arthur and Mildred. They begin, but Arthur's songs are melancholic, sentimental favorites that make everyone gloomier still. Sid lets out an apology between songs, which Nat and Essie accept out of hand, but he gets no response from Lily. Arthur sings another song, even sadder than the last, and at the finish Sid blurts out an apology to Lily for missing their engagement that evening. Lily says nothing; then, *"in a passion of self-denunciation,"* Sid agrees that what he did was unforgivable. He begins to weep, which is *"too much for Lily."* She rushes over to console him, *"swamped by a pitying love,"* then kisses him on his bald head and *"soothes him as if he were a little boy."* This perks Sid up, and *"the dawn of a cleansed conscience is already beginning to restore to its natural Puckish expression"* (3:71).

Arthur and Mildred begin an upbeat song, "Waiting at the Church," and Sid joins in with the line, "Can't get away to marry you today, My wife won't let me!" (3:71). Everyone laughs but Essie. Then Sid cheerfully reminds Lily of a time when they saw Vesta Victoria sing the song in New York; but the trip is a bad memory for Lily because of Sid's drinking, and she sadly responds that she does remember. Essie insists someone do something about Richard. Nat and Arthur have decided to look for him in the car when he stumbles through the screen door, his clothes disheveled and torn. Essie thinks he has gone mad, but Nat and Sid assure her that he is just drunk. Richard begins reciting poetry and lines from *Hedda Gabler*, as he had at the bar, but then *"his pallor takes on a greenish, sea-sick tinge,"* and he cries out to his mother as a little boy might, "Ma! I feel—rotten!" (3:74). Essie moves to him, but Sid steps in and, being "the kid who wrote the book," promises to take care of him. Sid and Richard go upstairs. Essie frantically wonders who "Hedda" is. "Oh, I know he's been with one of those bad women," she says, horror-struck. Nat tries to calm her, as *"Lily and Mildred and Arthur are standing about awkwardly with awed, shocked faces,"* and the curtain falls (3:74).

### Act 4, Scene 1

The same sitting room, around one o'clock in the afternoon. The Miller family has just finished lunch. Nat's face is set in *"frowning severity,"* and Essie's is *"drawn and worried."* Lily appears *"gently sad and depressed."* Sid is *"himself again,"* unconcerned about the night before. Mildred and Tommy are *"subdued, covertly watching their father,"* though Arthur acts *"self-consciously a virtuous young man against whom nothing can be said"* (3:75). Nat volubly expresses irritation for being dragged home on a workday to deal with Richard, who has been confined to bed. Tommy inquires why no one will tell him what Richard has done. His curiosity irritates Nat further, and Essie sends the children out of the room. Lily decides to take a walk, and Sid moves to join her, but Nat asks him to remain. Essie demands her husband punish Richard, but confuses him by expressing maternal concern and backhandedly relinquishing her son of guilt by blaming Nat's temper for the rebellion. She had interrogated Richard earlier about the woman "Hedda" and discovered that she is a character from a book (*Hedda Gabler* by Henrik Ibsen). She goes upstairs to bring him before his father.

Nat wakes up Sid, who had dozed off during Essie's recriminations. He shows Sid a note delivered to his office by a woman who, according to one of the mailroom boys, looked "like a tart." It accuses the bartender at the Pleasant Beach House of serving Richard, aware that he was underage. "If you have any guts," the note ends, "you will run that bastard out of town." Sid deduces correctly that "she's one of the babies" and "had a run-in with the barkeep and wants revenge" (3:78). Nat understands he must have a talk with Richard about sex. He says he did so with his older sons Wilbur, Lawrence, and Arthur, but Richard's innocence always shamed him out of it. Essie returns

with news that Richard is sleeping. Outwardly irritated but inwardly relieved, Nat heads back to his office.

Richard appears moments after his father's departure with an expression of *"hang-dog guilt mingled with defensive defiance"* (3:81). Essie accuses him of pretending to be asleep to avoid his father's wrath, but he shows a defiant lack of concern about punishment and expresses no remorse for what he did because it was "wicked or any such old-fogy moral notion." He has decided never to drink again; it made him feel sick and sadder than he was before, not happy like it does Sid. "Life is all a stupid farce!" he yells. "It's lucky there aren't any of General Gabler's pistols around—or you'd see if I'd stand it much longer!" (3:82; Richard refers to the suicide of the heroine of Ibsen's play). "You're a silly gabbler yourself when you talk that way!" she retorts, but she gives in to motherly concern after mention of suicide. Reminding him that he is not permitted to leave the house, she heads off to an appointment. Sid offers some cynical advice about drinking and women—"Love is hell on a poor sucker"—then falls back to sleep (3:83).

Mildred enters. She has a letter to Richard from Muriel. At first she tries to make him swear never to drink again, but her excitement over its contents takes over and she hands him the letter. In it, Muriel confesses that her father made her write the previous letter, which had broken off their engagement, and that she loves him and wants to meet him that night. She plans to sneak out to meet him, and he realizes he needs to leave that moment, while their mother is out. In spite of herself, Mildred admires his devotion to Muriel and looks at him with wonder as he makes his escape. Sid begins to snore as the curtain falls.

### Act 4, Scene 2

A beach on the harbor at almost nine o'clock that night. A grassy bank rises *"half-diagonally back along the beach, marking the line where the sand of the beach ends and fertile land begins"* (3:85–86); a painted white rowboat lies on the beach, and the boughs of two willow trees arch over the scene. The bow of the rowboat is darkened by the shadow of a willow, while the stern, along with a section of the beach, is illuminated by the *"soft, mysterious, caressing"* light of a new moon (3:86). A hotel orchestra can be heard in the far-off distance. Richard is discovered sitting on the rowboat, twirling his straw hat and impatiently awaiting Muriel. He haltingly confers with himself on the events of the previous night and his love for Muriel. Belle, he concludes, was "just a whore. . . . Muriel and I will go upstairs . . . when we're married . . . but that will be beautiful. . . ." He then recites from Oscar Wilde's "Panthea." Moved by the words, he muses over the beauty of the night. "I love the sand, and the trees, and the grass, and the water and the sky, and the moon . . . it's all in me and I'm in it . . . God, it's so beautiful!" (3:87). The town hall clock strikes nine—the hour Muriel designated for their meeting. He quotes from Algernon Swinburne's "Laus Veneris": "And lo my love, mine own soul's heart, more dear / Than mine own soul, more beautiful than God" (3:88).

Annoyed by his own sentimentality, Richard assumes a disaffected air. "Mustn't let her know I'm so tickled. . . . [I]f women are too sure of you, they treat you like slaves . . . let her suffer for a change" (3:88). Muriel appears on a path between the two willows. She calls out in a frightened voice, while Richard assumes a disaffected air. He pretends to have been thinking about "life," and that the time had passed quickly waiting for her. She asks him to come out of the moonlight. "Aw, there you go again," he retorts, "always scared of life!" (3:88). Muriel takes offense at this cavalier disregard for the risk she took to meet him. Threatening to leave, she starts back to the path, but Richard pleads with her to stay. Muriel is *"happily relieved—but appreciates she has the upper hand now and doesn't relent at once"* (3:89). When Richard tries to kiss her, she refuses but promises to kiss him at some point in the night—"maybe" (3:90). Richard coaxes her into the moonlight, and they sit together on the rowboat. She relates sneaking out of the house past her bedtime and tells him she must return before 10 o'clock, when her parents go to bed.

Richard gloomily blames her letter for what transpired the previous night. Withholding the details, he says her letter made him view life as a "tragic farce" (3:91). Muriel begs him to tell her what happened, but he continues that he even considered suicide. Eventually he admits he spent the money he saved to buy a gift for her at the Pleasant Beach House, the "secret house of shame." He lies that he went with a Princeton football star and that they entertained two chorus girls—one of whom tried to kiss him. At one point, he goes on, he fought a barkeep to defend the chorus girl's honor, then got drunk on champagne. She demands to know if he kissed her and starts to cry, shouting he is a liar when he says they did nothing. When she tries to run, he grabs her by the arm, begging her to listen, but she bites him and takes off toward the path.

In a tone of painful despair, Richard now insists she go home, which stops her. Working himself up over her accusation, he indignantly admits, "And what if I did kiss her once or twice? I only did it to get back at you!" (3:95). She relents that she will forgive him as long as he promises he did not fall in love, which he does. Again he tries to kiss her, and this time she shyly accepts. They complain about the long wait until marriage, and again he quotes Swinburne. Muriel—*"shocked and delighted"* at the line "more beautiful than God!"—scolds him lightly. They pledge mutual love for one another, and Muriel suggests they go to Niagara Falls for their honeymoon. "That dump where all the silly fools go?" Richard responds. "No, we'll go to some far-off wonderful place." Searching his mind for an alternative, he *"calls on Kipling to help him"*: "Somewhere out on the Long Trail—the trail that is always new—on the road to Mandalay! We'll watch the dawn come up like thunder out of China!" (3:97). "That'll be wonderful, won't it," she dreamily utters, her head on his shoulder, as the curtain falls.

### Act 4, Scene 3

The Miller family sitting room, Nat and Essie sitting contentedly in their chairs. Nat reads from a pile of Richard's books, which he has confiscated, while Essie contentedly sews her doily. Mildred has confessed to Richard's liaison with Muriel, so they are no longer worried. In fact, they sound quite forgiving, though he must be punished somehow. Nat praises George Bernard Shaw as a "comical cuss—even if his ideas are so crazy they oughtn't to allow them to be printed"; Algernon Swinburne has a "fine swing to his poetry—if he'd only choose some other subjects besides loose women"; and he likes the *Rubáiyát of Omar Khayyám* even better the second time around, "that is, where it isn't all about boozing" (3:98). Essie teases him for pretending to read them for Richard's sake, as he has been devouring them all evening.

Nat plans to bluff Richard into believing that he will no longer be permitted to attend Yale. Essie responds by complimenting their son on his "exceptional brain," the proof ironically in "the way he likes to read all those deep plays and books and poetry," which rouses a sly smile from her husband. She continues that Richard "could do worse" than Muriel, though she had a poor opinion of her in the past (3:99). She informs him that Arthur is with Elsie Rand, Mildred with her latest beau, and Sid and Lily have gone to listen to the orchestra. "Then, from all reports," Nat says, "we seem to be completely surrounded by love!" In addition, McComber apologized earlier that day, admitting that "kids would be kids," and Nat secured a profitable new advertiser for his newspaper. "It's been a good day, Essie—a damned good day!" (3:101).

Richard enters *"like one in a trance, his eyes shining with a dreamy happiness, his spirit still too exalted to be conscious of his surroundings, or to remember the threatened punishment"* (3:101). Essie expresses immediate concern, but her husband says, "No. It's love, not liquor, this time" (3:102). He asks her to leave them alone and tells Richard to take a seat. This snaps Richard out of his reverie. Chastising him for his drunken behavior, Nat reveals that he knows about the "tart" at the Pleasant Beach House. Richard swears he never went to bed with her. Nat believes him but asks how he met the lady; when Richard points out that his father would not want him to snitch, Nat agrees, then commenses to lecture him about PROSTITUTION. He informs his son that prostitutes do, in fact, serve a purpose—"it's human nature"—but that one must be careful. "You just have what you want and pay 'em and forget it" (3:104). His delivery becomes increasingly lame and faltering, and Richard finally breaks in, shocked that his father would suggest such a thing

when he plans to marry Muriel. Delighted at this, Nat still believes Richard needs punishment and threatens to forbid him from attending Yale. This backfires, as not going to college would allow Richard to marry Muriel faster. Nat insists, then, that he *must* go to Yale.

Richard calls his mother back inside, and they comment on the beautiful moonlit night. Richard asks if he might stay up and watch the Moon set, and his parents agree he can. Richard kisses his mother good night, then his father, and rushes out onto the porch. "First time he's done that in years," Nat says, bewildered. "I don't believe in kissing between fathers and sons after a certain age—seems mushy and silly—but that meant something!" (3:106). Nat asks Essie for permission not to say his prayers, as he is too tired; she agrees he should go straight to bed. She turns out the light, and the room fills with moonlight. He puts his arm around her while they both gaze out the window at their son. "There he is," Nat says, "like a statue of Love's Young Dream," and then he quotes from the *Rubáiyát*: "Yet, Ah, that Spring should vanish with the Rose! / That Youth's sweet-scented manuscript should close!" (3:107). They both express the notion that fall and winter can be beautiful too, as long as they are together. She kisses him, and they move silently toward the front parlor as the curtain falls.

## COMMENTARY

*Ah, Wilderness!* is most often read as a complicated wish-fulfillment fantasy on the part of its author—an idealized projection onto the stage that revisits O'Neill's tumultuous past and offers a subtextual commentary on his difficult present as a largely absentee parent and, more broadly, the tumultuous 1930s. That O'Neill means the Miller home to call to mind his own family's house, Monte Cristo Cottage in New London, Connecticut, is clear from his STAGE DIRECTIONS, in which the Millers' sitting room is nearly identical to that of the Tyrones' in his most autobiographical play *Long Day's Journey into Night*. Aside from having five chairs instead of four, along with a few small-town middle-class flourishes, the only substantial difference lies in the choice of books on the shelves: Richard Miller hoards his "advanced" literature in his room, whereas Edmund Tyrone, O'Neill's closest autobiographical avatar, has a bookcase reserved for his collection in the sitting room itself, books by Oscar Wilde, FRIEDRICH NIETZSCHE, and AUGUST STRINDBERG that starkly contrast with the more conventional fare of his father, James. The difference in time periods—1912 for the later play, 1906 for *Ah, Wilderness!*—is autobiographically significant as well. In 1912, O'Neill was diagnosed with tuberculosis, a lung disease he believed he had contracted during his rootless time drifting through waterfront dives in Manhattan and sailor towns around the globe. In that year as well, O'Neill had attempted suicide at JIMMY "THE PRIEST'S" bar. In 1906, on the other hand, his parents were traveling abroad on an international tour; O'Neill, like Richard, was about to matriculate into an Ivy League school (Princeton, not Yale), and he and his brother, JAMES O'NEILL, JR. (Jamie) had the run of the town—with its rather confusing blend of conventional pleasantries and debauched revelries. "If he ever had it," Travis Bogard writes of O'Neill's choice for *Ah, Wilderness!,* "the summer of 1906 was a time of freedom from pressure and pain" (359).

*Ah, Wilderness!* was a terrific success at the box office, and it remains one of O'Neill's most revived plays. Nevertheless, at the time of composition and well after, the playwright was struggling desperately with his "god play" DAYS WITHOUT END, a full-length experimental work that, after over two years of revision, disappointingly flopped when the Theatre Guild finally produced it in December 1933. O'Neill then sank into a depressive state that effectively isolated him from the stage for 12 years. (*Days Without End* has fallen into well-deserved obscurity and is rarely revived.) "From a biographer's point of view," Stephen A. Black suggests of the incongruity of composing such different plays in the same period, "the most important aspect of the composition of *Ah, Wilderness!* is that O'Neill could write it at all, especially at a time when writing *Days Without End* immersed him in unpleasant aspects of his relations with his mother and his wives. That it could spring fully formed from a night's sleep implies that in fundamental ways

he understood the family relations that allow the young to grow into their various selves and emerge from dependency" (379–380).

*Ah, Wilderness!* obscures most of the O'Neill family's dysfunctional aspects. O'Neill treats these in many plays, but they are vanquished from the Millers' dramatis personae through personality distribution (Bogard 360–361): His father JAMES O'NEILL's better qualities are discovered in Nat and his shortcomings in Sid; his brother Jamie's corrupting nature and streetwise sensibility can be found in Wint, Sid, and the salesman; and, if less obviously, his mother MARY ELLEN "ELLA" O'NEILL's maternal side has been conferred upon Essie and Lily Miller. O'Neill expressed a profound warmth toward these revised, fictional family members. "And do you like Pa and Ma and all the rest?" he asked his friend and editor Saxe Commins. "Fine people, all of them, to me. Lovable" (quoted in Alexander 179). His true love from New London, BEATRICE ASHE, who declined to marry O'Neill in 1916 for his drunkenness and lack of prospects, combines in Mildred (looks), Lily (unrequited love), and Muriel (exposure to licentious poetry by her intellectual boyfriend) (Alexander 175–178). It was, coincidentally or not, 16 years since Beatrice had broken off her engagement to O'Neill, as it is with Lily and Sid in the play.

O'Neill BIOGRAPHERS Arthur and Barbara Gelb find that *Ah, Wilderness!* and *Long Day's Journey* consist of "two sides of a coin—one a genial glimpse of what the O'Neill family, at its best, aspired to be, and the other a balefully heightened picture of his family at its worst" (192). The Gelbs and others find the source of the Miller family chiefly in O'Neill's boyhood friend Arthur McGinley's family, and many of their names are adapted for O'Neill's purposes. Nat Miller also resembles Frederick Palmer Latimer, a local judge who edited the *New London Telegraph* and encouraged O'Neill's writing career in the early 1910s. Latimer once remarked that O'Neill might one day exhibit "a very high order of genius" (quoted in Sheaffer 405). Fending off assumptions that the play was strictly autobiographical, O'Neill asserted that he personally had never enjoyed a childhood of any kind. "That's the way I would have *liked* my boyhood to have been," he said about the play. "It was a sort of wishing out loud" (quoted in Alexander 173).

O'Neill's title comes from one of his favorite poems, *The Rubáiyát of Omar Khayyám,* which Richard is startled to discover his family, even the priggish Aunt Lily, are familiar enough with to recite lines from memory. Omar Khayyám's lines, and the 11th–12th century Persian writer's body of work as a whole, reflects O'Neill's desire to mourn the loss of an innocent and fragile time but also to celebrate the joyful nature of life's sensual pleasures combined with romantic love. O'Neill derived the title *Ah, Wilderness!* from this quatrain, translated by Edward Fitzgerald:

A Book of Verses underneath the Bough,
A Jug of Wine, a Loaf of Bread—and Thou
Beside me singing in the Wilderness—
Oh, Wilderness were Paradise enow!

O'Neill's decision to replace *Oh* with *Ah* changes the meaning of the title more significantly than it may appear at first. He believed the interjection *ah* better expressed the sense of nostalgia he was looking for (Gelb 197), specifically a "nostalgia for our lost simplicity and contentment and youth" (quoted in Alexander 186). But if John Patrick Diggins considers *Ah, Wilderness!* "a testament to the country's character, especially the 'homely decency' of the much-maligned middle-class" (256), strangely, the title, as Thomas F. Van Laan has pointed out, places the emphasis squarely on the tragedy of life in the wilderness, not on the hopeful paradise now associated with the mythic American middle class (100).

Producers of the play's many revivals often misdirect their audiences' attention to "paradise," a phenomenon Doris Alexander considers "more than a desecration, by producers ignorant of the past, who tried to make it live as a lie about the nature of American life in the present" (188). It would be a travesty, for instance, for a production to adopt contemporary furnishings for the Miller home—or from any other time—as opposed to the carefully designated turn-of-the-20th-century look O'Neill specifies in his stage directions. O'Neill was, to use his character Cornelius "Con" Melody's favorite quote from Lord Byron in *A TOUCH OF*

*THE POET,* "among them, not of them." The "large small-town" folk represented in *Ah, Wilderness!* are meant to capture "the spirit of a time that is dead now," O'Neill explained to his son EUGENE O'NEILL, JR., "with all its ideals and manners & codes . . . a memory of the time of my youth—not *my* youth but of the youth in which my generation spent youth—" (quoted in Gelb 191).

Middle-class America generally stands as an oppositional sphere in American literature, particularly for modernists like O'Neill—a sphere in which the sensitive soul is torn asunder by those same "manners & codes" that radiate from the stage so compassionately in *Ah, Wilderness!* For example, in O'Neill's first full-length play, *BREAD AND BUTTER,* the autobiographical character John Brown's social philosophy more closely resembles the brand of PHILOSOPHICAL ANARCHISM (what one of O'Neill's favorite philosophers Max Stirner called "egoism") that O'Neill finally claimed as his own, rather than the communist anarchism of Emma Goldman that Richard Miller touts in *Ah, Wilderness!* In the latter play, Richard declares that rather than observe the Fourth of July holiday with the rest of the family, he will "celebrate the day the people bring out the guillotine again and I see Pierpont Morgan being driven by in a tumbrel!"—to which his father, Nat Miller, replies, "son, if I didn't know it was you talking, I'd think we had Emma Goldman with us" (3:13).

In *Bread and Butter,* on the other hand, John intones the egoist's line to his father that his unconventional sister's "duty to herself stands before her duty to you" (1:142). "Rot! Damned rot!" Brown rejoins, "only believed by a lot of crazy Socialists and Anarchists" (1:142). John continues with a line that might have come directly from Stirner, who held ownership of the self, what he called "ownness," above all other considerations: "You consider your children to be your possessions, your property, to belong to you. You don't think of them as individuals with ideas and desires of their own" (1:143). O'Neill once distinguished between comedy and tragedy as essentially based upon the actions of the characters in the end; as Doris Alexander notes: "Tragic characters are driven from within to violent conclusions; comic characters make comic compromises" (188). As such, John Brown commits suicide in the end of *Bread and Butter,* while *Ah, Wilderness!* concludes with Richard Miller gazing romantically at the moonlight.

O'Neill later applied John's parenting strategy to his own wayward son, SHANE O'NEILL, with whom, along with Eugene O'Neill, Jr., he had celebrated the Fourth of July at Casa Genotta, his Sea Island home, two months before conjuring *Ah, Wilderness!* in his sleep. "You must find yourself," he advised Shane, "and your own self. You've got to find the guts in yourself to take hold of your own life. No one can do it for you and no one can help you. You have got to go on alone, without help, or it won't mean anything to you" (quoted in Bowen 267). The significance of O'Neill assigning communist anarchism to Richard Miller and philosophical anarchism to John Brown is that Miller is the subject of a comedy, and his social philosophy makes him sound naïve in the idyllic, middle-class atmosphere of the Miller home; Brown, on the other hand, is a tragic figure, and his philosophy—O'Neill's—proves itself impotent against the malignant forces of middle-class social convention (Dowling 56). Ellen Campbell has suggested that in *Ah, Wilderness!* "our most distinguished, truth-telling dramatist explores the conventions of this sector of our culture [the middle class] and finds many of its values life-enhancing." If this is the case, O'Neill had clearly revised his thinking since *Bread and Butter* and, more importantly, since the birth of his children. By the 1930s, after three children, a world war, and the devastating effects of a depression, he seemed to have found surcease in a time, now dead, when family living seemed to make more sense than it had in the 1900s and 1910s.

"If there seems to be a large dash of sentiment," one reviewer promised her readers, "let us hasten to assure the more modern minded that they need have no fear. O'Neill's writing is always straight" (Wyatt 149). Richard's movement toward experience—his time at the ironically named Pleasant Beach Hotel, his exposure to prostitution and drunkenness there, his accompanying hangover, his deliriousness over Muriel's kiss, his exposure to his father's view on the nature of male sexuality, and so on—appears to move him toward the wilderness and away from paradise. But then he returns, perhaps more worldly-wise but even more contented to enjoy the beauty of the moon and the warmth of his loving family (symbolized by his kiss on Nat's cheek).

*Ah, Wilderness!* and *Long Day's Journey* are, in fact, two sides of a coin for O'Neill's recollections of family life in the early 20th century (comedy/tragedy), but those two sides exist within *Ah, Wilderness!* as well. Tommy's firecrackers to celebrate the Fourth, for instance, are comical but also add a sensation of outer violence juxtaposed with the sitting room's inner peace. At first they make the family *"jump in their chairs,"* but then Essie orders her son to take his noisemakers to the back of the house and says, "Now we'll have a little peace." *"As if to contradict this,"* O'Neill writes, *"the bang of firecrackers and torpedoes begins from the rear of the house, left, and continues at intervals throughout the scene, not nearly so loud as the first explosion, but sufficiently emphatic to form a* disturbing punctuation *to the conversation"* (3:8, emphasis mine).

Additionally, the scene with Belle is a cunning and perverse foreshadowing of Richard and Muriel's quarreling and lovemaking on the beach in act 4, scene 2. Richard's two scenes with young women—first Belle, the prostitute at Pleasant Beach, and then Muriel, the "proper" girl on an actual beach—present the adolescent young man with two options in sexual relations. In comedy, Thomas Van Laan specifies, "any deviation from the social norm is preposterous" (107), and so in the context of this play Richard inevitably repents and chooses Muriel. O'Neill at his age, and his avatar Edmund Tyrone in *Long Day's Journey,* had pursued the Belle option, and the need for repentance haunted the playwright for the rest of his life. O'Neill's subliminal wish fulfillment comes through clearly, then, when he moves Richard away from Belle. In actual life, the 16-year-old O'Neill would have gone upstairs, and Nat Miller, innocent and respectable as he appears on the surface, would have understood and forgiven.

O'Neill did find love in marriage, but it brought on the kind of all-consuming, alternating feelings of adoration and suffering we find in WELDED, a play about his relationship with his second wife, AGNES

BOULTON, that also includes a prostitution scene. (Timo Tiusanen aptly regards Richard and Muriel's dialogue on the beach as a parody of *Welded*, [243].) "The play is about ninety percent wish fulfillment and ten percent the real thing," writes Michael Manheim. "If anything, it is O'Neill's attempt to dramatize not his early life so much as his idealized recall of life before the Fall" (101). According to O'Neill's WORK DIARY, Richard's complacent acceptance of a stable middle-class existence will be short-lived, however. O'Neill, in fact, planned a sequel to *Ah, Wilderness!* in early September 1934. This time, the play would be a tragedy that would explicitly convey the sense of loss he meant audiences to experience with *Ah, Wilderness!*

O'Neill's sequel was to take place in either 1919 or 1921. In it, Sid has reformed because a doctor informed him he might die if he continued drinking (more echoes of O'Neill's brother Jamie, who did die of alcoholism), but he now takes on a hypocritical "puritanical disapproval of drink." Essie dies in 1919 from the shock of one of her sons' death while fighting in World War I. Tommy, whom O'Neill describes as "typical, restless, hard-drinking wild disintegrated 'lost generation'" (Floyd 1981, 241), was an aviator in the war and also dies in 1919. All we know of Lily is that she now runs the Miller household, while Mildred is on the verge of divorce, has taken a lover, and is a negligent parent of two. Richard has graduated from Yale, taken a position at Nat's paper, and then gone to war, returning "maimed, embittered, idealism murdered." Arthur is a loathsome businessman, a "smug, social-climbing country club, golfing success" who marries into a wealthy family and has children; like his sister, he takes a lover on the side. Nat Miller is "prostrated by the death of his wife—lost, bewildered in changed times—waiting for death—feels children alien, can't understand their view" (Floyd 1981, 242).

Since the premiere of *Ah, Wilderness!*, some critics curtly assert that given the play's quaint setting, sentimental plot, and complacent characters, if O'Neill had not been its author, "it would have faded into the oblivion it deserves" (quoted in Van Laan 100). Others contend that *Ah, Wilderness!* is far more complicated than it at first appears, a "nostalgic family comedy," yes, but one "whose true meanings exist in the currents of evil and despair beneath its bright and sparkling surface" (Kimbel 137). There can be no question of the play's sentimentality, as O'Neill made his intention in this respect perfectly clear: In his own words, the play's "whole importance and reality depend on its conveying a mood of memory in exactly the right illuminating blend of wistful grin and lump in the throat—the old tears-and-laughter stuff on exactly the right delicately caressing tone" (quoted in Alexander 186).

Van Laan identifies three clichés O'Neill adopts to his purposes: "sentimental stereotypes," the "Fourth of July myth of independence and equality," and the "notion of family life as the ideal form of existence" (Van Laan 101). Such clichés make the play as paradoxical in American literary history as it does in the O'Neill canon. (O'Neill did try his hand at a full-length comedy on the American middle-class much earlier with his 1916 play NOW I ASK YOU, which also shows the disaffected middle-class rebel entertaining suicide à la Henrik Ibsen's heroine Hedda Gabler.) O'Neill himself recognized that *Ah, Wilderness!* was "out of my previous line" and explained his mysterious deviation this way:

> My purpose was to write a play true to the spirit of the American large small town at the turn-of-the-century [sic]. Its quality depended upon the atmosphere, sentiment, an exact evocation of the mood of a dead past. To me, the America which was (and is) the real America found its unique expression in such middle-class families as the Millers, among whom so many of my own generation passed from adolescence into manhood. (quoted in Kimbel 137–138)

But deliberately or not, *Ah, Wilderness!* urges us to contemplate our own realities in the face of idealization, thus powerfully answering the question of why the "master of the misbegotten," America's most tragic dramatist, would write a comedy essentially romanticizing middle-class America. In *Ah, Wilderness!* everything turns out as it should, the most sacred convention of comedy—that is, right until you step out of the theater.

## CHARACTERS

**Bartender** Bartender at the Pleasant Beach Hotel. O'Neill describes him as a *"stocky young Irishman with a foxily cunning, stupid face and a cynically wise grin"* (3:51). In act 3, scene 1, the bartender serves Richard Miller and gets Richard very drunk in collusion with a prostitute from New Haven named Belle. When a salesman arrives, he advises the bartender to throw Richard out for being underage, which he does. When Belle reveals his name, the salesman identifies Richard as the son of Nat Miller. Fearing Miller will run him out of town, the bartender rails against Belle for not telling him beforehand; he then threatens to call the police. Belle swears revenge and later delivers a note to Richard's father, Nat Miller's, office accusing the bartender of knowingly serving Richard.

**Belle** A prostitute from New Haven. Belle is one of two prostitutes whom Wint Selby, a classmate of Arthur Miller's at Yale University, has invited to his town to celebrate the Fourth of July with sex. Wint had originally hoped Arthur Miller would entertain her while he went upstairs with the other, named Edith; but Arthur is previously engaged, so his younger brother Richard goes instead. O'Neill describes Belle as *"twenty, a rather pretty peroxide blonde, a typical college 'tart' of the period, and of the cheaper variety, dressed with tawdry flashiness. But she is a fairly recent recruit to the ranks, and is still a bit remorseful behind her make-up and defiantly careless manner"* (3:51). In act 3, scene 1, Richard and Belle perform a comic, though harshly realistic scene in which Belle attempts to seduce him upstairs for a sexual liaison that will cost him five dollars. Belle voices confusion about Richard when he refuses her advances; he seems innocent but also wealthy and fairly knowledgeable. When Belle turns against him viciously, he gives her the five dollars for nothing. This delights her but perplexes her further about his intentions. When a salesman enters the bar, Belle moves to his table, as Richard has annoyingly begun trying to reform her. The salesman identifies Richard as the son of the local newspaperman Nat Miller, and the bartender, fearful for his job, threatens to call the police if Belle refuses to leave. Belle swears revenge and delivers a note to Nat

Miller's office the following day, accusing the bartender of knowingly getting Richard drunk. Belle is one of many examples of prostitution in the O'Neill canon, though generally O'Neill's prostitutes are more nurturing and sympathetic characters.

**Davis, Sid** Essie Miller's brother and Nat Miller's brother-in-law. A ne'er-do-well newspaper reporter, Sid is 45 years old, *"short and fat, baldheaded, with the Puckish face of a Peck's Bad Boy who has never grown up"* (3:7). He dresses in once-fashionable but now faded and worn clothing. Though a talented reporter, he has recently been fired for drunkenness from his position on the *Standard* in Waterbury, Connecticut; however, Nat Miller will grant him a job at his paper. Sid has been in love with Lily Miller, Nat's sister, for 20 years, but she broke off their engagement 16 years prior to the action of the play because of his binge drinking. Nevertheless, they are still very much in love. "He's easily led," Essie says of her brother, trying to convince Lily to reconsider marrying him, "but there's no real harm in him" (3:29).

Sid gets drunk with Nat Miller at a picnic to celebrate the Fourth of July; when he returns to the Miller home for dinner, he amuses the family with his drunken antics and ribald sense of humor. Meanwhile, he has neglected to honor his promise to Lily to escort her to the fireworks show. When Essie eventually sends him away to sleep off his drunk, Lily accuses them all of enabling his alcoholism. After several hours, Sid returns to the sitting room, hungover and contrite. He begs Lily's forgiveness for missing their date; she ignores him at first, but once he begins weeping, she tenderly forgives him.

Sid epitomizes the word *avuncular*. It is Sid who nurses Richard Miller, after the teenager arrives home drunk, as in his own words, he "wrote the book" (3:74). He resembles O'Neill's father, James O'Neill, in his theatricality, steady drinking, and warmth; but he also represents the darker side of the play, calling to mind O'Neill's older brother, Jamie O'Neill—the failure of a roustabout punished too much as a child, bored with small-town existence, and rebelling in the only way he could. In act 4, scene 1, when he and Nat discuss

Richard's punishment for getting drunk, he says, "If you remember, I was always getting punished—and see what a lot of good it did me!" (3:79).

**McComber, David** Muriel McComber's father. A dry-goods merchant who advertises in Nat Miller's newspaper, McComber a typical small-town businessman dressed in plain black clothes whose appearance reflects his parochial views on love, literature, and life: *"He is a thin, dried-up little man with a head too large for his body perched on a scrawny neck, and a long solemn horse face with deep-set black eyes, a blunt formless nose and a tiny slit of a mouth"* (3:19). In act 1, McComber appears at the Miller home and attempts to coerce Nat Miller into putting an end to the brewing romance between his daughter Muriel and Nat's son Richard Miller. McComber considers Richard "dissolute and blasphemous" (3:19), a claim based chiefly on the letters Richard has written Muriel and the contaminating influence of the literature he exposes her to. When Nat takes offense at McComber's characterization of his son, McComber threatens to remove his advertising from his paper. Nat calls his bluff, saying that unless McComber apologizes, he will remove the advertisement himself and "encourage outside capital to open a dry-goods store in opposition to you that won't be the public swindle I can prove yours is!" (3:21). McComber leaves behind a letter from Muriel, one he coerced her to write that breaks off her relationship with Richard. McComber's "meek as pie" offstage apology that "kids would be kids" is one of the loose thematic threads that, in the convention of comedy, O'Neill ties neatly together in the end (101).

**McComber, Muriel** Richard Miller's girlfriend and David McComber's daughter. Muriel is a *"pretty girl with a plump, graceful little figure, fluffy, light-brown hair, big naïve wondering dark eyes, a round, dimpled face, a melting drawly voice"* (3:88). Richard has been accused by her father, David McComber, of corrupting her, and McComber threatens to remove his advertisement from Richard's father, Nat Miller's, newspaper if their relationship persists. He also forces Muriel to write Richard a letter breaking off the relationship herself. Although

we only meet Muriel in act 4, scene 2, her perceived betrayal fuels Richard's rebellious, spiritually wounded pose throughout the play. Muriel escapes from her parents' home at night to meet Richard on a moonlit strand of beach. She first appears *"in a great thrilled state of timid adventurousness"* (3:88). Throughout the scene, the two manipulate each others' emotions in the manner of adolescent love. When Richard quotes to her from Algernon Swinburne's "Laus Veneris"—"And lo my love, mine own soul's heart, more dear / Than mine own soul, more beautiful than God"—she is *"shocked and delighted"* but scolds him lightly for his blasphemy (3:97).

Muriel resembles the real-life Maibelle Scott, a young love of O'Neill's whom he wooed with rebellious literature; and John Patrick Diggins also finds her in O'Neill's early love interest Marion Welch, to whom O'Neill wrote romantic poetry in 1905 (161). In act 4, scene 1, Richard's sister Mildred Miller arrives with news from Muriel that she wishes to meet Richard that night. O'Neill and Scott also had a "go-between" named Mildred Culver; thus O'Neill uses the sister's name and the name of a family in the play who host a picnic that Mildred attends (Floyd 1985, 431–432).

**Miller, Arthur** Essie and Nat Miller's third son and Richard, Mildred, and Tommy Miller's older brother. Arthur is 19 and the eldest Miller child still living at home. A Yale student, Arthur is *"tall, heavy, barrel-chested and muscular, the type of football linesman of that period, with a square, stolid face, small blue eyes and thick sandy hair"* (3:6). Throughout the play, Arthur's *"manner is solemnly collegiate,"* and he dresses in the most fashionable college styles of the period. O'Neill portrays Arthur as a self-righteous and humorless small-town dullard, although a relatively harmless one compared to Edward Brown, Jr., in *Bread and Butter*. Arthur contributes little to the action of the play and is usually off with his girlfriend, Elsie Rand. There is some presence in his absence, however, as his classmate Wint Selby believes Arthur would be game to meet up with two "swift babies" from New Haven (3:34). This makes Arthur, who poses as a respectable young man beyond reproach, a hypocrite as well. His compassionate side emerges in act 3, scene 2, however, when he sings sentimental favorites to soothe his worried mother.

**Miller, Essie** Nat Miller's wife; Tommy, Mildred, Richard, and Arthur Miller's mother; and Sid Davis's sister. About 50 years old, Essie is *"a short, stout woman with fading light-brown hair sprinkled with gray, who must have been decidedly pretty as a girl in a round-faced, cute, small-featured wide-eyed fashion."* She commands other members of the household, especially her incompetent "second girl," Norah, in a *"bustling mother-of-the-family manner"* (3:7). Based on O'Neill's boyhood friend Art McGinley's mother, Evelyn "Essie" Essex McGinley (Sheaffer 405, Gelb 195), Essie is O'Neill's idealization of the middle-class mother figure: attentive to her children, stern but fair, innocently blind to the ways of the world, and somewhat illogical in her judgments, but in a charming and harmless way. Like her husband, Nat, to whom she is devoted, her love is so complete and unconditional that she can forgive nearly all of the family's minor transgressions—Richard's late-night, drunken behavior and secret liaison with his girlfriend Muriel McComber; her brother's heavy drinking; and even Norah's ineptitude. Critics compare her to Mrs. Brown in *Bread and Butter*, Margaret Anthony in THE GREAT GOD BROWN, and both Mrs. Light and Mrs. Fife in DYNAMO, among others, though she is even further idealized in the way that she devotes herself to her husband and children (Floyd 424). She resembles Mary Tyrone, who is based on O'Neill's mother, Mary Ellen "Ella" O'Neill, in many respects, though unlike Mary, Essie's "snobbery is short-lived, her guilt concerns her being over-weight, and her hysteria relates chiefly to her son's keeping late hours" (Manheim 101).

**Miller, Lily** Nat Miller's sister and Essie Miller's sister-in-law. Lily is 42 years old, *"tall, dark and thin. She conforms outwardly to the conventional type of old-maid school teacher, even to wearing glasses"* (3:7). She speaks softly and exudes a saintly air of kindness; although she is a spinster, she finds that her nieces and nephews (her brother Nat's children) and her students during the school year are sufficient to fulfill her maternal needs. Lily and Sid Davis, Essie's brother, fell in love 20 years before, but when he proposed to her, she refused on account of his regular drinking binges. Essie continues to urge her to marry Sid, as she knows the two love each other and has faith in Lily's ability to reform him.

Sid returns home drunk on the Fourth of July, having forgotten his promise to take Lily to the fireworks. At first she refuses to forgive him, but when guilt reduces him to tears, she comforts him reassuringly. Looking forward to Mary Tyrone, the avatar of O'Neill's mother in *Long Day's Journey into Night*, in the way Mary might have commented about her son Jamie (O'Neill's brother), Lily describes Sid as "irresponsible, never meaning to harm but harming in spite of himself" (quoted in Sheaffer 405). BIOGRAPHERS differ on who from O'Neill's childhood in New London, Connecticut, she might resemble most: Bessie Sheridan, a spinster schoolteacher (Sheaffer 195) or Lillian "Lil" Brennan (Gelb 195), both cousins of O'Neill's.

**Miller, Mildred** Essie and Nat Miller's daughter, and Tommy, Richard, and Arthur Miller's sister. Mildred is 15, vivacious, and romantic. O'Neill describes her as *"tall and slender, with big, irregular features, resembling her father to the complete effacing of any pretense at prettiness"* (3:6). Nevertheless, her lively manner and *"fetching smile"* make her considered attractive by all who know her. Mildred's character has a slight role in the play, and when she is not innocently spending time with local boys, she plays the role of childish observer to the more mature goings-on in the family. Although she does not approve of Richard's disobedience, she appears visibly impressed with his romantic side and at one point acts as a go-between for him and his girlfriend, Muriel McComber.

**Miller, Nat** Essie Miller's husband; Tommy, Mildred, Richard, and Arthur Miller's father; and Lily Miller's brother. O'Neill describes Nat as *"in his late fifties, a tall, dark, spare man, a little stoop-shouldered, more than a little bald, dressed with an awkward attempt at sober respectability imposed upon an innate heedlessness of clothes,"* with eyes that are *"fine, shrewd, humorous"* (3:7). Miller is the father of five sons and one daughter. The owner of the local *Evening Globe,* Nat is O'Neill's idealization of the middle-class head of household: a good provider, responsible, fair-minded, caring, intellectual when necessary, and extremely protective of his family. He drinks, but only socially, and spends most of his evenings home with his wife, Essie, whom he adores. In act 1, local dry-goods merchant David McComber comes to the Miller home and threatens to remove his advertisements from Nat's newspaper if Nat refuses to punish Richard for sending his daughter what he considers obscene poetry—Wilde, Swinburne, Omar Khayyám, among others. Nat responds by calling his bluff and, in turn, threatening to remove the advertisement himself and back an outside dry goods merchant to compete with McComber. When he discovers Richard has spent a night with a "tart," he falteringly explains to his teenage son that human nature demands prostitution, but to be careful not to entangle it in his life. This revolts Richard, since he plans to marry Mildred, and Nat happily drops the subject. Nat also delights in reading Richard's "advanced" literature, prompting Essie to tease him for pretending to read it to keep an eye on Richard, but actually enjoying it himself.

O'Neill's biographers have found three sources for Nat Miller from Eugene O'Neill's youth in New London: His character is a composite portrait of John McGinley, his boyhood friend Art McGinley's father; Judge Frederick Palmer Latimer, the editor of the *New London Telegraph,* whom O'Neill worked under for a time; and O'Neill's own father, James O'Neill (Sheaffer 405; Gelb 195). Nat Miller is, according to Thomas F. Van Laan, the most valued male figure in the context of the play, given that Nat is "a respectable, professionally successful, adult male with more common sense, wisdom, and self-discipline than the other adult males of the play" (104). Nat's character closely resembles James Tyrone, the character based on James O'Neill in *Long Day's Journey into Night.* But in contrast to the elder Tyrone, as Michael Manheim explains, "the pomposity is short-lived, the drinking controlled, the compulsion [for his profession] healthy, and the illusions—which concern a distaste for bluefish—the subject for a good deal of harmless family mirth" (101).

**Miller, Richard**    Essie and Nat Miller's fourth son; Tommy, Mildred, and Arthur Miller's brother. Richard is one of a long line of Eugene O'Neill's autobiographical avatars, including John Brown in *Bread and Butter,* the Poet in Fog, Robert Mayo in Beyond the Horizon, Stephen Murray in *The* Straw, and Simon Harford in More Stately Mansions, all of whom culminate in his intensely personal character of Edmund Tyrone in *Long Day's Journey into Night.* But unlike the others, Richard is innocent and curious, rather than prematurely experienced, tragic, and cynical. In appearance, Richard takes after both parents, as Edmund Tyrone does, but he differs in that he is *"of medium height, neither fat nor thin"* nor handsome, in contrast to the tall and wiry Edmund (and O'Neill). In temperament, however, he comes closer: *"There is something of extreme sensitiveness added—a restless, apprehensive, defiant, shy, dreamy, self-conscious intelligence about him. In manner he is alternately plain simple boy and posey actor solemnly playing a role"* (3:12).

Enamored by some of the same authors, poets, and playwrights who had influenced O'Neill as a young man—so-called advanced literature represented by such writers as Algernon Swinburne, George Bernard Shaw, and Oscar Wilde—Richard is given to quoting passages from these writers to help express his moods. He disdains the Fourth of July holiday as a "stupid farce." "I'll celebrate the day the people bring out the guillotine again and I see Pierpont Morgan being driven by in a tumbrel!" His tolerant father responds: "Son, if I didn't know it was you talking, I'd think we had Emma Goldman with us" (3:13). Richard Miller hoards his radical literature in his room, whereas Edmund Tyrone openly has a bookcase reserved for his collection in the sitting room. Unlike Edmund, Richard seems as yet incapable of expressing his feelings and desires in his own words. Consequently, one gets the impression that his adolescent romance with Muriel McComber seems fuelled more by romantic poetry than by love for the 15-year-old.

At 16, Richard is slated to attend Yale University, but his adoration of Muriel makes him wish he was heading straight for the workplace, specifically his father's newspaper, so they might be married sooner. Thus, when Nat Miller punishes him for ignoring a curfew by telling him he cannot attend Yale, Richard is delighted; so Nat comically reverses the punishment—now Richard *must* go to Yale. The structure of the play revolves around Richard's movement from innocence toward experience, a quest he consciously views as revenge against Muriel, whose father had forced her to write a letter breaking off their relationship. It begins when Richard accepts an invitation from his brother Arthur's college friend Wint Selby to go to the ironically named Pleasant Beach Hotel, where he is exposed to prostitution and gets drunk for the first time. The following day, he experiences his first hangover, which is mild, then defies his parents' punishment that he must stay home and meets Muriel at a moonlit beach, where they quarrel but eventually kiss. When Richard arrives home, Nat Miller explains his view on the nature of male sexuality—that prostitutes are essentially a product of human nature, and so the best thing is to "have what you want and pay 'em and forget it" (3:104). This philosophy disgusts Richard, who plans to be faithful to Muriel. Richard thus moves toward "wilderness" away from "paradise," then returns, perhaps slightly more worldly-wise but more contented to enjoy the beauty of the moon and the warmth of his loving family (symbolized in the final scene by his kiss on Nat's cheek).

**Miller, Tommy**  Essie and Nat Miller's youngest son; Arthur, Richard, and Mildred's brother. The first character to appear on the stage, Tommy is *"a chubby, sun-burnt boy of eleven with dark eyes, blond hair wetted and plastered down in a part, and a shiny, good-natured face"* (3:5). An irrepressible youth, Tommy's mild antics and sustained misbehavior exasperate his mother. In act 1, scene 1, Tommy goes outside before the others have left the dining room and begins lighting off firecrackers that add a touch of anxiety in the otherwise idyllic atmosphere of the Miller home. At first they make the family *"jump in their chairs,"* but then Essie orders her son to the back of the house and says, "Now we'll have a little peace." *"As if to contradict this,"* O'Neill writes, *"the bang of firecrackers and torpedoes begins from the rear of the house, left, and continues*

*at intervals throughout the scene, not nearly so loud as the first explosion, but sufficiently emphatic to form a disturbing punctuation to the conversation"* (3:8, emphasis mine). Tommy's presence throughout the play is one of impish observer, misbehaving son, and annoying little brother.

**Norah**  The Miller family's "second girl" (servant). O'Neill describes Norah in similar ways to Cathleen, the Tyrones' second girl in *Long Day's Journey into Night*, as a *"clumsy, heavy-handed, heavy-footed, long-jawed, beamingly good-natured young Irish girl—a 'greenhorn'"* (27). Norah adds an Irish touch to the play, along with some comic relief as she appears incapable of doing her job and consistently arouses Essie Miller's exasperation. In act 2, Norah considers Sid Davis's drunken performance very funny, which looks forward to Cathleen's defense of James Tyrone's drinking in *Long Day's Journey* as a "good man's failing" (3:774).

**Salesman**  Traveling salesman and customer at the Pleasant Beach Hotel. O'Neill describes him as a *"stout, jowly-faced man in his late thirties, dressed with cheap nattiness, with the professional breeziness and jocular, kid-'em-along manner of his kind"* (3:58). When the salesman enters the back room of the bar with a grin, he observes Richard Miller and a prostitute named Belle glowering sullenly at a table. He and Belle recognize their mutual needs for one another—sex and money, respectively—and Belle sallies over to his table. The salesman enjoys Richard's drunken recitation of poetry, though Belle laughs at Richard. When the salesman advises the bartender to throw Richard out, as he is drunk and obviously underage, the bartender does so. Belle then reveals that Richard's last name is Miller, and the salesman recognizes him as the son of the powerful newspaperman Nat Miller. He goes out to help Richard home, in respect to Nat, whom he considers "a good scout" (3:62). The salesman shares some traits with Jamie O'Neill, whose most successful role was in the play *The Traveling Salesman*. Nevertheless, Doris Alexander points out that with this salesman character, O'Neill reverses all that his brother had done to him in adolescence: Instead of coaxing him to drink, the salesman sends him out of the bar; instead of seducing him with prostitutes, he takes Richard's away; and in the end, rather than egging him on to further exploits, he leads him safely back home (3:182).

**Selby, Wint** A classmate of Arthur Miller's at Yale University. O'Neill describes him as a *"typical, good-looking college boy of the period, not the athletic but the hell-raising sport type. He is tall, blond, dressed in extreme collegiate cut"* (3:34). Wint has invited to town two prostitutes from New Haven named Belle and Edith, whom he refers to as "swift babies" (3:34), to celebrate the Fourth of July. Originally he hoped to match up Arthur Miller with Belle, but because Arthur is occupied with his girlfriend, Elsie Rand, Wint decides to take Arthur's younger brother Richard Miller instead. "I'm not trying to lead you astray, understand," he assures Richard disingenuously in act 2 (3:34). In this way, Wint resembles Jamie O'Neill, O'Neill's older brother, whom the playwright presents as having done precisely that—led him astray—through the character James "Jamie" Tyrone in *Long Day's Journey into Night*.

### BIBLIOGRAPHY

Alexander, Doris. *Eugene O'Neill's Creative Struggle: The Decisive Decade, 1924–1933.* University Park: Pennsylvania State University Press, 1992.

Black, Stephen A. *Eugene O'Neill: Beyond Mourning and Tragedy.* New Haven, Conn.: Yale University Press, 1999.

Bogard, Travis. *Contour in Time: The Plays of Eugene O'Neill.* Rev. ed. New York: Oxford University Press, 1988.

Bowen, Croswell, *The Curse of the Misbegotten: A Tales of House of O'Neill.* New York: McGraw-Hill, 1959.

Diggins, John Patrick. *Eugene O'Neill's America: Desire under Democracy.* Chicago: University of Chicago Press, 2007.

Dowling, Robert M. "On Eugene O'Neill's 'Philosophical Anarchism.'" *Eugene O'Neill Review* 29 (Spring 2007): 50–72.

Floyd, Virginia. *The Plays of Eugene O'Neill: A New Assessment.* New York: Ungar, 1985.

Floyd, Virginia, ed. *Eugene O'Neill at Work: Newly Released Ideas for His Plays.* New York: Ungar, 1981.

Gelb, Arthur, and Barbara Gelb. *O'Neill: Life with Monte Cristo.* New York: Applause Books, 2000.

Kimbel, Ellen. "Eugene O'Neill as Social Historian: Manners and Morals in *Ah, Wilderness!*" *Critical Essays on Eugene O'Neill*, edited by James J. Martine, 137–144. Boston: G. K. Hall & Co., 1984.

Manheim, Michael. *Eugene O'Neill's New Language Of Kinship.* Syracuse, N.Y.: Syracuse University Press, 1982.

Sheaffer, Louis. *O'Neill: Son and Artist.* Boston: Little, Brown, 1973.

Tiusanen, Timo. *O'Neill's Scenic Images.* Princeton, N.J.: Princeton University Press, 1968.

Van Laan, Thomas F. "Singing in the Wilderness: The Dark Vision in Eugene O'Neill's Only Mature Comedy." *The Critical Response to Eugene O'Neill*, edited by John H. Houchin, 152–160. Westport, Conn.: Greenwood Press, 1993.

Wyatt, Euphemia Van Rensselaer. "A Great American Comedy." *The Critical Response to Eugene O'Neill*, edited by John H. Houchin, 149–150. Westport, Conn.: Greenwood Press, 1993.

# *All God's Chillun Got Wings* (completed, 1923; first produced, 1924)

The PROVINCETOWN PLAYERS' production of Eugene O'Neill's two-act tragedy *All God's Chillun Got Wings* sparked one of the most controversial episodes in AMERICAN THEATER history. Such divergent organizations as the Societies for the Prevention of Vice and Crime, William Randolph Hearst's *New York American* newspaper, the Ku Klux Klan (KKK), and the municipal government of the City of New York all united against the Provincetown Playhouse's divisive premiere on May 15, 1924, in GREENWICH VILLAGE. The Provincetown Playhouse received poison-pen letters, bomb threats, warnings of race riots, and a host of other intimidations. The KKK in Long Island threatened to bomb the theater on opening night. "If you open this play," they warned O'Neill, "the theater will be bombed, and you will be responsible for all the people killed."

Another disturbing threat arrived in the form of a personal communication to O'Neill from the "Grand Kleagle" of the Georgia KKK: "You have a son [SHANE RUDRAIGHE O'NEILL]. If your play goes on, don't expect to see him again." In response, O'Neill scrawled a line across the bottom of the letter and sent it back at once. It read: "Go fuck yourself!" (quoted in Sheaffer 140).

Along with police protection, the Provincetown Players hired bodyguards to patrol the actors' dressing rooms on opening night. Hart Crane, the New York–based poet, wrote a friend that "there will be some kind of mobbing or terrors . . . and I expect to be there with my cane for cudgeling the unruly" (quoted in Sheaffer 142–143). The *New York Herald* set off this uproar when a reporter of theirs heard that the black actor PAUL ROBESON and the white actress Mary Blair would costar in the new O'Neill production. The basis of this outcry by the mainstream press and its largely white readership was that, as Hearst's *New York American* noted in a follow-up to the story, "the play requires that the white girl kiss the negro's hand on stage" (quoted in Sheaffer 135).

In accordance with municipal law, the Provincetown Playhouse submitted an application for a city permit to employ children as actors for the opening scene. Only a few hours before the show, however, the city turned them down with the dubious explanation that the children were too young, though they were early adolescents. The next week, a Broadway show was granted a permit to hire an eight-year-old, a clear message that the city wished to thwart the contentious O'Neill production. That night, either its director, James Light, or the stage manager, Harold McGee, read the children's scene out loud, and the show continued without further interruption. This solution, according to O'Neill in a letter to a Princeton University classmate, "enraged the police authorities, who not long after stirred up trouble for [O'Neill's play DESIRE UNDER THE ELMS]"; in spite of the commotion over *All God's Chillun*, O'Neill continued, "nothing at all happened, not even a single senile egg" (quoted in Clark 154n).

*All God's Chillun* is the second play of the Triumvirate, an experimental theater group that included O'Neill as playwright, KENNETH MACGOWAN as producer, and ROBERT EDMOND JONES for set design. It is one of many domestic dramas by O'Neill about the social and psychological complexities of marriage—including SERVITUDE, WELDED, the FIRST MAN, and notably LONG DAY'S JOURNEY INTO NIGHT—but this one appreciably stands out from the others, given the union is interracial. The plot charts the course of the relationship between a black man, Jim Harris, and a white woman, Ella Downey, from their preadolescent days as childhood sweethearts to their tumultuous marriage (significantly, each shares the first names of O'Neill's parents JAMES O'NEILL and MARY ELLEN "ELLA" QUINLAN O'NEILL. This interracial union, divisive for both black and white audiences of the early 20th century and beyond, ultimately destroys Jim's professional ambitions and sends Ella spiraling into violent psychopathology.

## SYNOPSIS

### Act 1, Scene 1

A street corner in lower Manhattan dividing a black ghetto from a white one. O'Neill describes the neighborhood, in which the action of the entire play is set, as *"a corner in lower New York at the edge of a colored district where three narrow streets converge"* (2:279). It is late in the day, and as the action moves forward, *"the street begins to grow brilliant with the glow of the setting sun"* (2:279). At left, the pedestrians are all white, and on stage right, they are all black. This ethnic contrast is vital to the scene: *"People pass, black and white, the Negroes frankly participants in the spirit of Spring, the whites laughing constrainedly, awkward in their natural emotion. Their words are lost. One hears only their laughter. It expresses the difference in race"*; a white tenor sings "Only a Bird in a Gilded Cage" in a *"high-pitched, nasal"* voice, and the blacks respond with a typical song of their own, "I Guess I'll Have to Telegraph My Baby" (2:279). Eight youngsters playing marbles on the sidewalk in the foreground are evenly divided in race and GENDER. Jim and Ella are the two outcasts of the group, taunted with the epithets "Jim Crow," "Sissy," and "Painty Face." Each admits they admire the other's color, Jim confessing that he drinks chalk with water to whiten himself, though "dat chalk only makes me feel kinder sick inside," and Ella responding, "I like black. Let's you and me swap" (2:282). After pledging to be sweethearts, Ella blows Jim a kiss, foreshadowing the scandalous kiss on his hand in the final scene of the play, and the curtain falls.

### Act 1, Scene 2

Nine years later on the same street corner, just after sunset. The pedestrians resume the racially distinct singing, speech, and laughter meant to starkly contrast the two ghettoes, but the *"street noises are now more rhythmically mechanical, electricity having taken the place of horse and steam"* (2:283). The whites are singing "Gee, I Wish That I Had a Girl," and the blacks sing "All I Got Was Sympathy." Shorty (white) and Joe (black), two teenage hoods, are talking about the boxing prowess of a prizefighter named Mickey. Mickey enters and boasts of his romance with Ella. All three had appeared as the sneering children in the previous scene. Jim enters, *"dressed in black, stiff white collar, etc.—a quiet-mannered Negro boy with a queerly-baffled, sensitive face"* (2:284). Jim has lost all the black dialect and street manners he had demonstrated in the first act, and he dreams of attending law school. Joe castigates him for meeting his requirements to graduate from high school. Haunted by their childhood romance, Jim has never fallen out of love with Ella and warns Mickey to "act square" with her; but Mickey, at first stunned by the challenge, returns the warning by accusing Jim, who has professional aspirations and whose father has done well in the trucking business, of "tryin' to buy white" (2:286).

Ella enters, having developed into a coarse and ill-mannered teenager. Jim asks whether she has turned into a bigot, since she has not talked to him in years; she responds in annoyance, "Haven't I been brought up alongside—Why, some of my oldest—the girls I've been to public school the longest with—" (2:287). Clearly she has. Jim tells Ella that if she ever needs "a true friend," she can find it in him; but before leaving, she contemptuously responds, "I've got lots of friends among my own—kind, I can tell you" (2:287). With nothing resolved between Jim or Ella, Joe berates Jim for being a race traitor. "What's all dis denyin' you's a nigger—an'

wid de white boys listenin' to you say it! Is you aimin' to buy white wid yo' ol' man's dough. . . ?" Jim submits to Joe's reasoning and reluctantly admits before departing for his graduation, "Yes. I am a nigger. We're both niggers" (2:288).

### Act 1, Scene 3

The same street corner five years later at night; the pedestrians' movements are slower, their voices softer, and their singing now halfhearted. Ella has given birth to, and subsequently lost to diphtheria, an illegitimate child by Mickey. Ella meets Mickey's friend Shorty, who offers her money on Mickey's behalf, but she refuses it because the child is dead. After Shorty accuses her of "travelin' around with Jim Crow," she tells Shorty that Jim is "the only white man in the world! Kind and white. You're all black—black to the heart" (2:291). Shorty exits after calling her a "nigger lover," and Jim, who has, O'Neill repeats, *"grown into a quietly-dressed, studious-looking Negro with an intelligent yet quietly-baffled face"* (2:292), appears looking shamefaced and exasperated. He has failed another class—his hard work and well-mannered aspect have done little to improve his poor performance in school. Jim has won Ella's heart, though she has not quite relinquished the racism of her upbringing. Ella consoles him with the backhanded line, "You've been white to me, Jim" (2:293). Jim cries out that his love runs so deep, he wants to be her slave—"yes, be your slave—your black slave that adores you as sacred!" (2:294). "Jim! Jim! You're crazy!" she shouts in alarm, "I want to help you, Jim—I want to help—" and the curtain falls (2:294).

### Act 1, Scene 4

On Jim and Ella's wedding day, outside an old brick church surrounded by a rusty iron gate on a *"bright sunny morning"* (2:295). Tenement buildings on either side of the churchyard evoke a *"stern, forbidding look,"* and their shades are *"drawn down, giving an effect of staring, brutal eyes that pry callously at human beings without acknowledging them"* (2:294–295). A Negro tenor sings repetitive stanzas, first with a *"contented, childlike melancholy"*—"Sometimes I feel like a mourning dove"; then a *"dreamy, boyish exultance"*—"Sometimes I feel like an eagle in the air"; and finally with *"a brooding, earthbound sorrow"*—"Sometimes I wish that I'd never been born" (2:295). The church bell rings once with a *"startling, metallic clang,"* and as if following a signal, white people pour from the tenements on the left and blacks from those on the right, then *"form into two racial lines on each side of the gate, rigid and unyielding, staring across at each other with bitter hostile eyes"* (2:295). Jim and Ella appear from the church door, which slams shut behind them. Terrified, Jim attempts to calm Ella by pointing out the sun's warmth and the deep blue sky. He calls out a taxi frantically to get them to a steamer to Europe, while Ella looks up at the sky *"with an expression of trancelike calm and peace"* (2:296), as the curtain falls.

### Act 2, Scene 1

Two years later at the Harris home, *"a flat of the better sort in the Negro district near the corner of Act One"* (2:297), on a beautiful spring morning. Jim's mother, Mrs. Harris, and sister Hattie Harris plan to give the apartment to Jim and Ella upon their arrival back in New York. The newlyweds had moved to France in an effort to live a life free from prejudice, but they decided to return home after only a year. Mrs. Harris is a hardworking, traditional woman who strives to improve her children's lifestyle; she is not overtly political, however. Though she missed her son while he lived in France, she also realizes that the French are more forgiving of a racially mixed couple than the less modern Americans and believes the couple would have lived a happier life abroad. Hattie, on the other hand, found the couple's departure from New York cowardly; they should have stuck to their guns amid the nation's racial turmoil as a political statement: "If they believe in what they've done, then let them face it out, live it out here, be strong enough to conquer all prejudice!" (2:299). The doorbell rings, and Mrs. Harris goes to answer it.

Jim enters, and the siblings warmly embrace. Jim explains that he and Ella decided to return to face their situation and allow Jim to return to law school. Though it was true that Ella's enlightened French neighbors had dismissed the mixed-race marriage, Ella herself could never accept it. While abroad, Ella turned anxious, isolated, morose, and

ashamed. She now suffers from nervous prostration, a condition that worsens precipitously over the course of act 2.

Ella enters with Mrs. Harris. Hattie's black pride is accentuated by a Congo mask she offers Jim and Ella as a housewarming gift—*"a Negro primitive mask from the Congo—a grotesque face, inspiring obscure, dim connotations in one's mind, but beautifully done, conceived in a true religious spirit. . . . It dominates* [the room] *by a diabolical quality that contrast imposes upon it"* (2:297). Ella responds to the present with open contempt. In spite of her marriage to a black man, which does not appear to have been consummated, she remains a racist. Jim offers to remove the mask, but Ella wants to keep it up for a laugh. Hattie accuses Ella of being a white supremacist, which she is, and for keeping Jim in his inferior status by discouraging him from returning to law school, which she has been. Ella screams for Jim to make Hattie leave. Jim demands that either she leaves, or he and Ella will. Hattie calmly agrees, and Mrs. Harris rushes from the room in tears.

Hattie pointedly announces that she and her mother "got a nice flat in the Bronx . . . in the heart of the Black Belt—the Congo—among our own people!" (2:304). Jim goes out to find his mother. Hattie and Ella scowl at each other in hatred, and then Hattie exits. From the window, Ella sees Shorty, now a pimp and a dope peddler, down on the street below. She calls to him, but he ignores her. The snub makes her recognize her situation; she calls for Jim, *"whimpering like a frightened child,"* then runs hysterically from the room (2:305).

### Act 2, Scene 2

The same apartment, early in the evening six months later. Ella has suffered a complete nervous breakdown. Her affliction stems from an inability to reconcile the love she has for her husband with her revulsion toward the black race. O'Neill symbolizes the onset of her insanity by shrinking the size of the room and lowering the ceiling, and the Congo mask now appears much larger. Jim is hunched over a pile of law books. Hattie tries to convince him to send Ella to an asylum for everyone's safety. While Ella sleeps, Hattie tells him, she raves, "Black! Black!"; while awake, she calls Hattie a "dirty nigger" (2:308). Jim appears to accept Ella's behavior, however. "I've got to be the whitest of the white," he tells his sister, in order to prove to Ella that he will stand by her. Hattie accuses him of being a traitor to his race and informs him that in one of Ella's raving fits, Ella admitted that she will not have a child with Jim because it will be black. In the end, unaffected by Hattie's argument, he pushes her gently out the door and states that from that point on, he will isolate Ella from everyone but the doctor.

Ella appears at the doorway clutching a carving knife menacingly. She moves toward him, prepared in her maniacal state to murder the only person who has stood by her. Jim catches her by the wrist, aghast at her murderous look. Ella then waffles from sounding like a meek child to abusively calling him a "dirty nigger," and back again (2:311). He persuades her to return to bed, but before exiting, *"her face is again that of a vindictive maniac,"* and she screams from the doorway, "Nigger!," and runs out, *"laughing with a cruel satisfaction"* (2:311). Now alone, Jim bows his head in agony as the curtain falls.

### Act 2, Scene 3
The same, six months later, just after sunset. The walls of the apartment appear closer still, the ceiling even lower. Ella enters holding the carving knife. *"She is pitifully thin, her face is wasted, but her eyes glow with a mad energy, her movements are abrupt and spring-like"* (2:311). She venomously addresses the mask, which looks even more magnified on the wall, pouring out a stream of racist invective with an intensity that surpasses any of her previous outbursts—"niggers, niggers everywhere. Hanging around, grinning, grinning—going to school—pretending they're white—taking examinations—" (2:312). This last thought stops her, and she cries out in terror that if Jim passes his exam, she will kill both him and herself. She projects Jim's ambitions upon the mask: "Be kind to you, treat you decent, and in a second you've got a swelled head, you think you're somebody, you're all over the place putting on airs. . . . What have you got against us? I married you didn't I? Why don't you let Jim alone?" She blames Jim's ambitions on the mask, which

she believes deliberately goaded him into following through with his professional ambition and, at the same time, prevented him from being "the whitest man that ever lived" (2:312).

Jim appears at the doorway with bloodshot eyes and an expression of *"crushed numbness"* (2:312). He holds a letter informing him he has failed the bar exam once again. Hearing the news, Ella *"grabs Jim by both hands and dances up and down,"* shouting perversely, "Oh, Jim I knew it! I knew you couldn't! Oh, I'm so glad, Jim! I'm so happy!" Taking down the mask *"with wild unrestraint,"* she sets it on the table and jams her knife through the center of it. "You devil!" Jim roars with his fists raised above his head. "You white devil woman!" (2:313). She assures him frantically that the "devil's dead" now, that she no longer needs to kill him or herself. "It couldn't live—unless you passed. If you'd passed it would have lived in you" (2:314).

Jim, now exhausted and resigned, pleads for her to stop, explaining he tried to "become a full-fledged Member" of the bar (i.e., the white race) so Ella might be proud of him. Ella prattles merrily in a childlike voice about the two of them playing the games they enjoyed as children—she blackening her face with shoe polish and he whitening his face with chalk—and kisses his hand, making him promise never to leave her. "Forgive me, God, for blaspheming You!" Jim shouts to the heavens *"in an ecstasy of religious humility."* "Let this fire of burning suffering purify me of selfishness and make me worthy of the child You send me for the Woman you take away!"

"I've only got a little time left and I want to play," Ella responds excitedly.

"Honey, Honey," he shouts, again in religious exaltation, "I'll play right up to the gates of Heaven with you!" and the curtain falls (2:315).

### CRITICAL COMMENTARY
Eugene O'Neill denounced the notion that *All God's Chillun* is primarily a race play, that it deals specifically with the American "negro problem" as opposed to standing on its own as a universal statement on love, marriage, and madness. O'Neill once submitted disingenuously that "the racial factor is incidental. The play is a character study of two

human beings" (quoted in Sheaffer 135). Indeed, he later considered producing a revival with a white Jim Harris to sidestep the race issue altogether. But it is difficult to imagine a white person at the time voicing the same complaints Jim does. Perhaps if the play were either produced or set in England, it is feasible that race would take a thematic back seat to socioeconomic CLASS, an issue of as paramount importance to that country as race is to the United States. Miscegenation, after all, was forbidden in 38 states in 1924. But more important, why include the initial expressionistic street scene that instantly establishes a powerful sense of New York's racial divide? Why the scene in which Joe demands that Jim admit he's a "nigger"? Why the marriage scene with its scowling church and the gauntlet of white and black separatists on the street out front? Why the Congo mask, and Hattie's strong activism and the pedantic tone of her conversation on race and marriage with Mrs. Harris? And so forth. As the play stands, if O'Neill honestly wished the racial factor to be "incidental," he could not have failed more utterly. But it is more likely that O'Neill made the statement to prevent his play from being considered solely a social protest play.

O'Neill's STAGE DIRECTIONS convey the play's expressionistic quality, though it is not pure EXPRESSIONISM. O'Neill's style in *All God's Chillun* is above the real but of it at the same time, an idiosyncratic brand of writing the playwright dubbed "super-naturalism." Most of what O'Neill creates is discernable in reality, though he adds stage directions that emphasize the psychological states his characters' environment engenders and heighten the contrasts that exist in actual life. As the walls grow ever closer in the final scenes, for instance, it calls to mind the various scene settings of *The* HAIRY APE. Travis Bogard writes, invoking the earlier play, that "the room is a cage, a cell to which the two are condemned" (195).

Act 1, scene 4, Jim and Ella's wedding day, steps up the play's expressionistic quality and powerfully highlights the "reality" of their situation. Neither side of the community approves of their union, much as neither whites nor blacks entirely condoned the play in actual life. Indeed, while the KKK and other racist groups harassed O'Neill and

the Provincetown group for putting on such a play, the black community also responded with a good deal of hostility. This was true partly because blacks found it demeaning to see a fellow black man so desperate to marry a white woman, and partly because Ella's character is morally and socially beneath Jim's, and thus their union affirmed the commonly held assumption of black inferiority—which, in fact, it did. In one *Nation* review, for instance, a critic wrote, "Why mate a first-rate Negro with a third-rate white woman? Because those are the facts. . . . Only this woman would have married a Negro in America today" (quoted in Miller 39). Nevertheless, W. E. B. DuBois, the most influential black activist of the era, championed *All God's Chillun,* writing that "Eugene O'Neill is bursting through [racial hatreds]. He has my sympathy, for his soul must be lame with the blows rained upon him. But it is work that must be done" (quoted in Sheaffer 138).

In the street scenes from act 1, O'Neill was possibly envisioning the intersection of Bleecker, Hudson, and Eighth Avenue, thus positioning his characters in the heart of Greenwich Village. O'Neill had by this time familiarized himself with both his adopted neighborhood and the AFRICAN AMERICANS who resided there. In his 1922 WORK DIARY, he jotted down the seed of the idea: "Play of Johnny T.—negro who married white woman—base play on his experiences *as I have seen it intimately*—but no reproduction, see it only as man's" (in Floyd 53, italics mine). The center (rather than the *"edge"*) of black life in lower Manhattan was traditionally located at the corner of Bleecker and Mercer, though by the mid-1920s, when the play appeared, the vast majority of blacks had already moved uptown to the Tenderloin district and Harlem. O'Neill's children in the first scene are most likely the angelic embodiments of the play's title, as they only show incipient signs of the racist worldview they will later adopt as adults—the "human race," as Jim calls it, rather than black or white, seems restricted to childhood. Hence Ella's need in the final scene to retreat back to their childhood in which interracial romance was an innocent, socially acceptable, and—importantly—nonsexual act.

Jim's scholastic difficulties, though O'Neill persistently decried any attempts at sociological criticism of the play, can be patently explained by the black sociologist and activist W. E. B. DuBois in his revolutionary study *The Souls of Black Folk* (1903). In this book, DuBois identifies the social psychology of "double consciousness" among African Americans, a condition in which blacks in the United States feel torn between two identities—American and black. The former is what they are, the latter what they are perceived to be. The most pernicious effect of this mental state is that with the white imposition of black low self-esteem, blacks often assume the lowly role whites project onto them. With the burden of nursing a racist, homicidal wife who will stop at nothing until her husband relinquishes his ambitions for equality, Jim again fails the bar exam. He cannot attain his ultimate goal, "to become a full-fledged Member" (2:315) of the legal community. "Passing" the exam and joining the bar are clear analogies for "passing" as white and gaining membership to the white race—and, ironically, he cannot because of his white wife and American society's mental sabotage.

Ella does love Jim, but the only way she can reconcile his "black" body with his "white" compassion is to refer to him often as "the whitest of the white" (2:291, 293, 304, 309, 312). By stabbing the mask in the final scene, as Travis Bogard phrases it, Ella has committed "symbolic genocide" (197). Jim might be considered an "Uncle Tom," or a black man who submits to white authority. O'Neill probably had this in mind, as in act 2, Ella, by that time thoroughly insane, refers to Jim as "Uncle Jim" (2:310). Jim also finds himself incapable, then, of fulfilling his true potential in a classroom filled with whites, though he has mastered the material, and his classmates and instructors show no open signs of racism:

It's all in my head—all fine and correct to a T. Then when I'm called on—I stand up—*all the white faces are looking at me*—and I can feel their eyes—I hear my own voice sounding funny, trembling—and all of a sudden it's all gone in my head ... and [I] give up—sit down—.... And it's the same thing in the written exams.... I learn it all, I see it, I understand it.... I know

each answer—perfectly. I take up my pen. *On all sides are white men starting to write.* ... but I can't remember any more—it fades—it goes—it's gone. (292–293, italics mine)

"Of course, the struggle between [Jim and Ella] is primarily the result of the difference in their racial heritage," O'Neill admitted in a 1924 interview to the *New York Times* critic Louis Kantor; but he insisted that "it is their characters, the gap between them and their struggle to bridge it which interests me as a dramatist, nothing else" (quoted in Kantor 46). *All God's Chillun* can be profitably read, in fact, as an early draft of O'Neill's intensely autobiographical masterpiece, *Long Day's Journey into Night*. Jim and Ella, the most apparent example, were O'Neill's parents' names, both of whom are depicted in *Long Day's Journey* as O'Neill remembered them in his early 20s. But the correspondences do not end there. Jim and Ella regress back into angelic childhood, just as Mary Tyrone, modeled on O'Neill's mother, MARY ELLEN "ELLA" O'NEILL, regresses back to her schoolgirl days at the Catholic seminary. Jim never achieves his goal to become a lawyer, just as James Tyrone/JAMES O'NEILL fails to reach Shakespearean stature on the stage. Both men are thwarted by the needs of their neurotic wives—Ella slowly driven to psychologically induced childhood by her own racism (O'Neill describes her kissing Jim's hand *"as a child might, tenderly and gratefully"* [2:315]), Mary driven back to childhood by a powerful morphine addiction. Both women lost a child to a fatal disease.

There is no doubt that, as T. S. Eliot wrote of O'Neill and his play, "He not only understands one aspect of the 'negro problem,' but he succeeds in giving this problem universality, in implying wider application" (quoted in Cargill et al. 169). But O'Neill's other statement that the race issue is "incidental" might lead some to forgo its racial aspect altogether. Wisely resisting this school of thought, Travis Bogard submits that "whatever O'Neill meant by the play's 'real intention,' what he has accomplished is, for 1924, a bold treatment of the social and personal problems that emerge from an interracial marriage" (193).

See also CENSORSHIP/FREE SPEECH.

## CHARACTERS

**Downey, Ella** Jim Harris's wife. In the opening scene, Ella, a white girl, accepts her black friend Jim Harris's invitation to be his sweetheart. Though Jim continues to love her through young adulthood, Ella becomes increasingly influenced by her prejudiced peers, and though she is never openly racist to Jim, she makes him feel ridiculous for continuing to see her as she was as a child. Ella has a child with the prizefighter thug Mickey, but the child, who never appears in the play, has died of diptheria by act 1, scene 3. Her life in disarray, she finally accepts Jim's overtures of love and eventually agrees to marry him, though she never fully accepts the social and psychological demoralization that comes with being married to a black man in the early 20th century. Over the course of their marriage, Ella's sanity slips away. At first, this is manifested in racist, homicidal tendencies, during which she makes every effort to thwart her husband's attempts to pass the bar exam and hence "pass" as white. In the final scene of the play, Ella regresses back into the angelic girl character in act 1, scene 1, a regression that speaks to the play's title: As a child, Ella is unaware of racial difference, but in adulthood, she has accumulated too much of the prejudices of those around her to live in partnership with a black man.

**Harris, Hattie** Jim Harris's sister. Hattie is a graduate-level, college-educated teacher in an all-black school who ardently disapproves of Jim's marriage to the white Ella Downey. She believes that Ella is determined to prevent Jim from successfully passing the bar exam, which is true, and when Ella grows increasingly insane, Hattie does her best to persuade Jim to have her institutionalized. Hattie is a combination of what W. E. B. DuBois called the "Talented Tenth," those 10 percent of educated blacks DuBois believed should lead the race to respectable standing, and the "primitivist" type of "New Negro" of the 1920s Harlem Renaissance, who had rejected white culture in favor of their African roots. Hattie is one of the strongest, arguably *the* strongest, female character in the O'Neill canon.

**Harris, Jim** Ella Downey's husband. Jim is a black man who, against the wishes of neighbor-

hood and family, marries his white sweetheart from preadolescence, Ella Downey. Through the course of the play, Jim attempts to pass the bar exam and become a lawyer, a clear metaphor for "passing" as white. He ultimately fails as a result of his low self-esteem, which he partly attributes to being surrounded by white test takers, and because his wife Ella makes every effort to thwart his dream. Given that Jim's radical activist sister, Hattie Harris, attended graduate school and became a successful teacher, it is clear that Jim's accommodations to the white world turn against him. In the end, Jim becomes an avuncular figure for his wife, who by the end of the play has regressed mentally to her more carefree and less prejudiced state as a child. Jim is resigned to professional failure by the end of the play and will most likely dedicate his life to nursing his schizophrenic, racist wife.

**Harris, Mrs.** Jim Harris and Hattie Harris's mother. Mrs. Harris is described in act 2, scene 1 as *"a mild-looking, gray-haired Negress of sixty-five, dressed in an old-fashioned Sunday-best dress"* (2:297), whose southern black propriety and strong dialect starkly contrast with her well-spoken and highly educated daughter Hattie. Like Hattie, Mrs. Harris disapproves of her son's marriage to Ella Downey, a white woman, but not for the political reasons espoused by her activist daughter. Mrs. Harris simply states, "De white and de black shouldn't mix dat close. Dere's one road where de white goes on alone; dere's anudder road where de black goes on alone—" (2:298). Above all, however, she wishes Jim to be happy, and though she believes they should have stayed in France, where the color line is less severely drawn, in a well-wishing gesture she gives over her apartment in lower Manhattan to her son and daughter-in-law and moves to the black section of the Bronx with Hattie.

**Joe** Joe represents the kind of black man Jim Harris might have become had he not persevered in school and attempted to transcend the racial gap his society has enforced. Jim's ambition offends Joe, who, though he demands a great deal of respect on the street, even among white toughs like Mickey and Shorty, has no self-respect concerning his race and no faith in black advancement, and who believes Jim "fakin' an' pretendin' and swellin' out grand an' talkin' soft and perlite," to "buy white" with the modest inheritance he received from his father, are an affront to him and the black race as a whole. In act 1, scene 2, Joe threatens to seriously harm Jim if he does not confess out loud to being a "nigger," which Jim resignedly does admit. "We're both niggers," he says at the end of the scene (2:288). Of course, Joe, in some ways, was right, at least in the context of the play and its conclusion, given O'Neill's clear doubts about the betterment of race relations in the United States.

**Mickey**  One of the children in the opening scene; he later becomes a prizefighter and street tough. Ella Downey is Mickey's "girl" in young adulthood, and Mickey's racism clearly affects her later psychological response to being married to the black Jim Harris.

**Shorty**  One of the children in the opening scene; he later becomes a pimp and the envoy between Mickey and Ella Downey (act 1, scene 3), who bears Mickey's child but loses it to diphtheria.

## BIBLIOGRAPHY

Bogard, Travis. *Contour in Time: The Plays of Eugene O'Neill.* Rev. ed. New York: Oxford University Press, 1988.

Cargill, Oscar, N. Bryllion Fagin, and William J. Fisher, eds. *O'Neill and His Plays: Four Decades of Criticism.* New York: New York University Press, 1961.

Clark, Barrett H. *Eugene O'Neill: The Man and His Plays.* Rev. ed. New York: Dover, 1947.

Floyd, Virginia, ed. *Eugene O'Neill at Work: Newly Released Ideas for His Plays.* New York: Ungar, 1981.

Kantor, Louis. "O'Neill Defends His Play of Negro." In *Conversations with Eugene O'Neill,* edited by Mark W. Estrin, 44–49. Jackson: University of Mississippi Press, 1990.

Miller, Jordan Y. *Playwright's Progress: O'Neill and the Critics.* Chicago: Scott, Foresman and Company, 1965.

Sheaffer, Louis. *O'Neill: Son and Artist.* Boston: Little, Brown, 1973.

# Ancient Mariner: A Dramatic Arrangement of Coleridge's Poem, The  (completed, 1923; first produced, 1924)

O'Neill's version of Samuel Taylor Coleridge's *The Rime of the Ancient Mariner* was written for the EXPERIMENTAL THEATRE at the Provincetown Playhouse (see PROVINCETOWN PLAYERS) in the later months of 1923. It opened on April 6, 1924, and closed on April 26, after 33 performances. It has not been professionally revived. *The Ancient Mariner* was originally envisioned as part of a double bill with another dramatic arrangement, *The Revelation of John the Divine.* O'Neill never completed the latter work, however, and *The Ancient Mariner* appeared along with Molière's *Georges Dandin*—a combination that *Theatre Magazine* compared to "serving a cream puff with a dish of cucumbers."

The play constitutes one of O'Neill's earliest uses of masks as they were employed in the choruses of GREEK TRAGEDY. It dramatizes the encounter between Coleridge's Mariner and Wedding Guest while a chorus of six sailors, "wearing the masks of drowned men" (O'Neill 169) pantomimes the action. Lines from the original poem are divided among the Mariner, the Wedding Guest, and the Chorus. Some original lines are also adopted as STAGE DIRECTIONS, and it is the expansion of these directions that constitutes the bulk of O'Neill's own contribution to the drama. In general, he works to make more explicit the original poem's biblical imagery: The Mariner is "like a prophet out of the Bible" (169), and the Albatross is "like a large Dove of the Holy Ghost" (172).

This procedure leads to occasional tension between O'Neill and Coleridge. For example, at the point of the play where the dead sailors are animated by spirits and rise in order to work the ship, O'Neill's direction tells us: "Their masks have changed. They now have those of holy spirits with haloes about their heads." Nevertheless, immediately afterward, in a line written by Coleridge, the Sailors themselves assert that they "were a ghastly crew" (181).

Critical response to the play was negative. *Theatre Magazine* concluded that it was "wearisome and far from entertaining." In the *New York Times*, John Corbin claimed: "Most people will probably find that Mr. O'Neill's 'dramatic arrangement' . . . is distinctly less thrilling than the poem as read." GEORGE JEAN NATHAN in the *American Mercury* complained about the production's "preoccupation with lighting and scenery at the expense of drama" (Nathan 244).

A month after the play's premier, O'Neill's partner KENNETH MACGOWAN made it a centerpiece in a defense of experimental theater published in the June issue of *Theatre Arts Monthly*. While acknowledging that "this business of trying out the limits of the theatre is a disturbing thing to most of our critics" (363), Macgowan characterized O'Neill's *Mariner* as "an attempt to formalize the stage almost to the point of the Japanese No drama" (357).

In addition to being a contribution to expressionist theater, O'Neill's *Mariner* can also be considered an interesting experiment in intertextuality. O'Neill wrote his script in the margins of a mass-market copy of Coleridge's poem. Since one of the most commented-on features of Coleridge's "Ancient Mariner" is the marginal gloss that the poet added in 1817—almost 20 years after the poem's first appearance—O'Neill must be seen as adding his own gloss to an already glossed work of literature. Some readers have seen Coleridge's gloss as the poet's anxiety-ridden attempt to constrain the metaphysical ambiguities of his poem. Perhaps one reason for the relative failure of O'Neill's play is that it can be seen to intensify this gesture of constraint.

Consider the status of the wedding in both works. O'Neill uses the wedding as a sign of debased worldliness out of which the Mariner would raise the chosen Guest. The two guests to whom the Mariner does not speak have "mask-like faces of smug, complacent dullness; they walk like marionettes" (169). The bride and groom who appear momentarily are similarly devoid of genuine life: "They smile but like two happy dolls, then kiss as dolls might" (171). Presumably it is the nascent capacity for something better, the hint of something "naturally alive" (169) in the face of the

chosen Guest, which leads the Mariner to single him out.

In the poetry of both Coleridge and that of his close collaborator William Wordsworth, weddings resonate with more positive associations and can be traced finally to the biblical trope of Christ as the bridegroom of the church. Both Coleridge and Wordsworth secularize this trope and use the wedding as a metaphor for the ideal union of the human mind and the natural world. For example, Wordsworth uses it to articulate the aim of *The Recluse*, the great, unrealized philosophical poem that he intended to write, to a considerable extent, under Coleridge's direction. Wordsworth asserts that utopian social arrangements would follow inevitably if only "the discerning intellect of Man" could be "wedded to this goodly universe / In love and holy passion"; his most ardent poetic ambition is to chant "the spousal verse / Of this great consummation" (Wordsworth 38–39). For his part, Coleridge described the joyful mind as the "wedding-garment" in which nature lived, and in *"Dejection: An Ode"* he bemoaned the psychic force of despair that could convert that garment into a "shroud" (Coleridge 156).

In Coleridge's *Rime of the Ancient Mariner,* the backdrop of the wedding suggests a way to call the Mariner's authority into question—to see him as a problematical figure who perhaps does not fully understand his own experience and story, and one whose impact on the Wedding Guest is, at best, ambiguous. Such ambiguity is nicely expressed in what may be the most interesting line from Coleridge that does *not* find its way into O'Neill's play: After his encounter with the Mariner, the poem says of the Guest, "A sadder and a wiser man, / He rose the morrow morn" (99). Since wisdom at the price of sadness is essentially the exchange that ushers Adam and Eve into the lapsed world, it is possible to see Coleridge's Mariner as an agent of the fall rather than redemption.

At the end of O'Neill's play, the stage directions suggest a radical disjunction between the Guest's and the audience's perception of the Mariner. The Guest flees the Mariner "as if running from the devil" (190) at the very moment when he (the Mariner) assumes his least ambiguous guise "as a prophet proclaiming truth" (189). Clearly, for O'Neill the Guest's flight signals his blameworthy failure to absorb the Mariner's lesson.

Such a judgment by O'Neill constitutes not so much a quarrel with the original poem as it does a choice of several plausible interpretations of it. George Jean Nathan was not alone among critics to complain of the production's essentially "leaving nothing to the imagination" (243), and this objection may suggest the limitations of the mode in which O'Neill was working. Staging the poem necessitates a narrowing of Coleridge's carefully crafted ambiguity. A "dramatic arrangement" of someone else's work is inevitably just another reading and, despite Macgowan's assertions, a fragile vessel in which to launch an experimental theater.

Two of O'Neill's earlier one-act plays, THIRST and FOG, are also indebted to Coleridge's *Mariner*.

### BIBLIOGRAPHY

Bogard, Travis. *Contour in Time: The Plays of Eugene O'Neill.* New York: Oxford University Press, 1972.

Coleridge, Samuel Taylor. *Coleridge's Poetry and Prose.* Edited by Nicholas Halmi, Paul Magnuson, and Raimonda Modiano. New York: WW Norton and Co.

Corbin, John. "The Play," *New York Times*, April 7, 1924, 15.

Cunningham, Frank R. "*The Ancient Mariner* and the Genesis of O'Neill's Romanticism." *Eugene O'Neill Newsletter* 3, no. 1 (1979): 6–9.

Gallup, Donald. "Eugene O'Neill's *The Ancient Mariner.*" *Yale University Library Gazette* 35 (1960): 61–86.

Macgowan, Kenneth. "Crying the Bounds of Broadway." *Theatre Arts Monthly* (June 1924): 355–364.

Nathan, George Jean. "The Theatre." *American Mercury* (June 1924): 240–245.

O'Neill, Eugene. "The Ancient Mariner." In *The Unknown O'Neill: Unpublished or Unfinished Writings of Eugene O'Neill*, edited by Travis Bogard, 167–190. New Haven, Conn.: Yale University Press, 1988.

———. *Thirst* and *Fog.* In *Complete Plays*, vol. 2, edited by Travis Bogard. New York: Library of America, 1988, 29–51, 95–112.

"Provincetown Playbill." *Theatre Magazine* (June 1924): 19.

Tiusanen, Timo. *O'Neill's Scenic Images.* Princeton, N.J.: Princeton University Press, 1968.

Wordsworth, William. "The Excursion: Preface to the Edition of 1814." In *The Poems*, vol. 2, edited by John O. Hayden, 35–40. London: Penguin Books, 1977.

Brian Folker

# *"Anna Christie"*: A Play in Four Acts (completed, 1920; first produced, 1921)

As late as 1941, 20 years after *"Anna Christie"* won Eugene O'Neill his second PULITZER PRIZE, he confessed to THEATRE GUILD cofounder Lawrence Langner that he "couldn't sit though it without getting the heebie-jeebies and wondering why the hell I ever wrote it—even if Joan of Arc came back to play 'Anna'" (quoted in Floyd 201n). Blanche Sweet starred in a silent FILM ADAPTATION in 1923, but the reference to Joan of Arc was probably an acknowledgment of Greta Garbo's highly acclaimed performance in the 1930 "talkie" version, when audiences heard the starlet's voice for the first time. Both films were symptomatic of the play's initial success on Broadway, and it was eventually made into the Broadway musical *New Girl in Town* in 1957.

A revision of O'Neill's 1920 play *Chris Christophersen, "Anna Christie"* (the quotes are meant to underscore its title character's street name, shortened from Anna Christopherson, and thus her PROSTITUTION) has fewer characters than *Chris*, and O'Neill reduced the original by two scenes. The newer play also reverses the character focus, as the titles suggest, from Chris Christopherson to his daughter Anna. Much of the dialogue from *Chris Christophersen* remains in *"Anna Christie,"* though its plot diverges significantly, and on the whole, *"Anna Christie"* was a major improvement.

On the day after its stage premiere on November 2, 1921, at the Vanderbilt Theater in New York

City, the drama critic KENNETH MACGOWAN, one of O'Neill's greatest promoters, wrote in his review that with *"Anna Christie"* O'Neill had made "dramatic history": "It is hard to think of any American play that is the superior of Eugene O'Neill's newest work in truth of life or in dramatic force" (quoted in Miller 27). At present, however, the play is sometimes not well regarded: O'Neill critic Virginia Floyd, for instance, characterizes *"Anna Christie"* as a "pseudo-tragedy with a happy ending. A source of embarrassment to the author in his lifetime, the play is merely an interesting failure today" (192).

## SYNOPSIS

### Act 1

The barroom of "Johnny-the-Priest's," a waterfront dive in Lower Manhattan. The curtain opens to two longshoremen ordering drinks from its owner, Johnny the Priest. Johnny's junior barman Larry enters to relieve him and is followed soon after by the Postman, who delivers a letter addressed to a "square-head," or Swede, the captain of a coal barge and a regular at Johnny's. The barmen surmise that the letter must be from Chris Christopherson's daughter out west, as the address is written in "woman's writing" (1:960). Chris arrives somewhat drunk after cavorting with an "Irish fallar" on the docks and begins singing a song he learned from an "Italian fallar" on another barge (1:961, 962). Chris has just landed from a trip down to Norfolk, Virginia, a "slow voyage—dirty vedder—yust fog, fog, fog, all bloody time!" (1:962). A bell rings from the back room, where the "family entrance," or ladies' entrance, is located. (In 1910, women were not permitted to enter most bars, even the lowest saloons, from the front entrance, and they had to ring a bell to be allowed in.) Chris remembers he left his companion Marthy Owen outside and runs to let her in.

Johnny reminds Larry to give Chris his letter and heads home. The letter announces the imminent arrival of his daughter Anna, whom he has not seen in 15 years. Larry jokes that Anna "'ll be marryin' a sailor herself, likely. It's in the blood" (1:964); a statement his counterpart makes in CHRIS CHRISTO-PHERSEN (1:805). This infuriates Chris, since that is precisely what he had been trying to protect her from by sending her out west. (Unlike the reunion scene in *Chris Christophersen*, Anna and Chris first meet at Johnny's, rather than on his barge.) Before Anna's arrival, Chris and Marthy Owen engage in some drunken conversation, including Chris's tale about leaving Anna in the care of his cousins in Minnesota, rather than "know dat ole davil, sea," or "know fader like me" (1:964).

Chris departs to sober up at a hash joint around the corner. This gives Anna, who enters a moment later, some time to relax with Marthy, who "got her number the minute [she] stepped in the door" (1:970). No longer the prudish typist we knew in *Chris*, Anna is visibly a woman of loose morals and coarse demeanor, *"showing all the outward appearances of belonging to the world's oldest profession"* (1:968). Anna explains to Marthy that she had been imprisoned for solicitation for a month and spent two subsequent weeks of recovery in a hospital bed. She goes on to say that before that, she was worked nearly to death on the Minnesota farm and was raped by her youngest cousin at 16. The experience led her not only to hate the family and escape to St. Paul, but to despise all men. Marthy assures her that not all men are bad and her father, Chris, is "as good an old guy as ever walked on two feet" (1:971). When Chris reappears, Anna's *"brilliant clothes, and, to him, high-toned appearance, awe him terribly"* (1:974). After a touching but restrained embrace, Chris convinces Anna to join him on a coal run up to Boston—"yust water all round, and sun, and fresh air, and good grub . . . see everytang dat's pooty. You need to take rest like dat. You work too hard for young gel already. You need vacation, yes!" (1:976–977) Anna accepts with the excuse that she does require rest after the long train ride from Minnesota, omitting to mention the prison sentence and her stay at the hospital.

### Act 2

Ten days later, Chris's barge *Simeon Winthrop* is at anchor, engulfed in a fog bank at night off Provincetown, Massachusetts (where O'Neill composed the play in summer 1920). The fog in *"Anna Christie,"* as in LONG DAY'S JOURNEY INTO NIGHT and other O'Neill plays, induces, druglike, a euphoric feeling of forgetfulness, spiritual cleanliness, and the blissful sensation of distance from life's tragedies. Anna is enamored of the fog and, by association, the SEA: "It makes me feel clean—out here—'s if I'd taken a bath. . . . And I feel happy for once—yes, honest!—happier than I ever been anywhere before!" (1:980, 982). Chris is devastated by this revelation, but chalks it up as another low, "dirty trick" of "dat ole davil, sea." He explains in discouraging tones that both Anna's brothers and two of his own were all lost at sea, along with so many other villagers from their hometown in Sweden. Anna asks, again foreshadowing her fate, whether all of the women from their family married sailors, and Chris, *"seeing his chance to drive home his point,"* responds, "Yes—and it's bad on dem like hell vorst of all. . . . Any gel marry sailor, she's crazy fool!" (1:981–982). Nevertheless, Anna feels a kind of atavistic sense of belonging at sea, one drawn from her heritage: "It's like I'd come home after a long visit away some place. It all seems like I've been here before lots of times—on boats—in this same fog" (1:982).

A crew of shipwreck survivors soon break the calm with shouts of "Ahoy!" They are half-dead from five days drifting in the open sea, and Chris orders Anna to bring whiskey to revive them. The Irishman Mat Burke is among them, and he and Anna promptly fall in love. They both speak in rough, immigrant dialects, though like Chris, Mat mistakes Anna for a "proper" lady: "what's a fine handsome woman the like of you doing on this scow?" (1:985) Mat is an insufferable boaster, taking full credit for rescuing his shipmates: "And only for me, I'm telling you, and the great strength and guts is in me, we'd be being scoffed by the fishes this minute!" (1:985) Mat tries to kiss Anna, but she pushes him to the floor and knocks him cold for a moment. He regains consciousness and, with full admiration for her strength, promises to make no such further advances. Again mistaking Anna for a lady, he says, "I'm a hard, rough man and I'm not fit, I'm thinking, to be kissing the shoe-soles of a fine, dacent girl the like of yourself" (1:987). Mat tells the story of his shipwreck with the blarney of an IRISH raconteur. Impressed with the tale, Anna tells him that all of the women in her family married sailors; Mat's response is in direct opposition to her father's: "Did they, now? They had spirit in them. It's only the sea you'd find rale men with guts

is fit to wed with fine, high-tempered girls (*then he adds half-boldly*) the like of yourself" (1:989). Mat then proposes rather ludicrously, but Chris breaks in angrily and tells him to get to bed, which he only does with Anna's insistence. Chris then shakes his fist at the sea, "Dat's your dirty trick, damn ole davil, you!" (1:992)

### Act 3

At port in Boston. Mat and Chris clash over Anna's well-being throughout act 3. The two disparage each other's ethnicities—Chris calling Mat an "Irish svine," while Mat calls Chris a "stock-fish-swilling Square-head." They also criticize their respective experiences at sea—Chris on the old windjammers, or "windbags" as Mat refers to them, and Mat on the new steamers where, according to Chris, "you got fallars on deck don't know a ship from a mudscow" (1:1,000). (This same conflict, among older sailors from the sail power days and the new generations laboring on the steamships, is drawn out between Paddy and Robert "Yank" Smith in O'Neill's *The* HAIRY APE.) Thrown into a rage by Mat's vow that he'll marry Anna that day, Chris lunges at him with a knife, and Mat easily disarms him. Anna steps in, happily greeting Mat, but then sees the strewn furniture on the floor and demands to hear what the fighting was about. Chris tells her it is the old sailor rivalry, but Mat tells her the full truth—that it started because he told Chris he loves her and wishes to marry her. Anna responds that she loves him too, but after kissing him full on the lips, she utters "good-by" (1:1,003). Uncomprehending at first, Mat demands an admittance from Chris that he has been beaten and wants to shake on it. Chris admits nothing of the sort, and Anna affirms that she will not marry Mat, though she loves him. Her pronouncement recharges the dispute between Chris and Mat, in which father and lover quarrel over who will orchestrate Anna's future. In the final scene, Anna defiantly proclaims, "Gawd, you'd think I was a piece of furniture! . . . I'll do what I please and no man, I don't give a hoot who he is, can tell me what to do! I ain't askin' either of you for a living. I can make it myself—one way or other" (1:1,007). She then confesses her past, including everything she had already told Marthy in act 1. She adds, knowing it is no use but desperately wanting Mat to understand, that her experience at sea has had a purifying effect and reversed her attitude toward life and men. Mat furiously calls her a "slut" and threatens to kill her with a chair (1:1,010). Chris jumps in the way to protect his daughter, but Anna pushes him aside and dares Mat to go ahead and kill her. Chris, railing against "dat ole davil sea," and Mat, in a rage over her betrayal, disembark to go on a "bat," or drinking spree, in the taverns of the Boston waterfront (1:1,011–1,012).

## Act 4

Two days later, still in Boston. Chris returns drunk and begs Anna's forgiveness for his part in her history. Anna tells him of her plan to return by train to New York the following morning. Chris begs her to reconsider and says if she is in love with Mat, and if marrying him would make her happy, then she should do it. She tells him there is no hope for that, and again he begs her forgiveness, which she vouchsafes by saying, "Don't bawl about it. There ain't nothing to forgive, anyway. It ain't your fault, and it ain't mine, and it ain't his neither. We're all poor nuts, and things happen, and we yust get mixed in wrong, that's all" (1:1,015). "You say right tang, Anna, py golly!" Chris rejoins. "It ain't nobody's fault! (*shaking his fist*) It's dat ole davil, sea!" (1:1,015) Once again, "dat ole davil, sea" is called out as the malevolent force controlling their lives. Chris has signed on to a British steamship *Londonderry* and has arranged for his earnings to be sent every month to Anna. Anna discovers a pistol in his pocket that he had planned to use on Mat, but he tells her he understood soon after buying it that Anna's condition was not Mat's "fault" (1:1,016), and it was never loaded.

Mat returns, inebriated as well but also bruised and disheveled from street brawling. His bloodshot eyes reveal an *"impotent animal rage baffled by its own abject misery"* (1,1,017). Anna, hearing his footsteps before he enters the cabin, hides in the corner with the unloaded revolver. Seeing no one inside, Mat suspects Anna has gone to shore to ply her trade and resolves to wait and "choke her dirty life out" when she returns (1:1,018). Anna steps

into the room and points the gun at him, but he is unfazed at the thought of his own death. He begs Anna to tell him it was all a lie, but she tells him it is no lie but that her love for him and the sea has changed her utterly. Mat informs her that he has signed on to the *Londonderry*—the same steamer her father has signed on to, though neither man knows it and the irony is not lost on her.

Anna accuses Mat of being no better than she is when sailing from port to port. It then comes out that Mat's true worry was that she loved the men she slept with as a prostitute, a revelation to Anna that, despite the ridiculous charge, all might be well. She tells him she will do anything to make him believe that she not only never loved her "johns," but hated them all. Mat makes Anna swear a "terrible, fearful oath" on a *"cheap old crucifix from his pocket,"* an oath in which she vows, in Mat's words, that "I'm the only man in the world ivir you felt love for" and to "be forgetting from this day all the badness you've done and never do the like again" (1:1,023–1,024). She does so gladly, and they decide to marry the following morning before he disembarks on the *Londonderry*, with Chris's mixed blessings. Mat finds himself ambivalent about her oath as well, since she is not Catholic, and in fact follows no religion. The final scene shows Chris taking in the view from the deck and melodramatically declaring, "Fog, fog, fog, all bloody time. You can't see vhere you vas going, no. Only dat ole davil, sea—she knows!" (1:1,027).

## COMMENTARY

Act 1 of *"Anna Christie"* takes place in "Johnny-the-Priest's," a waterfront dive closely resembling O'Neill's waterfront hangout JIMMY "THE PRIEST'S," a now-defunct bar in Manhattan located at 252 Fulton Street, where the playwright drowned his conscience in whiskey for months at a time. In the STAGE DIRECTIONS of act 1, O'Neill realistically describes the bar in minute detail, and his dialogue recreates the common slang and defiant attitudes of the waterfront figures he knew intimately. Arguably the finest passages of the play are to be found here, offering an early look at the extraordinary barroom dialogue in his later masterpiece, *The* ICEMAN COMETH.

O'Neill indicates that the action takes place around 1910, just before the time he spent loafing on the Manhattan waterfront and lived in the flophouse above Jimmy's for three dollars a month. Then in his early 20s, O'Neill effectively concealed from his family his ill-conceived marriage to KATHLEEN JENKINS, which led to his first son, EUGENE O'NEILL, JR. (whom O'Neill would not meet again for 10 years), as he coped with the still-reigning puritanical social order of the early 20th century. In an interview with the New York *Daily News* in 1932, remarking on the barroom setting of *"Anna Christie,"* O'Neill recalled that the regulars at Jimmy's were "a hard lot, at first glance, every type—sailors, on shore leave or stranded; longshoremen, waterfront riffraff, gangsters, down and outers, drifters from the ends of the earth" (quoted in Gelb 311).

Contemporary audiences, as Barbara Voglino has suggested, might feel "torn between the possibilities of [Anna's] self-determination and the implications of [Chris's] fatalism," but most audiences in the early 1920s chose the former. O'Neill wrote in a letter to theater critic GEORGE JEAN NATHAN that theatergoers mistakenly regarded the final scene as "a happy-ever-after which I did not intend" (O'Neill 148). He insisted that the moment when Mat discovers Anna is non-Catholic—not religious at all, in fact—the integrity of her "oath" to forget the past and never return to PROSTITUTION is slippery at best. Still, Anna is a precursor to many female characters in the O'Neill canon, including Cybel from *STRANGE INTERLUDE*; Nora Melody from *A TOUCH OF THE POET*; and, most important, Mary Tyrone from *Long Day's Journey into Night*: She is the forgiving mother figure, willing to accept and forgive the sins of her men with a naturalistic understanding that forces beyond human control dictate their fates.

Chris is spiritually adrift in the end as well. He has now lost his daughter to a sailor, which he swore he would never permit, and signs on in his old rank of boatswain (pronounced "bo'sun") for a steamship voyage to Cape Town, South Africa, after railing for years against the horrors of "dat ole davil, sea," which had claimed the lives of most of his family, including Anna's two older brothers and, indirectly, Anna herself.

Anna, too, should be apprehensive. She is marrying into the life of a coal stoker, essentially an industrial laborer, a type of seaman her father describes as "de dirtiest, rough gang of no-good fallars in world!" (1:994). Unlike Paul Andersen in *Chris*, as an uneducated, immigrant coal stoker, Mat Burke has little to no potential to achieve a captain's license, though a captainship is the only grade that would allow Anna to join him at sea. Anna, then, will be left behind in Boston to fend for herself as she has always done—"one way or other."

O'Neill wished his play to end with a figurative "comma at the end of a gaudy introductory clause, with the body of the sentence still unwritten"; at one point, he even toyed with naming it "Comma" (O'Neill 148; it was first copyrighted as "The Ole Davil"). Only *New York Times* critic ALEXANDER WOOLLCOTT appeared to "get it": "O'Neill seems to be suggesting to the departing playgoers," he wrote, "that they can regard this as a happy ending if they are short-sighted enough to believe it and weak-minded enough to crave it" (30). But if death and marriage are the mainstays of tragedy and comedy, it is understandable that audiences found in *"Anna Christie"* a pretext for enjoying the play as a comedy.

All the same, it is remarkable that audiences in 1920 would accept a respectable marriage as the "happy ending," in the comedic tradition, for a "girl gone bad." In 1905, GEORGE BERNARD SHAW's prostitution play *Mrs. Warren's Profession* was "shut down for obscenity"; and in 1911, Eugene Walter's *The Easiest Way*, which charts the course of a popular stage actress's descent into prostitution was prohibited from playing in Boston (Johnson 88). Not much earlier, the naturalist writer Theodore Dreiser, a contemporary of O'Neill's whom the playwright once claimed deserved his 1936 NOBEL PRIZE IN LITERATURE more than he, confounded the American reading public by having the title character of his first novel, *Sister Carrie* (1900), enjoy sexual relations, without the benefit of clergy, and thrive as an actress on the popular stage. That "happy ending" induced Dreiser's publishers to suppress their own novel. Indeed, according to Barrett H. Clark, the only censoring *"Anna Christie"* received in its national tour was in Dallas, where they demanded the word *God* be changed to *Gawd* and the word *house* (meaning Anna's brothel in St. Paul) to *place* (67).

Though critics disagree on this point, Anna Christopherson can be taken as an unrepentant former prostitute to the end, one who unapologetically lacks manners, religion, and, most important, remorse for her past actions. In the vein of literary NATURALISM, still controversial in the early decades of the 20th century, Anna soothes her guilt-ridden father by saying, "It ain't your fault, and it ain't mine, and it ain't his neither. We're all poor nuts, and things happen, and we yust get mixed in wrong, that's all." (1:1,015) Whether Anna was to blame or not for her louche existence would matter little to a middle-class American audience only a decade earlier. There is no repentance for her life as a prostitute—"I ain't sorry," she admits to Marthy in act 1 (1:972). If anything, it is quite the opposite. Prostitution was in many ways a saving grace for Anna, enslaved as she was through childhood on the brutal Minnesota farm.

However, audiences no doubt saw in Anna the figure, as critic Katie N. Johnson argues, of the "penitent prostitute," since she does "reform" in the end. "Such a story," Johnson suggests, "made great sense to Progressive reformers in what we might call the zenith of their work in 1921, when the battle against prostitution appeared to have been won. . . . Passing out of the Progressive Era, with its tedious reform policies, American audiences wanted, perhaps, to believe they were poet-prostitutes" (89, 100). With this in mind, though *"Anna Christie"* may be a failure as a work of art for O'Neill, the play marks a clear shift in the kind of subject matter American audiences were willing to accept—particularly since they misread it as a comedy—if not as the ambiguous "comma" O'Neill originally had in mind.

## CHARACTERS

**Burke, Mat**   Saved after a shipwreck in act 2 by Chris and Anna Christopherson's barge, the Irish seaman Mat Burke is nothing like his counterpart Paul Andersen in *Chris Christopherson*. If Andersen pretentiously displays all of the well-bred learning and manners of sophisticated rebelliousness, Burke is a perfectly natural character, boorishly singing his own praises in the manner of the protagonist from *The Hairy Ape*, Robert "Yank" Smith; both Yank and Mat have worked as coal stokers, and both are based on a drinking partner of O'Neill's named DRISCOLL, whom O'Neill knew from working as a seaman and his time at JIMMY "THE PRIEST'S." Mat speaks in an authentic Irish brogue and maintains his faith in CATHOLICISM. His Irishness is enormously important to the final act, as his doubts about Anna Christopherson's lack of religion make him feel cursed—"There's some divil's trickery in it, to be swearing an oath on a Catholic cross and you wan of the others" (1:1,024). In the name of love, Mat has forsaken the ethnic pride and religious faith that imbued him with the strength to endure the trials and prejudices that typified IRISH immigration to the United States.

**Christopherson, Anna ("Anna Christie")**   Anna is a realistically drawn victim of fate whose abandonment by her seafaring father led to disastrous consequences. After her mother's death 15 years before the action of the play, Chris sent Anna to be raised inland by his wife's family in Minnesota. During what historians refer to as the "Teutonic wave" of immigration in the 1870s and 1880s, Minnesota harbored tens of thousands of Scandinavian immigrant farmers who had emigrated from their homeland for the promise of cheap land. But what Anna encounters is far from the idyllic myth of rural America, those self-reliant, wholesome, hardworking Scandinavian farm communities of the western plains that most Americans envision—"them cousins," as Anna puts it to her father, "that you think is such nice people" (1:1,008). Instead, Anna is raped by one of her cousins at 16, exploited as a farmhand, and viciously abused in other ways until she escapes to the city of St. Paul. There she takes a job as a child's nurse, a post her independent spirit soon rejects, and within two years she turns to a life of prostitution.

Though Anna's character, again, demonstrates none of the idealism of New Womanhood her namesake espouses in *Chris Christophersen*, she is still a remarkably "modern" figure: She talks freely about her life of prostitution to Marthy Owen, she still speaks with a Swedish accent after 15 years stateside, she drinks whiskey by the glass (the first Anna, raised in England, scolded Chris for making a dreadful cup of tea), she never turns to religion for guidance or succor, and she has no respect for the patriarchal norm—indeed, she openly hates all men. Critics accuse O'Neill of writing too much explication in Anna's dialogue (allowing her, for example, to prematurely reveal her entire history to Marthy, and thus the audience, in the first act), though in one glowing review following its opening night in 1921, one cogent theater critic observed that "this ignorant, laconic, almost inarticulate girl [is] the mouthpiece of O'Neill's burning ironies" (quoted in Miller 30).

**Christopherson, Chris**   Friend of Eugene O'Neill and character in the plays *"Anna Christie"* and *Chris Christophersen.* Though the protagonists in *"Anna Christie"* are patently more realistic than those in *Chris Christophersen,* the character Chris is essentially unchanged. Chris is based on an actual Swedish regular at Jimmy "the Priest's" with the same name (O'Neill mistakenly spelled his name Chistophersen with an *e* instead of an *o,* like his friend's, which signifies a Norwegian or Danish name; he corrected this error in *"Anna Christie"*) who, like the fictional Chris, railed against the connivances of "dat ole davil, sea," as he famously repeats in the dialogue. O'Neill describes Chris in his stage directions for *Chris Christophersen* the way he remembered his Swedish friend, roommate for a time, and drinking partner: *"a short, squat, broad-shouldered man of about fifty with a round, weather-beaten face from which his light blue eyes peer short-sightedly, twinkling with a simple good humor"* (1:802).

The fictional Chris is the captain of a coal barge named the *Simeon Winthrop,* and the seamen at the bar berate him for relinquishing his true calling as a sailor. Chris's jarring dialect highlights his ethnic roots, which O'Neill artfully combines with an experienced seaman's command of waterfront argot. Also like the fictional Chris, O'Neill's friend accepted a job as captain of a coal barge, a sinecure for experienced seaman, docked in New York harbor. The actual Chris froze to death in 1917 following a Christmas Eve wetting down at Jimmie's after tumbling drunk onto an ice flow

wedged between the dock and his barge. Contrary to that man's undignified departure, O'Neill's character is thrust back to his old duties as a boatswain on a steamer called the *Londonderry;* thus O'Neill emphasizes the overpowering draw of the SEA that a true sailor cannot, no matter how in earnest, disengage for long.

**"Johnny-the-Priest"**   Johnny is based on Eugene O'Neill's friend and bartender James J. Condon, also called JIMMY "THE PRIEST," whose bar (located at 252 Fulton Street) O'Neill frequented, living for a time in a room above, in 1911–12, following his first voyage in the MERCHANT MARINE. "Johnny" is the saloon keeper in act 1, who O'Neill describes as a *"personage of the waterfront." "With his pale, thin, clean-shaven face, mild blue eyes and white hair, a cassock would seem more suited to him than the apron he wears. . . . But beneath all his mildness one senses the man behind the mask—cynical, callous, hard as nails"* (1:959).

**Larry**   Larry is a *"boyish, red-cheeked, rather good-looking young fellow of twenty or so"* who serves Chris Christopherson, Anna Christie, and Marthy Owens in "Johnny-the-Priest's" saloon in act 1. Larry foreshadows the final act by kidding Chris in act 1 of both plays that Anna "'ll be marryin' a sailor herself, likely. It's in the blood" (1:805, 964). Larry's boyishness and upbeat demeanor, along with his refusal to drink, emphasize by contrast the rough attitudes of the bar's patrons, but particularly the jolting appearance of Chris's daughter Anna, who clearly resembles a prostitute.

**Owen, Marthy**   Like Chris, Marthy is presented in both *"Anna Christie"* and *Chris Christophersen* with little modification. Marthy is Chris's female companion on his barge, who self-professedly has been "campin' with barge men the last twenty years" (1:966). Marthy *"might be forty or fifty. Her jowly, mottled face, with its thick red nose, is streaked with interlacing purple veins"* (1:962). She is dressed in ragged men's shoes and clothes. However, O'Neill suggests that *"in her blood-shot blue eyes a youthful lust for life which hard usage has failed to stifle, a sense of humor mocking, but good-tempered"* (1:962). A denizen of the waterfront all of her life, Marthy is, at bottom, a good-hearted woman who only wants what is best for Anna and Chris; her character is a clear attempt on O'Neill's part to transform the tragicomic stereotype of the drunken waterfront hag. As Margaret Loftus Ranald suggests, Marthy is a "Tugboat Annie" type (579), though the first Tugboat Annie appeared in *The Saturday Evening Post* on July 11, 1931, over a decade after O'Neill conceptualized his character.

## BIBLIOGRAPHY

Clark, Barrett H. *Eugene O'Neill: The Man and His Plays.* Rev. ed. New York: Dover, 1947.

Floyd, Virginia. *The Plays of Eugene O'Neill: A New Assessment.* New York: Ungar, 1985.

Gelb, Arthur, and Barbara Gelb. *O'Neill: Life with Monte Cristo.* New York: Applause Books, 2000.

Johnson, Katie N. "'*Anna Christie*': The Repentant Courtesan, Made Respectable." *Eugene O'Neill Review* 26 (2004): 87–104.

Miller, Jordan Y. *Playwright's Progress: O'Neill and the Critics.* Chicago: Scott, Foresman and Company, 1965.

O'Neill, Eugene. *Selected Letters of Eugene O'Neill.* Edited by Travis Bogard and Jackson R. Bryer. New Haven, Conn.: Yale University Press, 1988.

Ranald, Margaret Loftus. *The Eugene O'Neill Companion.* Westport, Conn: Greenwood Press, 1984.

Voglino, Barbara. *"Perverse Mind": Eugene O'Neill's Struggle with Closure.* London: Associated University Presses, 1999.

Woollcott, Alexander. "Second Thoughts on First Nights," *New York Times,* November 13, 1921. Reprinted in *The Critical Response to Eugene O'Neill,* edited by John H. Houchin, 29–30. Westport, Conn.: Greenwood Press, 1993.

# *Before Breakfast: A Play in One Act* (completed, 1916; first produced, 1916)

Eugene O'Neill wrote *Before Breakfast* in the now legendary summer of 1916, when the aspiring playwright first discovered Provincetown, Massachussetts, and the PROVINCETOWN PLAYERS first discovered him. The play premiered soon after on December 1, 1916, at the Playwrights' Theatre in New York City. *Before Breakfast* is a lengthy monologue that taxes its audience's emotional stamina. "How much are they going to stand of this sort of thing," O'Neill asked of his audience, "before they begin to break" (quoted in Gelb 589). He could have made the same query about LONG DAY'S JOURNEY INTO NIGHT, but much earlier the relative success of *Before Breakfast* convinced its author that The EMPEROR JONES, essentially a monologue itself, might be a success as well. O'Neill BIOGRAPHERS Arthur and Barbara Gelb note of *Before Breakfast*'s composition that O'Neill was secure in the fact that the Provincetown Players would provide an experimental venue to attempt such a radical departure from conventional American theater (589, 567).

## SYNOPSIS

The kitchen area of a small apartment on Christopher Street in GREENWICH VILLAGE. A clothesline hangs across the length of the room, two chairs and a table are in the center, and two windows look out onto a fire escape; wilting potted plants are in evidence on the sill. It is around 8:30 on a sunny morning. Mrs. Rowland, the only onstage character, emerges from a bedroom door to the right. Taking an apron from a wall peg, she awkwardly attempts to tie the knot in back, but her clumsy hands make it a difficult procedure, and she curses under her breath. Once the apron is secured, she fills a coffee pot, puts it on the stove, and, languidly dropping into a chair, self-pityingly places her hand on her forehead. She is hungover. She calls into the bedroom to make sure her husband, Alfred, is asleep. There is no reply, so she sneaks to the wooden cupboard and removes a bottle of Gordon gin from behind the dishes. She takes down a glass, pours a hefty drink, and tosses it back.

Much relieved, Mrs. Rowland again calls to her husband, this time in a half-whisper, and he remains unresponsive. She quietly takes down his jacket and vest, rifles through the pockets, and finds a letter in the vest. "I knew it!" she hisses, promptly reading it through. We are meant to understand that Alfred Rowland, her husband, has been having an affair. Mrs. Rowland's reaction to the letter signifies the type of woman she is: At first filled with rage, she then takes on the expression of *"triumphant malignity"* (1:392). The letter provides her with more ammunition against her husband, nothing more.

Now she wants Alfred awake in order to harass him in his vulnerable condition; he also is hungover. She shouts his name, and we hear a moan from the bedroom. From that point onward, the play is a monologue, a diatribe really, against the husband. She accuses him of being a lazy, philandering poseur who spends the money she earns as a seamstress on booze and loose women in the Village: "Heaven knows I do my part—and more—going out to sew every day while you play the gentleman and loaf around bar rooms with that good-for-nothing lot of artists from the Square" (1:393). She is referring to Washington Square, the center of Greenwich Village and a famed meeting place for musicians, writers, and artists for over a century. Though we never see Alfred, his wife's incessant ridicule and criticisms reveal a great deal. Alfred Rowland is a member of Greenwich Village's early bohemian crowd, an archetypal "starving artist" who maintains his integrity by not pandering to popular tastes: "All you do is moon around all day writing silly poetry and stories that no one will buy—and no wonder they won't" (1:393). She harangues him about his appearance— "How awful you look this morning! For heaven's sake, shave! You're disgusting!" (1:394) She hands him a cup of hot water for shaving, and a shaky, thin-fingered hand reaches from the bedroom door and, suffering from delirium tremens, spills some in the exchange. (This moment in the original production is noteworthy in that it was O'Neill's hand, also thin-fingered and shaky, making it the playwright's final performance on the stage.)

The sound of a razor being stropped comes from the bedroom, while Mrs. Rowland continues her tirade. We discover that Alfred's deceased father was a millionaire whose estate was devoured by creditors, thus leaving Alfred, a Harvard graduate and man-about-town, penniless after his death. Mrs. Rowland, a grocer's daughter, and Alfred mar-

ried after she became pregnant, though his father attempted to bribe her not to go through with the nuptials. Ironically, if tragically, the baby miscarried, and thus Alfred's attempt at doing the honorable thing was misspent. Mrs. Rowland harps, "It's lucky the poor thing was born dead, after all. What a father you'd have been!" (1:396)

Alfred cuts himself shaving and yelps in pain. Mrs. Rowland looks in and demands that he wipe his face, as the sight of blood revolts her. She informs him that she read the letter. Its author, Helen, has written that she is pregnant with Alfred's child. This would give Mrs. Rowland ample grounds for divorce, but out of pure spite, she has no intention of divorcing him. She voices some concern for Alfred's mistress but rejects her sympathies, since "She isn't any school-girl, like I was, from the looks of her letter. . . . She deserves to suffer, that's all I can say. I'll tell you what I think; I think your Helen is no better than a common street-walker, that's what I think" (1:397). A moment later, *There is a stifled groan of pain from the next room* (1:398). A dripping sound comes from the bathroom, then the sound of a chair being knocked over, followed by a loud crash. Mrs. Rowland runs to the bedroom door and looks down at the floor within. At first she is *"transfixed with horror,"* but the spell breaks, and she lunges at the front door, unlocks it, and rushes, *"shrieking madly,"* out into the hallway (1:398).

## COMMENTARY

One of O'Neill's most concisely written one-act plays, *Before Breakfast* is a nasty little monologue involving ALCOHOLISM, suicide, an extramarital affair, two illegitimate pregnancies, a miscarriage, and a termagant wife who "literally nags her husband to death" (Floyd 99). Indeed, O'Neill's father, JAMES O'NEILL, whom O'Neill invited to be a kind of adviser for the first production, is said to have asked the young playwright, "My son, why don't you write more pleasant plays?" (quoted in Gelb 588). "O'Neill didn't care about the success of the play," Provincetown Player Edna Kenton reflected on its first production, "he cared only about the reaction of the audience to monologue, trick shocks, trick relief. It was a deliberate experiment for a definite result—the endurance of the audience" (quoted in Bogard 79). In this way, it corresponds to O'Neill's attempt with his later play, WHERE THE CROSS IS MADE, to represent on stage what is happening in the mind of a psychotic and thus "see whether it's possible to make an audience go mad too" (quoted in Bogard 103). In addition, as the Poet in FOG discourses on how the Dead Child of the Polish Peasant Woman should be grateful it has died before reaching New York, Mrs. Rowland harps at her husband, "It's lucky the poor thing was born dead, after all. What a father you'd have been!" (1:396).

O'Neill's affair with LOUISE BRYANT, his friend JOHN REED's bride to be, was well under way by the time he had written his first draft, but there is no indication that any one couple inspired the torrid relationship it dramatizes, aside, perhaps, from some loose connections between the fictional couple and O'Neill and his first wife, KATHLEEN JENKINS. But the Rowlands have little in common with O'Neill's experience with Jenkins. O'Neill never lived with her for any meaningful time, and Jenkins, far from the shrewish Mrs. Roland, was mostly accepting of O'Neill's inability to settle down. "Like [August] Strindberg," Virginia Floyd observes, "he could be ruthless in making people and events in his own life serve a dramatic purpose, callously distorting people and events" (99).

Critics often list Mrs. Rowland—along with Ruth Atkins from BEYOND THE HORIZON, Maude Steele from BREAD AND BUTTER, and Ella Harris from ALL GOD'S CHILLUN' GOT WINGS—as one in a series of female "destroyers" in O'Neill's work that corresponds to those of his greatest influence, the Swedish playwright AUGUST STRINDBERG, specifically Strindberg's female monologue *The Stronger.* Obtaining a divorce from such a "destroyer" in the early 20th century, however, was a legal difficulty. A spouse had to justify a breakup by providing the court with evidence of wrongdoing. Like Alfred Rowland, O'Neill married Jenkins because she was pregnant with EUGENE O'NEILL, JR., and he did so out of a sense of duty as well. But his first act as a husband was to sail to Honduras on a gold-mining expedition; upon his return to New York, he staged being caught in the act with a prostitute at the HELL HOLE in lower Manhattan in order to obtain a divorce. The experience left him emotionally devastated, and he attempted suicide soon after. The weight of his guilt and discomfort over the affair is precisely the response O'Neill is after from his audience with *Before Breakfast.*

## CHARACTERS

**Rowland, Mrs.** Alfred Rowland's wife. Mrs. Rowland is in her early 20s but looks older. Nothing about her appearance is striking—her hair is an unkempt mass on her head; her body is medium-sized, *"inclined to a shapeless stoutness"*; her dress is *"shabby and worn"*; her eyes are *"pinched"* and *"of a nondescript blue"*; and her mouth is *"weak, spiteful"* (1:391). She is meant to be an eyesore—precisely the sort one would not wish to encounter before breakfast. As a schoolgirl, Mrs. Rowland was, according to her bitter and lengthy testimony, seduced by and became pregnant with the child of Alfred Rowland, a Harvard graduate and the only son of a bankrupted millionaire. They married, as Alfred considered that the honorable thing to do, but the child miscarried, and so they were both stuck in a miserable marriage for little reason. Mrs. Rowland will not grant Alfred a divorce, however, out of spite. The morning the action takes place, Mrs. Rowland recounts her litany of complaints against him: He is an unemployed alcoholic who writes poetry and hangs around the bohemian scene in Greenwich Village, while she works as a seamstress to make ends meet. In the mode of Swedish playwright August Strindberg's female "destroyer" figure (see Barlow 165), Mrs. Rowland is a constant drag on her husband's artistic ambitions—demanding that he adopt the role of "wage slave" over his goal of being a successful artist. In the final scene, once Mrs. Rowland has announced that she has read a letter from Alfred's mistress, who is pregnant with his child, and informed him that under no circumstances was she granting him a divorce, her husband commits suicide with a razor.

## BIBLIOGRAPHY

Barlow, Judith. "O'Neill's Female Characters." In *The Cambridge Companion to Eugene O'Neill,* edited by Michael Manheim, 164–177. New York: Cambridge University Press, 1998.

Bogard, Travis. *Contour in Time: The Plays of Eugene O'Neill*. Rev. ed. New York: Oxford University Press, 1988.

Floyd, Virginia. *The Plays of Eugene O'Neill: A New Assessment*. New York: Ungar, 1985.

Gelb, Arthur, and Barbara Gelb. *O'Neill: Life with Monte Cristo*. New York: Applause Books, 2000.

## *Beyond the Horizon: A Play in Three Acts* (completed, 1918; first produced, 1920)

One summer evening in 1917, Eugene O'Neill sat perched on a dock in Provincetown, Massachusetts, awaiting the arrival of a local fishing boat. A mentally retarded Provincetown boy named Howard Slade sat down and poignantly asked the young playwright, "What's out there, Gene?"

"Where?"

"Oh, way out there."

"The horizon," O'Neill responded simply.

"And what's beyond the horizon?"

(quoted in Gelb 635).

So the story goes. O'Neill chanced upon a title for the full-length play that would gain him his first PULITZER PRIZE for drama. *Beyond the Horizon* is perhaps the first distinctly American tragedy, a dramatic work that permanently embedded O'Neill in the public imagination as the nation's finest playwright. After its premiere on February 3, 1920, at the Morosco Theater in New York City, the *New York Times* review called *Beyond the Horizon* "an absorbing, significant, and memorable tragedy, so full of meat that it makes most of the remaining fare seem like the merest meringue" (Woollcott 19).

O'Neill includes a good deal of heavy-handed explication throughout *Beyond the Horizon*, in that characterization is developed less through action than through blatant pronouncements. Conversations consist of information the characters must have already known outside the action of the play, which makes much of the dialogue sound stilted and melodramatic. Over the last century, at least

two major O'Neill critics, Barrett H. Clark and Travis Bogard, have each disavowed its greatness: Bogard writes that "perhaps the play seemed more impressive than it is" (117), and Clark dismisses it as "over-praised" (98). Both share the opinion, however, that "in its time, it was a signal, the first important view of the American drama" (Bogard 117). "Was it not," Clark asked, "the most consistently sustained serious play yet written by an American?" (98).

### SYNOPSIS

*Act 1, Scene 1*

Farmland in New England, with stone walls, sectioned fields, and a winding road disappearing into the horizon. In the opening scene, Robert Mayo sits absorbed in a book of POETRY, silently mouthing the words to himself and gazing pensively over the horizon. Robert yearns to go abroad, a dream that could soon be realized, as he has signed on to a three-year voyage with his uncle, Captain Dick Scott. Robert's brother, Andrew Mayo, enters the bucolic scene filthy and exhausted but invigorated by hours of hard labor on the farm. Andrew, assuming his brother plans to make his fortune abroad, cannot relate to what Robert refers to metaphysically as his "quest of the secret which is hidden over there, beyond the horizon" (1:577); but still, as he has already remarked affectionately, "I guess I realize that you've got your own angle of looking at things" (1:576). Robert's "angle of looking at things" is strongly influenced by EAST ASIAN THOUGHT, as his "quest" is meant to answer the call of "the beauty of the far off and unknown, the mystery and spell of the East which lures me in the books I've read, the need of the freedom of the great wide spaces, the joy of wandering on and on" (1:577).

Before Andrew heads home, Robert expresses a vague concern over Andrew's girlfriend, Ruth Atkins. Andrew senses his brother's fondness for her but does not press the issue and heads home. Ruth enters soon after Andrew's exit. Robert repeats his passionate craving to discover the mysteries that lie "beyond the horizon," and Ruth is charmed by his ability to "tell things so beautifully" (1:581). In spite of Andrew's clear designs to marry Ruth, Robert professes his love for her, and she passionately responds in kind. Ruth pleads for him to stay (manipulatively bursting into tears when he equivocates), and Robert submits, thus tragically accepting the life role that is his brother's by right and natural inclination.

### Act 1, Scene 2

The sitting room of the Mayo farmhouse that evening. *"Everything in the room is clean, well-kept, and in its exact place, yet there is no suggestion of primness about the whole. Rather the atmosphere is one of the orderly comfort of a simple, hard-earned prosperity, enjoyed and maintained by the family as a unit"* (1:584–585). James Mayo; his wife, Kate Mayo; and Captain Scott are discussing Robert's imminent departure. Both James and Kate wish he would stay, but Captain Scott appears delighted. Andrew enters and voices his approval of Robert's decision then goes off to check on a cow. Robert then enters and reveals his intention to stay. James and Kate are dumbfounded but supportive, though Captain Scott expresses outrage and, more deeply, disappointment. "I've been cuttin' sure on havin' Robert for company on this vige [voyage]—to sorta talk to and show things to, and teach, kinda" (1:593).

Andrew returns and overhears the conversation; understanding what has happened with Robert and Ruth, though not letting on, he openly refutes his dream of settling on the farm and accepts his brother's berth on Captain Scott's vessel, with the excuse that he feels he "oughtn't to miss this chance to go out into the world and see things" (1:596). James accuses him of going because Robert won Ruth's love over him. Andrew insists he wishes to go, igniting a shouting match. Andrew swears he is no longer interested in farming, and James calls him a liar. The argument nearly comes to blows, but Robert jumps between them. James denounces Andrew, vowing to throw him out of the house even if he decides to stay, and storms out of the room. Kate follows him out in tears. Robert, in terrible throes of guilt, begs Andrew not to go. He also accuses Andrew of lying. Andrew admits to that but remains adamant about his decisions. He tries to soothe Robert's guilt over the matter and promises that "everything'll turn out all right in the end" before heading off to pack (1:601).

### Act 2, Scene 1

The sitting room of the Mayo farmhouse. By act 2, scene 1, the farm has slowly gone to waste, a direct result of Andrew's departure in act 1. James Mayo has died, and Robert lacks the work ethic and agricultural know-how to run a farm successfully. O'Neill describes the farmhouse in the STAGE DIRECTIONS for act 2, scene 1, as a site of growing disrepair and neglect: *"Little significant details give evidence of carelessness, of inefficiency, of an industry gone to seed"* (1:602). Robert has mortgaged the farm, and his farmhand Ben quits on the grounds that other hands in the area mock him for working such a failed venture. Andrew is expected back any time from his first voyage. At the end of the scene, Ruth has disavowed her love for Robert and admits that she had been in love with Andrew all along. Robert thus realizes he has thrown up his lifetime ambitions and embarked on a career for which he was entirely unfit, merely for a capricious romantic tryst. Andrew's voice comes up from the road, "Ahoy there!" Robert responds with *"forced cheeriness"* and walks out to greet him (1:617).

### Act 2, Scene 2

A hot day on the top of a hill on the farm at around 11 o'clock in the morning; a view of the sea is in the backdrop. The scene opens with Robert despondently caring for Mary and staring out at the horizon. Andrew's "angle of looking at things" has changed considerably over his three-year voyage around the globe. He has grown more cosmopolitan, but his practical side manifests a voracious materialism: "I feel ripe for bigger things than settling down here. The trip did that for me, anyway. It showed me the world is a larger proposition than ever I thought it was in the old days. I couldn't be content anymore stuck here like a fly in molasses" (1:626). Rather than sharing Robert's romantic quest for beauty and truth "beyond the horizon," Andrew is bent on empire-building as a speculator in BUENOS AIRES, ARGENTINA. He even insists that he had never truly loved Ruth. Ruth enters, suspicious that Robert told Andrew of her love for him. Robert leaves with Mary at Ruth's insistence, and she soon discovers that Andrew does not know about her admittance. Robert returns with Mary and Captain Scott. Though Andrew had planned to resurrect the farm and visit his family over a six-month period, Captain Scott has found a ship sailing to Argentina within a day, and Andrew will embark the following morning. In so doing, though not deliberately, he rejects a woman who loves him and abandons a brother who needs him.

### Act 3, Scene 1

The sitting room of the Mayo's farmhouse five years later; *"the whole atmosphere"* of the room, *"contrasted with that of former years, is one of an habitual poverty too hopelessly resigned to be any longer ashamed or even conscious of itself."* Robert is dying of pleurisy (corresponding with O'Neill's bout of tuberculosis from 1912–13), his daughter Mary has died, and Ruth's *"capacity for emotion has been exhausted"* (1:631). Ruth believes her daughter is "better off—being dead," foreshadowing the sense of release Robert experiences pending his own demise in the final scene and a dark sentiment O'Neill brings up earlier with the immigrant child in FOG and much later with the deceased night clerk in HUGHIE. And like the "black Irish" O'Neill claimed as his heritage, Robert has renounced any faith in God: "I could curse God from the bottom of my soul—if there was a God!" (1:634). Robert, as yet unaware that he has only a few hours to live, conjures a new vision. Admitting defeat as a farmer, he now wants to try his hand in the city, perhaps as a writer, "where people live instead of stagnating" (1:635).

Andrew reappears, back from a series of triumphs and failures as a speculator; his face has been *"hardened by the look of decisiveness"* and projects *"a ruthless cunning"* (1:639). Andrew's luck ran out in his last gamble in commodities trading. He is disgusted with himself and, as JAMES O'NEILL, JR., was in actual life, cynically resigned to his failure. He has sent for a chest specialist to treat his brother, but the doctor says that Robert's condition is too advanced for any meaningful treatment. In this scene, however, O'Neill offers a faint undercurrent of hope. Robert asks Andrew to marry Ruth, as "only with contact with suffering . . . will you awaken" (1:647). Though it is unclear what, precisely, Andrew is being asked to awaken from, we know that neither brother has followed his natural

path—suffering arises, O'Neill suggests, from living a life that does not conform to one's nature.

### Act 3, Scene 2

The same bucolic setting as act 1, scene 1. Robert has escaped from his convalescence out his bedroom window and climbed to the hilltop where he can watch the sunrise, dreaming one last time of what lies beyond the horizon. Ruth and Andrew follow, and his dying words to them speak to O'Neill's theme of death as endowing its victim the freedom to pursue his dreams at last: "You mustn't feel sorry for me. Don't you see I'm happy at last—free—free!—freed from the farm—free to wander on and on—eternally! . . . Look! Isn't it beautiful beyond the hills? I can hear the old voices calling me to co—(*exultantly*) And this time I'm going! It isn't the end. It's a free beginning—the start of my voyage! I've won to my trip—the right of release—beyond the horizon! Oh, you ought to be glad—glad—for my sake! . . . Remember Ruth—. . . Ruth has suffered—remember, Andy—only through sacrifice—the secret beyond there—. . . The sun! . . . Remember!" (1:652).

## COMMENTARY

A few months following the play's unexpected Broadway triumph, which propelled O'Neill to the height of his profession, O'Neill sent a letter to the *New York Times* explaining the play's original conception. In it, he recalled a Norwegian sailor from his time aboard the CHARLES RACINE who pined longingly for his family farm and cursed the day he first signed on to a ship (the character Olson in *The* LONG VOYAGE HOME is also based on him). At the time, O'Neill sensed that the Norwegian's complaints were disingenuous, as in his 20 years at sea, he had not once returned to his homeland. Contemplating his friend years later, O'Neill asked himself,

> What if he had stayed on the farm, with his instincts? What would have happened? But I realized at once he never would have stayed. . . . And from that point I started to think of a more intellectual, civilized type . . . a man who would have my Norwegian's inborn craving for the sea's unrest, only in him it would be con-

scious, too conscious, intellectually diluted into a vague, intangible wanderlust. His powers of resistance, both moral and physical, would also probably be correspondingly watered. He would throw away his instinctive dream and accept the thralldom of the farm for—why, for almost any nice little poetical craving—the romance of sex, say (quoted in Clark 94, 95).

The "more intellectual, civilized type" O'Neill envisioned is the highly autobiographical character Robert Mayo. Structurally speaking, each of the play's three acts contains two scenes: One takes place in the open air of the New England countryside and the other in the Mayo family sitting room. A simple enough, if experimental formula, this structure was enormously difficult to produce, as each set change required an enormous overhaul; in its first Broadway run, though only a three-act play, its performance time lasted nearly four hours (Bogard 118).

The farm's location might be either NEW LONDON, CONNECTICUT, or Truro, Massachusetts, on Cape Cod. It more probably takes place in Truro, near Provincetown, as O'Neill got the names Mayo and Atkins from two heroic members of the life-saving station at PEAKED HILL BAR that O'Neill's father bought him and AGNES BOULTON as a wedding present (Richter 167). Mayo and Atkins drowned during a rescue mission in 1880; their names were first memorialized in Provincetown folklore and then in the first great tragedy of the United States's first great tragedian. If Robert closely resembles O'Neill himself, and Andrew, if to a lesser degree, his brother James "Jamie" O'Neill, Jr., the elder Mayos also resemble the author's parents, JAMES O'NEILL and MARY ELLEN "ELLA" O'NEILL. This forms a connecting link from O'Neill's first major full-length play to his last—the intensely autobiographical LONG DAY'S JOURNEY INTO NIGHT. In the final scene of *Beyond the Horizon*, Andrew denounces his love for the farm, just as James, Jr., in *Long Day's Journey* denounces his father's stage trumpery as the "Count of Monte Cristo." The terrible argument between father and son that ensues is never reconciled.

*Beyond the Horizon* attempts to reconcile the tragic but spiritually sustaining power of life

dreams. Unlike the later "pipe dreams" spouted by O'Neill's dissipated characters in *The ICEMAN COMETH* or the consciously delusional aspirations "Erie" Smith conveys in *Hughie,* the dreams in this play, specifically those of the two brothers, Robert and Andrew Mayo, have every likelihood of being realized. But the draw of sex and the power of jealousy impel both brothers to enact a destructive role reversal that ends, fatally, in emotional bankruptcy for Andrew and poverty-stricken death for Robert. Autobiographically, as O'Neill biographers Arthur and Barbara Gelb note, the love triangle between Robert, Andrew, and Ruth is undoubtedly a rehashing of O'Neill's affair with LOUISE BRYANT, the fiancée and then wife of his Provincetown friend the radical journalist JOHN REED (635). Robert responds in the way O'Neill did when Bryant broke off their relationship in favor of Reed: "God! It wasn't that I haven't guessed how mean and small you are—but I've kept on telling myself that I must be wrong—like a fool!—like a damned fool!" And moments before Andrew's arrival, Robert violently thrusts her away from him and wakes the baby by yelling, "You—you slut!" (1:616)

No one in this play is a survivor. Each of O'Neill's characters' dreams are dashed irretrievably: Mrs. Mayo's vision of Robert settling down with a family on the farm ends with both the farm and the family's destruction; Mrs. Atkins, Ruth's termagant mother, is a "chronic invalid" who openly derides Robert's inability to run the farm and always believes her daughter made a grievous mistake by not marrying Andrew; James Mayo's assumption that the farm would, under Andrew's leadership, prosper into one of the finest in New England never comes to fruition; Ruth's romantic image of Robert is deflated after less than three years; Andrew's dream of marrying Ruth and working the farm is shattered, and, having next turned to speculation (the ultimate American Dream), he fails in that as well; the child Mary, the only source of Robert's happiness, is dead; and Robert only answers the pregnant call from "beyond the horizon" with his own death. Even the amiable Captain Scott, who had longed to serve as his nephew's mentor on the SEA, is rebuffed in the end by Andrew's materialism and innate distaste for the "sea's unrest."

O'Neill critic Barbara Voglino reads the ending of *Beyond the Horizon* as a rationale for O'Neill's abandonment of his first wife, KATHLEEN JENKINS, and his son EUGENE O'NEILL, JR., just nine years before its composition, "as preferable to a life of clipped wings like Robert" (32). Robert, she goes on, "merely made the wrong choice and was too weak to extricate himself from the consequences" (29). If one accepts this reading, Robert is simply "one of O'Neill's many self-deluded characters" (31).

Like Robert "Yank" Smith in *The* HAIRY APE, who finally achieves a sense of belonging in death, Robert is freed by death, after long imprisonment on the farm, to "wander on and on—eternally!" (1:652) "Discarding through death his individuating consciousness," Travis Bogard writes of Robert's tragic end, "ridding himself of the poet's awareness of the need for belonging, he moves through death into the mainstream of continuous life energy" (130). Indeed, the very last lines of O'Neill's stage directions demonstrate the author's dedication to what Arthur and Barbara Gelb call "tragedy's tonic effect" (638): "[Ruth] *remains silent, gazing at him dully with the sad humility of exhaustion, her mind already sinking back into that spent calm beyond the further troubling of any hope*" (1:653). Only after abandoning all hope can she free herself from disillusionment; only then can she relieve her suffering.

## CHARACTERS

**Atkins, Ruth**    Robert Mayo's wife. At the outset, Ruth Atkins invokes, somewhat like the character Josie Hogan in A MOON FOR THE MISBEGOTTEN, the robust self-reliance of a proud country woman: "*Her small, regular features are marked by a certain strength—an underlying, stubborn fixity of purpose hidden in the frankly appealing charm of her fresh youthfulness*" (1:578). We first meet Ruth wearing a white dress, and as O'Neill critic Virginia Floyd points out, "Ruth's white dress, like Mildred's in *The Hairy Ape*, signals a manipulatively virginal, but willfully destructive, nature" (143). Typical of O'Neill's depictions of tortured romances and unfulfilling marriages, Ruth Atkins, a woman, unwittingly distorts and destroys both Robert and

Andrew's quests to find happiness. At first, it seems to everyone, including Robert, that she is meant to marry Andrew. But in act 1, scene 1, we discover that Ruth is, in fact, enamored with Robert's poetic nature and begs him not to join his uncle Captain Scott on the voyage "beyond the horizon" he has always dreamed of. Apparently out of lust rather than love, Robert agrees to abandon his dream in order to be with her, a decision that goads his brother Andrew into taking his place at SEA. As such, Ruth is the first major female character in the O'Neill canon (the first is actually Maud Steele in BREAD AND BUTTER, which was never produced) to embody, as Judith Barlow phrases it, "the venerable myth that domesticity, even when freely chosen, kills the male of the species; woman is a trope for the bourgeois life, the insensitivity and materialism that annihilate the artistic soul" (165), if more sympathetically than other O'Neill female characters.

**Atkins, Mrs.**    Ruth Atkins's mother. Mrs. Atkins, a rough-spoken termagant, strongly protests her daughter's union with Robert Mayo and quite correctly, if abusively, insists that Ruth would have been better off married to Andrew. She suffers from partial paralysis and uses a wheelchair; as such, "*she has developed the selfish, irritable nature of the chronic invalid*" (1:602).

**Mayo, Andrew**    Robert Mayo's brother. O'Neill describes Andrew as "*an opposite type to Robert— husky, sun-bronzed, handsome in a large-featured, manly fashion—a son of the soil, intelligent in a shrewd way, but with nothing of the intellectual about him*" (1:573). Perhaps counterinstinctively, there is no resentment between them. Robert and Andrew fully respect each other's differences—Robert the intellectual dreamer, Andrew the practical laborer. Andrew transforms into a materialist wanderer, however, when he decides to take his brother's place aboard Captain Scott's bark the *Sundra*. O'Neill later and more fully explores the spiritually destructive power of materialism through his character Marco Polo in MARCO MILLIONS—which he originally conceived as "The Play of Andrew," a sequel to *Beyond the Horizon* (Floyd 1981, 30, 58)—as he also does in the character Anthony

Brown in *The GREAT GOD BROWN*. By choosing to go to sea in place of his brother Robert, the underlying assumption is that, like Robert, who stays on the farm, Andrew's fate is ironic: By following his brother's path, he tragically falls into a materialist trap bereft of the spiritual meaning Robert might have experienced had their positions been reversed.

**Mayo, James** James is a loving father with a strong head for business but uncompromising in his assumption that Andrew will "live and die right here on this farm, like I expect to" (1:588)—just as James O'Neill, Sr., assumed that his son Jamie would replace him as a matinee idol on the popular stage. And like the elder O'Neill, James Mayo feels that Andrew's decision to take his brother's place is a deliberate betrayal of their unwritten agreement that his oldest son would head the farm after him. Mayo dies two years prior to act 2 and never reconciles his dispute with Andrew, who was meant to take over his farm but instead went to sea and rejected his birthright as owner of the farm after hearing of Robert and Ruth's love for one another.

**Mayo, Kate** Mrs. Mayo is as loving and as long-suffering as MARY ELLEN "ELLA" O'NEILL, Eugene's mother; and as Ella accused her oldest son James for fatally infecting her infant EDMUND BURKE O'NEILL with measles, Mrs. Mayo blames Andrew's betrayal for her husband's death, which precedes the action of act 2.

**Mayo, Mary** Robert and Ruth Mayo's child, who dies by act 3 because of the mishandlings of a "quack" doctor (1:632)—a narrative device O'Neill also employs in *Long Day's Journey into Night* to blame on his mother's drug addiction (Mary Tyrone in the play) following his difficult birth.

**Mayo, Robert** Andrew Mayo's brother. Robert is an avatar of the playwright who also appears in earlier plays as the Poet in *FOG* and Michael Cope in *WELDED*, and later in heightened autobiographical forms such as Richard Miller in *AH, WILDERNESS!* and Edmund Tyrone in *Long Day's Journey into Night*, among others. Like O'Neill in his youth

and the character Paul Andersen in *CHRIS CHRISTOPHERSEN,* Robert spent a fruitless year in college and dreams of a vagabond's life at sea. A young, highly emotional, intellectual dreamer whose hopes are dashed in a variety of untenable ways, Robert Mayo, like the others, is the physical as well as psychological embodiment of his creator: *"He is a tall, slender young man of twenty-three. There is a touch of the poet about him expressed in his high forehead and wide, dark eyes. His features are delicate and refined, leaning to weakness in the mouth and chin"* (1:573). Through Robert, O'Neill perpetuates what O'Neill critic Travis Bogard called "Horizon Syndrome," an endemic American obsession with a drive toward what exists "beyond the horizon," connoting in fiction, drama, poetry, and elsewhere a "boundless aspiration for a somewhat vaguely defined freedom of spirit" (125). Bogard turns to the American playwright Edward Sheldon's *The High Road* (1912) as a probable source of such an aspiration. But O'Neill was also a lifelong admirer of Jack London, whose characters in his autobiographical novels *Martin Eden* (1909) and *The Valley of the Moon* (1913), like Robert Mayo, repeatedly called up the horizon metaphor to express their artistic and spiritual drive. His dream of viewing life beyond the horizon is dashed by his more powerful sex drive, and he initiates a romantic relationship with Ruth Atkins. Thus Robert suffers from an ironic fate in that he pursues a life course of rural domesticity meant for someone else—his brother Andrew.

**Dick Scott, Captain** Kate Mayo's brother and captain of the bark *Sundra.* Captain Scott is eager to mentor either of his nephews in seamanship. Though Robert originally signs on to ship out with him, his infatuation with Ruth overpowers him, and his heartbroken brother Andrew takes his place. Scott is based on a New London seaman, Captain T. A. Scott, O'Neill's boyhood sweetheart Maibelle Scott's grandfather (Richter 167).

### BIBLIOGRAPHY

Barlow, Judith. "O'Neill's Female Characters." In *The Cambridge Companion to Eugene O'Neill,* edited by Michael Manheim, 164–177. New York: Cambridge University Press, 1998.

Bogard, Travis. *Contour in Time: The Plays of Eugene O'Neill.* Rev. ed. New York: Oxford University Press, 1988.

Clark, Barrett H. *Eugene O'Neill: The Man and His Plays.* Rev. ed. New York: Dover, 1947.

Floyd, Virginia. *The Plays of Eugene O'Neill: A New Assessment.* New York: Ungar, 1985.

Floyd, Virginia, ed. *Eugene O'Neill at Work: Newly Released Ideas for His Plays.* New York: Ungar, 1981.

Gelb, Arthur, and Barbara Gelb. *O'Neill: Life with Monte Cristo.* New York: Applause Books, 2000.

Richter, Robert A. *Eugene O'Neill and Dat Ole Davil Sea: Maritime Influences in the Life and Works of Eugene O'Neill.* Mystic, Conn.: Mystic Seaport, 2004.

Voglino, Barbara. *"Perverse Mind": Eugene O'Neill's Struggle with Closure.* London: Associated University Presses, 1999.

Woollcott, Alexander. "Eugene O'Neill's Tragedy." In *Playwright's Progress: O'Neill and the Critics.* Chicago: Scott, Foresman and Company, 1965.

## *Bound East for Cardiff: A Play in One Act* (completed, 1914; first produced, 1916)

*Bound East for Cardiff* is widely hailed as one of Eugene O'Neill's finest one-act plays, unaccountably achieving so early in his career, according to O'Neill BIOGRAPHERS Arthur and Barbara Gelb, "that balance of realism, detachment and symbolism soon to emerge" (456). Indeed, they continue, of his first 20 plays written over a four-year period, 1913–17, only *Bound East* and *The* MOON OF THE CARIBBEES survive as "theater milestones" (639). The one-act SEA play also carries the distinction of being O'Neill's debut for the stage, followed closely by *THIRST* a month later. Though first produced for the PROVINCETOWN PLAYERS' second season at the WHARF THEATRE in Provincetown, Massachusetts, on July 28, 1916, O'Neill had written *Bound East for Cardiff* over two years earlier (winter 1914) under the title *Children of the*

*Sea* (which he later revised) at the Rippin family home in NEW LONDON, CONNECTICUT. He probably sent it, along with *ABORTION*, to Professor GEORGE PIERCE BAKER for admittance into Baker's famous English drama workshop at Harvard University. The slight revisions O'Neill made to the original script were undoubtedly due to Baker's tutelage (Voelker 209).

O'Neill's theatrical breakthrough is now the stuff of legend. While visiting Provincetown on a lark with his friend and mentor of PHILOSOPHICAL ANARCHISM, TERRY CARLIN (on whom the character Larry Slade in *The* ICEMAN COMETH is closely based), O'Neill read the play at Mary Heaton Vorse's house in front of an imposing audience of bohemian artists and writers, including Vorse, GEORGE CRAM "JIG" COOK, SUSAN GLASPELL, JOHN REED, LOUISE BRYANT, Harry Kemp, Hutchins Hapgood, Neith Boyce, and others (Alexander 222). Though accounts of the meeting differ (mostly depending on who is trying to take credit for his discovery), O'Neill later confirmed that he read the script to the group himself, and Harry Kemp recalled that O'Neill "delivered [the play] in his low, deep, slightly monotonous but compelling voice." After the final lines had been read, Kemp continued, everyone in the room

Production photo of *Bound East for Cardiff* by the Provincetown Players, The Wharf Theatre (Provincetown, Massachusetts), July 28, 1916. John Reed is second from left, and George Cram "Jig" Cook, playing Yank, lies "dying" on the lower bunk. *(Courtesy of the Museum of the City of New York)*

The Wharf Theatre in 1934, where O'Neill premiered as a playwright in 1916 *(Copyright Leona Rust Egan)*

understood that "here was a genuine playwright" (quoted in Gelb 556); Vorse concurred: "There was no one there during that reading who did not recognize the quality of this play. Here was something new, the true feeling of the sea" (quoted in Richter 106). A strong case can be made that this single evening permanently altered the course of AMERICAN THEATER.

By all accounts, the production was an enormous success. O'Neill both directed and took the one-line part of the second mate, while Jig Cook, who later directed many O'Neill plays for the Provincetown Players, played the dying sailor Yank. Susan Glaspell recalled of the premiere that "it seems to me I have never sat before a more moving production" (quoted in Gelb 569), and the *Evening Sun* wrote that "the play was real, subtly tense and avoided a dozen pitfalls that might have made it 'the regular thing'" (quoted in Gelb 584). Though *Thirst*, produced that August, did not earn such accolades, in an article entitled "Many Literary Lights among the Provincetown Players," the *Bos-*

*ton Sunday Globe* reported that "it begins to look as if the American drama may be richer for the fun and the work of the Provincetown Players this summer [1916]. They have put on two plays by Eugene O'Neil [sic], a young dramatist whose work was heretofore unproduced and who, they are confident, is going to be heard from in places less remote than Provincetown" (quoted in Gelb 573). Jig Cook knew full well the colossal importance of the play, telling the Chicago journalist Edna Kenton upon her arrival to Cape Cod:

> You don't know Gene yet. . . . You don't know his plays. But you will. All the world will know Gene's plays some day. Last summer this thing [the Provincetown Players] began. This year, on the night he first came to Provincetown and read us *Bound East for Cardiff*, we knew we had something to go with. Some day this little theater will be famous; some day the little theater in New York will be famous—this fall the Provincetown Players go into New York with *Cardiff* on their first bill. (quoted in Sheaffer 358)

That fall, on November 3, 1916, the Provincetown Players opened their first theater in New York, the Playwrights' Theatre at 139 MacDougal Street (later moved to 133, where it became the Provincetown Playhouse), and included *Bound East*, along with Louise Bryant's *The Game* and Floyd Dell's *King Arthur's Socks*, on its very first bill. Also that fall, Frank Shay published the play in pamphlet form with other Provincetown plays. *Bound East* was to be the first of O'Neill's SS GLENCAIRN series, which also includes *The* LONG VOYAGE HOME, *The Moon of the Caribbees*, and IN THE ZONE.

## SYNOPSIS

The seamen's forecastle (pronounced "fo'c'sle") of the British tramp steamer *Glencairn*, midway across the Atlantic Ocean heading from New York to Cardiff, Wales. Rows of bunks form a triangle at the far end. At right there are four portholes, and a doorway leads out at left front. Every minute or so, the blare of the ship's whistle drowns out all other sounds, indicating the ship is moving through a fog bank. Five men—Driscoll, Cocky, Davis, Scotty, and Olson—are discovered seated on a row of benches; four of them are smoking pipes, and the space is hazy with tobacco smoke. Paul, a Norwegian, is perched on the top bunk sporadically playing the accordion. On one of the lower bunks, Yank is lying motionless, perspiring heavily and looking extremely pale.

Cocky, who speaks in a cockney (or a British working-class) accent, is telling the others a tale of when, 10 years before, he hit a black woman, "greased all over with coconut oil," for making sexual advances toward him (1:187). The men laugh heartily at his expense, and Driscoll, a *"brawny Irishman,"* says, "a quane av the naygurs she musta been surely" (1:188). The others chime in that she was most likely a cannibal and, since the incident took place during the holiday season, one looking for Christmas dinner. Driscoll hushes the men when Yank groans and shifts in his bunk. He asks his friend if he needs water, but there comes no reply. Davis, another Irishman, reveals that Yank injured himself severely by falling down a hold. A longtime sailor, Yank barely whimpered

after falling and, with blood running from his mouth, tolerated being transferred to the forecastle in dignified silence. The captain attempted to diagnose Yank, but according to Driscoll, "all the toime he not knowin' whether 'twas cholery or the barber's itch was the matther wide Yank" (1:189). The men all praise Yank for a "good shipmate," and Driscoll recounts how he and Yank have sailed together as the best of friends for over five years. Olson, a Swede, voices concern that Yank has not yet eaten, which goads the rest into complaining about the food, *"forgetting the sick man in their sailor's delight at finding something to grumble about"* (1:190). Driscoll silences them ferociously and commands Paul to cease his accordion playing—at which point the fog whistle, as if mocking their attempts at a decorous end, *"sounds particularly loud in the silence"* (1:190).

Driscoll continues that he and Yank, on a foggy night such as this, once sailed together on a ship called the *Dover*, which went down. Calling to mind another of O'Neill's early sea plays, THIRST, Driscoll relates that he and Yank shared a lifeboat for seven days, during which time Yank kept his cool while Driscoll nearly went mad with thirst. At this, Yank opens his eyes. The men all question his condition, ask if he needs anything, and falsely pledge his quick return to health. Yank dismisses them as liars and replies that he accepts death as better than life at SEA.

It is time for Driscoll's watch, but Yank pleads with him to stay, and Driscoll promises not to abandon him. Smitty, an Englishman, and Ivan, a Russian, enter the forecastle after their watch, inquire about Yank, and promptly fall asleep in their bunks and begin snoring loudly. Yank howls with pain and spits blood. Driscoll moves to get the captain, but Yank implores him, again, to remain at his side, saying the captain cannot help him.

The captain and his second mate enter. The captain feels Yank's pulse, takes his temperature, and surmises his condition is worsening. After some further inspection, he informs Driscoll he can do nothing further, but he makes some lame assurances to Yank that he will be all right. Withering under Yank's knowing glare, he hastily exits with the mate. Driscoll echoes the captain's optimism, but Yank silences him and explains tenderly that he is unafraid of death. He confesses he had secretly wished that he and Driscoll could start a farm in Canada or Argentina, but never told him for fear of being made fun of. Driscoll admits he had the same aspiration. In a moment of mournful remembrance brought on by Yank's mention of Argentina, Driscoll recounts some of the picaresque experiences the two men shared at such exotic ports of call as BUENOS AIRES, Singapore, Port Said, Sydney, and Cape Town. Yank fearfully remembers a scrape in Cape Town, South Africa, when he stabbed a man to death, and he wonders whether he will be forgiven in the afterlife. Driscoll assures him the act was in self-defense, as the man attacked him from behind.

Envisioning his impending burial at sea, Yank wishes he could die out on deck with the stars and moon, as "it'd make it easier to go—somehow" (1:197). He tells Driscoll to divide his pay among the other men and take his only possession, his watch, for Driscoll's own. He also requests that he buy a box of candies for a barmaid in Cardiff named Fanny, who at one time loaned Yank money when he was broke. Yank now knows he is about to die and remarks that the fog seems to be pouring into the forecastle. He bids farewell to his friend and, staring straight ahead, asks, "Who's that?" Driscoll sees nothing. "A pretty lady dressed in black," Yank faintly whispers (1:198). Driscoll cries out for Yank, but he is dead.

Cocky enters and announces that the fog has lifted. He sees Driscoll praying softly on his knees and, about to rail him for "sayin' 'is prayers," recognizes Yank is dead and softly exhales, "Gawd blimey!" (1:199).

## COMMENTARY

At first glance, *Bound East for Cardiff* appears to be a fairly simple, perhaps even simplistic, representation of life at sea. Teachers and students alike might find it difficult, then, to identify the elements in the play that generated the level of critical praise it enjoyed in O'Neill's time and into our own. As late as 1934, O'Neill himself wrote the critic Richard Dana Skinner just two years before winning the NOBEL PRIZE IN LITERATURE,

*Bound East for Cardiff* (Very important, this play! In it can be seen—or felt—the germ of the spirit, life-attitude, etc. of all my significant future work—and it was written practically within my first half-year as a playwright, before I went to [George Pierce Baker], under whose influence the following year I did nothing worth 1/10 as original. Remember in these U.S. in 1914 *Bound East for Cardiff* was a daring innovation in form and content). (quoted in Richter 146–147)

Biographer Stephen A. Black identifies O'Neill's "particular genius" as an ability to "express the meaning of feeling . . . that is the way of *Long Day's Journey into Night* works, and the same can be said of most of O'Neill's good plays, even as early as *Children of the Sea*" (the play's first title, 159). As is the case with O'Neill's other "theater milestone," *The Moon of the Caribbees*, critic Heywood Broun noted of the play that its impact is due "more to the creation of mood and atmosphere than to any fundamentally interesting idea or sudden twist of plot" (quoted in Gelb 594). O'Neill strikes this mood with his use of the seamen's banter in foreign dialects, the realistic setting of the forecastle, the ship's whistle, and the elements of weather to provide atmosphere.

The play's reputation (to make, perhaps, too cynical a point) can also be attributed in part to the mythic opening night at the Wharf Theatre in Provincetown, Massachusetts. The Wharf was a fishing shack on a pier owned by Mary Heaton Vorse; the PROVINCETOWN PLAYERS converted it into a makeshift venue to air their theatrical experiments to the public. Given the first production's "lofty position in theater history," the scholar Zander Brietzke recently made a near-blasphemous remark that the first production was probably "pretty awful" (for one reason because O'Neill himself, a notorious victim of stage fright, had played the Second Mate) (44). Nevertheless, fellow PULITZER PRIZE–winning playwright and Provincetown Player Susan Glaspell famously remarked of the premiere:

The sea has been good to Eugene O'Neill. It was there for his opening. There was a fog, just as the script demanded, fog bell in the harbor.

The tide was in, and it washed under us and around, spraying through the holes in the floor, giving us the rhythm and the flavor of the sea while the big dying sailor talked to his friend Drisc of the life he had always wanted deep in the land, where you'd never see a ship or smell the sea. . . . It is not merely figurative language to say the old wharf shook with applause. (quoted in Gelb 569)

The juxtaposition of sea and land, which we also find in O'Neill's third *Glencairn* play, *The Long Voyage Home*, as well as BEYOND THE HORIZON and *"ANNA CHRISTIE,"* among others, presents the cyclical aspect of life at sea as one that imprisons its victims (sailors); hence O'Neill's title choice—"bound"—a pun that indicates not just the movement across the Atlantic to Wales, but also the notion that sailors are bound tightly to the sea without hope of escape (Brietzke 44).

*Bound East for Cardiff* is, as the critic Heywood Broun described it, a "mood play," one that deeply probes, in the mode of the Russian author Leo Tolstoy's novella *The Death of Ivan Ilich*, into the last thoughts and feelings of a dying man. Unlike the bourgeois Ilich, however, whose "most simple and most ordinary and therefore most terrible" existence middle-class audiences might readily relate to, O'Neill bears the challenge of inducing sympathy from an audience mostly unfamiliar with the sailor's life. Artistic strides had been made to introduce middle-class audiences to a realistic portrayal of the working CLASS in other media at least as early as the 1880s, but O'Neill's was a "new type of drama with a focus on the working-class subject as its crucial element" (Chura 526). The basis of this sympathy comes across through the companionship of the two men, Driscoll and Yank. In many ways, Driscoll has the hardest time confronting his friend's death, as he will be left without the one meaningful facet of his life—his relationship with Yank. Yank becomes terror-stricken at the thought of dying alone but says that though he has never been a religious man,

I know whatever it is what comes after it can't be no worser'n this . . . [J]ust one ship after another, hard work, small pay, and bum grub;

and when we git into port, just a drunk endin' up in a fight, and all your money gone, and then ship away again. Never meetin' no nice people; never gittin' outa sailor town, hardly, in any port; travelin' all over the world and never seein' none of it; without no one to care whether you're alive or dead. (*with a bitter smile*) There ain't much in all that that'd make yuh sorry to lose it, Drisc. (1:195)

Yank's only regret is leaving Driscoll behind. Unlike Yank's namesake in O'Neill's expressionistic full-length play *The HAIRY APE*, who in scene 1 explicitly rejects the other sailor's desire for a life on dry land—a home, a family, and female companionship—Yank longs for all of that. Ironically, he may have achieved it all if both men had been comfortable expressing their mutual desire. When Yank admits that he was afraid Driscoll would have laughed at the thought, Driscoll responds, "Laugh at you, is ut? When I'm havin' the same thoughts myself, toime afther toime" (1:196).

Along with its innovative portrayal of class, O'Neill biographer Louis Sheaffer notes that although the fiction writers Jack London and Joseph Conrad enjoyed enormous critical and popular success with their sea tales, up to that point no serious American playwright had adopted the sea as a subject. O'Neill's experience on the SS PHILADELPHIA, the SS NEW YORK, the CHARLES RACINE, and most important, the SS IKALA, the freighter on which O'Neill served in 1911 and on which the SS *Glencairn* is based, along with his cumulative knowledge of the theater after touring with his matinee-idol father, JAMES O'NEILL, made him the perfect writer to fill this literary gap. Of the *Glencairn* series, O'Neill wrote to the famed critic and editor H. L. Mencken that "they deal with merchant-sailor life on a tramp steamer as it really is—its sordidness inexplicably touched with romance by the glamour of the horizons" (quoted in Richter 146). In some ways, one might say the year 1916 marked a new era in representations of the sea, as not only did it see the premieres of *Bound East* and *Thirst*, it also signaled the end of the older generation, as Jack London, one of O'Neill's greatest literary heroes, died the same year.

Far more interested in self-actualization than social justice, however, O'Neill instills the "glamour" of his working-class subjects into his plays more than the radical political concerns his progenitors—such as the earnest socialist Jack London or even his fellow Provincetowner John Reed—expressed elsewhere. "The young O'Neill may have been engaged more by the Jack London romance of his subject," Joel Pfister suggests of the working-class elements in the *Glencairn* series, "than by the opportunity it afforded him for social criticism. He saw his own experience as a seaman (1910–1911) as an expression of his personal revolt against middle-class ways" (109). Travis Bogard attributes the ambience and philosophical treatment of sea life to another of O'Neill's great influences, the British novelist Joseph Conrad—specifically his novel *The Nigger of the Narcissus*, which O'Neill read in 1911 just before signing on to the *Ikala*. Bogard argues that Conrad was even more influential to the "reality" O'Neill constructs than his experience on the *Ikala* (38): "To enter the forecastle of the steamer *Glencairn* is to meet the brothers of the crew of the *Narcissus*" (39). Most significantly, Bogard discovered that O'Neill derived his original title from Conrad's novel, as Conrad at one point refers to the sailors as "the everlasting children of the mysterious sea" (quoted in Bogard 40).

Bogard further points to both the mood struck by Conrad and O'Neill respectively as more important than plot, and NATURALISM—the relinquishing of one's destiny to forces beyond one's control—resonates powerfully in both texts. Bogard continues that the "pretty lady dressed in black" who arrives to take possession of Yank's soul demonstrates a "positive assertion" not found in the other three *Glencairn* plays, in which O'Neill's "ironic fate crushes men" (43). In addition, unlike the invisible *"personification of the ironic life force"* the prostitute character Rose Thomas perceives in the final scene of O'Neill's *The WEB* (1:28), in *Bound East* the audience actually witnesses the entrance of the "pretty woman." This touch of EXPRESSIONISM in the final scene has been read in a number of ways: a residual hallucination of Fanny the barmaid, to whom Yank requests Driscoll to deliver a box of chocolates and who thus has the distinction

of being the subject of Yank's last wish; the cannibalistic "quane av the naygurs"; and the personification of death itself (Törnqvist 173–174). But given O'Neill's original title, *Children of the Sea*, the "pretty lady" is perhaps most clearly understood as the sea mother arriving to collect her child at the moment of his death. Bogard concludes his analysis of *Bound East* with the thought that the arrival of the sea mother "suggests that the sea is ultimately kind, that it receives its own gently and that it mourns for them. . . . [M]en are not alone because they belong to the sea" (41, 43).

## CHARACTERS

**Captain, The**   Captain of the tramp steamer SS *Glencairn*. Critic Robert Richter maintains that with this character whom O'Neill describes as *"an old man with gray mustache and whiskers"* (1:193), O'Neill "reveals his knowledge of medical care aboard ship" (Richter 150). At the time, it was the captain's duty to provide perfunctory medical care, though his only training consisted of "previous experience and a reference book" (Richter 150). The men all complain about the captain's medical abilities—ineffectually taking Yank's temperature, checking his pulse, and offering painkillers—yet at one point Driscoll, still groping at a hopeless hope, pleads desperately with the captain to help his dying friend Yank (1:194).

**Cocky**   British seaman on the tramp steamer SS *Glencairn*. O'Neill describes Cocky in the opening scene as a *"weazened runt of a man"* (1:187). Cocky has the first lines of the play, in which he relates to the other men of the forecastle that a "bloomin' nigger" woman at one port made sexual advances toward him, and he subsequently "fetched 'er a biff on the ear wot knocked 'er silly" (1:188). The men joke at Cocky's expense that the woman must have a "quane av the naygurs" and be a cannibal looking to make Cocky her Christmas dinner. O'Neill uses Cocky as an opening device to demonstrate his mastery of the seamen's banter, lore, and dialect. Cocky appears in all four *Glencairn* plays.

**Davis**   American seaman on the tramp steamer SS *Glencairn*. A *"middle-aged man with black hair* *and a mustache"* (1:188), Davis is a minor character who speaks in a mild Irish brogue. Davis witnessed Yank's fatal tumble down the hold and tells the men that although it was clear "he was hurt bad inside for the blood was drippin' from the side of his mouth," Yank bravely "never let a word out of him" (1:189). Davis also appears in *The Moon of the Caribbees* and *In the Zone*.

**Driscoll**   Irish seaman on the tramp steamer SS *Glencairn*. Driscoll, *"a brawny Irishman with the battered features of a prizefighter"* (1:188), is based on an Irish-born drinking partner of O'Neill's at Jimmy "The Priest's" bar, also named Driscoll, who worked on the same ship with O'Neill, the SS *Philadelphia*, as a coal stoker. The real Driscoll committed suicide, an unaccountable act to O'Neill's mind and one that later inspired him to write *The Hairy Ape*. In *Bound East for Cardiff*, Driscoll ministers to the needs of his best friend, Yank, who has fatally injured himself by falling down a hold. An otherwise coarse seaman, Driscoll nevertheless demonstrates an enormous amount of compassion and grief over the imminent death of his shipmate and closest friend of more than five years. Driscoll refuses to take his watch because Yank, though apparently unafraid of death, is terrified to be left alone while dying. Driscoll lies that his friend looks "as sthrong as an ox" (1:191) but knows that Yank will soon die.

   Over the course of the play, Yank and Driscoll sadly remember many of the adventures they had at sea and in the many waterfront districts of ports across the globe. At one point, Driscoll relates to the other seamen in the forecastle how Yank saved his life after a shipwreck. When Yank voices his fear that Driscoll might laugh at his dream to save up to buy a farm with Driscoll in Canada or Argentina, Driscoll responds, "Laugh at you, is ut? When I'm havin' the same thoughts myself, toime afther toime" (1:196). In the final scene, Driscoll's *"lips move in some half-remembered prayer"* and he *"makes the sign of the cross"* (1:198) as his friend passes away. Driscoll appears in all four *Glencairn* plays.

**Ivan**   Russian seaman on the tramp steamer SS *Glencairn*. O'Neill describes him as *"a dark burly fellow with a round stupid face"* (1:192). Ivan enters

with Smitty and, like Smitty, speaks a couple of lines and falls fast asleep on his bunk. Ivan's and Smitty's snoring, in the words of critic Egil Törnqvist, "together with the steamers whistle, form the ironic lullaby to Yank's lonely fight against the silent sleep that is in store for him" (1:172). Ivan also appears in *The Long Voyage Home* and *In the Zone*.

**Olson**   Swedish seaman on the tramp steamer SS *Glencairn*. Olson is based on a Norwegian seaman O'Neill worked with on the SS *Ikala* who, after 20 years at sea, pined for his farm back home (Gelb 290). His character was played by the world-renowned actor John Wayne in the director John Ford's film of *The Long Voyage Home* (1940), which adapts the whole SS *Glencairn* series into a sustained narrative. In *Bound East for Cardiff*, O'Neill simply describes him as a *"Swede with a drooping mustache"* (1:188). Olson plays a minor role in *Bound East* and *The Moon of the Caribbees*, but he is the shanghaied protagonist in *The Long Voyage Home*.

**Paul**   Norwegian seaman on the tramp steamer SS *Glencairn*. Paul entertains the men with his accordion. At one point, Driscoll demands that he stop playing: "Is that banshee schreechin' fit music for a sick man?" (1:190) Critic Egil Törnqvist makes the case that Driscoll's comparing the banshee of Irish legend to accordion music is significant, as "organ playing is what we expect at a funeral and a banshee, according to Irish popular belief, is a supernatural being who takes the shape of an old woman foretelling death by mournful singing or wailing" (Törnqvist 171). Paul also appears in *The Moon of the Caribbees* and *In the Zone*.

**Second Mate, The**   Second mate of the tramp steamer SS *Glencairn*. Although O'Neill often identified himself with the second mates of such sea plays as *The Personal Equation*, *Ile*, *Chris Christophersen*, *The Hairy Ape*, and the offstage character in *Thirst*, he describes this character as *"clean-shaven and middle-aged"* (1:193). Only 28 years old in the summer of its first run in Provincetown, O'Neill still chose to perform the role in the 1916 premiere of *Bound East for Cardiff* at the Wharf Theatre. The Second Mate has only one line in the play: "Isn't this your watch on the deck, Driscoll?" (1:194)

**Smitty** British seaman on the tramp steamer SS *Glencairn*. Described only as *"a young Englishman"* (1:192), Smitty is based on a sailor O'Neill once met at the Sailor's Opera Saloon in Buenos Aires, Argentina (Gelb 284; Yank also mentions the Sailor's Opera in the play, 1:196). In *Bound East for Cardiff*, Smitty is a minor character who speaks a couple of lines and then falls asleep on his bunk, but he plays a central role in two other plays from the SS *Glencairn* series, *The Moon of the Caribbees* and *In the Zone*. Smitty's and Ivan's snoring, Egil Törnqvist writes, "together with the steamers whistle, form the ironic lullaby to Yank's lonely fight against the silent sleep that is in store for him" (1:172).

**Yank** American seaman on the tramp steamer SS *Glencairn*. A *"dark-haired, hard-featured man"* (1:187) who drifts in and out of consciousness throughout the play, Yank is fatally injured after falling down a hold midway across the Atlantic. Yank's best friend, Driscoll, with whom he has served for over five years and experienced many adventures on land and at sea—at one point Yank saved Driscoll's life after a shipwreck—is ministering to his friend's needs as best he can and deceiving himself that Yank will make it through to Cardiff, where a doctor might cure him. Yank accepts death but fears dying alone. Death to Yank "can't be no worser'n this. . . . [J]ust one ship after another, hard work, small pay, and bum grub" (1:195). Though not a religious man, Yank still fears retribution in the afterlife, as he once killed a man in Cape Town, South Africa. Driscoll assures him the act was in self-defense: "I wisht I had nothin' blacker than that on my sowl. I'd not be afraid of the angel Gabriel himself" (1:197). Over the years, Yank secretly cultivated a pipe dream to leave the sea and make a life with Driscoll on a farm in Canada or Argentina, "to stay on dry land all your life and have a farm with a house of your own with cows and pigs and chickens, 'way in the middle of the land where yuh'd never smell the sea or see a ship" (1:195). In the final scene, Yank

apprehends a "pretty lady dressed in black" in the forecastle (1:198), a symbol of the sea mother who has come to take possession of her child. Yank also appears in *The Moon of the Caribbees*.

### BIBLIOGRAPHY

Alexander, Doris. *The Tempering of Eugene O'Neill.* New York: Harcourt, Brace, and World, 1962.

Black, Stephen A. *Eugene O'Neill: Beyond Mourning and Tragedy.* New Haven, Conn.: Yale University Press, 1999.

Bogard, Travis. *Contour in Time: The Plays of Eugene O'Neill.* Rev. ed. New York: Oxford University Press, 1988.

Brietzke, Zander. "*The Long Voyage Home*: A Vicious Cycle at Sea." *Eugene O'Neill Review* 28 (2006): 32–49.

Chura, Patrick. "'Vital Contact': Eugene O'Neill and the Working Class." *Twentieth Century Literature* (Winter 2003): 520–546.

Gelb, Arthur, and Barbara Gelb. *O'Neill: Life with Monte Cristo.* New York: Applause Books, 2000.

Pfister, Joel. *Staging Depth: Eugene O'Neill and the Politics of Psychological Discourse.* Cultural Studies of the United States. Chapel Hill: University of North Carolina Press, 1995.

Richter, Robert A. *Eugene O'Neill and Dat Ole Davil Sea: Maritime Influences in the Life and Works of Eugene O'Neill.* Mystic, Conn.: Mystic Seaport, 2004.

Sheaffer, Louis. *O'Neill: Son and Playwright.* Boston: Little, Brown, 1968.

Törnqvist, Egil. *Eugene O'Neill: A Playwright's Theatre.* Jefferson, N.C.: McFarland & Company, 2004.

Voelker, Paul D. "Eugene O'Neill and George Pierce Baker: A Reconsideration." *American Literature* 49, no. 2 (May, 1977): 206–220.

# *Bread and Butter: A Play in Four Acts* (completed, 1914; not yet produced)

Eugene O'Neill copyrighted his first full-length play, *Bread and Butter*, in early May 1914, though production notes indicate he began work on it the previous year. Written before O'Neill attended GEORGE PIERCE BAKER's playwriting workshop at Harvard University, the play has never been produced (though he copyrighted his first produced play, BOUND EAST FOR CARDIFF, less than two weeks after *Bread and Butter*), and O'Neill later disavowed it. Nevertheless, at the time O'Neill seemed confident in its artistic worth and innocently sent the script to the director and producer George C. Tyler soon after copyrighting it, expecting, in his words, "an immediate personal reading and reply within a week—possibly an acceptance" (O'Neill 125). The first and last acts of *Bread and Butter* take place in a parochial New England town called Bridgetown, most probably NEW LONDON, CONNECTICUT, though possibly Bridgeport, and the middle two acts occur in an artist's studio in Manhattan. In 1909, O'Neill shared a studio in the Lincoln Arcade Building at 65th Street and Broadway with a New London friend, Ed Keefe, and two young painters, George Bellows and Ed Ireland, who ushered him into their radical bohemian circle. Their art teacher, the famous Ashcan school painter Robert Henri, is reproduced in *Bread and Butter* as the character Eugene Grammont. O'Neill himself attended Henri's Ferrer Center, where he studied PHILOSOPHICAL ANARCHISM informally in 1915.

## SYNOPSIS

### Act 1

The Brown family sitting room. Edward Brown, his wife, and their eldest son, Edward Brown, Jr., are seated at a table in the center of the room. Edward, Jr., is a boorish snob whom his father, also a bore, is criticizing for having composed copy to advertise their hardware store that is "too wordy and solemn." Edward protests that he wishes to attract a "better class of people" to the family store. Brown, having grown up poor and worked his way up to the petty bourgeoisie, disabuses his son of the notion that wealthy patrons pay more than the working class, who "pay cash" (1:116). Changing the subject, Edward, Jr., complains that his father treats the youngest son, John Brown, too openly as the "pet of the family" (1:117), causing resentment among

the rest of the siblings. Brown makes no apologies but, rather, adds fuel to the fire by announcing his plan to send John, a recent Princeton graduate (and the only one of the five Brown children to attend college), to law school. Harry Brown, the dissipated but happy-go-lucky black sheep of the family, enters, having overheard the tail end of the conversation. He seconds his brother's resentful attitude but adds that John himself will never agree to go to law school, as his heart is in painting, not in a professional career. They move on to discuss John's budding romance with Maud Steele, the daughter of a local merchant whom Edward, Jr., had earlier asked to marry, though like Ruth Mayo in BEYOND THE HORIZON, Maud denied him in favor of his more romantic, sensitive brother.

The Brown daughters, Mary and Bessie, enter. Mary affirms the general resentment toward John, though Bessie, the prettier and livelier of the two, begs them all to leave John to follow his heart in both art and love. John furtively emerges from the doorway, and his appearance clearly contrasts with the rest of the Brown family, exposing a *"finer, more sensitive organization."* The family is visibly embarrassed, but Harry makes a joke of it, ushering John in with the lines, "Prisoner at the bar, you are accused [by Mary and Edward] . . . of being a flagrant member of the Idle Rich Class" (1:123), as well as of having asked Maud to marry him. John humors Harry's courtroom joke and confesses to being guilty on both counts. John also confirms his desire to pursue art rather than law: "My interest in life is different, and if I wish to be a man I must develope [sic] the inclinations which God has given me—not attempt to blot them out. . . . I am an artist in soul I know. My brain values are Art values. I want to learn how to express in terms of color the dreams in my brain which demand expression" (1:126). After this convoluted speech, all except Bessie believe he has been drinking. He further announces his desire to accompany his Princeton roommate to attend art school in New York City, a plan which, to his father's consternation, has met with the approval of Maud Steele's practical-minded father.

Richard Steele arrives. Once the family leave the two men alone, Steele convinces Brown that there is money in art if John enters the illustration and advertising end. Dubious that John would follow that track, Brown comments that "his ideas on the subject are lofty," but Steele assures him that "there's nothing like a year in New York to make him realize the importance of a bank account and settle down to brass tacks. . . . He'll come gradually to see the commercial aspects of the case—especially if you keep a tight hand on the pocketbook" (1:131). All the while John and Maud have been listening in. Once the two men exit to share a drink to their children's future matrimony, John and Maud enter the sitting room. The lovers are ecstatic that both fathers approve of their plan—John will go to New York to study art, and he and Maud will be married once he has made a name for himself in the art world. In the last lines, however, O'Neill demonstrates (rather too soon in the play's action) Maud's conventional expectations of John, the same sentiments her father expressed about commercializing his art. Maud picks up a magazine with a pretty girl on the cover, insinuating that this is the type of art John will create. After glancing at the image in disdain, John drops the magazine in the trash, which brings tears to Maud's eyes. John begs her forgiveness and explains that he wishes to accomplish "much finer things than that" (1:133). Maud forgives him, pretending to understand, and they kiss as the curtain falls.

## Act 2

A year and a half later in John's studio apartment in Manhattan. John shares the space with three other young men—Babe Carter and Steve Harrington, both painters, and Ted Nelson, a writer. John looks older, less confident, and his face exposes *"lines of worry"* and *"an unhealthy city pallor"* (1:135). He departs to meet his father at a hotel and promises to return with him directly. Babe searches the apartment for appropriate clothes to meet John's sister Bessie, with whom he is developing a relationship, against Edward Brown's wishes, back in Bridgetown. Eugene Grammont, the master of their art school, knocks and enters. Babe and Steve notify him that Brown is expected shortly and implore Grammont to convince him that John should stay on at art school. Grammont is doubtful of success,

particularly since John is still enamored with Maud, "the girl who was shocked at all your nudes—and said so" (1:138). Nevertheless, Grammont says of John, "Never in my long experience as a teacher have I met a young man who gave finer promise of becoming a great artist. . . . He has the soul, he has everything" (1:139). Grammont departs with assurances from Steve that he will retrieve him when the time comes to talk with Brown.

When John returns with his father, Babe has already left for Bridgetown, and Steve retreats to find Grammont. Brown is visibly irritated by John's acquaintances, and he informs his son that he knows of Babe and Bessie's relationship; when he forbade Bessie to see him, he continues, she moved into a hotel—a clear indication, though one lost on Brown, that Bessie and Babe are having premarital sexual relations as well. The conversation turns to John's future. Brown insists that he quit art school and take a job with Maud's father in his dry-goods store. He then points at a nude, first deriding it as unfinished—"That's Impressionism, I suppose. Rot!"—then chiding John that "there may be other attractions to this career of yours besides a lofty ideal" (1:144), meaning John's female model for the painting.

Ted Nelson, celebrating the publication of his first story, enters drunk with a cloak-and-suit model named Helene. Their raucous behavior scandalizes Brown. Steve and Grammont arrive, and John tells Steve to get rid of the drunken couple, which he does. John introduces Grammont to his father, and Brown acknowledges Grammont's established reputation in the art world—"I have heard of Mr. Grammont many times, although I'm not familiar with art matters" (1:147). John excuses himself, and the men sit to discuss John's career. After some perfunctory small talk, Brown accuses Grammont of retaining John for the tuition money. Deeply insulted, Grammont exits furiously as John returns. "Be true to yourself, John, remember!" he says as he departs. "For that no sacrifice is too great." Brown repeats his accusation against Grammont and characterizes the rest of John's milieu as "drunkards, old lunatics, and women of the streets" (1:148). He cuts John off from any allowance—"Starve awhile, and see how much bread and butter this high art will bring you!"—and departs with the warning that Steele's offer will be short-lived. "Oh, to hell with Steele!" John shouts as the door to the hallway slams shut (1:148–149).

### Act 3

Same setting as act 2, on a July afternoon of the same year. John, Steve, and Ted are there, and John, painting at his easel, now looks *"haggard and dissipated."* John works a low-paying job on the waterfront and drinks heavily; both activities have rattled his fragile constitution. He is exasperated with his artwork, believing it lacks "life" (1:150); equally exasperated, Ted grumbles, "I've written more short stories than Maupassant and O. Henry put together—and I sold *one.*" When Steve suggests that Ted turn to playwriting, Ted responds—echoing O'Neill's first short story, "TOMORROW," and the character Jimmie Tomorrow from *The* ICEMAN COMETH, based on O'Neill's friend JAMES FINDLATER BYTH—"I'm always going to start that play—tomorrow. . . . They ought to write on my tombstone: The deceased at last met one thing he couldn't put off till tomorrow" (1:151). John admits that Maud's letters reveal her impatience with his high-minded goals—"Oh, it's hell to love and be loved by a girl who can't understand; who, you know, tries to and cannot; who loves you, and whose life you are making miserable and unhappy by trying to be true to yourself" (1:152). Maud now wants John to return to Bridgetown and settle down, which his roommates admit is probably a good idea, given his poverty and growing disillusionment with his work. But John refuses on the grounds that he cannot return home a failure.

Babe and Bessie, now newlyweds, enter the studio. Bessie proposes that John is right to continue his studies and adds that marrying Maud would be a mistake. Bessie, Babe, and Steve depart, and Ted suggests they have a drink. John waffles between his desire to cure his hangover and wanting to continue painting.

There is a knock at the door, and Maud and Mrs. Brown enter. Maud is determined to rescue John from the "wicked old city," promising a position at her father's store and a beautiful house her father will give them as a wedding present (1:160).

Edward enters soon after, looking less self-conscious than in act 1 and scowling at John's disheveled and stained painting clothes. Edward also demands that John return to Bridgetown, if only to make Maud happy. John suspects that Edward still loves Maud and calls him out, accusing Edward of not wanting him to return so he might marry Maud instead. His brother does not deny the accusation but accuses John, in his turn, of associating with immoral women in New York. John punches Edward in a rage, and the group departs, leaving John weeping on the couch. Maud returns a few moments later and, seeing John on the couch, believes he still loves her and begs him once more to return. He relents, and, with the same tensions brewing between them we saw in act 1, they kiss as the curtain falls.

### Act 4

Two years later, in the sitting room of John and Maud's home in Bridgetown. They are now unhappily married. The room resembles the stodgy middle-class atmosphere of the Brown house in act 1, but with two impressionistic paintings hanging on the wall *"in startling incongruity"* to the rest of the room. Maud's good looks remain intact, though now she *"has lines of fretful irritation about her eyes and mouth and wears the air of one who has been cheated in the game of life and knows it; but will even up the scale by making those around her as wretched as possible"* (1:166). She and Edward, since elected the mayor of Bridgetown, enter from the front door, and she congratulates him on his successful bid for the district's congressional primaries. Edward openly observes Maud's unhappy aspect, which he blames entirely on his brother. John, for his part, has taken the position at Steele's shop and frequents low taverns with Harry, as O'Neill did with his own older brother JAMES O'NEILL, JR. (Jamie), and he is now a full-blown alcoholic. Edward also accuses John of consorting with "those low friends of Harry's,—women, I mean." Maud admits that all they do is fight now, their sex life is over, and fortunately they have not yet had a child. Edward, still holding a candle for Maud's affections, suggests she get a divorce, which she rejects outright on principle. "I have always held divorce to be the greatest evil of modern times," Edward agrees portentously, "and a grave danger to the social life of the nation" (1:169). But in this case he urges her to make an exception. Edward pledges his love to her, and she promises to consider his offer to move with him to Washington, D.C., as his wife.

John enters, having heard the last exchange, and sarcastically quotes the Ten Commandments to his pious brother: "Thou shalt not covet thy neighbor's wife" (1:170). Seemingly unconcerned, he exits the room. John returns once Edward has gone and finds Maud crying on the couch. They bicker over his drinking and the accusations Edward made about Harry and the company he keeps. "Harry's open about what he does and makes no pretense of being a saint," John says, "He's a lot better than those psalm-singing hyp-ocrites of whom my respected brother Edward is the leader" (1:172). John acknowledges that Maud hates him and pleads for a divorce. She refuses, this time because of the potential for scandal. Defeated, John changes the subject to Babe Carter, whose reputation has soared and is the subject of a posi-tive review in the newspaper. This sets Maud off again, and she voices the rumor that Babe and Bes-sie were "forced to marry . . . on account of their previous intimacy" (1:176).

The doorbell rings; it is Bessie, and Maud removes herself before John lets her in. Bessie, who is moving with Babe to Paris soon, entreats John to divorce Maud and join them in FRANCE to pursue his true calling; however, he insists that death is the only solution to end their marriage, given Maud's refusal to accept a divorce. When Bessie departs, Maud reenters in a furious state of hysteria. Emotionally out of control, she threatens to destroy Bessie's reputation. At this, John grabs her throat violently, but he releases her and rushes upstairs yelling, "There's an end to everything!" (1:183). These are his last words. From the ceil-ing we hear the muffled report of a gun and the sound of John's body falling to the floor. Maud slowly apprehends what John has done and runs shrieking out the front door—just as Mrs. Rowland does in BEFORE BREAKFAST when her artist husband commits suicide after her persistent nagging and refusal to divorce. The final image of the play is the spectacle of Maud running past the windows with her hands to her ears, screaming. Her screams fade away into the distance as the curtain falls.

## COMMENTARY

*Bread and Butter* is easily dismissed, with its heavy-handed themes and flat characterization, as a false start for "America's greatest playwright." But as KENNETH MACGOWAN wrote in 1929,

> O'Neill is a kind of chain-stitch playwright. I don't mean by this that you have only to yank at the thread of his story in some weak spot to see the whole thing ravel out. I mean that his ideas and materials and technique develop through a long chain of links bound inextrica-bly to one another. They develop slowly, per-haps spasmodically, but they develop inevitably from his first plays to his last. (449)

As such, *Bread and Butter*, which Macgowan proba-bly never read, is a satisfying read insofar as it estab-lishes, perhaps more so than any other of O'Neill's earliest plays, a number of key characterizations, settings, and themes for so many of O'Neill's later masterpieces: family strife, the American dream overwhelmed by the American nightmare, the cor-rosive effect of marriage or personal relations of any kind on the sensitive artistic sensibility, the feeling of alienation from social expectations, among oth-ers. This fact unequivocally demonstrates the pow-erful hold young adulthood had on the playwright throughout his life.

The play is, at bottom, a conflict between bour-geois expectations and modernist individualism. In the opening scene, O'Neill describes the Brown sitting room as hopelessly middle class, devoid of any artistic élan: "*This monotony of color is at well-regulated intervals monotonously relieved by preten-tiously stupid paintings of the 'Cattle-at-the-Stream', 'Sunrise-on-the-Lake' variety. These daubs are impris-oned in ornate gilt frames. . . . The room is sufficiently commonplace and ordinary to suit the most fastidious Philistine*" (1:115). The room partially resembles the O'Neill family room in MONTE CRISTO COT-TAGE, which O'Neill describes in more forgiving language in AH, WILDERNESS! and LONG DAY'S JOURNEY INTO NIGHT. Presumably O'Neill meant the room to achieve a horrifying effect on his target audience—bohemian artists revolting against bourgeois tastes—though it is unclear how, precisely, this effect would be understood in the ironic vein it was intended to convey. The bohemian setting of the New York studio—with broken-down furniture, piles of books and papers in disarray, expressionistic paintings on the wall, and an unfinished canvas clamped to an easel—stands in stark contrast to the Brown family home, just as the playfully intellectual banter among the young aspiring artists contrasts with the banal practicality of the Brown family discourse.

The structure of *Bread and Butter* is ambitious for its use of four acts, in the mode of HENRIK IBSEN's plays, though the end result is more muddling than illuminating. The play opens as a comedy, with the Browns appearing every bit as confident and complacent in their small-town preoccupations as the Miller family in *Ah, Wilderness!* Edward Brown, Jr.'s respectability is the butt of much of this humor—as in the lines when Harry declares that John wants to be a painter, and Edward responds, "There is room for a good painting business in this town with all the new summer homes being built along the shore" (1:119). Even after John moves to New York, though his appearance begins to degenerate, the playful banter of his bohemian roommates sustains the comedic elements of the first act. But by Edward Brown, Sr.'s arrival in New York, perhaps intentional on O'Neill's part, each of the main characters has become morbidly self-involved, tragic in their helpless need to take control of their swiftly crumbling dreams and desperately attempting to find order in the chaos that ensued from bad decisions.

John's social philosophy differs notably from Richard Miller's of *Ah, Wilderness!* Both young men are strongly influenced by anarchism, as O'Neill was at their age. But John's more closely resembles the brand of PHILOSOPHICAL ANARCHISM O'Neill finally claimed as his own, as opposed to the socialist anarchism of EMMA GOLDMAN, which Richard espouses. The most fundamental difference between the two is that the former is nonviolent and the latter accepts that the ends justify the means. BENJAMIN R. TUCKER, the owner of the

Unique Book Shop that first introduced O'Neill to philosophical anarchism, even had a falling-out with Emma Goldman over her lover Alexander Berkman's botched attempt to assassinate the steel magnate Henry Clay Frick. In *Ah, Wilderness!* Richard declares that rather than observe the Fourth of July, he'll "celebrate the day the people bring out the guillotine again and I see Pierpont Morgan being driven by in a tumbrel!" (3:13). His father, Nat Miller, replies, accurate in his construal of socialist anarchism, "Son, if I didn't know it was you talking, I'd think we had Emma Goldman with us" (3:13).

Philosophical anarchism, on the other hand, rejected all forms of authority in the interest of the individual, including any form of organized violence; its earliest proponent was the mid-19th-century German philosopher Max Stirner, whose book *The Ego and His Own* (1844) is a seminal anarchist text that O'Neill read avidly in his early New York years. Ed Keefe, a partial model for John Brown, recalled much later of their period in the studio when O'Neill introduced him to Tucker's bookshop that "I remember one book he made me buy: Max Stirner's *Ego and His Own*" (quoted in Gelb 243). In kind, John intones the egoist's line in act 2 that "[Bessie's] duty to herself stands before her duty to you." "Rot! Damned rot!" Brown rejoins, "only believed by a lot of crazy Socialists and Anarchists" (1:142). John continues with a line that might have come directly from Stirner, who held ownership of the self, what he called "ownness," above all considerations: "You consider your children to be your possessions, your property, to belong to you. You don't think of them as individuals with ideas and desires of their own" (1:143).

Grammont—closely based on the anarchist painter and founder of the Ashcan school of American painting, Robert Henri—accuses John's bourgeois family of being "worshipers of the golden calf . . . muddy souls, [who] will exert all their power to hold him to their own level" (1:139). In addition, the character Grammont pronounces himself an egoist—as the actual Robert Henri was—by telling John, "Be true to yourself . . . remember! For that no sacrifice is too great" (1:148). And finally, when John debates whether to join Ted in a drink at the end of act 3, Ted significantly remarks, "You're a slave of a fixed idea today" (1:157)—again calling to mind Stirner, who in *The Ego and His Own* rails against all "fixed ideas" (his term), such as "morality, legality, Christianity, and so forth" (quoted in Dowling 56), in much the same way Ralph Waldo Emerson denounced "foolish consistency." The significance of O'Neill using socialist anarchism for Richard Miller in *Ah, Wilderness!* and philosophical anarchism for John Brown in *Bread and Butter* is that Miller is the subject of a comedy, and his social philosophy is meant to make him sound a little naive in the idyllic atmosphere of the Miller home; John, on the other hand, is the subject of a tragedy, and his philosophy—O'Neill's—is to prove impotent against the malignant forces of social convention.

The first and last acts of *Bread and Butter* so closely resemble the setting and family structure of *Ah, Wilderness!* that O'Neill critic Virginia Floyd argues it can easily function as the comedy's sequel (60). Indeed, at 17, the character Richard Miller from *Ah, Wilderness!* is approaching his first year at Yale, while 22-year-old John Brown (O'Neill was 21 when he lived in the Manhattan studio depicted in the middle two acts) has just graduated from Princeton. As Floyd points out, "The creative aspirations of both young men are jeopardized by their infatuations with hometown sweethearts, pampered daughters of dry-goods merchants" (61)—Maud Steele in *Bread and Butter* and Muriel McComber in *Ah, Wilderness!* Travis Bogard notes that O'Neill endowed Maud with the same initials as O'Neill's hometown sweetheart, Mabelle Scott (37). One can argue, however, that John is a composite of O'Neill himself and Ed Keefe, O'Neill's longtime New London friend and roommate in the Manhattan studio, who was persuaded by his middle-class family to abandon a career in art and lived to regret it (Gelb 421). In fact, autobiographically the John Brown scenario would have been closer to O'Neill's early adulthood than the sequel to *Ah, Wilderness!* O'Neill actually planned this in his WORK DIARY, in which Richard becomes a newspaper city editor, fights in World War I, and returns "maimed, embittered, idealism murdered" (quoted in Floyd 242). And finally, if not exhaustively, Harry and Edward, John Brown's older brothers, combine, like

Eben Cabot's two brothers in DESIRE UNDER THE ELMS, to form a portrait of O'Neill's older brother Jamie—Harry the fraternal bad influence, Edward the class-conscious son (Floyd 61).

There is also a circumstantial connection in the play to O'Neill's divorce from his first wife, KATHLEEN JENKINS. "I'd gladly give you all the evidence you need [to obtain a divorce]" (1:175), John tells Maud. This calls to mind O'Neill's own divorce of Jenkins soon before he wrote the play, for which he staged extramarital relations with a woman, not coincidentally named Maude Williams (Gelb 421). The *"fluffy white summer frock"* in which Maud first appears will return as an indication of the hidden destructive force that lies behind seductive innocence, as with Ruth Atkins in BEYOND THE HORIZON, Mildred Douglas in *The* HAIRY APE, and Margaret Dion in *The* GREAT GOD BROWN. She resembles Mildred Douglas more than any other when we are introduced to her in the first act as having a *"continual pout of her small red mouth indicated the spoiled child even before one hears the note of petulance in her soft, all-too-sweet voice"* (1:132). More important, as the story progresses, Maud is a clear composite of Ruth Atkins and Margaret Dion. There are also connections to be made between John Brown and Anthony Dion and Edward Brown and William Brown (who obviously shares his last name) in *The Great God Brown.* Margaret, who also rejects her husband's sensitive interior life, leads him away from artistic and spiritual integrity toward commercial success, which eventually destroys him. In *Beyond the Horizon,* Ruth marries Robert Mayo for his poetic nature, but once married, she recognizes that the stability his practical brother Andrew offered is what she truly desired. Robert, like John, dies in the end (if by consumption rather than suicide), leaving Ruth to marry Andrew as Maud will no doubt marry Edward. The "fixed" bourgeois ideas embedded in the small-town minds of Bridgetown pose the greatest threat to John and eventually lead to his suicide. The expectation is that John will make a decent living in business, marry, have children, and settle down in Bridgetown civic life. These fixed ideas, the play tells us, inhibit creative thought, artistic integrity, and spiritual development.

## CHARACTERS

**Brown, Bessie** John Brown's older sister. Bessie is as enlightened a freethinker in the Brown family as her brother John. But unlike John, she successfully follows her own path by marrying John's artist roommate, "Babe" Carter, with whom she conducted a secret affair against her father's wishes. The two of them will eventually move to Paris to allow Carter's career to flourish. Bessie warns John in act 3 that marrying Maud and moving back to Bridgetown would be a mistake, as a "respectable" small-town existence with a closed-minded woman like Maud would be oppositional to John's true self. In act 4, when John is unhappily married to Maud, Bessie suggests that he join her and Babe in Paris, which he cannot do because Maud refuses to grant him a divorce.

**Brown, Edward** John Brown's father. O'Neill describes him as a "*tall, lean old man with a self-satisfied smile forever on his thin lips. He is smooth shaven, a trifle bald, fifty-eight years old, and dressed as becomes a leading citizen*" (1:116). Like JAMES O'NEILL and his avatar James Tyrone in *Long Day's Journey into Night*, Brown is a pitiable victim of the promises of the American dream, having moved up the socioeconomic ladder from the authenticity of the working class to the fakery of the petit bourgeoisie. In the play's opening scene, he tells Edward, Jr., "Remember your father was a working man and a farm hand, and all the education he's got beyond grammar school he picked up along the way" (1:117). Brown has high aspirations for his youngest son, John, and disapproves of his bohemian temperament. Richard Steele convinces him in act 1 that there is money to be made in art. After a year and a half at art school, however, John shows little promise to "make good," and Brown rejects his son's romantic dream outright.

**Brown, Edward, Jr.** John Brown's eldest brother. O'Neill describes him as "*tall and stout, pudgy-faced, dark-haired, small of eye, thick of lip and neck.*" Edward is dressed "*exactly as a small-town alderman should be dressed*" (1:116). Like his father, Edward Brown, Sr., Edward is meant to epitomize petit bourgeois superficiality and decorum. In the opening act, Edward is a local alderman with political ambitions; by the end, he has achieved the Bridgetown mayoralty and made a successful bid to run in the district's congressional primaries. In act 4, Edward pleads with Maud to divorce John and marry him, an offer she unwisely refuses in the name of social propriety. Like Andrew Mayo in *Beyond the Horizon*, Edward is in love, insofar as he is capable of love, with his brother's fianceé and later wife—Ruth Atkins in *Beyond the Horizon*, Maud Steele in *Bread And Butter*. Maud first rejects him, but by act 4, she realizes her mistake, just as Ruth does in act 2, scene 2 of *Beyond the Horizon*.

**Brown, Harry** John Brown's brother. Harry is a "*tall, dark, pleasant-looking young fellow of twenty-five with the good-natured air and breezy manners of a young-man-about-small-town. A bit of a sport, given to beer-drinking, poker parties and Kelly pool, if the foppish mode of his light check clothes be any criterion*" (1:118). Harry speaks with a youthful slang that contrasts with Edward, Jr.'s pompous diction: "On the level, Father, it isn't square for us to toil and sweat while fair young brother pulls that lily of the field stuff" (1:118). Like James "Jamie" O'Neill, Jr., and his avatar James Tyrone, Jr., in *Long Day's Journey into Night*, Harry introduces John to the underside of Bridgetown life as an escape from, and temporary defense against, middle-class ennui.

**Brown, John** Youngest Brown brother, whose looks and demeanor differ markedly from the rest of the Brown family. He has black hair and "*abnormally large dreamer's eyes*" (1:123) and is one in a long series of autobiographical avatars of the playwright himself, including the Poet in FOG, Robert Mayo in *Beyond the Horizon*, Richard Miller in *Ah, Wilderness!*, and Edmund Tyrone in *Long Day's Journey into Night*. After attending Princeton University, Brown decides to enter art school in New York against his father's wishes. His practical father, Edward Brown, Sr., wanted him to go to law school instead. In act 1, Brown is deeply in love with Maud Steele, and they plan to marry after he has succeeded as an art student and artist. But after two years of training under Eugene Grammont—a famous painter modeled after the

Ashcan school painter Robert Henri—Brown shows little success and has turned to drinking as a relief from the pressures of failure. Maud eventually persuades John to relinquish his artistic ambitions and take a job back in Bridgeport with her father, Richard Steele.

John never settles into married life in the provincial city and grows more and more morose and dissipated, frequenting low taverns with his brother Harry, who is based on O'Neill's older brother, James "Jamie" O'Neill, Jr. Both John's brother Edward and his sister Bessie want him to divorce Maud—Edward so that she might be free to marry him, and Bessie because she can see that John is not being true to himself. When Maud overhears Bessie's advice, she erupts in a fury and threatens to ruin Bessie's reputation. Pushed too far, John ends the marriage by committing suicide. Though philosophically a freethinker, John is caught in a web of social constraint: He cannot pursue a career in art because to do so means to sacrifice the respect and loyalty of his loved ones, he cannot do well at his job at Steele's store because his heart is not in it, and he cannot divorce Maud because the law stands in his way. In the end, as Travis Bogard sums up the final act, John "stands condemned as a man who has failed to follow his destined course and who thus has deserted his sole good" (38).

**Brown, Mary**   John Brown's eldest sister. Unlike her sister, Bessie Brown, Mary is a general prude and an adherent to the cult of respectability that predominates in Bridgeport. In the Brown family, she is Edward Brown, Jr.'s female counterpart in her unfashionable appearance and respectable worldview. Mary believes John is wasting his education, one that her father, Edward Brown, never offered her or the other Brown siblings.

**Brown, Mrs.**   John Brown's mother. She is an ineffectual middle-class mother, *"grey-haired, tired looking woman about fifty years old. . . . Her expression is meek and when she speaks the tone of her voice apologizes for the unseemly indulgence"* (1:115–116). Like Mrs. Townsend in ABORTION, she is a symbol of moral and intellectual female simplicity.

**Carter, "Babe"**   John Brown's roommate in a Manhattan studio and brother-in-law by act 3. Carter is a massive man with a deep voice and a pleasant, hearty laugh. He was John's roommate at Princeton and convinced John to join him at an art school in New York. Carter conducts a secret affair with John's sister Bessie, against her father's wishes, and marries her by act 3. Carter and Bessie will move to Paris to join Steve Harrington, who has made a successful career as an artist there.

**Grammont, Eugene**   The master painter at John Brown's art school in New York. Grammont is based on the Ashcan school painter Robert Henri, with whom O'Neill studied informally in 1915 (the year following the play's composition). Like Henri, Grammont is a proponent of philosophical anarchism, a nonviolent form of anarchism that places the self above all other concerns, such as social and familial expectations. Grammont believes that if John continues his studies, he could become a great painter, and in act 2, he engages John's father, Edward Brown, Sr., in a debate over John's future. After Brown accuses him of attempting to keep John in art school for the tuition money, he leaves angrily with the parting words to his pupil, "Be true to yourself, John, remember! For that no sacrifice is too great" (1:148).

**Harrington, Steve**   John Brown's roommate in a Manhattan studio. Harrington, possibly based on the Ashcan school painter George Bellows (with whom O'Neill shared an apartment in 1909), is an art student of about 28 years old, whose *"manner is reserved and quiet, but when he does speak his voice is low and pleasing"* (1:134). In act 4, Bessie Brown informs John, her brother, that Harrington has been a success in Paris "painting in the Salon and I don't know what else" (1:180) and that she and her husband "Babe" Carter, John's former roommate along with Harrington and Ted Nelson, will join him there to further Carter's career as well.

**Helene**   Ted Nelson's drinking companion in act 2 and a member of John Brown's bohemian circle in New York. She is a cloak-and-suit model and *"a renegade from the ranks of artists models, lured away* *by the brilliant inducement of wearing beautiful clothes instead of wearing none at all*" (1:145). Along with Nelson, she scandalizes John Brown, Sr., John's father, by appearing drunk at John's studio and indulging in coarse language.

**Nelson, Ted**    John Brown's roommate in a Manhattan studio. Nelson is an aspiring writer in acts 2 and 3 who we learn in act 4 has become a successful drama critic in Chicago. Nelson is introduced drunk with the cloak-and-suit model Helene in act 2 while celebrating his first publication. Though Nelson is a prolific writer—"I've written more short stories than Maupassant and O. Henry put together" (1:151)—he bemoans the fact that the only story he ever sold was his "rottenest, absurdist, and most totally imbecile story" (1:146) and that those are the only ones that sell.

**Steele, Maud**    John Brown's girlfriend in the first three acts and wife in the last. Maud is a "*remarkably pretty girl of twenty with great blue eyes, golden brown hair, and small delicate features*" (1:132). At first, Maud is enamored by John Brown's artistic sensibility, but her longings for security and respectability overwhelm her romantic side, and she manipulates him into a life of bourgeois ennui. Maud Steele's character is the first of a long line of O'Neillian female characters—most notably Ruth Atkins in *Beyond the Horizon* and Margaret Dion in *The Great God Brown*—who, in Judith Barlow's poignant words, symbolizes "the venerable myth that domesticity, even when freely chosen, kills the male of the species; woman is a trope for the bourgeois life, the insensitivity and materialism that annihilate the artistic soul" (165).

**Steele, Richard**    Maud Steele's father. Steele is a "*tall, stout, vigorous looking man of about fifty-five, with the imposing air of one who is a figure of importance in the town and takes this importance seriously*" (1:129). In act 1, Steele convinces Edward Brown, who highly respects his opinion, that John Brown can earn good money in art if he enters the commercial end of the trade. After John fails to make a name for himself as an artist in New York and

marries Maud, Steele provides the newlyweds with a house in Bridgetown, and John takes a job at his dry-goods store.

## BIBLIOGRAPHY

Barlow, Judith. "O'Neill's Female Characters." In *The Cambridge Companion to Eugene O'Neill*, edited by Michael Manheim, 164–177. New York: Cambridge University Press, 1998.

Bogard, Travis. *Contour in Time: The Plays of Eugene O'Neill*. Rev. ed. New York: Oxford University Press, 1988.

O'Neill, Eugene. *Selected Letters of Eugene O'Neill*. Edited by Travis Bogard and Jackson R. Bryer. New Haven, Conn.: Yale University Press, 1988.

Dowling, Robert M. "On Eugene O'Neill's 'Philosophical Anarchism.'" *Eugene O'Neill Review* 29 (Spring 2007): 50–72.

Floyd, Virginia. *The Plays of Eugene O'Neill: A New Assessment*. New York: Ungar, 1985.

Gelb, Arthur, and Barbara Gelb. *O'Neill: Life with Monte Cristo*. New York: Applause Books, 2000.

Macgowan, Kenneth. "The O'Neill Soliloquy." In *O'Neill and His Plays: Four Decades of Criticism*, edited by Oscar N. Cargill, Bryllion Fagin, and William J. Fisher, 449–435. New York: New York University Press, 1961.

# *Chris Christophersen: A Play in Three Acts*  (completed, 1919; first produced, 1920)

In a letter to GEORGE PIERCE BAKER, Eugene O'Neill's playwriting professor at Harvard University, O'Neill voiced a palpable optimism for the future of a play he had recently completed through the winter and spring of 1918–19 in Provincetown, Massachusetts: "I really have every confidence that, in spite of the fact that it is far removed in nature and treatment from the usual run of acceptable plays, it will eventually find a producer" (in Cargill et al. 39). His confidence was not misplaced, insofar as it would find a producer. The play's critical and financial success, however,

Chris Christopherson, the real-life model for the character in *Chris Christophersen* and *"Anna Christie"* *(Courtesy of the Sheaffer-O'Neill Collection, Charles E. Shain Library of Connecticut College)*

was minimal at best. *Chris Christophersen* saw an abysmal 19 performances in 1920, first in Atlantic City, New Jersey, premiering on March 8, 1920, at Nixon's Apollo Theatre, and then in Philadelphia, and its failure in those cities destroyed any hope for a run in New York. O'Neill held one of its directors, Frederick Stanhope, responsible for the disappointing reception in Atlantic City, since Stanhope had taken the liberty of performing unauthorized cuts to liven up an otherwise sluggish narrative (giving the play, in O'Neill's words, a "movie effect"); O'Neill then attributed its failure in Philadelphia to the fact that it was "miserably cast" (quoted in Clark 99). But a 1920 review in the *Stage* put the blame elsewhere: "The material is very slim, but the play carries itself along from sheer excellence of presentation. . . . Most of the credit [for its negligible entertainment value] goes to [the cast] and to Frederick Stanhope for his well directed staging" (in Cargill et al. 140).

## SYNOPSIS

### Act 1, Scene 1

Johnny "the Priest's" saloon, a sailors' dive near South Street on Manhattan's East Side waterfront in the year 1910. On the left is a double swinging door to the street. Across the back stretches a long bar with brass spigots that serve whiskey of the *"nickel-a-shot variety"* from wooden barrels; large mirrors hang above the bar, and untouched cases of more expensive liquor lie stacked below them. The proprietor, Johnny "the Priest," lolls behind the bar reading a newspaper; two men, Adams and Jack Burns, recline at one of two round wooden tables in front. Adams, a washed-up salesman, sits with head in hand, drunk, disheveled, and half asleep. He wears a tussled gray suit, and his face indicates a man "on a drunk." Burns wears a working man's checkered suit and is glaring at his companion *"with an amused leer of contempt"* (1:797). Burns wakens Adams by jerking his elbow off the table, shouting that since Adams persists in calling himself a "gentleman," he should buy him a drink. Adams refuses and snobbishly expostulates over his low state, consigned as he is to this "low, waterfront, barrel-house" (1:798).

Two longshoremen turn up at the bar and order whiskey with beer chasers; Larry, Johnny's replacement, enters close behind. Larry and Johnny exchange pleasantries. The longshoremen leave, and a postman arrives with a letter from Leeds, England, addressed to a "Christopher Christophersen." Johnny surmises the letter is for "Old Chris," a Swedish coal barge captain and regular at Johnny's. Adams chimes in that Chris is a "gentleman and a sport, and anyone that says different is a liar!" Johnny cuts Adams off and summarily orders him upstairs to "do a flop" (1:801).

Chris Christophersen enters. He is about 50 years old, wearing a blue shore suit and gray cap, and his face *"beams with a too-blissful happiness"* that indicates drunkenness. Johnny and Larry heartily welcome him; he orders whiskey and sings a few bars of a sailing shanty about a woman named Josephine. Chris grumbles that his latest voyage on the barge was slowed by a dense fog between Boston and New York—"yust fog, fog, fog all bloody time!" (1:803).

Larry hands the letter to Chris, who reads it with great difficulty, slowly mouthing the words as he goes; when finished, he announces that his daughter, Anna Christophersen, will be arriving in two days. Chris has not seen her in 15 years, since he sent her to live with relatives in England. Larry presciently deduces that, given Chris's seafaring heritage, Anna will no doubt marry a sailor. Chris balks at this idea and threatens to kill her himself if she gets caught up in "Dat damn, dirty SEA" (1:805). Chris boasts that she is a well-educated typist now, and that once he rids himself of his girlfriend Marthy, who stays with him on the barge, he will take his daughter on a voyage. Larry scoffs that he would be leading her right into a life on the sea. "Barge vas nutting," Chris rejoins, "It ain't sea or it ain't land eider" (1:806), and he insists that her voyage will be "yust nice and quiet—no rough vedder—plenty of fresh air, good grub, make her strong and healthy . . . so long's dat ole davil, sea, don't gat her" (1:806).

Two weathered sailors, Mickey and Devlin, enter the bar. Mickey recognizes Chris's voice as that of his old boatswain (pronounced bos'n) on one of the sailing vessels from the days of sail power. The three men sit together, drink whiskey, and nostalgically talk over old times. Remarking on the tragic transition from sail power to steam—a theme that O'Neill develops in "ANNA CHRISTIE," *The* HAIRY APE, and other plays—Chris declares that there "ain't no more fine ships like her on sea no more, py golly" (1:809). Mickey voices disgust after learning Chris is now a coal barge captain, considered one of the lowest positions for a sailor at the time. At first contrite, then contentious, Chris submits that it is a better life than that on the open sea. Mickey turns belligerent and demands that Chris redeem himself by joining him and Devlin on their next voyage—"We'll find a tall, smart daisy of a full-rigged ship with skys'ls—a beautiful, swift hooker that'll take us flyin' south through the Trades" (1:811). Temporarily taken in by this speech, Chris considers the offer, then wakes to the fact that the sea is up to its old tricks, getting him to return while he is drunk—even on land the sea has a powerful hold on sailors, O'Neill is saying, a supposition most clearly articulated in *The* LONG VOYAGE HOME. Chris rails against the sea and its tricks, recalling the family members he has lost at

sea. Mickey and Devlin relent, agreeing that it is "a dog's life" (1:813).

### Act 1, Scene 2

The interior of the cabin of Chris's barge, the *Simeon Winthrop*, around noon on the day of Anna's arrival. Chris and Marthy are in evidence; dressed in his best uniform, Chris slinks around, painstakingly cleaning his quarters and furtively checking his watch, while Marthy lounges in a rocking chair by the stove. Marthy "*is not beautiful*" (1:813): middle-aged and fat, with thick features and a mass of oily hair piled high on her head, she speaks her lines "*in a loud mannish voice, punctuated by explosions of hoarse laughter*" (1:813–814). Marthy suspects Chris is preparing to evict her and bullies him good-naturedly. When he informs her his 20-year-old daughter is expected to arrive that morning, Marthy capitulates understandingly—"Why didn't yuh tell me this b'fore, yuh thickhead?" (1:817)—and chides him for not meeting Anna at the boat. He explains that he does not have the proper clothes. The two bid farewell on good terms, but she returns, frantic. Anna is on the barge, and Chris needs to make a good impression. She loudly pretends to be a waterfront huckster and departs as Anna enters.

In contrast to Chris, the plainspoken Swede, Anna is entirely unlike her counterpart in "*Anna Christie*." She is a statuesque beauty with a distinctive air of self-confidence and a proper British accent; Chris is astounded that he has "so full grown, so well dressed, so modern" a daughter (1:818). Virtual strangers, separated by a gulf of socioeconomic and educational distance, Chris and Anna unaccountably hit it off. She scolds him lightly for making her go to "that awful dive," Johnny "the Priest's," to find him (1:820). She is critical of Chris's living quarters and the quality of his tea, but she is no typical Victorian lady. O'Neill means her to be an ideal of New Womanhood—independent, modern, liberated: "I don't even know what course I want to take, or what I eventually want to become. It's all—in the air (*intensely*) I only know I want to get away from being just a woman, to lead a man's life; to know as much as I can, and see and live as much as I can—to always have something new to work for. I won't grow stale—and married. I won't!" (1:825) Chris explains why he never visited her as a child in Sweden or as an adult in England, blaming it in part on his unrespectable job as a sailor, but more so on "dat ole davil, sea" (1:826). Chris is beckoned from outside to move his barge down the dock, and Anna prepares breakfast. When he returns, she proposes they rent a small house together on land. But Chris induces her to accompany him instead on his next trip. Anna demurs at first, given the conditions on board and her determination to find work, but she eventually accepts the offer—"It'll be such a lark!" (1:830)

### Act 2, Scene 1

Ten days later at midnight. The barge is caught in a heavy fog off the coast of Cape Cod, Massachusetts. Anna stands on deck wearing black oilskin weather gear, and her face exudes *"awed wonder"* over the dense fog (1:832). Chris appears through the cabin doorway wearing yellow oilskins. He implores her to go inside, but she dreamily insists on staying on deck, as she feels intoxicated by the sea—"out of the world altogether" (1:832). (The dialogue in most of this scene is nearly identical to act 2 of *"Anna Christie."*) Chris interprets his daughter's wonderment as another trick of "Dat ole davil, sea" and frantically attempts to fix their broken foghorn (1:833). Anna glories in the mystifying sensation the fog affords her, while Chris grows increasingly agitated and scared. "The trip has been wonderful," Anna muses, ignoring her father's desperation, "And now—drifting all alone in the fog—I wouldn't miss it for the world" (1:834). Chris informs her that their towline has broken and they are drifting out to deep sea (this indicates that Chris's boat is an "unrigged barge" rather than a "schooner barge," which has sails [Richter 178]). She dismisses her father's apprehensions. Chris mutters gloomily, "Ay tank maybe Ay'm damn fool for bring you on dis voyage" (1:836). Now it is he who suggests they might both find jobs in the countryside, a suggestion that falls on deaf ears.

Chris tells her that he is one of the few members of their clan who has not been drowned or lost at sea. "Dey're all fool fallar in our family. Dey all

work rotten yob on sea like dog for nutting. . . . Dey're damn stupid fallar don't know nutting but yust vork, don't vant for know, don't care nutting but yust gat big pay day in pocket, gat drunk, gat robbed, ship avay again on oder voyage. . . . And dat ole davil, sea, sooner later, she swallow dem up!" (1:839). Nevertheless, Anna repeats that she feels happier than she ever has. Chris curses himself as a "damn fool" for bringing her on the voyage. He soon hears a whistle in the distance and at first believes it is their tugboat searching for them. But then he recognizes it as the whistle of a steamship, and it is heading straight for them. At first panic-stricken, Chris swiftly adopts the attitude of a veteran sailor: He gives Anna a life preserver and tells her that the barge's lifeboat is prepared with supplies. The whistle gets increasingly louder, and Chris cries out to the steamship, "Ahoy! Ahoy dere!" There is no response. Chris orders Anna down to the dinghy and jumps in after. A cry is heard from the steamship—"Barge dead ahead!"—and at the curtain, the steamer's whistle *"seems to shatter the fog to fragments"* (1:844).

### Act 2, Scene 2

The main cabin aboard the British steamship *Londonderry*, heading from Boston to BUENOS AIRES, ARGENTINA (where O'Neill sailed in 1910, the year the play takes place), about 30 minutes after the collision. Captain Jessup enters the cabin and curses the fog. Mr. Hall, the first mate, reports that two survivors from the barge were spotted in a small boat before the impact. Jessup orders Hall to stay on course and summons the steward. The steward promptly appears and informs the captain that one of the survivors is a woman. The second mate, Paul Andersen, enters and reports that the damage to their ship is negligible. A handsome man in his mid-20s, Andersen is an avatar of the playwright himself. He substantiates the rumor that one of the survivors is a woman and adds, "She seems very well-educated. Spoke correct English without any accent. . . . As far as looks go—she's a corker" (1:848).

Jessup orders the survivors in. Chris is visibly shaken in the presence of what sailors call "the Old Man," but Anna is fully composed, confident, and evidently enjoying herself. Chris pleads with Jessup to let them ashore at the end of Cape Cod, but that is out of the question. Instead, he signs Chris on as a seaman and allows Anna to stay as a passenger. Andersen volunteers his quarters for Anna, and Chris glares at him with *"immediate jealous hatred"* (1:851). Chris is ordered to the forecastle (pronounced fo'c'sle"). Andersen delivers a cup of coffee for Anna, and Jessup leaves, warning Andersen as he departs, "No monkey business, now" (1:853).

A lengthy, flirtatious dialogue ensues. Anna is enamored by the young man, who seems to represent everything the sea does in her imagination. She tells him of her childhood inland and that she has never experienced the sea before the voyage on the barge (which makes little sense, considering how she arrived in New York). Andersen, for his part, comes from a farming family in Minnesota and chose life on the sea as a palliative to either farming or office work. Andersen's rhapsodic declaration of freedom from life's conventions draws Anna in, but he concludes by saying that for him, women are not meant for marriage but for loving freely, "women of all kinds and races—Woman!" (1:859) "That's stupid," she retorts, "It spoils all the rest" (1:859). A few lines later, he is back in her good graces. They say good night, but Andersen, unable to control himself, takes her in his arms and kisses her. She rebukes him, but he again apologizes, and she seems to accept. Chris enters and watches them say goodnight. After Andersen heads off, Chris frantically begs his daughter not to be taken in by Andersen's type. He ascertains that "dat ole davil, sea" has again encroached upon his life and fears she will marry this "sailor fallar" (1:862). She writes off his concerns as "crazy talk" and leaves him for the night. At the curtain, Chris shakes his fist at the sea, "Damn ole davil!" (1:863).

### Act 3, Scene 1

About a month later in the seaman's forecastle on the *Londonderry*; it is nine o'clock at night, and the ship is docked in Buenos Aires. Chris sits on a lower bunk deep in thought. Jonesy and Edwards, two young cockney, or British working-class, seamen are also present. Jonesy is writing a letter to his mother with great difficulty. Edwards, impatient for Jonesy to finish, turns his attention to Chris; he

accuses Chris of being too particular, that he sets his sights too high for Anna if he disapproves of Andersen. Chris evenly responds that "Ay don't vant King of England for Anna. Ay don't vant no man. Ay vant her myself. She's all Ay gat in vorld" (1:867). Edwards leaves Jonesy to his letter, and Glass enters. Glass is a conniving messroom steward who has contrived a practical joke against Chris. Chris knows Glass's reputation as a schemer but lets his guard down when the steward hints he knows something about the budding romance between Anna and the second mate. He describes Andersen as a drunken womanizer (which is basically true) and fabricates an incident in which Andersen publicly kissed a beautiful blonde at a casino in Buenos Aires. Glass considers Andersen a "good sport and a real seaman of the old school," but he is no gentleman for a proper lady like Anna. Chris again refers to Andersen as yet another of "dat ole davil sea's dirty tricks" (1:871). Glass provokes him further, going so far as to say, "You better get out your old pistol and shoot him" (1:872). He claims to have witnessed a tête-à-tête between the lovers in which Andersen proposed to Anna and she accepted. Chris takes him by the shoulders and roughly shakes him but regains self-control. Plainly taken in by Glass's story, he storms out of the forecastle. Glass and Jonesy chuckle over Chris's reaction, and Glass admits that everything was essentially true, aside from the casino incident and that Anna agreed to Andersen's proposal. In fact, she had denied him.

Glass departs, and Chris reenters a moment later with a look of determination on his face. Cursing "dat ole davil," he asks Jonesy for a sharper knife than his own. Jonesy, heedless of Chris's intent, tells him to get one from another sailor. Chris slowly heads off, and Jonesy, after a momentary sensation of foreboding, shrugs and says, "Ho, t'ell with 'im" (1:876).

### Act 3, Scene 2

The midship of the *Londonderry* nearly two hours later. Moonlight illuminates the scene. Lurking in a shadow between the ladder and the bulwark, the now homicidal Chris waits for Andersen. When Andersen appears, Chris, holding a knife in his right hand, positions himself to attack. The bell loudly chimes six times—11 o'clock. The cabin door opens, and Anna appears. Andersen takes her hand, but she releases his grasp. They stand for a moment admiring the night, with Chris crouching in the shadows; he has been trapped into eavesdropping but is curious just the same. Anna is distraught over the fact that she and her father will disembark the next day and resume the tedium of ordinary life. She adds that Chris now seems to hate her, and she and her father must "separate" (1:880). Andersen responds that Chris hates him and the sea, not her. He then accuses Chris, as Mat Burke does in *"Anna Christie,"* of having "swallowed the anchor," a seamen's term for losing faith in oneself, but he continues that both he and Anna are guilty of the same offense.

Andersen brings up the proposal he made the night before, and Anna once again rejects him, citing his love for the sea and need for continuous change, particularly with women. Chris's expression transforms from rage to elation as he realizes Glass's story was a lie. Andersen persists, admitting he has "played the damn fool, I know, but can't you see the change my love for you has made in me?" (1:883). He vows to relinquish his self-professed dream of "ambitionless ambition" (1:859) and strive for a captainship, a position that would allow Anna to accompany him on voyages. Now convinced, Anna accepts his proposal, and they agree to be married the following day. Chris despondently drops his knife, alerting them of his presence. He realizes that the sea has defeated him and wearily assents to their marriage.

From within the cabin, Captain Jessup calls for Andersen, and the two lovers retreat. Chris remains on deck and tosses his knife overboard. The captain comes out and discovers Chris brooding in the darkness. Predictably, he offers Chris, who had foresworn never again to work on the open ocean, the job of boatswain on the *Londonderry*. Chris accepts the berth with resignation. A change comes over him when the captain departs, however. He now looks at the sea with admiration: "Dat's your best dirty trick, ole davil! Eh, vell, you gat me beat for sure dis time" (1:889). He cheerfully sings his Josephine song as the cur-

tain falls. In the naturalistic tradition to which O'Neill belongs, the tricks and lures of the sea prove too powerful to effectively oppose.

## CRITICAL COMMENTARY

Today if *Chris Christophersen* is remembered at all, it is as the flawed rough draft of O'Neill's superior revision, *"Anna Christie,"* which appeared the following year and won him his second PULITZER PRIZE in 1922 (the first went to BEYOND THE HORIZON in 1920). O'Neill made *"Anna Christie"* two scenes shorter and with far fewer characters, but he retained much of the dialogue and mise-en-scène from the original. And as in *"Anna Christie,"* the first act takes place in an actual bar, JIMMY "THE PRIEST'S" (called Johnny "the Priest's" in the play), a West Side dive located at 252 Fulton Street, where O'Neill had squandered many months drinking, sleeping, and living off the dollar a day his father, JAMES O'NEILL, wired him intermittently as allowance. Two years after the action of the play (1910), O'Neill made a serious attempt on his life in a boarding room above the bar.

*Chris Christophersen*'s central conflict, as in *"Anna Christie,"* is the rift between Chris and Anna's divergent perceptions of the SEA. After years of work in the MERCHANT MARINE, many of which were spent as a deep-sea sailor on the old sailing ships, Chris superstitiously imagines the sea as a devilish force bent on swallowing up his life and the lives of everyone who dare oppose it. Indeed, he has fair proof for this: His two sons, his wife, and most of his relatives had all died, directly and indirectly, as a result of the family's maritime calling. Anna, on the other hand, embraces the freedom and inner peace the sea offers. The radical contrast between the working-class, dissipated father and the enlightened, highly educated daughter is also meant to emphasize the hereditary bridge between the Christophersens, a bridge that no amount of fine upbringing is capable of tearing down. The NATURALISM born of ancestral forces in the final two acts is foreshadowed by the bartender Larry's teasing assertion in act 1 that Anna will marry a sailor, as it is "in the blood" (1:805) and that taking her on a voyage is a mistake. Anna progressively rejects her professional ambitions in favor of the perilous but liberating maritime existence her Swedish family had pursued for generations. At bottom, however, the contrast between Anna and Chris is so stark that O'Neill loses sight of his own rejection of typecasting; the good-natured, working-class Swede and the well-bred British lady never form any meaningful, believable bond. The quintessence of modern New Womanhood, Anna longs to live a unique existence, one freed from the domestic drudgery she witnessed as a nursemaid in England. But once Chris's barge collide's with the steamship *Londonderry* in a fog bank, the fates of both him and his daughter drop into the hands of "dat ole davil, sea."

*Chris Christophersen* might be considered one of O'Neill's few dramas that end on an up beat, and there is no doubt, as Robert A. Richter writes, that "O'Neill is suggesting a new age for husband and wife, a new generation" (1:181). But it may also be wise to consider that the one female character in the O'Neill canon who does achieve Anna's dream to follow her captain husband around on deep-sea voyages—Mrs. Keeney from O'Neill's earlier one-act play ILE, a woman also frustrated with domestic restrictions, and one who also, like Anna, "used to dream of the fine free life" of the open seas (1:502)—went gradually insane.

## CHARACTERS

**Adams** A regular at Johnny "the Priest's" saloon. Adams, *"a man of fifty or so with grizzled hair, his face bloated and unshaven, his eyes puffy and bleary"* (1:797), was once a successful traveling salesman, like O'Neill's more notable character Theodore "Hickey" Hickman from *The ICEMAN COMETH*. But unlike Hickey, Adams's ALCOHOLISM prevents him from holding down a job. Adams has pretensions of being a respectable "gentleman," though no one at the bar treats this seriously.

**Andersen, Paul** The second mate on the steamship *Londonderry*. Andersen is an intellectually sophisticated, O'Neill-like romantic who has chosen a life at sea for the personal autonomy it affords. He comes from a Minnesota farming family, but like the character Robert Mayo in *Beyond the Horizon*, the young dreamer is ill-suited for the station-

ary existence of farm life. Too hastily, a leaden romance ensues between Andersen and Anna. In act 2, scene 2, Anna inquires if he has ambitions to become a captain, which Andersen quickly denies: "I'm not looking for material responsibilities. I'm doing my best to avoid them. . . . Freedom—that's life! No ties, no responsibilities—no guilty feelings," all of which Anna adoringly takes in until he adds, "Not love in the sense of a wife—marriage—an anchor—but love that is free—women of all kinds and races—Woman!" (1:858, 859). But once he falls in love, Andersen has a change of heart, and by the final scene, he repents his profligate history and vows to climb to the rank of captain, a berth that would allow Anna to join him on voyages. Only then does Anna agree to their union.

**Burns, Jack** A regular at Johnny "the Priest's" saloon. Burns, *"bull-necked and squat, with a battered, pushed-in countenance"* (1:797), is a middle-aged mail worker on the waterfront. In contrast to his drinking companion Adams's pretentiousness, Burns is a died-in-the-wool urban working man who resents Adams's complaints over losing his job: "Yuh're lucky not to have one" (1:798).

**Christophersen, Anna** Chris Christophersen's daughter. In contrast to the more believable streetwise prostitute we find in the play's revision, *"Anna Christie,"* Anna is a prim typist from Leeds, England, who speaks with a proper British accent and at first deplores her father's squalid lifestyle. Anna is a product of what historians refer to as the Cult of New Womanhood, a turn-of-the-century phenomenon that led women to reject the rigid, domestic lifestyles dictated by the mores of Victorianism: "I want to get away from being just a woman, to lead a man's life; to know as much as I can, and see and live as much as I can—to always have something new to work for. I won't grow stale—and married. I won't!" (1:825) But this "modern" resolve is somewhat undermined when she meets Paul Andersen, the second mate of the steamship *Londonderry*. When she and her father first collide with and are then rescued by the *Londonderry*, a British steamer on course for Buenos Aires, Anna falls in love with Andersen and consents to marry him, but only after he promises to work toward a captain's berth, a position that would permit her to sail with him on voyages.

**Christophersen, Chris** Captain of the coal barge *Simeon Winthrop* and Anna Christophersen's father. Chris's character, who also appears in "*Anna Christie*," is based on an actual Swedish regular at Jimmy "the Priest's" with the same name. (O'Neill mistakenly spelled his name Chistophersen with an *e* instead of an *o*, like his friend's, which signifies a Norwegian or Danish name; he corrected this error in "*Anna Christie*.") The actual Chris, like his fictional counterpart, railed against the connivances of "dat ole davil, sea," as his fictional counterpart repeats in the dialogue. O'Neill describes Chris in his STAGE DIRECTIONS the way he remembered his Swedish drinking partner and roommate: "*a short, squat, broad-shouldered man of about fifty with a round, weather-beaten face from which his light blue eyes peer short-sightedly, twinkling with a simple good humor*" (1:802). Chris's jarring dialect highlights his ethnic roots, which O'Neill artfully combines with an experienced seaman's command of waterfront argot. Also like the fictional Chris, the man accepted a job as captain of a coal barge, a sinecure for experienced seaman, docked in New York Harbor. The actual Chris froze to death in 1917 following a Christmas Eve debauch at Jimmy's after tumbling drunk onto an ice floe wedged between the dock and his barge. Contrary to that man's undignified departure, O'Neill's character is thrust back to his old duties as a boatswain on the deep-sea steamer *Londonderry*, thus emphasizing the overpowering draw of the sea that a true sailor cannot, no matter how in earnest, disengage for long.

**Devlin** A sailor at Johnny "the Priest's." When he and Mickey bump into Chris Chistophersen, Mickey's old shipmate, the two denigrate Chris for being a coal barge captain, but they relent after Chris relates his tragic family history at sea.

**Edwards** A seaman on the *Londonderry*. Edwards, "*a tall, lanky, dark-complected boy of eighteen*" (1:864), accuses Chris Christophersen of being snobbish about whom he will allow his daughter, Anna Chris-

tophersen, to marry, as he suggests to Chris that Paul Andersen, the second mate who is courting Anna, is generally well liked among the crew.

**Glass** The messroom steward on the *Londonderry*. A dark-complexioned man of about 25, Glass looks the part of the villain in the tradition of MELO-DRAMA: "*His thin face with its long pointed nose; its large mouth twisted to one side, the upper lip shadowed by a wisp of mustache; its sharp, mocking, pale blue eyes; has the expression of half-cruel, malicious humor which characterizes the practical joker*" (1:867). Glass convinces Chris Christophersen that Paul Andersen, who wishes to marry his daughter, Anna Christophersen, is a drunken rake. This goads Chris into plotting Andersen's murder.

**Hall, Mr.** The first mate on the *Londonderry*. Hall reports to the captain on the collision between their steamship and Chris Christophersen's coal barge.

**Jessup, Captain** The captain of the *Londonderry*. About 60 years ole, Jessup is an archetypical captain whose harsh commands are tempered by a proprietary compassion. Jessup allows Chris Christophersen to join the crew and his daughter, Anna Christophersen, to stay on as a passenger after the *Londonderry* collides with Chris's barge in a heavy fog bank. In the final scene, Jessup offers Chris the job of boatswain on the ship, which puts the finishing touch on the sea's final triumph over Chris, who had swore never to return to life on the deep sea.

**Johnny "the Priest"** Proprietor of Johnny "the Priest's" saloon. Johnny is based on Eugene O'Neill's friend and bartender James J. Condon, also known as Jimmy "the Priest," whose bar (located at 252 Fulton Street) O'Neill frequented, living for a time in a room above, in 1911 and 1912, following his three voyages in the merchant marine. O'Neill admiringly describes Johnny in both *Chris Christophersen* and "*Anna Christie*": "*With his pale, thin, clean-shaven face, mild blue eyes and white hair, a cassock would seem more suited to him than the apron he wears. . . . But beneath all his mildness one senses the man behind the mask—cynical, callous, hard as nails*" (1:797, 959).

**Jonesy**    A seaman on the *Londonderry*. Jonesy is *"a stout, heavy-faced, good-natured-looking young fellow"* (1:864) who appears in the seamen's forecastle writing a letter to his mother with great difficulty. Jonesy passively conspires with Glass against Chris.

**Larry**    A bartender at Johnny "the Priest's" saloon. A character in both *Chris Christophersen* and *"Anna Christie,"* Larry is a *"boyish, red-cheeked, rather good-looking young fellow of twenty or so"* who foreshadows Anna's fate by kidding Chris, in act one of both plays, that Anna "'ll be marryin' a sailor herself, likely. It's in the blood" (1:805, 964). Larry's boyishness and upbeat demeanor, along with his refusal to drink, emphasize the rough attitudes of the bar's patrons, but particularly the jolting appearance of Chris's daughter Anna, who clearly resembles a prostitute in *"Anna Christie."*

**Owen, Marthy**    A waterfront character and Chris Christophersen's companion on the *Simeon Winthrop* before his daughter, Anna Christophersen, arrives. Like Chris, Marthy's character is presented in both *"Anna Christie"* and *Chris Christophersen* with little modification. Marthy has been self-professedly "campin' with barge men the last twenty years" (1:966). Marthy, O'Neill writes in his stage directions, *"might be forty or fifty. Her jowly, mottled face, with its thick red nose, is streaked with interlacing purple veins"* (1:962). She is dressed in ragged men's shoes and clothes. However, O'Neill suggests *"in her blood-shot blue eyes [there is] a youthful lust for life which hard usage has failed to stifle, a sense of humor mocking, but good-tempered"* (1:962). A denizen of the waterfront all of her life, Marthy is, at bottom, a good-hearted woman who wants what is best for Anna and Chris; her character is a clear attempt on O'Neill's part to dismantle the tragicomic stereotype of the drunken waterfront hag. As Margaret Loftus Ranald suggests, Marthy is a "Tugboat Annie" type (579), though the first Tugboat Annie appeared in the *Saturday Evening Post* on July 11, 1931, over a decade after O'Neill conceived his character.

**Mickey**    An IRISH sailor at Johnny "the Priest's" and Chris Christophersen's former shipmate. Mickey recognizes Chris at Johnny "the Priest's"

and hails him as a fine seaman. When Chris informs him that he has taken a job as the skipper of a coal barge, Mickey demands that Chris join him and Devlin on a deep-sea voyage. Chris relates his tragic family history at sea, and Mickey assents that life at sea is a "dog's life" (1:813). O'Neill describes him as *"short and round-shouldered, monkey-like in the disproportionate length of his arms and legs"* (1:807); as such, it is likely that Mickey is a coal stoker, a position on steamships O'Neill treats at length in *The Hairy Ape*.

### BIBLIOGRAPHY

Cargill, Oscar, N. Bryllion Fagin, and William J. Fisher, eds. *O'Neill and His Plays: Four Decades of Criticism*. New York: New York University Press, 1961.

Clark, Barrett H. *Eugene O'Neill: The Man and His Plays*. Rev. ed. New York: Dover, 1947.

Ranald, Margaret Loftus. *The Eugene O'Neill Companion*. Westport, Conn.: Greenwood Press, 1984.

Richter, Robert A. *Eugene O'Neill and Dat Ole Davil Sea: Maritime Influences in the Life and Works of Eugene O'Neill*. Mystic, Conn.: Mystic Seaport, 2004.

# *Days Without End: A Modern Miracle Play* (completed, 1933; first produced 1934)

*Days Without End*, Eugene O'Neill's final experiment with masks, was arguably the greatest failure of his career. The first New York City production at the Henry Miller Theatre on January 8, 1934, received terrible reviews, some from critics who otherwise revered O'Neill as the finest playwright in the United States. One of O'Neill's close friends, the author Benjamin De Casseres, even wrote a lampoon of the play entitled "Drivel without End," a cruel prank that instantly destroyed their friendship (see De Casseres 2008). Other New York critics, some of whom O'Neill admired, called the play "heavy-handed and pretentious" (in Miller 80), "fakery preachment," "holy hokum," and "reactionary" (quoted in Alexander 1992, 207). Not only was

Production photo of the Theatre Guild's *Days Without End,* Henry Miller Theatre, New York City, 1934. Photo by Vandamm Studio (New York, N.Y.) *(Courtesy of the New York Public Library)*

it criticized as falling far below audiences' expectations of O'Neill's craftsmanship, but its seemingly pro-Catholic message offended his modern audience, revealing a crisis of atheistic faith and return to the CATHOLICISM of his youth. Ironically, the fact that the heroine is a divorcie offended many Catholics as well. Accusations of the play's pro-Catholic stance, though O'Neill denied them vehemently, might explain how it faired much better in the Catholic-dominated city of Boston at its premiere on December 27, 1933, and how the NOBEL PRIZE–winning IRISH poet William Butler Yeats successfully produced the play the following spring at Dublin's ABBEY THEATRE (April 16, 1934).

Given the play's critical reception, it might be surprising to learn that O'Neill struggled over this work perhaps more than any other, composing seven drafts and many title changes over more than a two-year period (late 1931 to early 1934). Also incongruously, in a one-month interlude during the agonizing period of its composition, O'Neill wrote the highly successful comedy AH, WILDERNESS!, which appeared earlier in 1933 to enormous praise from critics and audiences alike. *Ah, Wilderness!* remains a Broadway favorite, but *Days Without End* is rarely, if ever, revived today. In the years following its six-month run, O'Neill sank into a severe depression, compounded by increasing ill health, and he nearly suffered a complete nervous breakdown. No doubt his triumphant admission into the elite fellowship of Nobel Prize laureates in 1936 (as yet O'Neill is the only American dramatist granted this distinction) raised his spirits somewhat and fended off professional obscurity for a time.

Nevertheless, a 12-year period elapsed before his next play—one of his late masterpieces, *The ICE-MAN COMETH*—was produced in 1946.

## SYNOPSIS

### Act 1: Plot for a Novel

John Loving's office in the New York firm Eliot and Company on a cloudy spring afternoon in 1932. O'Neill's STAGE DIRECTIONS indicate that a circle of light should initially illuminate two figures at the table—John and his demon spirit Loving—and then as the action moves forward, the light slowly spreads across the room until the stage is entirely lit. Loving, whose dialogue is taken by the other characters as coming from John, wears a mask that bears a grotesque resemblance to John's face, as if it were *"the death mask of a John who has died with a sneer of scornful mockery on his lips. And this mocking scorn is repeated in the expression of the eyes which stare bleakly from behind the mask"* (3:113).

With the play set less than two years before its premiere, the historical realities of the Great Depression (1929–41) loom large over both characters and audience. John and his partner, William Eliot, have no clients or future prospects for any. John is in the process of outlining the plot of a novel and is engaged with his alter ego, Loving, in a battle of wills over the third and final part. Two parts have already been fleshed out. In the first, a teenage boy disavows his Catholic upbringing after his devout parents die of influenza; in the second, he discovers renewed faith through the love of an ideal woman. At some point, the protagonist commits an unnamed "terrible sin" against the woman—adultery. John argues that the third part should consist of his confession and her forgiveness. Loving mocks the character's (and by association John's) "ridiculous conscience" over the affair, and he cruelly suggests that the woman die in the end. Barely implicit is the assumption that John has committed adultery against his wife Elsa Loving, whom he loves fully, and he desires to work through his crisis of conscience by writing about it: "I want to get at the real truth and understand what was behind—what evil spirit of hate possessed me to make me. . . ." (3:115) Throughout John's quest to achieve spiritual fulfillment and

peace, Loving attempts to convince him, in the mode of what O'Neill called "philosophical Nihilism," that "There is nothing—nothing to hope for, nothing to fear—neither devils nor gods—nothing at all!" (3:115)

William Eliot, John's partner, enters the office, and he and John expound on the ill effect of the depression on their business. John admits that he is working on a novel—just dabbling, he lies, to pass the time. Eliot expresses kindhearted disbelief that John returned to writing after marrying his wife, Elsa. We learn that in his youth, John had written a flurry of articles denouncing the existence of Christ and touting atheistic political philosophies like socialism and ANARCHISM for the radical press. Eliot informs John that his family friend Lucy Hillman phoned the office, which makes John visibly nervous. Eliot exits, and John and Loving resume their quarrel over the novel's ending. Loving insists that John's protagonist denounce religion once and for all, while John passionately wishes his character might "find faith—somewhere!" (3:118).

Eliot reenters and announces that a priest, Father Matthew Baird, is waiting outside the office. Father Baird enters, and the three men discuss John's background. After John's parents died in the influenza epidemic, Father Baird, his uncle, became his guardian. John rebelled against his uncle's faith completely: While in college, he founded an atheist club, and afterward he became an outspoken critic of the church. Father Baird lists John's many replacements for his lost faith, including (in this order), socialism, anarchism, Marxism, mysticism, Buddhism, Pythagoras and numerology, and evolutionism (DARWINISM), none of which took hold. Apparently John at last found peace by renouncing all "isms" and marrying Elsa. After Eliot politely excuses himself, Father Baird admits that he had a vision in church while praying for John and believes his nephew is in "great spiritual danger" (3:126). The demonic Loving then goads John into relating the plot of his novel. The priest listens attentively, intermittently shocked at the blasphemy (at one point, the protagonist sells his soul to the devil) and sympathetic to the protagonist's tragic life, which he understands to be his nephew's. Throughout the dialogue, Loving appears visibly and audibly (to John) threatened by the priest, whom he despises for attempting to reestablish John's old faith. John himself, uncertain in his apostasy, mediates both sides.

Father Baird departs, promising to meet John and Elsa for dinner at their Manhattan apartment. The office telephone rings; it is Lucy Hillman. She asks whether she might visit Elsa, who has been trying to reach her. After hanging up the phone, John is clearly shaken at the prospect of Lucy and Elsa (best friends, as far as Elsa knows) reuniting, and Loving jeers at his reaction. "Your terrible sin begins to close in on you, eh? But then, it wasn't you, was it? It was some evil spirit that possessed you!" (3:131). John drops the subject abruptly, getting back to the novel plot, whereupon the demon maliciously suggests the wife die of influenza, a disease Elsa has recently contracted, which progresses into pneumonia.

## Act 2: Plot for a Novel (Continued)

John and Elsa Loving's living room in their duplex apartment in Manhattan, late afternoon of the same day. Elsa appears in a negligie and rings for her maidservant, Margaret, who appears soon after. Margaret scolds her mistress for not having taken a nap, but Elsa is too preoccupied with the arrival of John's uncle to sleep. Margaret announces Lucy Hillman, who enters looking dissipated and ostentatiously dressed. Elsa reproaches her old friend for being a stranger, and Lucy complains she has been attending too many parties with her philandering pseudo-bohemian husband, Walter. They talk about Lucy's growing cynicism, and we discover that Elsa had been married previously to a man named Ned Howell, whom she divorced on the grounds of adultery. Lucy loathes her husband, Walter, the marital state, and even motherhood, considering these centers of her life to be unfulfilling disappointments. Elsa, on the other hand, voices the true love she feels for John, considering him, as Nina Leeds does her three lovers in STRANGE INTERLUDE, "my child and father now, as well as being a husband and . . ." Lucy finishes the sentence—"lover"—and then accuses Elsa of being "incredibly Mid-Victorian" (3:137)—that is, restrained by respectable decorum. Lucy is evidently hiding something. At length, she admits to committing adultery, which shocks

Earle Larimore, Stanley Ridges, and Selena Royle as John, Loving, and Elsa Loving, respectively, in the Theatre Guild's 1933 production of *Days Without End* (Courtesy of the New York Public Library, Lincoln Center)

Elsa. The liaison had occurred at a soirée where her husband was openly flirting with another woman. In the spirit of vengeance, she seduced a man she knew to be happily married, an act of vengeance against both her husband's disloyalty and the other couple's happiness. When she describes the man as having two sides to his nature—one sweet and sympathetic, the other spiteful and sinister—she clearly indicates the demonic Loving's presence, "as if [the kind man] were no longer there. It was another man, a stranger whose eyes were hateful and frightening. . . . I seemed for a moment to be watching some hidden place in his mind where there was something as evil and revengeful as I was" (3:140).

After Lucy's partial confession, Elsa explains how John convinced her to marry him by describing their love as "a sacrament of faith in which each of us would find the completest self-expression in making our union a beautiful thing" (3:142). John enters the living room, with the sneering Loving close behind, and Lucy cowers in guilt by the couch. Elsa, oblivious to Lucy's anxiety, insists she remain to keep her husband company and leaves to check Margaret's progress with dinner. John's poker-faced smile instantly disappears. Lucy and John discuss the outcome of their treachery. John believes Lucy drinks too much to be capable of keeping the secret from her husband, whom she vengefully told of the affair if not the identity of the perpetrator. He threatens to confess his indiscretion to his wife, and Lucy pleads with him not to destroy Elsa's dream.

Lucy departs after Elsa returns from the kitchen. Elsa coaxes John into telling her what has been troubling him, and he lies that it is work-related and nothing more. Satisfied, Elsa exits to prepare for Father Baird's visit, and John and Loving resume their debate over the ending of the novel. Loving now suggests that the hero commit suicide. "There's always death to wash one's sins away—sleep, untroubled by Love's betraying dream!" (3:148).

### Act 3, Scene 1: *Plot for a Novel* (Continued)

John and Elsa Loving's living room. John, Loving, Father Baird, and Elsa are relaxing after dinner. Margaret serves them coffee and then exits. John voices concern over Elsa's health. She reassures him and coaxes him into relating the final part of his novel, which he reluctantly does: After the death of his parents, the protagonist became terrified by life and suicidal. He describes the experience of living with his demon, Loving, "as if he constantly sensed a malignant Spirit hiding behind life, waiting to catch men at its mercy, in their hour of secure happiness—Something that hated life!—Something that laughed with mocking scorn!" (3:151). He subsequently "believed," like John, "in one social or philosophical Ism after another, always on the trail of Truth!" (3:152). What finally provides the "truth" he had been seeking was through the love of an ideal woman. But his fear of her death, of her abandoning him as his parents had, made him resent their seemingly perfect love. So he sabotages the relationship by being unfaithful, if only once, and the experience torments him with guilt.

The story is identical to Lucy's, a point not lost on Elsa. Father Baird also understands that it is

autobiographical. Loving chimes in that they must think the superstitious notion of the hero "possessed by a demon" to be nonsense and adds that the affair was utterly meaningless and his hero's guilt misguided. John asks Elsa if she believes the woman could ever forgive his character. After a pause, she gravely responds, "No. She could never forgive him" (3:155). He begs her to consider the demon, that the act was out of his control, but she refuses. He continues that the next part of the plot involves the woman contracting influenza, which leads to pneumonia and eventual death. Elsa's anger now turns to fear. Father Baird silences John by warning him against the "fog of gloom" affecting Elsa (3:156). Elsa excuses herself as having a headache, and John and Father Baird start for the study. Before Elsa is gone, however, Loving cruelly remarks that outside it is cold and raining, thus taunting her into fulfilling his preferred ending of the novel's plot.

### Act 3, Scene 2

John Loving's study. To relieve his torment, John unleashes a stream of political protest at his uncle against capitalistic greed, the failed American dream, and the loss of individualism. He calls for a new savior, one who will teach them all how to live their lives in a true state of freedom and spiritual fulfillment in the mode of PHILOSOPHICAL ANARCHISM; Loving disclaims the vision, saying, "I'll grant you the pseudo-Nietzschean savior I just evoked out of my past is an equally futile ghost" (3:159). Father Baird suggests John continue his story. John tells of his hero's entering a church, seeking spiritual renewal there while at the same time challenging God to prove his existence. At one point, he finds faith, but it is soon overcome by what Loving refers to as the "mocking rational something in him that laughs with scorn" (3:160). Father Baird is again insulted by John's blasphemy, but John rejoins that only when the revelation comes to his hero that there is no God, and hence no meaning to life, can his character proceed with the business of living. "Once we have accepted it without evasion, we can begin to create new goals for ourselves, ends for our days!" (3:158). Father Baird challenges him to confess his sin, but John, roused from his reverie, dismisses the issue and excuses himself to check on

Elsa. A few moments later, he returns with the disheartening news that Elsa has gone out in the bad weather for a walk. Both men blame themselves— Father Baird for leaving her alone in a vulnerable state and John for telling his damning story.

Elsa appears in the hallway, enters dripping wet, and informs John that she knows of his betrayal. She curses him for destroying the "sacrament" they had built together: "And all that time I was loving you, you were only waiting for this chance to kill that love, you were hating me underneath, hating our happiness, hating the ideal of our marriage you had given me, which had become all the beauty and truth of life to me!" (3:164–165). Father Baird implores her to dry off and get to bed, but she responds sarcastically that to do so would disrupt the plot of John's novel. Nevertheless, she goes to her room, leaving John tortured with guilt. Father Baird begins to pray; John senses a "Presence" in the room and starts praying himself. Loving calls John a fool and, in a rage, screams at him, "I tell you there is nothing—nothing!" As the curtain falls, John unaccountably relents, and "(*stammers with a confused air of relief*) Yes—of course—what's the matter with me? There's nothing—nothing to fear!" (3:167).

### Act 4, Scene 1: End of the End

John's study, but now the interior of Elsa's bedroom is exposed at left. Elsa is prostrate in her bed, and John hovers above her in a sleepless, terrified state. Doctor Stillwell attends to her with a nurse, and Father Baird whispers something to the doctor. Loving stands behind the back of a chair, and "*the sinister, mocking character of his mask is accentuated now, evilly intensified.*" Elsa shouts out, delusional with fever, "John! How could you? Our dream!" (3:168). John's grief is extreme, and his irrepressible outbursts of anguish force the doctor and priest to send him out of the room. Stillwell informs Father Baird that Elsa could survive if she only had the will (3:172).

In the study, Father Baird implores John to retrieve his faith to save Elsa, but Loving's influence still holds strong. In a form of exorcism, Father Baird says, "It's the hatred you once gave your soul to which speaks, not you! (*pleadingly*)

I implore you to cast that evil from your soul! If you would only pray!" (3:173). Loving, for his part, cruelly rationalizes John's suicide if she dies: "There will remain only the anguish of endless memories, endless regrets—a torturing remorse for murdered happiness!" (3:175). John responds affirmatively that if she were to die, he would surely kill himself. When Elsa hears this, she gains some consciousness and pleads for him to stay. John slowly overcomes Loving's influence and heads off to a nearby church, as his protagonist does in the novel, to seek guidance at the foot of the cross. Elsa fully regains consciousness and, terrified he will kill himself, pledges forgiveness and understanding. The doctor checks her pulse and triumphantly announces that she will live.

### Act 4, Scene 2

The interior of a church in which a large, finely crafted wooden Christ on the cross serves as the centerpiece. Loving is walking backward in front of John to block his path (though O'Neill's stage directions specify that they never touch here or elsewhere in the play). John is now the more powerful of the two, and Loving's words fall on deaf ears. John kneels before the cross and begs Christ's forgiveness, imploring him to restore the lost spiritual love of his childhood faith. At the same time that John vows his loyalty to Christ, Loving curses the cross in wild desperation. Loving becomes increasingly weaker, until at last John intones, "Thou art the Way—the Truth—the Resurrection and the Life, and he that believeth in Thy Love, his love shall never die!" (3:179). With this, Loving collapses to the floor with arms outstretched in the attitude of a cross; his dying words are those begging for forgiveness. John and Loving have now merged into one man: John Loving. John Loving arises from his kneeling posture and stretches his arms apart to form a third cross on stage. Sunlight shines brightly through the crimson, green, and gold stained-glass windows; then the walls of the church and the face of the Christ figure light up. Father Baird enters the church and, recognizing the spiritual transformation in John, begins praying in thanks. He informs his nephew that Elsa will live, and John shouts, "I know! Love lives forever!"

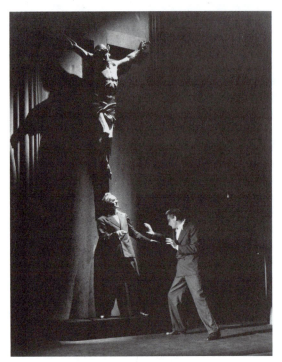

Final scene from *Days Without End* at the Henry Miller Theatre, New York City, 1934 *(Courtesy of the New York Public Library)*

He silences the priest, instructs him to listen, and then shouts in wild exultation, "Life laughs with God's love again! Life laughs with love!"—and the curtain falls (3:180).

## COMMENTARY

O'Neill intended *Days Without End* as a sequel to DYNAMO and thus the second play of a planned trilogy entitled *Myth Plays for the God-Forsaken* or *God is Dead! Long Live—What?* Each play, according to O'Neill, was to explore "the spiritual futility of the substitute-God search" (quoted in Floyd 1985, 406). The "substitute God" in *Dynamo* is technology and science; in *Days* it is love; and in *It Cannot Be Mad*, which he never wrote, it is the god of money. Selena Royle, the actress who first played Elsa, considered *Days* O'Neill's love poem to his third wife, CAR-LOTTA MONTEREY O'NEILL (the play is dedicated to her). In fact, Carlotta had requested he write her a love poem, and there is some evidence she wished

him to regain his lost Catholic faith, as John Loving does (Bogard 324; Alexander 206). This was not the first play in which O'Neill dramatized his love obsession of the moment: For his New London sweetheart, BEATRICE ASHE, it was SERVITUDE (1914), for his second wife AGNES BOULTON it was WELDED (1923), and now *Days Without End* for Carlotta (Alexander 189). With this in mind, O'Neill and Carlotta ferociously stood by the artistic and spiritual quality of this play against all critical odds. Carlotta herself responded in this way to O'Neill's friend SAXE COMMINS's disapproving comment that O'Neill had taken a step "backward":

> Gene and I nearly had a fit when we saw you had taken the end of the play quite from the wrong angle. It has *nothing* to do with *Christianity* or *prayer* that brings Elsa back—it is her *great & all consuming love for her husband!* Thro' her love she senses that her husband is in danger & that *love* gives her the strength to *come back* & live for him—We suppose *no one* will understand that tho'—that you didn't! (quoted in Shaughnessy)

Nevertheless, O'Neill critic Travis Bogard sums up the general opinion that "no play of O'Neill's is so lacking in action, so wasteful in construction, so filled with needless changes of scene and undeveloped and uninteresting characters" (327). Indeed, "the real drama," Bogard contends—a drama Stephen A. Black sets down thoroughly in his psychoanalytic biography—"was O'Neill's attempt to write the play" (328). O'Neill's proposed plot lines and considerations for the ending, which, like his fictional character, caused him considerable distress, can be found in Virginia Floyd's *Eugene O'Neill at Work* and Doris Falk's "The Many Endings of *Days Without End*." The most revealing passage in his work diary is his late notation to himself, "again reach same old impasse—play always goes dead on me here where it needs to be most alive or I go dead on it—something fundamentally wrong" (quoted in Alexander 1992, 202).

The year the play takes place, 1932, was significantly the worst year of the Great Depression, though Americans were terrified the country would sink even lower. O'Neill believed that the depressed economy reflected the spiritual enervation that American capitalism generated as well. However, like O'Neill's far more successful mask play, *The* Great God Brown, *Days* is primarily concerned with the Faustian duality of the soul, though it contains little of the thematic complexity of its precursor. One revealing interruption in the composition of this play was an essay O'Neill wrote for the *American Spectator* entitled "Memoranda on Masks" (November 1932). The essay's first section ends with a submission that clarifies his decision to use the Loving doppelgänger:

> Consider Goethe's *Faust,* which, psychologically speaking, should be the closest to us all of the Classics. In producing this play, I would have Mephistopheles wearing the Mephisophelean mask of the face of Faust. For is it not the whole of Goethe's truth *for our time* just that Mephistopheles and Faust are one and the same—*are* Faust? (O'Neill 1961, 118)

In addition, *Days Without End* charts the spiritual search for meaning through a return to faith in the mode of Francis Thompson's poem "The Hound of Heaven" (1888), which O'Neill read while being treated for tuberculosis at the Gaylord Farm Sanatorium in 1913. The "end" of the title signifies an end to John's spiritual quest—a line O'Neill significantly borrows from the Book of Common Prayer, "World Without End" (Bogard 326), meaning, as the play's Jesuit champion Gerard B. Donnelly, S.J., wrote, "Without belief in God our life is without purpose, our days are without an end" (quoted in Shaughnessy).

Though the play suffers from stilted dialogue, melodramatic plot devices, too much exposition, too little action, and an implausible ending, *Days Without End* is not without merit insofar as thematic content is concerned. O'Neill scholars Edward Shaughnessy and Albert Wertheim have both argued that the dominant themes—dualism and spiritual striving—make this otherwise poorly wrought work salvageable, at least for critics. Wertheim contends that *Days Without End* can be better appreciated if set against the backdrop of other "split character" plays in modern British and American drama from 1915 to the present, while Shaughnessy submits that since "faith was the deepest issue

of O'Neill's life, the only question that really mattered," we can read *Days Without End* as O'Neill's admittance that "faith can be recovered, whatever O'Neill may have intended."

The final two lines of the play emphasize that *Days* is, at bottom, a wish-fulfillment fantasy in matters of religion and love. Doris Alexander finds a parallel between the baffling ending of *Days* and one of O'Neill's earliest full-length plays, *Servitude* (1914). In both plays, she observes, O'Neill debunks his more sustained social philosophy of Nietzschean individualism by reconciling his abhorrence of the status quo with his desire to love. The only way to love, both plays seem to suggest, is by accepting convention as a necessary condition to achieve romantic love (Alexander 1961, 405). But still the question remains, why would O'Neill have chosen Catholicism in particular to represent the sacrifice of individualism in the name of love?

O'Neill himself attempted to disabuse critics that his intention was to promote Catholicism in any way, or indicate a personal turn back toward the religion of his youth—"*It is not Catholic propaganda!*" he declared when the Catholic Writers Guild hounded him to change Elsa from a divorcée to a widow if he wanted their preproduction endorsement. "If, after it comes out, the Church wants to set the seal of its approval on it," O'Neill continued, "well, that's up to them. But I don't give a damn whether they do or not—and I certainly will not make the slightest move to win that approval in advance!" (quoted in Alexander 1992, 206). In a letter to Sophus Keith Winther, a contemporary of O'Neill's anxious to include *Days Without End* in his 1934 book-length study of O'Neill's work, O'Neill writes:

> But the end [of the play] hardly means that I have gone back to Catholicism. I haven't. But I would be a liar if I didn't admit that, for the sake of my soul's peace, I have often wished I could. And by Catholicism I don't mean the Catholic church as a politically-meddling, social-reactionary force. That repels me. I mean the mystic faith of Catholicism whose symbols seem to me to approach closer than any other symbols to the apprehension of a hidden spiritual significance in human life. (O'Neill 1994, 433)

Indeed, given John Loving's lengthy exploration into the world's major philosophies, why did O'Neill choose Catholicism for the final redemption above all the others? His choice was clearly not arbitrary, given the MELODRAMA of the final scene. The simple answer might be that Catholicism offers certain comforts that none of the others do: promise of an afterlife; moral and spiritual certainty in the here and now; and most important given the love connection with Elsa, alleviation of guilt through confession. For these reasons, O'Neill answered one inquiry whether he had rediscovered his Catholic faith, "unfortunately, no" (quoted in Cargill 10).

The mother figure is of enormous thematic importance to the work as well, one not unrelated to the Catholic bias we see in the final scene. O'Neill sketched out the idea for one of his earlier drafts by having John kneel before the altar of the Virgin Mary and baby Jesus, rather than the Christ on the cross, and feel "identification of mother and Elsa with Her, himself with child, longing for reunion with them through Mother Goddess that really lures him to point of suicide before statue of Virgin" (quoted in Floyd *The Plays* 416). Elsa, then, is John Loving's "mother substitute" (quoted in Floyd 1985, 384), and his betrayal of her is akin to his betrayal of his devout mother by disavowing the church and subsequently adopting Loving—the hateful side of his nature—as his demonic muse. By embracing the church in the end, and thus killing off the demon, Loving, he has reunited with his mother and saved his wife's (mother's) life. Thus the "real drama" once again can be found in the composition of the play, as through the process of writing through his "sadistic wishes toward his mother (and his wives) made him sick and depressed. . . . [T]he act of composition carried him to the edge of a breakdown" (Black 385). The only means by which O'Neill could stifle the pain of such a "sadistic" revelation was to bring in the John Loving character as an author (distancing himself from the authorial role) and bury the REALISM under the abstract techniques of EXPRESSIONISM—masks, interior voices, "presences," and so on (Black 385).

An even deeper autobiographical solution might be found in the one figure in his life who did, in fact, return to the Catholicism of her youth, that "mystic faith" that provided "soul's peace"—his mother, MARY ELLEN "ELLA" O'NEILL. Indeed, Ella, who died in 1922, had successfully overcome a morphine addiction by returning to the spiritual succor only the church could afford her. Starting in June 1914, Ella ended her 26-year-old drug habit by entering a convent in Brooklyn and, when outside the convent, attending Mass each Sunday. Even when dealing with the pain and disfigurement of her mastectomy in 1919, she never returned to the drug (additional influences might have been the slowing of her husband JAMES O'NEILL's travel schedule; the 1914 Harrison Narcotic Act, which added a criminal element to her habit; and the onset of menopause, which would have relieved her of her intense fear of pregnancy [Black 155–156]). Indeed, though Ella still remained socially aloof, she was no longer alienated from the three most important men in her life, and after James's death, she found herself adept at managing her late husband's financial affairs. For O'Neill, his brother Jamie, and his father, the end to the 26-year nightmare at the heart of LONG DAY'S JOURNEY INTO NIGHT is the stuff of a "miracle play" if there ever was one.

Hence, the "old debt" that, as O'Neill wrote Lawrence Langner, he was paying by writing the play may be to the Catholic Church for saving his mother. In that letter, he refers to "any life-giving formula," no matter how archaic and restrictive, as being "as fit a subject for drama as any other" (O'Neill 1994, 424). Ella was destroyed by O'Neill's resolution to snub the Catholic Church at age 14, the same year he learned of Ella's morphine addiction. As Stephen A. Black argues in his biography, she "was said to have wanted Eugene to be a priest, and she took his apostasy very hard, perhaps as a sign of retribution for her sinful addiction" (383). Elsa's name is one letter off from Ella, and O'Neill's use of Catholicism to save her through forgiveness and faith strongly suggests his mother's experience as well.

John's experience at the cross corresponds to that of the historical character Juan Ponce de Leon before the Fountain of Youth in O'Neill's play *The FOUNTAIN*, and to Reuben Light's similar religious awakening before the electric dynamo in *Dynamo*, and Lazarus's expostulations in LAZARUS LAUGHED after Jesus raises him from the dead. All four characters outstretch their arms in prayer to a newly accepted god figure, and each incants a prayer or poem that acknowledges the cyclical flux of existence, what Juan Ponce de Leon calls the fountain's "rhythm of eternal life" (2:225) and Reuben the dynamo's "song of eternal life" (2:873). In a 1935 letter to Leon Mirlas, O'Neill himself explained his decision to end *Days Without End* with Catholicism as his hero's saving grace (quoted here in its draft form with the lines in brackets signifying lines crossed out, courtesy of Virginia Floyd):

> I chose Catholicism because it is the only Western religion which has the stature of a real Faith, because it *is* the religion of the old miracle plays and the Faustian legend which were the sources of my theme—and last and [blood] most simply because it happens to be the religion of my [Irish background, tradition, and] early training and therefore the one I know most about. As for propaganda, I need not tell you that [even if I were a believing Catholic (which, of course, I am not at all, I would] my plays never have been, and never will be, interested in converting anyone to anything except the possibility of the drama as an art. (quoted in Floyd 162–163)

If before *Days Without End,* as Doris Falk suggests, O'Neill "had always assumed that faith was itself a phenomenon of this world, the expression of a universal psychological need . . . [that belief] in the supernatural was an illusion, a 'pipe dream' to keep men alive when other values were gone" (423), then had he expressed the guileless quality of John Loving's spiritual transformation, the play may well have been a greater success. In the end, he would never contrive this kind of heavy-handed final scene again (Falk 423, Voglino 65).

## CHARACTERS

**Baird, Father Matthew**   John Loving's uncle and guardian. O'Neill sets up Father Baird's role as a spiritual guide by describing his appearance as exuding, at 70, "*health and observant kindliness— also the confident authority of one who is accustomed*

*to obedience and deference—and one gets immediately from him the sense of an unshakable inner calm and certainty, the peace of one whose goal in life is fixed by an end beyond* life" (3:119). Father Baird arrives at John Loving's office after having experienced a vision while praying in church that his nephew was in "great spiritual danger" (3:126). In act 1, Father Baird serves, along with John's business partner William Eliot, as John's expositor, informing us that following the deaths of John's parents, John sought spiritual salvation in a series of philosophies, none of which took hold. Father Baird listens attentively to the plot of John's novel and recognizes that it is autobiographical. Throughout the play, Father Baird attempts to convince John, in opposition to John's doppelgänger Loving, that spiritual salvation can only be won through acceptance of Christ as the savior. In the end, Father Baird prevails over Loving's denunciation of religion.

**Eliot, William**   John Loving's business partner. Eliot, whom O'Neill describes as "*about forty, stout, with a prematurely bald head, a round face, a humorous, good-natured mouth, small eyes behind horn-rimmed spectacles*" (3:115), serves little purpose in the play other than to exposit on John's former life as a radical journalist. It is interesting to note that the title of their firm, though they appear to be equal partners, is Eliot and Company; O'Neill probably left out John Loving's name to underscore the fact that John is not, by nature, overly concerned with the business of moneymaking.

**Hillman, Lucy**   Elsa Loving's close friend and John's onetime lover. Lucy, like Elsa, is about 35, "*but, in contrast to Elsa, her age shows, in spite of heavy make-up*" (3:134), and she smokes and drinks heavily to escape the pain of her unfulfilled home life. Lucy is overcome with guilt for having slept with her good friend's husband. Though Lucy never confesses to Elsa, she relates the story of her adultery, which exactly matches a scene in John's novel plot. Lucy resembles O'Neill's third wife, Carlotta Monterey O'Neill, in that Carlotta's ex-husband, Ralph Barton, like Lucy's ex-husband, Walter Hillman, humiliated Carlotta by philandering openly in their social set (Alexander 1992, 197). Lucy's affair with John was carried out partly to inflame her husband's jealousy and punish him for his own sexual misconduct, but also to seek vengeance on Elsa, whose "ideal marriage" was a source of great envy to the embittered Lucy (3:141).

**Loving, Elsa**  John Loving's wife. When Elsa first appears, she is noticeably ill with the flu but still radiates the beauty of *"that Indian Summer renewal of physical charm which comes to a woman who loves and is loved"* (3:133). Elsa divorced her first husband after discovering that he had committed adultery. This led to an extreme disillusionment with the marital contract, and she swore never to marry again. But John convinced her to marry by characterizing their relationship as a "a sacrament of faith in which each of us would find the completest self-expression in making our union a beautiful thing" (3:142). When she discovers John has committed adultery as well, she at first refuses him forgiveness and attempts suicide by exposing herself, sick with the flu, to the cold and rain of the streets. At one point, she cries out, as a character in *The Iceman Cometh* might, "I want my dream back—or I want to be dead with it!" (3:165). Lying in a semiconscious state, Elsa hears John swear to kill himself out of guilt, and she forgives him and instantly recovers.

O'Neill means Elsa's redemptive love to reflect Carlotta Monterey O'Neill's for him; Carlotta herself interpreted the play as expressing the sentiment that "Thro' her love she senses that her husband is in danger & that *love* gives her the strength to *come back* & live for him" (quoted in Shaughnessy). Elsa also brings O'Neill's second wife, Agnes Boulton, to mind, as in 1920, when O'Neill came down with influenza, Agnes implored him not to go out in the cold for fear he might contract pneumonia. Hence, as Doris Alexander suggests, O'Neill "associated [Elsa's] influenza with his own and Agnes' suicidal anguish at the thought of losing love" (1992, 195). In 1928, when he was with Carlotta in Shanghai, he again fell sick with influenza, and "his hatred of Agnes had overflowed against Carlotta" (195). One trouble with O'Neill's rendering of the Elsa character, one that makes her less than believable, is that, as Edward Shaughnessy has pointed out,

"on the one hand, she is supposed to be a mature woman well aware of the world's deceits. On the other, she holds expectations of marital bliss that place her grasp of reality in doubt."

**John**  O'Neill's most clearly drawn Faust character—the fabled scientist who sells his soul to Satan for knowledge and power. John closely resembles Dion Anthony of *The Great God Brown*, who was a more interesting articulation of virtually the same inner struggle—O'Neill's—between sneering cynic and loving saint, conventional businessman and free spirit, mother loathing and mother worship. Though John does not physically resemble his creator—having a *"rather heavy, conventional American type of good looks"* in the mode of the businessman Sam Evans in *Strange Interlude*—he does exhibit some features that do suggest O'Neill, a *"feminine sensitiveness, a broad forehead, blue eyes"* (3:113). Certainly O'Neill used the John character to reconcile many of his own inner conflicts and settled on a woman's love as the answer to his own loss of spirituality. John's last name can thus be explained by the Faust story, as *"Faustus* means fortunate or happy, and for O'Neill being happy and loving were one—hence his name for his modern John Faustus, 'John Loving'" (Alexander 1992, 195).

John had relinquished his faith in Catholicism after losing his parents to influenza when he was only 15 years old. After this, his uncle, Father Matthew Baird, took him in as his ward. Nevertheless, John continued to rebel against religion, founding an atheist club in college and over the course of his life trying out every philosophical "ism" available to fill the gap left by his apostasy: socialism, anarchism, Marxism, mysticism, Buddhism, Pythagoras and numerology, and evolutionism (DARWINISM). He found no "truth" in any of these, however, and this spiritual emptiness manifested itself in his Mephistophelean doppelgänger, Loving. As Harry Slochower remarks in the opening of an essay on O'Neill's philosophical "vacillations": "Through the character of John Loving in *Days Without End*, O'Neill recapitulated his own stormy development from anarchic defiance to pious recantation" (383). But John for a time finds peace in his marriage to his ideal woman, Elsa, a cosmic love he characterized as "a sacrament of faith in which each of us would find the completest self-expression in making our union a beautiful thing" (3:142).

Nevertheless, his inner Mephistopheles, Loving, thwarts his attempts at achieving happiness through love by instigating a sexual indiscretion with Elsa's good friend Lucy Hillman. John dramatizes his apostasy and subsequent act of adultery—which O'Neill considered the "great sin against love" (Alexander 1992, 196)—in the plot for a planned novel, which he hopes, if he can conceive of the right ending, will relieve him of his guilt and revive the spiritual peace he had felt with Elsa before the adulterous act. Elsa, apprehending John's betrayal, attempts suicide by exposing herself to the elements while ill with influenza at Loving's implicit suggestion. When it becomes clear that Elsa may not survive, John overcomes Loving's hold on him and returns to the church of his youth, while Elsa, through her love, forgives him. In the end, with the power of love and the grace of Christ, John and Loving merge into one complete whole—John Loving.

**Loving** John's doppelgänger. Originally conceived as a brother or a friend, Loving's character is John's "devil of hate" who haunts his soul and plays Mephistopheles to John's Faust. Loving wears a mask *"whose features reproduce exactly the features of John's face—the death mask of a John who has died with a sneer of scornful mockery on his lips"* (3:113). In a note to himself in an early stage of the composition of *Days Without End,* O'Neill characterized the doppelgänger Loving, or at least his original conception of him, as an avatar of his older brother JAMES O'NEILL, JR. (Jamie) as a "philosophical Nihilist" (quoted in Alexander 1992, 199). Though the Loving character eventually became a masked demon, rather than a brother or friend to the protagonist, John, O'Neill retained his philosophical nihilism. As such, in the first scene, when Loving jeers at John's terrible conscience, he says with a *"strange defiant note of exultance . . .* There is nothing—nothing to hope for, nothing to fear—neither devils nor gods—nothing at all!" (3:115). John, on the other hand, more closely resembles O'Neill's PHILOSOPHICAL ANARCHISM

when he complains to his uncle, Father Matthew Baird, that Americans "have lost the ideal of the Land of the Free. Freedom demands initiative, courage, the need to decide what life must mean to oneself. To them, that is terror. They explain away their spiritual cowardice by whining that the time for individualism is past, when it is their courage to possess their own soul which is dead—and stinking!" (3:158).

In this way, the demonic Loving resembles O'Neill's brother Jamie, who deliberately cultivated O'Neill's darker side. Though John often leans toward Loving's base cynicism, his more persistent resistance provides the play's central conflict. The character for which the world has the most meaning through the "grace of faith" (3:174) is John's uncle, Father Matthew Baird. John is essentially torn, then, between these two worldviews—Christian faith and philosophical nihilism. In the play's final scene, John relinquishes his evil spirit by praying in a church and receiving a blessed vision from the figure of Christ on the cross. When John shouts in a spiritual reverie, "Thou art the Way—the Truth—the Resurrection and the Life, and he that believeth in Thy Love, his love shall never die!" (3:179), Loving falls pleading for mercy and perishes at John's feet with arms outstretched in the humbled pose of the crucifixion.

**Margaret** John and Elsa Loving's maid. She is a doting, *"middle-aged Irishwoman with a kindly face"* (3:133) who serves little purpose other than to identify the Lovings as well-to-do, even at a time of severe economic depression. She also serves the function, intentional or not, of distancing John Loving from Irish Catholicism (Father Matthew Baird's name, not distinctively Irish-sounding, functions in the same way).

**Nurse** Dr. Herbert Stillwell's nurse. She is a *"plump woman in her late thirties"* (3:168) who cares for Elsa Loving after she has contracted pneumonia. She is the only character in the play with no lines.

**Stillwell, Dr. Herbert** Elsa Loving's doctor. Stillwell (the pun of his name is obvious and unnecessary) is *"in his early fifties, tall, with a sharp, angular face and gray hair"* (3:168). Stillwell believes that Elsa's condition is exacerbated by her lack of desire to live. His main function is to protect his patient from John's outbursts, which also aggravate her condition. Stillwell is not to be mistaken for one of the quack doctors O'Neill often includes in his plays, usually offstage, perhaps because in O'Neill's WORK DIARY he originally conceived of the Father Baird character, with whom the doctor frankly confers on Elsa's condition, as a brilliant country doctor.

## BIBLIOGRAPHY

Alexander, Doris. "Eugene O'Neill as Social Critic." In *O'Neill and His Plays: Four Decades of Criticism*, edited by Oscar Cargill, N. Bryllion Fagin, and William J. Fisher, 390–407. New York: New York University Press, 1961.

———. *Eugene O'Neill's Creative Struggle: The Decisive Decade, 1924–1933*. University Park: Pennsylvania State University Press, 1992.

Black, Stephen A. *Eugene O'Neill: Beyond Mourning and Tragedy*. New Haven, Conn.: Yale University Press, 1999.

Bogard, Travis. *Contour in Time: The Plays of Eugene O'Neill*. Rev. ed. New York: Oxford University Press, 1988.

Cargill, Oscar. Introduction to *O'Neill and His Plays: Four Decades of Criticism*, edited by Oscar Cargill, N. Bryllion Fagin, and William J. Fisher, 1–16. New York: New York University Press, 1961.

De Casseres, Benjamin. "'Denial without End': Benjammin DeCasseres's Previously Unpublished Satire of Eugene O'Neill's *Days Without End*." Edited by Robert M. Dowling. Forthcoming in the *Eugene O'Neill Review* 30 (Fall 2008).

Dowling, Robert M. "On Eugene O'Neill's 'Philosophical Anarchism.'" *Eugene O'Neill Review* 29 (Spring 2007): 50–72.

Falk, Doris. "The Many Endings of *Days Without End*." In *O'Neill and His Plays: Four Decades of Criticism*, edited by Oscar Cargill, N. Bryllion Fagin, and William J. Fisher, 415–423. New York: New York University Press, 1961.

Floyd, Virginia. *The Plays of Eugene O'Neill: A New Assessment*. New York: Ungar, 1985.

Floyd, Virginia, ed. *Eugene O'Neill at Work: Newly Released Ideas for His Plays*. New York: Ungar, 1981.

Miller, Jordan Y. *Playwright's Progress: O'Neill and the Critics*. Chicago: Scott, Foresman and Company, 1965.

O'Neill, Eugene. "Memoranda on Masks." In *O'Neill and His Plays: Four Decades of Criticism*, edited by Oscar Cargill, N. Bryllion Fagin, and William J. Fisher, 116–122. New York: New York University Press, 1961.

———. *Selected Letters of Eugene O'Neill*. Edited by Travis Bogard and Jackson R. Bryer. New York: Limelight Editions, 1994.

Shaughnessy, Edward L. "O'Neill's Catholic Dilemma in *Days Without End*." *Eugene O'Neill Review* (1991). Available online. URL: http://www.eoneill.com/library/on/shaughnessy/review91.htm. Accessed November 3, 2007.

Slochower, Harry. "Eugene O'Neill's Lost Moderns." In *O'Neill and His Plays: Four Decades of Criticism*, edited by Oscar Cargill, N. Bryllion Fagin, and William J. Fisher, 383–389. New York: New York University Press, 1961.

Voglino, Barbara. *"Perverse Mind": Eugene O'Neill's Struggle with Closure*. London: Associated University Presses, 1999.

Wertheim, Albert. "Eugene O'Neill's *Days Without End* and the Tradition of the Split Character in Modern American and British Drama." *Eugene O'Neill Newsletter* 6, no. 3 (Winter 1982). Available online. URL: http://www.eoneill.com/library/newsletter/vi_3/vi-3c.htm. Accessed July 2, 2007.

# *Desire under the Elms: A Play in Three Parts* (completed, 1924; first produced, 1924)

Eugene O'Neill's greatest play up to this point in his career and the finest American tragedy to be written until then, *Desire under the Elms* premiered on November 11, 1924, at the Greenwich Village Theatre in New York City. O'Neill informed Walter Huston, who played the lead as Ephraim Cabot in the premiere of *Desire under the Elms*, that he dreamed the entire plot one night between Christmas and New Year's Eve 1923. It was conceived during one of the most frantic periods in O'Neill's career, and he worked in fits and starts over the late winter and spring 1924, discontinuing work on his new script to oversee productions of WELDED, ALL GOD'S CHILLUN GOT WINGS, The ANCIENT MARINER (his adaptation of Samuel Taylor Coleridge's poem), and a revival of The EMPEROR JONES, with PAUL ROBESON taking CHARLES S. GILPIN's place as Jones. He completed the script on June 16, 1924, and its premiere on November 11 coincided with a revival of the SS GLENCAIRN series. Two months later, the production headed uptown to the Earl Carroll Theatre for a run on Broadway, and following that it went on a road tour across the country.

The play's "distresses," as one reviewer for the *New York Herald Tribune* reported, "range from unholy lust to infanticide, and they include drinking, cursing, vengeance, and something approaching incest" (Hammond 170). Such "distresses" led the New York district attorney Joab Banton to attempt its censorship by levelling charges of obscenity against the production. As with the premiere of O'Neill's *All God's Chillun Got Wings*, judges summarily cleared the play of all charges. Banton inadvertently advanced the play's profile, however, and long queues at the ticket counter followed the publicity.

*Desire under the Elms* made O'Neill a small fortune, and he sarcastically credited Banton for his good luck. Once, after paying his dentist, O'Neill reportedly laughed, "But don't thank me, thank that so-amiable District Attorney!" (quoted in Alexander 37) The play was also banned in England by the lord chamberlain, who succeeded in delaying its British premiere until 1940. Many cities across the United States banned it as well, even Los Angeles. In 1926, O'Neill wrote the notoriouss muckraker Upton Sinclair, "I hear they have 'pinched' my play 'Desire Under the Elms' in your Holy City, Los Angeles. Well, well, and so many of the pioneers are said to have come from New England! Boston has also banned it" (quoted in Alexander 38). During the Los Angeles trial, a judge ordered the touring group to perform scenes in the courtroom, after which they were duly exonerated.

Walter Huston as Ephraim Cabot in the Triumvirate's 1924 production of *Desire under the Elms* (Courtesy of the New York Public Library)

*Desire under the Elms* rises above the simple local-color piece on New England life it might appear superficially, though that function of the play should never be dismissed out of hand. With it, O'Neill artfully combines his most powerful themes and influences—GREEK TRAGEDY, father-son relations, the search for a mother god, the struggle between practical and sensual impulses. Moreover, the play also treats the Oedipus complex, a condition defined, if not invented (as O'Neill liked to point out), by the famed psychologist Sigmund Freud, in which sons feel a subconscious desire to kill their fathers in order to marry their mothers. The staging is also some of the most innovative of O'Neill's career. Though the set is permanent, O'Neill specified that only the rooms in which the action takes place should be visible at any given time, making the farmhouse replicate the systole and diastole of the four chambers of the human heart. It was the fourth production by what the press called the TRIUMVIRATE, an experimental trio that essentially replaced the PROVINCETOWN PLAYERS as the most audacious and forward-thinking theater group in the country; the group included O'Neill as playwright, KENNETH MACGOWAN as producer, and ROBERT EDMOND JONES for set design. With *Desire under the Elms*, the triumvirate powerfully answered the call of the nationwide Art Theatre Movement, "that a realistic play, to have value, must move toward a more profound realism, revealing the psychological essences and primitive mythic forces working in modern lives and attempting to reach a state of 'spiritual abstraction'" (Bogard 199). Since its first production, *Desire under the Elms* has sustained critical admiration, enjoyed many revivals (including, in 2009, a critically acclaimed production starrring Brian Dennehy as Ephraim Cabot at the Chicago's Goodman Theatre), and serves as the focus of a well-warranted body of scholarship.

## SYNOPSIS

### [Preface]

The Cabot farmhouse somewhere in New England on an early summer evening in the year 1850. Also on the permanent set stands a stone wall in front of the farmhouse with a wooden gate at center; a path leads around the right side of the house to the front door. Two windows are on the top floor and two on the bottom. One of the upper windows is the father's, Ephraim Cabot, and the other windows are his three sons'—Eben, Simeon, and Peter Cabot. The bottom left window looks into the kitchen, and the right right into the parlor. Two massive elms loom over each side of the house. Their branches hang down over its battered roof, and O'Neill symbolically describes them in womanly terms: "There is a sinister maternity in their aspect, a crushing, jealous absorption. They have developed from their intimate contact with the life of man in the house an appalling humaneness. . . . They are like exhausted women resting their sagging breasts and hands and hair on its roof, and when it rains their tears trickle down monotonously and rot on the shingles" (2:318). The trees emit a green glow that contrasts starkly with the house's tatty, gray exterior.

### Part 1, Scene 1

Eben Cabot, a fine-looking 25-year old with "*defiant, dark eyes [that] remind one of a wild animal's*

*in captivity*" (2:319), steps out from the house and loudly rings a hand-held dinner bell. "God! Purty!" he exclaims, looking up at the sunset; he then looks down, spits in disgust, and goes back inside. Eben's half brothers, Simeon and Peter, both in their late 30s, stand outside and also take note of the sunset's beauty. The yellow glow reminds Simeon of his long-deceased wife, Jenn, who had hair "yaller like gold" (2:320); Peter is reminded of the actual gold recently discovered in California. Together they discuss their prospects on the farm: Should they await the death of their 75-year-old father, who likes to brag that he will live another 25 years, to claim the farm as their own? Or should they light out to California and prospect for gold? Peter suggests that they might declare Ephraim legally insane. Overhearing the discussion from the kitchen window, Eben remarks he wished their father were dead instead, then calls them in for supper. Lured in by the smell of bacon, Simeon and Peter head like domestic cattle for the kitchen.

### Part 1, Scene 2

The kitchen. Austerely neat, the space contains little but a table with four chairs at center, a cook-stove in the right rear corner, and a poster advertising the gold rush in California hanging on the back wall. The brothers chide Eben for wishing their father dead. Eben asserts that Ephraim murdered his mother by working her too hard on the farm. Simeon enigmatically mumbles, "No one never kills nobody. It's allus somethin'. That's the murderer" (2:322). Eben blames his half brothers for not protecting his mother, whom he believes had rightful ownership of the farm, but they insist there was always too much work to worry over much else. When challenged, Eben reluctantly offers the same excuse. The brothers ponder over the motives behind their father's absence. A month earlier, Ephraim drove off in his buggy to "learn God's message t' me in the spring, like the prophets done" (2:325). The older brothers ridicule Eben for planning to call on a promiscuous local woman named Min, who is nearing 40; all three elder Cabot men have engaged in sexual relations with her. Eben storms out but pauses briefly to take in the brilliant sunset. "I don't give a damn how many sins she's sinned afore mine or who she's sinned 'em with," he cries out, "my sin's as purty as any one on 'em!" (2:326).

### Part 1, Scene 3

Nearing sunrise the following morning; the interior of the brothers' bedroom is visible. Eben returns and wakes the men with news from the village that their father has remarried a "female 'bout thirty-five—an' purty, they says." The brothers curse bitterly, "Everythin'll go t' her now" (2:327). Simeon and Peter settle on the move to California. Eben promises each of them 300 dollars from his mother's savings if they relinquish their shares in the farm, money that would enable them to travel to California by boat. Changing the subject, Simeon and Peter scoff at Eben's adventures with Min, and Eben responds with words that signify ownership rather than love: "What do I care fur her— 'ceptin' she's round an' wa'm? The p'int is she was his'n—an' now she b'longs t' me!" (2:329). Simeon derisively insinuates that Eben might try to "own" their father's new bride as well (foreshadowing the affair to come), but Eben responds contemptuously, "her—here—sleepin' with him—stealin' my Maw's farm! I'd as soon pet a skunk 'r kiss a snake!" Simeon and Peter mordantly speculate over what their "new Maw" will be like (2:329).

### Part 1, Scene 4

The brothers have relocated to the kitchen. The elder brothers eat heartily, while Eben's plate remains untouched. Simeon and Peter accept Eben's offer to buy them out; at the news, Eben is overcome *"with queer excitement"* (2:331). Now believing he has sole ownership, Eben vows to work the farm diligently, and he exits to inspect "his" farm with an *"embracing glance of desire"* (2:331). "It's purty! It's damned purty! It's mine! . . . Mine, d'ye hear? Mine!" (2:331). The other two remain in the kitchen drinking whiskey. At first, they vow not to work, but they soon grow restless, unable to relax after so many years of hard labor. They decide to join Eben with the chores, but he returns to announce their father's arrival. The older brothers exit to pack for the trip west. Now alone, Eben pulls up a floorboard under the stove where his father has hidden his mother's savings, then replaces the board

before the men reemerge with packed carpet bags. Eben ceremoniously pours 600 dollars in 20-dollar gold pieces on the kitchen table. Simeon hands Eben the paper that grants him their shares. They mumble disaffected, vaguely lamenting goodbyes.

At the kitchen table, Eben reads over the informal deed in a trance; the other two look down to the barn where their father, accompanied by his new wife, is unhitching his buggy. Simeon takes the wooden gate off its hinges and tucks it under his arm, shouting, "We harby 'bolishes shet gates, an' open gates, an' all gates, by thunder!" (2:334). But the brothers *"congeal into two stiff, grim-visaged statues,"* as Ephraim and Abbie Putnam come up the path. Abbie, ignoring the two men, gloats over her new property *"with the conqueror's conscious superiority"* (2:335). "I'll go in an' look at *my house*," she says after a perfunctory introduction to the brothers, who scornfully warn her not to take that attitude with Eben. The brothers proudly inform their father that they plan to leave the farm that day to seek gold in California; they circle around him, performing a gleeful Indian war dance. Ephraim backs away uneasily, assuming his sons insane and scolding them for their lust "fur the sinful, easy gold o' Californi-a" (2:336). Continuing their war dance, the brothers whoop and cheer over their newfound freedom, pick up stones and, at the count of three, hurl them through the parlor window. Cabot flies at them in a fury, and they race off singing a gold-rush song to the tune of "Oh, Susannah!"

Abbie's head appears from her new bedroom's window, expressing delight over her new home. She then enters the kitchen and takes in Eben's youthful good looks. Eben too feels a powerful sexual attraction to her, but scoffs at her claims to ownership. Though her possessiveness is unrelenting, she exposits on her mournful life story (see Characters section) and seductively pleads with Eben to befriend her. Eben stalks off, infuriated at his latest rival. Outside, Ephraim is cursing his older sons, and Eben contemptuously denounces Ephraim and his Puritan God. Father and son go off to work; Simeon and Peter are heard in the distance singing; and *"Abbie is washing* her *dishes"* as the curtain falls (2:340, emphasis mine).

## Part 2, Scene 1

An oppressively hot Sunday afternoon two months later. Dressed in her Sunday best, Abbie rocks languorously on the porch rocking chair. Eben's head appears from his bedroom window, and Abbie senses his presence. He glances around, spits in disgust, and disappears. A moment later he emerges outside, and, after some vicious repartee, *"They stare into each other's eyes, his held by hers in spite of himself, hers glowingly possessive. Their physical attraction becomes a palpable force quivering in the hot air"* (2:341). Abbie suggestively reflects on the heat: "Ye kin' feel it burnin' into the earth—Nature—makin' thin's grow—bigger 'n' bigger—burnin' inside ye— makin' ye want to grow—into somethin' else—till yer jined with it—an' it's your'n—but it owns ye, too—an' makes ye grow bigger—like a tree—like them elums" (2:342). Eben willfully defies Abbie's seduction and characterizes her marriage to his father as a form of PROSTITUTION.

Eben departs on a visit to see Min. Ephraim enters looking softer, younger, and healthier than in the previous scene. Abbie remarks that Eben is the "dead spit 'n' image" of Ephraim, though Ephraim believes, like his older sons, that Eben takes after his mother. The old man hints that his youngest son will eventually inherit the farm. Abbie wrathfully informs her husband that Eben has left to consort with Min and announces he tried to seduce her as well. In a rage, Ephraim threatens to "end" his son (2:345), but Abbie's resolution wavers, and she settles him down. She inquires if they were to have their own son whether he would leave the farm to her. He exultantly replies that if she gave him a son, he would do anything she asked. "'An' God hearkened unto Rachel'!" Ephraim joyfully quotes the Song of Solomon, "An' God hearkened unto Abbie!" (2:347).

## Part 2, Scene 2

Eight o'clock that same evening. The two upper bedrooms are now exposed. Ephraim and Abbie sit side by side on their bed, and Eben sits forlornly on his. Ephraim declares the farm requires the son. Abbie dully responds that it is she, not the farm, who needs a son. Eben rises from his bed and stares directly into the wall separating him from Abbie,

and *"Their hot glances seem to meet through the wall"* (2:348). He stretches out his arms to her, and Abbie, almost telepathically aware of his movements, rises from the bed. Eben flings himself down on his bed in agony. Ephraim details his personal history (see Characters section); throughout this impassioned monologue, Abbie is intent upon Eben on the other side of the wall. Ephraim, noting his wife's distraction, angrily accuses her of learning nothing. She promises to endow him with a son, which thrills him. Nevertheless, disturbed by "thin's pokin' about in the dark" of the house (2:350), he moves off to sleep with his cows, where he can find peace. Eben and Abbie continue staring hotly at each other through the wall. Abbie goes to his bedroom. They kiss passionately, but Eben abruptly pushes her away. They argue over Eben's attentions to Min and Abbie's possessiveness of the farm. She departs with an invitation for him to court her properly in the parlor. Eben cries out in dismay for his deceased mother, dresses, and heads for the door.

## Part 2, Scene 3

A few moments later in the parlor. O'Neill describes the space as a *"grim, repressed room like a tomb in which the family has been interred alive"* (2:352). Abbie is perched on the arm of a horsehair sofa. Candles light the gloomy space. Eben enters, hat in hand. They are both terrified. Abbie senses "somethin'" in the room, a presence that first disturbed her but seems to have softened with Eben's entrance. In his turn, Eben senses the spirit of his mother, whose remains were shown in that room after her death. Eben asserts that his mother would hate her replacement, but Abbie feels the spirit is kind to her and vows to emulate his mother's love. She embraces him with a *"horribly frank mixture of lust and mother love"* (2:354). They pledge mutual devotion, and *"their lips meet in a fierce, bruising kiss"* (2:355).

## Part 2, Scene 4

The exterior of the farmhouse at dawn. Now dressed in his work clothes, Eben appears from the house looking unusually contented and self-assured. Abbie's head pokes through the parlor window, and she calls out to him for one last kiss. Eben feels his mother's spirit can rest at last. He warns Abbie that Ephraim will soon return from the barn. She blows him a kiss and disappears into the house. Ephraim enters, staring at the sky. "Purty, hain't it?" he asks his son, who responds by mocking his father's old age and impaired eyesight. Ephraim interrogates him suspiciously. Eben tells Ephraim that he felt his mother's spirit go to its grave; he then orders his father to work. "I'm the prize rooster o' this roost," he says and boldly exits. Irritated by this encounter, Ephraim grumbles over Eben's soft-headedness— "Like his Maw" (2:357)—and goes in to breakfast as the curtain falls.

### Part 3, Scene 1

A night in late spring the following year. The upper bedrooms and kitchen are exposed. A cradle is set up in Ephraim and Abbie's bedroom. A party is brewing in the kitchen to celebrate the birth of Abbie's child. Eben sits despondently in his bedroom, head in hands. Benches are placed along the walls in the kitchen to accommodate the guests—a group of drunken farmers, their wives, and a number of young men and women from the neighboring farms. A small whiskey keg sits at the rear. Abbie and Ephraim are there. Abbie wears a shawl and looks pale and forlorn, desperately anxious for Eben's arrival. Ephraim appears drunk and excitable. Unbeknownst to the Cabots, the guests all know the child is Eben's, not Ephraim's, and they joke and wink to each other in barely concealed hilarity.

Ignorant of the guests' prodding remarks, Ephraim cajoles the fiddler into playing a danceable tune. The fiddler strikes up "Pop, Goes the Weasel." As the tempo rises, so too in speed and vigor does the now 76-year-old Ephraim's dancing steps. He boasts loudly over his physical prowess and the "Injuns" he has killed and scalped. At length, the fiddler stops, exhausted, while Ephraim appears barely out of breath. Upstairs, Eben goes into the adjoining bedroom to view the baby. *"His face is as vague as his reactions are confused, but there is a trace of tenderness, of interested discovery"* (2:362). Ephraim steps outside for air, and a woman declares loudly, "What's happened in this house is plain as the nose on yer face!" (2:362). Unconscious of the sniping guests, Abbie retreats upstairs to join Eben. The lovers worry over the possibility

of Ephraim finding out the baby is Eben's, then kiss passionately. Outside, Ephraim can feel the presence Eben and Abbie felt in the parlor in part 2, scene 3. "Even the music can't drive it out—somethin'" (2:363). He departs for the barn to rest; the fiddler begins "Turkey in the Straw," and the revelers intensify the celebration, this time over "the old skunk gittin' fooled!" (2:363).

### Part 3, Scene 2

The exterior a half hour later. Eben wistfully stares up at the sky. Ephraim enters from the barn looking tired and preoccupied. Once he sets eyes on Eben, his distracted manner changes to vindictive pride. He asks why Eben does not join the party, where he might find a future bride, and insinuates that by marrying he might inherit the farm. Eben contemptuously retorts that the farm was his mother's and now his by rights. Ephraim insists the farm will be Abbie's after his death; he then adds that she accused Eben of attempting to seduce her. In a rage, Eben thrusts Ephraim aside with the intent to murder Abbie, but he underestimates his father's strength. They grapple ferociously, and Ephraim swiftly gets the upper hand by grabbing Eben by the throat. Abbie emerges from the house and desperately attempts to separate them. Ephraim releases his grip and flings his son to the ground, assuring Abbie, "He ain't wuth hangin' fur" (another noteworthy foreshadowing; 2:365–366).

Ephraim rejoins the party, triumphant and laughing contemptuously over the thought of his defeated son. Eben accuses Abbie of seducing him to gain rights to the farm and threatens to inform Ephraim of the truth about their child and to head out west to join his brothers. "I wish he never was born!" he says of the baby, "I wish he'd die this minit!" (2:367). Abbie obtains Eben's halfhearted assurance that if she proves there was no scheme and rectifies their terrible situation, he will believe she loves him "better'n everythin' else in the world!" (2:368).

### Part 3, Scene 3

Before sunup the next morning; the kitchen and Ephraim's bedroom are visible. Eben sits despondently in the kitchen with his carpetbag on the floor. Ephraim is asleep upstairs, and Abbie is leaning over the crib, *"her face full of terror yet with an undercurrent of desperate triumph"* (2:369). She cries out in anguish but, seeing Ephraim stir, stifles her sobs and heads down to the kitchen. She throws her arms around Eben, who stands coldly aloof. "I done it, Eben! I told ye I'd do it!" she shouts. "I've proved I love ye—better'n everythin'—so's ye can't never doubt me no more!" Eben remains unmoved, but he admits his father should never know of the baby's true father, as Ephraim would be sure to "take it out on" the child (3:369). Abbie seems not to hear him, telling him that now there is no reason for him to leave. Eben slowly realizes she has killed someone, but at first assumes it is Ephraim. When he realizes she has killed their baby, he condemns her as a murderer and runs off in horror to inform the sheriff (2:371).

### Part 3, Scene 4

An hour later; the same rooms are shown as in the previous scene. *"The sky is brilliant with the sunrise"* (2:371). Abbie is doubled over the kitchen table with her head in her arms. Ephraim awakes in the bedroom with a start. He dresses and heads downstairs. In the kitchen, he prattles for a time in innocent chatter until becoming aware of Abbie's state. She confesses to the crime, and Ephraim races upstairs to verify it. He returns demanding an explanation, and she confesses hatefully that she loves Eben and that the child was theirs. "If he was Eben's," Ephraim declares after some contemplation, "I be glad he air gone!" (2:373) When Abbie tells him Eben has gone to get the sheriff, Ephraim declaims the injustice of his life—"God A'mighty, I be lonesomer'n ever!" (2:374).

Eben appears on the path. Ephraim warns him to quit the farm after the sheriff takes Abbie away "or, by God, he'll have t' come back an' git me fur murder, too!" (2:374). Once Ephraim is gone, Eben enters the house and throws himself at Abbie's feet, begging forgiveness. The sheriff has been notified, but Eben has had a change of heart, and he now wishes to escape with Abbie. She refuses, feeling her punishment will be well-deserved. He promises to accept responsibility as well. Ephraim returns. First mocking their romance, he announces he has set the farm animals free and plans to join Simeon and Peter out west. He opens the floorboard and discovers the money gone. Eben tells of the exchange in part 1, scene 4. Ephraim declaims the deterministic, puritanical view that "I kin feel I be in the palm o' His hand, His fingers guidin' me. . . . It's a-goin' t' be lonesomer now than ever it war afore—an' I'm gittin' old, Lord—ripe on the bough. . . . Waal—what d'ye want? God's lonesome, hain't He? God's hard an' lonesome!" (2:377).

The sheriff enters accompanied by two men to take custody of Abbie. Eben cries out that he "helped her do it. Ye kin take me, too" (2:377). Ephraim stares at his son *"with a trace of grudging admiration,"* then starts off to round up his cows. All three say strangely cordial good-byes; Eben and Abbie kiss. Eben comments, perhaps for the last time on the beautiful sunrise, and Abbie joins in his admiration. The sheriff takes a look about the farm and utters the final, ironic lines of the play: "It's a jim-dandy farm, no denyin'. Wished I owned it!" (2:378).

## COMMENTARY

*Desire under the Elms* is one of Eugene O'Neill's greatest achievements as a tragedian; others include MOURNING BECOMES ELECTRA, LONG DAY'S JOURNEY INTO NIGHT, THE ICEMAN COMETH, and A MOON FOR THE MISBEGOTTEN. Written well before these later masterpieces, *Desire under the Elms* exhibits O'Neill's full talent as a playwright relatively early in his career, though there had been many missteps along the way and several more to follow. *Desire under the Elms* builds upon the tragic elements of his early play *The ROPE*, in which a New England farmer named Abraham Bentley unsuccessfully attempts to will over 50 $20 gold pieces to Luke, his son by his second, much younger wife; but Luke's hatred for the bitter old New Englander prevents the truth of the father's benevolent intention from being revealed. *Desire under the Elms* also looks forward to *Mourning Becomes Electra* with its handling of New England tragedy and A TOUCH OF THE POET and MORE STATELY MANSIONS, the only surviving plays of his planned cycle on American acquisitiveness, A TALE OF POSSESSORS, SELF-DISPOSSESSED.

At the time of composition, O'Neill was dividing his time between New York and BROOK FARM, his home in Ridgefield, Connecticut. The region apparently inspired a melancholy in the playwright that sets the play's psychological tone: As he later wrote Lawrence Langner, "Ridgefield always drove me to hard cider, acidosis, and the Old Testament in the weepy, muddy, slush-and-snow days" (quoted in Alexander 33; a descriptive and telling personal sketch of O'Neill and his mood at Ridgefield can be found in Malcolm Cowley's "A Weekend with Eugene O'Neill"). A triumph of local color, *Desire under the Elms* is also a masterful expression of literary NATURALISM and a boldly modernist experiment all in one powerfully rendered yet compact articulation.

O'Neill's innovative set reflects the stony image of the New England farmer, as the stone wall can be read as a symbol for God's hardened will (Ephraim), imprisonment (Simeon and Peter), and a womblike partition from the outside world (Eben; see Ranald 1984, 175). The wall and the house behind it thus contrast effectively with the mournful elms and the "purty" glow of the sun as it rises and falls. In addition, the Cabots' dialogue is uncharacteristically restrained for an O'Neill play, and it is not exactly meant to replicate the early New England vernacular; rather, O'Neill was "trying," as he maintained, "to write a synthetic dialogue which in a way should be the distilled essence of New England" (quoted in Alexander 28). Most of the dramatic action is credible, though arguably the infanticide in the penultimate scene is a mistake. Critic Peter Hays finds that "the infant's death is largely a plot device, a shocking way for Abbie to prove her love and for Eben to prove his maturity in accepting part of the blame" (436). Given Abbie's discovery of her actual, untamable passion for Eben—the love that foils her plans for possession of the farm—it is difficult to imagine her killing their child, the ultimate bond between them and the symbol of their shared future. Conversely, killing off Ephraim, which would seem the most logical course of action if a character must die to prove one's love, would undermine O'Neill's acceptance of and near love for Ephraim's character. For O'Neill, the bitter old New Englander is the personification of struggle and hardship. One might even see Ephraim's death, if O'Neill had chosen to kill him off, as a kind of suicide. O'Neill himself once professed, "I have

always loved Ephraim so much! He is so autobiographical!" (quoted in Alexander 36).

O'Neill's portrayal of New England Yankees, members of the regional tradition whose lineages go back to the Puritan settlers, is a by-product of the local color tradition. There are great similarities between this work and James A. Herne's *Shore Acres* (1892), which also deals with a family squabble over the future of a New England farm, this time in Maine; as well as Sidney Howard's *They Knew What They Wanted*, the play that beat *Desire under the Elms* for the PULITZER PRIZE in 1924 and resembles O'Neill's plot to such an extent there was some question over PLAGIARISM by O'Neill (who had read the script several months before beginning work on his own project [Bogard 201–202]). Local color as a literary mode has often been condemned for its superficiality and lack of the inherent truths in staging "spiritual abstractions." But O'Neill posited that the setting and Yankee attributes of the characters are the most important aspects of the play: "What I think everyone missed in 'Desire' is the quality in it I set most store by—the attempt to give an epic tinge to New England's inhibited life-lust, to make its inexpressiveness poetically expressive, to release it" (quoted in Alexander 28). As such, critic Brenda Murphy aptly argues that "in developing this mode of dramatic representation, he opened a new level of meaning and a new way of meaning to the local-color realism traditionally associated with rural simplicity" (129).

New England Puritans were a religious group who practiced Calvinist theology and fled persecution in their homeland, England, by settling in the Massachusetts and Connecticut colonies in the 17th century. The *Harvard Encyclopedia of American Ethnic Groups* defines the essential characteristics of the Yankee, traits Ephraim epitomizes, as "discipline, work, and the permanence of the establishment" (Handlin 1,028). In addition, Puritan deserters who settled in the West were reportedly scorned by their countrymen: When Cotton Mather wrote in the early 1700s about "patriotism and love of country, he meant loyalty to New England" (Handlin 1,028); this calls to mind Ephraim's ephemeral flight to the plains and his contempt for Simeon and Peter's abandoning the farm "fur the sinful, easy gold o' Californi-a" (2:336). The Puritan God was a pitiless, wrathful figure, most famously described in Jonathan Edwards's blood-and-thunder sermon "Sinners in the Hands of an Angry God" (Handlin 1,741). This Calvinist theology informs the pious Ephraim's worldview: "God's hard, not easy! . . . I kin feel I be in the palm o' His hand, His fingers guidin' me. . . . God's hard an' lonesome!" (2:377). Throughout his life, Ephraim experienced periods of rebellion from his angry God, moving West where it was too "easy," courting Min, reveling in the celebration of his (presumed) son's birth, and growing "soft" over Abbie's matrimony with him. But each time God called him to task and, in Ephraim's eyes, reminded him that he was but a "servant o' His hand" (2:349). In the final scene, Ephraim's disaffected reaction to Abbie and Eben's deception is entirely predictable to Ephraim: "Waal—what d'ye want? God's lonesome, hain't he? God's hard an' lonesome!" (2:377).

In spite of the fact that O'Neill abandoned Irish CATHOLICISM early on, he also took a disdainful view of contentment and "soft" living, which is most probably what he meant by identifying Ephraim rather than Eben as being "so autobiographical." This is a point of confusion, as O'Neill's personality more evidently resembles Eben's contradictory consciousness. Nevertheless, O'Neill believed that a full life can only be achieved through trial, tragedy, and suffering. He publicly, if not always privately, equated contentment with bourgeois complacency and spiritual bankruptcy. In an article in the *Philadelphia Public Ledger* (January 22, 1922), for instance, he faced critics who considered his plays morbidly tragic with a dry note of sarcasm:

> Sure I'll write about happiness if I can happen to meet up with that luxury, and find it sufficiently dramatic and in harmony with any deep rhythm in life. But happiness is a word. What does it mean? Exaltation; an intensified feeling of the significant worth of man's being and becoming? Well, if it means that—and not a mere smirking contentment with one's lot—I know there is more of it in one real tragedy than in all the happy-ending plays ever written. (quoted in Clark 96–97.)

To O'Neill, the notion of tragedy as "unhappy" is a "mere present-day judgment" (quoted in Clark 97). According to him, the Greeks (and later the Elizabethans) understood the uplifting attributes of tragedy, and it was with this conviction that he wrote *Desire under the Elms*. Three Greek tragedies inform the play's dramatic action: Euripides' *Medea* and *Phaedra* and Sophocles' *Oedipus Rex*. In the first, the Colchian princess Medea marries Jason, who legendarily leads the Argonauts in search of the Golden Fleece, and she bears two of his children. Jason eventually falls in love with another princess, Creusa, and the vengeful Medea kills the princess along with her own two children. Medea is generally cast in a sympathetic light, however, thus emphasizing the intensity of her love rather than her infanticide, just as O'Neill does with the character Abbie Putnam.

In *Phaedra*, the title character, the minotaur's half sister and Theseus's wife, falls in love with her stepson Hippolytus. After Hippolytus rejects her, she commits suicide, but not before charging Hippolytus with rape. This resembles Abbie's false accusation (out of a similar desperation) that Eben attempted to seduce her. In *Oedipus Rex*, Oedipus, the king of Thebes, unknowingly marries his mother, Jocasta, after killing his father, Laius. In Sophocles' version, Jocasta hangs herself upon learning the truth, and Oedipus puts out his own eyes in symbolic punishment for his figurative blindness. (Ephraim's poor eyesight is brought up several times in *Desire under the Elms*.) No such shame appears in *Desire under the Elms*, only exaltation, though Abbie and Eben will undoubtedly be hanged for murder.

Sigmund Freud, the illustrious German psychologist, was just then gaining a wide following in the United States. Freud notoriously employed the Oedipus myth to describe the subconscious desire of all men to kill their father in order to marry their mother. Freud called this condition the "Oedipus complex." Because of Eben's intense attachment to the memory of his mother (a recurring motif in American drama; see Bogard 214–215), his hatred of his father, and his subsequent sexual relationship with his stepmother (which is technically incest, though they are not blood-related), many critics singled out Freud, rather than the Greek myth, as the guiding source for *Desire under the Elms.* But O'Neill dismissed this popular assumption: "To me, Freud only means uncertain conjectures and explanations about the truths of the emotional past of mankind that every dramatist has clearly sensed since real drama began. . . . I respect Freud's work tremendously—but I'm not an addict!" (quoted in Alexander 38). Thus, with *Desire under the Elms,* O'Neill "[demonstrates] one of his greatest strengths—as myth user rather than myth maker. Here and in *Mourning Becomes Electra* he combined ancient myths with modern psychology to examine American emotional and cultural equivalents," as Margaret Loftus Ranald has written (1998, 67).

This co-optation of Greek mythology in literature and psychology is a trend of modernism also employed by one of O'Neill's greatest philosophical influences, FRIEDRICH NIETZSCHE. As the tragic flaw in each of the borrowed mythical characters is the supremacy of internal desire over external reason, the larger struggle thus springs from this tension. Nietzsche, and later Freud, discovered a metaphor for this phenomenon in the struggle between the Greek gods Apollo, the sun god, and Dionysus, the god of wine and fertility, as outlined in Nietzsche's classic work *The Birth of Tragedy* (1872). The Apollonian impulse brings us full circle back to puritanical belief, typified in Ephraim Cabot's character, in "discipline, work, and the permanence of the establishment." We might also include reason, logic, order, and deference to social norms. The Dionysian impulse, in contrast, favors the irrational, the emotional, the creative, and the uninhibited spirit (Floyd 1985, 281), often acted out by the chorus (the revelers at Ephraim's party in the case of *Desire under the Elms*) in scenes of drunkenness, dancing, and music. Nietzsche contended that the most profound tragedies combined the Apollonian with the Dionysian impulses. But as the form of GREEK TRAGEDY developed, from the more openly imaginative Sophocles to the more naturalistic, or realistic, plays of Euripides, the Dionysian elements began to wane. Thus, Nietzsche called for a rebirth, or rebalancing, of the two. O'Neill answered this call with *Desire under the Elms* and soon after even more explicitly with *The GREAT GOD BROWN.*

Eben is caught between these two elements of his makeup—the "hard" and the "soft." While Ephraim symbolizes the Apollonian side (hard) and his mother and Abbie the Dionysian (soft), O'Neill shows the two collide in Eben, who strikes Ephraim as taking after his mother, and the brothers and Abbie as taking after his father. On the one hand, Eben expresses his Apollonian impulse in the form of his practical, if avaricious, desire for possession of the farm, his handling of his brothers more as competitors for real estate rights than as siblings, and his initial rejection of Abbie as a competitor for those rights. On the other, he betrays his Dionysian side in several ways: through his vision of the farm's beauty rather than its financial value; his passionate need for female companionship (first with his mother, then Min, then Abbie); his connection with the mother spirit that dwells in the parlor and more figuratively in the elms overhanging the sides of the house; and the ardent, near telepathic connection between him and Abbie in part 1, scene 4, and throughout her seduction of him. Eben thus experiences a heightened form of redemption by demonstrating his spiritual love for Abbie, one that conquers both his desire for the farm and his horror over the murder of their child.

O'Neill famously declared that "in all my plays sin is punished and redemption takes place" (quoted in Floyd 285). If one were to fully take him to task on this absolute, it might not stand up, but it certainly fits with *Desire under the Elms.* The sins of avarice, incest, and infanticide are redeemed in the final scene, in which the spiritual love inspired by Abbie prevails in the conflicted consciousness of O'Neill's tragic hero. And Abbie Putnam, though initially intending to seduce Eben for control of the farm, experienced a love so transcendent over all other desires that she willingly killed her own child to prove it.

Some might also read the play as centering on Ephraim rather than Eben, and thus his destruction of two wives through unendurable hard work, dispassionate neglect, and his inalterable belief in a "hard" God is redeemed through his fate to suffer the loneliness that had plagued him throughout his life. "Truth, in the theatre as in life," according to O'Neill, "is eternally difficult just as the easy is the everlasting lie" (quoted in Alexander 34). Ephraim's enduring strength enables him to discover "truth" in life, "hard an' lonesome" as it may be (2:377). Thereby the "somethin'" that is the organizing principle of the play, the puritanical God figure, might be read as the naturalistic forces determining the fate of all characters, Abbie's natural desire, Eben's mother, or a wraithlike manifestation of Ephraim's haunted past.

## CHARACTERS

**Cabot, Eben**   Ephraim Cabot's son and Simeon and Peter Cabot's half brother. Eben is 25 years old in the opening scene, where O'Neill describes him as *"tall and sinewy. His face is well-formed, good-looking, but its expression is resentful and defensive. His defiant, dark eyes remind one of a wild animal's in captivity. Each day is a cage in which he finds himself trapped but inwardly unsubdued."* Eben's fierce, predatory qualities are highlighted by his black hair, a mustache, and a *"thin curly trace of beard"* (2:319), contrasting with his half brothers' more bovine characteristics. Unlike Simeon and Peter, Eben is strongly attached to the Cabot farm, partly because he has the strong, acquisitive nature of his father, and partly because he is powerfully connected to the memory of his deceased mother, who died 10 years before. This split in his nature can be understood as a combination of the Dionysian (his mother's maternal warmth) and Apollonian (his father's strict adherence to Puritanical theology and hard living). Friedrich Nietzsche, O'Neill's great literary and philosophical influence, argued in *The Birth of Tragedy* that together these impulses form the basis of the best of ancient Greek tragedy.

Eben believes that the farm is rightfully his, as his mother had some legitimate claim on its ownership. At the same time, he demonstrates a much stronger bond with the land and the natural order of things than any other character in the play, with the possible exception of Abbie. Along with his two half brothers, whose mother was Ephraim's first wife and who was also worked to death on the farm, he loathes his father and wishes him dead. In part 1, scene 3, Eben offers to buy his brothers' shares of the farm for 600 dollars in gold coins that his mother had saved and that his father was hid-

ing. The brothers depart with their small fortune to strike out for California and join the gold rush that has just begun there. Once their departure is settled, Eben is confronted with a new competitor for rights to the farm—Ephraim's third wife, Abbie Putnam.

At first Eben hates Abbie, who is 35, for her intrusion on his plans to co-opt the farm from his father. Abbie attempts to seduce him to form an alliance against Ephraim, but in spite of her covetous designs, she falls in love with him. He eventually returns her love, and they have a child together, one that Ephraim believes is his. Their incestuous relationship calls to mind that of the Greek character Phaedra (Abbie), who attempts to seduce her stepson Hippolytus (Eben). He also plays Oedipus, the Greek tragic hero who kills his father Laius (Ephraim, though Ephraim survives) and marries his mother, Jocasta (Abbie). Abbie goes on to kill their child to prove her love to Eben, calling to mind a third Greek myth, Medea, in which Medea kills her own children when Jason's infidelity is revealed. O'Neill offers a more redemptive ending than it might appear on the surface, in that the love shared between Eben and Abbie surmounts the avaricious tendencies the characters displayed in the play's first two parts. In the final scene, Eben and Abbie admire the sunrise as the sheriff and his men lead them away to the gallows. Ephraim will maintain the farm and live the rest of his days in a terrible state of perpetual loneliness like Lavinia Mannon in *Mourning Becomes Electra*.

**Cabot, Ephraim**   A New England farmer in his mid-70s; Eben, Peter, and Simeon Cabot's father and Abbie Putnam's husband. O'Neill describes Ephraim as *"tall and gaunt, with great, wiry, concentrated power, but stoop-shouldered from toil. His face is as hard as if it were hewn out of a boulder, yet there is a weakness in it, a petty pride in its own narrow strength. His eyes are small, close together, and extremely nearsighted, blinking continually in the effort to focus on objects, their stare having a straining, ingrowing quality"* (2:334–335). Ephraim is the quintessential New England Yankee, possibly the most affecting example in all of American drama: He is a hardworking, God-fearing Puritan fated to suffer his life in a state (largely of his own construction) of severe loneliness. He is also representative of the Apollonian impulse (the practical), as opposed to the Dionysian (the creative). As such, critics point to Ephraim Cabot as an avatar of O'Neill's father, JAMES O'NEILL, who similarly equated hard work and property ownership with salvation and would also have been 76 (Ephraim's age in the final part) had he still been alive. Oddly enough, O'Neill himself considered Ephraim one of his favorite creations because he is "so autobiographical!" (quoted in Alexander 36).

Ephraim has worked the same farm for 50 years, survived two wives (three soon after the action of the play, as Abbie will go to the gallows for killing her son), and warded off the acquisitive desires of his three sons to take over the farm. A month before the opening scene, Ephraim rode out "t' learn God's message t' me in the spring" (2:325). His return comes in part 1, scene 4, wherein he brings "hum" a new wife, Abbie Putnam. Forty years his junior, Abbie has married in order to take the farm as her own after his death. His son Eben is her only competitor, as Ephraim's other two sons, Simeon and Peter, desert the farm upon her arrival to prospect for gold in California. Abbie and Eben soon fall in love and secretly carry on a relationship behind Ephraim's back.

Ephraim's monologue in part 2, scene 2, a speech to Abbie that Margaret Loftus Ranald considers the "great key to the theology of the play" (1984, 175), exposits his entire life history, including the theological lessons learned along the way: He came to the farm 50 years earlier and worked himself to the bone removing stones to make a workable farm. Others in the area either died or moved west; Ephraim remained, hardening physically, emotionally, and spiritually. At one point, he too emigrated west. Life farming the plains proved too "easy," however, and he heard God's voice scold him for his indolence: "This hain't wuth nothin' t' Me. Git ye back t' hum!" (2:349). Obediently returning to New England, Ephraim soon married. Before his first wife's untimely death, she bore Simeon and Peter. Over time, he grew lonesome and married again; this was Eben's mother, whose parents contested his claim to the farm. Sixteen years later, she died as well, and his hatred for his sons grew as

they made their own claims on the farm. God spoke to him again, ordering him to find a new wife, and he did—Abbie. Throughout Ephraim's monologue, Abbie and Eben appear to exchange love messages telepathically through the wall separating their bedrooms, and to assuage Ephraim's anger over her distraction, she promises to endow him with a boy. When a child arrives the following spring, Ephraim, unaware the child is Eben's, throws a celebration in which the townspeople all share the knowledge that the child is the product of the incestuous relationship between Eben and Abbie, and they joke about it behind his back. In the final scene of the play, Abbie confesses the child was Eben's and that she killed it to prove her love to Eben. Resigned to end his years in loneliness, Ephraim heads off to work as the lovers head off to the gallows.

**Cabot, Peter** Ephraim's Cabot's second son, Simeon Cabot's brother, and Eben Cabot's half brother. Peter is 37 years old. O'Neill describes him, like his brother Simeon, in terms of comparison with Eben: *"built on a squarer, simpler model, fleshier in body, more bovine and homlier in face, shrewder and more practical"* (2:319). Peter, like Simeon, has a bovine quality that connotes the hard-working, dispassionate New England Yankee, *"their bodies bumping and rubbing together as they hurry clumsily to their food, like two friendly oxen"* (2:321). Unlike his father Ephraim, whom he loathes, Peter is willing to abandon both the farm and New England for the more profitable venture of prospecting for gold in California. In this respect, along with whiskey drinking and father envy, both brothers resemble O'Neill's brother JAMES O'NEILL, JR. (Jamie), who moved to California with their mother, MARY ELLEN "ELLA" O'NEILL, to oversee James O'Neill, Sr.'s real estate interests after his death. In part 1, scene 4, he sells his share of the farm to Eben for 300 dollars in gold pieces. Peter articulates his and Simeon's view of the farmhouse as a form of imprisonment and the stone wall in front as a symbol of that condition: "Here—it's stones atop o' the ground—stones atop o' stones—makin' stone walls—year atop o' year—him 'n' yew 'n' me 'n' Eben—makin' stone walls fur him to fence us in!" (2:320). When Ephraim returns with his new wife,

Abbie Putnam, he and Simeon celebrate their new-found freedom by performing an Indian war dance around their father and throwing stones through the parlor window. They depart singing a gold-rush song to the tune of "Oh, Susannah!"

**Cabot, Simeon**  Ephraim's Cabot's eldest son, Peter Cabot's brother, and Eben Cabot's half brother. Simeon is 39 years old, and he lost his wife, Jen, 18 years before. O'Neill describes both Simeon and Peter in the same terms of comparison with Eben: *"built on a squarer, simpler model, fleshier in body, more bovine and homlier in face, shrewder and more practical"* (2:319). Simeon, like Peter, has a bovine quality that connotes the hardworking, dispassionate New England Yankee, *"their bodies bumping and rubbing together as they hurry clumsily to their food, like two friendly oxen"* (2:321). Unlike his father, Ephraim, whom he loathes, Simeon is will-ing to abandon both the farm and New England for the more profitable venture of prospecting for gold in California. In this respect, along with whiskey drinking and father envy, both brothers resemble O'Neill's brother James O'Neill, Jr. (Jamie), who moved to California with their mother Mary Ellen "Ella" O'Neill to oversee James O'Neill, Sr.'s real estate interests after his death.

In part 1, scene 4, Simeon sells his share of the farm to Eben for 300 dollars in gold pieces. He sym-bolically removes the wooden gate from the stone wall in front of the house, which symbolized to both him and his brother the imprisonment of Ephraim's reign. When Ephraim returns with his new wife, Abbie Putnam, Simeon and Peter celebrate their newfound freedom by performing an Indian war dance around their father and throwing stones through the parlor window. They depart singing a gold-rush song to the tune of "Oh, Susannah!"

**Putnam, Abbie (Abbie Cabot)**  Ephraim Cabot's third wife and Eben Cabot's lover. Abbie arrives on the farm, the newlywed bride of Ephraim, in part 1, scene 4, and she instantly displays her desire to claim ownership of the farm. Her first line in the script reads, "Hum!. . . It's purty—purty! I can't believe it's r'ally mine" (2:335). Abbie is 35 and thus Ephraim's junior by 40 years. Like Cybel in *The*

*Great God Brown* and Josie Hogan in *A Moon for the Misbegotten*, Abbie represents an earth mother, sensual and close to nature, *"buxom, full of vitality"* (2:335). Though she marries Ephraim for the practi-cal purpose of achieving a sense of ownership, she shares Eben's *"unsettled, untamed, desperate quality."* Upon their first meeting, after appraising her rival's strength, *"her desire is dimly awakened by his youth and good looks"*; Eben also is *"physically attracted"* to his new challenger for rights to the farm (2:338).

At their first encounter, Abbie attempts to win Eben over by confessing her life. She has no memory of her mother, who passed away when she was very young. As an orphan, Abbie worked as a domestic servant until marrying a "drunken spreer" with whom she had a child that died in infancy (2:339). Her hus-band later died as well, and though she celebrated her freedom for a time, she was soon back working in domestic servitude. She envied her employers' homes but had given up hope of achieving one of her own until Ephraim appeared. She married him with his assurance that his "hum" would be part hers.

Abbie initially intends to seduce Eben in order to form an alliance against Ephraim, but they soon fall in love. In part 2, scene 3, they meet in the parlor where Eben's mother was shown after her funeral. The two lovers apprehend "somethin'" in the room (2:354). According to Eben, it is his mother's spirit, which at first seems malevolent to Abbie but softens once Eben appears and the two consummate their love. Abbie vows to take Eben's mother's place in his heart, thus emphasizing the incestuous nature of their relationship and equat-ing her with the mythic Greek characters Phaedra, who attempts to seduce her stepson Hippolytus, and Jocasta, who marries her son Oedipus, who had killed his father. They have a child together, though Ephraim believes the child is his. When Ephraim tells Eben that Abbie "says, I want Eben cut off so's this farm'll be mine," (2:365) Eben accuses Abbie of playing him for a fool. She there-fore kills their son to prove her love to him, now evoking the Greek tragedy character Medea, who killed her two children for vengeance against her husband, Jason, for leaving her. Abbie also rep-resents the sensual, life-affirming impulse of the Greek god Dionysus, the god of fertility and wine, whom the German philosopher Friedrich Nietzsche argued was a necessary component in tragedy to offset the more practical god of the sun, Apollo. In the end, after Eben had rushed off to inform the sheriff of her murderous act, he returns and embraces her love for him, willing to share her punishment over the murder of their son. As the two are being led away by the sheriff and his men to the gallows, O'Neill combines all of these mythological elements, allowing the Dionysian to supplant the lovers' hard and acquisitive Apollonian impulses.

**Sheriff (Jim)** The sheriff, who is addressed as "Jim." He arrives with two men and his pistol drawn in the final scene to take Abbie and subsequently Eben into custody for the murder of their child. Jim has the final, ironic lines of the play: "It's a jim-dandy farm, no denyin'. Wished I owned it!" (2:378). His acknowledgement of the farm's beauty echoes the sentiments of the Cabot family; at the same time, his envy is clearly misplaced, given the tragedies that have occurred there. Jim is one of several lawmen who conclude O'Neill's plays with an ironic line, including *The WEB* and *The Great God Brown*.

### BIBLIOGRAPHY

Alexander, Doris. *Eugene O'Neill's Creative Struggle: The Decisive Decade, 1924–1933.* University Park: Pennsylvania State University Press, 1992.

Bogard, Travis. *Contour in Time: The Plays of Eugene O'Neill.* Rev. ed. New York: Oxford University Press, 1988.

Clark, Barrett H. *Eugene O'Neill: The Man and His Plays.* Rev. ed. New York: Dover, 1947.

Cowley, Malcolm. "A Weekend with Eugene O'Neill." In *O'Neill and His Plays: Four Decades of Criticism,* edited by Oscar Cargill, N. Bryllion Fagin, and William J. Fisher, 1–16, 41–49. New York: New York University Press, 1961.

Floyd, Virginia. *The Plays of Eugene O'Neill: A New Assessment.* New York: Ungar, 1985.

Hammond, Percy. "Desire under the Elms," *New York Herald Tribune,* November 12, 1924. In *O'Neill and His Plays: Four Decades of Criticism,* edited by Oscar Cargill, N. Bryllion Fagin, and William J. Fisher, 170–171. New York: New York University Press, 1961.

Handlin, Oscar. "Yankees." In *Harvard Encyclopedia of American Ethnic Groups,* edited by Stephen Thernstrom, 1,028–1,030. Cambridge, Mass: Belknap Press of Harvard University Press, 1980.

Hays, Peter. "Child Murder and Incest in American Drama." *Twentieth Century Literature* 36, no. 4 (Winter 1990): 434–448.

Murphy, Brenda. *American Realism and American Drama, 1880–1940.* New York: Cambridge University Press, 1987.

Ranald, Margaret Loftus. *The Eugene O'Neill Companion.* New York: Greenwood Press, 1984.

———. "From Trial to Triumph (1913–1924): The Early Plays." In *The Cambridge Companion to Eugene O'Neill,* edited by Michael Manheim, 51–68. New York: Cambridge University Press, 1998.

# *Diff'rent: A Play in Two Acts* (completed, 1920; first produced, 1920)

Eugene O'Neill completed *Diff'rent* on October 19, 1920, and the PROVINCETOWN PLAYERS immediately accepted it for production at their Provincetown Playhouse in New York City. After a lackluster two-month run following its premiere on December 27, *Diff'rent* moved uptown to the Times Square Theatre, where the Selwyn group billed it as a "daring study of a sex-starved woman" (quoted in Wainscott 59). *Diff'rent* intermingles two of the playwright's lifelong obsessions: the destructive effects of puritan morality and the (incompatible) substitution of material and sexual desire for religious cant in the American mind. It is notably the first play to initiate the playwright's association with Freudian psychoanalysis (Bogard 145). Though a penetrating study of one woman's desperate attempt to be "diff'rent" in a cynical world, audiences mainly dismissed the play as a torturous exercise in Freudian force-feeding. "Even with the help of the censor who tried to stop it," O'Neill chronicler Barrett Clark sardonically wrote, the play was "never a great success in the theater" (79).

By the fall and early winter of 1920, O'Neill had won his first PULITZER PRIZE for BEYOND THE HORIZON, and the Provincetown Players' production of The EMPEROR JONES, starring the inimitable CHARLES S. GILPIN, electrified critics and audiences alike. "Yet the unescapable impression of anyone who remembers *The Emperor Jones* and its fine imaginative quality, its color, and its spiritual power, and compares it with *Diff'rent*," KENNETH MACGOWAN wrote in his *Vogue* review of *Diff'rent*, "must be that the newer play is a step backward for its author" (148). *Diff'rent* received mixed to bad reviews, but its poor reception had little effect on O'Neill's confidence as a burgeoning playwright; at one point he told the theater critic GEORGE JEAN NATHAN, "Well, this is rather reassuring. I had begun to think I was too popular to be honest" (quoted in Clark 79).

## SYNOPSIS

*Act 1*

The parlor of the Crosby home in a New England fishing town. It is mid-afternoon on a day in late spring 1890. The room is low-ceilinged, with dark, stolid furniture and conservative decor. A screen door leads to the front lawn and beyond that an elm-lined street; a window looks out on a vegetable garden, and sunlight pours in from two other windows and the screen door. The room contains a bookcase, a horsehair couch, plush-covered chairs, an old-fashioned piano, and a fireplace; on the mantelpiece is a marble clock and a Rogers group (a classical-style plaster statuette). An unwieldy marble-topped table is at center; a large China lamp, a Bible with brass clasps, and *"several books that look suspiciously like cheap novels"* lie on the table. Hanging on the walls are a number of *"enlarged photos of strained, stern-looking people in uncomfortable poses,"* and the windows are framed by stiff white curtains. *"Everything has an aspect of scrupulous neatness"* (2:3). Emma Crosby, a thin, plain-looking 20-year-old woman with *"soft blue eyes"* that disclose a *"romantic dreaminess,"* is seated on the couch with her fiancé, Caleb Williams, a tanned, powerfully built SEA captain of 30. They are both dressed in simple black "Sunday best" clothing, and Caleb's hand rests lovingly on Emma's wrist (2:4).

The engaged couple happily discuss their marriage, which is two days away. In his excitement, Caleb lets out a curse. Emma softly scolds him, remarking that her father, Captain John Crosby, and her brother Jack, also sailors, are not responsible for using coarse language, "But you're diff'rent. You just got to be diff'rent from the rest" (2:4). Caleb rejects the idea he acts unlike other sailors. For her sake, he vows to try, but warns that "sailors ain't plaster saints . . . not a darn one of 'em ain't!" (2:5). Caleb has spent the last three years at sea and has finally earned enough to marry her. They talk over sailors' experiences on shore leave, particularly with the "naked heathen" women of the South Sea islands (2:7). He takes her in his arms and lovingly kisses her goodbye.

Jack Crosby, Emma's 25-year-old brother, enters wearing a fisherman's sou'wester (oilskin coat) and carrying a string of cod heads. He takes in the tender scene with a mocking grin. Jack looks every bit the handsome sailor Caleb is, though *"his small blue eyes twinkle with the unconsciously malicious humor of the born practical joker"* (2:8). "Belay, there!" he shouts, startling the pair. Emma reproaches him for sneaking in and then for the type of women he runs with. "Ho-ho!" he laughs sarcastically. "Caleb's one o' them goody-goody heroes out o' them story books you're always readin', ain't he?" (2:9). He then insinuates that Caleb's first mate Jim Benson has been telling a story about town that contradicts her dream of Caleb's purity. Emma turns on Caleb suspiciously. Caleb storms out to "give that Jim Benson a talkin' to he won't forgit in a hurry" (2:10). Emma demands to know the story, and Jack tells her.

On Caleb's last voyage, an island girl fell in love with him. As a joke on their prudish captain, the other sailors told her that Caleb awaited her on the ship, and she swam out to him naked; Caleb then brought her on board. The following day, the native woman howled in despair as the sailors prepared to disembark. Caleb ordered the men to pry her off the side of the ship and when that failed, to shoot warning shots into the water. The whole time, Jack recounts, Caleb cowered in his cabin while the crew laughed at the great joke. When Jack finishes the tale, Emma announces that the wedding is off. Taken aback, Jack admonishes her: "Jealous of a brown, heathen woman that ain't no better'n a nigger?. . . Why, them kind o' women ain't women like you. They don't count like folks. They ain't Christians—not nothin'!" (2:13–14). "He'd ought to have acted diff'rent," she says bitterly and refuses to reconsider. Jack stalks off to find their mother, Mrs. Crosby. Emma throws herself on a chair and begins to cry.

Caleb's sister Harriet Williams calls in from the doorway. Harriet and Alfred Rogers enter. Harriet is 20-years old, dark-featured, and plain, but with a *"certain boldly-appearing vitality of self-confident youth"* (2:14); Alfred, a fisherman, is four years older, stocky, and wearing his Sunday best. He and Harriet, who are engaged, exchange flirtatious barbs until Harriet notices Emma has been crying. Emma informs her that she intends to break off her engagement. Mrs. Crosby, highly energetic in spite of weighing more than 200 pounds, enters with Jack at her heels. Jack and Alfred go off to the other room and are soon heard howling with laughter offstage. Mrs. Crosby admits she heard the story about Caleb but never took it seriously; she failed to inform Emma because she knew her daughter "was touchy and diff'rent from most" (2:17). Harriet becomes increasingly agitated by Emma's accusatory tone toward her brother and tells her she "ought to realize what men be." Harriet knows, for instance, that Alfred has fooled around with other women. "If you're looking for saints," she quips, "you got to die first and go to heaven" (2:18). Mrs. Crosby agrees and tries to talk her daughter into going through with the wedding.

Jack and Rogers reenter, grinning broadly. They joke back and forth with Harriet about the women they have known, and they all leave together talking and laughing. Harriet stops at the doorway and assures Emma that Caleb would never have done it if he were married, then exits. Mrs. Crosby informs her that Emma's own father, Captain Crosby, also had liaisons with other women, but she must understand "men is men the world over." Emma responds that she knows her father is a good man, but she still insists that "Caleb always seemed diff'rent." Captain Crosby, a short, powerful, bowlegged sailor of 60, enters in a misshapen suit. He jokes good-naturedly that it is the "the fust time ever I heerd good o' myself by listenin'!" (2:21). Jack has informed him of Emma's plan, and Crosby holds the same view as the others—a man's a man. "Thunderin' Moses, what the hell d'you want Caleb to be—a durned, he-virgin, sky-pilot?" (2:22). Mrs. Crosby takes him into the next room to talk it over.

Caleb shyly enters. *"His face is set emotionlessly but his eyes cannot conceal a worried bewilderment, a look of uncomprehending hurt."* He admits the story is true but tells her that in the South Seas women are "diff'rent" (2:23), then contritely explains that the island woman took him by surprise. After their encounter, he locked her out of the cabin and felt miserable for having broken his fidelity to Emma. Emma forgives him but still refuses to go through with the marriage. "Ever since we was little I guess I've always had the idea that you was—diff'rent. . . . You've busted something way down inside me—and I can't love you no more." She vows never to marry, and he wonders whether time might heal her pain. "It ain't a question of time, Caleb," she says, "It's a question of something being dead. And when a thing's died, time can't make no diff'rence" (2:25). He tells her he will wait 30 years if he must. When she heads off to lie down, Caleb implores her to remember what he said about waiting. She disappears without offering a reply; he turns slowly to the door, his expression a *"mask of emotionlessness,"* as the curtain falls (2:26).

**Act Two**
Early spring 1920—30 years later. It is late afternoon, and the setting is the same as act 1, but the parlor has been hideously modernized. The whole atmosphere has *"a grotesque aspect of old age turned flighty and masquerading as the most empty-headed youth."* Garish rugs have replaced the staid, dark rugs of the previous act; the curtains are now orange and the walls no longer brown but a *"cream color sprayed with pink flowers."* A Victrola plays JAZZ, and a brand new piano has replaced the old-fashioned one. Emma's *"books that look suspiciously like cheap novels"* have now been replaced by *"installment plan sets of uncut volumes."* Only the Bible on the table and the marble clock on the mantelpiece remain.

Emma and Benny Rogers, Harriet and Alfred's 23-year-old son, are discovered. Benny, a loutish replica of his deceased father—*"coarser, more hardened and cocksure"*—is a veteran of World War I and wears the khaki uniform of a private in the army. He reenlisted after the war but returned home after his second tour. Emma, now a *"withered, scrawny woman,"* looks the personification of her newly renovated room—*"there is something revoltingly incongruous about her, a pitiable sham, a too-apparent effort to cheat the years by appearances"* (2:27). Her cheeks are covered in rouge, eyes penciled with mascara, hair died an unnatural black against her sallow skin; she wears a ridiculously youthful dress for her age, with high-heeled pumps and silk stockings. *"Above all there is shown in her simpering, self-consciously coquettish manner that laughable—and at the same time irritating and disgusting—mockery of undignified age snatching greedily at the empty simulacra of youth. She resembles some passé stock actress of fifty made up for a heroine of twenty"* (2:27–28).

Once the MUSIC stops, Benny turns off the Victrola and applauds Emma's selection. She admits the record was bought for him, but she prefers the newer songs: "They put life and ginger in an old lady like me—not like them slow, old-timey tunes." Benny, who refers to her as Aunt Emma, calls her "the only live one in this dead dump" (2:28). He teases her about the rumor that she and his uncle Caleb, whom he considers "a darn stingy, ugly old cuss," almost got married (2:29). She quickly denies it. Benny continues that Caleb has made a great deal of money whaling, but only saves more and spends less, especially on Benny. We find through exposition that Benny's father, Alfred Rogers, and Emma's brother, Jack, drowned at sea, leaving him and his mother, Harriet, under Caleb's financial care. Benny wants 100 dollars to go on a spree in Boston with a friend, but Caleb has refused. "Here I'm sweatin' blood in the army after riskin' my life in France and when I get a leave to home, everyone treats me like a wet dog." Emma remarks coquettishly that she barely recognized him when he returned so "big and strong and handsome" (2:31). This makes Benny uncomfortable, and he makes to leave. Emma pleads with him to remain, admitting she modernized

the house for his sake; then she jealously inquires about his relationship with a local woman with a loose reputation named Tilly Small. Benny admits to this, but only because Tilly serves him liquor. Emma promises to keep liquor at her house, which delights him. A remark about French women he consorted with during the war arouses a *"hectic, morbid intensity in her"* (2:34). She feverishly inquires about precisely what the women did for him, but he refuses to tell, jokingly referring to Emma as too young for such information. When he moves to go, she pleads with him once more to stay, and soon Harriet Rogers can be heard in the distance calling Benny's name. As Harriet approaches the house, Emma rushes upstairs to change, chirping coquettishly, "Them French girls ain't the only ones knows how to fix up," and *"flounces out."* Benny looks after her with a *"derisive grin of contempt"* (2:35).

Harriet enters. She appears substantially older, with a *"fretful, continuously irritated expression. Her shoulders stoop, and her figure is flabby and ugly"* (2:35). She reproaches Benny for not answering her call and informs him she told Caleb about money he had stolen. She then chastises him for his open assignations with Tilly Small and for "makin' a silly fool out of poor Emma Crosby" (2:35). "How can I help it if she goes bugs in her old age and gets nutty about me?" he retorts, then tries to wangle her into the joke by describing Emma as "all dolled up like a kid of sixteen and enough paint on her mush for a Buffalo Bill Indian" (2:36). Harriet calls him a "worthless loafer" and warns him not to get between Emma and his uncle, who has waited for Emma for 30 years. He irritably vows to prevent their union, and Harriet tells him he should reenlist and not come back until he has stripped away the "meanness and filth that's the Rogers part of you and found the honesty and decency that's the Williams part" (2:37). She exits in a fury. Now alone, Benny has an idea and calls for Emma. He bids her goodbye, informing her that Caleb has cut him off financially and he must reenlist. This terrifies Emma, who offers to let him stay with her. She also promises to have a talk with Caleb. Benny warns that Caleb is still in love with her. He pretends to be jealous, then suggests they get married. Overwhelmed by the proposal, she gleefully accepts.

Caleb knocks at the door. Emma kisses Benny passionately on the lips, and he runs off to the other room. Caleb greets her cautiously and peers around at *"the garish strangeness of everything"* (2:41). *"His face wears its set expression of an emotionless mask but his eyes cannot conceal an inward struggle, a baffled and painful attempt to comprehend, a wounded look of bewildered hurt"* (2:41–42). Emma asks how he likes the new decor. "You've changed, Emmer," he insists disapprovingly, "changed so much I wouldn't know you, hardly" (2:42). He curtly derides her excessive use of makeup and dyed hair, which reminds him of "the kind of women I've seed in cities" (2:43). When she breaks down, weeping, he comforts her apologetically, *"looking at her with the blind eyes of love"* (2:44). He asks if she remembers his vow to wait 30 years and if she might forgive him. Evasively, she promises to "think it over" (2:45).

Caleb brings up the rumors about Benny, and she defends Benny ferociously. Confused that she would now give Benny the benefit of the doubt but not *him* 30 years before, Caleb refers to his nephew as "Alf all over again—on'y worse!" (2:46). He had hoped the army would make Benny a better man, but it only made him worse; he then reveals that Benny never engaged in battle but only loaded and unloaded supplies for the quartermaster. He heard Benny has been making a fool of her, telling the whole town how he takes her money and that she rearranged her house for his sake. She accuses him of being jealous, which confounds Caleb, who always thought of her as a second mother to Benny. Emma shouts that she and Benny love each other and will be married the following day. Caleb is thunderstruck. He vows to prevent the marriage and moves to leave; on his way out, he considers either allowing them to marry, out of spite, or paying Benny off. Emma falls to her knees, wraps her arms around his legs, and begs him not to harm Benny. He assures her angrily he will not hurt anyone. "Folks be all crazy and rotten to the core and I'm done with the whole kit and caboodle of 'em. I kin' only see one course out for me and I'm goin' to take it" (2:49). Emma always considered herself "diff'rent from the rest o' the folks," he says, but she

is only "madder'n they be" (2:49). He storms out, and the door slams shut behind him.

Emma cries out Caleb's name as Benny sneaks in silently from the other room. Eating almonds and brazenly littering the floor with shells, he commends her for defending him and boasts he could take Caleb in a fight. When he openly considers accepting Caleb's bribe, Emma is devastated by the betrayal. "Why, you're as old as Ma is, ain't you, Aunt Emmer? (*He adds ruthlessly*) And I'll say you look it, too!" (2:51). Weeping hysterically, Emma screams at him to leave, but he scoffs at her ridiculous attempt to look and act younger than she is. A knock comes at the door, and Benny makes his escape. It is Harriet looking for Benny. Emma tells her he is in the next room. Benny reenters, annoyed at Emma's disloyalty, and Harriet takes him away to investigate a strange sound from their barn. Emma's face goes blank. With steady determination, she tears down the orange curtains, gold-framed pictures, colorful cushions, and the other modern decorations, heaping them with deliberate speed in a pile on the floor. *"She does all this without a trace of change in her expression—rapidly, but with no apparent effort"* (2:53). Benny lurches into the room and frantically announces that Caleb has hanged himself in the barn. He needs Emma to help calm his hysterical mother. Emma says she needs take care of something at her own barn first. Irritated by this, Benny rushes out to find someone else. Emma howls Caleb's name, then whispers, "Wait, Caleb, I'm going down to the barn" (2:54). The curtain falls as she disappears out the rear door.

## COMMENTARY

Nearly all critics agree that *Diff'rent* contains serious flaws—the starkest being the far-fetched contrast between the Emma Crosby of act 1 and act 2. But they hesitate before writing it off as yet another of O'Neill's experimental failures. "For one thing," Travis Bogard writes, "there is an intensity about the writing, a quality not quite to be defined that keeps it from the ludicrous" (145). For another, the seeming lack of authorial manipulation—a potentially fatal shortcoming—allows some audiences to feel as if they were "present at a situation which is determined by human beings," rather than experiencing a contrived plot with carefully constructed characterizations (Clark 80). In terms of O'Neill's development as a playwright, *Diff'rent* also exhibits "some deep thought about the realistic depiction of character that was to stand O'Neill in good stead later on" (Murphy 122). Finally, a series of major O'Neill themes begin to emerge in *Diff'rent*, themes O'Neill would later expand upon in Desire under the Elms, Mourning Becomes Electra, and *The Iceman Cometh*, among others. These include, respectively, Puritanical influence on the fate of New England characters driven to moral turpitude by a restrictive social environment; the masklike use of facial expressions, makeup, and stage props to hide the inner self from themselves and others; and the fatal consequences of destroying life-sustaining pipe dreams.

At the time of its first production, O'Neill was embattled by the general view, most strongly voiced by adherents to feminism, that Emma was an unconvincing female character. "*Diff'rent* seems to have aroused the ire of all the feminists against me," he complained to the journalist Louis Kantor, "it could have been woven with equal truth about a man, with a different reaction, of course" (quoted in Diggins 168). "Whatever its faults may be," O'Neill defensively elaborated in an article for the *New York Tribune*, *Diff'rent* "has the virtue of sincerity. It is the truth, the inevitable truth, of the lives of the people in it as I see and know them.

> Whether it is psychoanalytically exact or not I will leave more dogmatic students of Freud and Jung than myself (or than Freud and Jung) to decide. It is life, nevertheless. I stick out for that—life that swallows all formulas. Some critics have said that Emma would not do this thing, would undoubtedly do that other. By Emma they must mean "a woman." But Emma is Emma. She is a whaling captain's daughter in a small New England seacoast town—surely no feminist. She is universal only in the sense that she reacts definitely to a definite sex-suppression, as every woman might. The form her reaction takes is absolutely governed by her environment and her own character. Let the

captious be sure they know their Emmas as well as I do before they tell me how she would act (O'Neill 105).

O'Neill casts little doubt on Virginia Floyd's contention that O'Neill's New England plays treat the dark historical truth about America's Puritan heritage: "Had New Englanders not evolved into the stiff, repressed individuals he depicts . . . their society would have had fewer moral aberrations" (211). But John Patrick Diggins even finds fault in O'Neill's interpretation of New England Puritanism. True Puritans, he contends, would never assume, as Emma does, that an individual could rise fully above carnal sin. Puritans also, perhaps counterinstinctively, have the capacity to forgive (168). With this in mind, the other characters in *Diff'rent* (and perhaps Nat Miller, Richard Miller's father from Ah, Wilderness!) might stand as more realistic Puritans, ones who express understanding and forgiveness in the face of men's pursuit of carnal satisfaction.

In the context of the play, it is difficult to believe that Emma could have been shaped exclusively by the environment of her "small New England seacoast town." Each character, with the glaring exception of Emma, appears to accept, even applaud, men's sexual adventures on voyages. "If you're looking for saints," Harriet Rogers warns Emma, "you got to die first and go to heaven" (2:18). Harriet offers an exception, however, when she chastises Benny for his affair with Tilly Small. But Tilly Small resides in their town, rather than being "dark" natives of a romanticized foreign land. South Seas women in the 1920s, as Kenneth Macgowan notes of the type in his *Vogue* review, are "much celebrated today" as a result of the "fact and fiction of the Gauguin revival" (148; Macgowan refers to the sensation created by the impressionist painter Paul Gauguin's series of seminude portraits of Tahitian women). In fact, the South Seas islands—a region O'Neill also contrasts favorably against New England in *Mourning Becomes Electra*—always remain in the back of one's mind in *Diff'rent*. Caleb's monologue at the end of act 2 describing the "diff'rent" life in the South Seas— the singing, the nakedness, the eternal beauty—is the most powerful writing in the play and echoes the lyrical mise en scène of his early one-act play from the SS GLENCAIRN series, *The MOON OF THE CARIBBEES*. It is in "such strong and uplifting lyricism," Macgowan predicts, that American dramatists will find "the future of the theater": "There lie imagination and vision based upon reality, but springing upward into the strange and mysterious reaches of the soul which modern psychology has opened for us" (149).

Above all, the play fails, according to Travis Bogard, because audiences are "unable *clearly* to define the nature of the dream, and because Emma's tawdry substitute for the dream has pathos without real substance" (147, emphasis mine). Take one reviewer's response to the radical shift that takes place over the two acts: "When we discovered Caleb and Emma sitting on the couch, he holding her chastely in his arms . . . it was all so sweet and tender that, for a moment, it occurred to us that here might be a play by Eugene O'Neill with a happy ending" (quoted in Wainscott 62). O'Neill's obscured purpose is found chiefly in the STAGE DIRECTIONS, where he embeds these clues in the text, such that if an audience member blinked they might consider what follows implausible. Emma's eyes, for example, offer the only evidence that she has act 2 buried in her psychology. They have an *"incongruous quality of absent-minded romantic dreaminess"* that belie the Puritan aspect of her character and offer the only foreshadowing of her "incongruous" transformation in act 2, when O'Neill again specifies that *"there is something revoltingly incongruous about her"* (2:27). On the walls of the parlor in act 1, her Puritan influence is further disclosed in the hanging portraits of *"strained, stern-looking people in uncomfortable poses"* (2:3). The word *diff'rent*, too, is used no less than 11 times in the first 17 speeches, and in his monologue at the end of act 1, Caleb uses the word five times; O'Neill specified that the word "should always be read in the same uninflected tone" (quoted in Wainscott 61). And lastly, though not exclusively, Emma's sustained incongruity turns from "romantic" to "revolting"—in the way that her *"books that look suspiciously like cheap novels"* in act 1 have been replaced by *"installment plan sets of uncut volumes"* in act 2 (2:3, 27). Audi-

ences are not to blame for missing O'Neill's intertextual explanations, but it might make for a good case that *Diff'rent* is better to be read than seen.

*Diff'rent* is notably one of Eugene O'Neill's most deliberate forays into NATURALISM—a genre in which the fate of characters, often leading to death or worse, is dictated by the caprices of environmental and biological forces beyond their control (see Floyd 211). If natural human sex drive can be considered Emma's (and, presumably, Caleb's) most potent biological enemy, two serious environmental forces appear to inform and distort Emma's moral outlook, leading to what O'Neill called her "clearly inevitable" suicide (105): her outward Puritanism and the sentimental inner life she leads as a reader of *"several books that look suspiciously like cheap novels"* (2:3). Jack's main defense of Caleb—all men, really—is that no one can live up to the moral standards of "goody-goody heroes out o' them story books you're always readin'" (2:9). Although it is no doubt true that Emma "had demanded the spiritual, nonsexual love idealized in her Puritan society" (Floyd 218), the pure love she unfairly demands of Caleb might just as easily have come from "them story books"; it is perhaps more likely, in fact, given the context of the townspeople's general acceptance of the "men will be men" rationalization of male sexuality. Thus, her pipe dream of Caleb's moral perfection derives, unevenly, from both romantic and spiritual sources; and when excruciating disillusionment follows—"You've busted something way down inside me—and I can't love you no more" (2:25)—Emma constructs another in the figure of Benny Rogers. "She must," as O'Neill phrased it, "re-create her god in this lump of mud. When it finally is brought home to her that mud is mud, she cries for the real Caleb, seeing him now for the first time" (O'Neill 105).

Between 1890 and 1920, a colossal upheaval took place in American culture that established consumerism as the new religion. Joel Pfister contends of *Diff'rent* that if the marketplace replaced the church during this 30-year period (the working title of the play was "Thirty Years"), "[t]he changing pattern of her behavior followed the resignification of sexuality in America's modern 'therapeutic' culture of consumption" (189). It is the tension between her combined Puritan and romantic expectations and her actual need for sex that leads to Emma's frenzied consumption of modern products as an avenue for achieving sexual gratification. Over the decade of the 1920s—O'Neill's most experimental period—such radical historical "time shifts" as we find in *Diff'rent* reappear, with varying degrees of success, in such plays as *The FOUNTAIN*, *MARCO MILLIONS*, and *STRANGE INTERLUDE* (Wainscott 63). *Diff'rent* is probably the least successful because the ending offers none of the catharsis of real tragedy. Indeed, the influential theater critic ALEXANDER WOOLLCOTT regarded Caleb and Emma's suicides as merely "dull and conventional" (quoted in Wainscott 63). "To kill them off at the end is an act of mercy," Barrett Clark explains, "and O'Neill's mood here was anything but merciful." Instead, Clark maintains, O'Neill should have made them "go on living in quiet desperation" (81). O'Neill did so later with the repressed character Lavinia Mannon; Lavinia and the other major characters in *Mourning Becomes Electra* do not commit suicide, in spite of the fact that they are "more clearly justified in killing themselves than Caleb and Emma" (81). Christine and Orin Mannon do, however, kill themselves in O'Neill's unfinished sequel *MORE STATELY MANSIONS*.

## CHARACTERS

**Crosby, Emma**   Captain John and Mrs. Crosby's daughter, Jack Crosby's sister, and Captain Caleb Williams's fiancé. In act 1, Emma Crosby is an energetic, thin, plain-looking 20-year-old of medium height. She has large blue eyes that betray *"an incongruous quality of absent-minded romantic dreaminess."* On her parlor table rests reading material that signifies two sources of her romantic idealism—*"several books that look suspiciously like cheap novels"* and a Bible (2:3). From these emerges a dual predilection for, as her brother Jack Crosby calls them, "goody-goody heroes out o' them story books" (2:9) along with Puritan moral rigidity. Her Puritan background is further emphasized by O'Neill in his stage directions by portraits of *"strained, stern-looking people in uncomfortable poses"* hanging in her parlor (2:3). Emma is engaged to Captain Caleb Williams, a successful young sea captain whom she has known all

her life and considers "diff'rent" from the other sailors in their New England seacoast town. When it becomes apparent that he had a sexual liaison with a native island woman in the South Seas—the result of a practical joke on Caleb by his crew—she breaks off their engagement and vows never to marry. She admits he is not blame, but the truth has "busted something way down inside me—and I can't love you no more" (2:25). This rejection of Caleb's true self results in the tragedy of act 2. As Ronald H. Wainscott suggests, "This fixation to be 'diff'rent,' this superhuman rigidity, is the instrument of her destruction" (2:62).

Act 2 takes place 30 years later, during which time Emma has undergone a grotesque transformation. No longer a prim, puritanical maid, Emma is now *"a withered, scrawny woman,"* who applies gross amounts of makeup, dyes her hair an unnatural black, and wears clothing much too frilly for her age. Still "incongruous," Emma now appears as *"a pitiable sham, a too-apparent effort to cheat the years by appearances"* (2:27). She has fallen in lust with Benny Rogers, Caleb's insidious 23-year-old nephew who has returned home from a boondoggle as an army private in the quartermaster's office during World War I. At one point, Emma breathlessly requests that he frankly describe his sexual encounters with French girls in Europe; as Virginia Floyd argues, "Deprived of information on sexual matters all her life, she craves a glimpse of the dark, unknown, forbidden pleasures that lie beyond her world" (215). Benny mocks her openly for her pathetic attempt to woo him by trying to act and appear younger than her 50 years. Benny proposes they get married, but he does this for her money.

Once Emma informs Caleb that she plans to marry his despicable nephew and not him—after he had waited 30 years hoping she would forgive his indiscretion—Caleb commits suicide by hanging himself in his barn. Benny, meanwhile, has overheard his uncle considering the bribe and, unaware that Caleb will soon be dead, decides to accept the offer. Overwhelmed by Benny's betrayal, and recognizing her disastrous mistake with Caleb, Emma first destroys the modern renovations in her parlor and then, moments after discovering Caleb has killed himself, commits suicide in her own barn offstage. With Benny, O'Neill clarifies in an explanatory article, Emma wished to "re-create her god in this lump of mud. When it finally is brought home to her that mud is mud, she cries for the real Caleb, seeing him now for the first time" (O'Neill 105).

**Crosby, Captain John** Mrs. Crosby's husband and Emma Crosby's father. O'Neill describes the 60-year-old sailor as a *"squat, bow-legged, powerful man, almost as broad as he is long . . . with a great, red, weather-beaten face seamed by wrinkles"* (2:21). Crosby is a happy-go-lucky prankster whom both his wife and daughter think of as a good man with faults. But when Emma discovers her fiancé, Captain Caleb Williams, had a sexual liaison with an island woman in the South Seas, she breaks off her relationship. When she refuses to accept Captain Crosby's rationale that that is the way men naturally behave at sea, he shouts in bewilderment, "Thunderin' Moses, what the hell d'you want Caleb to be—a durned, he-virgin, sky-pilot?" (2:22).

**Crosby, Jack** Crosby Captain John Crosby and Mrs. Crosby's son and Emma Crosby's brother. O'Neill describes the 25-year-old sailor as a *"hulking, stocky-built young fellow. . . . His heavy face is sunburned, handsome in a coarse, good-natured animal fashion. His small blue eyes twinkle with the unconsciously malicious humor of the born practical joker"* (2:8). Jack arrives in act 1 wearing a fisherman's sou'wester (oilskin hat) and carrying a string of cod heads. He shares with his sister Emma a story about her fiancé, Captain Caleb Williams: While on a voyage in the South Seas, Caleb's crew played a practical joke on him by sending a naked native woman to their ship. Caleb, known as a strictly devout man faithful to Emma, apparently had a sexual experience with the woman. Jack and the rest of the townspeople find this hilarious. But Emma, to Jack's consternation, breaks off her engagement with Caleb, as she always considered him "diff'rent" from other sailors. Jack cannot fathom the idea of stopping a marriage over jealousy for a South Seas woman. "Jealous of a brown, heathen woman that ain't no better'n a nigger? . . . Why, them kind o' women ain't women like you. They don't count like folks. They ain't Christians—not nothin'!" (2:13–14).

**Crosby, Mrs.** Captain John Crosby's wife and Emma and Jack Crosby's mother. O'Neill describes the 50-year-old as a *"large, fat, florid woman. . . . In spite of her two hundred and more pounds she is surprisingly active, and the passive, lazy expression of her round moon face is belied by her quick, efficient movements"* (2:15). Before her appearance in the middle of act 1, Mrs. Crosby's son Jack tells her daughter Emma the story of a sexual liaison that Emma's fiancé, Captain Caleb Williams, had with a South Seas island woman. Emma consequently breaks off her engagement with Caleb, and Mrs. Crosby attempts to persuade her daughter to change her mind. Her rationale is that "men is men the world over" (2:21) and that Emma's father, Captain John Crosby, is a good husband regardless of his faults. Emma refuses to accept this: Although she loves her father and considers him a good man, she had always considered Caleb "diff'rent."

**Rogers, Alfred** Harriet Williams's fiancé and later husband, and Benny Rogers's father. In act 1, Alfred is *"a husky young fisherman of twenty-four"* (2:14) engaged to Harriet Williams. When Harriet voices disbelief that Emma Crosby has refused to marry her brother Captain Caleb Williams because of Caleb's sexual encounter with a South Seas woman, Alfred advises her with a *"man-of-the-world attitude of cynicism"*: "Don't take it so dead serious, Harriet. Emmer'll git over it like you all does" (2:15)—meaning all women eventually "git over" the fact that men will roam sexually. By act 2, 30 years later, Alfred has drowned at sea, and Caleb Williams describes Alfred and Harriet's ne'er-do-well son Benny Rogers as "Alf all over again—on'y worse!" (2:46).

**Rogers, Benny** Alfred and Harriet Rogers's (née Williams) son and Captain Caleb Williams's nephew. Twenty-three years old and a *"replica of his father in Act One, but coarser, more hardened and cocksure,"* (2:27) Benny has survived his father Alfred Rogers, who drowned at sea following the action of act 1. He and his mother have since been supported by his uncle, Caleb Williams. Benny, a ne'er-do-well alcoholic and womanizer who worked an army boondoggle in the quartermaster's office during World War I, considers Caleb a "tightwad," as he refuses to give him money to spend on sprees to Boston, liquor, and women. James Tyrone, Jr., in LONG DAY'S JOURNEY INTO NIGHT—a highly autobiographical play based on O'Neill's own family—uses the same word, *tightwad*, to describe his father, James Tyrone. Benny's mother, Harriet, additionally refers to him as a "worthless loafer" (2:36), an epithet Tyrone levels on his son. An overall bad seed, Benny resembles Jamie Tyrone, who is based on O'Neill's brother JAMES O'NEILL, JR. (Jamie), in other ways as well, but without Jamie Tyrone's depth and sympathetic charm. While Caleb was away at sea before the action of act 2, Benny has allowed Emma Crosby, Caleb's now 50-year-old former fiancé, to flirt with him. When he hears his uncle will cut him off financially, he proposes to marry her, but only for her money. But when Benny overhears his uncle consider bribing him not to marry Emma, he viciously informs Emma that he will accept the offer. Caleb commits suicide after Emma tells him she will marry Benny, but when Benny ruthlessly discards their marriage for Caleb's bribe, she realizes her mistake and commits suicide as well.

**Williams, Captain Caleb**  Harriet Williams's brother, Benny Rogers's uncle, and Emma Crosby's fiancé. Caleb Williams is a successful sea captain in a small coastal town in New England. In the opening scene of act 2, O'Neill describes the 30-year-old Caleb as having *"black hair, dark eyes, face rugged and bronzed, mouth obstinate but good-natured"* (2:4). After a three-year whaling voyage, Caleb has earned enough money to marry Emma Crosby, whom he has known all his life and always loved. Two days before the wedding, however, Emma's brother, Jack Crosby, lets slip a story about Caleb that has been circulating around town: While anchored off an island in the South Seas, Caleb's crew played a practical joke on him by having a native island girl swim out naked to their vessel. Caleb brought her on board, and although he had always been faithful to Emma, the two had a sexual encounter. This shatters Emma's dream of Caleb as being "diff'rent" from other sailors, and she breaks off the engagement. In the most moving

speech of the play, Caleb desperately attempts to explain himself by describing life in the South Seas as "diff'rent" (2:23–24). Emma forgives him but still maintains he has "busted something way down inside me—and I can't love you no more" (2:25). Caleb vows to wait 30 years for her, and his visage at the end of act 1 *"sets in a concealment mask of expressionlessness"* (2:26).

Act 2 takes place 30 years later, and Caleb has arrived home from his latest voyage. When he visits Emma in her parlor, he discovers that she has undergone a grotesque transformation. Her parlor is now decorated in a garish modern style, and she has taken to wearing too much makeup and dying her hair an unnatural black. Confused and disgusted, Caleb remarks that she resembles "the kind of women I've seed in cities" (2:43). Once she begins crying, however, his love returns stronger than ever. Emma reveals that while he was gone, she fell in love with Caleb's loutish nephew, Benny Rogers. When she informs him they will be married the following day, Caleb goes to his barn and hangs himself. Benny then makes it clear to her that he only wanted her for money, and she joins Caleb by hanging herself in her own barn.

In an article on *Diff'rent*, O'Neill explains that Caleb "dies because it is not in him to compromise. He belongs to the old iron school of Nantucket–New Bedford whalemen whose slogan was 'A dead whale or a stove boat.' The whale in this case is transformed suddenly into a malignant Moby Dick who has sounded to depths forever out of reach. Caleb's boat is stove, his quest is ended. He goes with his ship" (O'Neill 105). Caleb's "old iron school" type of New England captain can also be found in the characters Captain David Keeney in *ILE* and Captain Isaiah Bartlett in WHERE THE CROSS IS MADE and GOLD.

**Williams, Harriet (Mrs. Harriet Rogers)**  Alfred Rogers's fiancée and later wife and Caleb Williams's sister. In act 1, Harriet is astonished to learn that Emma Crosby has refused her brother Captain Caleb Williams's hand in marriage because of a sexual liaison he experienced with a South Seas island woman. Harriet becomes annoyed by Emma's moral superiority and the presumption that

Caleb ever took the native island woman seriously: "I hope you ain't got it in your head my brother Caleb would sink so low as to fall for one of them critters?" (2:17); she then says, "Caleb ain't no plaster saint and I reckon he's as likely to sin that way as any other man" (2:18). By act 2, 30 years later, Harriet has aged into a bitter, stoop-shouldered, *"flabby and ugly"* woman with a *"fretful, continuously irritated expression"* (2:35). Her husband, Alfred, has drowned at sea, and Caleb takes financial care of her and her ne'er-do-well son, Benny Rogers. She scolds Benny, who is 23, for making a fool of Emma by flirting with her for money. When Caleb returns from his last voyage and commits suicide over the news that Emma has decided to marry Benny, Harriet becomes hysterical. Benny tries to enlist Harriet to calm her, but Emma goes off to her barn offstage to join Caleb by hanging herself.

## BIBLIOGRAPHY

Bogard, Travis. *Contour in Time: The Plays of Eugene O'Neill.* Rev. ed. New York: Oxford University Press, 1988.

Clark, Barrett H. *Eugene O'Neill: The Man and His Plays.* Rev. ed. New York: Dover, 1947.

Diggins, John Patrick. *Eugene O'Neill's America: Desire under Democracy.* Chicago: University of Chicago Press, 2007.

Floyd, Virginia. *The Plays of Eugene O'Neill: A New Assessment.* New York: Ungar, 1985.

Macgowan, Kenneth. Review of *Diff'rent.* In *O'Neill and His Plays: Four Decades of Criticism,* edited by Oscar Cargill, N. Bryllion Fagin, and William J. Fisher, 147–149. New York: New York University Press, 1961.

Murphy, Brenda. *American Realism and American Drama, 1880–1940.* New York: Cambridge University Press, 1987.

O'Neill, Eugene. "Damn the Optimists!" In *O'Neill and His Plays: Four Decades of Criticism,* edited by Oscar Cargill, N. Bryllion Fagin, and William J. Fisher, 104–106. New York: New York University Press, 1961.

Pfister, Joel. *Staging Depth: Eugene O'Neill and the Politics of Psychological Discourse.* Chapel Hill: University of North Carolina Press, 1995.

Sheaffer, Louis. *O'Neill: Son and Artist.* Boston: Little, Brown, 1973.

Wainscott, Ronald H. *Staging O'Neill: The Experimental Years, 1920–1934.* New Haven, Conn.: Yale University Press, 1988.

# *Dreamy Kid: A Play in One Act, The* (completed, 1918; first produced, 1919)

In April 1918, Eugene O'Neill reunited in GREENWICH VILLAGE with a cadre of former drinking partners from his old West Side haunt, the HELL HOLE. By this time, O'Neill had completed more than 20 plays; seven of these had already been produced on stage. All of the characters in *The Dreamy Kid* are African American. Bucking against the long-standing tradition of using white actors in black face, the PROVINCETOWN PLAYERS hired an all-black cast for the PLAYWRIGHTS' THEATRE'S premiere on October 31, 1919, giving them a precedent for employing black actors. African Americans were cast in leading roles for *The EMPEROR JONES* and *ALL GOD'S CHILLUN GOT WINGS* in the years following. (*The Emperor Jones* and *The Dreamy Kid* were later revived in 1925 in the earliest stages of the Harlem Renaissance).

O'Neill was just then sketching out ideas for his first tour de force, *BEYOND THE HORIZON*, which would win him his first PULITZER PRIZE in 1920. One of his Hell Hole associates was Joe Smith, a black man whom O'Neill's second wife, AGNES BOULTON, described as "the boss of the Negro underworld near the Village [whose] tales were startling." Smith regaled O'Neill with the story of a black New York gangster with the perverse street moniker "Dreamy." "I remember Gene speaking that name almost lovingly and then laughing," Boulton wrote, a "Negro gangster named Dreamy—so Joe had spoken of him. *Why Dreamy?*" (quoted in Floyd 154). Boulton and O'Neill returned to Provincetown the following month, and O'Neill began work on *The Dreamy Kid.* The *why* of Dreamy's name not only served to inspire the play, but O'Neill employed it as a narrative device to drive the plot forward as well. The answer to the mystery of the name reveals both the provenance of the title character's schizophrenic mind, struggling between the competing moral forces of southern black spirituality and northern urban criminality and his family's experience in the early years of a black exodus to northern cities in what is now known as the Great Migration.

## SYNOPSIS

The play is set in Mammy Saunders's apartment on Carmine Street, a two-block byway that connects Seventh Avenue South and Sixth Avenue in the mazelike core of Greenwich Village. In the opening scene, Mammy is on her deathbed; Ceely Ann, her caretaker, promises to find her grandson Abe, or "Dreamy," before she dies. Mammy is under the illusion that Dreamy is "de mos' innercent young lamb in de worl'" (1:678). Ceely, on the other hand, understands what Dreamy has become: "I knowed with all his carryin's-on wid dat passel er tough young niggers—him so uppity 'cause he's de boss er de gang—sleepin' all de day 'stead er workin' an' Lawd knows what he does in de nights—fightin' wid white folks, an' totin' a pistol in his pocket—" (1:678). Irene enters after Mammy drifts off to sleep. She reluctantly informs Ceely that the police are hunting him down. Ceely, harshly judgmental of Dreamy and Irene, had put the word out that Mammy is dying, thus putting Dreamy in danger. Irene disappears onto the street to implore her lover not to heed his Mammy's dying wish.

Soon after Irene exits, Dreamy creeps into the apartment armed with a revolver, with looks that do nothing to explain his implausible nickname: "*He is a well-built, good looking young negro, light in color. His eyes are shifty and hard, their expression one of tough, scornful defiance. His mouth is cruel and perpetually drawn back at the corner into a snarl. He is dressed in well-fitting clothes of a flashy pattern*" (1:680).

O'Neill thrusts the plot forward with two narrative devices. The most obvious is that Dreamy's decision to go to Mammy places him in great danger. He has killed a white man. Despite the fact that he acted in self-defense, it is a capital crime, and he will be executed by the electric chair if he is caught. Dreamy begs his grandmother to keep quiet, obsessively checking the window to the street; but apparently unaware of Dreamy's position, Mammy

ruminates loudly about death, the afterlife, and the love she feels for her grandson. The second device is, as O'Neill's first conception of the play tells us, how the title character became known as "Dreamy." Midway through the play, O'Neill stimulates interest in the name's incongruity when Mammy asks, "Does you know how yo' come by dat nickname dey alls call yo'—de Dreamy? Is I ever tole yo' dat?" (1:684). Lying to appease her, he responds with a tolerant, "No, Mammy," and she begins a tale that he, if not the audience, has probably heard many times.

Hearing footfalls outside the door, Dreamy shushes her before she can finish. The intruder is Irene, who informs Dreamy that she saw a policeman hiding in a doorway across the street. She pleads with him to escape, but he roughly declines, revealing a new aspect of his personality that resonates with the superstitions of Old Southern black culture: "I can't beat it—wid Mammy here alone. My luck done turn bad all my life, if I does" (1:687). Mammy affirms this, crying out in terror, "Yo' ain't gwine leave me now, Dreamy? Yo' ain't, is yo? . . . Yo' promise yo' sacred word yo' stay wid me till de en'. (*with an air of somber prophecy—slowly*) If yo' leave me now, yo' ain't gwine git no bit er luck s'long's yo' live, I tells yo' dat!" (1:688). Irene disregards the warning in the mode of the pragmatic northerner, but Dreamy submits that his grandmother's curse, no matter the consequences, cannot be ignored. Irene finally escapes after Dreamy persuades her to inform his gang of the situation, though he knows they are powerless to help.

Dreamy now sees three policemen, and they evidently know he is there. In a deft piece of dialogue, O'Neill intersperses Dreamy's frantic outcries with Mammy reliving her experiences in the Old South and ethereally providing an answer to the *why* of Dreamy's nickname:

MAMMY—Down by de crik—under de ole willow—whar I uster take yo'—wid yo' big eyes a-chasin'—de dun flitterin' froo de grass—an' out on de water—. . .

DREAMY— . . . Dey don' git de Dreamy alive—not for de chair! Lawd Jesus, no suh! . . .

MAMMY—An' yo' was always—a-lookin'—an' a-thinkin' ter yo'se'f—an' yo' big eyes jest a-dreamin'—an' dat's w'en I gives yo' dat nickname—Dreamy—Dreamy—. (1:690)

As the police climb the stairs, Dreamy holds his grandmother's hand with one of his own and points his revolver at the door with the other. Mammy is *"faltering"* in her speech, as Dreamy rails against being caught alive. However, rather than concluding the play with the sensational gun fight audiences might expect, O'Neill ends with the STAGE DIRECTIONS, *"There is another slight sound of movement from the hallway,"* and the curtain falls (1:691).

## COMMENTARY

In a letter to John Peter Toohey, who had written a congratulatory note about the production, O'Neill responded, "I'm glad you liked [it] and that it was done so well. Of course, I by no means rate it among my best one-act plays for genuine merit, but I did think that it would prove theatrically effective and go over with a bang to an audience—thanks partly to the trick, which I acknowledge" (O'Neill 95). O'Neill does not make clear what "trick" he refers to, but two obvious possibilities come to mind. The first is that *The Dreamy Kid* had an all-black cast, which at the time would certainly draw audiences as a curiosity. The second might be the final scene, which is enormously powerful in its contrasts between the dying Mammy and her fugitive grandson. Rather than sensationally end the play with sounds of gunfire, there is only a *"slight sound of movement from the hallway"*—a pretty good theatrical "trick" in its own right.

O'Neill critic Virginia Floyd elegantly argues that Dreamy's name "signifies the one side of man that society cannot touch or corrupt, the spiritual side of Dreamy that triumphs when all else collapses" (154). But what we now call the Great Migration of rural southern blacks fleeing the horrors of Jim Crow and the outbreak of public lynchings to northern cities had just begun picking up steam when O'Neill composed *The Dreamy Kid*. This allows for a historical explanation as well. Though it is true, as Floyd professes, that

O'Neill offers "no solution" to the race problem, he is following a tradition in African-American literature—carried forth by Paul Laurence Dunbar, Charles W. Chesnutt, Pauline Hopkins, James Weldon Johnson, and Jean Toomer, among many others—of the hapless southern negro migrating to the northern cities where, seduced by city life, they free-fall into depravity.

In the early years of the 20th century, native New Yorkers—black and white—regarded the handful of southern black migrants in their city as "rovers," "wanderers," "vagrants," "a hoodlum element," "criminals in search of a sporting life" (Osofsky 21). As such, Dreamy more closely resembles Paul Laurence Dunbar's character Joe Hamilton in his naturalistic novel of black migration *The Sport of the Gods* (1902)—a guileless country boy who evolves from well-meaning son and brother in the South to gambling addict, violent drunk, and murderer in New York—than he does the homicidal Bigger Thomas in Richard Wright's novel *Native Son* (1940).

This tradition of which O'Neill became a member, consciously or not, re-created the southern blacks' tendency to convert themselves into caricatures of urbanity and thus reject the positive moral foundation of the rural South—the family, the church, the local community—for that of the fashionable New York sporting set, those who, like Dreamy, dressed in *"well-fitting clothes of a flashy pattern"* (1:680). Few if any black writers offered much in the way of a "solution" to this problem either (at least not before the Harlem Renaissance)—"I confess that I can see no practicable [remedy] now," Dunbar wrote (265)—aside from casting a warning at the South, where so many blacks were taken in by the "dream" of New York City, and about what they might find when they got there.

## CHARACTERS

**Abe, "The Dreamy Kid"** Two decades before Richard Wright invented his terrifying character Bigger Thomas in *Native Son* (1940), whose childhood on the streets of Chicago shaped him into a violent criminal, O'Neill's Dreamy Kid personifies and perpetuates white assumptions of the pernicious influence southern blacks had on northern life and vice versa. Also like Bigger Thomas,

Dreamy is not entirely unsympathetic: Though a fugitive murderer on the run, Dreamy does return to his grandmother's deathbed and sweetly holds her hand, soothing her fears of dying and remaining by her side as she gradually expires. As ALEXANDER WOOLLCOTT professed in his *New York Times* review following the opening night, "It is interesting to see how, just as [Theodore] Dreiser does in [his play] *The Hand of the Potter*, so here the author of 'The Dreamy Kid' induces your complete sympathy and pity for a conventionally abhorrent character" (in Cargill 134).

**Ceely Ann**   Mammy Saunders's caretaker. Ceely Ann is symbolic of the traditional Christian morality of southern black culture and is deeply critical of the criminal sporting life Abe, or "Dreamy," has chosen for himself. She is determined, however, to grant Mammy's final wish: to speak with her beloved grandson, Abe, one last time before her death.

**Irene**   Abe's girlfriend. Irene is a prostitute whom O'Neill had originally envisioned as white, but he figured theatergoers would never accept an interracial relationship. Irene continually tries to convince Dreamy that he cannot stay with Mammy Saunders, as the police, knowing their relationship, are sure to find him there. Dreamy rebuffs her efforts, believing that to abandon his grandmother on her deathbed would be bad luck.

**Saunders, Mammy**   Mammy is a 90-year-old southern black woman who migrated north with her grandson, Abe, or "Dreamy," after her daughter, Sal, died while Dreamy was still an infant. Mammy is on her deathbed and pleads to see her grandson one last time before she dies. Dreamy does come, though he is a fugitive murderer, and afraid of the bad luck that would ensue if he were to abandon her, he remains at her bedside to the end.

## BIBLIOGRAPHY

Cargill, Oscar, N. Bryllion Fagin, and William J. Fisher, eds. *O'Neill and His Plays: Four Decades of Criticism.* New York: New York University Press, 1961.

Dunbar, Paul Laurence. "The Negroes of the Tenderloin." In *The Sport of the Gods and Other Essen-*

*tial Writings,* edited by Shelley Fisher Fishkin and David Bradley, 264–267. New York: Modern Library, 2005.

Floyd, Virginia. *The Plays of Eugene O'Neill: A New Assessment.* New York: Ungar, 1985.

O'Neill, Eugene. *Selected Letters of Eugene O'Neill.* Edited by Travis Bogard and Jackson R. Bryer. New Haven, Conn.: Yale University Press, 1988.

Osofsky, Gilbert. *Harlem: The Making of a Ghetto, Negro New York, 1890–1930.* New York: Harper Torchbooks, 1968.

# *Dynamo* (completed, 1928; first produced, 1929)

O'Neill completed *Dynamo*, the first of a planned trilogy entitled "Myth Plays for the God-forsaken," or "God Is Dead! Long Live—What?," in October 1928, during a traumatic period of self-exile in FRANCE with his soon-to-be third wife, CARLOTTA MONTEREY O'NEILL. O'Neill and Carlotta were biding their time during his tumultuous divorce from AGNES BOULTON. After the resounding success of *STRANGE INTERLUDE*, which won O'Neill his third PULITZER PRIZE, the THEATRE GUILD enthusiastically accepted *Dynamo* for production, which premiered on February 11, 1929. The run lasted 50 performances, just enough to cover the Guild's subscribers, and in the end the play turned out to be a total critical failure. The next two plays of the trilogy were 1934's DAYS WITHOUT END, also a failure, and *It Cannot Be Mad?*, which O'Neill never finished. The playwright told KENNETH MACGOWAN that he meant his trilogy to "dig at the roots of the sickness of today as I feel it—the death of an old God and the failure of science and materialism to give any satisfying new one for the surviving primitive religious instinct to find a meaning for life in, and to comfort its fears of death with" (quoted in Clark 120).

Macgowan leaked news of O'Neill's planned trilogy, and of *Dynamo* as its first installment, to the press during preproduction. This led critics, according to O'Neill, to miss the intended "human" and "psychological" aspects of the play by concentrating too closely on the God-replacement theme. Not one critic, O'Neill complained, "got what I thought my play was about" (quoted in Alexander 147).

*Dynamo* tells the story of a modern-day prodigal son who returns to his Puritan New England home with a messianic desire to replace the Christian God of his youth with a new god of electricity. The critics, then, cannot be blamed for the misinterpretation. Along with the script itself, which is overwritten and thematically muddled, two personal issues undoubtedly contributed to its failure. The first was O'Neill's devastating divorce proceedings with Boulton, a period in which he suffered from extreme guilt feelings and self-hatred over the loss of his family (Manheim 75). The second was his rare absence during rehearsals, which had the unfortunate consequence of actors playing roles and speaking lines that neither they nor their director, Philip Moeller, entirely understood. Many critics viewed *Dynamo* as a kind of death knell for O'Neill's theatrical career, but they were utterly

Glenn Anders and Claudette Colbert as Reuben Light and Ada Fife in the Theatre Guild's 1929 production of *Dynamo* *(Courtesy of the New York Public Library)*

mistaken. His triumphant rebound would come in less than two years with his astonishing psychological drama MOURNING BECOMES ELECTRA.

## SYNOPSIS

### Act 1, Scene 1

An evening in May 1928 or 1929 ("the present day") in a small Connecticut town. The exterior of two houses face a street upstage; the Fifes' house is at left and the Lights' at right. "The lilacs are in bloom, the grass is a fresh green" (2:821). Muffled thunder can be heard in the distance, and faint flashes of lightning occasionally illuminate the scene. The interior of the Lights' sitting room on the ground floor and Reuben Light's bedroom upstairs are exposed. Reuben, a boyish and sensitive 17-year-old, is discovered upstairs, and the Reverend Hutchins Light, in his early 60s, and his younger wife, Amelia Light, in her 40s, are seated downstairs in chairs to the left and right, respectively, of a table at center. One kerosene lamp lights the room, which looks worn and faded, though everything is "*spotlessly clean*" (2:823); the furniture, including Hutchins Light's small desk, appears old but well maintained. Hutchins begins with an inner monologue expositing bitterly that their new neighbor, Ramsay Fife, has joked that that he might mistake Reuben's "odor of sanctity" for a skunk's and shoot him. Hutchins begs God to tell him why He has not yet stricken down the atheistic blasphemer.

Mrs. Light remarks aloud that Reuben will be graduating this spring, then inwardly thinks the boy has no interest in a ministerial position. "I'd rather see him dead," she adds, "than go through the poverty and humiliation I've had to face!" (2:825). She calmly voices this concern to Hutchins, who responds that it is God's will that Reuben follow in his footsteps. Reuben's inner monologue reveals that Ramsay Fife had challenged his father to a debate over the existence of God, at one point defying God to strike him dead. He has arranged a secret liaison that night with Fife's daughter Ada, and the Lights worry they might be romantically involved. Reuben hears JAZZ coming from the Fifes' Victrola, the sign she is ready. He sneaks downstairs and out of the house just as Amelia goes up to his room. She looks out his window, and a flash of lightening exposes him hiding in the lilac bushes between the houses. Amelia gasps in disbelief, "Oh, Reuben . . . you've never noticed girls!" (2:828), and the stage goes dark.

### Act 1, Scene 2
No time has elapsed. The walls of the Light home have been replaced, and the interior of the Fife home is now exposed. The Fifes are seated on chairs, again to the left and right of a table at the center of the downstairs sitting room. Ramsay Fife is a 50-year-old Scotch-Irishman who superintends the local electricity plant; May Fife is about 40, a dreamy, sentimental woman who weighs over 200 pounds. Their sitting room is brightly lit with electric bulbs, and everything has a feel of *"glaring newness."* Ada, a 16-year-old "flapper" with bobbed hair, is fixing herself up in front of a mirror in the bedroom upstairs. May Fife remarks inwardly that she believes Ada is falling in love, then remembers to remind her husband to start wearing his summer underwear. Ramsay's inner dialogue tells of the resentment he feels having to read a journal on hydroelectric engineering, though he knows far more than the official engineers at his plant. He compares his wife to a cow, though he recognizes he has "never seen her equal anywhere" (2:831). May wistfully dreams of when they first met. He was a linesman for the plant, and her parents warned her against linesmen, but she fell in love and married him against their will.

Ada looks at herself vainly in the mirror. She likes Reuben well enough but thinks him too much of a "Mama's boy" (2:832). When she goes downstairs, Ramsay begins fuming over a story in the newspaper. A midwestern man had killed another man in a fight over a woman and received a 20-year sentence. The woman helped him escape, and they fled to the West Coast, where they had a daughter who fell in love with a minister's son. When the two became engaged, the man confessed his crime to the future son-in-law, who promptly called off the marriage and turned the man over to the authorities. Ramsay warns Ada of getting involved with such people, boys like Reuben who come from the "Bible-punching breed." He considers Reuben "yellow" and dares Ada to bring the boy to him. She accepts the challenge (2:833).

When Ada goes outside to meet Reuben, she asks him over to meet her father. Amelia Light watches the scene from Reuben's window next door. Reuben tries to kiss Ada, and Ada rebuffs his advance, but Amelia believes she kissed her son, "the brazen little harlot!" Reuben has *"a look of growing dread on his face"* as they go into the Fife house (2:835). Ramsay is wracking his brain to come up with a "good scheme" to pull on Reuben, then roughly orders his wife out of the room. She passively moves to leave, but Ramsay looks down at the news headline and shouts he has devised the perfect ruse. Amelia enters the yard between the houses, hoping to spy on the couple. "That nasty wicked boy!" she thinks, "he'll be punished good for this!" (2:836), and the stage goes dark.

### Act 1, Scene 3
No time has elapsed, but the wall of the Fifes' bedroom has now been replaced, and the sitting rooms are exposed. Hutchins Light looks down at a Bible, but he is preoccupied by Reuben's romance with Ada. May Fife dreams of her love for the power plant and its dynamos, which to her are "always singing about everything in the world." Ramsay Fife is waiting impatiently for Reuben, whom he plans to make think he is "the devil himself" (2:837). Ada and Reuben enter the Fife sitting room, and Ramsay welcomes him with *"exaggerated cordiality"* (2:837). He inquires whether Reuben's father plans to carry out their debate on the existence of God. Reuben proclaims that he would debate if he were his father but admits he has no calling for ministerial work. Ramsay notes that Lucifer is the god of electricity, so God would not call through an electric device. Lightning flashes, visibly unnerving Reuben. Mrs. Light is exposed in the lilac bushes, hoping not to have been seen, but she hears Reuben talking with the blasphemer Fife. Ramsay demands to know Reuben's intentions with his daughter and warns him not to get her pregnant. Scandalized, Reuben insists that he plans to marry Ada.

The trap is set. Ramsay confesses to having murdered Amelia's fiancé and escaped from prison. Reuben, shocked and enormously conflicted, eventually tells him he will not inform the police. Ada is delighted, but Reuben continues that Ramsay should turn himself in and repent in the eyes of God. Ramsay scoffs, "Your hell and God mean no more to me than old women's nonsense when they're scared of the dark!" (2:843). This blasphemy ignites Reuben's religiosity, and he threatens to turn Ramsay in if his sacrilege persists, then withdraws hurriedly. Ada chokes back tears, but she regains control and excuses herself to study. Hutchins Light fearfully jumps to his feet as another flash of lightning strikes; he scolds himself for his nerves and goes upstairs. The thunder from the last lightning strike booms loudly when the stage briefly goes dark.

### Act 1, Scene 4

No time has passed, but the light is now very dim, *"as if the moon were behind the clouds"* (2:844). Now only Reuben's bedroom is exposed. May Fife is leaning out her bedroom window, musing over the beauty of the stormy sky while Amelia Light waits for her to go inside. When May does so, slowly, Amelia creeps back into her house. Reuben emerges from the Fife house, questioning whether Ramsay Fife's sin had gone unpunished because there was no God. A terrible flash of lightning lights up the stage. Convinced the lightning is God's wrath, he admits he is afraid of God, and then the thunder booms. Hutchins Light enters Reuben's bedroom and calls in alarm for his wife and son. Ramsay Fife pokes his head out of the sitting-room window.

Amelia runs into Reuben's room, says she overheard Reuben ask Ada to marry him and shoves Hutchins into Reuben's closet to get the truth from their son. Reuben enters, his thoughts of secrecy bringing on another flash of lightning. Amelia convinces him to explain what happened by appealing to his fear of God's wrath, and the thunder booms. He tells her Ramsay's story but insists he still loves Ada. Hutchins appears from the closet with a belt. Reuben realizes that his mother wants him to be punished and vows not to show pain. After Hutchins whips the boy, lightning strikes again, and Hutchins cringes in terror. Reuben notices this and inwardly denounces his father for his cowardice. Hutchins throws down the belt and announces he will inform the police. Reuben condemns them all for harboring cowardice in the family blood. "But

I'll get him out of my blood, by God!" he shouts at his mother. "And I'll get you out, too!" He curses her treachery and then pulls on the bedroom door, which he finds locked (2:849).

Hutchins appears outside, and Ramsay calls for his daughter to watch the fun. Hutchins swears to avenge himself by turning Ramsay in. Ramsay, *"enjoying himself hugely,"* keeps up the story until Ada tells Hutchins the truth. Reuben breaks down the bedroom door and rushes outside. Ada accuses him of being a "yellow rat," and she never wants to speak to him again. Realizing the whole thing was a lie, Reuben screams, "It's you who're the rat, Ada! You can go to hell!" (2:851). Conscious now of the joke played on him, Hutchins threatens to whip Reuben for humiliating him, but Reuben yells, "I'm not scared of you or your God any more!" Lightning flashes, but Reuben just laughs at the sky mockingly. "Shoot away, Old Bozo! I'm not scared of you!" (2:852). Terrified of their son, the Lights rush inside, while Reuben walks off left shouting, "There is no God! No God but Electricity! I'll never be scared again! I'm through with the lot of you!" (2:852). The sound of wind and rain fill the theater as the curtain falls.

### Act 2, Scene 1

Same as act 1, 15 months later, early on a hot August morning. The interior of the Light sitting room is revealed. May Fife is leaning out her downstairs window, basking in the sun and musing dreamily about Amelia Light's recent death, then death in general. Ada's head comes through the next window, and she scoffs at her mother's sentimentality over Amelia Light, who hated them. May Fife urges her to make up with her father, whom she has barely spoken to since Reuben left.

Hutchins Light enters his sitting room. He looks much older, desperately lonely, and suffering from a profound state of mourning. Next door, May Fife continues that although Ramsay Fife does not show it, he is "really the kindest man in the world" (2:855). Ada responds scornfully, then warmly calls her mother the kindest in the world. She disappears into the house, and Reuben strides in from the left carrying six books tied in a strap. The frightened boy of act 1 is gone. Reuben looks stronger now, more self-assured, and *"consciously hard-boiled"* (1:855). "Home, Sweet Home!," he thinks sardonically, "the prodigal returns!" (1:856). He and May Fife finally notice each other, and May expresses delight at his return. Reuben tells her he has been studying electrical sciences, and he is grateful to Ramsay for waking him up to the truth. Electricity is now his god. He asks if she ever heard the sound of dynamos. May says she loves them and imitates their humming sound. Reuben is impressed and says so. May tells him to hide so they can surprise Ada, and he runs behind the lilac bushes.

Ada appears at the window, but Reuben, ashamed of his latent boyishness, emerges from the bushes. His appearance scares Ada at first, but he kisses her full on the lips and tells her to admit she loves him. She does, and Reuben tells her about his new love of science and that when he left he had gone to the top of a hill and stared at the lightning for hours. After that, he never felt fear again. He has traveled the country, studying science and always working jobs that pertain to electricity. He asks if she can convince her father to give him a job. She tells him she will try. He makes off to see his mother with a promise to take Ada for a walk to the hill later. Ada cannot bring herself to tell him Amelia is dead, and he enters his house unawares.

Reuben enters the sitting room. His father stares at him in a bewildered silence, not fully recognizing his son. But soon the anger rises, and he accuses Reuben of killing his mother. Reuben demands to know where she is. When Hutchins tells him she is dead, he takes the news with some regret but little emotion. Amelia died of pneumonia, but Hutchins blames Reuben. "You killed her as surely as if you'd given her poison, you unnatural accursed son!" (2:863). Hutchins's rage turns to sorrow, and he admits that her last words were "don't be a fool," taken from Reuben's occasional postcards that read "We have electrocuted your God. Don't be a fool" (2:865). Reuben perceives this as a sign that he converted her to his new religion. He agrees to stay a few nights but tells his father he will soon be working at the electrical plant. "Electricity is God now," he says and mockingly vows to convert his father as he had

his mother. He departs, but as he walks down the road, *"the callousness has gone from his face, which is now very like that of Act One"* (1:866). Ada tells him from the window her father will hire him as a floor man at the plant. She asks for a kiss, and he moves toward her but then, remembering his mother's hatred of her, steps away and tells her he will be back that night. *"She looks after him, bewildered and hurt,"* as the curtain falls (2:866).

### Act 2, Scene 2

The same scene, at around 11:30 at night. Reuben's bedroom is now exposed, and the wall to the Lights' sitting room has been replaced. Ada and Reuben enter from left. They have just had sex, and Ada feels scared but in love and exhilarated. "Up on the hill when we—oh, I felt I was just you, a part of you and you were part of me!" (2:867). Reuben acts preoccupied, uninterested in Ada's love talk, believing he will never be satisfied until he has discovered "the truth about everything." She expresses her fear and asks if he loves her, if their evening meant as much to him as it does her, and he callously retorts, "What people call love is just sex—and there's no sin about it!" (2:867). She asks whether he still wants to get married, and he rejects the idea of having a Christian marriage. "We're married by Nature now" (2:868). He tells her that when he visited his mother's grave, he began to pray. Then he remembered there was nothing to pray to, except possibly electricity. Ada asks whether his mother might forgive them, and he says she never would, but who cares, and bids her goodnight. Ada stands outside her house for a moment, crying softly over the change in Reuben, then moves off left. Reuben lights the lamp in his bedroom and reflects on his mother's betrayal there. He then considers the night with Ada, coldly asserting she will be "handy" to have around (2:869). He questions the relationship between love and sex and remembers his mother and father had sex to conceive him. "God that seems lousy somehow! . . . I don't want to think of it" (2:869). His thoughts return to the possibility of praying to electricity, and he decides to visit the dynamos at the electrical plant. He blows out the light and walks out.

## Act 2, Scene 3

A half hour later at the Light and Power Company's hydroelectric plant. The sounds of rushing water and the humming dynamo fill the air. The plant is red brick with two sections. The dynamo room is at left, wider than the other but one floor shorter. The dynamo room is *"brilliantly lighted by a row of powerful bulbs in white globes"* and exposed by an open door and a large window. The dynamo itself is *"huge and black, with something of a massive female idol about it, the exciter set on the main structure like a head with blank, oblong eyes above a gross, rounded torso."* An upper window looks into the room at right, which is filled with the *"mathematically ordered web of the disconnecting switches, double busses, and other equipment"* that lead out through the roof to transmission towers (2:871).

Reuben enters from the right, stands for a moment looking at the dynamo, and then notes its resemblance to a "great dark" female idol that pagans used to worship, "only it's living and they were dead." But he reflects that does not resemble a girl's figure; rather, he shouts in revelation, it is "a great, dark mother! . . . that's what the dynamo is! . . . that's what life is!" (2:871). He reverently listens to its humming and quotes May Fife, "always singing about everything in the world." He kneels and prays to the dynamo, feeling his mother urging him to, and begs the "Mother of Life" for his own mother's forgiveness and for her to reveal the truth to him. He slowly rises to his feet, with a new look of *"calm and relief,"* feeling now that he has been forgiven (2:872), and walks back home to sleep in peace.

## Act 3, Scene 1

The hydroelectric plant, four months later. The door to the dynamo room is closed, muffling the humming sound and accentuating the sound of rushing water from the dam. Reuben and May Fife enter from left. Reuben has brought May, whose *"moony dreaminess is more pronounced,"* to witness a miracle at the dynamo. Reuben now believes that the dynamo's song is "the poem of eternal life" (2:873). The song brings back memories of his peaceful childhood with his mother; May promises to be a mother to him and Ada. Reuben has

renounced his relationship with Ada to appease the will of the dynamo. He tells May of his revelation of the oneness of the universe, that life on earth emerged from the ocean with electricity at its core, "the Great Mother of Eternal Life, Electricity, and Dynamo is her Divine Image on earth!" (2:874). He now believes he has been chosen as its savior on earth, but he must relinquish the desires of the flesh in spite of his growing love for Ada. At home, he beats himself with a belt to waylay his sexual impulses, and he has successfully avoided Ada for over a month.

Sensing the dynamo calling him, Reuben tells May to wait outside until Ramsay Fife has left work; he then enters the dynamo room. Fife appears from the doorway, inwardly cursing Reuben for his "queer look" and maltreatment of his daughter. After a moment, he sees his wife and scoffs at her habit of "staring at the dynamos and humming like a half-wit" (2:875). He asks if she believes Reuben and Ada have slept together, and she says they have, just like she and Ramsay when they first met. Ramsay vows to beat some decency into the boy and storms off. May opens the door to the dynamo room, revealing Reuben on his knees praying with his arms outstretched before the dynamo. Ada enters from left looking for Reuben. Reuben believes no miracle has occurred because he still must fully renounce Ada. He goes out to look for her and is superstitiously struck by the coincidence of finding her outside. She humors him soothingly about his belief in the impending miracle. Taking her arm too roughly, he guides her over the dam and into the dynamo room from a door on the roof. Terrified, Ada cries out, "Rube! I don't want to go—" (2:879). He slams the door shut behind them, and the stage briefly goes dark.

## Act 3, Scene 2

No time has elapsed. The dimly lit interiors of the upper and lower switch galleries are exposed. The lower gallery's oil switches resemble *"queer Hindu idols tortured into scientific supplications"* (2:879). The upper gallery contains *"a fretwork of wires, steel work, insulators, busses, switches, etc., stretching upward to the roof"* (2:880). Reuben and Ada are standing just inside an upper-gallery door leading to the roof of the dynamo room at left. Ada stares about her, terrified, commenting that the morass of electrical engineering equipment looks alive. "Alive with the mighty spirit of her eternal life!" Reuben shouts, and he tells her not to press close to him, as they are now in a temple. He believes the dynamo mother is no longer angry with Ada, since Ada has come to believe (2:880). Reuben asks her to pray to the dynamo mother with outstretched arms, all the while fighting his impulse to have sex with her. Ada obeys and takes a position under the switches with arms outstretched. Questioning the dynamo mother's wishes, Reuben demands to know if Ada truly believes in her. She swears she does, and Reuben kisses her passionately. But his sexual desire overwhelms him; he cries out her name and bends her to the floor, and the stage goes dark (2:881–882).

### Act 3, Scene 3
A short time has elapsed. The interiors of all the rooms in the power plant are revealed, including a small switchboard room to the right of the dynamo room in which Jennings, a man of around 30 and the operator on duty, is seated at a desk. Mrs. Fife is in the dynamo room, humming while she stares dreamily at the dynamo. Reuben, still with Ada in the upper gallery, is on his knees, sobbing, with head in hands. Reuben believes he has betrayed his mother and that the miracle will never happen. Ada tells him she loves him, and in an attempt to comfort him, she gently pats his back; he pulls away and shouts for her not to touch him. "*A terrible look of murder comes into his face*" (2:883).

Reuben refuses to kill Ada with his hands, flesh on flesh, so he rushes to the switchboard room to get a revolver from the desk drawer. He forces the operator into a rear office and walks determinedly back to Ada. "*His face is as drained of all human feeling as a plaster mask.*" He convinces himself that this will be an execution, not a murder, which calms his nerves. But when he hears her voice calling to him, he jumps up the stairs, screams "Harlot!" and fires two shots into her. Gaping down at Ada's body, Reuben realizes what he has done, then begs his mother to show him a sign. He rushes through the switchboard room and downstairs to

the dynamo, "*stretching out his arms to the exciter head of his Dynamo-Mother with its whirling metal brain and its blank, oblong eyes*" (2:883).

May Fife asks about the gunshot sound. Reuben ignores her, pleading to the dynamo like a child, renouncing his desire to know the truth and begging his mother to hide him. When he clasps the carbon brushes of the dynamo, there is a flash of bluish light, all of the lights go dim, and the dynamo hum perceptibly weakens. "*Simultaneously Reuben's voice rises in a moan that is a mingling of pain and loving consummation, and this cry dies into a second sound that is like the crooning of a baby and merges and is lost in the dynamo's hum*" (2:884). His body falls limply to the floor, and May runs to him. May scolds the dynamo for not being nice; the dynamo's hum picks up, and the lights go on again. May beats the steel casing of the dynamo, yelling "*in a fit of childish anger,*" "You hateful old thing you!" (2:885). Her hands in too much pain to continue, she stops and cries softly as the curtain falls.

## COMMENTARY

*Dynamo* is a play with a great deal of potential, but it fails mainly because of its strained convergence of two disparate themes: the evangelistic Christian battle with the modern god of electricity and, as O'Neill described it, "the boy's psychological Mother-struggle-ending-in-girl-sacrificed-to-Mother-God" motif (quoted in Alexander 144). O'Neill intended audiences to focus on the latter, but it was the former that received the attention. According to Doris Alexander, O'Neill "thought he had shown that banal conflict as simply laughable in the comic arguments between Fife and the minister" (146–147). O'Neill blamed the mistake on producer Kenneth Macgowan's premature press release that described *Dynamo* as the first of a planned trilogy entitled "Myths for the God-forsaken," or "God Is Dead! Long Live—What?" In fact, this is precisely what he told Macgowan: *Dynamo* was to be a "symbolical and factual biography of what is happening in a large section of the American (and not only American) soul right now. It is really the first play of a trilogy that will dig at the roots of the sickness of today as I feel it—the death of an old God and the failure of science and materialism to give any satisfying new one for the surviving primitive religious instinct to find a meaning for life in, and to comfort fears of death with" (quoted in Clark 120).

Nowhere does O'Neill mention his later intention, though he still complained later that no critic understood the overarching theme of the play:

> It certainly seems damn queer to me—although knowing what most of the critics are, it shouldn't—that no one seems to have gotten the real human relationship story, what his mother does to the boy and what that leads to in his sacrifice of the girl to a maternal deity in the end—the girl his mother hated and was jealous of. [sic]—that all that was the boy's real God struggle, or prompted it. This all fits in with the general theme of American life in back of the play, America being the land of the mother complex. (quoted in Barlow 136)

"Not a damn one mentions it," he continued, "They were so damned hot on the general religious theme that they couldn't see the human psychological struggle" (quoted in Floyd 356). His first note on the play in 1926 helps further clarify his intentions, however muddled: "Play of Dynamos—the despairing philosopher-poet who falls in love with balance equilibrium of eternal energy—his personification of it—his final marriage with it—the consummation ending with his destruction" (quoted in Alexander 129).

Doris Alexander finds the root of O'Neill's "general theme of American life" in the psychoanalytic theories of Carl Jung, who wrote in his *Psychology of the Unconscious* (1912) that "Americans, as a result of the extreme detachment from their father, are characterized by a most enormous mother complex" (quoted in Alexander 137). Other distinctly American themes emerge in the play as well. The Christian fundamentalist battle with science, for example, had been sensationally played out in the press during the famous Scopes Monkey Trial, in which a high school teacher in Tennessee was indicted in 1925 for teaching Darwin's theory of evolution to his students. O'Neill's nod to the controversy over DARWINISM appears in Ada's teasing her father over his foul temper while reading

the newspaper: "What's the bad news, Pop? Has another Fundamentalist been denying Darwin?" (2:832). In another big news event of the 1920s, the novelist Sinclair Lewis notoriously opened a speech to a Kansas church group by saying that if there were a God, He would strike Lewis dead for what he would say in the next 15 minutes. As the press reported the incident, Lewis stood on the pulpit with watch in hand and challenged God to kill him within 15 minutes, just as Ramsay Fife challenges Hutchins Light (Alexander 130). Travis Bogard, along with Brenda Murphy and William Wasserstrom, have also pointed to Henry Adams's chapter in his classic autobiography *The Education of Henry Adams* (1918), "The Dynamo and the Virgin." In the modern image of the dynamo, Bogard writes, Adams suggests "a particularly American manifestation of the life force seen in earlier times in Europe as the worship of Venus and the Virgin" (319).

Certainly O'Neill's tortured relationship with his own mother and the immensity of his disappointment over his failed marriages to KATHLEEN JENKINS and Agnes Boulton took a terrible toll on the playwright, a toll we find dramatized in Reuben Light's experience with the most important women in his life. When Reuben questions the relationship between love and sex and remembers his mother must have had sex to conceive him, he thinks, "God that seems lousy somehow! . . . I don't want to think of it" (2:869). This line strongly speaks to O'Neill's early CATHOLICISM. Director JOSÉ QUINTERO, for instance, believed that one reason he felt such a strong affinity for O'Neill's work is that he understood "the guilt that all men of the Western world, particularly those raised Catholic, have over the fact that their mothers had to have sex to have them" (quoted in Murphy 17). Mother-figure worship among Catholic men, related to the idolatry of the Virgin Mary, is a prevailing theme in the O'Neill canon—along with *Dynamo*, it also figures importantly in *The GREAT GOD BROWN, STRANGE INTERLUDE, A MOON FOR THE MISBEGOTTEN,* and *LONG DAY'S JOURNEY INTO NIGHT,* among others— and the pain that ensues when the mother abandons her child is a traditional obsession among men raised in Catholicism. The connection between the Virgin Mary and the dynamo was reinforced when

O'Neill, researching *Dynamo*, visited a General Electric power plant north of Danbury, Connecticut, in late September 1927, and saw firsthand that "the horizontally mounted generators . . . actually looked like women" (Alexander 140).

Reuben Light, rather than suffering a tragic fate like Anthony Dion in *The Great God Brown* or even Yank in *The HAIRY APE*, appears to have gone insane in the last scenes rather than having been driven to suicide or death (and murder in the case of Reuben) by any naturalistic forces beyond his control. O'Neill never mentions whether he meant Reuben to be mad, but it is difficult to accept the character any other way. On the other hand, though Barbara Voglino quite rightly points out that "no sane person would kneel down and pray to a generator" (59), if this was a play meant to be one of O'Neill's "God-forsaken," as the title of his planned trilogy suggested, the later character John Loving kneeling before the Cross in the final scene of *DAYS WITHOUT END* (the other completed play of the trilogy) appears no less insane than Reuben before the dynamo (58). Either way, the themes fall apart if the god figure of the dynamo is a psychological delusion brought on by mental collapse rather than the bona fide and realistic "mother struggles" we see years later in *A Moon for the Misbegotten* and *Long Day's Journey into Night*. No real meaning can be taken from it. Even the historical character Juan Ponce de Leon in O'Neill's earlier play *The FOUNTAIN*, who experiences a similar religious awakening before the Fountain of Youth, appears more believable since he was at death's door when he experienced his epiphany. All three characters in *The Fountain*—Juan, Reuben, and John—outstretch their arms in prayer to a newly accepted god figure; each incants a prayer or poem to the new god as articulating for them the cyclical flux of existence, what Juan Ponce de Leon calls the "rhythm of eternal life" (2:225) and Reuben the dynamo's "poem of eternal life" (2:873).

O'Neill seems to have taken up in *Dynamo* where he left off in *Strange Interlude*. In the final scene of the latter, Nina Leeds shouts, "Yes, our lives are merely strange dark interludes in the electrical display of God the Father!" (2:817). O'Neill also borrowed his "thought-asides method" from *Strange Interlude*, though he later regretted this decision. "That was what principally hurt 'Dynamo,'" he admitted of its first production, "being forced into thought-asides method which was quite alien to essential psychological form of its characters. . . . [I] saw this when I re-read it after return from East—too late!" (quoted in Alexander 145). He would never use the technique again.

In *Dynamo*, O'Neill revisited many theatrical techniques that had made him famous over the previous decade. The first is the episodic structure, consisting of a series of very short scenes that culminate in a final scene that destroys the doomed, truth-seeking protagonist, successfully applied with *The EMPEROR JONES* and *The Hairy Ape*. The Crocodile God in *The Emperor Jones* and the gorilla in the final scene of *The Hairy Ape* both resemble the destructive, expressionistic force of the dynamo in this play, which also appears to be a living being. Act 1 of the play resembles *DESIRE UNDER THE ELMS* in its use of replaceable walls. Act 3 of the play, which takes place at a power plant, is O'Neill's answer to the period's industrial ethos and borrows from the imagery we find in the period's futuristic paintings and Fritz Lang's film of the same era, *Metropolis* (1927; Manheim 71). But the set also, like the house and trees in *Desire under the Elms*, gave expressionistic emphasis to the lost mother figure's lingering presence and continued influence on the young men. (Eben Cabot and Reuben Light, who both desperately want the forgiveness and acceptance of their dead mothers, are two letters away from sharing the same first name.)

O'Neill scholars and BIOGRAPHERS have since attributed *Dynamo*'s overbearing "shallowness and adolescent pretentiousness" (in Wainscott 255) to O'Neill's own tumultuous life at the time of composition. He wrote the play during a period when he was experiencing deep guilt feelings, primarily brought on by his divorce from Agnes Boulton. "O'Neill saw in his tragedy an opportunity to come to grips with the cataclysm in his own life," Doris Alexander argues. "It had been shattered when 'something' inside him found out in *Strange Interlude* that his love for Agnes was doomed" (132). But the divorce also apparently brought back to his conscience his abandonment of his first wife and child, Kathleen Jenkins and EUGENE O'NEILL, JR. He applied the biblical tale of the prodigal son to his early one-act play *The ROPE* following the experience with Jenkins. (The only minor character in the play, "Jennings," significantly calls to mind that of his first wife, and both Ada and Amelia share the A of Agnes.) Then he returned to it when his marriage to Boulton fell apart (Alexander 135). But these experiences were highly personal, Virginia Floyd aptly states, and did not necessarily speak to a larger American spiritual crisis: "He tries to provide a lesson for godless America in *Dynamo* but fails when he uses a page from his own life to do so" (366).

O'Neill published *Dynamo* in book form soon after the production in an attempt to rewrite it closer to his original meaning. But even he acknowledged he could not capture his vision either on the stage or in print. "I like it better now," he wrote of the published version, "but not enough. I wish I'd never written it—really—and yet I feel it has its justified place in my work development. A puzzle" (quoted in Alexander 148). And so it does, and so it is.

## CHARACTERS

**Fife, Ada** Ramsay and May Fife's daughter. In act 1, Ada Fife is a vivacious and pretty 16-year-old "flapper" with blue eyes and bobbed hair whose *"speech is self-assertive and consciously slangy"* (2:830). She has begun a youthful romance with the more proper, religious-minded Reuben Light, whom her prankster father Ramsay Fife, an atheist, disapproves of as a "yellow," "Bible-punching" type (2:833). Though she thinks of Reuben as too much of a "Mama's boy" (2:832) to fall in love with at first, Ada defends Reuben's integrity. Her father then challenges her to bring the young man to him, believing he will expose Reuben as "yellow." Ada agrees and that night convinces the reluctant Reuben to meet Ramsay. Ramsay has concocted a hoax in which he pretends to be a murderer who escaped from prison. Although Reuben initially promises not to turn him in, he goes back and tells his mother. When Ada finds out, she calls him a "yellow rat" (2:851). He responds by denouncing her for betraying him with the lie and runs away from home.

Reuben returns after 15 months of studying science. Ada, now 18, admits she still loves him, and they have sex. But Reuben has changed drastically during his time away. He has rejected his old god and adopted a new religion in which electricity is his new god and he the savior of the human race. Ada, still in love and wanting to marry him, humors his new belief and joins him at the dynamo to witness the miracle he believes will take place there. No miracle occurs; instead, unable to control his physical desire, he makes love to Ada in the power station. After this, he believes his betrayals of his mother, Amelia Light—who hated Ada and died while he was away—and the electricity god embodied by the dynamo have prevented the miracle from taking place. He kills Ada to demonstrate his allegiance to his mother and the electricity god, then commits suicide by clutching the carbon brushes of the operating dynamo.

Ada's character changes too drastically to be credible from the first to third acts, but the father-daughter relationship between Ramsay and Ada closely parallels that of Josie and Phil Hogan in O'Neill's late play *A Moon for the Misbegotten.*

**Fife, May** Ramsay Fife's wife and Ada Fife's mother. May is around 40 years old, *"tall and stout, weighing well over two hundred pounds."* In spite of her weight, her face retains a *"girlish naïveté and fresh complexion"* (2:830). May's expression always betrays a moony dreaminess, and her tone of voice is *"sentimental and wondering"* (2:830). Throughout the play, May's thoughts reveal a meandering, delusional mind that sees the best in everything and everyone around her. May continually refers to her husband as the "the kindest man in the world" (2:855), for instance, in spite of his surly, cantankerous personality. In her more distant thoughts from reality and nostalgic recollections of her marriage to Ramsay, she calls to mind the morphine-addled Mary Tyrone of *Long Day's Journey into Night,* a character closely based on O'Neill's mother, MARY ELLEN "ELLA" O'NEILL ("May" is one letter away from "Mary").

Doris Alexander has made an interesting connection between May and the mother of O'Neill's first wife, Kathleen Jenkins. Mrs. Jenkins once said of O'Neill's flight from her daughter and family, "There would have been no 'mother-in-law' about it, either, and he knew that. I felt toward him as if he were my own son" (quoted in Alexander 136). For her part, May tells Reuben Light, an autobiographical avatar of O'Neill, "I'll be your mother—yours and Ada's" (2:873). Given to humming along with the dynamos, which she adores, she accepts Reuben Light's new religion of an electricity god out of hand and apprehends none of the latent insanity it entails. She is one of O'Neill's "earth mothers," like Cybel in *The Great God Brown* and Josie Hogan in *A Moon for the Misbegotten.* In some ways, May is the most enigmatic character in the play, as it is largely unclear whether O'Neill means her to be read as a prophet of the new electricity god or the simple "half-wit" her husband takes her for (2:875).

**Fife, Ramsay** May Fife's husband and Ada Fife's father. Fife is a *"small wiry"* 50-year-old Scotch-Irishman *"with a sharp face and keen black eyes." "His thin mouth is full of the malicious humor of the practical joker. He has a biting tongue, but at bottom is a good-natured man except where the religious bigotry of his atheism is concerned"* (2:829). The superintendent of the local power plant, Ramsay has challenged his neighbor, Reverend Hutchins Light, to publicly debate the existence of God. He is also a prankster who establishes the comedy of act 1 by concocting a scheme to show up Reuben Light—whom his daughter is enamored with but he considers a sanctimonious "Bible-punching" type (2:833)—as "yellow" by telling him that he (Ramsay) murdered a man and subsequently escaped from prison. Ada agrees to the hoax, as she believes Reuben would not turn against her father. As Ramsay predicted, Reuben immediately informs his mother. Hutchins Light, whom Amelia Light had hidden in the closet during Reuben's confession, sees the story as an opportunity to avenge Ramsay's blasphemous talk against him. When Ada Light tells Hutchins and Reuben the truth, the minister is once again humiliated. Ramsay's hoax convinces Reuben that his mother and Ada, the two most important women in his life, have betrayed him, and he runs away from home. When he returns,

Ramsay offers him a job at the plant but grows uneasy at Reuben's strange behavior—behavior that eventually leads to Reuben's murder of Ada and his suicide.

Michael Manheim connects Fife's "taunting, iconoclastic" character in the form of James "Jamie" Tyrone, Jr. in LONG DAY'S JOURNEY INTO NIGHT, based on O'Neill's older brother James "Jamie" O'Neill, Jr., and Hutchins Light as Jamie's father, the "puritanical . . . condemning" James Tyrone, Sr., based on O'Neill's father JAMES O'NEILL (Manheim 73).

**Light, Amelia** Reverend Hutchins Light's wife and Reuben Light's mother. Amelia is in her mid-40s, significantly younger than her husband Hutchins; her *"stout figure is still firm and active, with large breasts and broad, round hips"* (2:823). Inwardly resentful of the "poverty and humiliation" she has faced as the wife of a minister (2:825), In act 1 Amelia attempts to help her son avoid entering his father's profession. Nevertheless, she shares her husband's puritanical attitude toward sexuality and is horrified to discover that Reuben and Ada Fife, whom she considers a "brazen little harlot" (2:835), are conducting a secret romance. When Reuben returns from Ada's house, he makes his mother swear on the Bible not to tell his father what he learned. Ada's father, Ramsay Fife, concocted a hoax with which he wanted to expose Reuben as "yellow" by sharing the fraudulent secret that he (Ramsay) is a murderer who escaped from prison. But Amelia had told her husband to hide in Reuben's closet before his return, so Hutchins hears the tale from Reuben, not Amelia.

Reuben feels betrayed by his mother and runs away from home. When he returns 15 months later, she has died, and his father accuses him of having killed her "as surely as if you'd given her poison" (2:863). O'Neill also considered his own mother, Mary Ellen "Ella" O'Neill, had betrayed him when she succumbed to her morphine addiction; there are many parallels between that relationship and the mother-son relationship of Amelia and Reuben, as well as in their corresponding characters, Mary and Edmund Tyrone, in O'Neill's highly autobiographical *Long Day's Journey into Night.*

**Light, Reuben** Hutchins and Amelia Light's son. In act 1, Reuben is 17 years old, tall and slim, with his father's red hair, weak mouth, strong jaw, and gray-blue eyes. *"His natural voice has an almost feminine gentleness,"* but he shares his father Hutchins's tendency when engaging the outside world to boom at people *"self-protectively"* (2:824). Although he does not feel the calling to be a minister like his father, he superstitiously fears, like Hutchins, that the lightning and thunder in act 1 are the wrathful voice of an angry God. Reuben is smitten with Ada Fife, the daughter of Ramsay Fife, an atheistic superintendent of the local power plant who has waged an ongoing battle with his father over the existence of God. To prove to his daughter that Reuben is "yellow," Ramsay concocts a scheme in which he tells Reuben that he is a murderer who escaped from prison. Reuben believes him, and though at first promising to keep the secret to himself, he goes home and tells his mother, Amelia. Before he arrives, however, his mother, having seen Reuben and Ada have a secret liaison, orders her husband to hide in Reuben's closet so she can get a full confession. Upon hearing Ramsay's bogus story, Hutchins beats his son and then goes off to tell Ramsay he will inform the authorities. Ada explains the joke to Hutchins, which humiliates him but also makes Reuben believe he has been betrayed by both his mother and Ada—the two most important women in his life—and he leaves home angry and disillusioned.

Fifteen months later, Reuben returns a changed man, *"hardly recognizable as the Reuben of Act One."* He has renounced the old puritanical God of his parents in favor of the new god of electricity and science, and *"his manner is now consciously hard-boiled"* (2:855). Amelia has died, and his father openly accuses him of killing her with his absence. Her last words were from Reuben's postcards: "Don't be a fool." "We have electrocuted your God," his postcards read, "Don't be a fool!" (2:865). Reuben interprets her last words as a conversion to his new faith. Reuben reacts coldly to the news at first, but then he experiences a mounting sense of loss, one that turns into a maniacal obsession over the dynamo at the local electric plant. Ada still loves him, regardless of his transformation and strange beliefs. She gets him a job with her father at the

power plant, and the two make love on the hill to where Reuben first fled in act 1. But Reuben becomes messianic in his belief in the electricity god, and his mother's death exacerbates the sense of urgency to have the new god reveal to him true knowledge at the dynamo—which he sees as a kind of mother figure—and proclaim him the savior of the human race. He therefore breaks off relations with Ada, whom his mother hated, but feels he must flagellate himself with a belt to negate his unrelenting sexual urges.

In the end, Reuben believes that his sexual relations with Ada betrayed his mother and prevented the miracle of the dynamo that he believed would make him the savior of the human race. (In his worship of the dynamo, he finds a strange bedfellow in the character of May Fife, Ramsay's wife.) He thus kills Ada as proof of his allegiance to his mother, then grabs hold of the live carbon brushes of the operating dynamo and, renouncing his desire to understand truth and wanting only to hide, kills himself to reunite with his mother.

Reuben's "mother struggle," extremely oedipal in nature and therefore closely related to the psychoanalysis of Sigmund Freud, is far less realistic than that which we encounter in O'Neill's later autobiographical plays *Long Day's Journey into Night* and *A Moon for the Misbegotten.* His experience at the dynamo corresponds to that of the historical character Juan Ponce de Leon before the Fountain of Youth in O'Neill's earlier play *The Fountain* and John Loving's similar religious awakening before the cross in the later play *Days Without End.* All three characters outstretch their arms in prayer to a newly accepted god figure, and each incants a prayer or poem that acknowledges the cyclical flux of existence, what Juan Ponce de Leon calls the fountain's "rhythm of eternal life" (2:225) and Reuben, the dynamo's "poem of eternal life" (2:873). Finally, Reuben Light's conversion is so extreme as to lead audiences to believe he simply went insane, as opposed to a character filled with self-contempt, feelings of betrayal, and mother-longing, as O'Neill was at the time of composition.

**Light, Reverend Hutchins** Amelia Light's husband and Reuben Light's father. Hutchins is in his early 60s, red-haired, of medium height, and *"ponderously built"* with a *"stubborn jaw weakened by a big indecisive mouth."* *"His voice is the bullying one of a sermonizer who is the victim of an inner uncertainty that compensates itself by being boomingly overassertive"* (2:823). Hutchins is involved in a dispute with his neighbor Ramsay Fife, an atheist who has challenged him to a debate on the existence of God. Hutchins wonders to himself why God has not yet struck down the blasphemer, who once challenged God to strike him down within five minutes' time. Like his son Reuben, he fears that the lightning and thunder in act 1 are the wrathful voice of an angry God. When Hutchins hears from Reuben that Ramsay is a murderer who escaped from prison—a hoax played on Reuben by Ramsay to prove to his daughter Ada that the young boy is "yellow"—he threatens to turn his enemy over to the authorities. Ada tells Hutchins the truth, which humiliates Hutchins and leads Reuben to run away from home.

When Reuben returns 15 months later, Amelia has died, and Hutchins has become an old man, *"his whole face is a mask of stricken loneliness"* (2:854). He blames Reuben's disappearance for his wife's death—"You killed her as surely as if you'd given her poison, you unnatural accursed son!" (2:863)—but clearly still loves his son. This complicated pattern of uncertainty, condemnation, and love reflects the father-son relationships of the Tyrone family in O'Neill's highly autobiographical masterpiece *Long Day's Journey into Night.* There is also a correlation between the Lights and Mary and James Tyrone, who are based on O'Neill's parents, James O'Neill and Mary Ellen "Ella" O'Neill. James Tyrone (who also speaks in "overassertive" tones to compensate for his "inner uncertainty") uses the word *poison* to describe the morphine his wife takes, and Mary voices a disgust over her family's financial situation that is similar to Amelia's disgust.

## BIBLIOGRAPHY

Alexander, Doris. *Eugene O'Neill's Creative Struggle: The Decisive Decade, 1924–1933.* University Park: Pennsylvania State University Press, 1992.

Barlow, Judith. *Final Acts: The Creation of Three Late O'Neill Plays.* Athens: University of Georgia Press, 1985.

Bogard, Travis. *Contour in Time: The Plays of Eugene O'Neill.* Rev. ed. New York: Oxford University Press, 1988.

Clark, Barrett H. *Eugene O'Neill: The Man and His Plays.* Rev. ed. New York: Dover, 1947.

Floyd, Virginia. *The Plays of Eugene O'Neill: A New Assessment.* New York: Ungar, 1985.

Manheim, Michael. *Eugene O'Neill's New Language of Kinship.* Syracuse, N.Y.: Syracuse University Press, 1982.

Murphy, Brenda. "Fetishizing the Dynamo: Henry Adams and Eugene O'Neill." *Eugene O'Neill Review* 16, no. 1 (1992): 85–90.

Voglino, Barbara. *"Perverse Mind": Eugene O'Neill's Struggle with Closure.* London: Associated University Presses, 1999.

Wainscott, Ronald H. *Staging O'Neill: The Experimental Years, 1920–1934.* New Haven, Conn.: Yale University Press, 1988.

Wasserstrom, William. "Notes on Electricity: Henry Adams and Eugene O'Neill." *Psychocultural Review* 1 (1977): 161–178.

# *Emperor Jones, The* (completed, 1920; first produced, 1920)

*The Emperor Jones* is the first international triumph of EXPRESSIONISM by an American playwright; with it, Eugene O'Neill single-handedly introduced experimental AMERICAN THEATER to Europe and established his reputation as the United States' preeminent playwright. The November 1, 1920, premiere at the Provincetown Playhouse in New York City was a groundbreaking literary achievement for AFRICAN AMERICANS as well. *The Emperor Jones* was the first play to have a black man, CHARLES S. GILPIN, perform the leading role for a white theater company. On the day following its premiere, the *New York Times* reported astonishing news: Gilpin, along with being an "uncommonly powerful and imaginative performer . . . is a negro" (quoted in Miller 21). Moreover, though written by a white author, mostly in black dialect, and loaded with

Charles S. Gilpin as Brutus Jones in the Provincetown Players' production of *The Emperor Jones* at the Playwrights' Theatre, November 1, 1920 *(Courtesy of the Yale Collection of American Literature, Beinecke Rare Book and Manuscript Library)*

racial epithets, stereotyping, and unabashed repetition of the word *nigger*, the play was embraced by the black artistic community as well. James Weldon Johnson, one of the most influential promoters of African-American culture at the time, importantly observed that no previous effort to establish African-American actors and themes in the theater world "so far as the Negro is concerned, evoked more than favorable comment. . . . But [with] O'Neill's *The Emperor Jones* . . . another important page in the history of the Negro was written" (183–184).

## SYNOPSIS

### Scene 1

The main room of an emperor's palace, with porticos in the background that reveal tropical views of a small, unidentified Caribbean island. A native black woman furtively enters from the right. She carries a bundle bound to a stick and moves toward the main door with the clear intention of escape. Smithers materializes from under the portico. Smithers is a cockney, or British working-class, confidence man with a treacherous, ferretlike appearance; he is wearing the stereotypical garb of the adventurer colonialist—white riding suit, put-

tees, white cork helmet, a revolver, and an ammunition belt strapped to his waist. At first, the native woman does not see him, but when she does she makes a break for the door. Smithers lunges to intercept her and holds her fast by the shoulders. He interrogates the terrified woman and discovers that while the title character, Brutus Jones—formerly a Pullman porter of 10 years, but now the island's emperor—was sleeping, the natives have escaped to the hills and are plotting a rebellion, led by Jones's political enemy, Lem. Smithers receives this information with *"immense, mean satisfaction"* (1:1,032): "Serve 'im right! Puttin' on airs, the stinkin' nigger! . . . I only 'opes I'm there when they takes 'im out to shoot 'im" (1:1,033). No matter his views, Smithers profits from Jones's reign, and he whistles shrilly to alert him. The woman runs off the moment his back is turned.

Brutus Jones enters, enraged by the disturbance. In the STAGE DIRECTIONS, O'Neill describes Jones's appearance as *"typically Negroid, yet there is something decidedly distinctive about his face—an underlying strength of will, a hardy, self-reliant confidence in himself that inspires respect. His eyes are alive with a keen, cunning intelligence"* (1:1,033). Smithers hints around that the palace is unusually quiet, enjoying the rare moment when he knows something Jones, clearly his superior, does not. The repartee between the two thieves includes a good deal of exposition revealing details about them both. Before his arrival on the island, Jones served time for stabbing a man who had used loaded dice against him in a crap game and was imprisoned for the murder. He escaped prison by killing another man, his chain gang's prison guard. Now a fugitive on the run, Jones fled to the Caribbean. Smithers, in contrast, has lived on the island eight years longer than Jones but had accomplished nothing. Prior to the play's action, Jones gained his emperorship by convincing the native islanders he was supernatural. His one political rival, the island native Lem, had hired an assassin to kill him, but the assassin's gun misfired, and after Jones shot the killer dead, he declared to the bewildered crowd—whom Jones significantly considers, as white colonialists might, "low-flung, bush niggers"—that only a silver bullet could kill him. In order to substantiate the bluff, Jones had a silver bullet crafted for him, proclaiming to the natives that "I'm de on'y man in de world big enuff to git me" (1:1,036). "Oh Lawd," he laughs, showing his acceptance of an alien white religion followed by subtle slave imagery, "from dat time on I has dem all eatin' out of my hand. I cracks de whip and dey jumps through" (1:1,036). His motivation for tricking the natives has already been made clear: "De fuss and glory part of it, dat's only to turn de heads o' de low-flung, bush niggers dat's here. Dey wants de big circus show for deir money. I gives it to 'em an' I gits de money. (*with a grin*) De long green, dat's me every time!" (1:1,035).

Smithers chides Jones, who professes religious convictions, for never having converted the island natives to the Baptist Church; he then informs Jones what the old native woman has told him—that a rebellion led by Lem is brewing in the hills above the palace. The faraway sound of a tom-tom softly fills the air; its rhythm matches that of the normal human pulse, 72 beats a minute; in the stage directions, O'Neill instructs that the tom-tom beat should continue "*at a gradually accelerating rate from this point uninterruptedly to the very end of the play*" (1:1,041). Jones hears the tom-tom, and when Smithers explains it is part of a native war ritual to bolster their courage against a common enemy, Jones knows his game is up. "So long, white man," he tells Smithers and, self-assured that he will survive the insurgency, flees into the island's jungle forest (1:1,043). Prepared ahead of time for his inevitable ousting, Jones has memorized the island's labyrinthine jungle paths, stored caches of food along the way, and made plans to evade the rebel band by escaping to Martinique on a French gunboat.

### Scene 2

The edge of the "Great Forest." Now on the run, Jones is exhausted from the journey but relaxed and self-congratulatory. However, his sinecure as emperor has ill-trained him for the grueling trek through the jungle. Jones foreshadows what lies ahead by bolstering his resolve with the words, "Cheer up, nigger, de worst is yet to come" (1:1,044; remarkably, these are the same words [excluding the racial epithet] Mark Twain once wrote to his wife in response to her fears

of impending bankruptcy, though apparently O'Neill got the line from his friend TERRY CARLIN). Jones comes to realize his surroundings are unfamiliar and fails to locate the store of food he purposefully hid under a white stone, as the one stone has inexplicably proliferated into many. The first of a series of nightmares manifests itself as a jumble of "Little Formless Fears." O'Neill describes the ghostly creatures as "*black, shapeless, only their glittering eyes can be seen. If they have any describable form at all it is that of a grub-worm about the size of a creeping child*" (1,045–46). They laugh at him with a sound "*like a rustling of leaves,*" and Jones, startled, fires a shot into the trees. Their ethereal laughter ends, and Jones, "*with renewed confidence . . . plunges boldly into the forest*" (1:1,046).

### Scene 3

Deep in the thick canopy of the Great Forest. Moonlight offers Jones some visibility. His Panama hat is now gone, and his uniform is torn. He comes across a triangular clearing; an eerie clicking noise comes from the brush. The native rebels' unrelenting tom-tom continues to beat, only now a little louder and more rapidly. He has lost track of time and is growing tired, but he remains sanguine: "Never min'. It's all part o' de game. Dis night come to an end like everything else" (1:1,047). He whistles cheerfully but stops himself abruptly, fearful he might expose his location. In the moonlit triangle, the spectral form of the negro gambler Jeff, the man he had murdered for cheating, gradually comes into view. Jeff is wearing a Pullman porter's uniform and is found shooting craps on the jungle floor, "*casting them out with the regular, rigid, mechanical movements of an automaton*" (1:1,047). At first, Jones truly believes Jeff is alive, and he voices sincere delight that his victim survived the stabbing. But Jeff offers no response. Jones panics, firing into the bizarre apparition, which instantaneously disappears. The tom-tom beats louder and faster, and Jones, fearing the rebel band is closing in, runs headlong into the underbrush (1:1,048).

### Scene 4

Along a dirt road in the forest. Jones's uniform is now severely damaged. A road stretches from right front to left rear. Under the moonlight, the road appears *"ghastly and unreal"* (1:1,049). The heat is overwhelming, and Jones tears off his coat, revealing his bare torso, and takes off his spurs. As each item is symbolically discarded, so too is his identity as emperor. Continuing his monologue, Jones calms his fear of the "ha'nts," or ghosts, by recalling his parson's instruction to him that ghosts do not exist, that they are the purview of "ign'rent black niggers" (1:1,049); apparently, then, Jones has a predisposition to have such visions. He convinces himself that Jeff was just a figment of his overdeveloped imagination, that his fatigue and hunger are making him see things.

A prison chain gang enters from stage right. They are shackled, wear the striped black and white uniforms of convicts, and carry picks and shovels. A white man in a prison guard uniform carrying a Winchester rifle and a whip follows close behind. At the silent crack of his whip, the prisoners begin working on the road. *"Their movements, like those of Jeff in the preceding scene, are those of automatons,—rigid, slow, and mechanical"* (1:1,050). The prison guard cracks his whip again, this time at Jones, who obediently joins the gang in the subservient mindset of an institutionalized being. While Jones is at work, the guard lashes him on the back, causing him to wince. When the guard turns his back, Jones murderously raises his shovel high above the man's head. But the shovel unaccountably disappears, and Jones instead shoots the guard in the back, thus killing his life's two murder victims again and wasting a third bullet. The tom-tom continues beating, louder and faster.

### Scene 5

Another clearing, though this time its shape is circular. Importantly, this scene marks Jones's psychological shift from his personal guilt feelings to the racial ancestry he had treacherously denied by enslaving his African kinsmen on the island. His clothes are in their last stages of utter disrepair. He sits on a stump with his head in his hands, rocking back and forth praying in anguish, asking Jesus to absolve him of his sins and cease his tormenting visions. Jones then turns his attention on his patent leather shoes, which are destroyed.

From all sides, a group of Southern planters, *"young belles and dandies,"* and an auctioneer at a slave auction appear. Again, like Jeff and the members of the chain gang, *"There is something stiff, rigid, unreal, marionettish about their movements"* (1:1,053). The auctioneer silently orders Jones to mount the auction block to allow the planters a clear view of his body. The auctioneer gestures to Jones's terrific build and well-behaved demeanor. In a fear-driven rage, Jones shoots the auctioneer twice. The stage drops into darkness, and all we hear are Jones's screams as he flees again into the woods and the beat of the tom-tom, faster and louder. He now has only his silver bullet left to protect him from further paranormal apparitions.

### Scene 6

Another clearing, which is enclosed by creeping vines and arched tree trunks that give the impression of the hold of an old sailing ship. Jones's imagination has sent him further back in history to a slave ship loaded with captured Africans. The moon no longer illuminates the jungle floor, and Jones enters left on his hands and knees, groaning over his lost ammunition, the darkness of the forest, and his state of complete exhaustion. The stage gradually lightens to reveal two rows of captured slaves, who rock back and forth, simulating the movement of a ship on the open sea. From his prostrate position, Jones sees the ghastly scene, and he throws himself back down with his head in the dirt to hide from this terrifying group of apparitions (1:1,055). The slaves moan in unison, reaching a crescendo, seemingly directed by the sound of the tom-tom coming ever nearer, then settling down to a low murmur, then back up again repeatedly. Jones's voice involuntarily joins the others in this song of sorrow and pain. Again, the light fades into darkness, and Jones plunges wildly into the jungle (1:1,056).

### Scene 7

At the foot of a tree on the banks of a great river; an altar made from boulders lies near the base of the tree. Scene 7 takes Jones fully back to Africa, where a witch doctor sings and dances about a stone altar. The witch doctor's ritualistic pantomime fully indicts Jones for his crimes, and Jones instinctively ascertains that *"the forces of evil demand a sacrifice.*

*They must be appeased. . . . Jones seems to sense the meaning of this. It is he who must offer himself for sacrifice. He beats his forehead abjectly to the ground, moaning hysterically"* (1:1,058). In a peculiar bit of stage direction, O'Neill sends the witch doctor to the river's edge to call from its depths an African god in the form of a crocodile, whose enormous head emerges from the river bank; evidently the river is the Congo, since O'Neill specifically calls him a *"Congo witch-doctor"* in the stage directions (1:1,057).

The witch doctor then taps Jones with his wand and points to the river. The crocodile lifts himself onto the riverbank, and Jones wriggles toward him. Jones penitently accepts the sinful nature of the crimes he committed on the island, as while he moves in the direction of the crocodile, he cries out for Jesus' mercy for "dis po' sinner" (1:1,058). In his final lines, Jones prays to "Lawd Jesus" to save him, starkly contrasting the white god of the enslavers with the pagan god of his African ancestry (1:1,059). Jesus does rescue him, for the time being, as he is snapped out of a horror-stricken reverie by his own pious rant and remembers the silver bullet is still left. He fires at the crocodile, which drops back into the water. The witch doctor jumps behind the tree, and Jones *"lies with his face to the ground, his arms outstretched, whimpering with fear"* while the tom-tom beats fill the air with a *"baffled but revengeful power"* (1:1,059).

### Scene 8

Dawn the following morning, again at the edge of the Great Forest, the same as scene 2. Smithers appears among a group of native rebel soldiers, led by Jones's political nemesis, Lem. The opportunistic Smithers has now joined the rebels, and he and Lem dispute Jones's fate. Smithers, with sustained respect for Jones's abilities, refuses to believe the group of islanders could catch him—"Aw! Garn! 'E's a better man than the lot o' you put together. I 'ates the sight o' 'im but I'll say that for 'im." Lem insists in the stereotypical dialect of a "savage," "We cotch him" (1:1,060). Rifle shots are heard in the jungle. Lem informs Smithers that he armed his men with silver bullets to overcome Jones's magic. The rebel soldiers come through the forest carrying Jones's dead body. The mythic nature of Jones's

demise in itself inspires admiration, even from his enemies. "Silver bullets!" Smithers exclaims with an ironic smirk in the final line of the play, "Gawd blimey, but yer died in the 'eighth o' style, any'ow!" (1:1,061).

## COMMENTARY

On the 50th anniversary of Eugene O'Neill's death, Cornell West, one of the United States' preeminent black studies scholars, referred to O'Neill as "the great blues man of American theater." In an interview on National Public Radio, West compared him to Martin Luther King, Jr., because his plays were meant, as King's speeches, "to redeem the soul of America"; to the jazz great Charlie Parker because both had created art in "blood, sweat, and tears"; and to a fellow recipient of the NOBEL PRIZE IN LITERATURE, Toni Morrison, because like her, he was determined to show the humanity of African Americans through literature, certainly in *The Emperor Jones* but also in *The* DREAMY KID and *ALL GOD'S* CHILLUN GOT WINGS (West 2003).

Starting with the Napoleonic figure of Brutus Jones the emperor, O'Neill's deliberate project was to strip away layer upon layer of civilization to reveal humanity's most basic instincts. With a black protagonist at the center of the drama, a radical departure in American theater, O'Neill's goal was nothing less than to present to his audiences, as West phrased it, "the unmasking of civilization." Indeed, when only 18 years old, the Harlem Renaissance poet Langston Hughes published one of his earliest poems the year after *The Emperor Jones* appeared, "The Negro Speaks of Rivers" (1921). This poem so unmistakably echoes O'Neill's meaning, as well as referencing the riverbank upon which Jones is metaphorically slain, that it bears quoting here in its entirety:

I've known rivers:
I've known rivers ancient as the world and
    older than the flow of
    human blood in human veins.

My soul has grown deep like the rivers.

I bathed in the Euphrates when dawns were
    young.

I built my hut near the Congo and it lulled me
    to sleep.
I looked upon the Nile and raised the pyramids
    above it.
I heard the singing of the Mississippi when
    Abe Lincoln
      went down to New Orleans, and I've seen its
    muddy bosom turn all golden in the sunset.

I've known rivers:
Ancient, dusky rivers.
My soul has grown deep like the rivers.

The Emperor Jones was not the first American
play to rise above the grotesque distortions of 19th-
and early 20th-century minstrelsy, the enormously
popular and overtly racist variety shows that carica-
tured the shuffling "happy darky" for white American audiences. (James Weldon Johnson credits the
black dramatist Ridgely Torrence with that distinction—by 1917, Torrence had already produced three
one-act plays with the Coloured Players at Madison
Square Garden.) In fact, two of O'Neill's early plays,
*The* MOON OF THE CARIBBEES and *The Dreamy Kid*
had black characters; but the 1918 production of
*Moon* had an all-white cast, and the cast of *The
Dreamy Kid,* produced the following year, was all
black. Furthermore, Edward Sheldon's *The Nigger,*
a highly controversial answer to Thomas Dixon's
profoundly racist *The Clansman* (1905; later made
into the 1915 silent film *The Birth of a Nation* by D.
W. Griffith), also preceded *The Emperor Jones.* But
Johnson submits that while Torrence and O'Neill
may not have been the first American playwrights
"to experiment with the Negro as a theme for theatre . . . they were the first to use the Negro and
Negro life as pure dramatic material" (185), rather
than as political or racist polemical devices.

Just as he would with its immediate successor,
*The* HAIRY APE, O'Neill structured *The Emperor
Jones* in eight scenes. The middle six, as O'Neill
critic Virginia Floyd describes them, "form one prolonged dramatic monologue, part dialogue . . . part
soliloquy" (205): The first three—scenes 2–4—
delve into Jones's burdensome conscience, which
is deftly symbolic of black life after enslavement;
the next three—scenes 5–7—take us back through
the black collective consciousness (thus adopting

the approach of psychologist Carl Jung, whose work
in the burgeoning field of psychoanalysis made a
great impression on O'Neill) of Africans during and before their enslavement. Scenes 1 and 8
bracket the expressionism of the middle six scenes
with comparatively realistic settings and dialogue.
The *"Little Formless Fears"* of scene 2 symbolize
the everyday, indistinct anxieties that virtually
all people suffer, though few of us recognize their
provenance. But as the play moves forward, the
nightmares become more distinctive, referencing
specific causes for the external stimuli that trigger
traumatic psychological responses.

O'Neill applies Jung's theory of a dark "shadow"
lurking within our psyches here. Jung believed that
the shadow side of our psyches should be considered
"evil," but the more we consciously acknowledge
our shadow, the less it manifests itself in destructive
behavior on ourselves and others. In his later experimental play LAZARUS LAUGHED, we find one of the
most Shakespearean lines in the O'Neill canon, one
that reflects Carl Jung's shadow concept and explains
the "formless little fears." Lazarus explains that "men
are too cowardly to understand" the meaning of eternity, "And so the worms of their little fears eat them
and grow fat and terrible and become their jealous
gods they must appease with lies!" (2:611).

Brutus Jones's ghostly avatars from the past—
his "han'ts," as he calls them—reflect the bizarre
distortions of expressionistic theater that employed
grotesque and exaggerated effects to highlight
characters' psyches. Eerily, none of the "han'ts"
are given dialogue; The movements of Jeff and the
members of the chain gang are *"those of automatons—rigid, slow, and mechanical"* (1:1,050); the
southern slave owners are *"marrionettish"* (1:1,053),
like the Fifth Avenue pedestrians in scene 5 of
*The Hairy Ape*; and the characters seem to regress
toward their natural origins as Jones moves backward in time, away from the modern black world of
prison and enslavement.

O'Neill innovatively employs two additional stage
techniques that propel the action forward. One is the
use of a tom-tom drum, which begins near the end of
scene 1 at the normal pulse of the human heart, 72
beats per minute, but *"continues at a gradually accelerating rate from this point uninterruptedly to the very end*

*of the play*" (1:1,041). The drumbeat gets faster as the rebels close in on Jones's position and while Jones's nightmares increasingly horrify him. Before writing *The Emperor Jones*, O'Neill read about "religious feasts in the Congo" where tribal members begin drumming at 72 beats per minute; then the beat "is slowly intensified until the heartbeat of everyone present corresponds to the frenzied beat of the drum. . . . There was an idea and an experiment," O'Neill continued, "how would this sort of thing work on an audience in the theater?" (quoted in Clark 104). This drum technique, however, was not unique. The American dramatist Austin Strong used virtually the same idea in his 1915 MELODRAMA *The Drums of Oude* (Clark 105). But when the drums combine with the terrifying imagery of Jeff, the chain gang, the auction, the slave galley, and the crocodile god—along with the lights progressively dimming as we dive ever-deeper into Jones's conscience and his African lineage—the dramatic effect, if done well, is spellbinding.

The play's potential to expand the boundaries of experimental theater are limitless. Most recently, the Wooster Group shocked audiences by having a white woman (Kate Valk) play Brutus Jones in blackface. Along with the disturbing fact that blackface was still able to provoke racial outrage by the late 1990s, this potentially odious idea, Johan Callens argues, is meant to demonstrate "the unstable, homologous positions of the so-called hierarchical and immutable differences underlying the racial (and gender) ideology, exposing the latter as a case of the 'primitive' mythological thinking which the black emperor supposedly substantiates" (46). With this in mind, Nathan Irvin Huggins, the prominent historian of black America, is particularly instructive when he remarks of Brutus Jones's character that "here was no stereotype of the negro character. Emperor Jones' ultimate fall, although superstition is involved, occurs because the artifices that have propped him up have been removed. So, exposed and defenseless Jones—like any other man—falls victim to his fear and his essential, primitive nature" (quoted in Shaughnessy 162n).

Along with the more evident race issues in the play, many of O'Neill's political ideas stem from his early education in PHILOSOPHICAL ANARCHISM. There is no good or evil, the founding father of

Kate Valk, a white woman in blackface, playing Brutus Jones in the Wooster Group's production of *The Emperor Jones*. Photo by Paula Court *(Courtesy the Wooster Group)*

philosophical anarchism Max Stirner insisted in his treatise *The Ego and His Own*, as one can murder freely so long as it is *legal*, which makes "morality nothing else than *loyalty*" (65). But he continues that "according to our theories of penal law, with whose 'improvement in conformity to the times' people are tormenting themselves in vain, they want to punish men for this or that 'inhumanity'; and therein they make the silliness of these theories especially plain by their consistency, *hanging the little thieves and letting the big ones run*" (153, emphasis mine), a line Jones applies to his own brand of criminality in scene 1 (1:1,035).

*The Emperor Jones* is O'Neill's most resonant imaginative enacting of this worldview. Smithers' is greedy, treacherous, and lazy, not coincidentally the three characteristics most commonly associated with blackness in the white mainstream American mind but also, in the context of philosophical anarchism, with the business interests that propel corrupted states (and to the anarchist, all of them are) forward. In scene 1, Smithers has informed Jones of a native revolt against his sovereignty, and Jones is preparing to flee into the jungle forest, with a plan to escape by boat:

SMITHERS—(*with curiosity*) And I bet you got yer pile o' money 'id safe some place.

JONES—(*with satisfaction*) I sho' has! And it's in a foreign bank where no pusson don't ever git it out but me no matter what come. You didn't s'pose I was holdin' down dis Emperor job for de glory in it, did you? Sho'! De fuss and glory part of it, dat's only to turn de heads o' de low-flung, bush niggers dat's here. Dey wants de big circus show for deir money. I gives it to 'em an' I gits de money. (*with a grin*) De long green, dat's me every time! (*then rebukingly*) But you ain't got no kick agin me, Smithers. I'se paid you back all you done for me many times. Ain't I pertected you and winked at all de crooked tradin' you been doin' right out in de broad day. Sho'. I has—and me makin' laws to stop it at de same time! (*He chuckles.*)

SMITHERS—(*grinning*) But, meanin' no 'arm, you been grabbin' right and left yourself, ain't yer? Look at the taxes you've put on 'em! Blimey! You've squeezed 'em dry!

JONES—(*chuckling*) No, dey ain't all dry yet. I'se still heah, ain't I?

SMITHERS—(*smiling at his secret thought*) They're dry right now, you'll find out. (*changing the subject abruptly*) And as for me breakin' laws, you've broke 'em all yerself just as fast as yer made 'em.

JONES—Ain't I de Emperor? De laws don't go for him. (*judicially*) You heah what I tells you, Smithers. *Dere's little stealin' like you does, and dere's big stealin' like I does.* For de little stealin' dey gits you in jail soon or late. For de big stealin' dey makes you Emperor and puts you in de Hall o' Fame when you croaks. (*reminiscently*) If dey's one thing I learns in ten years on de Pullman ca's listenin' to de white quality talk, it's dat same fact. And when I gits a chance to use it I winds up Emperor in two years. (1:1,035, emphasis mine)

Significantly, the only line that survives in the 1933 Hollywood adaptation with Paul Robeson as Jones is the Stirnerian line *"Dere's little stealin' like you does, and dere's big stealin' like I does."* The idea that it was white businessmen on the Pullman trains who taught him "big stealin'" is omitted.

Contemporary African political theorists contend that the most important explanation for the continent's current ongoing turmoil—the police states, corruption, AIDS, religious persecution, and genocide that have plagued the continent since the end of the colonial period—is that once freed from European rule, the only models African nations had to emulate were the police states, corruption, rape, religious restrictions, and random acts of murder that colonial powers had employed to control African nations for decades. Jones is, at bottom, a race traitor, lending some connection to his treacherous namesake—Brutus, Julius Caesar's betrayer. Keeping this in mind, along with Jones's misguided adoption of white methods of dominance, it is reasonable to read O'Neill's ending as a warning to African Americans not to take on white political, religious, and cultural forms to replace or deny their African roots. By not sacrificing himself to the god of his ancestors, Jones is, after all, destroyed by the victims of white colonialism and the silver currency that motivated them both.

## CHARACTERS

**Jones, Brutus** Former Pullman porter and convicted murderer, Jones betrays his race by taking on the role of a white colonialist and securing, through deception, the emperorship of a small Caribbean island. Jones is no ordinary criminal, however. Once audiences get past the heavy black dialect—which they would mainly associate with the minstrelsy figures of the popular stage—it becomes plain that Jones is a resourceful, self-confident, and intelligent character, far more sympathetic than Smithers, the Cockney trader and confidence man who also lives there. Jones is clearly the more intelligent of the two. After only two years, he learned the local dialect, began teaching the native islanders English, and successfully crowned himself emperor of the island's population. When an assassin's gun misfired, Jones convinced the natives that only a silver bullet could kill him.

When Jones realizes there is a native revolt against his sovereignty, he flees into the jungle forest with a plan to escape the island by boat. Over the course of his flight, he encounters a series of bizarre apparitions that lead him down through the history of African oppression. In the end, he is tracked down by the island natives, who shoot him dead with silver bullets. As O'Neill critic Virginia Floyd writes of this ending, "even in death Jones evokes awe and respect. He had died as he desired, perpetuating the myth that made him emperor" (208).

O'Neill drew much of Brutus Jones's character from a NEW LONDON personality named Adam Scott, an African American who served as bartender, bodyguard, and spiritual guide to O'Neill and his radical New London circle in 1912. In spite of Scott's morally questionable line of work, each Sunday he put away his apron and towel and took on the rather contradictory role of elder at a local Baptist church. O'Neill BIOGRAPHERS Arthur and Barbara Gelb have traced some of Scott's witticisms directly to Brutus Jones. Given his ungodly profession, O'Neill and his friends used to razz Scott, a respected friend and incisive mentor, for being at the same time a bartender and an elder at the church. Scott's response, for his part, was that "after Sunday, I lay Jesus on the shelf" (Gelb 349) while Jones responds to Smithers, "it don't git me nothin' to do missionary work for de Baptist Church. Is'e after de coin, an' I lays my Jesus on de shelf for de time bein'" (1:1,042).

O'Neill's chief historical source for Jones was the murderous Haitian dictator Vilbrun Guillaume Sam. According to O'Neill, an "old circus man" once told him the story of how Sam had spread a rumor among the Haitian people that only a silver bullet could kill him and that if it came to it, he would be the one to pull the trigger (quoted in Clark 104). The concept appealed to O'Neill as a theatrical device, so much so that the play's working title was "The Silver Bullet." Sam's political fate clearly reflects the plot of *The Emperor Jones*. Before completing the first year of his dictatorship, Sam was hunted down by a vengeful mob. After discovering the impudent tyrant hiding behind a curtain in the French embassy, the throng of rebels gruesomely dismembered his body and paraded his remains through the poverty-stricken streets of the Haitian capital.

**Lem**  Brutus Jones's political rival on the island. Lem hired an assassin to kill Jones, but the assassin's gun misfired, and Jones claimed that only a silver bullet could harm him. Lem believed this but continued to stir up a rebellion and armed his band of rebels with silver bullets. In the end, Lem's men find and kill the fugitive emperor.

Lem is a colonialist caricature of native savagery. O'Neill describes him as a "*heavy-set, ape-faced old savage of the extreme African type, dressed only in a loin cloth*" (1:1,060), and he speaks in a way that calls to mind both Tarzan and Tonto at once: "Lead bullet no kill him. He got um strong charm. I cook um money, make um silver bullet, make um strong charm, too" (1:1,061). This dialect, as Joel Pfister points out in his historical look at O'Neill's work, is reminiscent of the accent Charles S. Gilpin was required to adopt when playing a black preacher in John Drinkwater's *Abraham Lincoln* (1919). As James Weldon Johnson remarked of the part, the dialect was one "such as no American Negro would ever use . . . a slightly darkened pidgin-English or the form of speech a big Indian chief would employ in talking with the Great White Father at Washington" (quoted in Pfister 132). Nevertheless, Lem's struggle, in the end, is a just one. Though he superstitiously accepts Jones's assertion that he is supernatural, he recognizes Jones for what he is: a colonialist exploiting the islanders for his own personal gain. That he is successful in thwarting Jones is both a warning to white colonialists and possibly to black Americans to avoid such racial treason.

**Smithers, Henry**  A cockney, or working-class, British trader. Smithers is greedy, treacherous, and lazy, not coincidentally the three characteristics most commonly associated with blackness in the white mainstream American mind of the early 20th century. Smithers is an unsuccessful confidence man who drinks too much and is far too lazy to accomplish what Jones has done, though he has lived on the island eight years longer than Jones. To

Smithers's credit, though he felt Jones was "puttin' on airs" as a black emperor, he recognized Jones's superior abilities (1:1,033).

## BIBLIOGRAPHY

Callens, Johan. "'Black is white, I yells it out louder 'n deir loudest': Unraveling the Wooster Group's *The Emperor Jones.*" *The Eugene O'Neill Review* 26 (2004): 43–69.

Clark, Barrett H. *Eugene O'Neill: The Man and His Plays.* Rev. ed. New York: Dover, 1947.

Dowling, Robert M. "On Eugene O'Neill's 'Philosophical Anarchism.'" *Eugene O'Neill Review* 29 (Spring 2007): 50–72.

Floyd, Virginia. *The Plays of Eugene O'Neill: A New Assessment.* New York: Ungar, 1985.

Gelb, Arthur, and Barbara Gelb. *O'Neill: Life with Monte Cristo.* New York: Applause Books, 2000.

Johnson, James Weldon. *Black Manhattan.* Reprint. New York: Da Capo Press, 1991.

Miller, Jordan Y. *Playwright's Progress: O'Neill and the Critics.* Chicago: Scott, Foresman and Company, 1965.

Pfister, Joel. *Staging Depth: Eugene O'Neill and the Politics of Psychological Discourse.* Chapel Hill: University of North Carolina Press, 1995.

Shaughnessy, Edward L. "O'Neill's African and Irish-Americans: Stereotypes or 'Faithful Realism'?" In *The Cambridge Companion to Eugene O'Neill,* edited by Michael Manheim, 148–163. New York: Cambridge University Press, 1998.

Stirner, Max. *The Ego and His Own: The Case of the Individual against Authority.* Reprint, translated by Steven T. Byington with an introduction by J. L. Walker. New York, Benjamin R. Tucker, 1907.

West, Cornell. Interview, *The Tavis Smiley Show,* National Public Radio, November 26, 2003.

# *Exorcism: A Play of Anti-Climax* (completed, 1919; first produced, 1920; destroyed)

Eugene O'Neill's destroyed one-act play *Exorcism* is a dramatization of the night on New Year's Eve 1911, or some time in the first weeks of January 1912 at JIMMY "THE PRIEST'S" bar in New York City when O'Neill attempted suicide by self-administering an overdose of Veronal. As closely autobiographical as *The STRAW* and *LONG DAY'S JOURNEY INTO NIGHT,* the action in *Exorcism* would come chronologically just before *Long Day's Journey,* which takes place in summer 1912, and a year before *The Straw,* which recounts O'Neill's battle with tuberculosis in fall 1912 and spring 1913. A terrific loss for O'Neill scholars, *Exorcism* would have been, biographer Louis Sheaffer believes, "the most reliable index of Eugene's frame of mind after his suicide attempt" (1968, 214). O'Neill wrote the one-acter in the summer or early fall of 1919, the same period when he wrote *Honor among the Bradleys* and *The Trumpet,* neither of which survive. After *Exorcism*'s premiere at the Provincetown Playhouse in New York City on March 26, 1920, O'Neill abruptly cancelled the production. Some time later, he contacted the Provincetown Players' secretary, M. Eleanor "Fitzi" Fitzgerald, and requested all extant copies of the script, which he destroyed upon receipt. In 1922, he wrote to the GREENWICH VILLAGE bookstore proprietor Frank Shay, "'Exorcism' has been destroyed . . . and the sooner all memory of it dies the better" (quoted in Sheaffer 1973, 12).

O'Neill BIOGRAPHERS suspect that his decision to destroy the play came from the fact that it was either too revealing or too flawed. This last is doubtful, as much worse writing survives; the first is closer to the truth, though Stephen A. Black probably comes closest when he speculates that of O'Neill's autobiographical works, *Exorcism* probably would have produced a devastating reaction from his parents. In *Exorcism,* O'Neill's protagonist, Ned Malloy, overdoses on morphine, not Veronal. Given his mother's long addiction to morphine, one that effectively devastated O'Neill's family life for more than two decades and the vital tragic revelation of *Long Day's Journey* (which O'Neill never wanted produced), along with his father's recent stroke, one can hardly blame the playwright for striking it from his oeuvre (Black 257, Gelb 332).

Most critics disliked this tell-all account of O'Neill's suicide attempt at Jimmy "the Priest's," though the critic ALEXANDER WOOLLCOTT's review in the *New York Times* praised *Exorcism* as "interesting all the way through . . . an uncommonly good play by Eugene O'Neill" (quoted in Cargill et al. 142). This review and a series of interviews conducted by biographer Louis Sheaffer with actors Jasper Deeter, who played Ned Malloy, and Alan MacAteer, whose role closely resembled O'Neill's friend and flophouse roommate JAMES FINDLATER BYTH—the model for James Anderson in "TOMORROW" and "Jimmy Tomorrow" in *The ICEMAN COMETH*—provide all that we know of the plot. Deeter recollected that the protagonist, Ned Malloy, felt embattled by his wife, who was filing for divorce, and by a prostitute he hired for adultery charges to be substantiated by witnesses (Sheaffer 1968, 210). This precisely follows O'Neill's tormenting experience with KATHLEEN JENKINS, his first wife, who received a divorce based on O'Neill's having hired a call girl to bed down with him while witnesses looked on (New York State law required proof of cause for divorce); it was a humiliating experience that prompted O'Neill's attempted suicide.

Perhaps a more probing question than why O'Neill destroyed the play, then, is why he would have written it in the first place. Louis Sheaffer provides a powerfully convincing explanation that deserves to be quoted at length:

> O'Neill's action in writing and then tearing up the too autobiographical "Exorcism" testifies to a duality in his nature. One of the most withdrawn of individuals, he was at the same time subject to a force of virtually equal strength to bare himself, to tell all, from a need to explain and justify himself. This need, this drive, was at the bottom of his turning playwright; properly speaking, he did not choose to become a playwright but was driven to it. (1968, 210)

In his review, Woollcott describes Ned Malloy as having come from a "substantial and correct family," a middle-class young man "so full of contempt for [his parents] that he has walked out, head high, and fallen into the gutter" (quoted in Cargill et al. 142). O'Neill's surviving STAGE DIRECTIONS describe the play as set in the middle of March and taking place in a filthy room littered with books, old newspapers, splintered furniture, and cigarette butts. The room

exactly describes his own at Jimmy "the Priest's," being on the "top story [of] a squalid rooming house occupying the three upper floors of a building on a side street near the downtown waterfront, New York City—the ground floor being a saloon of the lowest type of grog shop" (quoted in Floyd *at Work* 7). Ned Malloy's personal demons plague him, and he rejects his parents' advice to go west and work on a farm. He swallows a presumably lethal dose of morphine, dispassionately utters what he believes will be his last words, "That's over" (Woollcott 142), and assumes a fetal position on his bed. After he lies unconscious for 24 hours, two friends from the bar burst into his room and revive him, as James Byth and others had for O'Neill. Ned awakens, witnesses his "two drunken friends, who are bibulously pleased with themselves for having yanked him back from the brink of the grave" (Woollcott 142), and experiences a revived appreciation and acceptance for life. He has symbolically returned from the grave, his demons "exorcised."

After his own suicide attempt, Louis Sheaffer writes, "like his protagonist, he felt that he had exorcised his 'devils'; at last he was free to leave [Jimmy "the Priest's"] and make his peace with his family" (1968, 214). Furthermore, Stephen Black remarks that O'Neill would then "spend the rest of his life trying to understand and express the way the world looked when one subjectively accepted mortality, and he would eventually create numerous characters who take themselves to the brink of death and then react to what they have seen" (1968, 122). Travis Bogard regards Ned Malloy as O'Neill's "first Lazarus" (1968, 109)—the biblical figure Jesus Christ brings back to life. O'Neill explores this theme head-on in his 1926 full-length play *LAZARUS LAUGHED*. O'Neill himself experienced yet another "rebirth" a year later after being diagnosed with tuberculosis and spending the first half of 1913 in the GAYLORD FARM SANATORIUM for tubercular patients.

Upon his release from Gaylord on June 3, 1913, O'Neill was informed that his friend James Byth, one of his saviors in 1912, had died after falling from his bedroom window at Jimmy "the Priest's." It was a tragedy, possibly accidental (Alexander 22), that O'Neill always believed was suicide.

Three years later, still haunted by his friend's death, he wrote a short story about the incident, "Tomorrow." Another friend's suicide took place much closer to the time of *Exorcism*'s composition. On January 22, 1918, his longtime companion and entrée into Greenwich Village bohemian circles, Louis Holladay, overdosed on heroin. Like Byth, questions exist as to whether it was a suicide or a mistake, but Holladay's death was undoubtedly caused by the fact that he was drinking alcohol on top of the drug—a lethal combination. These harrowing incidents held sustained importance in O'Neill's mind until his death in 1953. *Exorcism* would be O'Neill's last one-act play until HUGHIE, one of the world's great masterpieces of the form, in 1942.

## BIBLIOGRAPHY

Alexander, Doris. *Eugene O'Neill's Last Plays: Separating Art from Autobiography.* Athens: University of Georgia Press, 2005.

Black, Stephen A. *Eugene O'Neill: Beyond Mourning and Tragedy.* New Haven, Conn.: Yale University Press, 1999.

Bogard, Travis. *Contour in Time: The Plays of Eugene O'Neill.* Rev. ed. New York: Oxford University Press, 1988.

Cargill, Oscar, N. Bryllion Fagin, and William J. Fisher, eds. *O'Neill and His Plays: Four Decades of Criticism.* New York: New York University Press, 1961.

Floyd, Virginia, ed. *Eugene O'Neill at Work: Newly Released Ideas for his Plays.* New York: Ungar, 1981.

Gelb, Arthur, and Barbara Gelb. *O'Neill: Life with Monte Cristo.* New York: Applause Books, 2000.

O'Neill, Eugene. *The Iceman Cometh.* In *Complete Plays,* vol. 3, 1932–1943, edited by Travis Bogard. New York: Library of American, 1988, 561–711.

———. "Tomorrow." In *The Unknown O'Neill: Unpublished or Unfinished Writings of Eugene O'Neill,* edited by Travis Bogard. New Haven, Conn.: Yale University Press, 1988, 313–331.

Sheaffer, Louis. *O'Neill: Son and Artist.* Boston: Little, Brown, 1973.

———. *O'Neill: Son and Playwright.* Boston: Little, Brown, 1968.

# First Man: A Play in Four Acts, The (completed, 1921; first produced, 1922)

Eugene O'Neill began writing *The First Man*, with the working title "The Original Man," in the summer of 1920, just after receiving his first PULITZER PRIZE for BEYOND THE HORIZON. His wife, AGNES BOULTON, had given birth to a son, SHANE RUDRAIGHE O'NEILL, the previous year (on October 30, 1919), and though Shane was O'Neill's second child, the infant was the first to require any degree of parenting on the playwright's part. (He had not seen his first son, EUGENE O'NEILL, JR., since 1911 if he had at all and would not get to know him for another year.) The story of an obsessive workaholic who revolts against his servile wife's desire to have a child, *The First Man* is the most searing self-authored indictment of O'Neill's inability to endure the personal and professional sacrifices that parenthood demands. For its sardonic look at traditional family values and structural reasons as well, the play received lackluster reviews at best. It was first produced at the Neighborhood Playhouse in New York City on March 4, 1922, and O'Neill himself was never particularly enthusiastic about the work, saying first that he was "at least satisfied" with the play (quoted in Estrin 74), as opposed to "ANNA CHRISTIE" (which he never liked, though it won him a second Pulitzer) and later admitted he wished he had destroyed it along with three others—GOLD, The FOUNTAIN, and WELDED (Estrin 105). Perhaps the most astonishing feature of this prosaic work of REALISM is that he wrote it within a year of The EMPEROR JONES and The HAIRY APE, two of the most innovative expressionistic dramas ever to appear on the American stage.

## SYNOPSIS

### Act 1

Curtis and Martha Jayson's living room at their house in Bridgetown, Connecticut (probably NEW LONDON, but possibly Bridgeport), on a late afternoon in the fall. The Jaysons are entertaining Edward Bigelow, Curtis's best friend from his college days at Cornell University. Martha and Bigelow talk about his children as Curtis, a renowned anthropologist, reads a scientific journal. We find through exposition that Martha was raised in the mining camps of Nevada. Curtis and Martha met while he was working as a mining engineer (a vocation inspired by the western tales of Bret Harte). He then had a stint as a prospector, then a geologist, and finally settled on anthropology; all of these professions, we are to understand, speak to his powerfully romantic spirit. Curtis announces his plan to accept an offer from a high-profile anthropological expedition in the Tibetan highlands to seek out evidence of the "First Man," popularly known as the "Missing Link." Martha is visibly disappointed by the news but stifles her feelings. Curtis talks about the "chance in a million" to find the First Man before he departs to let Bigelow continue his "confessions of a fond parent"; when Bigelow responds good-naturedly that his old friend knows nothing about parenthood, Curtis grimly retorts that Bigelow is "forgetting" something (2:60) and goes to his study. When they were in Nevada, the Jaysons lost two children to pneumonia, and that tragedy ostensibly instigated a 10-year anthropological tour of the world and a compact between Curtis and Martha never to have children again.

Curtis's youngest sister, Lily Jayson, enters the room. Bigelow departs, promising to collect Martha later for a drive with the children. Lily warns Martha that the Bridgetown scandalmongers, with the Jayson family in the lead, have begun talking about how much time she spends with Bigelow, a reformed rake. Martha resents the insinuation, but Lily assures her that, along with herself, "you'll have to make compromises, too—if you want any peace" (2:63). She adds that perhaps having children would put a stop to the rumor mill, particularly if it was a boy, since Curtis's siblings have as yet only produced girls. Martha is 38 years old, and Lily continues that if Martha were to break her promise to Curtis, she must do so immediately—"If you want my advice, you go right ahead and don't tell Curtis until it is a fact he'll have to learn to like, willy-nilly" (2:65–66). Martha's contrite expression reveals that she has already done just that. She is, in fact, two months pregnant.

The doorbell rings, and Lily instructs Martha to be brave, as the entire Jayson clan has come to visit. Mrs. Davidson, the grande dame of the family and Curtis's great-aunt, enters, followed by Curtis's sister Esther and her husband, Mark Sheffield. Lily cruelly informs them that Martha had forgotten the visit and has made plans with Bigelow to go for a drive with his children. Next she throws a cutting remark at Mark, a corporate lawyer, and Mrs. Davidson scolds her for her impetuousness with advice that she needs "a husband and the responsibility of children" (2:67); the aunt then turns to Martha and pointedly asks whether she does not agree that "every woman who is able should have children" (2:67). Martha halfheartedly concurs.

Curtis enters and asks for Martha's help with work. The two retreat into Curtis's adjoining study. John Jayson, John, Jr., and Dick—Curtis's father and two brothers—enter with John, Jr.'s, wife, Emily, filling the room with a total of eight Jaysons (if one includes the in-laws Mark and Emily). Lily recklessly informs the tribe that Martha is two months pregnant. Mrs. Davidson is overjoyed, particularly at Lily's insistence that it will be a boy; the rest begin doing the math and skeptically wonder over the timing of conception, as Curtis was in New York around the time. Martha enters, and the atmosphere grows chilly.

After some strained discussion about Curtis's work, a car outside honks loudly. Martha calls for Curt to relieve her and exits to join Bigelow. Irritated by the interruption but compliant, Curtis announces he has just received authorization for Martha to join the expedition, and he will surprise her with the news the next day, her birthday. The family realizes he is unaware of Martha's pregnancy, which heightens their suspicion all the more. They hint it would be unwise for Martha to travel to the Far East if she were pregnant, and he explodes, "No, I tell you! It is impossible!" (2:76). He leaves the room to change shoes for a walk, and the curtain falls with a vacuous comment from Jayson, Sr.: "Well, if I were sure it would all blow over without any open scandal, I'd offer up a prayer of thanks" (2:77).

### Act 2

The following morning in Curtis Jayson's study. The room is haphazardly strewn with books, manuscript papers, and journals, but it is also strikingly adorned with trophies and skins from a menagerie of exotic animals—*"tiger, polar bear, leopard, lion, etc."* (2:78). Curtis and Bigelow are listening to Martha play with the Bigelow children outside. Bigelow reinforces Lily Jayson's warning in act 1 that Martha is caught in a desperate social whirlpool that she must not navigate alone. He reminds Curtis, who has been too preoccupied with work to notice, that the scandal Bigelow caused before his wife's death and subsequent devotion to his children caused Bridgetown to devote "its entire leisure attention to stinging me to death" with scandal and alienation (2:79). His reformation is sincere, however, as since his wife's death he has devoted his life fully to his children. Martha enters, exhausted from playing. Once Bigelow exits, Martha pleads with Curtis not to follow through with the expedition. She whispers in his ear that she is pregnant. Curtis, appalled that he was never consulted, cannot contain his *"disappointment and aversion"* (2:83); he reveals his own news about her going on the expedition and chides her for betraying the memories of their dead children. "If you had just the tiniest bit of feminine in you," she responds forlornly, "but you're so utterly masculine, dear!" (2:85)

Martha confesses in a lengthy monologue that while camping among natives in China's Yunnan Province, she experienced a revelation that "all the wandering about the world, and all the romance and excitement I'd enjoyed in it, appeared an aimless, futile business, chasing around in a circle in an effort to avoid touching reality" (2:86). She relates a moment when she saw an ugly local woman with a child in her arms who made the woman look more beautiful than Martha considered herself. Curtis retorts with a monologue of his own (one containing no less than 15 first-person pronouns): He relies on her for his work, he says, which along with her love and devotion is the only thing that provides his life with meaning; as such, he refuses to allow a "stranger" to interfere with the life (his life) they had built together (2:87). He suggests she get an abortion, but Martha grows helplessly dejected and concludes, "I've spoiled you by giving up my life so completely to yours" (2:88). Curtis asks if his love is not enough for her, to which she

responds, "Yes, you love me. But who am I? You don't know" (2:89). Curtis cries out in heartbroken torment, "Martha! Stop! This is terrible!" (2:89). The curtain falls with the two staring at each other in mutual apprehension.

### Act 3

The same setting at three o'clock in the morning the following spring. John Jayson, Sr., is staring blankly into the flames of the study's fireplace. Dick comes through the door with terrifying sounds of pain and misery trailing in after him from the rooms above. Dick, a World War I veteran, submits that Martha's labor is more difficult to bear than soldiers' screams from "No Man's Land," the contested space between occupied trenches at the front. The family still suspects that Bigelow is the father, and Jayson guiltily voices his preference for the baby to die rather than face the public backlash that such a scandal might engender. Dick solemnly agrees.

Lily comes in, looking as harrowed as Dick after witnessing over 24 hours of Martha's terrible trial in labor; she pronounces herself "a life-member of the birth-control league" (2:91). Esther, Emily, and John, Jr., join them. "I thought I went through something when mine was born," Esther says in horror, "but this is too awful" (2:92). Martha's blood-curdling screams reverberate throughout the scene. Dick and Lily leave. Emily reports that Curtis has declared he "hates" the child, which further deepens their suspicion the child is not his. Fearing a scandal, John, Sr., orders them not to express their opinions in public. Mark Sheffield appears from the garden and informs them that Curtis is phoning Bigelow, which terrifies them all. Curtis enters, *"incredibly drawn and haggard, a tortured, bewildered expression in his eyes"* (2:94); he demands they leave and wonders aloud why they are opposed to Bigelow's joining him. They all depart. Listening to his wife screaming in agony, Curtis paces the room in a mixture of horror for his wife and unbridled anger at the child.

Bigelow appears. He tries to console his friend, but Curtis accuses him of being responsible. Exposing Martha to his children, he charges, inspired her to break her vow. He then damns "all children" and expresses unadulterated hatred for "it," the as yet unborn child upstairs. Bigelow admonishes him for having such a "horrible" attitude, but Curtis does not relent. He says that when he visited Martha in the room upstairs, he tried desperately to conceal the hatred burning in his eyes, but she saw it nonetheless and screamed, pushing him away. The DOCTORS then barred him from the room. Curtis confesses that, like his father and brother in act 2 but for different reasons, he wished the child would die. "For the love of God," Bigelow reproaches him, "if you have such thoughts, keep them to yourself" (2:99).

The Jayson family files back into the study. Martha's screaming has at last stopped—it is a son. In *"a horrible cry of rage and anguish,"* Curtis cries out, "No! No!" The family reacts to this heartless display *"in fright and amazement"* (2:100). A nurse enters and informs Curtis that Martha has requested to see him, and he rushes excitedly from the room. He returns moments later, however, looking *"like a corpse"* (2:101): Martha is dead. The baby's weight, 11 pounds (O'Neill's birth weight), killed her in childbirth. Before dying, Martha whispered for Curtis's forgiveness, which further sparks the family's suspicions. He once again expresses his hatred for the child and now considers "it" his wife's murderer and storms back to Martha. As the curtain falls, Emily, jealous of Martha's boy and the most destructive scandalmonger of the family, blurts out, "(*putting all her venomous gratification into one word*) . . . Well!" (2:102).

## Act 4

The Jaysons' living room three days later. The whole family arrives from the funeral dressed in mourning. All of them, with the exception of Mrs. Davidson, who is sincerely crying, reveal faces that are *"strained . . . irritated, worried, or merely gloomy"* (2:103). Lily admonishes the family for their false show of bereavement at the funeral. Curtis, who made a desperate attempt to leap into Martha's grave, has still not seen his son, which makes them think he is "deliberately flaunting this scandal in everyone's face" (2:104). Taken as a whole, their postulation of the child's illegitimacy is based on the evidence that (1) Curtis had said it was "impossible," (2) they believed Curtis was probably away when it was conceived, (3)

Curtis swore he "hated" the child, and (4) Martha had asked his forgiveness on her deathbed. They collectively surmise that his continued friendship with Bigelow is a ruse to avert scandal. "Oh, I hate you, all of you!" Lily shouts, "I loathe your suspicions—and I loathe myself because I'm beginning to be poisoned by them, too" (2:104). Dick spots Curtis and Bigelow coming in from the garden, and the family quickly withdraws to Curtis's study.

Curtis and Bigelow enter. Curtis mulishly plans to set out for the expedition that afternoon, and Bigelow pleads with him not to go through with it. Enraged by his friend's callousness, Bigelow vows to quit their friendship; but assuming Curtis is mad with grief, he apologizes just before parting. The Jaysons enter silently from the study. Sheffield, the self-appointed "spokesman" of the group, advises Curtis that in order to save appearances for the family, he must remain with the baby for at least a month. "This is a small town, Curt," he says, "and you know as well as I do, gossip is not the least of its faults" (2:111). "You're not playing the game, Curt," his brother Dick agrees. Emily adds that Curtis would never act this way if he really loved Martha, to which Curtis responds, recalling the title of O'Neill's first full-length play, BREAD AND BUTTER (which also takes place in the fictional Bridgetown), "What do you know of love—women like you! You call your little rabbit-hutch emotions love—your bread-and-butter passions" (2:112). Emily strikes back by insinuating the illegitimacy of the child along with Martha's presumed adultery. Curtis grasps now what the family has believed all along. "Bigelow? Big? Pretending he's as much my friend. . . . Oh, you—you—you—filth!" (2:114). Scanning their faces, he sees that they all believe he has been cuckolded by Bigelow. Disgusted, he races up the stairs to the child.

Mrs. Davidson, oblivious to the conflict swirling about her, declares she has reconciled her dislike for Martha and now loves and respects her for dying "in the performance of her duty" (2:115). Curtis reenters and announces that he has seen the child, recognizes Martha in his eyes, and proclaims him his own son. He then announces his intention to go ahead with the expedition, but he places the boy in his great-aunt's care on the condition that she is "never to let him know this obscene little world" (2:116). Overjoyed with her new charge, Mrs. Davidson vows to honor his wish. After his departure, with the exception of Lily and John, Sr., the family appears relieved to be rid of both Curtis and the possibility of scandal.

## COMMENTARY

While intriguing for its candor, *The First Man* is otherwise one of O'Neill's most commonplace plays. In 1928, O'Neill told the New York *Sun* that he did not like *The First Man*, along with other works of realism from the period like "*Anna Christie*," and when the critic GEORGE JEAN NATHAN lambasted its first production, O'Neill concurred, saying with a smile, "You let it down too easy. . . . It is no good" (Estrin 83, 177). One reason for this is that O'Neill had been successfully weaning himself off realism and toward the new EXPRESSIONISM that he single-handedly introduced to AMERICAN THEATER. *The First Man*'s only artistic experiment, if one can call it that, is the blood-curdling cries of childbirth that fill the air in act 3. But it is hard to imagine this coming off well in a theater.

Originally intended as a modern retelling of the myth of Jason and the Argonauts (hence "Jayson") and the quest for the Golden Fleece, *The First Man* wound up being O'Neill's personal foray into the GENDER wars. Curtis Jayson is the stereotypical man, or, as the famous psychoanalyst Carl Jung terms it, the "animus"—"intellectually creative, idealistic, egotistical, and aggressive"; Martha, then, is the "anima"—"physically creative, realistic, unselfish, and passive" (Falk 76). Aside from this rather stale method of sexual categorization, the chief problem with this play is that had O'Neill stuck to gender conflict—more specifically the question of bearing children—it may have been a more sustainable drama. This theme, however, as Margaret Loftus Ranald describes it, makes the play only "little more than the unthinking acceptance of Strindberg's view of the battle between the sexes" (222). The second major conflict, equally important in the text and thus deflating the impact of the first, is the battle between modern individualism and small-town puritanism.

In good part, *The First Man* stands as an indictment of the NEW LONDON "gentry" O'Neill despised

in his youth. This certainly described the Chappells, a hyper-conventional family from New London who, according to one of its younger members, "considered the O'Neills shanty Irish . . . and we associated the Irish with the servant class" (quoted in Sheaffer 49). Ironically, O'Neill's earliest full-length drama, *Bread and Butter*, written eight years earlier and never produced, is a far clearer (if not cleverer) treatment of American parochialism (it also takes place in Bridgetown/New London); the Jayson family, as they file on and off stage in all their numbers, are more distracting than enlightening, though it is true, as O'Neill's contemporary Sophus Keith Winther wrote, that the family demonstrates how "in their obedience to a fixed ethical theory they have exactly reversed the good and the evil" (2:136).

In the memoir written by O'Neill's second wife, Agnes Boulton, *Part of a Long Story* (along with many less-subjective testimonials), it is painfully clear that O'Neill had little interest in fatherhood as a reality if not a concept. Nor did he ever develop such an interest. He complained that PEAKED HILL BAR, their home in Provincetown, Massachusetts, reeked of diapers and milk. Indeed, as Louis Sheaffer notes in his biography, Curtis Jayson's monologue defending a childless existence sounds a good deal like a dream O'Neill described to Agnes Boulton in the first days of their courtship:

> Curtis: Haven't we been sufficient, you and I together? Is not that a more difficult, beautiful happiness to achieve than—children? Does not it mean anything to you that I need you so terribly—for myself, for my work—for everything that is best and worthiest in me? (quoted in Sheaffer 48).

> O'Neill to Boulton: You had seemed to me alone and virginal and somehow—with nothing but yourself. I wanted you [Agnes] alone . . . in an aloneness broken by nothing. Not even by children of our own. I don't understand children, they make me uneasy, and I don't know how to act with them. (quoted in Boulton 68)

> Agnes: To be alone with me—that was what he wanted; we had everything—work, love and companionship. Never, *never* let anything interfere with work or love! (quoted in Sheaffer 48)

Even more telling is an early letter from 1914 in which O'Neill turned down a trip to the beach (one of his favorite recreational activities) upon hearing children would be present: "When I found out the children were to be taken along I backed out. A long trolley ride with a couple of playful brats is my idea of one of the tortures Dante forgot to mention in the Inferno" (quoted in Gelb 408).

After the unwanted entrance of Shane to their otherwise idyllic bohemian lives, perhaps further aggravated by the birth of their daughter OONA O'NEILL, O'Neill grew embittered at home and stayed away as much as possible. (Agnes was no great nurturer either; her daughter lived with her parents in the first years of marriage to O'Neill and receives only perfunctory mention in Boulton's *Part of a Long Story*.) O'Neill biographer Stephen A. Black reasons that O'Neill's "reluctance to become a father may have been partly the result of identification with his mother's inability to tolerate the possible loss of another child after the baby Edmund died. Jayson seeks immortality in anthropology rather than fatherhood, and Eugene sought it in play-writing" (268). Therefore, though Martha Jayson's death is treated as a tragedy, the play appears to end on a cynical high note: Curtis Jayson can have his cake and eat it too. Not only is he free to carry on with his expedition without the distracting guilt of leaving behind his wife and child for five years, he can also enjoy fatherhood once the boy is "old enough" (no diapers, less milk) "to know and love a big, free life" (2:116).

Both Louis Sheaffer and Travis Bogard write off O'Neill's premise that the mourning father of two would be so resistant to having another child as, respectively, something "one cannot accept" (48) and being "beyond rational explanation" (150). Though O'Neill certainly projected his own distaste of parenthood on his character, as far as we know there is one significant discrepancy between the O'Neills and the Jaysons: Martha tricked Curtis into impregnating her, overstepping his rightful decision in the matter by assuming, as his sister Lily does, that "in his inmost heart, he'll be tickled to death" (2:66). With this in mind, Curtis Jayson's difficulty in accepting parenthood does not seem entirely beyond reason. Is it necessarily true that "if

he had really loved his young, he most likely would have been eager for others to replace those he and his wife had lost" (Sheaffer 48)?

Martha, for a time under the illusion that she had elected to make his work hers as well (as O'Neill's mother MARY ELLEN "ELLA" O'NEILL acquiescently had for JAMES O'NEILL), could well have divorced him. The fact that she chose to pursue her own desires above those of her husband hardly runs counter to modern marriage; presumably this is why O'Neill (almost literally) poured the decidedly unmodern Jayson clan into the roux. It would have been far more beneficial to her, it seems, to have divorced Curtis and married Bigelow, as the townspeople suspected she might. So was it by a sense of social duty she made this decision? Her character as O'Neill wrote it, blind as she is to the requirements of social convention, does not lend much to that theory. But then there is always love, O'Neill's great stumbling block to individual advancement. O'Neill most probably included the two dead children in order for Curtis not to appear as the "beyond rational" child hater he has been labeled nonetheless, though this was precisely the portrait he wished to draw in a sympathetic light. In his early play SERVITUDE, O'Neill deliberately intended the neglectful father and husband David Roylston to find his way under the audience's skin; in *The First Man*, O'Neill almost gleefully, though he eventually came to regret it, let loose his demons.

## CHARACTERS

**Bigelow, Edward**   Curtis Jayson's college friend and a good friend to Martha Jayson. Bigelow, "*a large, handsome man of thirty-nine . . . [whose] face shows culture and tolerance, a sense of humor, a lazy unambitious contentment*" (2:57), is a recent widower; before his wife's death, he was well known as a shameless philanderer and man-about-town. After her death, however, he reformed and devoted himself to raising their children. The Bridgetown community refuses to accept his reformation, however, and a rumor spreads that he and Martha are having an affair. Later, when Martha's pregnancy becomes public knowledge, the new assumption is that the child is his. Bigelow attempts to persuade

Curtis Jayson not to follow through with his quest to find the remnants of the "First Man," or "Missing Link," as he refers to it, but to stay at home with Martha, protect her from the scandalmongering community that destroyed his life, and raise their child together.

**Davidson, Mrs.**  Curtis Jayson's great-aunt and the matriarch of the Jayson clan in Bridgetown, Connecticut. O'Neill describes her as "*seventy-five years old—a thin, sinewy old lady, old-fashioned, unbending and rigorous in manner. She is dressed aggressively in the fashion of a bygone age*" (2:66). Mrs. Davison is an old flibbertigibbet who demands that her family live up to the expectations of small-town propriety. Before the play's action, she had desperately hoped that one of her nieces or nephews would provide the clan with a boy. There is a distinct shift between Mrs. Davidson in the first act and in the last. In the first, we are to understand that she represents all of the old-school stuffiness of small-town Victorian culture. But after Martha gives birth to a boy in act 3 and, as Mrs. Davidson puts it, subsequently dies "in the performance of her duty" (2:115), she becomes far more nurturing and trustworthy. In the final scene of the play, Curtis hands his son over to her care with assurances that she will not allow the child to be influenced by the very culture she herself had cultivated, a condition to which she happily agrees.

**Jayson, Curtis**  A famous anthropologist obsessed with his work and Martha Jayson's husband. Clearly based in part on his creator, Curtis Jayson is a "*tall, rangy, broad-shouldered man of thirty-seven. . . . His square-jawed, large-featured face retains an eager boyish enthusiasm in spite of its prevailing expression of thoughtful, preoccupied aloofness*" (2:57). After graduating from Cornell University with a degree in mining engineering, Curtis found a job in a Nevada mining town. While there, he met his future wife, Martha, and they had two children together, both of whom died of pneumonia when a negligent nurse allowed them to play outside in the winter cold. After the death of their children, Curtis and Martha swore to each other they would never again have children and set off on a 10-year anthropo-

logical tour of the world. Curtis wrote several books based on their experiences abroad with a great deal of help from Martha. Curtis's real calling is in actual experience, however, and to him book writing is a necessary evil.

Two years before the play's action, the Jaysons moved back to Bridgetown, Connecticut, Curtis's hometown, to allow Curtis to finish his latest book. The townspeople, particularly the larger Jayson clan, disapprove of their vagabond lifestyle and apply pressure on them, but especially Martha, to settle down with children. Jayson appears unaccountably ignorant of his family's parochial scandalmongering. Though Martha does not hold the Jayson clan's conventional views, she nevertheless feels an irrepressible urge to bear children regardless of her vow to Curtis. Meanwhile, he has been granted permission to bring her along on an anthropological expedition to the Tibetan highlands to find the remains of the "First Man," popularly called the "Missing Link." When he discovers that she became pregnant and waited to tell him until it was a "fact," he rails against the prospect of giving up his expedition. He also feels that a child will destroy the "link" between him and Martha: "Can you expect me to be glad when you propose to introduce a stranger who will steal away your love, your interest—who will separate us and deprive me of you! No, no, I can't! It is asking the impossible. I'm only human" (2:87).

Despite Curtis's proposal that Martha get an abortion, she goes ahead with the childbirth. After a terrible ordeal in labor, Martha dies giving birth to an 11-pound baby (O'Neill's birth weight). Curtis initially renounces the child as his wife's murderer but then accepts him after hearing that his family believes the boy is his friend Edward Bigelow's son, not his. Disgusted with his family's persnickety ways, he hands the child over to his aunt, who always wanted a boy in the family, and sets off to the Tibetan highlands with promises to return when the boy is "old enough . . . to know and love a big, free life" (2:116).

Curtis shares traits of the woebegone artist John Brown in his earliest full-length play, *Bread and Butter*, and the obnoxious, self-centered novelist and playwright David Roylston in *Servitude*.

Indeed, O'Neill pays homage to the former here, when Curtis's sister-in-law Emily accuses him of not caring for Martha, and he retaliates with anti-establishment language nearly lifted from the earlier play: "What do you know of love—women like you! You call your little rabbit-hutch emotions love—your bread-and-butter passions" (2:112). Ultimately, like Martha, he is a Jungian prototype of his gender—"intellectually creative, idealistic, egotistical, and aggressive" (Falk 76). Not given to nurturing anything other than his art, O'Neill quite obviously projected his own misgivings about the birth of his son Shane Rudraighe O'Neill in 1919, just before he conceived of the idea, onto the Curtis Jayson character. As Louis Sheaffer has noted, Curtis's monologue in act 2, in which he pleads with Martha not to go through with the birth, is strikingly similar to words he used to convince Agnes Boulton not to trample their idyllic marital "aloneness" (quoted in Sheaffer 48). And like Curtis, O'Neill's work superseded everything in his mind, including—perhaps especially—children.

**Jayson, Emily**    Curtis Jayson's vindictive sister-in-law and John Jayson, Jr.'s wife. Emily is the least sympathetic character in the play, as she symbolizes all that small-town parochialism meant to O'Neill—the scandalmongering, the pettiness, the strictly held codes of conduct, and the ostentatious materialism. When Martha has a boy, she expresses inhuman jealousy, as she only produced girls and Mrs. Davidson, the family matriarch, wanted a male grandnephew. Emily clearly led the charge against Edward Bigelow in the community and planned to do so again with her sister-in-law, Martha Jayson. We can see this in Curtis Jayson's attack on her when she accuses him of not loving his wife: "What do you know of love—women like you! You call your little rabbit-hutch emotions love—your bread-and-butter passions" (2:112).

**Jayson, John**    Curtis Jayson's father and a successful banker in Bridgetown. O'Neill describes Jayson, a 65-year-old father of five, as a "*typical, small-town, New England best-family banker, reserved in pose, unobtrusively important—a placid exterior hid-*

*ing querulousness and a fussy temper*" (2:68). Initially, at least, O'Neill portrays Jayson as caring far more about the town's perception of his family than his son's well-being—at one point, he even announces his preference for Martha and Curtis Jayson's baby to die in childbirth than face the scandal that might follow. By the end of the play, however, he is one of the few characters who develop. In the final scene, after Curtis has departed for the Tibetan highlands, leaving his child behind in the care of his great-aunt, Jayson's son Dick voices relief that the scandal has been avoided; Jayson snaps back with the final line of the play: "Keep your remarks to yourself, if you please!" (2:117). He is a less-developed Edward Brown, Sr., from O'Neill's first full-length play, *Bread and Butter*.

**Jayson, John, Jr.**    Curtis Jayson's brother and Emily Jayson's husband. O'Neill describes John, Jr., who is about 40, as "*his father over again in appearance, but pompous, obtrusive, purse-and-family-proud, extremely irritating in his self-complacent air of authority, emptily assertive and loud*" (2:68–69). John, Jr., is one of the most judgmental members of the clan and places the family's reputation above individual concerns even more than his father. He is an only slightly reworked Edward Brown, Jr., from O'Neill's first full-length play, *Bread and Butter*.

**Jayson, Lily**    A brazen college student and Curtis's younger sister. Lily is a "*slender, rather pretty girl of twenty-five. . . . She rather insists on a superior, intellectual air, is full of nervous, thwarted energy*" (2:61–62). Lily looks down on Bridgetown provincialism, and yet she is a victim of it. Though she sympathizes with Martha Jayson, who is rumored incorrectly to be conducting an affair with Edward Bigelow, Curtis Jayson's best friend from college, Lily cannot entirely shake off the small-town restrictions. Her rebellious attitude actually acts in opposition to her professed individualism (presumably what she learned in school), and her actions and words generally do more harm than good. Her character is summed up in act 4 when she admits that though she hates the family's scandalmongering, she equally hates herself, as she feels "beginning to be poisoned by them, too" (2:104).

**Jayson, Martha**   Curtis Jayson's wife. Born and raised in the mining communities of Nevada, Martha is *"a healthy, fine-looking woman of thirty-eight. She does not appear this age for her strenuous life in the open has kept her young and fresh. She possesses the frank, clear, direct quality of outdoors, outspoken and generous"* (2:57). She and Curtis met while he was working as a mining engineer in the West; she bore two children, both of whom died of pneumonia while under the charge of a careless nurse. After this tragedy, Martha and Curtis made a pact never to have children again and devoted their lives to travel and the quest for knowledge. Martha is an independent-minded, self-reliant character, but she nevertheless accommodated her anthropologist husband's romantic expeditions and helped him write anthropological treatises based on their experiences. Though for most of their journeys, Martha had convinced herself that their vagabond existence appealed to her and that she shared her husband's dogged struggle to attain knowledge, at one stop in China, she spied a native woman holding a child and had a revelation that "all the wandering about the world, and all the romance and excitement I'd enjoyed in it, appeared an aimless, futile business, chasing around in a circle in an effort to avoid touching reality" (2:86).

After two years working with Curtis on his latest book in Bridgetown, Connecticut, Curtis's hometown, Martha becomes pregnant and does not tell Curtis for two months. When the Jayson family discovers the news, they assume she has been conducting an affair with Curtis's old friend Edward Bigelow and that it is his child. Meanwhile, Curtis has been granted permission to bring Martha along on an expedition to find the "First Man," popularly called the "Missing Link," in the Tibetan highlands. Before he informs her of the news on her birthday, however, she confesses that she is pregnant. Alarmed by her dismissal of their vow, he tells her about the expedition, pleads with her not to go through with the pregnancy, and appeals to their love as recompense for their lack of children. "Our life seems to mean your life to you, Curt—and only your life," she replies, "I have devoted fifteen years to that. Now I must fight for my own" (2:87). Her labor turns out to be dreadfully long

and painful, and she dies—but not before asking his forgiveness—after giving birth to an 11-pound boy (O'Neill's birth weight). Curtis eventually gives over the child to his aunt, Mrs. Davidson, and follows through with his quest with promises to return when the boy is old enough to take his mother's place in his adventures.

Martha is an interesting admixture between the long-suffering wives one finds in the characters Alice Roylston in *Servitude* and Nora Melody in *A Touch of the Poet*. But she rises above their marital subservience to their egoistic husbands and appears more like the characters Cybel and Margaret Dion in *The Great God Brown*, respectively, a nurturing earth mother and devoted Faustian Marguerite combined in one (Falk 76). On the other hand, Cybel and Margaret were content to devote themselves to providing the artist Anthony Dion with spiritual and motherly succor (though Margaret ultimately caves in to convention). Martha, however, is determined to carry out her own life's desire and have a baby against Curtis's wishes. In this way, she is a less carefully drawn portrait of the well-meaning but spiritually destructive Ruth Atkins in *Beyond the Horizon* and Nina Leeds in *Strange Interlude*. Ultimately, like Curtis, she is a Jungian prototype of her gender: "physically creative, realistic, unselfish, and passive" (Falk 76). In the end, she appears to have been repentant of her decision to go ahead with the pregnancy, as her dying words were those begging Curtis's forgiveness.

**Jayson, Richard "Dick"**   Curtis Jayson's brother and Emily Jayson's husband. Dick *"is a typical young Casino and country club member, college-bred, good-looking, not unlikable"* (2:69). Dick accepts the parochialism of Bridgetown but clearly understands its destructive capability. Nevertheless, he seems prepared to toe the line in order to maintain his privileged existence. He is a less-dissipated version of Harry Brown from O'Neill's first full-length play, *Bread and Butter*.

**Sheffield, Esther**   Curtis Jayson's sister and Mark Sheffield's wife. O'Neill describes her, rather benignly in contrast to the other characters, as *"a stout, middle-aged woman with the round, unmarked,* sentimentally-contented face of one who lives unthink-ingly from day to day, sheltered in an assured posi-tion in her little world" (2:66). Esther is a snob who describes the westerner Martha Jayson as some-one who "shows her breeding" (2:74), but she is basically harmless compared to the others. Her pointless dialogue makes one wonder why O'Neill included her character at all.

**Sheffield, Mark**   Curtis Jayson's brother-in-law and Emily Sheffield's husband. Mark is a cor-porate lawyer in his mid-40s and a custodian of Bridgetown's standards of conduct; his face is *"alert, shrewd, cautious, full of the superficial craftiness of the lawyer mind"* (2:66). The Sheffields are quintessen-tial small-town gentry, such as that which O'Neill experienced in New London, Connecticut. One such family from his time there were the Chappells, a hyper-conventional family who, according to one of its younger members, "considered the O'Neills shanty Irish . . . and we associated the Irish with the servant class" (quoted in Sheaffer 49). Mark is the self-appointed "spokesman" of the Jayson clan who informs Curtis of the rumors about Martha and Edward Bigelow having an affair and the belief that the child is theirs.

### BIBLIOGRAPHY

Barlow, Judith. "O'Neill's Female Characters." In *The Cambridge Companion to Eugene O'Neill*, edited by Michael Manheim, 164–177. New York: Cam-bridge University Press, 1998.

Black, Stephen A. *Eugene O'Neill: Beyond Mourning and Tragedy*. New Haven, Conn.: Yale University Press, 1999.

Bogard, Travis. *Contour in Time: The Plays of Eugene O'Neill*. Rev. ed. New York: Oxford University Press, 1988.

Boulton, Agnes. *Part of a Long Story: Eugene O'Neill as a Young Man in Love*. Garden City, N.Y.: Doubleday & Company, 1958.

Estrin, Mark, ed. *Conversations with Eugene O'Neill*. Jackson and London: University Press of Missis-sippi, 1990.

Falk, Doris V. *Eugene O'Neill and the Tragic Tension: An Interpretive Study of the Plays*. New Brunswick, N.J.: Rutgers University Press, 1958.

Ranald, Margaret Loftus. *The Eugene O'Neill Compan-ion*. New York: Greenwood Press, 1984.

Sheaffer, Louis. *O'Neill: Son and Artist*. Boston: Little, Brown, 1973.

Winther, Sophus Keith. *Eugene O'Neill: A Critical Study*. New York: Random House, 1934.

# *Fog: A Play in One Act* (completed, 1914; first produced, 1917)

*Fog* was first produced, three years after its composi-tion, in GREENWICH VILLAGE by the PROVINCETOWN PLAYERS on January 5, 1917, at the Playwrights' Theatre in New York City. Composed two years following *Titanic*'s disastrous voyage, *Fog* is set on an oarless lifeboat adrift off the Grand Banks of Newfoundland. The STAGE DIRECTIONS are highly ambitious for a playwright with as yet no produc-tions to his name, as O'Neill demands fog, a rising sun, falling ice, rolling swells, and two boats, among other effects. *Fog* is, as Margaret Loftus Ranald has asserted, "O'Neill's first foray into the eerie world of supernatural fantasy" (53). More important, per-haps, is that the two main characters, a Poet and a Man of Business, along with a Dead Child (who has no lines but is listed as a character), emerge as on- and offstage characters in dozens of O'Neill's later plays. O'Neill introduces many of his favorite themes in this play as well, including what he calls the "genius" of fog, environmental determinism (DARWINISM), and the moral and spiritual death that comes with financial success, among others.

### SYNOPSIS

The curtain rises at dusk to *"a menacing silence [that], like the genius of the fog, broods over every-thing"* (1:97). Three dark figures sit barely visible in a lifeboat enshrouded by the fog. As daylight breaks through the fog's thickness, a towering iceberg appears, one resembling *"the façade of some huge Viking temple"* (1:109). The lifeboat carries a sun-dry party of survivors: a Poet, a Man of Business, and a sleeping Polish Peasant Woman who cradles her Dead Child, whom O'Neill lists as a character. It is a striking image that calls to mind both the Crucifixion, with the Poet as the good thief and the Man of Business as the bad, and the *Pieta* at once. Presumably to emphasize the thickness of the fog, O'Neill first identifies the two men onboard as A Man's Voice and Another Man's Voice and then as First Voice and Second Voice; as the dialogue gradually reveals their true selves, he calls them Dark Man and Other Man, Dark Man and Business Man, and finally Poet and Business Man.

At first they discuss the sinking of their passenger steamer, which had collided with a "derelict." The Man of Business (currently the First Voice) is initially optimistic about their odds for survival, as one of the ship's officers informed him that many ships had responded to their call for help. Because he owns a house on the Connecticut shore, as O'Neill's father had, he also insists that fog banks generally burn off with the sun. The pessimistic but soon valiant Poet (here the Second Voice) rebuffs the Man of Business's confidence, saying, "You forget we are now near the Grand Banks, the home of fog" (1:98).

The lifeboat's occupants each recount the trials of the previous day, revealing that the child in the woman's arms died while they were cast adrift. The Poet questions whether the child's death was, in fact, tragic, given the poor standard of living an immigrant family was sure to suffer upon arrival as new immigrants to the United States. "What chance had the poor child? Naturally sick and weak from underfeeding, transplanted to the stinking room of a tenement or the filthy hovel of a mining village, what glowing opportunities did life hold out that death should not be regarded as a blessing for him?" (1:99) "I see you're a bit of a reformer," the now amused Man of Business rejoins. But the Poet, like O'Neill, is no reformer; he believes in social determinism, the belief that our social environment shapes and directs human life, not the widely held American ideologies of self-determination and the power of individual will.

It is gradually getting lighter as the conversation continues. When the Poet (now identified as the Dark Man) assumes the Man of Business (the Other Man) had never seen the woman on the ship, the Man of Business responds that unlike many of the first class passengers aboard, he had no interest in "slumming" in the steerage. The Poet explains that he spent much of his time down there because he "found the people in the steerage more interesting to talk to than the second class passengers" (1:102). Though here suggesting the kind of PHILOSOPHICAL ANARCHISM that informs much of O'Neill's drama, such slumming in the steerage or stokehole is a dangerous symbolic act in his later work—one most powerfully employed to shatter the "fireman" character Robert "Yank" Smith's inflated ego in The HAIRY APE. While they recount each others' stories, the Poet explains that he saw the calamity as an opportunity to end his disillusioned life and go down with the ship; but in the steerage he saw the terrified Polish Peasant Woman clutching her child and was moved to lead them to safety, thereby rescuing him (from himself) in return. In contrast to the valiant Poet, we soon find that the initially rather likable Business Man is a coward willing to risk the lives of others to save his own.

The two hear the distant sound of a steamer's whistle; but the lifeboat is drifting toward a massive iceberg. The Poet understands that if they call attention to themselves, the steamer might hit the iceberg, and they would all die. The whistle becomes louder and louder, the Business Man is about to cry out for help, but the Poet overpowers him. Soon they apprehend the sound of falling ice and realize the iceberg is breaking apart in the morning sun. The Business Man, in a fit of uncontrollable terror, nearly jumps into the water to avoid being crushed by the ice, but the Poet saves him once more. In an odd twist of supernatural romanticism, a rescue party from a passing steamship is led to the castaways by the sound of the Dead Baby's crying. As the Polish Peasant Woman had inadvertently saved the Poet from committing suicide back on the ship—which the Poet sees as "an omen sent by the Gods to convince me my past unhappiness is past and my future will change for the better" (1:104)—the Dead Baby's crying saves both the Poet and the Business Man. The final tragedy has Christian overtones as well, then, since the true saviors must meet a sacrificial death.

## COMMENTARY

Fog is an immensely important mystifying element in O'Neill's work, perhaps most resonantly in this play, but he also brings the "genius" of fog to bear on characters in *"Anna Christie"* and, most powerfully, in Long Day's Journey into Night. We know O'Neill was strongly influenced by Samuel Taylor Coleridge's *The Rime of the Ancient Mariner,* which he later adapted for the stage (see *The Ancient Mariner),* and Travis Bogard argues that Coleridge's lyrical ballad is the basis for *Fog*'s mystifying mise en scène (27). O'Neill was well aware of the lethal Grand Banks fog from his experiences as a seaman on the SS New York and SS Philadelphia, along with his familiarity with fishermen from New London, Connecticut and Rudyard Kipling's *Captains Courageous* (Richter 144).

Though demonstrating O'Neill's future promise, *Fog* conforms poorly to the structural standards of a one-act play. As with the short story, a one-act play must treat one action, one revelation, or one turning point and probe into that subject or theme as cohesively as time allows. Instead, *Fog* is really two separate plays: The first is a drama of social protest in which the Poet and the Man of Business argue over immigration, capitalism, and the myth of the American Dream. The second part looks ahead to the expressionism and what O'Neill called "Supernaturalism" of his middle plays. As the fog lifts, the two men make out a massive iceberg looming over them. Soon after, they hear the whistle of a steamship, which presents a moral dilemma: Do they shout for help and risk the ship colliding with the iceberg or say nothing and most likely freeze to death? The Man of Business, a success in the financial world, opts for the former but is thwarted by the Poet. This symbolic act equates material success with moral cowardice, a theme that, again, carries over into many O'Neill plays—most memorably in the figure of *Long Day's Journey into Night*'s James Tyrone (based on his highly successful but, in O'Neill's mind, overly acquisitive father, James O'Neill).

Unlike the Captain in *Thirst,* who commits suicide rather than face the fact that the shipwreck was his responsibility and Lavinia Mannon in Mourning Becomes Electra, who refuses to do so because

it would free her from punishment, suicide in *Fog* is a way to maintain one's innocence in the face of inhumanity. As he explains to the Business Man, the Poet had planned to kill himself as the ship went down but chose to save the immigrant woman and her baby instead. He later regretted it, however, saying that "death was kind to the child. It saved him for many a long year of sordid drudgery," and "if I had known the sufferings that poor woman was to undergo as a result of my reckless life-saving I would have let her go down with the ship and gone myself" (1:99, 104). The tie that binds this play is that the social paradox the Poet explicitly voices—material success depends on the suffering of others—metaphorically broadens to include the even more sweeping assertion that success (material or otherwise), survival, and happiness can only come when others experience their reverse.

## CHARACTERS

**Dead Child, A**   The dead son of the Polish Peasant Woman. Through the play's action, the child lies dead in his mother's arms. The happiness that both mother and child exuded in the ship's steerage moved the Poet to find a free lifeboat, lower it down to the water, and help guide them to relative safety. In the play's final scene, the Poet and the Man of Business are rescued by a group of steamship sailors who tell them that they were led through the fog to their lifeboat by the sound of the Dead Child's crying. Dead children become a strong motif in many O'Neill plays, most often explained by his survival guilt over his older brother Edmund O'Neill's untimely death at age two.

**Man of Business, A   (First Voice, The Other Man, Business Man)**   The Man of Business, or Business Man as he is referred to in the play itself, is a character who forms the basis of many materialistic, naive men of success in the O'Neill canon, such as Anthony Brown in *The Great God Brown,* Marco Polo in Marco Millions, Sam Evans in Strange Interlude, and T. Stedman Harder in A Moon for the Misbegotten, who touts *"sterling patriotic principles,"* and asserts the rags-to-riches paradigm that "everyone has a chance in this world; but we've all got to work hard, of course" (1:99). Most of O'Neill's success stories, like this Man of Business, are well-meaning but ultimately superficial and doomed to live soulless, unfulfilled lives.

**Poet, A (Second Voice, The Dark Man)**  With the character, Eugene O'Neill introduces a staged alter ego that would appear in many of his later plays, most unmistakably as Robert Mayo in BEYOND THE HORIZON, Stephen Murray in *The* STRAW, and, most famously, Edmund Tyrone in *Long Day's Journey into Night*: the romantic figure of the dark-haired, maudlin poet with suicidal tendencies and radical social ideas but no faith in mankind to carry them out; a watered-down version of this character is Richard Miller in AH, WILDERNESS! Like O'Neill, the Poet is a self-described "humanist" rather than a more politically ideological "Socialist" (1:102). This character is not simply the by-product of a 25-year-old's naive idealism, however, for as the playwright matured, he never abandoned this avatar of himself. The Poet is a firm believer in social determinism, or Social DARWINISM, asserting the naturalistic line that poverty is "a hereditary ill that only the most vital men are able to shake off" (1:99). As such, he morbidly contends that "death was kind to the child" (the Dead Child). "What glowing opportunities did life hold out," he asks, "that death should not be regarded as a blessing for him? . . . Surely his prospects of ever becoming anything but a beast of burden were not bright, were they?" (1:99).

**Polish Peasant Woman, A**  A character with no lines who acts as a symbol for the horrors of eastern European immigration in the early decades of the 20th century. According to the Poet, the woman along with her child's fates are sealed: They will live in squalor and labor for capitalists in the cities or industrialists in the mining towns. Saved from being crushed by mobs of frightened immigrants in steerage, the woman's child has died after a day adrift on the open SEA. Through the play's action, the woman sits at the end of the boat holding the Dead Child in her arms, calling to mind the *Pieta* image of the Virgin Mary holding her dead son after the Crucifixion. By the time the boat is rescued, she too has died.

**Third Officer of a Steamer, The**  A young officer who successfully steers a lifeboat through the fog and rescues the *Starland* survivors. After hailing the castaways, he inquires as to the whereabouts of the child whose crying indicated their location. Back on the bridge of his steamer, he and his first officer heard the child's cries—"weird too it sounded with everything so quiet and the fog so heavy" (1:111)—and realized it would probably lead them to survivors of the shipwreck. According to the officer and his crew, the cries lasted for as long as it took to locate the survivors, then abruptly stopped when the fog rose. In the final scene, the Third Officer and the Man of Business cast some doubts on their respective stories—that the child's cries helped the crew find them and that the child had died 24 hours before.

## BIBLIOGRAPHY

Bogard, Travis. *Contour in Time: The Plays of Eugene O'Neill*. Rev. ed. New York: Oxford University Press, 1988.

Ranald, Margaret Loftus. "The Early Plays." In *The Cambridge Companion to Eugene O'Neill*, edited by Michael Manheim, 51–68. New York: Cambridge University Press, 1998.

Richter, Robert A. *Eugene O'Neill and Dat Ole Davil Sea: Maritime Influences in the Life and Works of Eugene O'Neill*. Mystic, Conn.: Mystic Seaport, 2004.

# *Fountain: A Play in Eleven Scenes, The* (completed, 1922; first produced, 1925)

Eugene O'Neill wrote his epic play *The Fountain* in Provincetown, Massachusetts, between the summers of 1921 and 1922. It was copyrighted on the same day as his more realistic drama *The* FIRST MAN, October 13, 1921. *The Fountain*, his first major historical drama, charts the voyage of the Spanish colonial explorer and soldier Juan Ponce de León (1460–1521), who joined Christopher Columbus on the Italian explorer's second voyage

Walter Huston as Ponce de Leon, in 1926. *(Courtesy of the Sheaffer-O'Neill Collection, Charles E. Shain Library of Connecticut College)*

to the New World. Ponce de León's personal mission was to expand the Spanish empire. Following his promotion as the first governor of Porto Rico (which became Puerto Rico four centuries later) in 1506, he embarked upon his famous quest to discover the Fountain of Youth in what is now Florida. O'Neill explained in his program note that he was less interested in historical reality than "the recurrence in folklore of the beautiful legend of a healing spring of eternal youth. . . . The play is only incidentally concerned with the Era of Discovery in America" (quoted in Clark 101).

Even veteran O'Neill producers balked at the enormity of the project, and after several rejections the play languished unproduced until the EXPERIMENTAL THEATRE, INC. accepted it in 1925. Directed and designed by ROBERT EDMUND JONES, *The Fountain* premiered on December 10, 1925, at the GREENWICH VILLAGE Theatre, New York, with an abysmal run that lasted just over two weeks. By this time, however, O'Neill had

entirely lost interest in the project. Nevertheless, he insisted it go on as further rewrites, he believed, would diminish rather than improve the quality of the play (Wainscott 171). O'Neill's *The GREAT GOD BROWN*, also directed by Jones, was only a month away from a comparatively successful if more controversial production at the Greenwich Village Theatre. During rehearsals, O'Neill considered *The Great God Brown* "worth a dozen *Fountains*" (quoted in Bogard 238). Nevertheless, in the character of Juan Ponce de Leon, we find a major theme from the O'Neill canon: the tension that forms when professional ambition clashes with spiritual fulfillment, love of beauty, and human compassion.

## SYNOPSIS

### Part 1
*Scene 1*

Early night, 1492, in the courtyard of the Moorish chieftain Ibnu Aswad's palace in Granada, Spain. The courtyard forms a right triangle with the apex at rear right. A large porte cochere (passageway) opens out to the street at left center, and the courtyard is filled with courtly, Moorish architectural flourishes—arches, marble columns thickly decorated with arabesques, and a massive fountain of green marble at center. Only the sound of the fountain's water can be heard. Ibnu Aswad enters with an expression "*of great pride borne down by sorrow and humiliation*" (2:169). That day the Moors had been defeated by the Spaniards. Aswad goes through the porte cochere and reenters with Juan Ponce de Leon and his servant Pedro. The Moor praises Juan for his valor on the battlefield, welcomes him to his palace, and tells him the Spanish victory was "the will of Allah" (2:169). Juan respectfully informs him his friends will soon arrive. Aswad exits with a bow.

Maria de Cordova enters wearing a black veil. Her husband is Juan's "brother in arms" Vicente de Cordova (2:170), but Maria pledges her love to him. Juan rejects the sentimental notion of romantic love—the only meaningful achievement for him is glory for Spain. She leaves Juan with a warning about his dual self—"soldier of iron—and dreamer. God pity you if those two selves should ever clash!" (2:173). Juan's old friend, the noble-man Luis de Alvaredo, enters a little drunk and teases Juan for his indiscretions with other men's women. Luis, a poet and dreamer, has rescued a Moor minstrel named Yusef from certain death by the cruel Franciscan monk Diego Menendez. He goes out to Yusef and returns with him and Menendez, Vicente de Cordova, and three vicious warrior nobles—Oviedo, Castillo, and Mendoza—following close behind. Menendez protests against the pagan Yusef's presence, but Juan permits him to stay. The Spaniards drink to victory, and Luis sings a song of what Juan will later call "eternal recurrence": "Love is a flower / Forever blooming / Life is a fountain / Forever leaping . . . Failing, falling, / Ever returning / To kiss the earth that the flower may live" (2:175). Juan scoffs at his senti-mentality and announces he will join Christopher Columbus through the Western Passage to the East, a voyage that might lead to heights of glory matching the Venetian merchant Marco Polo's. The other nobles mock Columbus for his belief that the world is round.

Yusef sings in Arabic, and Luis, the only Span-iard present who speaks the language, translates the song as a tale of a Fountain of Youth from which chosen pilgrims drink and "the years drop from them like a worn-out robe." The fountain, he reports, lies in a "sacred grove where all things live in the old harmony they knew before man came" (2:177). Juan uses the tale to rile Vicente about his age, 45, then implies that Vicente's wife, Maria, nearing 40, might appreciate a drink from the fountain as well. Vicente prepares to duel when a *"harsh shriek"* comes from the rear: Menendez has killed Yusef. Juan dispatches the noblemen and promises to finish his business with Vicente the following day. Luis is grief-stricken by the death of his bard, and Juan lamely comforts him by making light of Yusef's tale of the foun-tain. "Juan, why do you always sneer at beauty," Luis retorts, "while your heart calls you a liar?" (2:179). They resume drinking and talk of their future travels with Columbus. As their spirits lift, Juan toasts jokingly, "Sir Lying Poet!," to which Luis responds, "Sir Glory-Glutton!," and the cur-tain falls (2:179).

## Scene 2

About a year later. Early morning on the deck of Christopher Columbus's flagship heading west across the Atlantic Ocean. Multiple decks and ladders are packed with sleeping noblemen, soldiers, Franciscan monks, and converted Indians from Columbus's pre-vious voyage. Luis, Oviedo, Castillo, and Mendoza are playing dice. Juan is discovered next to the pilot. Luis loses and asks Juan to lend him money. Juan plays for him instead and loses—a bad omen for one who has never lost at dice. The men expound on the duel between Juan and Vicente de Cordova, a victory for Juan that caused a great scandal in the court. But Juan is happy to hear that Maria is preg-nant and that her relationship to Vicente seemed to strengthen after the duel.

Juan and Columbus are at odds, as Columbus views the journey as a new crusade for Christianity and Juan as an imperial mission for glory and the expansion of Spanish lands. Columbus appears on the higher deck to the poop, *"A commanding figure of noble presence, the face full of the ardent, fixed enthusiasm of the religious devotee"* (2:183). Address-ing Menendez, Columbus curses the noblemen on the voyage as looking upon the journey as "an esca-pade in search of easy riches, not a crusade for the glory of God" (2:183). Juan and Luis overhear him condemning Juan for his scandalous duel; then, in a lengthy monologue, Columbus calls the voyage "the Last Crusade" (2:184).

From the darkness, Juan dares Columbus to "govern with tolerance" (2:184). Columbus demands to know the identity of the eavesdrop-per, and Juan reveals himself. He climbs the lad-der to face Columbus when the shout of "Land Ho" is heard from the mainmast head. The sun comes out, and all the men rush to the sides to view what they believe is Cathay (China). Colum-bus commands the Christian cross to be raised and the men to kneel. Juan ignores this and jams his sword into the deck, forming a military-style cross; other noblemen and soldiers follow his example. The monks chant, while the rest, save Juan, sing a hymn, *"their pent-up excitement giving to the hymn a hectic, nervous quality."* Columbus shouts up to the heavens, "Te Deum!"—and the curtain falls (2:186).

## Part 2

### Scene 3

About 20 years later. Late afternoon in the court-yard of the governor's palace in Porto Rico (Puerto Rico). The stage is lush with flowers, palms, and fruit trees, and a decorous fountain resembling the one in scene 1 stands at center. Doors leading into the house are at right and left, with the entrance to the courtyard from the road at rear center. The day is scorching hot. Juan, now over 50 and governor of Porto Rico, is discovered sitting on a bench in front of the fountain. *"His eyes stare straight before him blankly in a disillusioned dream,"* his face is now *"aged, lined, drawn,"* and his hair and beard have turned gray (2:187). Luis, now a Dominican monk, appears from the left rear. Juan resents his con-version and scorns the now-deceased Columbus's political legacy as a "ruinous error" (2:187)—his brutal insistence on conversion and acceptance of slavery having made the conquered native people a burden on Spanish rule. Luis informs him the Spanish fleet has arrived.

Three men enter the scene: Oviedo, a Franciscan named Friar Quesada, and Nano, a tall, noble-look-ing Indian chief under guard. Quesada and Oviedo protest that Nano's tribe refuses to pay their taxes and Nano refuses to convert to Christianity. Juan dismisses Quesada and tells Oviedo he dislikes slav-ery, considering it wasteful and counterproductive. Oviedo hints that circumstances will change when Menendez returns from Spain, and he exits. Juan questions Nano about Cathay and the Fountain of Youth. Nano, who came to Porto Rico as an orphan child, says he knows about the fountain, which his people call the Spring of Life, but tells him only, "Those the Gods love can find it" (2:190). Juan orders him off to prison but promises not to execute him for any charge save rebellion.

Juan curses the late Columbus, whose cruelty resulted in an insurrection among the conquered natives; Columbus also did not mention him in his reports to Spain, thus condemning Juan to "obscu-rity" (2:191). He admits he is too old now to find the route to Cathay. Menendez enters. He has since been promoted to bishop and looks the part of an *"oily intriguer of Church politics"* (2:192). Menendez deviously hints that Juan will discover the Foun-tain of Youth, but after he departs, Luis warns that Menendez wants to get Juan out of the picture.

Beatriz de Cardova enters. A strikingly beautiful girl of about 18, Beatriz introduces herself as Juan's new ward; she is the child of the now deceased Maria and Vicente de Cordova. Beatriz carries a patent from the king for Juan to locate Cathay. Before dying, Beatriz tells Juan, her mother asked her to bring him "'tenderness . . . [t]hat will repay the debt I owe him for saving me for you'" (2:194). Juan curses the memory of his lost youth but then gallantly kisses Beatriz on the hand and welcomes her to Porto Rico.

### Scene 4

Early evening three months later in Menendez's study in the palace—a large room with high ceilings and a massive cross hanging on the rear wall. *"The color scheme is dark and gloomy, the atmosphere that of a rigid, narrow ecclesiasticism"* (2:194). Quesada enters to inform Menendez that the Spanish citizens held a meeting and decided Juan must resign as gov-ernor unless he sails to Cathay at once. He continues that Juan has held secret meetings with the chieftain Nano, and the Spaniards believe the Indian chief must burn at the stake. But Menendez, furious at Quesada for goading the Spanish settlers to rebel, had plotted a peaceful revolt against Juan, not a mob-run insurrection. As punishment, he orders Quesada to join Juan on the voyage to Cathay.

Flames light the sky where the Spanish are burning local villages. Juan enters, looking much older. *"Beneath the bitter, mocking mask there is an expression of deep, hidden conflict and suffering on his face as if he were at war with himself"* (2:196–197). Menendez is shaken by the thought that Juan may have overheard the conspiracy. Realizing this did not happen, he accuses Juan of being too immersed in Beatriz's affairs to govern and demands to know why he has not sailed for Cathay. Juan angrily insists he will wait for Nano to help him locate Cathay and takes offense at the insinuation Beat-riz might look upon him as a father. He exits in a fury. Realizing that Juan is under Beatriz's spell, not Nano's, Menendez summons her.

Beatriz enters. Menendez terrifies her with the prospect of rebellion, accusing her of inciting revolt by convincing Juan to embolden the Indians. He tells her Juan has become a frail old man, and the only thing to save him is the quest for Cathay—his life's ambition. Oviedo enters and insists their only hope is to join forces with the rabble against Juan. Beatriz calls him a coward. Menendez orders her to change Juan's mind. Once she is gone, he assures Oviedo they will triumph if she succeeds.

*Scene 5*

A dungeon cut into natural rock with a stone staircase leading to a trapdoor in the vaulted ceiling. Nano is semiconscious and hangs limp, his body *"thin and wasted,"* from iron chains attached to the back wall (2:201). At center, a soldier stokes a fire, in which several irons are heating. Juan comes through the trapdoor and asks if Nano has agreed to talk. He has not, and Juan orders the soldier outside. He exposits that Porto Rico has erupted into a state of rebellion. "What matter?" he says helplessly, "I could pray that it might be a deluge annihilating mankind—but for Beatriz" (2:202). He begs to know what enables Nano to withstand suffering so courageously. "What values give you your loan of life?" (2:202). But his anger rises as Nano refuses to disclose the route to the Fountain of Youth. He threatens Nano with the hot irons but drops them despondently to the floor. He then draws his sword and vows to end Nano's life, but the chieftain's family having been slain by the Spanish and his tribal lands vanquished, he is unafraid of death. Juan promises to bring Nano back to his old home, which rouses the Indian's interest. Nano does not trust him, but after Juan swears to Nano's god rather than his own, he agrees to guide Juan to the fountain. Beatriz's voice can be heard above, and Juan rushes happily to meet her. Nano lifts his eyes to the ceiling and intones, "Great Spirit, forgive my lie. His blood shall atone!"—and the curtain falls (2:204).

*Scene 6*

Same as scene 3—the courtyard of the governor's palace. It is twilight, and the sky is dark with clouds. Beatriz and Juan meet at center, and Beatriz is taken aback by Juan's harried appearance. She warns him about the rebellion, but he *"makes a gesture of contempt with his sword as if brushing*

*all revolutions aside"* (2:204). He asks whom she dreams of as her lover, and she admits shyly it is his younger double, someone like the dashing Juan of her mother's stories. He admits he had been incapable of love then but that her tenderness has cured him. She implores him to sail for Cathay to restore him to health. Juan announces his plan to sail at once and asks for a kiss and her promise to wait for his return before marrying; she assents. He makes to kiss her on the lips but instead kisses her forehead as a father might.

Luis enters with word that rebels are calling for Nano's blood and that Juan has lost control as governor. Juan vows to protect Nano. Beatriz departs to share Juan's plan with Menendez. Luis calls his friend's search for the fountain "merely a fable, legend, the dreams of poets," but then Juan shocks him with the blasphemous suggestion that Christ's story is no more real (2:208). Luis sees that Juan has fallen in love with Beatriz. Juan admits that, for him, she is the "Spirit of Youth, Hope, Ambition, Power to dream and dare" (2:209).

Beatriz returns with the news that Menendez is powerless to stop the mob, and Juan prepares for a fight. Menendez enters, pleading with Juan to hand Nano over to the mob. Nano is dragged in by soldiers. The mob pours into the courtyard, led by Quesada and calling for Nano's blood. Juan strikes down four men, and the rest back away fearfully, shouting that Juan is bewitched by the Indian chieftain. Juan proclaims that the fleet will sail the following day, but he requires Nano to pilot them to Cathay. He then orders Nano to tell them of his homeland, which he does in a *"clear monotonous voice, with expressionless face"* (2:211). The mob shouts their approval and disperses singing a chantey of gold and glory. "Now you must find the golden cities!" Beatriz exclaims; but Juan responds, "I only care for the one—the golden city of Youth, where you are queen" (2:212). She looks into his face, bewildered, as the curtain falls.

**Part 3**

*Scene 7*

Four months later on a strip of beach in Florida. Bright moonlight illuminates the sand, but the forest is a *"black shadow"* in the night (2:213). An

Indian chief is discovered looking out to SEA. Armed with a tomahawk, a knife, and an unslung bow, he motions for his Medicine Man. A withered old man appears from the forest with a painted face and ornaments dangling from scant clothing. More Indians emerge from the darkness, and the chief orders them to prepare for a fight.

Nano comes up the beach, dripping wet. He identifies himself as a son of a former chief from their tribe and tells them he swam from the Spanish warship to warn them of the impending Spanish raid. The white men are not gods, he explains, but their weapons are powerful. As evidence of their brutality, he describes the crucifixion of Christ. "They see only things, not the spirit behind things," he goes on, and their only true god is gold. He recounts tricking Juan into believing he could find the Spring of Life, which "Only Gods can reveal" (2:214). The chief agrees to meet him the next day at a nearby spring. Nano will tell Juan it is the Spring of Life, and they will ambush the Spanish there. But when Nano swims away, the Medicine Man counsels the chief to "first try to propitiate their devils" (2:215). The chief orders a meeting of the council, and the Indians disappear into the forest.

*Scene 8*
The same beach at noon the following day. The sun beats down on the hot sand, and the forest is now "a matted green wall" (2:216). Led by the Medicine Man, the Indians are constructing a makeshift altar on a large rock with a bowl made of bark to fill with gold nuggets. They plunge a cross made of branches into the sand but mistakenly plant it upside down. They hear the boom of a warship's canon and shrink back in terror. The Medicine Man bolsters their resolve, convinced that if they pretend to worship the same god, the Spanish will leave them in peace. They form a circle around the shrine and dance ceremonially.

Juan enters, followed by Luis, Nano in chains, soldiers, monks led by Quesada, and a group of armored noblemen. Quesada takes in the upside-down cross and shoots the Medicine Man for blasphemy. The rest of the Indians flee in a panic. When Quesada has turned away, the Medicine Man heaves himself up, plunges his knife into Quesada's back, and they both fall dead. The men roar with anger and make to pursue the others, but Juan commands them to stay. He questions Nano's description of the land as "a land of flowers," though the landscape is "dead, preserved in some colorless, molten fluid" (2:216). Nano explains the flowers are inland by a spring. With Juan's go-ahead, the men plant the banners of Castile and Aragon, then kneel as Juan officially annexes the land, which he names Florida (the land of flowers).

Noting the men's impatience, Luis urges Juan to his feet. A noble sees the gold, and they spill the bowl's contents in a chaotic scene of unhinged greed. Juan orders them back in formation, then shouts for everyone to sing the "Te Deum." There is a dead silence, and "all nature seems to lay upon these men a mysterious spell, a sudden exhausted recognition of their own defeat" (2:219). The Franciscans sing the "Te Deum" "mechanically and spiritlessly," and the others half-heartedly join in as the curtain falls.

*Scene 9*
Around midnight in the Florida jungle. Flowering vines twist around massive tree trunks, Spanish moss hangs down thickly from the branches, and a spring gurgles in the midst of a grassy clearing. The Indians are hiding on the periphery. A bird call can be heard, and then an Indian appears; the chief comes out to greet him. The Indian reports that Juan and Nano have entered the forest. They hide; the chief is ready to give Nano the signal when it is time for the ambush.

Juan and Nano enter. Nano identifies the spring as the Spring of Life, and Juan again voices disappointment and suspicion over the lack of flowers and beautiful maidens. Nano has led him to several springs on their voyage through the islands to Florida, including one with an old hag instead of maidens, but Nano insists this is the spot. A whistle comes from the forest, and Nano assures Juan it is a bird. Juan's emotions get the better of his suspicions as he dreams of Beatriz. "You are everywhere and nowhere—part of all life but mine!" (2:221). Nano goads him to continue, and after a final prayer to Beatriz and eternal youth, Juan kneels and drinks.

Nano disappears into the forest and orders the Indians to kill Juan when he rises. Eyes closed, Juan builds the courage to look at his reflection. He groans in anguish, then jumps to his feet and draws his sword. The Indians shower him with arrows, and he falls to the ground. Nano checks the body, then commands them to attack the Spanish camp. The Indian warriors plunge back into the woods. In the distance is heard the terrified howls of dying Spaniards as the curtain falls.

*Scene 10*

The same scene, a few hours later. "*As the curtain rises, there is a pitch-blackness and silence except for the murmur of the Spring*" (2:222). Juan is struggling to get to his feet, but he falls back to the ground. Wondering if he is dead, he begs to God for a sign, "a second's vision of what I am that I should have lived and died!" At that moment, a "*strange unearthly light*" illuminates the clearing. The figure of a woman rises from the spring, "*like a piece of ancient sculpture, shrouded in long draperies of a blue that is almost black.*" She stares forward, arms at her sides, palms turned outward, "*with a stony penetration that sees through and beyond things*" (2:222). Juan demands to know who she is—death? an angel?—but receives no response. He calls for Beatriz, and suddenly her voice comes from the darkness singing Luis's song of "eternal recurrence" from scene 1.

Light pours over the spring, and it transforms into a colorful fountain whose water merges with the land and the sky. The form of Beatriz emerges from the water, and she dances as if communicating the "*spirit of the fountain.*" Juan alternates between anger, defiance, and desperation at the mystical spectacle, then sinks to the forest floor. Beatriz vanishes, and the figure of a Chinese poet appears; he is writing on a block with a brush, "*absorbed in contemplation.*" Juan perceives him to be the "poet from the East who told his father the Fountain lie" in Yusef's tale from scene 1 (2:223).

Yusef appears, followed by Nano, at whom Juan shouts in uncontrollable rage. Luis is next, and his presence calms and comforts him. The four apparitions join hands in a circle, and Juan guesses they signify the cycle of life "from old worlds to

new," then laughs derisively, "cheating the old and wounded—Ha!" (2:224). Beatriz's singing can once again be heard, and the forms of the four men disappear into the fountain. They soon reappear, dressed in clothing representative of leaders of their respective religions and holding "*the symbol of his religion before him*" (2:225), then fade back into the fountain. "All faiths," Juan says in confusion, "they vanish—are one and equal—within—." The form of the old Indian hag from the earlier fountain appears, reaching out to him. He wishes her away, then changes his mind and allows her to sit with him, upon which she transforms into Beatriz. "Beatriz!" he shouts in ecstasy. "Age—Youth— They are the same rhythm of eternal life!" (2:225).

Beatriz and the original figure disappear into the fountain, and then Beatriz's form rematerializes in the water. She is tall now, "*majestic, vibrant with power.*" Her arms are raised upward; she "*soars upward. A radiant dancing fire, proceeding from the source of the Fountain, floods over and envelops her until her figure is like the heart of its flame.*" Juan stares at the vision, then shouts in religious ecstasy, "I see! Everlasting, time without end! Soaring flame of the spirit transfiguring Death! All is within! All things dissolve, flow on eternally!" (2:225). Beatriz's singing continues, this time triumphantly, then stops. The stage goes dark, and Juan loses consciousness.

Dawn comes up, and Luis and another Dominican enter. Luis shouts joyfully that Juan has survived the assault. Juan awakes in a semiconscious state, murmuring about his new state of enlightenment. Luis and the other monk carry him out.

*Scene 11*

Some months later in the courtyard of a Dominican monastery in Cuba. The walls are unadorned but for several Christian symbols displayed in the wall's niches—a crucifix, figures of the Holy Family and Saint Dominic—and the lush, tropical plants and sky can be seen through the entranceway and over the walls. Juan lies asleep in a chair, and the Father Superior, "*a portly monk with a simple round face, gray hair and beard,*" stands nearby. Luis enters and informs the Father that a caravel (a small Spanish sailing ship) has arrived carrying sad news for Juan. Juan wakes up, and the Father Superior leaves to prepare vespers. Luis tells him of the arriving caravel and of an Indian insurrection on Porto Rico that killed Menendez. Beatriz has come from there on the caravel to nurse him. Juan tells his friend that the experience at the fountain was "the one time Beauty touched my life" (2:228). Luis looks *"more and more troubled"* and at length informs him that his nephew, also named Juan, is accompanying Beatriz.

Beatriz and Juan's nephew enter with their servants, who go into the monastery. Luis tenderly squeezes Juan's hand and departs. Beatriz expresses relief that Juan survived. The nephew, *"a slender, graceful young cavalier,"* introduces himself. He echoes Juan's early pronouncement that gold does not interest him, only the expansion and glory of Spain. "Brave dreams!" Juan says, "Echoes blown down the wind of years" (2:229). Beatriz describes the nephew proudly as the noblest defender of the settlement during the insurrection, her image of the older Juan from her mother's stories. "Then you have found him at last—my double?" Juan asks (2:229). She shows some embarrassment, but Juan shouts exultantly that they love each other. He blesses them with his hands, then falls back into his chair.

Beatriz and the nephew depart, but their voices are soon heard singing the song of eternal recurrence outside the walls. Luis enters and, annoyed by the young people's singing, starts off to scold them. "No!" Juan shouts. "I am that song! One must accept, absorb, give back, become oneself a symbol! . . . Oh, Luis, I begin to know eternal youth! I have found my Fountain! O Fountain of Eternity, take back this drop, my soul!" (2:231). Luis bows his head and weeps as his old friend dies. Father Superior reenters to announce vespers. He asks if Juan is dead, and Luis cries, "No! He lives in God!" They pray over his body. The Fountain of Youth song fills the air, and then the chants of vespers begin. *"For a moment the two strains blend into harmony, fill the air in an all-comprehending hymn of the mystery of life,"* and the curtain falls (2:231).

## COMMENTARY

*The Fountain* is the first of three mythic-historical dramas Eugene O'Neill wrote through the 1920s,

the others being MARCO MILLIONS, about the famed Venetian explorer Marco Polo, and *LAZARUS LAUGHED*, regarding the biblical character Lazarus. *The Fountain*, though deeply flawed, directly addresses a major theme of O'Neill's: the tension that forms when professional ambition clashes with spiritual fulfillment, love of beauty, and human compassion. Throughout most of the dramatic action, Juan Ponce de Leon closely resembles Captain David Keaney from O'Neill's early one-act sea play *ILE*, Anthony Mayo from BEYOND THE HORIZON, and Marco Polo from the epic drama *Marco Millions*. In the character of James Tyrone, closely based on his father JAMES O'NEILL, this tension between love and ambition culminates, as most of his major themes do, in his late masterpiece LONG DAY'S JOURNEY INTO NIGHT. *The Fountain* also importantly looks forward to O'Neill's planned cycle A TALE OF POSSESSORS SELF-DISPOSSESSED, which meant to condemn Western corporate greed and imperialism as the harbinger of what he considered a failed society. In the Western world, O'Neill fiercely argued, the unstoppable force of materialism had destroyed the promise of mankind in general, and the United States in particular.

Maria de Cordova first introduces the motif of Juan's conflicting consciousness when she warns him in scene 1 about the dangers of a dual self—"soldier of iron—and dreamer. God pity you if those two selves should ever clash!" (2:173). This spiritual "clash" generates the tension of each scene shift, and it builds considerably until its culmination in the "ecumenical mystical experience" (Floyd 235) Juan finds at the Fountain of Youth. What he discovers there is a deep spiritual enlightenment that he calls it "eternal becoming"—"O God, Fountain of Eternity, Thou art the All in One the One in All—the Eternal Becoming which is Beauty!" (2:226). O'Neill also introduces this rather vague concept of recurrence and unity with Luis's song in scenes 1, 10, and 11:

> Love is a flower
> Forever blooming
> Life is a fountain
> Forever leaping . . .
> Failing, falling,
> Ever returning
> To kiss the earth that the flower may live. (2:175)

Luis (the poet) and Maria (the lover) represent the angel-like side of Juan's divided self, while the scheming clergymen, avaricious nobles, and bloodthirsty soldiers pull at him possessively from the opposing side. Another significant historical division is that of church and state as represented in the feud between Juan and Christopher Columbus. Columbus's stated goal is to "crusade for the glory of God," as opposed to spearheading "an escapade in search of easy riches" for the nobles aboard his ship (2:183). Juan, in contrast, wishes to usher in "a new era of world empire" for Spain (2:184). Once Juan embraces the coexisting, cyclical life forces of love, religion, mankind, and nature through his love for Beatriz and renounces his perverse quest for glory and power, he may die in a blissful state of peace and forgiveness.

*The Fountain* might be considered one of O'Neill's early ventures into EXPRESSIONISM, given its weighty romanticism and free-form episodic structure (Bogard 232–233), though many scenes come across as mere MELODRAMA. In the play's action, O'Neill frees himself to present an explicit manifestation of a god figure in the "Fountain of Eternity" as the natural world, religious ecstasy, unity, beauty, and love, all represented by the benign spirits of the fountain rather than as the abstract God entity of his Catholic upbringing. But O'Neill muddles this point, along with other forms of natural philosophy and Taoism that seem to inform the play but remain elusive in the text. (For example, is "eternal becoming" meant to call to mind or build upon FRIEDRICH NIETZSCHE's notion of "eternal recurrence"?) Travis Bogard helps explain the convolution; "God *is*, as Nature *is*, and man need only recognize his presence to be caught up in the force of life at its most profound. Once the force is known, once the vision is made real, man is in harmony with his world" (236). Bogard continues that O'Neill later shaped the dramatic action of ALL GOD'S CHILLUN' GOT WINGS and WELDED in a similar way by offering his protagonists a state of "religious ecstasy" in the final scene (2:238), though this structure reaches jarring levels in his most overtly religious "God play" DAYS WITHOUT END, which many mistakenly took, if understandably, for O'Neill's return to CATHOLICISM.

Doris Falk sums up *The Fountain* this way: "Amid all the pseudo-historical intrigue of the plot, the real action of the play unfolds in the progress of Juan from soldier to poet, from cynical militarist to devout believer in 'eternal becoming'" (79). No one denies the ambitious thematic scope of this work, though what lessons have actually been learned remain a mystery. How does Juan open himself up to revelations of "eternal becoming"? By falling in love with Beatriz? O'Neill leaves such crucial questions unanswered. If they are meant to be unanswerable, as some critics maintain, then Juan's grandiloquent attempts to articulate his revelation sound like more gushing water on the stage. The play's most historical scenes provide its most intriguing moments—the shipboard scene with Columbus, the political infighting at Porto Rico, the native response to Spanish imperialism, the conflict between spirituality and materialism in the Catholic church—in spite of O'Neill's insistence that historical facts are "incidental" to this drama. But it is in the historically grounded moments that O'Neill relinquishes his vague, lyrical spiritualism and allows his immense talent for dialogue to offset the poetical bombast. "As an action adventure, it succeeds," Virginia Floyd notes bluntly. "As serious drama, it fails" (235).

The director Robert Edmund Jones of the Experimental Theatre, Inc., showcased dazzling sets for the exotic locales and engineered a series of arresting stage and sound effects, particularly in the fountain scene (scene 10). Given *The Fountain*'s "lush romanticism" (Floyd 226), extravagant time shifts stretching over a 20-year period, an enormous cast, and extremely demanding scene shifts—including Moorish and Spanish courtyards in Spain and Porto Rico, respectively; a Florida beach and jungle; and a Dominican monastery in Cuba—Jones clearly accomplished something remarkable.

The blame for its failure, then, was placed squarely on its author. After the New York premiere, critics complained that *The Fountain* was too long and impossibly dull in spite of the remarkable, widely acknowledged visual tour de force Jones had brought off at the Greenwich Village Theatre. Though a veteran impresario of set design, Jones had his work cut out for him, and the fountain scene, along with the constant and radical scene shifts throughout, took an enormous amount of fancy creative footwork and cost more money than the company could make back. "As usual," the *New York Times* reported, "Mr. O'Neill has made [the stage designers'] task none too easy" (quoted in Wainscott 176). Ronald H. Wainscott has gleaned from contemporary accounts of Jones's production that the fountain scene, "Filled with music, song, and dance in a rapidly shifting cacophony of sight and sound . . . suggested a modern-day masque" (175). This may be one reason it is rarely, if ever, revived today.

The play's major failings include its lack of action, its seemingly interminable length, and a bombastic poetical writing style that lacks any tangible substance. "There is something labored in his purple patches," wrote Barrett Clark of the play's pretentious lyricism (102). According to O'Neill, however, what critics believed distasteful in the writing was a deliberate stylistic decision, if admittedly a failed one. "So many folk have objected to the blank verse rhythm in [*The Fountain*] on the grounds, seemingly, that it is not beautiful verse," he explained to GEORGE JEAN NATHAN,

> Whereas, of course, I used to gain a *naturalistic effect of the quality of the people and speech of those times,* to place them, with little care for the original poetic beauty save in the few instances where that is called for. I wanted to make ordinary speech of ordinary thoughts stilted, bigoted, narrow, sentimental and romantic, pretentiously ornate. (162, emphasis mine)

Ironically, the dialogue is sadly lacking for precisely those reasons. In fact, O'Neill originally intended the entire play to be performed in his own blank verse; given his lifelong lack of talent in writing POETRY, it is well he changed course in the final draft. *The Fountain*'s length would tax any audience's patience. With a running time of well over three hours, "the monotony," complained *Bookman* of the 1925 premiere, "became positively painful" (quoted in Wainscott 174). O'Neill as historian, wrote the *Wall Street Journal,* has "lately rediscovered Mr. Ponce de Leon and embalmed him" (quoted in Wainscott 171).

O'Neill actually researched the history of the Spanish conquest quite carefully. As represented in the play, the Spaniards customarily kidnapped native chiefs to disrupt the tribal leadership structure and forced natives to convert to Christianity and perform menial labor, and O'Neill renders much of Ponce de Leon's life with historical accuracy as well (Floyd 230n and 233n). But according to O'Neill, the actual history of Ponce de Leon only concerned him "incidentally," as he explained in his program note, "without pretending to any too educational accuracy in the matter of dates and facts in general."

> The characters, with the exception of Christopher Columbus, are fictitious. Juan Ponce de Leon, in so far as [sic] I've been able to make him a human being, is wholly imaginary. I have simply filled in the bare outline of his career, as briefly reported in the Who's Who of histories, with the conception of what could have been the truth behind his "life-sketch" if he had been the man it was romantically—and religiously— moving to me to believe he might have been! Therefore, I wish to take solemn oath right here and now that *The Fountain* is *not morbid realism*. (quoted in Clark 101, emphasis mine)

Nevertheless, O'Neill took great pains to research the period and his subject, reading anything that might help him, in his words, "in the way of atmosphere, mood, method or myth" (quoted in Sheaffer 52). Over the course of his study, he drew back his efforts, however, as "the more I ponder over this play . . . the more I feel that the less I know of the real Juan Ponce, the better. I want him to be my Spanish noble, none other—not even his historical self. . . . I am afraid too many facts might obstruct the vision I have and narrow me into a historical play of spotless integrity but no spiritual significance. Facts are facts, but the truth is beyond and outside them" (quoted in Sheaffer 53).

Juan's experience at the fountain corresponds to that of the character Reuben Light before the electric dynamo in DYNAMO and John Loving's similar religious awakening before the cross in the later play *Days Without End*. All three characters outstretch their arms in prayer to a newly accepted god figure, and each incants a prayer or poem that acknowledges the cyclical flux of existence, what Juan Ponce de Leon calls the fountain's "rhythm of eternal life" (2:225) and Reuben the dynamo's "song of eternal life" (2:873). *The Fountain*, in the end, stands as O'Neill's largely failed attempt to create, paradoxically, an outsized type of theater that transcended the melodrama of the previous generation with a "naturalistic effect" while at the same time rejecting "morbid realism" (ironically, a style O'Neill can be largely credited with inventing for AMERICAN THEATER). In the end, the epic quality of *The Fountain* more closely resembles the "romantic extravaganzas of his father's theater" than the kind of psychological NATURALISM audiences had grown to expect from the man who, by the mid-1920s, was reputedly America's greatest playwright.

## CHARACTERS

**Alvaredo, Luis de**   Juan de Ponce de Leon's close friend, a Spanish nobleman and later a Dominican monk. *"His face is homely but extremely fetching in its nobility, its expression of mocking fun and raillery"* (2:173). When we first meet the good-natured Luis, he is *"slightly drunk"* and, though dressed as a courtly nobleman, looks *"dissipated"* (2:173). A poet by nature and temperament, Luis sings a song in the courtyard at Granada in scene 1 that forms the play's leitmotif (Floyd 227): "Love is a flower / Forever blooming / Life is a fountain / Forever leaping . . . Failing, falling, / Ever returning / To kiss the earth that the flower may live" (2:175). He has temporarily saved the life of the Moorish minstrel Yusef, who sings a song of the fabled Fountain of Youth that only Luis can translate. Juan, a pragmatic militarist, scoffs at the sentimental, poetic undertones of the fountain myth.

After the Franciscan Diego Menendez kills Yusef offstage, Juan lamely tries to comfort the stricken Luis by sarcastically insinuating that Luis may reunite with the Moor at his mystical fountain. "Juan," Luis replies, "why do you always sneer at beauty—while your heart calls you a liar?" (2:179). By scene 3, over 20 years later, Luis has joined the Dominican order, which Juan, a firm opponent to Christian meddling in the New World, considers

an act of treachery. They remain friends, however, and Luis appears as an apparition during Juan's revelation at the Fountain of Youth in scene 10. By dancing and singing with an Indian Medicine Man, a Buddhist, and a Moor, Luis symbolizes one link in the integrated religious vision that Juan experiences there.

**Aswad, Ibnu**   Moorish chieftain of Granada. O'Neill describes him as *"an elderly, noble-looking Moor, the lower part of his face covered by a long, white beard"* (2:169). Aswad welcomes the victorious Juan Ponce de Leon into his palace in Granada after Juan has vanquished the Moorish armies and secured southern Spain for the Spanish crown. Aswad believes the defeat was the will of Allah. "Whosoever the victor," he proclaims to Juan, "there is no conqueror but Allah!" (2:170).

**Columbus, Christopher**   Spanish explorer and Juan Ponce de Leon's commander on the expedition to Porto Rico. In scene 2, he is commanding a vessel on his second journey to the New World with Juan, his political rival, onboard. O'Neill describes Columbus as having *"long, white hair"* and *"a commanding figure of noble presence, the face full of the ardent, fixed enthusiasm of the religious devotee"* (2:183). Columbus's stated goal is to "crusade for the glory of God" as opposed to spearheading "an escapade in search of easy riches" for the nobles aboard his ship (2:183). Juan, in contrast, wishes to usher in "a new era of world empire" for Spain (2:184). Personal ideologies aside, Juan respects Columbus initially as a man whose enterprises have "served Spain well" (2:182), even though, he admits, the two explorers are "by nature antagonistic" (2:183). By scene 3, 20 years later, Columbus has died, and Juan curses him for having antagonized the natives with his Christian rhetoric along with ignoring Juan's "services" in his reports to Spain and thus condemning him to "obscurity" (2:191).

**Cordova, Beatriz de**   Maria and Vicente de Cordova's daughter and Juan Ponce de Leon's ward in Porto Rico. The 18-year-old Beatriz arrives at Porto Rico 20 years after Juan's voyage with Christopher Columbus. Juan is now the governor of the island,

and Beatriz announces she has been made his ward after her parents' passing. Her striking resemblance to her mother, Maria, who had loved Juan in Spain, inspires Juan to continue his search for Cathay with hopes of discovering the Fountain of Youth. Beatriz's name resembles the 13th-century Florentine poet Dante Alighieri's great love and poetic muse, Beatrice, who inspired the poet to understand the everlasting nature of life. In O'Neill's play, as in Dante's poetry, Beatriz is *"a beautiful young girl . . . the personification of youthful vitality, charm and grace"* (2:193).

Juan rapidly falls in love with Beatriz, though she loves him as a father figure and dreams of finding his youthful double for marriage. This provokes Juan to resume his quest for the Fountain of Youth in the jungles of Florida. There, in scene 10, Beatriz's beautiful form miraculously appears in the fountain. Her singing and dancing, along with those of the apparitions of a Chinese poet, Yusef the Moorish minstrel, Nano the Indian chief, a Buddhist priest, the Dominican monk Luis de Alvaredo, and a woman "figure" representing the fountain itself, reveal to him the mystery of life and grant him the knowledge of a unifying matrix of religion, nature, and love.

In the final scene, Juan is being nursed at a Dominican monastery in Cuba after the Indians attacked him in Florida. There the actual Beatriz introduces Juan to his nephew, who not only shares his name but looks like his youthful self and aspires to conquer lands in the name of Spain as his uncle had. Rather than be distressed over Beatriz's lover, as his friend Luis de Alvaredo feared he might, the elder Juan blesses the young couple, then dies in peace. Beatriz, rather than a well-rounded character in her own right, apparently symbolizes the love and beauty required to experience spiritual enlightenment.

**Cordova, Maria de**   Vicente de Cordova's wife and Beatriz de Cordova's mother. Maria, *"a striking-looking woman of thirty-eight or forty,"* appears in the opening scene to meet Juan Ponce de Leon. Her face betrays a marked expression of *"discontent and sorrow"* (2:170); she loves Juan but understands that his ambition prevents him from returning her

affection. Recalling the desires of Mary Tyrone in O'Neill's masterpiece *Long Day's Journey into Night*, a character based closely on the playwright's own mother, she admits to Juan that she prays "to become worthy again of that pure love of God I knew as a girl" (2:171); she believes her inability to bear a child has been God's punishment to her for loving Juan.

Juan announces his plan to join Christopher Columbus on his next voyage to the New World, which rouses her into confessing her true feelings for him. "You are noble," she tells him, "the soul of courage, a man of men." She then articulates the play's central theme: "You will go far, soldier of iron—and dreamer. God pity you if those two sides should ever clash!" (2:173). Twenty years later, Maria has died, and her daughter Beatriz de Cordova becomes Juan's ward in Porto Rico. Before dying, her mother bade her daughter "bring him tenderness. . . . That will repay the debt I owe him for saving me for you" (2:194). Juan falls in love with Beatriz, but she loves him as a father and desires to marry a man who matches her mother's descriptions of Juan.

**Cordova, Vicente de**   Maria de Cordova's husband, Beatriz de Cordova's father, and Juan Ponce de Leon's fellow soldier and rival. Vicente, *"a gray-haired, stern, soldierly noble of forty-five,"* arrives at the Moorish courtyard in scene 1 to celebrate the Spanish victory, only to be ridiculed by Juan. We find that Vicente's wife, Maria, is in love with Juan, but Vicente does not know it, which adds dramatic irony to the action. When Juan suggests Maria may appreciate a drink from the Fountain of Youth, Vicente challenges him to a duel, which causes a great scandal in the Spanish court and tarnishes Juan's reputation. Nevertheless, Juan later voices some satisfaction when he hears that Vicente and Maria's marriage has strengthened and that she had borne a baby girl—Beatriz de Cordova.

**Juan**   Juan Ponce de Leon's nephew. Juan arrives in the play's final scene as Beatriz de Cordova's suitor. Though Juan Ponce de Leon fell in love with her, Beatriz, whose mother, Maria de Cordova, had been in love with Juan in Spain, always considered him a father figure. At one point she tells him that she wishes to find a younger double of him.

Beatriz announces the arrival of Juan's nephew at a Dominican monastery in Cuba. She praises the young man as "you were in my mother's tales," and the older Juan responds wistfully, "Then you have found him at last—my double?" (2:229). The younger Juan, the only nobleman brave enough to fight during a native insurgency on Porto Rico, is a *"slender, graceful young cavalier"* with the goal, like his uncle before him, "to plant Spain's banner" on the citadels of the Golden Cities of Cathay. "Brave dreams!" Ponce de Leon responds, remembering his own youthful ambitions. "Echoes blown down the wind of years" (2:229). Beyond jealousy, Juan blesses the union between the two lovers and dies in peace.

Juan is the personification of the cyclical nature of life. As his uncle dies, Juan will adopt his role and then, presumably through Beatriz's love, arrive at a similar enlightenment to his uncle.

**Medicine Man**   The medicine man of the Indian tribe Juan discovers in Florida while searching for the Fountain of Youth. O'Neill describes him as *"incredibly old and shrunken, daubed with many insignia in paint, wearing many ornaments of bone and shell"* (2:213). When the captured Indian chief Nano escapes from the Spanish vessel and warns his former tribe of the impending Spanish invasion, the Medicine Man advises his chief to "first try to propitiate their devils," rather than ambush them as Nano recommends (2:215). The Medicine Man arranges for a Christianlike shrine to be erected on the beach when the Spanish arrive, but they mistakenly place a makeshift cross upside down, and the Franciscan Friar Quesada stabs him to death for blasphemy. With a last burst of strength, the Medicine Man stabs Quesada in the back, and they both die together.

**Menendez, Diego**   A Franciscan priest, later bishop, and a contemporary of Juan Ponce de Leon and Luis de Alvaredo. O'Neill describes him, like Friar Quesada, as having *"a pale, long face, the thin, cruel mouth, the cold, self-obsessed eyes of a fanatic"* (2:174). Though a clergyman, he is a political ani-

mal, hungry for power and murderous. At the end of scene 1, Menendez kills Yusef the Moorish minstrel, whom Luis had tried to protect, and later attempts to supplant Juan as governor of Porto Rico. Menendez wants to convert the natives by force, but Juan, as governor, prevents him. Unlike Menendez, Juan believes enslavement is an institution that places a burden on Spain rather than providing an effective labor force. The scheming Menendez convinces Beatriz to encourage Juan on his quest to Cathay to get Juan out of the way. Eventually killed during a native insurrection, Menendez, like Quesada, symbolizes the Catholic Church's brutality and greed during Europe's imperialistic expansion in the New World.

**Nano**   A tribal chieftain in Porto Rico but formerly of Florida ("Land of Flowers"). O'Neill describes him as *"a tall, powerfully built Indian of fifty or so"* (2:188). Once the Spanish conquer Porto Rico, Nano bravely refuses to convert or pay tithes, causing the Franciscan monks Quesada and Menendez to demand that Juan Ponce de Leon, then governor of Porto Rico, execute him. Nano's wives and children, along with many others, were brutally killed by the Spanish invaders. Juan refuses to permit the execution, and the monks scheme to coerce Juan to continue his quest for Cathay (China), thus allowing them free reign. Quesada foolishly incites insurrection when he makes the Spanish soldiers believe that Nano has bewitched Juan. Meanwhile, Nano tells Juan that he knows about the cities of Cathay and the Fountain of Youth, but he refuses, even under torture, to reveal how to get there. When Juan offers to take him back to his original home, however, Nano perceives an opportunity for revenge and agrees to help him. Nano then accompanies Juan on a wild goose chase through the Caribbean. When they finally arrive off the shores of Florida, he slips away and warns his tribe of the Spaniards' brutal designs on their land. He suggests a plan to ambush them by a stream he will identify as the Fountain of Youth, a plan they carry out once the tribesmen witness the Spaniards' cruelty. After the ambush, he believes Juan has been killed and does a *"wild dance of savage triumph"* (2:221).

Nano appears again in scene 10 as an apparition at the Fountain of Youth. By dancing and singing dressed as a medicine man with a Moor, a Buddhist, and a Christian, he symbolizes one link in the integrated religious vision Juan experiences there.

**Oviedo, Alonzo de** A Spanish nobleman. O'Neill describes Oviedo with Castillo and Mendoza as *"the type of adventurous cavaliers of the day—knights of the true Cross, ignorant of and despising every first principle of real Christianity—yet carrying the whole off with a picturesque air"* (2:174). Oviedo, the only one of the three who has any significant role, turns against Juan de Ponce de Leon upon Juan's refusal to execute Nano and implement, through brute strength, the conversion and forced labor of the natives on Porto Rico.

**Ponce de Leon, Juan** General, explorer, and later governor of Porto Rico. In scene 1, Juan, *"a tall, handsome, Spanish noble of thirty-one,"* arrives at the Moorish palace of the chieftain Ibnu Aswad (2:169). He has defeated the Moors in battle and thus captured southern Spain for the Spanish crown. He is loved by Maria de Cordova, the wife of his "brother-in-arms" Vicente de Cordova, though he is too pragmatic and ambitious to return her love. However, Juan reveals a romantic spirit to those who know him best. O'Neill signals this division in the first STAGE DIRECTIONS when he describes the character as *"haughty, full of romantic adventurousness and courage; yet he gives the impression of disciplined ability, of a confident self-mastery—a romantic dreamer governed by the ambitious thinker in him"* (2:169). When Juan meets Maria in the Moorish palace, she warns him of the dangers of living with a dual self—"soldier of iron—and dreamer. God pity you if those two selves should ever clash!" (2:173). Then, when he scoffs at the fable of the Fountain of Youth, reputedly located in Cathay (China), his old friend Luis de Alvaredo exposes his duality, saying "Juan, why do you always sneer at beauty, while your heart calls you a liar?" (2:179).

Another conflict forms in scene 2, one symbolized in Juan's fractious relationship with his rival, Christopher Columbus. Though neither man values material wealth, Juan joins Columbus on his second voyage to gain glory for Spain through conquest, which Columbus sees as a "crusade for the glory of God" (2:183); thus, O'Neill treats the disjunction between church and state as well.

Twenty years after Juan arrives in the New World, he has been promoted to governor of Porto Rico, though he had initially dreamed of finding the Western Passage to the East, where he might conquer the glorious cities of Cathay as the Venetian Marco Polo had before him. Both the Catholic clergymen and the Spanish settlers in Porto Rico turn against him, thinking him too easy on the natives and bewitched by the Indian chief Nano. Maria de Cordova's beautiful daughter Beatriz de Cordova arrives in Porto Rico and announces that her parents have died and she has been made his ward. Now in his early 50s, Juan has become prematurely aged by disillusionment, his face now *"aged, lined, drawn,"* and his hair and beard have turned gray (2:187). Juan falls in love with the 18-year-old Beatriz and hopes the Fountain of Youth will return him to his former self.

Juan persuades Nano to pilot him to the "Land of Flowers," where the Indian lies that the Fountain of Youth can be found. They sail not to Cathay but to Florida, where a native Indian tribe ambushes him, under Nano's urging, at a stream purported to be the Fountain of Youth. They leave him for dead, but Juan awakens and experiences a sublime revelation. A mystical fountain rises out of the stream and presents him with the apparitions of a woman figure from antiquity and Beatriz, who sings the fountain song originally sung by Luis in scene 1, that represents the leitmotif of "eternal becoming"—a spiritual revelation of the mystery of the universe. Apparitions of a Muslim (the Moorish minstrel Yusef), a Buddhist (a Chinese poet), a Christian (his friend Luis de Alvaredo), and a pagan (Nano), all dressed as priests, next reveal to him the unity of all religious faiths and thus of humankind as a whole.

In scene 11, Juan is dying from his wounds at a Dominican monastery in Cuba. Beatriz has fallen in love with his nephew, also named Juan and ambitious to expand the Spanish empire, like his uncle before him. Juan blesses their union and dies in peace while Beatriz and her lover sing the fountain song and Dominicans chant at vespers. The combined sound fills the air with "an all-comprehending hymn of the mystery of life" (2:231).

**Quesada, Friar**   A Franciscan monk. Much like his elder, Diego Menendez, Quesada has *"the burning eyes of a fanatic"* (2:188). Quesada appears in scene 3 demanding justice against the tribal chieftain Nano, who refuses to convert and whose tribe refuses to pay the Spanish tithe. In scene 4, Quesada informs Menendez that he attended a meeting of the Spaniards, and they all demand that Juan Ponce de Leon resign as governor of Porto Rico and that Nano, who they believe has bewitched Juan, should be executed. Menendez admonishes Quesada for sparking a foolish rebellion, then punishes him by sending him with Juan to Florida in search of Cathay and the Fountain of Youth. Once in Florida, Quesada kills the Indian Medicine Man for mistakenly placing a makeshift cross (meant to appease the Spaniards) upside down. But the Medicine Man, with his last effort before dying, stabs Quesada in the back, and they die together. Like Menendez, Quesada symbolizes the Catholic Church's brutality and greed during Europe's imperialistic expansion in the New World.

**Yusef**   A Moorish minstrel. In scene 1, Yusef appears in the courtyard of Ibnu Aswad's palace in Granada just after the Spaniards have conquered southern Spain. O'Neill describes him as *"a wizened old Moor dressed in the clothes of the common people, but wearing the turban signifying that he has made the pilgrimage to Mecca"* (2:174). His hatred of the Spanish is apparent in his eyes, but, like Aswad, he looks *"resigned to his fate"* (2:174). Juan Ponce de Leon's poetic friend Luis de Alvaredo, the only Spaniard who speaks Arabic, has taken a liking to him and saved him from the Franciscan monk Diego Menendez. He sings a song describing the Fountain of Youth, from which, Luis translates for Juan, chosen men "drink, and the years drop from them like a worn-out robe" (2:177). Soon after, Menendez kills him offstage. Yusef appears again in scene 10 as an apparition at the Fountain of Youth. By dancing and singing with an Indian Medicine

Man, a Buddhist, and a Christian, he symbolizes one link in the integrated religious vision Juan experiences there.

## BIBLIOGRAPHY

Bogard, Travis. *Contour in Time: The Plays of Eugene O'Neill.* Rev. ed. New York: Oxford University Press, 1988.

Clark, Barrett H. *Eugene O'Neill: The Man and His Plays.* Rev. ed. New York: Dover, 1947.

Falk, Doris V. *Eugene O'Neill and the Tragic Tension: An Interpretive Study of the Plays.* New Brunswick, N.J.: Rutgers University Press, 1958.

Floyd, Virginia. *The Plays of Eugene O'Neill: A New Assessment.* New York: Ungar, 1985.

O'Neill, Eugene. *Selected Letters of Eugene O'Neill.* Edited by Travis Bogard and Jackson R. Bryer. New Haven, Conn.: Yale University Press, 1988.

Sheaffer, Louis. *O'Neill: Son and Artist.* Boston: Little, Brown, 1973.

Wainscott, Ronald H. *Staging O'Neill: The Experimental Years, 1920–1934.* New Haven, Conn.: Yale University Press, 1988.

# *Gold: A Play in Four Acts*
## (completed, 1920; first produced, 1921)

Eugene O'Neill's full-length play *Gold* completes a project begun with WHERE THE CROSS IS MADE. A one-act "ghost" play produced by the PROVINCETOWN PLAYERS in their 1918–19 season, *Where the Cross Is Made* contains virtually the same setting, characters, and plot, with some revisions, as the final act of *Gold*. In summer 1918, O'Neill's second wife, AGNES BOULTON, wrote a draft of a short story idea entitled "The Captain's Walk." O'Neill then co-opted the project for himself, first writing up a four-act scenario and then turning the last act into *Where the Cross Is Made* (Boulton 191), before finally returning to the original structure for *Gold*.

*Gold*'s first producer, John D. Williams, advertised the play in newspapers as "Eugene O'Neill's greatest drama . . . the greatest dramatic event of the year!!" (quoted in Wainscott 67). In hindsight, Williams's excessive optimism sounds a good deal like a "sustaining lie" that might readily apply to any number of delusional protagonists in O'Neill's canon. These buoyant press releases, perhaps simply false advertising, were instantly undermined after opening night (delayed three times) at the Frazee Theatre in New York City on June 1, 1921. *Variety* magazine called *Gold* "talky, balky, tiresome and impossible" (quoted in Wainscott 69), and the *Nation* quipped that the play was derivative from popular MELODRAMA and O'Neill's own writing. "We cannot rid ourselves of the feeling that we have heard all this before" (Lewisohn 26).

Ronald H. Wainscott, in his comprehensive production history of O'Neill's premieres, submits that regardless of many aborted failures over the course of the playwright's career, "With the possible exception of *The* FIRST MAN, *Gold* was the worst first production of a full-length O'Neill play" (74). O'Neill placed the blame squarely on the shoulders of its leading man, Willard Mack, an actor well known for his histrionics. In a letter written on the date of its premature closing, O'Neill wrote to writer and filmmaker Ralph Block, "I feel like paraphrasing Rolla's line into: 'Don't cry, my child, and I will take you to see an actor boiled in oil'" (O'Neill 156). The production closed after only 10 days and 13 performances, and it has probably never been revived. Nevertheless, *Gold* importantly developed several themes that inform O'Neill's greatest masterpieces—domestic conflict, the "inscrutable force" of the SEA, the life-sustaining "pipe dream," and the tension between material greed and spiritual well-being.

## SYNOPSIS

### Act 1

A desolate coral island at the southern tip of the Malay Archipelago. A palm tree casts a circular shadow around its trunk, the only protection from intense sunlight; a lagoon can be seen in the distance over long hummocks of sand. Abel, the cabin boy of the sunken whaling ship *Triton,* lies sleeping in the shade. His body quivers erratically, suggesting terrible nightmares. The ship's cook, Butler, who had been shanghaied by the *Triton* in Oak-land, California, rushes onstage from the far right, rear. He places his hand upon the boy's forehead, and Abel wakes up, apprehensively looking about (1:893). Butler offers the boy water from a flask he secured before the ship went down. Everyone on the island is dying of thirst. Abel begs for more, but Butler roughly refuses, telling him the remaining water will save him and the boy, while the others, who have treated them both brutally, will justly die. Butler explains that Captain Isaiah Bartlett; his boatswain (pronounced bos'n), Silas Horne; a crewman, Ben Cates; and an islander, Jimmy Kanaka, found a chest of brass trinkets and other junk they assume is gold and emeralds. When Butler tried to set them straight, they made after him as if to kill him (1:895–896).

The sailors enter with the heavy chest. All of them are parched and sunburned, their lips cracked and tongues swollen from thirst, *"But there is a mad air of happiness, of excitement, about their scorched faces"* (1:897). The men cry desperately for water. Captain Bartlett retorts, "Ye ought to be singin' 'stead o' cryin'—after the find we've made. . . . Gold! Enough of it is your share alone to buy ye rum, and wine, and women, too, for the rest o' your life!" (1:897–898). "No more hard work on the dirty sea for ye, bullies," Bartlett promises his crew, "but a full pay-day in your pockets to spend each day o' the year" (1:898). For his part, Bartlett plans to return to his son, Nat; his daughter, Sue; and his wife, Sarah, in California and never go whaling again. Bartlett's voice becomes *"more and more that of a somnambulist"* (1:898) as he tells the story of a Spanish sailor in New Bedford who asked to charter his ship to claim a stash of gold in South America using a map with a cross where it was buried. The captain refused the sailor and always regretted it. He turns on Butler, calling him a liar and demanding that he acknowledge the worth of the "treasure." Butler looks down at a *"heavy anklet encrusted with colored glass"* and humbly agrees that he was mistaken. The captain strikes him to the ground for his earlier "lie," and the boy runs off. Butler follows, roaring back at the crew that the gold is nothing but brass and junk. Jimmy offers to knife him, but the captain orders him to stay his hand.

Jimmy spots an approaching sailing vessel. Bartlett orders the men to bury the treasure and draw a treasure map so as not to forfeit a portion of their shares to the rescuing ship. Fearing Butler and Abel know where they buried the gold, the men implore Bartlett to order their deaths before the ship arrives. Bartlett says nothing, but Jimmy looks in his face, and, *"seeming to read the direct command there"* (1:905), he goes after the cook and the boy. They hear the two murdered offstage, and Bartlett, now desperate with guilt, demands reassurance from his crewmen that he never gave the word to kill. They assure him only Jimmy would be punished if the bodies were discovered. Jimmy returns, and Bartlett orders him to dig their graves so "none'll see" (1:906). The men rush off to greet the oncoming ship, and Bartlett says, "Gold! I've been dreamin' o' it all my life!. . . Lay safe, d'ye hear. For I'll be back for ye! Aye—in spite of hell I'll dig ye up again!" (1:907). His crew's joyful shouting comes from offstage as the curtain falls.

## Act 2

Late afternoon six months later in Captain Bartlett's boat shed on his wharf on the California coast. The shed is strewn with *"old anchors, ropes, tackle, paint-pots, old spars, etc."* (1:908). Bartlett and Silas Horne are discovered, and though Horne looks fully recovered from their ordeal in the South Seas, Bartlett's hair has turned white, and his eyes reveal an inner conflict between weakness, fear, and determination. Bartlett and his crew have rigged another vessel with which to return to the island and claim their treasure. They plan to leave the following day when the tide is highest, but the ship has not yet been christened, an unthinkable omission that would bring certain bad luck to the voyage. Indeed, Horne remarks, she should have been christened when launched a month before. Bartlett vows to name the ship after his wife, Sarah Allen, and that she will christen it herself. Bartlett confesses he suffers from nightmares in which Abel and Butler return to haunt him. The two share a glass of rum, and Horne convinces Bartlett he did the right thing by killing them.

Mrs. Sarah Bartlett enters. She looks feeble with sickness but determined, and *"there is something*

*accusing in her stare"* (1:911). She wants to speak with Bartlett alone, but he storms out, swearing she will christen the ship with her name. She defiantly refuses. Their 20-year-old-daughter, Sue, enters with her 30-year-old fiancé, Daniel Drew, a ship's officer. Sue scolds her sick mother for leaving her bed. Mrs. Bartlett informs her of Bartlett's departure the following day and repeats her refusal to christen the ship. Sue and Drew assist her out, then reenter. Sue recounts the night her father began sleeping in the shed. Neither parent will reveal what happened, and she believes her 18-year-old brother, Nat, an apprentice ship designer, has been acting strangely as well. She feels "he's caught the disease," as he wants to ship with their father on the new schooner. Nat enters. He looks much like his father, but *"appears an indoor product"* (1:915) rather than a hardened sailor. Sue informs him that their father leaves the next day, and he voices a strong desire to join him. Sue tries to talk him out of it but fails, and she heads back to the house with Drew.

Bartlett enters. Nat hints he knows something about his father's mysterious quest. Bartlett jokes, "Ye'll be tellin' me next it's buried treasure I be sailin' after . . . and a map to guide me with a cross marked on it where the gold is hid! And then they be ghosts guardin' it, ben't they—spirits o' murdered men?" (1:918). "No, not that last," Nat says, but he suspects the first part may not be far off. Bartlett explodes in anger and tells him to stay home with the women. "I'll stand alone in this business and finish it out alone if I go to hell for it," he says, intoning the words *"with a sort of somber pride"* (1:919). Nat relents, and he makes to go. His mother enters at the same time and orders him up to the house.

The Bartletts discuss the evening before Captain Bartlett moved to the shed, when he had recounted the events of act 1. She begs him to stay at home and confess his sins of murder and greed. He remarks that she looked forward to the money he might have made had he discovered ambergris (a valuable substance made in a sperm whale's intestines that contains a chemical used in perfume), but she retorts that his actions are her punishment. She tells him the gold is "cursed with the blood o' the man and boy ye murdered" (1:921). Though he "spoke no word" (gave no direct order) to kill them, she responds that he might have stopped the killing nevertheless. She pleads with him to confess his sins to "God and men, and make your peace and take your punishment" (1:922). He stubbornly refuses and again demands she christen the ship. Once he threatens to bring Nat along, she concedes. As she exits, Bartlett awkwardly attempts to comfort her, but, horror-stricken by the curse, Mrs. Bartlett shouts, "No. Don't you touch me!" (1:924), and she looks fearfully over her shoulder as she rushes through the door. The curtain falls.

### Act 3

Outside the Bartlett home on the following morning at dawn. An iron platform at left connects to a steel ladder down to the wharf. Jimmy, Cates, and Horne look down on the Bartletts' progress with the christening. Mrs. Bartlett's wails can been heard below. "He's still out o' his head, d'ye know that, Cates?" Horne says (1:925). They now regard Bartlett as insane and refer to Jimmy under their breath as a "nigger" (1:926). They have begun a plot to claim the treasure for themselves alone. Bartlett comes up the ladder in a mood of *"triumphant exaltation"* (1:927). He orders the men to prepare the ship for departure; Cates and Horne go down, but Jimmy pauses, questioning whether Sarah placed a spell on the ship. Bartlett laughs mockingly and orders him down.

Mrs. Bartlett, Sue, Drew, and Nat come around the house from the right. Drew and Nat support Mrs. Bartlett, who is *"in a state of complete collapse"* (1:927). Bartlett shouts down to the men at the wharf, and Sue silences him as the men assist her mother inside, scolding him for coercing her to christen the boat. He mulishly informs her he will disembark that morning, no matter the doctor's prognosis. Sue swears her mother will die if he leaves, and he covers his ears shouting, "No! Ye lie!" (1:931). Drew appears in the doorway. When he challenges Bartlett's manhood, Bartlett draws back his fist in a rage, but Sue stops him. Bartlett reluctantly agrees to see Mrs. Bartlett once more before departing and storms into the house. Sue follows. Horne and Cates emerge from the ladder

and discuss the situation with Drew. They all think Bartlett has gone insane, but the crewmen are still determined to go through with the voyage, though neither man can navigate.

Sue returns from the house. She has overheard the conversation and pleads with Drew, who has just received his captain's license, to take her father's place. Drew accepts, and the two go into the house to prepare for his voyage. Horne and Cates conspire to kill Drew at sea. Drew and Sue reenter. Drew orders the men to the wharf, kisses Sue goodbye, and follows them down the ladder. Nat returns from a doctor's appointment and asks whether their father has left. When Sue tells him he is still inside, he offers himself as a replacement. Sue argues that "Ma would lose her mind" if he left (1:936). Nat notices the sails are set to depart and spots Drew onboard. She explains Drew's offer and waves down to him.

Bartlett emerges from the house. He notices the schooner has already disembarked and is heading out to the point. Sue assures him Drew only wants to test the boat, which quiets him until he sees it heading for the open sea. Only then does Sue tell her father of Drew's plan. Bartlett curses her meddling, and Mrs. Bartlett emerges from the house. She praises God for having saved Bartlett from the evil voyage and curses the ship. Sue protests to her mother, and Bartlett lunges at Mrs. Bartlett to strike. Mrs. Bartlett collapses into Sue's arms, and she and Nat take her inside. Bartlett goes quickly to the iron platform and shouts between his cupped hands, "Ahoy! Ahoy! Sarah Allen! Put back! Put back!" (1:939).

### Act 4

Nine o'clock at night exactly one year later in Bartlett's *"look out post"* (1:940), a room at the top of the Bartlett house that perfectly resembles a sea captain's cabin with portholes, lantern, cot, floating ship's compass, etc. Sue sits dressed in black and looking much older, with Doctor Berry at a table at center. Mrs. Bartlett is dead. Sue extracts a letter from Drew, who has written from a hospital in Rangoon, that tells of the *Sarah Allen's* destruction and his close escape from the murderous crew: They stabbed him and left him for dead on an island, where the natives nursed him back to health and sent him on to Rangoon. He then caught a fever and nearly died. Nat has already gone to San Francisco to determine the schooner's fate. The doctor entreats Sue to admit Bartlett, who obsessively keeps watch for the schooner from his lookout, into an asylum. "Your father won't let himself look the facts in the face. If he did, probably the shock would kill him. That darn dream of his has become his life" (1:941).

Footsteps are heard ascending the stairway, and Nat, who also looks older and careworn, enters the room. In San Francisco, he found firsthand witnesses who saw the derelict. Nat admits he feels glad about the fate of the ship and has decided to move away. He expresses astonishment when Sue hands him the letter from Drew. After reading it, he criticizes Drew for allowing the crewmen to get the better of him and not reveal their secret. The doctor bids them goodnight. Nat and Sue talk about their father's condition and go downstairs.

Bartlett enters from a companionway above. *"The madness which has taken almost complete possession of him in the past year is clearly stamped on his face, particularly in his eyes, which seem to stare through and beyond objects with a hunted, haunted expression. His movements suggest an automaton obeying invisible wires"* (1:945). He spreads out his map and proclaims that he ordered the men home within the year, and they should signal their arrival with a green and a red light on the main mast. He conjures Butler and lambastes him for regarding the treasure as junk; then Silas Horne, reminding him that he never gave the order to kill; and finally Mrs. Bartlett, for telling him she was going to die and making him promise to confess his sins. Nat reenters, informs his father that the *Sarah Allen* is destroyed, and finally persuades Bartlett to tell him the story of the gold. Bartlett assures him the schooner will arrive that night. Surprisingly, Nat reassures his father he did the right thing by killing Butler and Abel.

Bartlett goes back up the companionway and shouts, "Sarah Allen, ahoy!" (1:950). Nat looks through one of the portholes and sees nothing. His father reenters and tells him to look again. Nat now sees the vessel. "A red and a green—clear as day!"

(1:951). They hear the men lower the boats and arrive at the front door. Nat throws open the door, and Sue enters, *"looking with amazement and horror from father to brother"* (1:951). Nat has succumbed to his father's madness and rushes downstairs to greet the men. Sue accuses Bartlett of driving his son to insanity; she demands he tell Nat the truth. Bartlett pulls himself once again up the companionway. Nat reenters. *"His pale face is set in an expression of despair"* (1:952). He drops his head in her lap and sobs that he found nothing on the wharf. He shows her the map to prove that their father was not lying about the gold and vows to outfit a new schooner to sail back to the archipelago.

From above, we hear Bartlett's triumphant shout once more, "Sarah Allen, ahoy!" (1:954). He rushes down, announcing that his ship has arrived. Nat begins to believe again. Sue takes Bartlett's face in her hands and begs him to stop for Nat's sake. He grapples with conflicting thoughts but finally relents—"Nothing there, boy!" Bartlett confesses that, in his mind at least, he had made the order to kill—"I murdered 'em in cold blood" (1:954). Nat protests, and Bartlett's mind again swings between righteousness and guilt; his body appears to fight the battle raging within, as *"he makes to force the sustaining lie out of his brain"* (1:954), and his sanity reemerges to save his son. He produces the anklet from his pocket, something he had kept with him but never authenticated, fearing Butler was right and his dream lost. Nat identifies it scornfully as "the cheapest kind of junk—not worth a damn!" (1:955). Bartlett takes the map, tears it to pieces, and sags back into a chair. Sue orders Nat to find the doctor and checks Bartlett's pulse, crying out, "Oh. Nat—he's dead, I think—he's dead!" (1:955). The curtain falls.

## COMMENTARY

At the time of its premiere, most critics found *Gold* depressing and tedious. O'Neill's omission of avant-garde experimentation, the playwright's most famous contribution through the 1920s, might partially explain why. O'Neill's STAGE DIRECTIONS only vaguely suggest the expressionistic devices he had successfully employed the previous fall, in 1920, to dramatize the psychology of extreme guilt in *The*

EMPEROR JONES; even *Where the Cross Is Made*, which garnered only slightly better reviews than *Gold*, ends with the ghosts of Cates and Horne returning to haunt Bartlett in his lookout.

The stage directions for the barren island, too readily evoking Robert Louis Stevenson's *Treasure Island*, might lead us at first to take *Gold* as another experiment in this direction: *"The intensity of the sun's rays is flung back skyward in a quivering mist of heat-waves which distorts the outlines of things, giving the visible world an intangible eerie quality, as if it were floating submerged in some colorless molten fluid"* (1:893). Only occasionally after this does O'Neill provide directions that hint at this "intangible eerie quality"—for instance, Bartlett's voice in act 1 while he dreams of abandoning the sea and speaks increasingly like a *"somnambulist"* (1:898), and when he descends from the companionway in the final act like *"an automaton obeying invisible wires"* (1:945). Clearly these hints were not sufficient, and the stage designer for the premiere, a traditionalist named Joseph Physioc, staged the production realistically, including using real sand for the *"long hummock a few feet above sea level"* in act 1 (1:893; see Wainscott 71). The play is neither an example of NATURALISM like *"ANNA CHRISTIE,"* which would be produced the following November and win him his second PULITZER PRIZE, nor is it EXPRESSIONISM like *The Emperor Jones*. As such, the high emotional tenor of the Bartletts' monologues strike the false note of MELODRAMA that typified what O'Neill detested about his father's generation of AMERICAN THEATER.

O'Neill's first chronicler, Barrett H. Clark, defends the play somewhat, stating that although "in no other early play are his basic shortcomings more strikingly evident" (109), "what a magnificent idea there is in it!" (106). The social and psychological forces that drive Isaiah Bartlett's greed are, indeed, signature O'Neill: the complexities of family life; the vindictiveness of the sea on its defectors; the steady conflict between material acquisitiveness and spiritual fulfillment; and the human need for a life-sustaining "pipe dream," involving money, religion, or personal ambition. O'Neill would develop these thematic fixations over the entirety of his career, though generally distilling them in separate works until they all came together powerfully in his late masterpiece, LONG DAY'S JOURNEY INTO NIGHT.

O'Neill overplayed his hand with *Gold*, however, and his ideas muddle together in half-baked scenes that contain gross improbabilities: Why would Bartlett's henchmen believe in the gold's value in the first place? If they were mad, as Butler suggests, how did they regain their sanity and not Bartlett? Why would Daniel Drew take on Bartlett's mad quest in just a moment's notice without even knowing what they were looking for? Why would Sue (the practical one), who was highly suspicious of the crew, ask him to take such a risk in the first place? If Bartlett died of shock, as Dr. Berry's diagnosis indicates, why does he have *"an expression of strange peace"* before he dies (1:955)? How and why, exactly, does Mrs. Bartlett die, given that he stayed? What is the basis for Nat's insanity—genetic predisposition?

Each member of the Bartlett family personifies an idea rather than a well-rounded character in and of him- or herself. These "ideas" are also implausibly mixed: Bartlett, the abusive scoundrel driven to insanity by his acquisitiveness; Mrs. Bartlett, a religious fanatic who mysteriously dies from the knowledge of her husband's evil-doing; Nat, the whiny invalid who dreams of escape; and Sue Bartlett, the supposedly sensible one who sends her fiancé off on a cursed six-month voyage through the South Seas. Sue is the only Bartlett grounded in the real world, a metaphor for O'Neill's "reality principle" (Engel 27). Dedicated as she is to "truth," Sue comes across as O'Neill's voice of the female GENDER, domesticated practicality in the mode of another failed female character, Alice Roylston in SERVITUDE. Certainly we can see soundings of James and Mary Tyrone in *Long Day's Journey* in the elder Bartletts, who can be read as avatars of O'Neill's actual parents, JAMES O'NEILL and MARY ELLEN "ELLA" O'NEILL, and Nat might be an incipient Edmund Tyrone (O'Neill himself). Louis Sheaffer has pointed out that O'Neill changes the schooner's name from *Mary Allen* in *Where the Cross Is Made* to *Sarah Allen* in *Gold*. This change is significant in that O'Neill appears to have replaced his mother's name, Mary Ellen "Ella"—a religious woman whom O'Neill "lost" to morphine as Bartlett lost the *Sarah*

*Allen* and his eponymous wife—with his childhood nurse's name, Sarah Sandy (1968, 431). Sheaffer speculates that the change was likely made to avoid his mother making the connection.

O'Neill had already written several plays on the cruel fate of sailors who abandon the sea—all four of the SS GLENCAIRN plays, CHRIS CHRISTO-PHERSEN, and its superior revision *"Anna Christie"* are some obvious (and generally more successful) treatments of this theme. Rather than adopting the life of a waterfront loafer with a lifetime supply of "rum and wine and women," as his men choose to do, Bartlett plans to join his family, similar to the doomed character Olson in the *Glencairn* play *The* LONG VOYAGE HOME, and "rest to home 'til the day I die" (1:898). O'Neill probably intended the scene changes to reflect this movement "home" and away from the sea, moving as they do from the island, which symbolizes the sea as it does in another *Glencairn* play, *The* MOON OF THE CARRIBBEES, to the wharf, to the house, and finally to his upper-floor lookout. Each step takes him farther from the sea and closer to death. (These disruptive scene shifts fuelled discontent among audiences, as they had with BEYOND THE HORIZON; Wainscott 72). Daniel Drew is the only sailor who never forswears his devotion to maritime life; thus, he will survive.

John Williams's press release described *Gold* as a "study in conscience" (quoted in Wainscott 67). Starting with Bartlett's first assertion in act 1 that he never gave "the word" to kill Butler and Abel, he cannot fully relieve himself of guilt until "confessing" to Nat in act 4. As such, O'Neill's character development of Bartlett lies somewhat fallow. Here is a man who, prior to the play's action, made a practice of shanghaiing sailors (as he had Butler) along with beating and terrorizing his crew (including his 15-year-old cabin boy), all the while perfectly sane. It is tricky, then, to deduce how we are to share his wife's presumption of Bartlett's inherent goodness and where his daughter derives her love for him. Another underdeveloped motive behind his "sustaining lie" is that his desire to find gold stems from his sense of obligation to Mrs. Bartlett to give up whaling, attend church, and "keep up with the Joneses":

I'll give up whalin' like ye've always been askin' me, Sarah. Aye, I'll go to meetin' with ye on a Sunday like ye've always prayed I would. We'll make the damn neighbors open their eyes, curse 'em! Carriages and silks for ye—they'll be nothin' too good—and for Sue and the boy. I've been dreamin' o' this for years (1:898).

Mrs. Bartlett, then, is nearly as guilty as Bartlett himself, and she confesses as much in act 2, saying, "That was my sin o' greed that I'm bein' punished for now" (1:921). In O'Neill's world, her equal need for social acceptance and religious belief must end tragically (with the bizarre exception of his late "God play" DAYS WITHOUT END). Among the Bartlett household, Sue's "reality principle" emerges, Edwin A. Engel submits, "as a concept in contradistinction to the role of Mrs. Bartlett, who represented the conscience, which is the product of fanatical religion and therefore as mad as Bartlett's 'lies'" (27). Mrs. Bartlett's "false idol" of Christ on the cross, as O'Neill more subtly implies in *Where the Cross Is Made*, can be equated with Bartlett's false gold. Both delusions share the same tragic fate. Mrs. Bartlett still represents Bartlett's moral conscience, which, after battling with his "lies," melodramatically wins out in the final scene; but as Dr. Berry had prophesied, her moralizing kills him in the process.

Two other one-act plays O'Neill wrote in 1918, *The* ROPE and *The* DREAMY KID, also deal with the life-sustaining pipe dream that would eventually suffuse the entirety of his late masterpiece *The* ICE-MAN COMETH (Sheaffer 1973, 106). The loss of one's "sustaining lie," or "pipe dream," in those plays also ends in tragedy, but without the *"strange peace"* Bartlett experiences in the final scene of *Gold* (1:955).

## CHARACTERS

**Abel**  Captain Isaiah Bartlett's cabin boy on the whaler *Triton*. O'Neill describes Abel as a *"runty, under-sized boy of fifteen, with a shriveled old face, tanned to parchment by the sun"* (1:893). O'Neill presumably named Abel after the biblical son of Adam and Eve who was killed by his wicked brother, Cain. Abel is dying from thirst in act 1, and Butler shares his last drops with him, as he had also been treated abusively by Bartlett and his men. Jimmy Kanaka kills him before the rescue ship can arrive, so they will not have to share what they assume is gold treasure.

**Bartlett, Captain Isaiah**    Captain of the whaler *Triton*. Captain Bartlett is a massively built man with a small mustache and *"iron-gray hair"* (1:896) who speaks in a heavy accent redolent of a hardened sailor. Before the play's action, Bartlett hears a tale of hidden treasure from a Spanish sailor in New Bedford, Massachusetts. For years after, he regretted his decision not to sail with him and began obsessing over the possibility of finding his own treasure. After his whaler, the *Triton*, is wrecked off a coral island in the Malayan archipelago, he and his crew—his mate, Silas Horne, his boatswain, Ben Cates, and an islander, Jimmy Kanaka—discover a chest full of Malayan brass trinkets and, mad with thirst, believe them to be gold and jewels. When a rescue ship arrives, Bartlett silently orders Jimmy Kanaka to kill Butler, his cook, and Abel, the cabin boy, so they cannot take the gold for themselves. He buries the chest and draws a map with plans to reclaim the gold after outfitting another ship at home.

Bartlett returns to his home in California, where his wife, Sarah, is driven to sickness and death by his evil deed (which he admitted to her soon after his arrival). His son Nat shares his desire for gold, and his daughter Sue attempts to save them all from insanity. When hearing that Sue persuaded her fiancé, Daniel Drew, to take the voyage in his stead, Bartlett's mental obsession worsens. After a year, he expects the ship back and confesses to his son what happened on the island. Nat joins in his obsession until Sue convinces her father to tell his son the truth. He shows Nat an anklet that he saved but never authenticated and confesses that he murdered his two crewmen in thought if not word. Once Bartlett's confession is complete and thus his dream shattered, he penitently dies in his daughter's arms.

Bartlett is one of several examples in the O'Neill canon who harbor an obsession with material wealth that proves destructive to themselves and those around them— Abraham Bentley from *The Rope*, Captain David Keeney of ILE, Marco Polo in

MARCO MILLIONS, and James Tyrone in *Long Day's Journey into Night* are some other examples. O'Neill believed that his father, James O'Neill, the model for James Tyrone, sold his great acting talent for cash by buying the rights to and taking the lead role in the moneymaking melodrama *The Count of Monte Cristo*. Bartlett's motives to make himself and his family rich are complicated by his silent order to kill Abel and Butler. But his wife's intense religious zealotry provokes a crisis of conscience. The struggle between morality and greed torments him to madness until he finally confesses his sins; he dies soon afterward with *"an expression of strange peace"* (1:955).

**Bartlett, Nat**    Captain Isaiah Bartlett's son. Nat, who is 18 years old, closely resembles his father in appearance, but *"there is no suggestion . . . of the older man's physical health and great strength. He appears an indoor product, undeveloped in muscle, with a sallow complexion and stooped shoulders"* (1:915). Nat works as a ship designer, though he aspires to go to sea like his father. Nat offers to take his father's place on the voyage back to the Malay Archipelago, but his sister Sue defies his wish by sending her fiancé, Daniel Drew, instead. After their mother dies, Nat goes to San Francisco to investigate the fate of Captain Bartlett's ship, the *Sarah Allen*. He returns with evidence that it sank and plans to leave home to start life anew. Unlike Nat's counterpart, Ned, in *Where the Cross Is Made*, whose vulnerability to sharing his father's insanity creates the tension of that play, Nat is a background figure in *Gold*, and his acceptance of his father's fantasy of hidden treasure seems perfunctory. In the end, Sue convinces her father to tell Nat the "truth," that he murdered his men, and Nat discovers that the treasure is nothing but brass trinkets; he then says, "What a damn fool I've been!" (1:955), his last line in the play.

**Bartlett, Mrs. Sarah Allen**    Captain Isaiah Bartlett's wife. Mrs. Bartlett is physically slight, and although *"sickness, or the inroads of a premature old age, have bowed her shoulders, whitened her hair, and forced her to walk feebly with the aid of a cane,"* she stands firmly against her husband's desire to return to claim his "treasure" and carries herself with an air of *"fixed determination"* (1:910). Mrs. Bartlett grows increasingly ill over the course of the middle two acts and finally succumbs, presumably a death caused by Bartlett's murderousness and avarice. When he requests that she christen his new schooner with her name, *Sarah Allen,* she refuses until he threatens to take their son with him. Mrs. Bartlett calls on her husband to "Confess to God and men, and make your peace and take your punishment" (1:922) for killing his cabin boy, Abel, and cook, Butler, in the Malay islands to ensure they would not take his treasure. When he accuses her of sharing his materialism, she retorts, "That was my sin o' greed that I'm bein' punished for now" (1:921). Mrs. Bartlett is an intensely religious woman, a character who, Edwin A. Engel argues, "represented the conscience, which is the product of fanatical religion and therefore as mad as Bartlett's 'lies'" (27). Her Christ on the cross is his gold treasure, equally false idols in Eugene O'Neill's worldview.

**Bartlett, Sue**    Captain Isaiah Bartlett's daughter. O'Neill describes Sue as *"a slender, pretty girl of about twenty, with large blue eyes, reddish-brown hair, and a healthy, sun-tanned, out-of-door complexion."* Like her mother, Mrs. Sarah Bartlett, her slight frame contrasts with her demeanor, in Sue's case, a *"suggestion of great vitality and nervous strength"* (1:911). Sue is the only member of the Bartlett family who demonstrates no signs of insanity or obsessive compulsion, such as her father's and brother's fantasy of the *Sarah Allen* returning with gold or her mother's religious zealotry. With her combination of practicality and love, Sue takes on a series of lost causes in an attempt to hold her family together. She convinces her fiancé, Daniel Drew, to take her father's place as captain of the *Sarah Allen* and make the voyage to the South Seas in pursuit of Bartlett's secret; he does so and is nearly killed, first by a murderous crew, then a South Asian fever. Sue attempts to make her mother stay in bed; Mrs. Bartlett does not do so and eventually dies. Sue convinces her father to throw off his pipe dream of gold and tell Nat the "truth"; he does so and dies moments

later. She successfully staves off her brother's momentary insanity, but there is no indication he will be better off for it.

**Berry, Doctor**    The Bartlett family physician. Dr. Berry is about 60 years old with a kindly demeanor; his *"whole manner . . . is that of the old family doctor and friend, not the least of whose duties is to play father-confessor to his patients"* (1:940). Dr. Berry submits to Sue that Captain Isaiah Bartlett "won't let himself look the facts in the face. If he did," he presciently adds, "probably the shock of it would kill him" (1:941). He believes Bartlett should be placed in an asylum. His diagnosis comes too late, as once Bartlett's fantasy begins to take hold of Sue's brother, Nat, she begs her father to tell his son the truth. Once he does, he fulfills Dr. Berry's prophecy and dies, but with *"an expression of strange peace"* (1:955). Nat scornfully accuses Dr. Berry, as many O'Neill characters do, of "always looking for trouble where there isn't any" (1:943).

**Butler**    Captain Isaiah Bartlett's cook on the whaler *Triton.* Butler was shanghaied by Bartlett and his crew in Oakland, California. Bartlett and his men treated the cabin boy, Abel, abusively throughout their voyage. When the *Triton* sank, Butler, Abel, the captain, and three other crew members—Ben Cates, Silas Horne, and Jimmy Kanaka—found their way to a coral island at the southern end of the Malay Archipelago. Butler had secured a small flask of water from the ship and will only share it with Abel. As a result, neither Butler nor Abel go mad with thirst, as the others do, and Butler identifies the "treasure" the captain and his men find as "all sorts of metal junk . . . . Nothing but brass and copper, and bum imitations of diamonds and things—not worth a damn!" (1:895). Bartlett calls him a liar and demands he retract his statement, which Butler does under threat of physical harm. But he runs away and repeats his assessment defiantly, which eventually leads Bartlett to allow Jimmy Kanaka to find him and Abel and kill them.

**Cates, Ben**    Crew member on the whaler *Triton.* O'Neill describes Cates as *"squat and broad* *chested, with thick, stumpy legs and arms. His square, stupid face, with its greedy pig's eyes, is terribly pock-marked. He is gross and bestial, an unintelligent brute"* (1:896). Cates conspires with Silas Horne, the Captain's boatswain, to claim the false treasure for themselves. In action not seen onstage, they stab Daniel Drew, Sue Bartlett's fiancé, after he takes Bartlett's place at the helm of the new schooner *Sarah Allen*, and leave him for dead at a "native settlement" (1:942). They presumably drown with Jimmy Kanaka (whom they had also planned to kill) when the *Sarah Allen* is wrecked. His character appears as a ghost in the final scene of *Where the Cross Is Made*.

**Drew, Daniel**   Sue Bartlett's fiancé and acting captain of Captain Isaiah Bartlett's schooner, *Sarah Allen*. O'Neill describes him as *"a well-step-up, tall young fellow of thirty. Not in any way handsome, his boyish face, tanned to a deep brown, possesses an engaging character of healthy, cheerful forcefulness that has its compelling charm. There would be no mistaking him for anything but the ship's officer he is. It is written on his face, his walk, his voice, his whole bearing"* (1:912). Drew is devoted to Sue Bartlett; so much, in fact, that he accepts her proposition that he take over as captain of the *Sarah Allen* in her father's stead. Drew does so without Captain Bartlett's permission, ignorant of the *Sarah Allen's* errand to the South Seas. He writes a letter to Sue from a hospital in Rangoon and reports that while in the South Seas, the boatswain, Silas Horne, and the crew members Ben Cates and Jimmy Kanaka stabbed him and left him for dead at a "native settlement" (1:942). The islanders nursed him back to health, but he took a ship to Rangoon, where he caught a fever and nearly died.

**Horne, Silas**   Captain Isaiah Bartlett's boatswain (pronounced bos'n) on the whaler *Triton*. O'Neill describes him as *"a thin, parrot-nosed, angular man, his lean face marked by a life-time of crass lusts and mean cruelty"* (1:896). Horne masterminds the plot, with Ben Cates as his accomplice, to take over the *Sarah Allen* on its voyage to recover the buried "treasure" on the coral island in the southern end of the Malay Archipelago. In action not

seen onstage, they stab Daniel Drew, Sue Bartlett's fiancé, after he takes Bartlett's place at the helm of the new schooner *Sarah Allen*, and leave him for dead at a "native settlement" (1:942). They presumably drown with Jimmy Kanaka (whom they had also planned to kill) when the *Sarah Allen* is wrecked. His character appears as a ghost in the final scene of *Where the Cross Is Made*.

**Kanaka, Jimmy**   Crew member on the whaler *Triton*. O'Neill describes him as *"a tall, sinewy, bronzed young Islander. He wears only a loin cloth and a leather belt with a sheaf-knife"* (1:896). Jimmy stabs the cook, Butler, and the cabin boy, Abel, on Captain Bartlett's unspoken order. Silas Horne, the boatswain, and his lackey, Ben Cates, regard him as a "nigger" (1:926) and plan to kill him, along with Daniel Drew, when they return to claim the "treasure." In action not seen onstage, he goes down with Horne and Cates on the *Sarah Allen* after stabbing Drew and leaving him for dead at a "native settlement" (1:942). His character appears as a ghost in the final scene of *Where the Cross Is Made*.

## BIBLIOGRAPHY

Boulton, Agnes. *Part of a Long Story: Eugene O'Neill as a Young Man in Love.* Garden City, N.Y.: Doubleday & Company, Inc., 1958.

Clark, Barrett H. *Eugene O'Neill: The Man and His Plays.* 1929. Rev. ed. New York: Dover, 1947.

Engel, Edwin A. *The Haunted Heroes of Eugene O'Neill.* Cambridge, Mass.: Harvard University Press, 1953.

Lewisohn, Ludwig. "*Gold.*" Review (1921). In *The Critical Response to Eugene O'Neil*, edited by John H. Houchin, 26–27. Westport, Conn.: Greenwood Press, 1993.

O'Neill, Eugene. *Selected Letters of Eugene O'Neill.* Edited by Trowis Bogard and Jackson R. Bryer. New Haven, Conn.: Yale University Press, 1988.

Sheaffer, Louis. *O'Neill: Son and Playwright.* Boston: Little, Brown, 1968.

———. *O'Neill: Son and Artist.* Boston: Little, Brown, 1973.

Wainscott, Ronald H. *Staging O'Neill: The Experimental Years, 1920–1934.* New Haven, Conn.: Yale University Press, 1988.

# Great God Brown, The
## (completed, 1925; first produced, 1926)

Eugene O'Neill's most enigmatic "mask play," perhaps the most enigmatic play of his career, generated a universal feeling among critics that the celebrated American dramatist had overreached, but brilliantly. The *New York Post* called the play "a superb failure," and *New York Times* critic BROOKS ATKINSON remarked that by making the play so complex—emotionally, psychologically, dramaturgically, and philosophically—O'Neill had placed "a responsibility upon his audience too great and far too flattering" (quoted in Miller 51, 53). Indeed, Atkinson himself found that "to place within the limits of a newspaper review an intelligible account of the details of so involved a play is, of course, quite impossible" (quoted in Miller 53). The actress Leona Hogarth, who played the character Margaret Anthony, complained that ROBERT EDMUND JONES, the play's director, proved incapable of making their roles "intelligible" to his cast; she noted that "there was so much talk of overtones and subtle meanings that the cast was tied up tight as knots. The last act was always obscure and the more Jones tried to explain it the more clouded it grew" (quoted in Sheaffer 192).

O'Neill fully understood critics' potentially negative reaction to the play's complexity, so on the day of the premiere at the GREENWICH VILLAGE Theatre—January 23, 1926—he and his production crew took preemptive action. They rushed copies of the script to a team of transcribers to ensure that critics received a hard copy to review before publishing their pieces the following Monday. (Opening night was deliberately planned for a Saturday so that reviewers would have the following Sunday to decide what to write.) Nevertheless, audiences far less sophisticated than Atkinson, and entirely unprepared for what they were about to see, sat through the play "night after night . . . silently attentive" (Sheaffer 194). Given its experimentalism—with masks, EXPRESSIONISM, symbolism, philosophy, psychology, and religion—it might surprise

Leona Hogarth, as Margaret, and Robert Keith, as Dion Anthony, in the 1926 production of *The Great God Brown* (Courtesy of the Museum of the City of New York)

contemporary readers that *The Great God Brown* was a popular success, especially once it moved uptown to Broadway. Legend has it that two shopgirls were overheard commenting on the play after the third act: One turned to the other and said, "Gee, it's awful artistic, ain't it?" The other replied, "Yes, but it's good all the same" (Clark 163).

## SYNOPSIS

### Prologue

A moonlit night in June on a casino pier in an unidentified location. In an early draft, O'Neill referred to the city as New Caledonia, Connecticut (probably NEW LONDON). The set is meant to evoke a courtroom, with benches on three sides and a railing across the back of the pier. William A. Brown appears with his parents. They are celebrating William's, or Billy's, high school commencement, and a school quartet plays "Sweet Adeline" in the background. With the courtroom atmosphere in place, Billy's father acts as judge and jury, condemning the youth to a future of becoming a partner in his contracting firm as an architect (2:474).

Dion Anthony enters after the Browns exit to join the dance, and it is the audience's first glance at the masks that make the play experimental. Dion's parents are unmasked, while Dion wears a mask that *"is a fixed forcing of his own face . . . into the expression of a mocking, reckless, defiant, gaily scoffing and sensual young Pan"* (2:475). Dion's parents also play judge and jury, first condemning him to "slave" like his father had to, without the benefit of a college career, a course of action that would, his father vociferates, "teach him the value of a dollar!" (2:475, 476). Upon hearing from his wife that the Browns plan to send Billy to college, however, the father's petty resentment over the Browns' success turns him against his own principles: "Then you can make up your mind to go, too! And you'll learn to be a better architect than Brown's boy or I'll turn you out in the gutter without a penny!" (2:476). Dion himself has no such aspirations. In the mold of the Dionysian creative spirit, he wants to be an artist. His response to his parents' designs for him are arbitrary, mocking, though he vaguely utters ejaculations that mean little to his spiritually bankrupt parents. He exits doing *"a grotesque caper, like a harlequin and darts off, laughing with forced abandon"* (2:477).

Margaret then enters. She also wears a mask, but this one is *"an exact, almost transparent reproduction of her own features, but giving her the abstract quality of a Girl instead of the individual, Margaret"* (2:477). Billy follows close behind, unmasked and *"humbly worshipping."* As Billy pledges his love to Margaret, she removes her mask and, ignoring Billy entirely, speaks wistfully to the moon about her love for Dion. They exit separately, with Billy resigned to her passion for Dion.

Dion enters again, and we see both masked and unmasked avatars of his personality—the sad ascetic (unmasked) and the cynical sensualist (masked). Unmasked, he cries out, "Why was I born without a skin, O God, that I must wear armor in order to touch or to be touched?" But then, donning his mask his voice becomes *"bitter and sardonic,"* and that self retorts, "Or rather, Old Graybeard, why the devil was I born at all?" (2:480). Billy enters

again briefly to inform Dion of Margaret's love for him and departs. Margaret enters, and though they both pledge their love to one another, Margaret is terrified and revolted whenever Dion removes his mask. Clearly the soul-searching, fearful Dion, the Dion behind the mask, is not the Dion she has fallen in love with. "All's well," Dion resentfully assures her after replacing the mask, "I'll never let you see again" (2:483).

### Act 1, Scene 1

Dion and Margaret Anthony's sitting room seven years later. The Anthonys live in the same small town in one half of a two-family house. They are now married with three sons and have returned home after living abroad for five years. Like Jim and Ella Harris from ALL GOD'S CHILLUN GOT WINGS, Dion and Margaret had assumed that living abroad would broaden their horizons and allow them to escape the limiting expectations of American society; but also like Jim and Ella, living abroad simply prolongs their inevitable return to face their demons. Dion's mask hangs just below his face, *"giving the effect of two faces."* A self-professed failure as an artist, Dion's actual face looks older and more tortured, though its priestly quality has amplified over time. His mask, however, has distorted from its original Pan-like mischievousness to resembling Mephistopheles and betraying *"the ravages of dissipation"* from years of gambling and alcohol abuse (2:484). The room, like the casino pier, is meant again to suggest a courtroom atmosphere.

Unlike the conflicted figure of Dion, Margaret enters as the classic matron—*"mature and maternal . . . fresh and healthy but there is the beginning of a permanently worried, apprehensive expression about the nose and mouth"* (2:484–486). It is four o'clock in the afternoon, and Margaret chides Dion for having slept so late. "The Ideal Husband!" Dion retorts, calling to mind Oscar Wilde's play of that title. The reference to Wilde might also recall Wilde's novel *The Picture of Dorian Gray* (1890), in which the Irish author also employs a face transfigured from dissipation, but on the painted portrait of his subject rather than a mask. The two engage in spousal repartee—Dion making cynical observations of domestic life and Margaret plead-

Great God Brown, The   195

ing he be more available to the family—in which he sardonically sums up the nature of relationships as "This domestic diplomacy! We communicate in code—when neither has the other's key!" (2:485). Still, Margaret treats him in a motherly fashion, calling him "my poor boy!" while he intones scripture to signify his desperate internal struggle. She then pleads with him to speak to Billy Brown about employment. We learn that Billy has become a successful architect—"his career itself already has an architectural design," Dion scoffs, "One of God's mud pies!" (2:487)—though he remains unmarried and probably still in love with Margaret.

### Act 1, Scene 2
Billy Brown's office at his architectural firm. In contrast to Dion, Billy has *"grown into a fine-looking, well-dressed, capable, college-bred American business man, boyish still and with the same engaging personality"* (2:488). Billy is looking over a blueprint when Margaret enters to inquire about the availability of a position for Dion, since her husband is too proud and dissipated to do so himself. She lies, however, about her husband's state, calling him a "hopeless family man." Billy knows the truth and is *"painfully embarrassed by her loyalty and his knowledge of the facts"* (2:490). Dion had sold his father's holdings in the firm to Billy's father, but Billy is aware that Dion's skills as an illustrator would be an asset to the firm and decides to offer him a job.

### Act 1, Scene 3
The brothel parlor of Cybel, a prostitute. Cybel has found Dion drunk on her doorstep and taken him in to avoid attracting the police. There is no hint of a courtroom here, as Cybel's great quality is that she is judgmental only about those who are untrue to their inner selves—that is, their unmasked selves. Dion lies passed out on one of her sofas, his mask on his chest, as a nickel-in-the-slot piano plays *"a sentimental medley of 'Mother-Mammy' tunes"* (2:492).

Cybel awakens Dion. At first disoriented and fearful (in his unmasked state), he swiftly puts on his mask and is all cynicism and bluster. In retaliation, Cybel takes up her own mask, which casts her with the *"rouged and eye-blackened countenance of the hardened prostitute"* (2:493). She makes clear that if

Dion wants to be nasty and coarse, she is well-practiced in that game. He gives up and removes his mask, revealing, once again, the vulnerable ascetic. She takes her mask off in turn, and they agree to be friends.

The doorbell rings, the two reflexively put on their masks, and Billy Brown enters. He has been searching for Dion to offer him the job. Dion accepts, saying, in the mode of his Mephistophelean persona, "One must do something to pass away the time, while one is waiting—for one's next incarnation" (2:495). Dion then recites a monologue in which he recalls watching his mother's death, and he reflects that Margaret, her replacement, is really three mothers in one—a notion that Margaret will affirm in act 4, scene 2, and the epilogue. Dion sarcastically forsakes his belief in God in favor of becoming a follower of "the Great God Mr. Brown." "Shut up, you nut!" Brown responds, not comprehending the spiritual sacrifice Dion is about to make, "You're still drunk" (2:496).

### Act 2, Scene 1
Cybel's parlor in springtime, another seven years later. Cybel and Dion are both playing solitaire without masks, and Dion's face, again, *"is that of an ascetic, a martyr, furrowed by pain and self-torture, yet lighted from within by a spiritual calm and human kindliness"* (2:497). Cybel is by this time Billy Brown's kept woman, but she loves Dion. She informs Dion that Brown wants the piano out, and when she mentions his name, Dion puts on his mask in a jealous rage. By now it has lost any resemblance to the old Pan mask from the prologue. Rather, it *"is now terribly ravaged. All of its Pan quality has changed into a diabolical Mephistophelean cruelty and irony"* (2:498). Dion's doctor has warned him that one more drop of alcohol will kill him, but Dion continues to drink. Nevertheless, he has been a success at Brown's firm, and it is clear he feels he has betrayed himself spiritually. Interestingly, this is the only scene where the masks are explicitly discussed, though it could be a commonplace expression when Cybel scolds Dion, "Haven't I told you to take off your mask in the house?" Dion exits in a masked fury when Cybel tells him they will not see each other for "a long, long time" (2:500). She

has apparently had a premonition that Dion will die soon.

Brown enters. He is infatuated with Cybel but ascertains that, like Margaret, Dion has won her heart. Brown asks her what women see in Dion, and she responds, "He's alive!" (2:502). Brown confesses his love for her, and makes her promise she will stop seeing Dion, she assures him, again prophetically, that she will never see Dion again.

### Act 2, Scene 2

The drafting room in Brown's office. Dion sits perched on a stool reading from Thomas à Kempis's *Imitation of Christ*. Recalling Robert "Yank" Smith's search for belonging in *The HAIRY APE*, part of Dion's recitation includes the words, "'Keep thyself as a pilgrim, and a stranger upon the earth, to whom the affairs of the world do not—belong.'" Margaret finds Dion there, and she hides behind her back the mask *"of the brave face she puts on before the world to hide her suffering and disillusionment"* (2:503). He has been missing on a drunken "bat," and Margaret is relieved to find him all right. Dion knows his time is short and wants Margaret to recognize him for his true self. Before pulling off his mask, thus breaking his promise from the prologue, he begs her to look at his actual face: "Behold your man—the sniveling, cringing, life-denying Christian slave you have so nobly ignored in the father of your sons! Look!" (2:504). He removes his mask and, kneeling and kissing the hem of her dress, begs her forgiveness before his assured end. Lifting her own mask to protect herself from the unmasked Dion, Margaret shouts for help before fainting in outright horror. Their nameless boys run into the room as a cohort. Dion departs to Brown's house, leaving Margaret in their care.

### Act 2, Scene 3

Brown's home library. Brown is sitting, reading an architectural journal. His servant answers the doorbell, and Brown hears Dion say, "Tell him it's the devil come to conclude a bargain." Dion enters wearing his mask, which now projects *"the appearance of a real demon, tortured into torturing others"* (2:506). In a tone of *"deadly calm,"* he explains to Brown the cause of his duality. When the two of them were four years old, Brown had come up

from behind Dion, who was drawing in the sand, and, envious of Dion's artistic gifts, battered him over the head with a stick and maliciously rubbed out his drawing. Dion began crying, not because of the act but because of who performed it—his best friend, Billy Brown. "Everyone called me a cry-baby, so I became silent for life and designed a mask of the Bad Boy Pan in which to live and rebel against that other boy's God and protect myself from his cruelty" (2:506–507).

At Brown's invitation, Dion begins drinking heavily and further explains why his mask has enacted such a grotesque transformation. When the god Pan, a fertility god, is denied the sunshine, he grows "sensitive and self-conscious and proud and revengeful" and hence transforms into the "Prince of Darkness" (2:508). Dion rants that the cathedral he designed for Brown's firm is his final act in life, and he goads Brown into confessing that he had always wished Margaret had chosen him. When Brown says yes, he has always loved her, Dion insists that love is "merely the appearance"—that, in fact, Brown has always loved him, not Margaret, "because I have always possessed the power he needed for love, because I am love!" (2:510).

As Dion is dying of alcohol poisoning, however, his mask slips away, and he begs Brown's forgiveness. Similar to his unmasked pleadings to Margaret in act 2, scene 2, Dion kisses Brown's feet and dies with the unfinished prayer "Our Father" (2:510). Once Brown sees Dion's actual face, he realizes that it was the mask that Margaret loved.

Margaret knocks on the door, and Brown hides Dion's body. Margaret and the three boys enter, and Brown lies that Dion is upstairs sleeping off a drunk. He goes to the bedroom and reenters wearing Dion's mask and clothes. Margaret is fooled, and she expresses delight in the fact that Dion (now Brown) looks so much healthier. They kiss passionately and go back to the Anthony home as a family.

### Act 3, Scene 1

The draftsmen's workroom at left and Brown's office at right. Two draftsmen, one older and one younger, gossip about why Brown had fired Dion so suddenly, given Dion's clear success with a cathedral design. Margaret enters, again looking for Dion. Brown follows close behind and assures her that Dion is hard at work on the design for a new state capitol building and cannot be disturbed. Brown is keeping Dion's death a secret in order to play Dion. However, Dion's mask has turned Brown's actual face *"ravaged and haggard . . . tortured and distorted by the demon of Dion's mask"* (2:516). Brown now has a separate mask to hide his face's distortion, a mask that closely resembles the man he had been all along—*"the self-assured success"* (2:515).

Desperate to end his torment and the charade of living as Dion, Brown, as Brown, declares to Margaret that he has always loved her. Revolted by Brown's disfigurement and betrayal of Dion, Margaret bluntly rejects him. He meekly tells her that she should never return to the office again. Soon after Margaret exits, a client comes in and requests that Brown liven up the architectural plan for his house, "make it fancier and warmer"; for as it stands, the plan is "too cold, too spare, too like a tomb . . . for a livable home" (2:517). Brown assures him that he will hand the job over to his now-celebrated assistant, Dion Anthony.

### Act 3, Scene 2

Brown's home library, about eight o'clock the same night. Brown sets his new mask beside Dion's masks and stares into the latter's eyes. He talks to the mask in conspiratorial tones, plotting to send Brown off to Europe to make way for Brown's, now Dion's, marriage to Margaret. He will wait until Margaret fully falls in love with the new Dion and then unmask himself before her and tell her the truth of his identity. Apparently delusional, he believes Dion's mask is taunting him, telling him that Margaret will never "believe," "see," or "understand" the truth. Brown dismisses the mask's goading and treats it like a partner, making further plans for their happiness. Reinforcing Dion's homoerotic declaration in act 2, scene 3, Brown kisses the mask before putting it on, declaring "I love you because she loves you! My kisses on your lips are for her!" (2:519).

### Act 3, Scene 3

The sitting room of the Anthony household a half hour later. Margaret—who insists that Brown, whom she now believes is Dion, call her Peggy as

Dion used to when they were young lovers—tells Brown how much happier she has been since his transformation. Before that, she tells him, "You were always so strange and aloof and alone, it seemed I was never really touching you. But now I feel you've become quite human—like me—and I'm so happy dear!" Brown is overwhelmed with joy. "Then—that justifies everything!" (2:520). Margaret informs him of Brown's overtures in act 3, scene 1. Brown swears he will kill him, which shocks Margaret at first, but she apparently writes it off as a romantic gesture, and Brown gets back to work on the capitol design. Brown has now fully embraced the Dionysian side of Dion's personality, laughing maniacally that he will create a design that will "adroitly hide old Silenus [one of Dionysius's followers] on the cupola! Let him dance over their law-making with his eternal leer!" (2:523).

### Act 4, Scene 1

The drafting room in Brown's architectural office. Brown is wearing Dion's mask and has just finished the capitol design. Brown appears to be suffering from a nervous breakdown, as he jeers at the design's surface practicality: "Only to me will that pompous façade reveal itself as the wearily ironic grin of Pan as, his ears drowsy with the crumbling hum of past and future civilizations, he half listens to the laws passed by his fleas to enslave him! Ha-ha-ha! (*He leaps grotesquely from behind his desk and cuts a few goatish capers, laughing with lustful merriment*) . . . Oh, how many persons in one God make the good God Brown? Hahahaha!" (2:524). The draftsmen in the other room assume that he is drunk. Taking off the Dion mask in order "to become respectable again," his actual face is revealed to the audience, *"now sick, ghastly, tortured, hollow-cheeked and feverish-eyed"* (2:525).

Margaret enters, looking *"healthy and happy,"* though *"her face wears a worried, solicitous expression"* (2:525). Margaret accuses Brown, who has donned his Brown mask, of working Dion too hard. She fears he might be suffering from a nervous breakdown. Brown assures her that the project is finished and that he, Brown, will be destroyed before long. He removes himself to reappear almost instantly, still wearing the same clothes, as Dion.

The committee overseeing the capitol building project enters. Brown disappears again to reenter with the Brown mask on. He rips the plan into four pieces, unaccountably to the committee and Margaret, but with the excuse that the plan is an insult to himself, the committee, and God. After Margaret shrieks and snatches up the pieces, Brown disappears into the office again to instantly reemerge as Dion. He struggles to placate them, but the effort to remain stable is too great, and, moving slowly toward the exit, Brown places his finger to his lips and whispers to the draftsmen, "Sssh! This is Daddy's bedtime secret for today: Man is born broken. He lives by mending. The grace of God is glue!" (2:528). He then tells a draftsman that Brown is dead in the next room. They rush into the office and return carrying Brown's mask as if it were his dead body. They all assume that Dion has murdered him, and the younger draftsman calls the police (2:529).

### Act 4, Scene 2

Brown's home library the same day. Dion's mask is on the table facing the audience. Brown is naked except for a white loin cloth, calling to mind the character Brutus Jones's nakedness in scene 7 of *The Emperor Jones*. Writhing in agony and praying *"in agonized supplication,"* Brown begs for God's mercy (2:529); but recognizing that God has forsaken him, he calls to God to let the whole world, including Margaret, suffer as he suffers.

Cybel enters wearing her mask, a black kimono, and slippers. She glances at the mask and understands why he has avoided her—"You are Dion Brown!" "I am the remains of William Brown," he responds, pointing to Dion's mask, "I am his murderer and his murdered!" (2:530). She warns him that the police are hunting him down, that they are in the garden, and there is no escape route. Brown puts on Dion's mask and gains new strength. He giddily mocks the authorities outside, "Welcome, dumb worshippers! I am your great God Brown! I have been advised to run from you but it is my almighty whim to dance into escape over your prostrate souls!" (2:531). The police fire through the window and shoot him down.

Cybel takes off the Dion mask and puts it on a table under the light of a floor lamp. The police rush into the room with guns drawn, and Margaret follows close behind with the shredded capitol plans clutched to her chest. Cybel identifies him as "Billy" and suggests that the police leave them alone so she can find out more. As he dies, he calls her "Mother" and asks what prayer she had taught him. Suggestively framing the answer as a question, she responds *"with calm exultance,"* "Our Father Who Art!" He answers that he has discovered the answer, presumably from the Bible in Matthew, Book 5—"I know! I have found Him! I hear Him speak! 'Blessed are they that weep, for they shall laugh'! . . . Only he that has wept can laugh!" (2:532). Brown dies, and Margaret, after Cybel places his body carefully on the couch and kisses him, takes up Dion's mask and kisses it, saying, "My lover! My husband! My boy! . . . You will live forever! You will sleep under my heart! I will feel you stirring in your sleep, forever under my heart!" She kisses the mask once more, and the police captain enters, inexplicably speaking toward the audience, "Well, what's his name?"

"Man!" Cybel responds.

"How d'yuh spell it?" he asks (2:533).

### Epilogue

The same casino pier as in the prologue, also in June, but four years after the last scene. Margaret and the Anthony boys, now in their teens, enter on right. The boys boast about their girlfriends to Margaret, hoping she will agree that one or the other is best. They all resemble the *"tall, athletic, strong and handsome-looking"* appearance of the William Brown we knew in the prologue. Margaret reminisces to them about her youth and the June months she spent at the resort. She makes them promise they will not forget their father, Dion. Not wanting them to miss out on the magic of June, she sends them off to the dance. As she had in the prologue, Margaret sets her mask on one of the benches and looks up at the moon. She removes Dion's mask from her cloak and, echoing her words in act 4, scene 2, "My lover! My husband! My boy!," passionately kisses the mask *"on the lips with a timeless kiss"* (2:535).

## COMMENTARY

*The Great God Brown* is one of Eugene O'Neill's most philosophical plays, and most philosophically muddled—so much so, in fact, that he was compelled to publish an "explanation" to the play in the *New York Evening Post* (February 26, 1926). In it, the author admits to a "mystical pattern which manifests itself as an overtone in [the play], dimly behind and beyond the words" (quoted in Clark 160). O'Neill explains the symbolism of each character, a mode of explication that reveals the extent to which the characters are barely characters at all, but rather walking, talking symbols acting as catalysts to ignite others' desires and fantasies. The play is a dissertation on the tension between FRIEDRICH NIETZSCHE's duality of restraint and reason, signified by the "Apollonian" character William A. (Apollo) Brown, and the creative, intuitive life-lust of our "Dionysian" side, Dion (Dionysus) Anthony. While writing the play, O'Neill was reading Sigmund Freud's book *Group Psychology and the Analysis of the Ego* (1921), in which, O'Neill biographer Stephen A. Black notes, Freud employs the Pan god as "expressing and denying sexual impulse" (322)—hence Anthony's Pan mask explains his simultaneous attractiveness to Margaret and denial of sexuality with Cybel.

The use of masks was not particularly experimental, as they were regularly employed to "typify" characters (Bogard 266) the way Margaret's "good girl" facade does. The mask symbolizes the external public self that one presents to the world, and the unmasked self represents a character's authentic inner self. But the way in which Dion's mask transforms and becomes, as O'Neill phrased it, "distorted by morality from Pan to Satan" (quoted in Clark 160) is highly experimental and possibly untried up to that point.

O'Neill brings a fair amount of autobiographical material to bear in the play as well, written as it was "in tears! Couldn't control myself!" (quoted in Sheaffer 167). Indeed, O'Neill considered it "very near—and dear—to me, that play—(I'm not sure it isn't the best beloved of them all" (quoted in Alexander 79) Dion Anthony can be seen as an avatar of O'Neill himself, as can Brown, but more so in

Dion, as Louis Sheaffer writes, "the situation of Artist versus Society activated the adolescent strain in O'Neill's emotional make-up; he conceived Dion chiefly in terms of romantic self-pity and narcissistic self-dramatization" (169). Stephen Black argues that since O'Neill was desperately trying to give up drink at the time of its composition, with the transformation of the alcoholic Dion into the teetotaling Brown, O'Neill "experimented with temperance to see how it might feel" (327). In addition, Dion sells out to corporate interests and disintegrates morally and physically as a result. Being a "sellout" was always a fear of O'Neill's, and through Dion he shows his conviction never to do so. But O'Neill also had a pragmatic side that ultimately ensured his professional success in the mode of William Brown. In this case, we can also see some of his brother JAMES O'NEILL, Jr. (Jamie) in the fatalism, ALCOHOLISM, and reliance on prostitutes as surrogate mothers that Dion enacts. Dion's monologue in act 1, scene 3, in particular recall Jamie's surrogate Jamie Tyrone's life-destroying experience at his own mother's deathbed as he recounts in *A MOON FOR THE MISBEGOTTEN* (3:930).

At bottom, the philosophical, near-theological message O'Neill conveys through the tortured lives of Dion Anthony and William Brown is that human suffering is a sublimely life-renewing, redeeming act in all fulfilling lives; "Both are portrayed at their deaths," as Virginia Floyd argues, "as suffering, redemptive Christ-figures" (316). Dion Anthony and William Brown die tragically—Anthony from alcoholism, Brown by trigger-happy police officers—but it is only through the tragic circumstances that led up to their respective ends, O'Neill insists, that the human race can obtain spiritual redemption.

## CHARACTERS

**Anthony, Dion** Margaret Anthony's husband and William A. Brown's friend. Dion Anthony is the Dionysian side of Nietzschean duality—the Apollonian is represented by William Brown—that represents living by instinct and sensuality, rather than restraint and reason. Behind the mask, however, Dion's actual face is "*dark, spiritual, poetic, passionately supersensitive, helplessly unprotected in its* *childlike, religious faith in life"* (2:475), an ascetic, moral face O'Neill regards as one requiring cynical protection from outside view—hence the character's last name, evoking the "masochistic, life-denying spirit of Christianity as represented by St. Anthony" (quoted in Clark 160) that O'Neill intended to convey in this character.

Dion marries Margaret and has three sons, but his lack of artistic success leads him to sink deeper and deeper into alcoholism. As it becomes clearer that his ascetic side will never be accepted by either his wife or society at large, his Dionysian Pan-god mask transforms slowly into a Satanic, or Mephistophelean, face. When he dies of alcoholism in Brown's study in act 2, scene 3, Brown snatches up his mask and, for a time, successfully passes himself off as Dion. In his monologue in act 1, scene 3, Dion also resembles James "Jamie" O'Neill, Jr., O'Neill's older brother, who was also by his mother's side when she died—but who then transferred her back to the East Coast on a train in which he scandalously drank himself into a stupor with a prostitute. Dion also resembles O'Neill himself, as O'Neill was well aware of the professional hazard of denying the creative spirit in order to make monetary gains.

**Anthony, Margaret** Dion Anthony's wife. Margaret, appearing in the prologue in a *"simple white dress,"* is the symbol and image of the American "good girl," but she longs for the passionate romance only Dion Anthony, the Pan god, can offer. As with her deliberate namesake, Marguerite from the Faust legend, she is so blinded by her desire to have children that she almost encourages her husband's transformation into Mephistopheles. Through most of the play, she wears a mask that evokes *"an exact, almost transparent reproduction of her own features, but giving her the abstract quality of a Girl instead of the individual, Margaret"* (2:477). After marrying Dion, Margaret accepts her husband's dissipated habits of gambling and alcoholism, but ultimately not his professional idleness. She convinces William Brown to provide him with a job as an architectural designer and thus precipitates his downfall. Devoted to him to the end, in the epilogue Margaret carries Dion's mask under her cloak next to her heart.

**Brown, William A.** Dion Anthony's friend. William "Billy" Brown is first described as *"a handsome, tall and athletic boy of nearly eighteen. He is blond and blue-eyed, with a likable smile and a frank good-humored face"* (2:473). Billy will grow up to be the representative figure of the American success story; he exudes the modest air of someone who knows his good fortune is due, in part at least, to a combination of luck and his privileged background. O'Neill's successful businessman character Sam Evans also adopts this pose in STRANGE INTERLUDE. But perhaps more important for O'Neill, Brown also represents the Apollonian side of Friedrich Nietzsche's duality of Apollonian versus Dionysian, which is played by the Dion Anthony character. As O'Neill signals in his STAGE DIRECTIONS, Billy Brown's face in the prologue already shows *"a disciplined restraint"* (2:473), and "restraint" is a key Apollonian personality trait, along with reason and practicality. When Dion dies, however, Brown steals his identity by putting on his mask. For some time, Brown successfully poses as Dion, as both husband and designer, but Dion's Mephistophelean mask proves too tormenting for Brown. After the police mistake Brown's own mask for Brown himself, he is finally cut down by the police.

**Cybel** A prostitute for William Brown and a mother figure to Dion Anthony. Cybel is both Dionysian and borne of O'Neill's interest in EAST ASIAN THOUGHT, as *"her large eyes dreamy with the reflected stirring of profound instincts . . . [and] she chews gum like a sacred cow forgetting time with an eternal cud"* (2:492). Cybel's name, according to O'Neill, "is an incarnation of Cybele, the Earth Mother doomed to segregation as a pariah in a world of unnatural laws, but patronized by her segregators, who are thus themselves the first victims of their laws" (quoted in Clark 160). Unlike Margaret, Cybel is accepting of Dion's ascetic, unmasked persona. She believes in being true to one's self, and she shares Dion's Dionysian pursuit of life for life's sake. As a prophet, she foresees Dion's death and is in compassionate attendance at Brown's. Buxom and curvy, Cybel performs the role of *"an unmoved idol of Mother Earth,"* much like Abbie Putnam in DESIRE UNDER THE ELMS, and a figure later elaborated upon and perfected in the character Josie Hogan in *A Moon for the Misbegotten*.

## BIBLIOGRAPHY

Alexander, Doris. *Eugene O'Neill's Creative Struggle: The Decisive Decade, 1924–1933.* University Park: Pennsylvania State University Press, 1992.

Black, Stephen A. *Eugene O'Neill: Beyond Mourning and Tragedy.* New Haven, Conn.: Yale University Press, 1999.

Bogard, Travis. *Contours in Time: The Plays of Eugene O'Neill.* Rev. ed. New York: Oxford University Press, 1988.

Clark, Barrett H. *Eugene O'Neill: The Man and His Plays.* Rev. ed. New York: Dover, 1947.

Floyd, Virginia. *The Plays of Eugene O'Neill: A New Assessment.* New York: Ungar, 1985.

Miller, Jordan Y. *Playwright's Progress: O'Neill and the Critics.* Chicago: Scott, Foresman and Company, 1965.

Sheaffer, Louis. *O'Neill, Son and Artist.* Boston: Little, Brown, 1973.

# *Hairy Ape: A Comedy of Ancient and Modern Life in Eight Scenes, The* (completed, 1921; first produced, 1922)

Audiences confront much that is disturbing in Eugene O'Neill's *The Hairy Ape,* beginning with the title itself—and as the play moves forward, we are hard-pressed to find any evidence of the "comedy" O'Neill promises in its subtitle. When it was first produced on March 9, 1922, by the Provincetown Players at the Provincetown Playhouse on MacDougal Street in Greenwich Village (the play later moved uptown to Broadway), *The Hairy Ape* starkly divided the critics. The *Freeman* called it "without question not only the most interesting play of the season, but the most striking play of many seasons," while *Billboard* caustically accused the play of smelling "like the monkey house in the Zoo, where the last act takes place and where

the play should have been produced" (in Miller 35). Members of the audience were generally convinced, and this goes for nearly all of O'Neill's plays through the 1920s, that they had either just witnessed a work of unfettered genius or were the butt of a complicated prank. Nevertheless, O'Neill's convincing use of dialect; his blending of Naturalism and Expressionism, which would later become the hallmark of "American style" theater; and his powerful psychological treatment of alienation in the modern world, all arguably combine to make *The Hairy Ape,* though definitely not his best work, one of the most revolutionary plays of its time.

## SYNOPSIS

### Scene 1

The firemen's forecastle (pronounced "fo'c'sle") of a transatlantic steamship, which disembarked from New York Harbor one hour before the scene's action. The firemen are unable to stand upright, a condition which, along with their vocations as coal shovellers, make the men resemble *"those pictures in which the appearance of the Neanderthal Man is guessed at"* (2:121). Robert "Yank" Smith, the strongest and most apish-looking of them, is seated in the foreground, with the rest of the men loudly but respectfully situated behind him. Virtually all of the (white) nations of the earth are meant to be represented there—Irish, German, French, Swedish, and so on—much like Harry Hope's saloon in O'Neill's late play *The Iceman Cometh.* Long, a socialist who speaks "Cockney," or working-class British dialect, attempts to open the men's eyes to the capitalist, un-Christian exploitation of industrial laborers like themselves. Yank quickly disabuses Long of any hope to convert him to socialism, or to politics of any kind: "De Bible, huh? De Cap'tlist class, huh? Aw nix on dat Salvation Army—Socialist bull. Git a soapbox!" (2:125). His self-deluding position is that they, the firemen, are the driving force of the ship and are therefore more powerful than the officers and owners above them.

Another argument erupts between Yank and Paddy, an older Irish seaman with experience on the sailing ships that were discontinued in the first decade of the 20th century. "'Twas them days [before steam power] men belonged to ships not

Carlotta Monterey (later O'Neill) and Louis Wolheim in the first production of *The Hairy Ape* *(Courtesy of the Sheaffer-O'Neill Collection, Charles E. Shain Library of Connecticut College)*

now," he insists, "'Twas them days a ship was part of the sea, and a man was a part of a ship and the sea joined all together and made it one" (2:127). Yank rebuts with a lengthy monologue describing his self-perceived role in the steam, smoke, coal, and steel of the industrial age. The ship's bells sound, indicating it is time for their shift in the stokehole. Paddy decides to ignore the bells and indulge himself, "sittin' here at me ease, and drinking, and thinking, and dreaming dreams" (2:130). Yank exits in disgust while Paddy lies back in his bunk, humming contentedly to himself.

*Scene 2*

The promenade deck of the same ship. The setting is in extreme contrast to scene 1. Mildred Douglas, a dabbler in sociology whose father owns the steamship line and a major steel mill company called Nazareth Steel, and her aunt recline elegantly on

the ship's promenade deck. Mildred is as deluded as Yank in scene 1, though in a way, she "belongs" even more than Yank, given that her father owns both the ship itself and the steel mills that made it. She sees herself as capable of relating to and uplifting the lower class, when in reality her world is so utterly alienating to them, and theirs to her, that, as the aunt caustically points out, her presence is only destructive to their self-esteem and sense of purpose: "How they must have hated you . . . the poor that you made so much poorer in their own eyes" (2:131). And now, her aunt continues, by threatening to visit Whitechapel in London as she did the tenements of New York, she's turning her "slumming international." "Please do not mock at my attempts to discover how the other half lives," she rejoins to her aunt, "Give me credit for some sort of groping sincerity in that at least." Her grandfather started work as a "puddler," a steelworker who puddles pig iron to make wrought iron, in steel mills and achieved the American dream by working his way to ownership of a steel company. But at what cost? Mildred admits that she has "neither the vitality nor integrity [of her grandfather]. All that was burnt out in our stock before I was born" (2:131). It is her underlying contention that by experiencing "how the other half lives," a popular expression of the time and the title of Jacob Riis's widely read urban reform tract of 1890, she will "put [her heritage] to the test" by visiting the ship's stokehold (2:132).

Mildred orders the second engineer to escort her on an expedition, which he accepts reluctantly. The officer warns her against wearing her white dress and offers her his old coat to prevent her white dress from getting soiled by oil and dirt, advice she dismisses out-of-hand, since she owns 50 more like it. It is clear to him from the first that her desire to go slumming is a foolish exercise. "There's ladders down there that are none too clean—and dark alleyways," he says, which only encourages her (2:134). Apparently he is afraid for their well-being among the firemen; he brings along the fourth engineer because, he tells Mildred, in the stokehold "two are better than one" (2:133). As Mildred and the engineers depart for the "dark alleyways" of the stokehold, her aunt repeatedly accuses her of being a "poser" (2:134).

## Scene 3

The stokehole (stokehold or boiler room). Paddy and Yank continue their feud, Paddy complaining the watch is too long while Yank embraces the hard labor. In his STAGE DIRECTIONS, O'Neill describes the scene in terms that evoke images of hell: *"The fiery light floods over their shoulders as they bend round for the coal. Rivulets of sooty sweat have traced maps on their backs. The enlarged muscles form bunches of high light and shadow"* (2:135–136). The firemen work in unison, adding a savage, ritualistic quality to the expressionistic scene. A whistle sounds intermittently, signaling the firemen to shovel faster so the engines can pick up steam. At first Yank accepts the challenge of the whistle and goads the rest to follow his backbreaking pace. But when Mildred enters, just behind Yank, the whistle blows once too often. Yank then *"brandishes his*

*shovel murderously over his head in one hand, pounding on his chest gorilla-like"* and roars a series of foul oaths at the whistle and the officers who blow it (2:137). He sees the rest of the men staring behind him and turns toward Mildred's ghostly figure. For a moment, he glares at her ferociously. *"As for her,"* O'Neill writes, *"during his speech she has listened, paralyzed with horror, terror, her whole personality crushed, beaten in, collapsed, by the terrific impact of this unknown, abysmal brutality, naked and shameless"* (2:137). She lets out a petrified wail that snaps Yank out of his furious rage; he looks dumbfounded, and Mildred faints outright. Just before losing consciousness, she whimpers to the engineers, "Take me away! Oh, the filthy beast!" With this one puncturing utterance (repeated by Paddy in scene 4 as "hairy ape"), Yank's self-inflated identity collapses. "God damn yuh!" he yells after the engineers carrying the unconscious form of Mildred, and he wildly hurls his shovel at the closing door. The scene ends with the whistle blowing another *"long, angry, insistent command"* (2:138).

## Scene 4

Back in the firemen's forecastle, same as scene 1. The men relax after their shift. All faces have been perfunctorily washed except Yank's, which gives him the distinctive appearance of a figure from blackfaced minstrel shows and heightens his designation as an "ape." While the other firemen try to convince Yank to wash, he is perched on a bench in the pose of Rodin's famous sculpture *The Thinker*. Paddy jokes that Yank has fallen in love with Mildred. "Love, hell!" he responds, "Hate, dat's what. I've fallen in hate, get me?" (2:139).

Long voices the complaint Mildred's aunt had warned her of—that her presence before them was an insult, and the engineers (the management) are equally at fault for "exhibitin' us's if we was bleedin' monkeys in a menagerie" (2:139). A deck steward had informed him of her father's identity, and he holds to his anticapitalist line, likening their condition to that of slavery, with Mildred and her father as the masters. Long suggests they take her to court, to Yank's disgust—"Hell! Law!"—and together the others respond, expressionistically, as a chorus from GREEK TRAGEDY, "Law!" "Hell!

Governments!" Yank says, "Governments!" Hell! God!" "God!" (2:140). Paddy continues to make light of Yank's reaction and the whole "touching" scene in the stokehold, remarking that it looked "as if she'd seen a great hairy ape escaped from the Zoo!" "Say," Yank says, "is dat what she called me—a hairy ape?" "She looked it at you if she didn't say the word itself," Paddy answers (2:141). Insisting repeatedly that she does not belong and he does, Yank swears violent revenge on Mildred and her kind for this slight. Bent on immediate reprisal, he runs at the door, but all the men join together to stop him. The scene closes with Yank at the bottom of the pile, howling with rage, "I'll show her who's a ape!" (2:143).

## Scene 5

A Sunday morning in New York three weeks later. Yank and Long go slumming in their own right among the "respectable" citizens of Fifth Avenue. The most affluent street in Manhattan, Fifth Avenue is significantly located in the exact center of the island, as far as possible from either waterfront. Along the avenue are expensive fur and jewelery displays with tags announcing outrageous prices that hang visibly from each item. *"The general effect,"* O'Neill describes in his stage directions, *"is of a background of magnificence cheapened and made grotesque by commercialism, a background in tawdry disharmony with the clear light and sunshine on the street itself"* (2:144). Long hopes their excursion will spark Yank's "class consciousness" and convince him that Mildred is only one representative of a larger social evil: "There's a 'ole mob of 'em like 'er, Gawd blind 'em!' (2:146). "Observe the bleedin' parasites," Long instructs him; but sensing Yank's brutish purpose, he warns him to "'old yer 'orses" (2:147). Church soon lets out, and if O'Neill describes the stokers as resembling *"those pictures in which the appearance of Neanderthal is guessed at,"* the pedestrians on Fifth Avenue are equally grotesque, *"a procession of gaudy marionettes, yet with something of the relentless horror of Frankensteins in their detached, mechanical unawareness"* (2:147).

In this scene, O'Neill steps up the play's expressionistic quality. In fact, the costume designer, Blanche Hays, proposed to the playwright in rehearsal

that the pedestrians wear masks to heighten the dehumanizing effect of commercialism on the characters, a proposition O'Neill agreed to enthusiastically (Egri 90). Along the street, voices are heard preaching the conservative ideas of the day. Yank fiercely provokes the men in the crowd to fight, while Long tries to settle him down, but the genteel pedestrians are surreally unresponsive to his outbursts. Fearing police intervention, Long grabs Yank to stop his provocations, but Yank pushes him to the ground. Long *"slinks off"* stage left (2:148). Yank then makes a vulgar advance on one of the matrons, who continues walking as if he were invisible.

Yank roars his creed of belonging to the steel and steam of the technological age, but still no one appears to either see or hear him, which only exacerbates his fury. A woman yells out, "Monkey fur!" and they all rush to the storefront window. Yank first attempts to pick up the street curb to hurl at them, then tries to rip a lamppost from its foundation to use as a club. While Yank is struggling with this, a fat gentleman in spats and top hat rushes past him to catch a bus, and Yank is temporarily knocked off balance. Desperate for a fight, Yank lunges and *"lets drive a terrific swing, his fist landing full on the fat gentleman's face."* But the gentleman unaccountably *"stands unmoved as if nothing had happened"* (2:149). Yank had made him miss his bus, however, and he calls for a policeman—the only response Yank receives from the Fifth Avenue crowd. A platoon of policemen overwhelm him, and the pedestrians continue their bizarre promenade. The policemen club Yank into submission, and a patrol wagon's gong is heard clanging loudly offstage. The crowd, still gawking at the window display, remains wholly oblivious to the disruption.

## Scene 6

A cellblock on Blackwell Island (now Roosevelt Island), a notorious prison located on the East River between the boroughs of Queens and Manhattan. Yank is now perched on the cot in a prison cell, as he was on the bench in the forecastle in scene 4, *"in the attitude of Rodin's 'The Thinker,'"* but this time with a bloody bandage draped about his head. The set design is, again, highly expressionistic, as the line of cells disappear into the background, *"as if they ran on, numberless, into infinity"* (2:150). Roaring over the noise of the other prisoners and rattling the bars of his cell menacingly, Yank sees the prison as a zoo, his cell as a cage, and himself, now, as a captured "hairy ape."

Like the firemen in the stokehole, the prisoners represent many ethnicities. Yank tells the inmates of his encounter with Mildred and again swears revenge on her and her class. One prisoner suggests that if Yank wants to get back at Mildred and the industrialists, he should consider joining the anarchist labor organization INDUSTRIAL WORKERS OF THE WORLD (IWW), or "Wobblies," as they were called. He had been reading about them in the *Sunday Times,* and a Senator Queen's description of them impresses Yank: "There is a menace existing in this country today which threatens the vitals of our fair Republic—a foul menace against the very life-blood of the American Eagle . . . . I refer to that devil's brew of rascals, jailbirds, murderers and cutthroats who libel all honest working men by calling themselves the Industrial Workers of the World; but in light of their nefarious plots, I call them the Industrial *Wreckers* of the World!" (2:152; Senator Queen is most probably a send-up of Attorney General Mitchell A. Palmer, who staged a series of raids against radicals in 1919 and 1920 in response to a bomb attack on his home [Pfister 137]). "Wreckers, dat's de right dope!" Yank responds. "Dat belongs! Me for dem!" (2:152). The inmate hands him the paper, and Yank again assumes the pose of *The Thinker.* From this posture, he leaps up to the bars of his cell, grabbing one bar with both hands with his feet on the adjacent bars for leverage, and at the mercy of Yank's superhuman strength, *"the bar bends like a licorice stick under his tremendous strength"* (2:154). The guards sense a jailbreak and drag a riot hose into the cellblock. The curtain falls with the sound of a tremendous crash of water.

## Scene 7

About a month following scene 6, the inside of an IWW chapter office, with the street outside in plain view. Inside there are a group of longshoremen and ironworkers who encircle a secretary in green eyeshades hunched over a table. Two men are playing checkers. In stark contrast to what one might expect from Senator Queen's strident report, the scene is tranquil and professional. On the street, Yank approaches the door to the office with caution, awed by the ominous silence within. Yank finds nothing like the "gang of blokes—a tough gang" (2:152) that the prisoner had oversimplistically and Senator Queen had hyperbolically described them. Yank's disappointment stems from the fact that the IWW has little resemblance to the group that, as Queen said, "plot[s] with fire in one hand and dynamite in the other" (2:153). On the contrary, O'Neill portrays them as staid and bureaucratic, expressionistically juxtaposed against Yank's imposing ferocity.

Scene 7 is the most anomalously realistic of the play, and as such, it is arguably the most brilliant. Since the American press had already envisioned an expressionistic view of the organization, O'Neill counters these popular assumptions by making the IWW scene the only truly realistic one in the play. Yank offers to bomb a Steel Trust factory in their name, which marks a reversal in his attitude toward steel and steam: "I mean blow up de factory, de woiks, where he makes steel. Dat's what I'm after—to blow up de steel, knock all de steel in de woild up to de moon" (2:158).

In the end, the men at the IWW also consider Yank a "brainless ape," possibly a spy from the Secret Service or one of the private agencies like Burns and Pinkerton, which the trusts notoriously used to hire to bust strikes organized by the IWW. They roughly dispatch him to the street. With his ego deflated once again, Yank sits on the cobblestoned street contemplating his next move, again in the posture of *The Thinker.* He looks up and begs the "Man on the Moon" for advice. A policeman working the street beat strolls by and orders him to move along. "Say, where do I go from here?" he asks. The policeman answers with a shove and says, "Go to hell" (2:160).

## Scene 8

The gorilla cage at the Central Park Zoo. The gorilla's enormous features can just be made out, and he is seated like Yank had been in previous scenes—in the pose of *The Thinker.* Yank enters stage left, and his presence causes a chattering reaction among the monkeys offstage. The gorilla's eyes move left, but he makes no sound or other movement. Yank speaks admiringly to the gorilla about his physique, but the ape offers no discernable reply. Yank's monologue shows sympathy and fraternal sentiment; he feels as if, with this ape in the cage, he might at last have found a place where he belongs. Originally, O'Neill planned to have Yank return to the stokehold, a place where he basically did belong. Another alternative was to successfully integrate him into the Wobblies. Instead, he sends him to the zoo, where Yank testifies openly on his alienated condition to a caged gorilla that will soon kill him: "I ain't on oith and I ain't in heaven, get me? I'm in the middle tryin' to separate 'em, takin' all de woist punches from bot' of 'em. Maybe dat's what dey call hell, huh? But you, yuh're at de bottom. You belong! Sure! Yuh're de on'y one in de woild dat does, yuh lucky stiff!" (2:162).

The ape reacts to Yank's fraternal advances with alternating growls, roars, and rattles of his cage. Yank mistakes this for comprehension or agreement and jimmies open the lock. The gorilla slowly exits the cage, and Yank holds out his hand to shake, promising to take him for a stroll down Fifth Avenue. The gorilla lunges at him and wraps him in a *"murderous hug"* (2:163). We hear the sound of Yank's ribcage cracking before the gorilla flings him bodily into the cage and shuts the door behind him. Yank is thus suffocated to death by a fellow primate, an actual "hairy ape." This was the last type—out of the stokers, the Fifth Avenue pedestrians, the prisoners, and the members of the IWW—that he meets during his identity quest with whom Yank felt he might "belong."

## COMMENTARY

Like its highly acclaimed predecessor, *The* EMPEROR JONES (1920), *The Hairy Ape* is framed in eight scenes. The first four take place on a transatlantic ocean liner and the second four in New York City while its protagonist Robert "Yank" Smith is on shore leave. In all eight scenes, O'Neill expressionistically juxtaposes his title character, an aggressive, brutish "fireman," or "stoker," with a series of contrasting agents. These contrasts are often mistaken for romantic MELODRAMA, since harshly

drawn oppositions—rich/poor, good/evil, etc.—are the stuff of melodrama. But in fact, O'Neill was experimenting with expressionism, a new type of German drama that reached the United States in the 1920s. O'Neill later insisted that *The Emperor Jones*, also a work of expressionism, was a stronger influence on *The Hairy Ape* than anything that came out of Europe. One can also see the seeds of this work having been planted even earlier in his play *The* PERSONAL EQUATION, which was written for GEORGE PIERCE BAKER's Harvard playwriting workshop in 1915 and also offered "observations on the state of radical politics" and the plight of the working class (Diggins 65).

O'Neill's own often-quoted report to KENNETH MACGOWAN upon completing the play explains a great deal about the playwright's intentions:

> *The Hairy Ape*—first draft—was finished yesterday. . . . I don't think the play as a whole can be fitted into any of the current "isms." It seems to run the whole gamut from extreme naturalism to extreme expressionism—with more of the latter than the former. I have tried to dig deep in it to probe in the shadows of the soul of man bewildered by the disharmony of his primitive pride and individualism at war with the mechanistic development of society. And the man in the case is not an Irishman, as I at first intended, but more fittingly, an American—a New York tough of the toughs, a product of the waterfront turned stoker—a type of mind, if you could call it that, which I know extremely well. . . . Suffice it for me to add, the treatment of all the sets should be expressionistic, I think. (quoted in Egri 77)

The most pronounced expressionistic technique O'Neill employs is cage imagery, which dominates this play: the bunks in the forecastle that, the stage directions expressly note, *"cross each other like the framework of a steel cage"* (2:121); the stokehold, in which the firemen *"are outlined in silhouette in the crouching, inhuman attitudes of chained gorillas"* (2:135); Fifth Avenue, lined as it is in *"adornments of extreme wealth"* making a *"background in tawdry disharmony with the clear light and sunshine on the street itself"* (2:144); the prison cell's *"heavy*

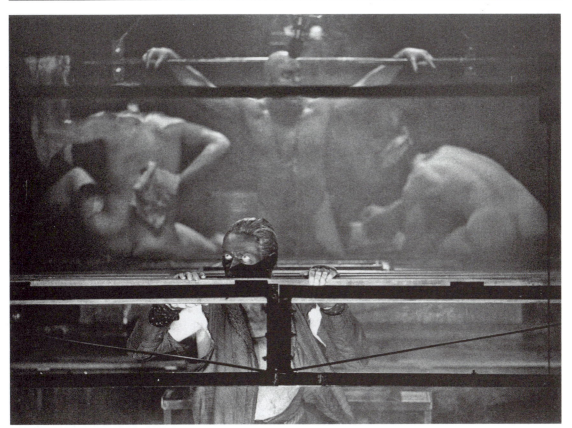

Willem Dafoe as Robert "Yank" Smith in the Wooster Group's production of *The Hairy Ape*. Photo by Mary Gearhart *(Courtesy The Wooster Group)*

*steel bars"* (2:150); the gorilla cage at the zoo; and finally the *"crackling snap"* of Yank's crushed ribcage (2:163). There is enormous potential for directors and set designers to treat O'Neill's expressionistic stage directions innovatively. Indeed, ALEXANDER WOOLLCOTT, in his *New York Times* review immediately following the premiere on March 9, 1922, applauded the Provincetown Players for, "in one of the real events of the year," transforming "that preposterous little theatre . . . one of the most cramped stages New York has ever known [and creating] the illusion of vast spaces and endless perspectives" (quoted in Miller 32, 31). The Wooster Group's production of the late 1990s highlighted the industrial nightmare O'Neill conceived by constructing massive, cagelike scaffolding, which allowed Yank (fiercely played by Willem Dafoe) to climb about the cage with his coal-blackened face resembling noth-

ing less than the primal ancestor, heavily influenced as it was by DARWINISM, that O'Neill envisioned.

The transition from sail to steam power in the last years of the 19th century was a painful one in the MERCHANT MARINE. Recalling the dispute between Chris Christopherson and Mat Burke (who is also based on O'Neill's friend DRISCOLL) in act 3 of "ANNA CHRISTIE"—Chris representing the old windjammers, or "windbags," and Mat the steamships—O'Neill's character Paddy indicts the new, industrialized, steam-powered factories of the sea Yank lords over with such outlandish conceit:

Oh to be scudding south again wid the power of the Trade Wind driving her on steady through the nights and days! Full sail on her! . . . 'Twas them days men belonged to ships, not now. 'Twas them days a ship was part of the sea, and a man was part of a ship, and the sea joined all together and made it one. (*Scornfully*) Is it one wid this you'd be, Yank—black smoke from the funnels smudging the sea, smudging the decks—the bloody engines pounding and shaking—wid devil a sight of sun or a breath of clean air—choking our lungs with coal dust—breaking our backs and hearts in the hell of the stokehole—feeding the bloody furnace—feeding our lives along with the coal, I'm thinking—caged in by steel from a sight of the sky like bloody apes in the Zoo! (2:127).

Paddy's monologue makes clear that O'Neill's experience on the Norwegian bark CHARLES RACINE, one of the last square-riggers (Richter 40), was by far a more fulfilling voyage than his work on industrialized steamers like the SS PHILADELPHIA. This transition from sail to steam power was a fait accompli by the early 1910s. Sailors were no longer the skilled adventurers of the past but became associated instead with the less-glamorous industrial workforce. Nonetheless, Yank holds to his dearly held belief that modern technology is the thing of the future, that he is intrinsically a part of the new industrial age, and that Paddy and his generation are historical deadweight.

I belong and he don't. He's dead but I'm livin'. Listen to me! Sure I'm part of de engines! Why de hell not! Dey move, don't dey? Dey're speed, ain't dey! Dey smash trou, don't dey? Twenty-five knots an hour! Dat's goin' some! Dat's new stuff! Dat belongs! . . . I'm de end! I'm de start! I'm somep'n and de woild moves! It—dat's me!—de new dat's moiderin' de old! I'm de ting in coal dat makes it boin; I'm steam and oil for de engines; I'm de ting in noise dat makes yuh hear it; I'm smoke and express trains and steamers and factory whistles; I'm de ting in gold dat makes it money! And I'm what makes iron into steel! Steel, dat stands for de whole ting! And I'm steel—steel—steel! I'm de muscles in steel, de punch behind it! (2:128–129).

The word *belong* is used 43 times in the play (with variations on parts of speech) and 10 times in Yank's final monologue in scene 8 alone. Jean

Chothia, in a powerful study of O'Neill's use of dramatic language, writes that "the word 'belong' is repeated by Yank until it becomes an emblem of his quest and, because of this first striking usage, we are alert to the ambiguities inherent in that quest" (78). The motif of belonging is punctuated by Yank's last line of scene 1, where he turns to Paddy and growls, "Aw, yuh make me sick! Yuh don't belong!" (2:130).

In scene 1's opening stage directions, O'Neill announces that "the treatment of this scene, or of any other scene in the play, should by no means be naturalistic" (2:121). What the playwright means by this is that *The Hairy Ape* is openly *not* intended to be a social protest play, or any kind of social realism at all, though its protagonist is a stoker on a steamship, and the first two of many conflicts are of major historical importance. The first conflict, between Yank and Long, is a relatively minor one, but O'Neill gives it more weight in the highly expressionistic scene 5. The setting of scene 1 is in the firemen's forecastle of a steamship—one that recalls the forecastle in O'Neill's earlier play *The Personal Equation* (Egri 78)—an oppressive, cage-like dwelling in the bowels of the ship. Similar to Ella and James Harris's tenement apartment in ALL GOD'S CHILLUN GOT WINGS, which O'Neill specifies should shrink around them as the scenes progress to connote the sensation of imprisonment, the ceiling of the forecastle "*crushes down upon the men's heads*" (2:121).

O'Neill's subtitle, *A Comedy of Ancient and Modern Life*, is an accurate introduction to the play insofar as *ancient* calls to mind Yank's clear connection to Homo sapiens's natural heredity, our Darwinian ancestry, incredibly only three years before the famous Scopes ("Monkey") trial of 1925. Yank is also a "tragic hero," a figure from ancient GREEK TRAGEDY doomed by a fatal personal flaw—nearly always hubris, or unwarranted and excessive pride. O'Neill suggests in the final line of his (notoriously complex) stage directions that "*perhaps*" it is only in death that "*the Hairy Ape at last belongs*" (2:163). Indeed, death provides the sole escape from the cages thrown up around us by modern times—a proposition O'Neill incessantly defends in the body of his work.

The distinctly "modern" conclusion of this play, then, is dark and existential: The dehumanizing effects of a modernized, industrialized world make it impossible to sustain any authentic feelings of self-pride, self-worth, individuality, or belonging. That O'Neill calls *The Hairy Ape* a "comedy" might be irony without adulteration, or it might be a reference to the "happy ending" of Yank's finally fitting in—far more subtle than the uncertain marriage proposal that concludes *"Anna Christie"*—if only in death.

## CHARACTERS

**The Aunt** Mildred Douglas's aunt. Mildred's aunt appears with her niece in scene 2. Lounging on the promenade deck of the ship, the two women form a stark contrast to the fireman in the forecastle of the previous scene. O'Neill describes the aunt as a *"pompous and proud—and fat—old lady"* (2:130), specifying that she is a "type"—the meddling, henpecking aunt—right down to her double chin and lorgnettes, and she dresses in a way that betrays her pretentious need to indicate a sense of superiority over others. The aunt mocks her niece's "morbid thrills of social service work on New York's East Side" and subsequent desire to make her "slumming international" with a visit to Whitechapel, a working-class slum in London (2:131). She considers her niece "artificial" and in her final lines repeatedly calls her a "poser" (2:134). Mildred contemptuously responds by slapping her aunt across the face and then laughs as she joins the Second Engineer down to the stokehold of the ship. Although O'Neill is clearly critical of this character type from the United States' ruling class, Mildred's aunt voices some of the playwright's own views—and foreshows Robert "Yank" Smith's violent reaction to Mildred in the following scene—when she scornfully remarks to her niece, "how they [the poor of New York's East Side] must have hated you, by the way, the poor that you made so much poorer in their own eyes!" (2:131).

**Douglas, Mildred** An upper-CLASS young woman who has studied sociology in college and expresses an interest (without sincerity) in discovering "how the other half lives," first on New York's Lower East

Side and then, fatefully, in the steamship's stoke-hole (2:131). Philanthropic slumming, or "friendly visiting," was a popular activity among frustrated, dynamic Victorian women who were tired of the subjugation the codes of domestic respectability imposed. It was a means to head off impending boredom and at the same time an attempt to generate some spiritual uplift in an increasingly cynical urban environment. Unlike the maritime slumming expeditions espoused in O'Neill's early one-act play *Fog*, where the Poet sincerely considered life in the steerage more interesting than on the promenade, here Mildred's inclinations are almost purely selfish—a means by which to rid herself of the mounting ennui brought on by having everything in life except self-fulfillment.

Mildred's father owns a line of steamships, along with a company called Nazareth Steel, but her grandfather was a "puddler" in the steel mills. In an attempt to connect with her past—impossibly distanced by time and station—she demands that an engineer accompany her to the stokehold. Once there, she glimpses Robert "Yank" Smith, whose rough mannerisms, filthy body, and vile language trigger a fainting spell. Before losing consciousness, however, she screams out "Oh, the filthy beast!" (2:137). That one line disillusions Yank, who had always taken great pride in his work and his sense of belonging on the ship, to a point of no return. For her part, Mildred must also suffer disillusionment, as Peter Egri argues, given her original desire to cure herself of ennui by reestablishing a connection with her working-class heritage; Yank is O'Neill's tragic hero, and we are not meant to feel too much sympathy for Mildred, as in the context of the play at least, "her spiritual death will only make itself felt as a living insult in Yank's soul" (Egri 86).

**Long** Long is a cockney, or British working-class, socialist agitator and coal stoker aboard Robert "Yank" Smith's ship who rails openly and often against the capitalist class. Long attempts to direct Yank's rage against Mildred Douglas toward social activism, rather than personal revenge. In scene 4, after Mildred visits the stokehold, Long voices outrage over the engineers "exhibitin' us's if we was bleedin' monkeys in a menagerie" (2:139). In scene 5, he accompanies Yank to Fifth Avenue, the wealthiest street in New York, with the intention of convincing Yank that Mildred's insult was social and economic, not a personal matter, and to "awaken [Yank's] bloody class consciousness" (2:146). Yank dismisses Long's political rhetoric and favors individual action—violent revenge—over Marxist politics and class consciousness. Long slinks away, afraid of the police, when he fails to control Yank's violent outbursts against the wealthy pedestrians.

**Paddy**   Paddy is an elderly IRISH seaman aboard Robert "Yank" Smith's ship who speaks in a thick Irish brogue and argues with Yank about the relative merits of sail (skilled) versus steam (unskilled) seamanship: "'Twas them days [of clipper ships] men belonged to ships, not now," he contends, "and a man was part of a ship, and the sea joined all together and made it one" (2:127). O'Neill describes Paddy as *"an old, wizened Irishman"* whose face is *"extremely monkey-like with all the sad, patient pathos of that animal in his small eyes"* (2:123). Paddy's monologue on the natural beauty of sail power in scene 1 directly contradicts Yank's elevated view of their steamship's 25-knot speed and ferocious power. This point of view is also argued by the character Chris Christopherson in *"ANNA CHRISTIE,"* O'Neill's earlier full-length play of the SEA. At the end of scene 1, Paddy, who consciously seeks to retain his individuality in the face of meaningless industrial work, refuses to heed the call of the work bell, defiantly telling the other men, "Let them log me and be damned. I'm no slave the like of you. I'll be sittin' here at me ease, and drinking, and thinking, and dreaming dreams" (2:129–130).

**Second Engineer**   The Second Engineer is *"a husky, fine-looking man of thirty-five or so"* (2:133). In scene 2, he appears on the promenade deck to escort Mildred Douglas down to the stokehold. He warns her that the soot in the stokehold will blacken her white dress, to which she curtly responds, "It doesn't matter. . . . I have fifty dresses like this. I will throw this one into the sea when I come back" (2:133–134). When the Second Engineer exits to find the Fourth Engineer to join them, Mildred describes him as "an oaf—but a handsome, virile oaf" (2:134). He

appears again in scene 3, when he and his Fourth accompany Mildred into the stokehold, and the two of them carry her out after she faints at the sight of Robert "Yank" Smith. Long condemns the engineers in scene 4 for "exhibitin' us's if we was bleedin' monkeys in a menagerie" (2:139).

**Smith, Robert "Yank"**   A stoker on a steamship and the tragic antihero of O'Neill's play. Yank Smith is likely, with the possible exception of Theodore "Hickey" Hickman from *The Iceman Cometh,* the most difficult role for an actor to portray successfully in all of O'Neill's repertoire, as the character's monologues are frequent and lengthy and must be performed with an impeccable Brooklyn accent. (Yank's father worked as a trucker on the Brooklyn waterfront.) Line after line of bluster is shoveled out to the audience while the firemen in the stokehold, for their part, rhythmically shovel coal into the furnace; the latter action is meant to keep the ship and the play's tension moving forward, the former to keep Yank's sense of "belonging" stable and prop up the crew's self-esteem, as associated with him, in a foul, heavily industrialized work environment.

Yank's character is based on a drinking partner of O'Neill's at JIMMY "THE PRIEST'S" bar named Driscoll, who worked as a coal stoker on the SS *Philadelphia.* Driscoll, according to O'Neill in a 1922 interview with *American Magazine,* "committed suicide by jumping overboard in mid-ocean." O'Neill himself had attempted suicide in spring 1912. "It was the why of Driscoll's suicide that gave me the germ of the idea [for *The Hairy Ape*]" (quoted in Clark 128).

*The Hairy Ape* charts the course of Yank's identity quest, as his preferred sense of "belonging" was shattered by Mildred Douglas in scene 3. When Mildred faints during her expedition down to the stokehold, calling Yank a "filthy beast" before losing consciousness, Yank takes it as a personal insult rather than a social one, as Long did (2:141). That one act tears Yank's worldview apart and leads him on a journey from one social group to another in an effort to discover where, in fact, he "belongs." His quest ends at the Central Park Zoo, where he unlocks the gorilla cage and is crushed to death by the animal inside. Hence, as O'Neill writes in the final line of the stage directions, "*perhaps* [only in death], *the Hairy Ape at last belongs*" (2:163).

## BIBLIOGRAPHY

Chothia, Jean. *Forging a Language: A Study of the Plays of Eugene O'Neill.* New York: Cambridge University Press, 1979.

Clark, Barrett H. *Eugene O'Neill: The Man and His Plays.* Rev. ed. New York: Dover, 1947.

Diggins, John Patrick. *Eugene O'Neill's America: Desire under Democracy.* Chicago: University of Chicago Press, 2007.

Egri, Peter. "'Belonging' Lost: Alienation and Dramatic Form in Eugene O'Neill's *The Hairy Ape.*" In *Critical Essays on Eugene O'Neill,* edited by James J. Martine, 77–111. Boston: G. K. Hall & Co., 1984.

Miller, Jordan Y. *Playwright's Progress: O'Neill and the Critics.* Chicago: Scott, Foresman & Company, 1965.

Pfister, Joel. *Staging Depth: Eugene O'Neill and the Politics of Psychological Discourse.* Chapel Hill: University of North Carolina Press, 1995.

Richter, Robert A. *Eugene O'Neill and Dat Ole Davil Sea: Maritime Influences in the Life and Works of Eugene O'Neill.* Mystic, Conn.: Mystic Seaport, 2004.

# Haunting, The

See MOURNING BECOMES ELECTRA.

# Homecoming, The

See MOURNING BECOMES ELECTRA.

# Hughie (completed, 1941; first produced, 1958)

Eugene O'Neill's last one-act play and the only one he had completed since EXORCISM over 20 years earlier (destroyed by O'Neill), *Hughie* is universally acknowledged as one of the finest if not *the* finest one-act play in AMERICAN THEATER history. Written in a mere three weeks with little revision at O'Neill's California home, TAO HOUSE, in April 1941, *Hughie* has enjoyed many successful revivals since its world premiere at the Royal Dramatic Theatre in Stockholm, Sweden, on September 18, 1958. Three standout productions include one with JASON ROBARDS, who starred in the 1964 American premiere directed by JOSÉ QUINTERO during the EUGENE O'NEILL RENAISSANCE; another with Al Pacino in 1996; and, most recently, a production starring Brian Dennehy in 2008. All played the leading role of the small-time gambler and racketeer "Erie" Smith.

*Hughie* was to be the "last in time" for a planned series of between six and nine one-act plays O'Neill called *By Way of Obit,* the first taking place in 1910 (O'Neill 532). "In each," he wrote to GEORGE JEAN NATHAN, "the main character talks about a person who has died to a person who does little but listen" (531). Set in 1928 in the lobby of a dingy third-rate hotel in Manhattan's theater district, *Hughie* examines the inner and outer lives of the hotel's night clerk (the listener) and that of a small-time Broadway hustler (the talker). O'Neill completed one other *By Way of Obit* installment involving an Irish chambermaid, but he destroyed it on February 2, 1944, along with several scenarios for others, including one dramatic obituary for his beloved dog Silverdene Emblem "Blemie" O'Neill, later published as an essay.

## SYNOPSIS

The lobby of a third-rate hotel in close vicinity to the "*Great White Way sector*" (Broadway and Times Square) on the West Side of Midtown Manhattan. It is between three and four o'clock in the morning during the summer of 1928. Charlie Hughes, a night clerk in his early 40s, sits languidly on a stool behind the desk, blankly staring in front of him. A switchboard, a honeycomb of mailboxes, and a clock adorn the wall at his back. Footsteps are heard from the street entrance offstage left. The night clerk automatically assumes his patent "*The-Patron-Is-Always-Right-grimace*" (3:832).

Erie Smith enters. Erie has "*the same pasty, perspiry, night-life complexion*" as Charlie; he is slightly older but looks younger and deliberately dresses and carries himself with the bearing of a typical *"Broadway sport and a Wise Guy"* (3:832). In reality, Erie is a small-time racketeer and gambler. A regular at the hotel, Erie has spent the last several days on a drinking bender following the funeral of the hotel's late-night clerk, Hughie. At first, Erie outwardly resents Charlie as an inferior replacement for Hughie. Taking his key for room 492, he warms to the night clerk after discovering the similarity of the clerks' names. He regrets having gone "on a bat" as he finds himself liable to "get careless" and expose himself to enemies. "Don't never know nothin'," he advises Charlie, "Be a sap and stay healthy" (3:833).

Charlie has worked as a hotel clerk for over 10 years; his experience has deadened him to arrogant, self-involved customers like Erie. His mind trails off, and the sounds that pour in from the street supply his only diversion. He deliberately pays just enough attention to Erie's banter to respond politely when asked a direct question. Erie correctly guesses that Charlie is married with children, as Hughie had been, and that his age is 43 or 44, though the apathetic Charlie is not sure which himself. Erie also deduces that Charlie comes from the "sticks," and he has—Saginaw, Michigan. Erie himself grew up in "Erie, P-a," the reason street associates assigned him the nickname. Erie goes on that a woman from his hometown named Daisy claimed she was pregnant with his child, though she was notoriously promiscuous. Erie "took a run-out powder" to Saratoga Springs, then on to New York City. There he remained for over 20 years, traveling occasionally to play the "bangtails" (horses) at the racetracks in Saratoga Springs, Belmont, and elsewhere.

Not listening to his clients' expositions—what Charlie terms *"The Guest's Story of His Life"* (3:835)—is an art the night clerk has perfected over the years. In fact, Charlie *"is not listening so intently he misses his cue until the expectant silence crashes in his ears"* (3:836). He gambles on an affirmative response, and Erie *"bitingly"* accuses him of dozing off, then coaches him on how to be a good listener by explaining Hughie's example.

Erie boasts how he used to tease Hughie, a prudish married man, by persuading sleazy women he brought back to the hotel to entice Hughie with racy overtures. This anecdote prompts Erie to brag about the "queens" from "the Follies, or the Scandals, or the Frolics" he has "made" (3:837). Charlie listens intently to garbage men outside emptying and banging the metal cans on the street. According to the STAGE DIRECTIONS, he dreams of working as a garbage man: *"'A job I'd like. I'd bang those cans louder than they do! I'd wake up the whole damned city!'"* (3:837). Erie senses Charlie's distraction. "Jesus, what a dummy!" he roars and heads to the elevator downstage right. But when Charlie bids him a deferential good night, Erie stops abruptly and jiggles his room key, harping over the "crummy dump" and decides not to go to bed quite yet. *"The clerk's face would express despair, but the last time he was able to feel despair was back around World War days when the cost of living got so high and he was out of a job for three months."* Erie admits that something indefinite worries him. Charlie responds *"in the vague tone of a corpse which admits it once overheard a favorable rumor about life,"* while his thoughts return to the garbage cans (3:837).

Erie confesses that ever since his "pal" Hughie's death, both his luck and his confidence in gambling have vanished; he understands death is "part of the game" but misses the former clerk terribly (2:838). The garbage men are no longer heard, but an elevated train passes by, offering Charlie a kind of existentialist sense of hope. Each train that passes signals to him that *"the night recedes, too, until at last it must die and join all the other long nights in Nirvana, the Big Night of Nights"* (3:838). Erie resents Charlie's unresponsiveness but is encouraged when the clerk agrees to call him by his first name. He continues his eulogy to Hughie, bragging about cheating the clerk in dice and describing him, albeit affectionately, as a "sucker"—"the kind of sap you'd take to the cleaners a million times and he'd never wise up he was took" (3:839). He also escorted Hughie to the horse races at Belmont; the clerk describes the thoroughbreds there as "the most beautiful things in the world" (3:840). Erie agrees. "I'll tell you, Pal, I'd rather sleep in the same stall with old Man O' War than make the whole damn follies." *"The Clerk wonders what horses have to do with anything—or for that matter, what anything has to do with anything—then gives it up"* (3:840). The next day, Hughie stole two dollars from his wife's purse to bet on horses, but Erie protectively refused to lead him into the gambling life. "Boy Scouts got nothin' on me, Pal, when it comes to good deeds," he says ruefully. "That was one I done. It's too bad I can't remember no others." But Charlie's mind, again, *"has left the premises"* (3:841).

Erie tells of his first meeting with Hughie after a "big killing" in Tijuana, Mexico; Hughie had just been hired and spoke little for the first few nights. Erie persisted, regaling him with tall tales of gambling exploits and sexual conquests; soon Hughie perceived him as a "sort of dream guy" (3:844). Hughie also came from a "hick burg": "He'd read somewhere—in the Suckers' Almanac, I guess— that all a guy had to do was come to the Big Town and Old Man Success would be waitin' at the Grand Central [train station] to give him a key to the city. What a gag that is! I even believed it once, and no one could ever call me a sap." Hughie eventually settled on his job as a hotel night clerk, met a "sales girl in some punk department store," and got married.

The garbage men move on, and Charlie now counts the footsteps of a police officer outside. *"If only he'd shoot it out with a gunman some night!,"* he rails inwardly in profound frustration, *"'Nothing exciting has happened in any night I've ever lived through!'"* (3:841). Erie asks Charlie a question, forcing the clerk to probe his consciousness—it has something to do with his wife, and Charlie offers a dull response. "Better lay off them headache pills, Pal," Erie says in disgust, "First thing you know, some guy is going to call you a dope." But Charlie's mind is off once more, thinking now of the car passing by (3:842).

Erie regains his affability and recounts a time when Hughie invited him to dinner. Not one to dine in a family setting—"I was thinking, I'd rather be shot" (3:842)—Erie found the experience less abhorrent than he assumed. "And his kids wasn't the gorillas I'd expected either." At the table, he started in on a bawdy horseracing story to entertain the children, provoking Hughie's wife to rush them off to bed before he could finish. "She had

me tagged for a bum, and seein' me made her sure she was right" (3:843). When Hughie apologized for his wife and explained she was brought up in a strict household, Erie changed the subject "on purpose," comparing Hughie's marital problems with a time when a Broadway prostitute demanded more money than he thought she was worth. Erie quotes the coarse dialogue with the streetwalker, thus conducting a conversation within a conversation within a conversation. An ambulance's siren can be heard in the near distance, and Charlie imagines himself in a dialogue with the doctor treating the patient.

Erie lets out a *"forced chuckle."* Charlie, drawn out of his reverie, misreads the embarrassed chuckle as laughter and congratulates him on the great joke. Twirling his room key and staring at the ground, Erie *"for a moment is so hurt and depressed he hasn't the spirit to make a sarcastic crack"* (3:844). He turns toward the elevator again but fails once more and turns on Charlie and accuses him of being deaf. Still unresponsive, Charlie is now engrossed in the sound of a fire engine's wail. *"'Where's the fire?,'"* he asks an imaginary fireman in his head. *"'Is it a real good one this time? . . . 'I mean, big enough to burn down the whole damn city?'"* The fireman responds; *"'Sorry, Brother,'" "'but there's no chance. There's too much stone and steel'"* (3:844). Erie abandons his effort, *"twirling his key frantically as if it were a fetish which might set him free"* (3:844).

Erie still cannot summon the willpower to go to his room. "Christ, it's lonely," he swears bitterly. He feels a powerful urge to regale someone with tall tales of gambling and gangster life, but Hughie's absence makes this impossible. "He thought gambling was romantic," Erie says "He thought gangsters was romantic. . . . Yeah, Hughie lapped up my stories like they was duck soup, or a beakful of heroin" (3:844, 845). Starved for excitement, if only in his imagination, Hughie expressed a fascination with Legs Diamond, and Erie complied by fabricating a relationship between himself and the famous gangster. He insists his lies hurt no one but meant a great deal to Hughie.

Erie tells of a "big horseshoe of red roses" he sent to Hughie's funeral, a symbol to him of their mutual need for one another—Erie to feel like a big shot and Hughie that he was in the game. Erie commissioned the wreath to include the line, printed in forget-me-nots, "Good-by, Old Pal" (3:847). The street outside descends into a deep silence, offering Charlie no escape from "492." He begins to regret not having listened. Perhaps Erie might be useful after all, his *"one possible escape"* (3:847). His mind gropes about desperately for a word or phrase from Erie's verbal torrent and recalls a mention of gambling. It is a compelling topic for him, and the notorious Jewish mobster Arnold Rothstein had always fascinated him. He asks Erie with *"almost lifelike eagerness"* if he knows the famous criminal. Erie has now entered his own trancelike state, as he continues mourning the loss of his friend and with him his "dream guy" self. But Charlie's reverie over Rothstein arouses real emotion in the clerk's mind. *"Beatific vision swoons on the empty pools of the Night Clerk's eyes. He resembles a holy saint, recently elected to Paradise"* (3:848). When Erie, like the Poet in O'Neill's early one-acter *Fog* discussing the death of an immigrant child, admits Hughie is "better off" and "out of the racket" of life, Charlie uncharacteristically agrees, referring to life as a "racket" and to Erie vocally as "492." "But we might as well make the best of it," he says, granting Erie access to an inner aggression only expressed to that point in the stage directions. "Well, you can't burn it all down, can you? There's too much steel and stone" (3:848).

The outburst irritates Erie at first, but he accepts whatever solace the clerk might provide. He chastises him coldly for the remark but quickly returns to the horseshoe of flowers, insisting the cost, 100 dollars, is not an exaggeration, and that he borrowed the money from dangerous hustlers. His ability to pay back these debts worries him, as he might "get beat up and maybe sent to a hospital" (3:849). Charlie still focuses on *"the Big Ideal"* and asks if Eric knows the infamous gambler and gangster Arnold Rothstein. "What's he got to do with it?" Erie demands. "He wouldn't loan a guy like me a nickel to save my grandmother from streetwalking" (3:849). Returning to the problem of the horseshoe, Erie assumes he could pay back money with a few wins at gambling. But without Hughie he has lost both luck and confidence.

Oblivious to Erie's desperation, the night clerk reiterates his singular interest in Arnold Rothstein. Erie again demands to know what Rothstein has to do with anything. But after a pause, *"his face lights up with a saving revelation"* (3:850). They have connected at last. Erie assumes his dream-self persona, acknowledges a (fantasy) friendship with Rothstein, and recounts a series of outlandish tales of gambling and womanizing. Charlie accepts each word as fact, no longer perceiving Erie merely as "492" but now reverently as *"the Gambler in 492, the Friend of Arnold Rothstein"* (3:850). Erie pushes a couple of dollars and some change across the counter toward the clerk, produces a pair of dice, and inquires slyly whether Charlie wants to inspect the dice. "What do you think I am?" the clerk responds, adding, "I know I can trust you" (3:851). Erie smiles, remarking that his mourning period for Hughie might be shorter than he thought. *"His soul is purged of grief, his confidence restored"* (3:851). Erie tosses the loaded dice and begins winning. Chuckling to himself, he chalks his streak up to "luck" and "know how" and assumes *"the slyly amused, contemptuous, affectionate wink with which a Wise Guy regales a sucker"* (3:851).

## COMMENTARY

Drama critics universally regard *Hughie* as a "perfect dramatic poem" (Bogard 419) and probably "the finest American one-act play" (Floyd 555). This deceptively simple late work marks a watershed American-style contribution to the modernist and existentialist European writing of the first half of the 20th century. European playwrights and authors such as Bertholt Brecht, Samuel Beckett, Albert Camus, and Jean-Paul Sartre began representing the deep search for meaning in a lonely and hostile modern world through this period (Harold Pinter is the most outstanding contemporary example), but certainly no American had yet achieved the depth of feeling and mastery of stagecraft we find in this one-act play.

In his review of the 1958 Swedish premiere, Henry Hewes writes that "unfortunately, some of the best things in the play have been written in the stage directions," but he nevertheless rated this long-unproduced one-acter as "top-drawer O'Neill

. . . a perfectly-constructed work" (224, 226). Zander Brietzke notes that *Hughie*, unlike much of the O'Neill canon, is a "minimal play in every respect: minimal set, minimal cast, minimal length, minimal dialogue" (235); in fact, O'Neill wrote *Hughie*, in the playwright's own words, "more to be read than staged" (O'Neill 531). He makes this clear through his multifaceted, strikingly written stage directions. The night clerk, Charlie Hughes's inner monologue can only be found in those passages, hidden as they are from a live audience: In them, the outwardly soft-spoken and deferential night clerk reveals an excitable, often violent imagination. Charlie's reveries would be very difficult to stage effectively. But O'Neill BIOGRAPHER Louis Sheaffer reports that O'Neill told his third wife, CARLOTTA MONTEREY O'NEILL, that he envisioned a production that might incorporate voiceovers for Charlie's inner monologue, along with a streaming film of the New York City street life that electrifies his imagination—clear evidence of the playwright's "visionary" ability to foresee the "mixed-media theater of later decades" (523).

*Hughie* represents a fascinating departure in length and scope from O'Neill's previous two plays, also masterpieces: LONG DAY'S JOURNEY INTO NIGHT and The ICEMAN COMETH. But many thematic and stylistic parallels remain between them, along with his next and final play, A MOON FOR THE MISBEGOTTEN. *Hughie* comes closest to *Iceman*, not only in its sordid urban setting and low-life characters but also thematically, and it can be read as "a kind of epilogue" to *Iceman* (Bogard 418). Each of the characters in both plays relies on a false "pipe dream" about themselves or their future that provides otherwise desperate lives with meaning and larger significance. "The only obstacle to happiness in [the plays'] scheme of things," Laurin Porter suggests, "arises when a member of the 'family' refuses to play by the rules, challenging the validity of the dream and breaking its soporific spell" (178). Betrayal arrives in the form of the illusion-breaker Hickey in *Iceman* and Hughie's death in *Hughie*. Porter significantly distinguishes between the two New York plays by characterizing *Hughie*, in contrast to *Iceman*, as a more intimate "pipe dream for two" (178). If the mélange of characters

we find in *Iceman* demonstrates a small universe of down-and-out psychologies, the two characters in *Hughie* complement each other perfectly—Erie demonstrating inward despair and outward aggression, Charlie outward apathy and inner hostility. Kurt Eisen argues that they respond to one another's "performing self" (outer) and "perceiving self" (inner) just as Theodore "Hickey" Hickman and Larry Slade do in *Iceman* (182). O'Neill biographer Stephen A. Black points out that Erie is more introspective and less caught up in the arrogance of his pipe dream than Hickey. Along with demonstrating his ability to mourn sincerely, unlike Hickey after murdering his wife, Erie fully comprehends the effect his behavior might have on other people—rejecting Hughie's bid to join him in gambling, for instance. "Rather than face up to his behavior," Black writes, "Hickey would simply have gone off on a drunk" (452).

In *Hughie*, O'Neill challenged himself to reconcile the oppositional poles of Erie and Charlie's characters into a mutually compassionate unit of "kinship" (see Manheim). Erie finds meager solace in gambling and alcohol, short-term solutions to the long-term problems of isolation, alienation, and disillusionment. Charlie, for his part, tunes everything out but the street, imagining that nearly any menial job would be more exciting than his own. But Erie understands that his drinking benders and money problems compromise his "know how" and personal safety, and he requires a "sucker" like Hughie to infuse him with confidence and luck. For this reason, the play's action revolves around Erie's desperate attempts to break through Charlie's "invisible wall of indifference" (Floyd 558). Charlie's aggressive inner desires are fruitless because, like Robert "Yank" Smith in The HAIRY APE, "there's too much stone and steel" to destroy the city and feel a part of something important and exciting, however destructive. Only when the street sounds die away does Charlie recognize the value of Erie's "dream guy" persona. Only then can he relinquish his "invisible wall of indifference" and satisfy Erie's need for what O'Neill referred to as "The Good Listener" (quoted in Floyd 558).

Another remarkable attribute of both *Iceman* and *Hughie* is the empathy with which O'Neill renders the tormented inner lives of America's "misbegotten"—small-time gamblers, saloon keepers, sleazy racketeers, prostitutes, and pimps—with only artful hints of the MELODRAMA or supernatural forces we find in many of his early plays. "The Night Clerk character," he told George Jean Nathan, "is an essence of all the night clerks I've known in bum hotels—quite a few! 'Erie' is a type of Broadway sport I and my brother [JAMES O'NEILL, JR.] used to know by the dozen in far-off days. I didn't know many at the time the play is laid, 1928, but they never change. Only their lingo does" (O'Neill 531–532). Thus critics often compare Erie to O'Neill's brother Jamie, the model for James Tyrone in *A Moon for the Misbegotten*, given their similar use of Broadway "lingo" and close association with Broadway hustlers, showmen, and prostitutes.

The rationale behind moving the time period forward, as opposed to setting it in the more familiar 1910s—a decade when O'Neill and his brother actually wandered the Theater District and the Tenderloin together—appears in the opening stage directions: Built between 1900 and 1910, the hotel has suffered hard times while the rest of the nation enjoys, as O'Neill describes it, *"the Great Hollow Boom of the twenties,"* now known as the Roaring Twenties. *"The Everlasting Opulence of the New Economic Law has overlooked it,"* and the hotel *"manages to keep running by cutting the overhead for service, repairs, and cleanliness to a minimum"* (3:831). O'Neill openly and with pointed sarcasm castigates the United States and its arrogant optimism by capitalizing on the fashionable terms at the time that successful people used, terms that not only avoided bitter truths like the lives led by Charlie and Erie but denied them access to the boom as well. Economic expansion, in short, has left O'Neill's characters in the dustbin of American society.

Erie and Charlie, and Hughie before them, rely upon mutually constructed fantasies impossible to sustain without the other. The final scene of *Hughie* implies that these fantasies will only perpetuate a never-ending cycle of delusion. "No possibility of transcendence," Porter submits, "no viable means of breaking through the limitations of time and space, no discovery of ultimate mean-

ing or value" (187). Nevertheless, simple human interaction—albeit necessarily male interaction (or the occasional prostitute) in *Hughie* and elsewhere in the O'Neill canon, no matter its dependence on the lies we construct about ourselves—emerges in the final scene as the necessary ingredient to a bearable life. Henry Hewes concludes his review of the premiere by stating that with *Hughie*, O'Neill "had come to believe that the interdependence of human beings, even when it is selfishly motivated, contains a divine element of love" (226).

See also EAST ASIAN THOUGHT.

## CHARACTERS

**Hughes, Charlie (Night Clerk)**   The Night Clerk at a rundown hotel in the theater district of New York City. Charlie is either 43 or 44 years old, not being sure himself, tall and thin with a *"jutting Adam's Apple. His face is long and narrow, greasy with perspiration, sallow, studded with pimples from ingrowing hairs"* (3:831). All of his facial features are unduly large but otherwise unexceptional. Charlie moved to New York from Saginaw, Michigan, but has lived long enough in the City to consider himself a New Yorker. He moved east to achieve the American dream and before long wound up working as a night clerk, a job he considers the most boring in the City. He married a termagant named Jess, with whom he gets along "all right" (3:842), and they have three children.

As the play begins, we find Charlie seated behind the lobby's desk. *"He is not thinking. He is not sleepy. . . . Behind horn-rimmed spectacles, his blank brown eyes contain no discernible expression. One would say they had even forgotten how it feels to be bored"* (3:831). Charlie's imagination, as O'Neill reveals in the stage directions, is remarkably active. His character thus deepens if one reads the text of *Hughie* as opposed to only seeing it acted out on the stage. When "Erie" Smith arrives at the hotel from a four-day bender, Charlie adopts a *"The-Patron-Is-Always-Right-grimace"* (3:832) but is entirely lost in his own, often violent, imaginings. Mourning the loss of the previous night clerk, Hughie, Erie desperately requires a replacement, a "sucker" who can boost his confidence and bring him luck. Through most of the play's action, which consists mainly of Erie's monologue, only the noise of ambulance sirens, garbage collectors, cops walking the beat, and elevated trains activate Charlie's fecund imagination. Occasionally Charlie's thoughts acknowledge Erie's presence. He calls him "492," after his room number, a significant designation that Laurin Porter argues suggests Christopher Columbus's arrival in the New World in 1492. "The allusion is ironic," she writes, "there are no discoveries in Charlie's world" (182).

Erie drones on for over three-quarters of an hour, while Charlie envisions himself, among other things, as a garbage man waking the city with his can-banging and the city burned to the ground (though he concludes, calling to mind Robert "Yank" Smith's struggle for identity in *The Hairy Ape*, that *"there's too much stone and steel"* [3:844]); he conceives of the passing elevated trains as symbolic of time passing toward death, *"Nirvana, the Big Night of Nights"* (3:838). Charlie eventually recognizes Erie as his *"one possible escape"* (3:846) from the silence that, by four o'clock in the morning, has fallen upon the now desolate street. He recalls that "492" mentioned something about gambling, and Charlie wonders whether Erie knows Arnold Rothstein, the notorious Jewish gangster who "fixed" the 1919 World Series. Erie mordantly admits that Rothstein "uses [him] to run errands when there ain't no one else handy" (3:849), but then he realizes that Charlie has, however inadvertently, offered himself up as a replacement for the deceased Hughie, his dream-affirming "sucker" and "Good Listener" (Floyd 558). In the final scene, Erie challenges Charlie to a crap game with loaded dice. Together they create a mutually beneficial pipe dream—Erie, the great Broadway sport and gambler, and Charlie, who might now live vicariously through his tall tales.

**Smith, "Erie"** A small-time New York gambler and racketeer. Erie resides in a seedy hotel on a side street in New York City's theater district. He is 45 years old, with the same *"pasty, perspiry, night-life complexion"* as the night clerk, Charlie Hughes. O'Neill vividly describes Erie as a New York type who acts *"consciously"* like a *"Broadway sport and a Wise Guy—the type of small fry gambler and horse*

*player, living hand to mouth on the fringe of the rackets. Infesting corners, doorways, cheap restaurants, the bars of minor speakeasies, he and his kind imagine they are in the Real Know, cynical oracles of the One True Grapevine"* (3:832). Erie owes his nickname to the fact that he grew up in Erie, Pennsylvania. When he was 18 years old, a promiscuous local girl named Daisy accused him of impregnating her; Daisy's father then sought Erie out, triggering him to take "a run-out powder" to Saratoga Springs, then on to New York City (3:835). Erie's room number at the hotel is 492, a designation Charlie Hughes assigns him in his inner thoughts. The number calls to mind 1492, the year Columbus "discovered" the New World (Porter 182). Erie, then, is a kind of mock Christopher Columbus, and his lackluster life on the edge of civilization symbolizes for O'Neill the dismal failure of the American experiment.

When Erie enters the hotel lobby a few moments after the play begins, he is recovering from a four-day bender in commemoration of the death of the previous night clerk, Hughie. When Hughie died, Erie lost a friend but, more importantly for him, a symbol of his own self-importance—the "sucker" or the "sap," a guileless listener who would believe his tall tales, let him cheat and win at dice, and satisfy his longing to view himself as more important than he actually is. In fact, all three men—Erie, Hughie, and Charlie Hughes—hail from the "sticks" and had figuratively read in the "Suckers Almanac," Erie says, "that all a guy had to do was come to the Big Town and Old Man Success would be waitin' at the Grand Central [train station] to give him a key to the city" (3:841). Over the course of the play, Erie eulogizes Hughie's memory in long monologues directed at, but failing to penetrate, Charlie Hughes's conscious mind. Actually, what Erie requires to survive is someone to act, as O'Neill phrases it in his WORK DIARY, as "The Good Listener" (Floyd 558), a "perceiver" to Erie's "performer" self (Eisen 182). Without it, his "pipe dream" of being the ultimate *"Broadway sport"* fades away, and reality overwhelms him: He is a failed gambler who lives hand-to-mouth in a hostile and lonely modern world.

Erie at first grows despondent as his efforts to replace Hughie with Charlie prove futile.

He jangles his key obsessively, *"as if it were a fetish which might set him free"* (3:844), terrified of returning to his room and feeling somehow that if he does, the perceptible loss of his "dream guy" self (3:844) might solidify into a permanent condition and possibly death. For the bulk of the play, only the noises of sirens, garbage men, and elevated trains from the outside successfully ignite the night clerk's imagination. But around four o'clock in the morning, after a little under an hour, the noises are silenced, and Charlie recognizes that accepting Erie's advances would fill the void. He is fascinated by the fact that Erie knows the notorious gangster Arnold Rothstein and apparently oblivious to Erie's confession that he only occasionally runs minor errands for the Big Shot. But Erie apprehends in Charlie the mutual need, however unconscious, to fuel a fantasy state that eludes the morbid, bitter truth of their misbegotten lives. In the final scene, Erie produces a pair of loaded dice and resumes his role of largeness. For his part, Charlie looks on at the "friend of Arnold Rothstein" and lives vicariously through his tales of gambling, gangsters, and sexual conquest. Together, they create "an oasis in the desert of their days" (Sheaffer 522).

## BIBLIOGRAPHY

Black, Stephen A. *Eugene O'Neill: Beyond Mourning and Tragedy.* New Haven, Conn.: Yale University Press, 1999.

Bogard, Travis. *Contour in Time: The Plays of Eugene O'Neill.* Rev. ed. New York: Oxford University Press, 1988.

Brietzke, Zander. *The Aesthetics of Failure: Dynamic Structure in the Plays of Eugene O'Neill.* Jefferson, N.C.: McFarland & Company, 2001.

Eisen, Kurt. *The Inner Strength of Opposites: O'Neill's Novelistic Drama and the Melodramatic Imagination.* Athens: University of Georgia Press, 1994.

Floyd, Virginia. *The Plays of Eugene O'Neill: A New Assessment.* New York: Ungar, 1985.

Howes, Henry. "Hughie." In *O'Neill and His Plays: Four Decades of Criticism,* edited by Oscar Cargill, N. Bryllion Fagin, and William J. Fisher, 224–226. New York: New York University Press, 1961.

Manheim, Michael. *Eugene O'Neill's New Language of Kinship.* Syracuse, N.Y.: Syracuse University Press, 1982.

O'Neill, Eugene. *Selected Letters of Eugene O'Neill.* Edited by Travis Bogard and Jackson R. Bryer. New York: Limelight Editions, 1994.

Porter, Laurin. "*Hughie*: Pipe Dream for Two." In *Critical Essays on Eugene O'Neill,* edited by James J. Martine, 78–88. Critical Essays on American Literature. Boston: G.K. Hall & Co., 1984.

Sheaffer, Louis. *O'Neill: Son and Artist.* Boston: Little, Brown, 1973.

# Hunted, The

See MOURNING BECOMES ELECTRA.

# Iceman Cometh, The
## (completed, 1939; first produced, 1946)

Eugene O'Neill's reputation as the United States' "master of the misbegotten" culminates in his late masterpiece *The Iceman Cometh.* The action takes place in a downtown Manhattan saloon and "Raines-Law" hotel called Harry Hope's and covers two days in the life of a motley assortment of anarchists, prostitutes, pimps, and war veterans, among a host of other "lost souls" hiding behind pipe dreams and ALCOHOLISM to shield themselves from the terrorizing realities of modern-day life. "In bomb shelters," writes Travis Bogard, "men do not behave very differently, perhaps, from the way they behave in *The Iceman Cometh*" (421–422).

O'Neill wrote *The Iceman Cometh* at TAO HOUSE, his home in Danville, California, between June 8 and November 26, 1939, and completed a near-final draft in December 1939—one of the most horrifying periods in modern history: Hitler's army invaded Poland and commenced a policy of genocide against Jews and other populations of Europe, Great Britain and FRANCE subsequently declared war on Germany, the United States was still caught in the devastating throws of the Great Depression, and the Far East had plunged into a gruesome conflict that would end with the atomic devastation of Hiroshima and Nagasaki five years later. "The war news," O'Neill wrote his daughter OONA O'NEILL after completing *The Iceman Cometh*, "has affected my ability to concentrate on my job. With so much tragic drama happening in the world, it is hard to take theatre seriously" (O'Neill 508). Two weeks later, however, O'Neill wrote to producer Lawrence Langner: "I'm working again on something . . . after a lapse of several months spent with an ear glued to the radio for war news. You can't keep a hop head off his dope for long!" (510). O'Neill coyly refers here to his tragic masterpiece LONG DAY'S JOURNEY INTO NIGHT.

O'Neill understood that *The Iceman Cometh* was probably the best play he had ever written, and he deliberately delayed production until after the war's conclusion. In the war's aftermath, he projected, the American public would experience a hangover of disillusionment on a national scale. Only then, he argued in a letter to his friend Dudley Nichols, could audiences comprehend the thesis of *The Iceman Cometh*—that mankind requires life-sustaining "pipe dreams" to endure the devastating realities of modern life:

No, *The Iceman Cometh* would be wrong now. A New York audience could neither see nor hear its meaning. The pity and tragedy of defensive pipe dreams would be deemed unpatriotic, and uninspired by the Atlantic Charter [Churchill and Roosevelt's vision of a postwar world order], even if the audience did catch that meaning. But after the war is over, I am afraid from present indications that American audiences will understand a lot of *The Iceman Cometh* only too well (O'Neill 537).

Unfortunately, the THEATRE GUILD premiere on October 9, 1946, at the Martin Beck Theater in New York City—O'Neill's first since his DAYS WITHOUT END debacle in 1934 (a period that came to be known as the "silence")—came too early and received mixed to poor reviews. (My own grandfather, James Kellock, returned home exasperated from the premiere and grouched to my preteen mother, "Well, the Iceman cameth, and who gives a damn.") *Time* magazine quipped that "as drama . . . for all its brooding, *The Iceman* was scarcely deeper than a puddle" (quoted in Diggins 62). Some critics, such as the novelist Mary McCarthy, struck an even more mean-spirited chord in their estimation: Likening the four-and-a-half-hour play to "some stern piece of hardware . . . ugly, durable, mysteriously utilitarian," McCarthy expanded her attack to include an ad hominem critique of O'Neill as an artist generally: "The return of a playwright who—to be frank—cannot write is a solemn and sentimental occasion," and she went on to compare O'Neill with other American writers such as Theodore Dreiser and James T. Farrell (both of whom O'Neill respected enormously), whose work "can find no reason for stopping, but go on and on, like elephants pacing in a zoo" (50).

Director and critic Eric Bentley—who, incredibly, directed the German-language premiere of *The Iceman Cometh*—went so far as to call O'Neill stupid, if indirectly: "I still maintain that O'Neill is no thinker. He is so little a thinker, it is dangerous for him to think. To prove this you have only to look at the fruits of his thinking; his comparatively thoughtless plays are better. For a non-thinker he thinks too much" (48). In the face of such attacks, stalwart champions of O'Neill's such as GEORGE JEAN NATHAN took pains to defend the play's artistry and power:

With the appearance of *The Iceman Cometh*, our theatre has become dramatically alive again. It makes most of the plays of other American playwrights produced during the more than twelve-year period of O'Neill's absence look comparatively like so much damp tissue paper. It is, in short, one of the best of its author's works and one that again firmly secures his position not only as the first of American dramatists but, with Shaw and O'Casey, one of the three really distinguished among the world's living (133).

Such accolades must have provided little comfort to the playwright, but 10 years later, three years after O'Neill's death and the same year that *Long Day's Journey into Night* premiered, director JOSÉ QUINTERO

Production photo of the 1946 Theatre Guild's *The Iceman Cometh*. "Play's climactic scene, his long confessional."
(Courtesy of the New York Public Library)

revived *The Iceman Cometh* in a now-legendary production with a brilliant cast, starring JASON ROBARDS as Theodore "Hickey" Hickman. Staged in the intimate atmosphere of the Circle in the Square Theatre, a former GREENWICH VILLAGE nightclub, this production lasted a full 565 performances (a record for O'Neill), effectively reviving O'Neill's reputation as the finest American dramatist and igniting, along with the premiere of *Long Day's Journey*, a EUGENE O'NEILL RENAISSANCE over the following decade. A number of well-regarded productions have been staged since, including the critically acclaimed Broadway production directed by Howard Davies and starring Kevin Spacey as Hickey (1999).

## SYNOPSIS

O'Neill's script begins with an unusual introductory paragraph describing the setting, Harry Hope's saloon. He specifies that the location is a Raines-Law hotel on "the downtown West Side of New York." New York's Raines Law provided a loophole for serving liquor after hours and on Sundays at saloons like Harry's that were located on the ground floor of tenement buildings if they offered rooms for rent on the upper floors and served food (see Raleigh "Historical Background" 1968, 59–60). The Raines Law was signed in 1896 as a measure to curb drinking and deviancy. Ironically enough, given there were rooms upstairs, the legislation inadvertently encouraged binge drinking and PROSTITUTION. At Harry Hope's, "a cheap ginmill of the five-cent whiskey, last-resort variety," the food consists of "a property sandwich in the middle of each table, an old desiccated ruin of dust-laden bread and mummified ham or cheese" reserved only for "the drunkest yokel from the sticks." The Raines Law also stipulated that during off hours, booze must be served in a back room. Harry circumvents this by rigging a black curtain separating the rear of the barroom from the back room (3:563).

## Act 1

An early morning in the summer of 1912 at Harry Hope's saloon on the ground floor of a five-story tenement on the Lower West Side of Manhattan. A dingy black curtain separates the bar proper from the back room, in which circular bar tables are crammed tightly together. A sign on the door to the toilet in the left corner reads, "This is it." Another door leads to the hallway back center. Its walls and ceiling are *"now so splotched, pealed, stained and dusty that their color can best be described as dirty"* (3:565). The bar stretches along the back wall, and the barroom contains one table with four chairs. A dull morning light glows softly from the windows in the rear right, and wall-bracketed lighting illuminates the back room.

The seats and tables in the back room are occupied by a motley group of mostly middle-aged barflies, including Larry Slade, a 60-year-old IRISH AMERICAN and former leader in the anarchist movement who falsely claims he awaits the peaceful oblivion of death; Hugo Kalmar, an Eastern European has-been anarchist who deludes himself that he continues to hold a vital role in "the Movement"; Piet "The General" Wetjoen, a former Boer (Dutch colonialist) commander in the Boer War (1899–1902, South Africa), who dreams of returning home to a hero's welcome; Cecil "The Captain" Lewis, Wetjoen's former enemy from the British army but now his close friend who shares the Boer's dream; James "Jimmy Tomorrow" Cameron, a former war correspondent in the Boer War who insists he will sober up and resume his journalism career "tomorrow"; Joe Mott, the only African American in the group and a onetime gangster and proprietor of a black gambling establishment who boasts of the time he will reopen his business; Pat McGloin, a corrupt member of the police force who was fired for accepting bribes but still believes he will be reinstated; Ed Mosher, McGloin's good friend, Harry Hope's brother-in-law, and a former circus man who ostensibly longs to rejoin the free and open life of the circus; Harry Hope, a onetime Tammany official (see Raleigh "Historical Background" 1968, 56–58) and proprietor of the bar who boasts of his connections in local politics and vows to take one last walking tour of his old neighborhood; and Wil-

lie Oban, a Harvard Law School graduate in his late 30s whose father was a notorious bucket-shop racketeer (fraudulent stock trader) and believes the city district attorney will one day hire him.

Larry Slade is the only one conscious. Rocky Pioggi, an Italian-American bartender in his late 20s, steps through the curtain from the bar at right. *"A tough guy but sentimental in his way, and good-natured,"* Rocky sneaks Larry a free drink, warning him not to wake up his boss, Harry Hope. The night before, Harry had ordered no more free drinks "'beginnin' tomorrow,'" but Larry grins sardonically and acknowledges that Harry's weakness for his friends is stronger than his desire for profit. Harry's threats about "tomorrow" reflect the general attitude of the barroom habitués, who all, according to Larry, share "a touching credulity

Terry Carlin, the real life anarchist Larry Slade *(Courtesy of the Sheaffer-O'Neill Collection, Charles E. Shain Library of Connecticut College)*

concerning tomorrows" (3:569). Larry considers this "Tomorrow Movement" a kind of religion, in which "the lie of a pipe dream is what gives life to the whole misbegotten mad lot of us, drunk or sober" (3:569–570). Larry, "the Old Foolosopher," gave up on the "pipe dream" of the anarchist movement long ago, finally recognizing the bitter truth that "men didn't want to be saved from themselves, for that would mean they would have to give up greed, and they'll never pay that price for liberty." Hugo awakes briefly. "Don't be a fool! Loan me a dollar!" (3:570) he screams at Larry, and promptly passes out.

Sleeping off their drunk from the previous night, they all await the arrival of Theodore "Hickey" Hickman, a traveling salesman, or "drummer," who shows up each year to celebrate his old friend Harry Hope's birthday. Universally adored by the patrons at Harry's, Hickey buys them all drinks and elevates their spirits with his salesman's wit and tall tales from the open road. In a repeated gag, Hickey weeps over a picture of his wife and then, Rocky explains, "springin' it on yuh all of a sudden dat he left her in de hay wid de iceman" (3:571).

Willie Oban cries out in his sleep, "It's a lie!" and "Papa! Papa!" (3:572). Rocky roughly shakes him awake, but Harry Hope comes to and, contradicting his previous instructions, rebukes Rocky for not giving Willie a drink. Joe Mott awakens next and inquires about Don Parritt, an 18-year-old with ties to Larry and the "Movement" who rented a room at Harry's the previous night. Joe hopes Parritt might buy him a drink; when Larry says he is "broke," Joe and Rocky testify that Parritt had a roll of money but denied it and refused to buy anyone a drink, an unpardonable offense that earned him the epithet "tightwad." Larry and Parritt's mother, Rosa, were comrades in the "Movement." Larry explains that several people were killed in an anarchist bombing on the West Coast, and Rosa was captured by the police; Larry predicts she will be condemned to life in prison. Parritt claims to have escaped capture in order to seek refuge and companionship with Larry. Though he still respects Rosa, Larry claims he cares nothing for her, the "Movement," Parritt's trouble, or anything else.

Parritt enters with a "*shifting defiance and ingratiation in his light-blue eyes and an irritating aggressiveness in his manner*" (3:576). Larry introduces him to the bar. "It's the No Chance Saloon," Larry says, "It's Bedrock Bar, The End of the Line Café, The Bottom of the Sea Rathskeller," filled only with men who cling desperately to "a few harmless pipe dreams about their yesterdays and tomorrows," though he singles himself out as "the exception" (3:577, 578). Larry suspects an insider in the "Movement" must have betrayed Rosa Parritt. When Parritt claims he "got wise [the Movement] was all a crazy pipe dream," Larry inwardly feels there is something about this newcomer that "*isn't right*" (3:582).

Hugo reawakens briefly and recites his favorite lines from Ferdinand Freiligrath's poem "Revolution": "The days grow hot, O Babylon! 'Tis cool beneath thy villow trees!" (3:583). He salutes Parritt, inquires about his mother (whom he also knew in the "Movement"), demands that Parritt buy him a drink, and passes out. Larry describes each member of the "family circle of inmates" (3:585). Willie awakens and scolds Larry for leaving him out of his "Who's Who in Dypsomania" (3:585); Willie then expounds on his privileged background, superior education, and the tactics of his criminal father who sent his son to law school in order to have a legal expert in his bucket-shop operation. He then belts out a bawdy folk song, awakening all the drunks and infuriating Harry. Threatened with removal, Willie pleads to stay and claims his room is haunted. Harry relents, once again blaming Rocky for his own threats.

Gradually gaining consciousness, the men begin to define their respective roles in the cloistered society of the bar. They all defer to Harry, whose truculent, irascible temperament is a facade that conceals a deep affection for his friends. Since his wife, Bessie, died 20 years before, Harry has never stepped foot outside the bar. Harry's friends all know that Bessie was a horrible nag and that all Harry ever wanted was to drink with his barroom pals as much as he pleased and never again face the outside world.

Each character talks passionately about his respective pipe dream. Each jibes the others good-naturedly about their delusions but takes offense if someone challenges his own. Pearl and Margie, "*typical dollar street walkers*," enter the bar from their night's work. Rocky is their pimp, but his pipe dream emerges in the presence of the two prostitutes—he takes issue with being regarded as a "pimp" and considers himself a legitimate bartender; the women for their part consider themselves "tarts, but dat's all" (3:602). Margie and Pearl relate an anecdote wherein two men picked them up that night, then got embroiled in a political argument—one being a "Bull Mooser" (Progressive Party followers of Theodore Roosevelt) and the other a "Republican" (3:601; the Bull Moose party split from the Republicans after William Howard Taft beat Roosevelt for the Republican nomination)—and the hotel detective chased them away. They discuss Harry's other bartender, Chuck Morello, who periodically goes on drinking benders and gets into brawls, and Cora, another prostitute. They scoff at "dat old pipe dream" of Chuck and Cora's "about gettin' married and settlin' down on a farm" (3:602). Cora and Chuck enter. Parritt complains about the bar being a "hooker hangout" and declares he hates "every bitch that ever lived" (3:604). Parritt appeals to Larry for approval after such outbursts, but he never gets it. "I don't want to know a damned thing about your business," Larry grumbles (3:604).

Cora relates a story about "rolling" a drunken tourist, then informs the group that she and Chuck met Hickey outside on the street corner, "'just finishin' figurin' out,' he told them, 'de best way to save dem and bring dem peace'" (3:606). Cora adds that Hickey appears uncharacteristically sober. Harry orders Rocky to fetch him and believes Hickey is planning a practical joke. They all agree to play along.

Rocky reenters with Hickey. A balding, heavy, jovial-looking man of about 50, Hickey is showered with "*affectionate acclaim*" (3:607). "Hello, Gang!" he responds merrily. Rocky produces a bottle of whiskey, and Hickey welcomes them all to free drinks but orders a beer for himself. Harry mocks him as a member of the Salvation Army and the newly elected president of the W.C.T.U. (the Women's Christian Temperance Union). Hickey assures his old friends he has no interest in reforming them,

adding significantly that he quit drinking because he "finally had the guts to face myself and throw overboard the damned lying pipe dream that's been making me miserable" (3:609). He insists it is not booze he wishes to liberate them from, but rather their pipe dreams. Throughout his monologue, the gang stares at him with "*an uneasy resentment*" (3:610).

"Be God, you've hit the nail on the head, Hickey!" Larry finally responds. "This dump is the Palace of Pipe Dreams!" (3:611). His enthusiasm dies out, however, when Hickey suggests that Larry, "The Old Grandstand Foolosopher," is no exception with his lies of welcoming death (3:611). Parritt howls in agreement, and Hickey regards the stranger for the first time. He sizes Parritt up as "members of the same lodge" (3:612) for reasons he cannot account for. Having walked all the way from his home in Astoria, Queens, he begins yawning and soon falls asleep. The men erupt into a fierce discussion of Hickey's peculiar transformation. "He'll be a fine wet blanket to have around at my birthday!" Harry quips. "I wish to hell he'd never turned up!" (3:614). But Ed Mosher assures him Hickey is simply overworked and will snap out of it; he recounts an amusing anecdote about a quack doctor whose lifelong goal was to sell enough of his "miraculous cure" that there "wouldn't be a single vacant cemetery lot left in this glorious country" (3:616). The group howls with laughter at the punch line that the doctor is dead but most probably selling snake oil on a street corner in heaven. "That's the spirit," Hickey says groggily, "don't let me be a wet blanket—all I want is to see you happy." Their "*puzzled, resentful and uneasy*" glares resume as Hickey falls back to sleep, and the curtain falls (3:616).

### Act 2

Harry Hope's back room, just before midnight on the eve of Harry's birthday. The tables are arranged for a banquet, with 17 chairs and place settings; ribbons hang from the light brackets, and a birthday cake with six candles (one for each decade of Harry's life) sits on a separate table right front. Cora, Chuck, Hugo, Larry, Margie, Pearl, and Rocky are discovered. Cora arranges a vase of flowers while Margie and Pearl sort Harry's presents and fuss over the cake. Hugo is passed out, and Larry sits facing front, with a whiskey before him, *"in frowning, disturbed meditation"* (3:617). They all want Harry's party to come off well, but no one feels genuinely festive. Hickey has been irritating them all with passive-aggressive "hintin' around" about each of their pipe dreams. Harry and Jimmy Tomorrow, in particular, have been "run ragged" by Hickey's expostulations, and the rest are still hiding in their rooms. Hickey's influence has caused Rocky and Chuck to refer openly to the women as whores. When the women call Rocky a pimp, he slaps them both hard. Larry *"bursts into a sardonic laugh"* (3:622). The sound awakens Hugo, and Larry warns him not to miss out on the revolution started by "the great Nihilist Hickey! He's started a movement that'll blow up the world!" (3:622). Hugo fumes over Hickey's interference, then passes out.

Joe Mott enters with an air of defiance. "Listen to me, you white boys!" he shouts, "Don't you get it in your heads I's pretendin' to be what I ain't, or dat I ain't proud to be what I is, get me?" (3:625). Joe's anger subsides, and he blames Hickey for his ill humor. Larry assumes Hickey stopped drinking to hide the real reason for his conversion. Hickey silently enters and startles the group by bellowing, "Well! Well!! Well!!!" He carries a load of presents for Harry, and Margie and Pearl help to arrange them on the table. Hickey refutes Larry's theory, redirecting the topic to Larry's own pipe dream of longing for death. Rocky breaks Hickey's spell—"Aw, hire a church!" (3:627). Hickey resumes an infectious celebratory mood, bragging about buying treats that "will please the whores more than anything" (3:627); he upsets the women by referring to them as "whores," but an earnest apology brings them back around. Chuck and Rocky leave and reenter with Hickey's basketful of champagne bottles.

Hickey turns on Hugo, backhandedly scoffing at his revolutionary cant. "Leave Hugo be!" shouts Larry, "He rotted ten years in prison for his faith! He's earned his dream! Have you no decency or pity?" (3:628). Hickey contends that a true act of pity would relieve Hugo of his dream, just as it would for Larry—"all the grandstand Foolosopher bunk and the waiting for the Big Sleep stuff is a pipe dream." When his dream dissolves, Hickey

goes on, "You'll say to yourself, I'm just an old man who is scared of life, but even more scared of dying. So I'm keeping the drunk and hanging on to life at any price, and what of it? Then you'll know what real peace means, Larry" (3:629). "Be God," Larry retorts, "if I'm not beginning to think you've gone mad! (*with a rush of anger*) You're a liar!" (3:629). Hickey switches the topic to Parritt. Larry instinctively knows the source of the young man's guilt but refuses to share it or admit he cares.

Willie enters, sober and *"in a pitiable state"* (3:632). Now a Hickey convert, he plans to buy new clothes with Hickey's money and then approach the district attorney for a position. Larry advises he start drinking, which tempts Willie, but then he blurts out, "That's fine advice! I thought you were my friend!" (3:632), and he sulkily takes a seat alone. Joe and Cora are at the piano; Joe is teaching her how to play "The Sunshine of Paradise Alley." Parritt enters, also complaining about Hickey, but with a paranoia not shared by the others. When Larry calls him a fool for listening, Parritt levels Hickey's charge against him but guiltily lets up. Parritt believes Larry is the only man his mother truly loved, though she practiced "free love" with countless partners, making Parritt feel as if he grew up in a brothel. Larry excoriates Parritt for dishonoring his mother and threatens to leave. Parritt begs him to remain and returns to the subject of Hickey. "There's something not human behind his damned grinning and kidding" (3:635); but he returns to his own case and begins to confess his treachery. He rationalizes that studying American history made him realize that ANARCHISM was "a damned foreign pipe dream" that might destroy American democracy. Larry refuses to believe such high-minded principles motivated Parritt, but he repeats his lack of concern.

A fight erupts in the hallway. Rocky rushes to investigate and reenters with Lewis and Wetjoen, both of whom are relatively sober. Hickey's insinuations have led them to clash with one another; each accepts Hickey's line about the other's pipe dream but violently defends his own. Ed Mosher and Pat McGloin enter, complaining about Hickey's effect on Harry; nevertheless, they have also resolved to actively pursue their dreams. Harry enters with Jimmy Tomorrow. They all cheer in a "*spiritless chorus*" (3:640). Jimmy looks terrified, and Harry's phony grouchiness has transformed into real bitterness. Hickey starts pumping his hand in congratulations, but Harry pulls away in a fury. He laces into Hickey, calling him a "sneaking, lying drummer" (3:641), then turns his wrath on the rest of the party. He eventually lets up, and they happily forgive him.

When Jimmy recounts his tale of losing his wife, Marjorie, to another man during the Boer War, Hickey disabuses him of the pipe dream by telling him he was surely delighted to be rid of her so he could drink as much as he liked. Larry jumps at this, suspecting Hickey's transformation was precipitated by the iceman story coming to fruition. Hickey verbally beats Larry into submission by remarking that if all their stories eventually come true, then Larry's "Big Sleep" might too.

Rocky and Chuck serve schooners of champagne, and Hickey makes a sincere toast to Harry but ruins it by toasting the end of all pipe dreams. He then calls for a speech from Harry. The old proprietor begins modestly, but his anger uncontrollably rises. "I'm not running a damned orphan asylum for bums and crooks! Nor a God-damned hooker shanty, either! Nor an Old Men's Home for lousy Anarchist tramps that ought to be in jail! I'm sick of being played for a sucker!" (3:646). He concludes by vowing to take his walk through the neighborhood. Hickey cheers him on, then apologizes for having been "a damned busy body" since his arrival. But he tells them he is "slated to leave on a trip" and wanted to help them before his departure. Larry demands to know if it was his wife leaving him that converted him to "this great peace" (3:648). They all jeer at Hickey, believing Larry's theory. Hickey accepts the attack good-naturedly, then reveals that his wife is dead. Guilt descends upon the crowd, and they beg his forgiveness, but he declares he feels no remorse, that she was better off without "a no-good cheater and drunk" like him. Everyone gapes at Hickey in "*bewildered, incredulous confusion*" as the curtain falls (3:650).

## Act 3

Harry Hope's barroom in the middle of the morning the following day. A section of the back room is still visible, and the tables and chairs have been returned to the cluttered disarray of act 1. Above the mirror behind the bar hang photographs of the Irish Tammany leader Richard Croker and the Bowery politician "Big Tim" Sullivan, as well as lithographs of the professional boxers John L. Sullivan and "Gentleman Jim" Corbett. Joe sweeps the floor sullenly, ignoring the others, then begins slicing bread at the free lunch counter. Hugo is passed out, and Larry, Rocky, and Parritt look tense and exhausted. Hickey kept everyone awake after the party, relentlessly preaching about their pipe dreams. Rocky challenges Larry to jump from his fire escape if he truly welcomes death. Parritt seconds that, calling Larry a "yellow old faker" (3:653). Rocky threatens to oust Parritt, but Larry calls him off. "He don't belong," Rocky says; then he yawns loudly and drifts off to sleep.

Parritt talks again about Larry's importance to him in childhood. At one time he wondered if Larry was his father. He confesses to his betrayal, perversely admitting that his only reason was money—"I got stuck on a whore and wanted dough to blow in on her and have a good time! That's all I did it for! Just money! Honest!" (3:654). Larry roughly shakes him by the shoulders, demanding that Parritt stop involving Larry in his life. This awakens Rocky, and the conversation turns back to Hickey. "I'm damned sure he's brought death here with him," Larry somberly remarks. "I feel the cold touch of it on him" (3:655). Larry then insinuates that if Parritt had any "guts or decency" (3:655), he would leap from his own fire escape. Rocky recounts an argument with Pearl and Margie, who went on strike and left for Coney Island.

Chuck enters wearing a "*Sunday-best blue suit*" and banded straw hat (3:656). At Hickey's insistence, he and Cora have decided to marry that day. Rocky sneers at their pipe dream, and the two bartenders square off for a fight. When Joe tries to break it up, they tell him to keep out of it. They call him "a black bastard" and a "doity nigger" (3:658), and he lunges at them with his bread knife. Chuck grabs a whiskey bottle and raises it to strike, while Rocky pulls from his pocket a short-barreled, nickel-plated revolver. Larry intervenes by laughing and pounding his fist on the table at the bitter irony of Hickey's success. Hugo returns briefly to consciousness, calls Hickey a "Gottamned liar," and passes out. Joe takes the drink he earned from his chores, then smashes the glass on the floor. "I's on'y savin' you de trouble, White Boy. Now you don't have to break it soon's my back's turned, so's no white man kick about drinkin' from de same glass" (3:659–660). He announces he will find money to reopen his gambling house, "If I has to borrow a gun and stick up some white man" (3:660), and stumbles out the door.

Willie Oban enters, completely sober and dressed in *"an expensive, well-cut suit, good shoes and clean linen,"* but shaking terribly from withdrawal. He desperately wants a drink but cannot go to the district attorney's office smelling of whiskey. Lewis enters, also clean, nicely dressed, and suffering from *"katzenjammer"* (a hangover; 3:661). He refers to Hickey as an "interfering ass" and regrets having befriended "that stupid bounder of a Boer" (meaning Wetjoen; 3:661). Wetjoen enters with the same spruced-up appearance and ill condition as the previous two. He and Lewis mock each other's inability to extricate themselves from the bar, then attack their respective reputations during the Boer War. Lewis claims Wetjoen was a known coward, and Wetjoen that Lewis embezzled regimental money to gamble and drink. Larry sardonically compliments Hickey on his ability to "raise the dead," which silences them. Both men make to leave the bar but take positions at either window and wearily stare out at the street (3:664).

Willie approaches Parritt and proposes he retain Willie's legal services. Parritt disabuses him of the notion that he requires a lawyer, then pleads with Larry to believe that it was only a "few lousy dollars to blow in on a whore" that compelled him to betray his mother. Larry orders a drink on Hickey, though he had vowed not to accept one. "I'd get blind to the world now if it was the Iceman of Death himself treating!" (3:666–667). Larry wonders why he conjured that image, then laughs: "Well, be God, it fits, for Death was the Iceman Hickey called to his home!" (3:667).

Ed Mosher and Pat McGloin enter; they have been arguing as well and bitterly denounce Hickey's interference. Cora and Chuck enter and announce

their plan to get married in New Jersey that afternoon. No one takes them seriously. The couple bickers drunkenly then hears Hickey approach and makes a hasty exit. Harry, Jimmy Tomorrow, and Hickey appear at the doorway. Harry and Jimmy are also dressed in their finest clothes and are desperately hungover—their unsteady walk *"suggests the last march of the condemned"* (3:669). Hickey prods the two along and gives another speech about the fear men experience when they "face the truth," but that "it's exactly those damned tomorrow dreams which keep you from making peace with yourself. So you've got to kill them like I killed mine" (3:670, 671). He cajoles Lewis and Wetjoen into leaving first. Mosher and McGloin follow, with Willie close behind. They all thank Harry as they depart. Jimmy Tomorrow is next, but he pleads, "Tomorrow! I will tomorrow!" He finally relents, but he screams at Hickey, "You dirty swine!" before rushing from the bar (3:672). Larry protests when Hickey turns on Harry. Harry lets out a stream of excuses—rheumatism, automobiles, the weather, the respect to Bessie's memory. None of them pass muster with Hickey, who openly defies Harry's pipe dream about his wife. "She was always around your neck," he says, "making you have ambition and go out and do things, when all you wanted was to get drunk in peace" (3:674).

Harry at first pretends he cannot hear, but then, in a burst of fury, he exits the bar. Rocky stares out the window in disbelief. "I'll bet yuh he's comin' back," he says. "Of course, he's coming back," Hickey responds. "So are all of the others. By tonight they'll all be here again. You dumbbell, that's the whole point" (3:674). But Harry continues to move away from the bar, and Rocky excitedly reports each step. Larry turns to Hickey: "And now it's my turn, I suppose? What is it I'm to do to achieve this blessed peace of yours?" (3:674). "Just stop lying to yourself," Hickey replies. "I sit here," Larry says, "with my pride drowned on the bottom of a bottle, keeping drunk so I won't see myself shaking in my britches with fright, or hear myself whining and praying: Beloved Christ, let me live a little longer at any price! . . . You think you'll make me admit that to myself?" Hickey chuckles, "But you just did admit it, didn't you?" (3:675). Parritt cheers on Hickey, who grants that Parritt would be fit to take his place as Larry's dream destroyer.

Rocky, observing Harry's progress, shouts that Harry stopped in the middle of the street. Harry runs back to the bar. Paralyzed with fear, he frantically claims that a reckless driver almost ran him over (automobiles had not yet been invented the last time Harry left the bar). Hickey goads Harry into admitting there was no car. Harry does so dejectedly and accidentally bangs his bottle down next to Hugo's head. Hugo mutters superstitiously that Harry appears to be dead and moves to another table, thrusting *"his head down on his arms like an ostrich hiding its head in the sand"* (3:677). "Another one who's begun to enjoy your peace!" Larry shouts. Hickey assures him they will be fine after "the first shock" (3:677). "Close that big clam of yours, Hickey," Harry orders. "Bejees, you're a worse gabber than that nagging bitch, Bessie, was" (3:678). Dumbfounded by this admittance, Rocky agrees with Hugo that Harry looks dead. "It's the peace of death you've brought him," Larry hisses. Hickey loses his temper for the first time, but he quickly collects himself. Harry complains the liquor has lost its "kick" and blames Hickey's meddling. Larry insists Hickey disclose what happened to his wife, Evelyn Hickman. Hickey says she took "a bullet in the head" (3:679). When Larry suggests he drove her to suicide, Hickey clarifies that she was murdered, and the police have not found the killer. "But I expect they will before very long" (3:679). Harry bets the iceman murdered her, then says in exasperation, "But who the hell cares? Let's get drunk and pass out" (3:680). Parritt continues to stare at Larry, demanding that he end his guilt.

Hugo reawakens, fear-stricken this time. Hickey ignores him and attempts to comfort Harry. "It's time you began to feel happy," he says uncertainly and the curtain falls (3:680).

## Act 4

Same as act 1 at 1:30 the following morning. Larry, Hugo, and Parritt sit at a table in the back room, left front. Parritt glares at Larry with *"sneering, pleading challenge"* (3:681). Cora, Lewis, McGloin, and Wetjoen sit at one table, and Willie, Harry, Mosher, and Jimmy Tomorrow sit at another. Two

bottles of whiskey and water pitchers stand on each table. Everyone sits *"like wax figures, set stiffly on their chairs, carrying out mechanically the motions of getting drunk but sunk in a numb stupor which is impervious to stimulation"* (3:681–682). Joe is passed out on the bar side, and Rocky, who now resembles a *"minor Wop gangster"* (3:682), roughly attempts to send him to the back room where he can drink legally. Chuck enters, drunk and disheveled from a fight. Back from a "periodical" (drinking binge), Chuck complains that alcohol no longer produces its desired effect. He now understands that Hickey was right to call his and Cora's engagement a pipe dream. "On'y it was fun," he admits forlornly, "me and Cora kiddin' ourselves" (3:683).

When Chuck asks Rocky where the "son of a bitch" Hickey is, Rocky responds, "De Chair, maybe dat's where he's goin'. I don't know nuttin', see, but it looks like he croaked his wife" (3:683). Rocky admits he is a pimp and that he too finds drinking no longer helps. He recounts how Joe confessed in tears that he "wasn't a gamblin' man or a tough guy no more" (3:684). Joe regains consciousness and moves dejectedly into the back room. Rocky and Chuck follow. Cora hands Chuck a roll of bills, but otherwise no one moves. Parritt shouts that Larry wants him to "take a hop off the fire escape" to repent for his sin. "God damn you!" Larry responds. "Are you trying to make me your executioner?" (3:686). Rocky says, "Sure. Why don't he? Or you? Or me? What de hell's de difference? Who cares?" (3:686). The rest join him in a dismal chorus— "The hell with it!" "Who cares?" (3:686). Rocky tries to entice Parritt and Larry to become pimps, "and not be lousy barflies" (3:687). "The peace Hickey's brought you," Larry responds. "It isn't contented enough, if you have to make everyone else a pimp, too" (3:687). He adds that Hickey will return, as he has lost confidence that the "peace he's sold us is the real McCoy" (3:688).

Hickey appears in the doorway at the back of the bar and angrily rejects Larry's assertion. Harry accuses him of having taken the "life out of" the whiskey, and the men all cry out, "We can't pass out! You promised us peace!" With a mix of sadness and anger, Hickey retorts, "By rights you should be contented now, without a single damned hope or lying dream left to torment you! But here you are, acting like a lot of stiffs cheating the undertaker!" (3:689). He announces that by two o'clock, his time will have run out, and he again pleads for them to appreciate the loss of their delusions. "Don't you know you're free now to be yourselves, without having to feel remorse or guilt, or lie to yourselves about reforming tomorrow? Can't you see there is no tomorrow now? You're rid of it forever! You've killed it!" (3:689).

Hickey confesses that he murdered his wife, Evelyn, to save her from forgiving him again for philandering and drunkenness. *"There is a second's dead silence as he finishes—then a tense indrawn breath like a gasp from the crowd, and a general shrinking movement"* (3:690). Parritt compares his own state with Hickey's by saying, "It's worse if you kill someone and they have to go on living. I'd be glad of the Chair!" Agitated by the comparison, Hickey replies, "There was love in my heart, not hate" (3:691). He takes up his narrative again, but Harry cries out, "Who the hell cares? We don't want to hear it. All we want is to pass out and get drunk and a little peace!" (3:691). Pounding the tables with their glasses, the group all join in chorus—"Who the hell cares? We want to pass out!" (3:692). Jimmy emerges from his stupor and, *"in a precise, completely lifeless voice,"* admits to no one in particular, "It was all a stupid lie—my nonsense about tomorrow" (3:692). He was glad when his wife left him—it made it easier to get drunk without the guilt.

Two detectives, Moran and Lieb, silently enter the barroom. Moran shows Rocky his badge and demands to see Hickey. When they tell Rocky it was Hickey who called them, he points to the back room. "And if yuh want a confession," he says dully, "all yuh got to do is listen. He'll be tellin' all about it soon" (3:693). Lieb blocks the exit, and Moran stands at the curtain while Hickey continues his story.

Hickey's father was an evangelical minister in Indiana, but Hickey never fell for his "religious bunk" (3:693). His home, school, and "hick town" all felt like prison to him. He began smoking, drinking, and visiting local brothels. Nothing shook his resolve to rebel, and he hated everyone "except Evelyn." The daughter of well-to-do Methodist

parents, Evelyn was the one person in town who believed in Hickey's goodness. "I loved Evelyn. Even as a kid. And Evelyn loved me" (3:694). She refused to believe he was beyond reform, and she forgave him no matter how egregious the crime against her. "No, sir, you couldn't stop Evelyn. Nothing on earth could shake her faith in me. Even I couldn't. She was a sucker for a pipe dream" (3:694). The madam of the brothel believed in Hickey's ability to become a salesmen and lent him money to move away and start a career. Against Hickey's advice, Evelyn promised to stay loyal and wait for him to send for her. "Who the hell cares?" Harry says, "What's she to us? All we want is to pass out in peace, bejees!" Again, the chorus erupts from the crowd—"What's it to us? We want to pass out in peace!" (3:695).

Oblivious of the disruption, Hickey continues that his knowledge of other peoples' pipe dreams made him an instant success as a salesman, and he eventually sent for Evelyn. On the road, he would become homesick, and since he never drank on the job, he turned to women to satisfy his loneliness. Aware of his infidelities, Evelyn always forgave him. At one point, he even infected her with a sexually transmitted disease. She pretended to believe his story about contracting it from a cup on the train. "Christ, can you imagine what a guilty skunk she made me feel! If she'd only admitted once she didn't believe any more in her pipe dream that some day I'd behave!" (3:698). He reaches for her photograph but remembers he tore it up. Parritt announces that he tore up his picture of his mother as well because "her eyes followed me all the time. They seemed to be wishing I was dead!" (3:698).

Hickey's indiscretions grew more regular and despicable, but Evelyn's forgiveness never waned. "There's a limit to the guilt you can feel and the forgiveness and the pity you can take!" (3:699). He knew he would have to withstand another act of forgiveness once Harry's birthday party came around. "Who the hell cares?" Harry chants. "We want to pass out in peace!" Again the chorus repeats his call and bangs their glasses on the tables (3:700). "So I killed her," Hickey says, and Moran and Lieb move toward him. Parritt confesses that he turned in his mother because he hated her. Still ignoring him, Hickey goes on that he killed Evelyn to grant her peace. But he remembers starting to laugh while looking down at her corpse, then yelling, "'Well, you know what you can do with your pipe dream now, you damned bitch!'" (3:700). The force of this admission startles him, *"as if he couldn't believe what he just said"* (3:700). Parritt again chimes in, "Yes, that's it! Her and that damned old Movement pipe dream!" (3:701).

In a state of *"frantic denial,"* Hickey begs Harry to believe he had to have been insane. "Who the hell cares?" Harry blurts out, but then he realizes the potential of Hickey's admission. "Insane? You mean—you went really insane?" (3:701). The detectives believe Hickey is trying to establish an insanity defense, and they arrest him. "Do you suppose I give a damn about life now?" Hickey protests to Moran. "Why, you bonehead, I haven't got a single damned lying hope or pipe dream left!" (3:703). As they lead Hickey away, Harry jeers at them and shouts words of encouragement to his old friend.

Hickey's voice can be heard down the hall as the detectives usher him out. On Harry's cue, the men all raise their glasses, hoping the whiskey will now have "the old kick" (3:703). "May the chair bring him back to peace at last, the poor tortured bastard!" Larry shouts. Parritt resumes his comparison to Hickey: "You know what you can do with your freedom pipe dream, don't you, you damned old bitch!" (3:704). Larry drops his facade of dispassion and agrees that Parritt should end his life. Parritt thanks him and exits. Larry sullenly remains in his seat, solemnly listening for the inevitable.

Harry and the gang proceed to get very drunk. One by one, their pipe dreams resume: Rocky assures Harry that an automobile stopped him from taking his walk; Cora and Chuck reflect that they cannot get married until they have a farm first; Lewis and Wetjoen and McGloin and Mosher recommence their friendships. All the while Hugo calls fearfully to Larry, but ultimately he gives it up and joins in the resurrectional party.

Margie and Pearl enter. Rocky hails them warmly, tells them Hickey's story, and threatens to "knock de block off" anyone who calls them whores (3:709). Larry loses patience and rises from

his seat angrily. He stops at the sound of Parritt's body whirring past the window, *"followed by a muffled, crunching thud"* (3:710). Larry drops back into his seat and puts his head in his hands. "Life is too much for me! I'll be a weak fool looking with pity at the two sides of everything till the day I die. . . . May that day come soon! (*He pauses startledly, surprised at himself—then with a sardonic grin*) Be God, I'm the only real convert to death Hickey made here. From the bottom of my coward's heart I mean that now!" (3:710). Unlike the rest of them, his pipe dream has come true.

Harry's party resumes, and everyone drunkenly begins singing different songs at once. They all stop abruptly and break into fits of laughter, while Hugo loudly booms the French revolutionary song "Carmagnole." He then screams out his usual cant, "Capitalist svine! Stupid bourgeois monkeys!" They all holler together, "'Tis cool beneath thy willow trees!" (3:711), pounding their glasses and laughing wildly. In the midst of the bedlam, Larry sits staring vacantly in front of him as the curtain falls.

## COMMENTARY

In an interview following the 1946 premiere of *The Iceman Cometh*, Eugene O'Neill told the *New York Times* about his cast of barroom characters: "I knew 'em all. . . . I've known 'em all for years. . . . The past which I have chosen is one I knew. The man who owns this saloon, Harry Hope, and all the others—the Anarchists and Wobblies and French Syndicalists, the broken men, the tarts, the bartenders and even the saloon itself—are real. It's not just one place, perhaps, but it is several places that I lived in at one time or another . . . places I once knew put together in one" (quoted in Raleigh Introduction 1968, 25). O'Neill based the setting of *The Iceman Cometh*—Harry Hope's bar—on three gin mills he had frequented in Manhattan from 1907 to the late 1910s, before Prohibition (1920–33) effectively dried them up: JIMMY "THE PRIEST'S," located at 252 Fulton Street off the West Side waterfront; the taproom of the Garden Hotel on the northeast corner of Madison and 27th Street across from Madison Square Garden; and Tom Wallace's HELL HOLE, officially the Golden Swan, at Fourth Street and 6th Avenue in Greenwich Village. O'Neill's memories of these three bars and the men and women who inhabited them inspired *The Iceman Cometh,* one of the most thematically complex and forcefully authentic plays in AMERICAN THEATER history.

O'Neill first boarded at Jimmy "the Priest's" in 1911. He had just returned to New York City with 12 dollars in his pocket from BUENOS AIRES, ARGENTINA, on the steamship SS IKALA. He probably began drinking there four years earlier, in 1907, when he worked for the Chicago Supply Company office around the block (Alexander 2005, 7). Jimmy's was the setting of his short story "TOMORROW." The story's protagonist, James Anderson, is based on the alcoholic press agent and former Boer War correspondent JAMES FINDLATER BYTH, who appears in *The Iceman Cometh* as James "Jimmy Tomorrow" Cameron. O'Neill's play *EXORCISM* (which he destroyed) and the first acts of "*ANNA CHRISTIE*" and *CHRIS CHRISTOPHERSEN* also take place at Jimmy's. The waterfront flophouse offered shared rooms upstairs for three dollars a month, free soup for lodgers, and whiskey or a schooner of beer for a nickel (Raleigh Introduction 1968, 4–5). In January 1912, O'Neill attempted suicide with an overdose of Veronal in his room at Jimmy's. Byth, his roommate, was one of the friends who saved his life. O'Neill dramatized this traumatic event in *Exorcism* and in a more hidden autobiographical way with the guilt suicide of Don Parritt (see Sheaffer 499).

O'Neill drank often at the Garden Hotel taproom with his brother JAMES O'NEILL, JR. (Jamie), and he got drunk there to bolster his resolve before staging a liaison with a prostitute, which gave him grounds to divorce his first wife, KATHLEEN JENKINS (Alexander 2005, 8). O'Neill discovered the Hell Hole just after completing his drama seminar with GEORGE PIERCE BAKER in 1915. There he met numerous characters who influenced him in one way or another, including the Hell Hole's proprietor, Tom Wallace, the model for Harry Hope; the Irish philosophical anarchist TERRY CARLIN, immortalized in the character Larry Slade; and Joe Smith, the black gambler and small-time gangster who inspired O'Neill to write *The DREAMY KID* and who appears as Joe Mott. From the composite portrait of these three low venues sprang what O'Neill

called in his first note for the idea, "the Jimmy the P.—H. H.—Garden idea" (Floyd 1981, 260), which became *The Iceman Cometh.* In the same note, he jotted down, "and N.L. [New London]. family one"—*Long Day's Journey into Night.*

Describing the purview of the bar before Hickey's arrival, O'Neill wished to articulate, in his words, "the atmosphere of the place, the humour and friendship and human warmth and *deep inner contentment* at the bottom" (quoted in Eisen 156). For this reason, without the play's novelistic, lengthy introduction to the characters—"as if you'd read a play about each of them," he wrote in defense of the rambling quality of act 1—"you would find the impact of what follows a lot less profoundly disturbing" (quoted in Eisen 156, 157). In 1912, the year the play is set, O'Neill was an able seaman, would-be poet, and son of the great matinee idol JAMES O'NEILL; as such, he intimately related to his characters. Harry Hope's gang erect a fortress around themselves as protection from existential misery with alcohol, pipe dreams, and friendship, as O'Neill had done at Jimmy's in 1911–12 and later at the Hell Hole in the winter of 1915–16. Only at the bar, O'Neill emphasized in a letter to KENNETH MACGOWAN, could the men experience the *"deep inner contentment,"* or what Kurt Eisen calls a "befogged equivalent of happiness," the men display in act 1 and in the final scene after Hickey is taken away (Eisen 154, 156–157).

O'Neill's initial title for *The Iceman Cometh* was *Tomorrow,* the title of his 1916 short story (the only one published in his lifetime) and the seed for the late play. The next day, however, he came up with *The Iceman Cometh,* "which I love," he wrote George Jean Nathan, "because it characteristically expresses so much of the outer and the inner spirit of the play" (O'Neill 501). Although the joke of the title—Hickey's tearfully producing a picture of his wife and then revealing he left her in bed with the iceman—is not particularly funny (as Mary McCarthy is quick to point out; 52), the actual joke is quite good: A man yells upstairs to his wife, "Has the iceman come yet?" and his wife calls back, "No, but he's breathing hard" (quoted in Berlin 99). O'Neill may have been relying on the audience's awareness of this old joke and chose not to include it for the same reason he wrote the dialogue "in exact lingo of place and 1912, as I remember it—with only the filth expletives omitted" (O'Neill 502).

"The philosophy" of the play, O'Neill told the press before the 1946 premiere, "is that there is always one dream left, one final dream, no matter how low you have fallen, down there at the bottom of the bottle" (quoted in Alexander 2005, 56–57). *The Iceman Cometh* is also a nostalgia play that expresses the sense of longing O'Neill felt in his later years for the men he befriended in his 20s, and in their turn the men's nostalgia for the "good old days" which may or may not have existed in their former lives (see Raleigh "Historical Background" 1968, 55). As such, it is primarily a play about memory and the ability to reconstruct one's past in a positive light in order to bear the terror of an unknown future. Put another way, the work grapples with "the existential theme of being asked to face life when there is no meaningful life to be found" (Diggins 64). Certainly O'Neill's wistful remembrance of his early days slumming in New York is itself a "pipe dream," as by all accounts he was not a happy young man. Indeed, it is difficult to single out a period in his life when he was truly happy. That knowledge, O'Neill seems to be saying, requires a certain level of memory tampering, particularly in one's later years when death (the iceman) comes to claim you. Perhaps more than any other O'Neill play, given his age at the time of composition, *The Iceman Cometh* is a product, as Doris Alexander phrases it, of "O'Neill's own need to come to terms with death" (2005, 15).

O'Neill's theme of the pipe dream—what he also termed the "hopeless hope"—first appeared in his 1919 full-length play *The* STRAW (1:793). A highly autobiographical account of O'Neill's time at the GAYLORD FARM SANATORIUM, *The Straw* introduces the newspaper man Stephen Murray (O'Neill), who understands that the tuberculosis patients at the sanatorium all claim they are not "really sick," which he acknowledges is the "pipe dream that keeps us all going" (1:733). In the final act, Murray's nurse Miss Gilman defines the "hopeless hope" as "some promise of fulfillment,—somehow—somewhere—in the spirit of hope itself" (1:793–794).

Even stronger parallels exist between *The Iceman Cometh* and A TOUCH OF THE POET, in which O'Neill's protagonist, Con Melody, for better or worse, sheds his pipe dream of British nobility in favor of his "bogtrotter" Irishman persona. But O'Neill deepens this sentiment in *The Iceman Cometh*, asserting that as the future cannot be trusted and the present is a painful manifestation of the past, only a fictionalized past can grant peace and inspire a "hopeless hope" for the future. "It's all very true," Doris Alexander hypothesizes an audience's reaction, "that a group of drunken bums like those in Harry Hope's saloon must cherish their illusions or perish, but what has all this to do with me?" (1953, 366). O'Neill's torment over the horrors of World War II caused an increasing despair over the future of humanity in the playwright, a pessimistic view that might not hold up in better times. In a powerful way, then, as mentioned in the introduction, the timing of the production had a strong impact on its reception.

O'Neill told his eldest son, EUGENE O'NEILL, JR., that Hitler's blitzkrieg, particularly as it led to the fall of France (July 1940), sank him "deeper and deeper into a profound pessimistic lethargy" (O'Neill 509). He shelved his planned cycle, A TALE OF POSSESSORS SELF-DISPOSSESSED, because, as he wrote his daughter Oona O'Neill in July 1940, "the Cycle I have been writing will have little meaning for the sort of world we will probably be living in by the time I finish it" (O'Neill 508). A few days later, he wrote to his friend Lawrence Langner: "To tell the truth, like anyone else with any imagination, I have been absolutely sunk by this damned world debacle. The Cycle is on the shelf, and God knows if I can ever take it up again because I cannot foresee any future in this country or anywhere else to which it could spiritually belong" (O'Neill 510).

Certainly from his historical viewpoint, O'Neill had every right to imagine the rest of the world sharing his bleak vision of the future, but he underestimated the patriotic fervor that infused the citizenry of what, almost overnight, rose up as the world's greatest superpower. Perched on a stool at the stage bar at a rehearsal for *The Iceman Cometh*, the embittered playwright told the journalist and later O'Neill biographer Croswell Bowen,

Of course, America is due for a retribution. There ought to be a page in the history books of the United States of America of all the unprovoked, criminal, unjust crimes committed and sanctioned by our government since the beginning of our history and before that, too. There is hardly one thing that our government has done that isn't some treachery—against the Indians, against the people of the Northwest, against the small farmers. . . . This American Dream stuff gives me a pain. . . . Telling the world about our American Dream! I don't know what they mean. If it exists, as we tell the whole world, why don't we make it work in one small hamlet in the United States? If it's the constitution they mean, ugh, then it's a lot of words. If we taught history and told the truth, we'd teach school children that the United States has followed the same greedy rut as every other country. We would tell who's guilty. The list of the guilty ones responsible will include some of our great national heroes. Their portraits should be taken out and burned. . . . [And] the big business leaders in this country! Why do we produce such stupendous, colossal egomaniacs? They go on doing the most monstrous things, always using the excuse that if we don't the other person will. It's impossible to satirize them, if you wanted to (quoted in Bowen 83–84).

Larry Slade announces this central theme of historical delusion in *Iceman*'s opening scene: "To hell with the truth! As the history of the world proves, the truth has no bearing on anything. It's irrelevant and immaterial, as the lawyers say. The lie of a pipe dream is what gives life to the whole misbegotten mad lot of us, drunk or sober" (3:569–570). Along with "pipe dreams," the expression *misbegotten* is a vital one in the O'Neill canon, a term the playwright evocatively used in the title of his final play, A MOON FOR THE MISBEGOTTEN. Although *misbegotten* generally describes an illegitimate child (born out of wedlock), in O'Neill's imagination it might best be understood as someone who feels they should never have been born at all. This theme most resonantly enters *Iceman* when Larry Slade quotes Heinrich Heine's poem about morphine:

"Lo, sleep is good; better is death; in sooth, The best of all were never to be born." As O'Neill biographer Louis Sheaffer points out, these lines "were not lightly chosen by Slade's creator" (499), given O'Neill's mother, MARY ELLEN "ELLA" O'NEILL's, longtime morphine habit and O'Neill's guilt that the addiction directly resulted from his birth. O'Neill dramatized the psychic pain that ensued in his next play, *Long Day's Journey into Night.*

Audiences and critics alike commonly refer to the men at Harry's as "derelicts," "barflies," "deadbeats," "drunken bums," "lowlifes," "ne'er-do-wells," "little men," and so on. Of course, they are all of these insofar as their lives at Harry's saloon are concerned, but each in his own way (aside, perhaps, from the bartenders and prostitutes) actually led rather remarkable lives before their retreat to the lower depths: Larry Slade was an anarchist leader during the movement's heyday in the 1870s, '80s and '90s; Harry Hope was a locally respected Tammany Hall politician; Ed Mosher traveled with a circus; Cameron, Lewis, and Wetjoen all served in life-threatening capacities, if not always honorably, in the Boer War; Joe Mott was the proprietor of his own gambling club and a respected gangster among whites at a time of unbridled racial discrimination; Willie Oban, the youngest and most desperate alcoholic in a throng of serious alcoholics, graduated from Harvard Law School, and his father was one of the most powerful confidence-trick men in Manhattan; and so on. As critic BROOKS ATKINSON noted in his review of the 1956 production, "These are creatures that once were men—very pungent and picturesque creatures too, for O'Neill was a good deal of a romantic" (34).

Scholars vary on this point, but the play is generally read as a work of REALISM or NATURALISM, and the characters are little modified from O'Neill's experience with their true-to-life counterparts (see Alexander 1953). From an outsider's perspective, it might be understandable to think of the bar and its denizens as romantically portrayed. But the romantic spirit that inspired O'Neill to pursue a career in literature led him to explore the lives of many extraordinary, if tortured, individuals and go on to become an extraordinary, tortured individual himself. O'Neill symbolically infuses his characters with corrupt, ultraviolent, and criminal pasts that he believed formed the roux of modern society. But he adds the ironic twist that these men could never be considered legitimate members of the society that created them. Paradoxically, criminals and outcasts become more terrorized by everyday modern existence and the human condition than the "respectable" citizens who shape it.

Given all this, O'Neill biographer Stephen A. Black asks an extremely important question of the play and its creator: "Does O'Neill intend us to take seriously the idea that the bums with their pipe dreams have the right dope after all?" (427). The author of a psychological approach to O'Neill's life and work, Black's answer is remarkably astute and stands, to my mind, as the finest explanation of O'Neillian pipe dreams we have. Black reads the pipe dreams of the men at the saloon as an externalized display of what psychoanalysts call "intrapsychic defenses," a difficult-sounding concept but one that addresses the practical functionality of living in a world of pipe dreams more concretely than any other. Black refers to the need for every person to create internal "defenses to protect against thoughts and feelings that threaten their psychic equilibrium." "To imagine life without defenses," Black explains, "recall a terrifying nightmare. Imagine being awake while the nightmare went on; imagine being unable to tell whether the terrifying thing is real or 'only a dream,' as we say; imagine being unable to awaken from the dream and have it go away" (428). If we accept this need to shield ourselves mentally, "then those of us (in the audience) who say we are normal may not have any very great claim to superiority over the bums who are dependent on alcohol and yea-saying friends to get through life's waking hours." Here we find the heart of O'Neill's pessimism: Though "normal" people may escape alcoholism and be capable of taking on many of life's challenges in the outside world, O'Neill shows that it is only a matter of degree, and they "may nevertheless find themselves in exactly the same situation as Hope's people when face to face with what Larry calls the stench of death" (428).

Audiences should not accept Hickey's plea of insanity unless insanity means living a lifelong lie.

O'Neill contends that we all must, in our own ways, construct defensive pipe dreams to maintain sanity in the face of devastating psychological and social realities. After all his pronouncements about the importance of shattering illusions, Hickey emerges in the final scene as the most delusional character of all. But for one horrifying moment, he understands the intense hatred he felt toward his wife, Evelyn. Her incessant ability to forgive drove him to unbearable guilt, for which he could escape only through her death and ultimately his own. Unable to bear the truth, Hickey cowers behind the lie of insanity. The other characters (even Larry, at the end, who had always considered himself an exception) consciously acknowledge their pipe dreams as pipe dreams until the final scene, when they deliberately return to the comforts afforded by self-delusion.

By tearing down these "intrapsychic defenses," Hickey propels the men, however briefly, into a living nightmare from which they cannot awaken, sleep through, or drink themselves out of. Don Parritt is one of two exceptions. His boyish defenses—manifested first in his declaration that he betrayed his mother after studying American history, then that he simply wanted to pay for sex—were so weak, he never for a moment believed them himself. Larry, on the other hand, as Hickey's "only real convert to death" (3:710), is destined to live his life yearning for the end, formerly his innermost fear but now his only escape from the terror of living. Given the play's creator was a writer who dedicated his career to conquering truth in one way or the other, we can apprehend Parritt as an avatar of the younger O'Neill, who faced his demons—in the face of his mother's addiction and his father's absenteeism—and as a result attempted to end his life in a waterfront flophouse. Larry represents the other side of O'Neill, the one that "pretended to accept it all while sitting in dour, pessimistic judgment on himself and the world" (Black 424). In this configuration, Hickey might be the Jamie O'Neill whom O'Neill depicts in *Long Day's Journey into Night*—the teller of truths no one cares to hear.

Earlier in O'Neill's career, particularly in the SS *GLENCAIRN* cycle, O'Neill relied upon the SEA, the forecastle, and the stokehold as his "safe zone" rather than a bar (unless the bar, as in *The* LONG VOYAGE HOME, acts as a surrogate for the sea). When one recalls Robert "Yank" Smith's fate in *The* HAIRY APE after he abandons the protection of his ship, we can see Harry Hope's as a haven from such a fate. "The bar, like the ship, is a safe zone where the men are completely free," Zander Brietzke writes. "Free from worry, free from responsibility, free from family, free from friends, free from commitment, free from love, free from all pain, and thus free from all things that might make life worth living" (45). And like the firemen in Yank's stokehold, Harry Hope's bar resembles nothing less than the American melting pot—perhaps even, as one critic phrased it, a "microcosmic reflection of the great world" (Raleigh Introduction 1968, 8; see also Floyd 1985, 521). In it, O'Neill interweaves CLASS, race, GENDER, and ethnicity into the same tragic fabric of his thesis: that "truth" is too difficult to accept on its own terms and that one must devise a protective dream about oneself to carry on. In O'Neill's sea plays, the sea claims as victims those who oppose it, and the same is true of Harry's bar. Those who deny its protection—Hickey, Parritt, and eventually Larry—must face death head on without the solace of pipe dreams, alcohol, or friendship.

The Swedish playwright AUGUST STRINDBERG's work powerfully influences the gender conflicts in the play, as it does throughout the O'Neill canon. Strindberg's "woman destroyers" appear in the offstage characters of Evelyn Hickman, Rosa Parritt, Marjorie Cameron, and Bessie Hope, who, along with many other women characters in the O'Neill canon, "precipitated, either intentionally or culpably," the physical and spiritual death of their men. Such a view of women constitutes, according to Sheaffer, "additional evidence of a misogynistic strain in O'Neill" (Sheaffer 500; see also Berlin 103). O'Neill's offstage women in *The Iceman Cometh* have been read in two important ways: Virginia Floyd makes autobiographical connections, showing how the major offstage women characters "form a composite picture of O'Neill's mother," Mary Ellen "Ella" O'Neill. In this reading, Evelyn (whose name closely resembles "Ella") represents

the "long-suffering but forgiving wife"; Rosa is the "detached mother," as distracted from her maternal duties by the "Movement" as Ella was by morphine; Bessie is the "pious, nagging, intolerant shrew"; and James Cameron's Marjorie is "the attractive but unfaithful spouse" (Floyd 1985, 530).

Bette Mandl, in one of the finest essays on the topic, "Absence as Presence: The Second Sex in *The Iceman Cometh*," demonstrates the extent to which all the men's pipe dreams are somehow interrelated to women; thus, in the context of this O'Neill play, "as in so many others, the women tend to be merely representative of that which men struggle with and against in enacting their destinies" (185). Hickey "must face judgment," and Parritt must commit suicide as a result of their mixed hatred and love for the most important women in their lives; and the disgust Larry feels concerning Rosa's promiscuity appears to have been a significant factor—possibly *the* significant factor—for his abandonment of the "Movement." Rosa's ghost, Mandl argues, is exorcised from his conscience the moment his pipe dream falls away (190; see also Glover).

Scholars identify two key European plays that inform much of the thematic structure of *Iceman*: HENRIK IBSEN's *The Wild Duck* (1884) and Maxim Gorky's *The Lower Depths* (1902). In *The Wild Duck*, an outsider named Gregers Werle intrudes upon a seemingly harmonious family, the Ekdals. Werle, like Hickey, has a messianic compulsion to destroy the family's illusions. The play ends with the Ekdal daughter, Hedvig, committing suicide after discovering that the father might not be her own, which calls to mind Parritt's jump from the fire escape and his confusion over Larry's role as his own potential father. Had the illusions remained, Ibsen implies, the family may well have remained intact. As Werle's antagonist, Dr. Relling, tells him at one point, "to rob the average man of his life lie . . . is to rob him of his happiness" (quoted in Manheim 1; see also Floyd [1985] and Brustein). Gorky's *The Lower Depths* presents a comparable mise en scène (in four acts, like *The Iceman Cometh*): a low rooming house filled with alcoholic boarders. Another outsider, Luka, arrives to bolster their otherwise desperate lives by constructing illusions of grandeur around each. Upon Luka's departure, however, the illusions melt away, and reality once again sets in. Again, a disillusioned character commits suicide, though the play inverts O'Neill's schema (see Muchnic).

Additional sources can be found in GREEK TRAGEDY, with O'Neill's use of the chorus in act 4 (Tiusanen 28–31) and the unity of the play's time and place (Berlin 103; see also King). FRIEDRICH NIETZSCHE, O'Neill's "literary idol," informs much of Larry Slade's nihilistic philosophy, which also resembles O'Neill's only self-professed philosophy, PHILOSOPHICAL ANARCHISM. The 12 men at Harry's birthday party recall the Last Supper with Hickey's 12 disciples, Parritt as Judas, and the three prostitutes as the three Marys (see Day *passim* and Bogard 412n; Ibsen applies a similar motif in *The Wild Duck*). Strong parallels have been made between Harry Hope's bar and Plato's metaphor of the cave as well, in which prisoners chained to the inner wall of a cave see only shadows until they exit to face the blinding sunlight of reality; Plato's philosophers, however, achieve enlightenment when their eyes adjust, whereas O'Neill's characters confront a tragic, sometimes fatal, awareness (Raleigh Introduction 1968, 14).

Finally, though certainly not exhaustively, Brenda Murphy has identified two American plays written in the two years before O'Neill completed *The Iceman Cometh* with similar themes, settings, and characters: Philip Barry's *Here Come the Clowns* (1938) and William Saroyan's PULITZER PRIZE–winning *The Time of Your Life* (1939). Placed side by side with *The Iceman Cometh*, Murphy argues, the three plays form an "American saloon trilogy," as "all three plays present a group of characters in the grip of paralyzing idleness that faces a threat from an outside character who tries to enforce his will and values on the community" (215).

Paradoxically, what distinguishes *The Iceman Cometh* from these sources, important as they are for understanding the complexity of the work, is that element that the play's admirers find most ingenious about it and detractors its greatest flaw: O'Neill's unremitting repetition of dialogue. Some obvious examples are Hugo Kalmar's near-identical, often prolonged outbursts between periods of alcohol-induced slumber and the repeated use of the term *pipe dream* by nearly all the characters. Eric Bentley, the most prominent critic of this repetition, considered them a needless expressionistic device; indeed, when he directed the play in German, he cut a full hour's worth of dialogue (Bentley 42). Other critics contend that this repetition heightens the sense of O'Neill's profound compassion for his characters, and that furthermore the technique approximates a classical symphony with its traditional four movements (acts). Travis Bogard submits that the play "should be heard as music is heard with an understanding that it progresses in patterns of sound, as much as in patterns of narrative action" (409; see also Floyd 1985, 513). The play's most famous director, José Quintero, the architect of the Eugene O'Neill renaissance in the 1950s and 1960s, most likely succeeded where its first production failed through his understanding of O'Neill's dialogic rhythms. "It [the play] resembles a complex musical form," he wrote, "with themes repeating themselves with slight variation, as melodies do in a symphony." Quintero ironically found that directing the rambling play taught him "the meaning of precision in drama" (quoted in Berlin 103). Hickey's monologue in act 4, then, the longest O'Neill ever wrote, might be considered a kind of instrumental climax.

Critics acknowledge that O'Neill's second, far more significant allusion in the title is biblical, and thus his rationale behind adding the archaic form of "comes": "At midnight there was a great cry made, behold, the bridegroom cometh!" (Matthew 25:6). In the Bible, the bridegroom is Jesus Christ, who arrives to bring salvation and a symbolic "victory over death" (Raleigh "Historical Background" 1968, 81). Hickey, a messianic figure with promises of salvation, arrives only to bring death to the contented—the literal death of his wife, Evelyn, Parritt, and himself, and the figurative death of the men's pipe dreams and thus their will to live. "I'd get blind to the world now if it was the Iceman of Death himself treating!" Larry declares. "Well, be God, it fits, for death was the Iceman Hickey called to his home!" (3:666–667). Virginia Floyd connects O'Neill's sentiment to a line by the Finnish poet Uno Kailas, who wrote, "I have but two doors, but two: to dream and to death." The swinging saloon door, then, is a door to death for characters that exit into modern day realities and, inversely, the door to dream upon entry (Floyd 1985, 526).

By understanding the meaning of the title, we can also grasp the play's overall thematic structure. The bawdy joke transforms from the comedy of act 1 into the mounting terror in acts 2 and 3, and back again. The exceptions are the three victims of Death—Larry, Hickey, and Parritt. So should we see *The Iceman Cometh* as a comedy or tragedy? Perhaps we should rely on its author's definition of the work as "a big kind of comedy that doesn't stay funny very long" (quoted in Raleigh Introduction 1968, 11).

See also EAST ASIAN THOUGHT.

## CHARACTERS

**Cameron, James "Jimmy Tomorrow"**  Boarder at Harry Hope's saloon and former Boer War correspondent. O'Neill describes Jimmy as nearly identical to Hugo Kalmar in appearance and dress, but with a face *"like an old well-bred, gentle bloodhound's . . . his eyes are intelligent and there once was a competent ability about him. His speech is educated, with a ghost of a Scotch rhythm in it. His manners are those of a gentleman. There is a quality about him of a prim, Victorian old maid, and at the same time of a likable, affectionate boy who has never grown up"* (3:567). O'Neill based Jimmy's character on James Findlater Byth, his father, James O'Neill's former press agent and a close friend and roommate of O'Neill's at Jimmy "the Priest's" bar. O'Neill used Byth as the protagonist in his short story "Tomorrow," and he also appeared in *EXORCISM* (destroyed by O'Neill). Byth is one of the men at Jimmy "the Priest's" who saved O'Neill's life in 1912 when the latter took a potentially lethal dose of Veronal (dramatized in *Exorcism*). In 1913, Byth either jumped or fell to his death from the fire escape at Jimmy's; though O'Neill believed he committed suicide, news reports and logic (suicide from a third-story window?) indicate that he more probably fell (Alexander 2005, 22). Before his death, O'Neill said, Byth was "always my friend—at least always when he had several jolts of liquor—[and] saw a turn in the road tomorrow. He was going to get himself

together and get back to work. Well, he did get a job and got fired. Then he realized that this tomorrow never would come. He solved everything by jumping to his death from the bedroom at Jimmy's" (quoted in Raleigh Introduction 1968, 5).

In *Iceman*, Jimmy Tomorrow holds, to Larry Slade's mind, the dubious distinction of being the "leader of our Tomorrow Movement" (3:584). Jimmy once served as a war correspondent for "some English paper" (3:584) and dreams that someday he will sober up and return to his journalism career. Among the denizens at Harry's bar, he has always claimed that while he was working in South Africa, his wife, Marjorie, had an affair—his excuse for leading a dissipated lifestyle. Theodore "Hickey" Hickman convinces him to try getting a position as a journalist, but he returns with his tail between his legs and confesses, "I discovered early in life that living frightened me when I was sober" (3:692). Marjorie was unfaithful because Jimmy was a drunkard, not the other way around. Rather than drowning his heartbreak in a bottle, as he had always claimed he was "glad to be free—even grateful to her, I think, for giving me such a good tragic excuse to drink as much as I damned well pleased" (3:692). Doris Alexander suggests that this admission resembles that of Smitty to the Donkeyman in *The MOON OF THE CARIBBEES* (1953, 365).

**Cora**  Prostitute and Chuck Morello's perpetual fiancée. Cora is a *"thin peroxide blonde"* (3:604) with a *"round face . . . with traces of a doll-like prettiness"* (3:604–605). Chuck and Cora's pipe dream is that they will get married and move to either Long Island (her idea) or New Jersey (his). Cora tells an amusing anecdote about "rolling" a drunk from the "sticks." When Theodore "Hickey" Hickman arrives at Harry Hope's bar intending to end all pipe dreams, Cora and Chuck head off to New Jersey to get married. Cora drinks too many sherry "flips," her favorite cocktail, and Chuck leaves her in disgust to get drunk and fight. Once the police arrest Hickey for murdering his wife and the bar returns to normal, Cora laughs, in self-delusion, that they cannot get married until they have picked out a farm.

**Hickman, Theodore "Hickey"**   Traveling hardware salesman and regular at Harry Hope's bar. Hickey is around 50 years old, mostly bald, slightly under average height, with a boyish demeanor, and *"a stout, roly-poly figure"* (3:607). O'Neill characterizes him as having *"the salesman's mannerisms of speech, an easy flow of glib, persuasive convincingness"* (3:607). Hickey is the product of a strict Methodist upbringing in Indiana, where in his adolescence he rebelled by drinking and visiting the local brothels. Although he rapidly gained a reputation for badness, his future wife, a prim local girl named Evelyn, never stopped believing in his essential goodness. Hickey borrowed money from a local madam in order to escape the doldrums of small-town life and launch his career as a salesman. Once he had earned enough, he sent for Evelyn. They moved together, now married and very much in love, to Astoria, Queens. In spite of Hickey's compulsive philandering and periodic drinking binges—from which he would return home, in his words, "like something lying in the gutter that no alley cat would lower itself to drag in—something they threw out of the D.T. ward in Bellevue along with the garbage, something that ought to be dead and isn't!" (3:697)—Evelyn always forgave him and never relinquished her pipe dream that he could reform. Travis Bogard relates the Hickmans' relationship to that of Dion and Margaret Anthony in *The Great God Brown* insofar as, like Margaret, "Evelyn cannot see what is behind Hickey's face, even when he forces her brutally to look upon it" (417).

Each year Hickey arrives at Harry Hope's bar on a "periodical" to join its group of regulars and celebrate his old friend Harry's birthday. Over most of the first act, the men at the bar await Hickey's arrival with great anticipation; the group at Harry's bar universally adore him for his striking wit and generosity. He is known for a gag in which he produces a picture of his wife with tears in his eyes, then says he has left her in bed with the iceman. When Hickey arrives, he arouses a chorus of hail-fellow greetings all around, but then announces that he has both stopped drinking and renounced his pipe dreams. Ever since, he tells them, he has achieved true happiness and peace. "Just the old

dope of honesty is the best policy," Hickey describes his new credo. "Just stop lying about yourself and kidding yourself about tomorrows" (3:610). Hickey's proselytizing has a terrible effect on the alcoholics at the bar: As their pipe dreams begin to vanish, they sink into a miserable state of involuntary sobriety (those who have not stopped drinking find the whiskey no longer has its old kick), and infighting erupts among close friends.

In the final scene of act 2, Hickey informs the gang that Evelyn is dead. He shocks them further by admitting he feels "glad" she died, since only then could she find peace after years of loving "a no-good cheater and drunk" like him (3:650). Although the members at the bar revolt against him, he succeeds in convincing them to recant their life lies, and their moods increasingly darken. By the end of act 3, he begins to question his method of conversion, believing Harry in particular, who failed to take a walk around the block (his pipe dream), should feel happy and relieved. In act 4, in the longest monologue O'Neill ever wrote, Hickey recounts his life story and confesses that he murdered Evelyn. Earlier, Hickey had called the police to turn himself in, and two detectives—Moran and Lieb—enter the bar quietly during his confession.

Don Parritt, an outsider who before the action of the play betrayed his anarchist mother and thus sentenced her to a life in prison, interjects during the monologue with comparisons between his guilt over his betrayal and Hickey's murder of his wife. Hickey dismisses the similarity. "There was love in my heart, not hate" (3:691). But as his confession continues, it becomes increasingly clear that hatred was at the heart of the murder. "There's a limit to the guilt you can feel and the forgiveness and the pity you can take!" (3:699) he cries out, an admission that suggests his gag about the iceman was a wish-fulfillment fantasy that, if true, might have relieved him of his guilt. In his first real moment of clarity, the most chilling scene of the play, Hickey blurts out that he stood over Evelyn's body, laughed out loud, and shouted, "'Well, you know what you can do with your pipe dream now, you damned bitch!'" (3:700). As the detectives take him away, Hickey swears he must have been insane. His old friend Harry seizes upon this as a rationale for reversing everything that had transpired: Hickey was insane all along, and they can now resume their comfortable existence living in the dream world of tomorrows. With Hickey gone, no doubt to the electric chair, the whiskey begins to take effect, and the gang all sings together in paroxysms of friendship and drunkenness. Parritt has learned a great deal about himself through Hickey's speech, realizing he must commit suicide to relieve himself of guilt, and he heads off to the fire escape.

Hickey has several fictional predecessors in the O'Neill canon, including the "drummer" Adams from *Chris Christophersen* (Barlow 17; Bogard 410n) and, most evidently, Lazarus in LAZARUS LAUGHED. O'Neill biographer Louis Sheaffer points out that Lazarus, too, "sought to free his disciples of guilt and fear but succeeded only in plunging them into darker depths" (498). Unlike most of the characters in *The Iceman Cometh*, scholars find the model for Hickey in O'Neill's actual life difficult to place. On the one hand, O'Neill wrote Kenneth Macgowan, "What you wonder about Hickey: No, I never knew him. He's the most imaginary character in the play. Of course, I knew many salesmen in my time who were periodical drunks, but Hickey is not any of them" (quoted in Floyd 517). On the other, just after finishing his final draft, he wrote to George Jean Nathan that "there was a periodical drunk salesman, who was a damned amusing likable guy. And he did make that typical drummer [salesman] crack about the iceman, and wept maudlinly over his wife's photograph, and in other moods, boozily harped on the slogan that honesty is the best policy" (O'Neill 501).

Louis Sheaffer believes that Hickey is based on Charles E. Chapin, the city desk editor of the *New York Evening World*, who in 1918 "shot his wife in the head as she slept and insisted afterward that he had been motivated by love, by concern for her welfare" (494). Numerous scholars have made the correlation between Hickey's personality and O'Neill's older brother, Jamie's—the drinking, the garrulous banter, the womanizing, and so on (see Black 422)—along with other details they share, such as Jamie's attending religious school in Indiana and that his most successful acting experience was his starring role in *The Traveling Salesman*.

Sheaffer has offered an autobiographical approach as well. Although Hickey is the complete antithesis of his creator in both physical appearance and personality, "O'Neill, burning to voice through Hickey some of his darkest impulses, took pains to mislead anyone trying to follow his biographical facts in his writing" (502).

**Hope, Harry**   Proprietor of Harry Hope's saloon and rooming house and a former small-time Tammany politician. Harry runs a Raines Law hotel, which can legally offer alcohol to its customers during off hours in a back room as long as there are rooms for rent and food available. Harry's bar is a composite of three of Eugene O'Neill's actual haunts in New York City—Jimmy "the Priest's," the taproom of the Garden Hotel, and the Hell Hole. One of O'Neill's more intimate portraits, Harry is based on Tom Wallace, the proprietor of the Hell Hole (officially, the Golden Swan), a bar on Fourth Street and Sixth Avenue in Greenwich Village. O'Neill befriended scores of radicals and bohemians there in fall 1915 (including Terry Carlin, the model for Larry Slade), along with small-time gamblers, politicians, and a West Side gang called the Hudson Dusters. He continued drinking at the Hell Hole until Prohibition closed it down. Wallace knew the politician Richard Croker (whose portrait hangs above Harry's bar), a corrupt boss of Tammany Hall—the Democratic political machine that effectively ran New York politics from the 1870s to the early 1900s. O'Neill describes Harry as "*sixty, white-haired, so thin the description 'bag of bones' was made for him*" (3:568). With a face like "*an old family horse*," Harry explodes in anger when provoked. No one at the bar takes these outbursts seriously, and everyone adores him for his generosity and congeniality: "*Hope is one of those men whom everyone likes on sight, a softhearted slob, without malice, feeling superior to no one, a sinner among sinners, a born easy mark for every appeal*" (3:568).

Harry's late wife was a nagging termagant named Bessie Mosher (Ed Mosher's sister). Harry refers to her often with affection, but everyone at the bar knows Bessie's death liberated him from responsibility and allowed him to drink with his friends in peace. Bessie forced Harry to take political advantage of his position as a local bar owner, which he did while she was alive. But since her death 20 years earlier, Harry has never once stepped foot outside his bar. Nevertheless, he habitually voices his pipe dream to take a walk through the neighborhood. When his old friend Theodore "Hickey" Hickman arrives to celebrate his 60th birthday, Hickey wishes to convince Harry and his friends to destroy their illusions about themselves. Though Hickey's mission infuriates Harry, he eventually does, after great protestation, dress up and walk out of the bar. Only making it to the corner, and using reckless automobile drivers as an excuse for his failure, Harry is in fact terrified of life outside the bar. When Hickey confesses that he killed his wife, laughed over her dead body, and called her a "damned bitch" (3:700), he begs Harry to agree that he must have been insane to say such a thing (though in fact he killed her out of hatred for her guilt-inducing ability to forgive). As Hickey is led away by detectives, Harry seizes on this false admission as a means by which to revert the bar back to its former, comfortable state of oblivion. Harry's last name can thus be taken two ways: either the loss of hope or the retention of it, depending on one's reading of the character and the play as a whole.

**Kalmar, Hugo**  Boarder at Harry Hope's saloon, former editor of a radical journal, and has-been activist in the anarchist movement. The description of Hugo in the STAGE DIRECTIONS exactly matches that of O'Neill's Czech anarchist associate, Hippolyte Havel. Havel was an editor at the anarchist *Revolt* magazine when O'Neill worked there, and he was also the basis for the character Hartman in The PERSONAL EQUATION, as well as former lover of EMMA GOLDMAN. In *Iceman*, Hugo *"has a head much too big for his body, a high forehead, crinkly long black hair streaked with gray, a square face with a pug nose, a walrus mustache, black eyes which peer from behind thick-lensed spectacles"* (3:565–566). Like Havel, Hugo dresses impeccably, wears a black Windsor tie and a threadbare black suit, and bears the *"stamp of an alien radical, a strong resemblance to the type Anarchist as portrayed, bomb in hand, in newspaper cartoons"* (3:566). O'Neill biographer

Louis Sheaffer suggests that his name, Kalmar, is a reduction of "Karl Marx" (495). Hugo spent 10 years in prison for his anarchist activities abroad, and although the movement abandoned him years before, he still considers himself a major political figure.

Director and critic Eric Bentley wrote a famously disparaging essay on *The Iceman Cometh* (which he himself directed at one time), pointing to Hugo's character as too indicative of EXPRESSIONISM—too much a "literary concept"—for a realistic play like *The Iceman Cometh* (quoted in Alexander 1953, 362). In actual fact, as Doris Alexander points out in rebuttal, Hippolyte Havel's personality has been described in precisely the same way as O'Neill describes Hugo. One telling example is the radical socialite Mabel Dodge Luhan's description of Havel's response to a conversation between Goldman and "Big Bill" Haywood of the INDUSTRIAL WORKERS OF THE WORLD: "'They talk like goddam bourgeois,' suddenly cried Hippolyte Havel in a high, peevish voice, glaring around through the thick lenses of his spectacles. . . . 'My little sister!' he exclaimed to me later that evening, in his sweet whining voice. 'My little goddam bourgeois capitalist sister!' And tears ran over his spectacles" (quoted in Alexander 1953, 362). Hugo recurrently recites the lines, "The days grow hot—oh, Babylon! 'Tis cool beneath thy willow trees," which come from Ferdinand Freiligrath's poem "Revolution" about the exiled revolutionaries of the 1848 uprisings throughout central Europe (published in English in the March 1910 issue of Emma Goldman's radical journal *Mother Earth*). Doris Alexander provides several readings of O'Neill's intended use of the poem in *Eugene O'Neill's Last Plays* (2005, 33).

**Lewis, Cecil "The Captain"**  Boarder at Harry Hope's bar and former captain in the British infantry during the Boer War. O'Neill describes him *"as obviously English as Yorkshire pudding and just as obviously the former army officer"* (3:567). Close to 60, with white hair and a military mustache, Lewis is introduced passed out and shirtless, with a scar on his shoulder indicating a war wound. He and Piet Wetjoen, who was a commando leader for the Boers during the war, met while working in the Boer War spectacle at the 1904 St. Louis World's Fair. The former enemies have been, according to Larry Slade, "bosom pals ever since" (3:584). O'Neill probably met their counterparts through James Findlater Byth, the model for James "Jimmy Tomorrow" Cameron, who worked as a press agent for the Boer spectacle in New York.

Lewis's pipe dream is to be welcomed home to Great Britain as a war hero. But when Theodore "Hickey" Hickman arrives at the bar and challenges them to follow through with their pipe dreams, Wetjoen and Lewis fall out of friendship, and Wetjoen accuses him of having destroyed his reputation by gambling his regiment's money away. Lewis insists that a friend of his at the British Consulate will give him a position as a clerk for the Cunard shipping company, but Wetjoen cruelly responds that the men at the consulate who offered him a job did so on the spot to be rid of him and avoid a scandal. Lewis and Wetjoen reconcile after both realize that their pipe dreams will never come true. Lewis rejoices with the others when Harry agrees with Hickey that he must have been insane when Hickey murdered his wife—a false diagnosis that allows Joe and the rest to reinstate their pipe dreams and get drunk in peace.

**Lieb**  Plainclothes detective who, with his partner Moran, arrests Theodore "Hickey" Hickman for killing his wife. Lieb is 20-something, and he and his middle-aged partner *"look ordinary in every way, without anything distinctive to indicate what they do for a living"* (3:692). O'Neill biographer Louis Sheaffer notes that *lieb* is German for love, and his partner's name, Moran, calls to mind "morgue" or "mourning." Sheaffer suggests the two names symbolize O'Neill's twin themes of love and death and that O'Neill hints at Hickey's fate by having Moran do the talking for both detectives (495).

**Margie**  Prostitute at Harry Hope's bar. Margie's pimp is Harry Hope's night bartender, Rocky Pioggi. Just over 20 years old, with brown hair, hazel eyes, and too much makeup, Margie is *"a slum New Yorker of mixed blood"* (3:600). Margie's pipe dream is that she is a "tart," not a "whore." When

Theodore "Hickey" Hickman descends upon Harry Hope's to strip away their pipe dreams, Rocky calls her and her fellow prostitute Pearl "whores," and the two go "on strike" to Coney Island. When they return, Hickey has been arrested, the bar has returned to normal, and Rocky gallantly declares he'll "knock de block off anyone calls you whores!" (3:709).

**McGloin, Pat**  Boarder at Harry Hope's bar and former corrupt police lieutenant. In his 50s with dusty blond hair and sagging jowls, McGloin has the look of his former profession *"stamped all over him.... His face must once have been brutal and greedy, but time and whiskey have melted it down into a good-humored, parasite's characterlessness"* (3:567). McGloin was fired under corruption charges, and he dreams of clearing his name and rejoining the force. He and Ed Mosher are good friends, and he humors the former Harvard Law School graduate Willie Oban that Willie can some day defend him in court. Though he claims he "took the fall for the ones higher up," McGloin longs for the "fine pickings" he hears of the graft the police are collecting (3:596). When Theodore "Hickey" Hickman arrives to celebrate Harry Hope's birthday and challenge each man to confront his pipe dreams, McGloin and Mosher argue, as do all the other Hickey-agitated inmates at the bar. McGloin calls Mosher a "crooked grifter" (3:671), and Mosher calls him a "flannel-mouth, flat-foot Mick" (3:667). McGloin attempts to talk over his case with the police chief, but he returns in defeat. When detectives arrest Hickey for killing his wife, Harry Hope chalks up the disruption to Hickey's self-diagnosis of insanity. Once the detectives arrest Hickey, McGloin, along with the rest, resumes his friendship with Mosher and his pipe dream. In the final scene of the play, when all of the men sing separate nostalgic songs, McGloin sings "Tammany," which John Raleigh considers an appropriate choice by O'Neill, as the song is "an affectionate but lively satire on Tammany politics" ("Historical Background" 1968, 62).

**Moran**  Plainclothes detective who, with his partner Lieb, arrests Theodore "Hickey" Hickman for killing his wife. Moran is middle-aged, and he and his younger partner *"look ordinary in every way, without anything distinctive to indicate what they do for a living"* (3:692). O'Neill biographer Louis Sheaffer notes that the name Moran calls to mind "morgue" or "mourning," and his partner's name, Lieb, is German for love. Louis Sheaffer suggests the two names symbolize O'Neill's twin themes of love and death and that O'Neill hints at Hickey's fate when Moran "does all the talking" for both men (495).

**Morello, Chuck** Bartender at Harry Hope's bar and Cora's pimp and perpetual fiancé. Chuck arrives late in act 1 and is not a particularly well-rounded character compared to the others. He is a healthy, *"tough, thick-necked, barrel-chested Italian-American, with a fat, amiable, swarthy face"* (3:604). O'Neill introduces him wearing *"a straw hat with a vivid band, a loud suit, tie and shirt, and yellow shoes"* (3:604). Although he is Cora's pimp, the two share the pipe dream that they will buy a farm in New Jersey and get married. Chuck goes on drunken "periodicals" and often gets into brawls, while Cora is an alcoholic prostitute and thief. When Theodore "Hickey" Hickman descends upon the bar, they accept his challenge to get married and go off together. On the way to the ferry, however, Cora gets drunk on sherry "flips," and Chuck abandons her in disgust. He also gets drunk and winds up in a fight. Realizing that their betrothal is just a pipe dream, Chuck admits, "Yeah. Hickey got it right. A lousy pipe dream. . . . On'y it was fun, kinda, me and Cora kiddin' ourselves" (3:683). After Hickey is led off by the police for killing his wife and the bar returns to normal, Chuck and Cora resume their dream. Cora laughs, in self-delusion, at the thought of moving to New Jersey when they still needed find an appropriate farm.

**Mosher, Ed** Boarder at Harry Hope's bar, former ticket salesman in a traveling circus, and Harry Hope's brother-in-law. Nearing 60 and overweight, Mosher *"has a round kewpie's face—a kewpie who is an unshaven habitual drunkard"* (3:567–568). His clothing and accoutrements reflect his former career in the circus, with gaudy clothes, fake rings, and a gold chain without a watch. He has a touch of the confidence man about him, but he has always been *"too lazy to carry crookedness beyond petty swindling"* (3:568). Mosher is most likely based on Jack Croke, a regular at the Garden Hotel and the circus ticket man who gave O'Neill the idea for The EMPEROR JONES (Alexander 2005, 47). Mosher sucks up to Harry even more than the others, mainly out of habit as a social parasite, though he is really no more a freeloader than any of Harry's other boarders. His pipe dream is to return to the traveling life of the circus, though he has no real desire to leave Harry's.

Mosher is, ironically, a close friend of the corrupt ex-policeman, Pat McGloin. McGloin and Mosher have a falling-out when Theodore "Hickey" Hickman arrives at the bar to celebrate Harry's birthday and wipe away the men's pipe dreams, thus disrupting the natural rhythms of the bar's social order. But like the others, they reconcile once Hickey is taken away by the police for murdering his wife, and they rationalize Hickey's talk as having been that of a madman.

In the final scene of act 1, Mosher relates the story of an 80-year-old "snake oil salesman" pretending to be a doctor. Mosher's punch line is that the "doctor" died regretting that he could not fulfill his dream of spreading his "miraculous cure" so there "wouldn't be a single vacant cemetery lot left in this glorious country" (3:616). Judith Barlow suggests that Mosher's con-artist doctor is a "picture in miniature of Hickey," and she gives the anecdote more significance than it may appear to deserve, since O'Neill expanded his original story by 200 words, and like Hickey, the quack doctor is "peddling death" (30).

**Mott, Joe** Boarder at Harry Hope's bar and former proprietor of a Negro gambling house. The only black person among the denizens of the bar, Joe is around 50, *"brown-skinned, stocky,"* and wears clothes that once were sporty but are now falling apart. *"His face is only mildly Negroid in type"* (3:566). Joe is based on Joe Smith, a small-time gangster O'Neill met at the Hell Hole who told him the story that inspired *The Dreamy Kid*. O'Neill's second wife, AGNES BOULTON, describes Smith as "the boss of the Negro underworld near

[Greenwich] Village [whose] tales were startling" (quoted in Floyd 154). Joe performs odd jobs for Harry and the bartenders to pay for drinks and dreams of once again taking his place as the proprietor of a respectable all-black gambling establishment. Regardless of his race, Joe is an insider at the bar, though during the upheaval of Theodore "Hickey" Hickman's intervention, the men shout racist epithets at him. Joe offers perhaps the clearest articulation of Hickey's method of conversion: "Listen to me, you white boys! Don't you get it in your heads I's pretendin' to be what I ain't, or dat I ain't proud to be what I is, get me?" (3:625).

Harry's other regulars generally consider him "white"—a racist vernacular term from the period that connotes both personal integrity and racial superiority. Doris Alexander points to Joe's pipe dream as one of the first conceived by O'Neill. In his WORK DIARY notes for the summer of 1921, he considers a play titled either "White" or "Honest Honey Boy": "'Joe'—tragic-comedy of negro gambler (Joe Smith)—8 scenes—4 in N.Y. of his heyday—4 in present N.Y. of Prohibition times, his decline" (quoted in Alexander 2005, 46). Joe leaves Harry's in a fit of anger, vowing to raise the money to open a new establishment "if I has to borrow a gun and stick up some white man" (3:660). Joe returns to the bar defeated, but he rejoices when Harry agrees that Hickey must have been insane when he murdered his wife—a false diagnosis that allows Joe and the rest to reinstate their pipe dreams and get drunk in peace.

**Oban, Willie**  Boarder at Harry Hope's bar, a graduate of Harvard Law School, and son of Bill Oban, "King of the Bucket Shops." Willie is in his late 30s and despite his age is one of the worst alcoholics in the bar, possibly the worst. O'Neill describes him as generally filthy in appearance and dressed in clothes that *"belong to a scarecrow"*; his long, unkempt hair straggles over a *"haggard, dissipated face"* (3:568). Willie's father is based on Al Adams, a high-end racketeer whom O'Neill's father, James O'Neill, befriended in the taproom at the Ansonia Hotel at Broadway and 73rd Street in New York City. Adams served time in Sing Sing, a prison north of the city. The scandal humiliated his sons, who had no idea he made his money through bucket shops (illegal stock-trading establishments). Adams eventually committed suicide out of guilt and, possibly, fear of more prison time. As is the case with Willie, Adams's sons attended the best schools money could buy, but they were ostracized when the truth about their father became public (see Alexander 2005, 9–15). As Willie describes his stay at Harvard, "I was accepted socially with all the warm cordiality that Henry Wadsworth Longfellow would have shown a drunken Negress dancing the can can at high noon on Brattle Street." "Harvard," he continues, "was my father's idea," as Bill Oban wanted his son to gain the finest legal education he could and learn the loopholes (3:585). Rather than committing suicide, Willie's father died serving a life sentence.

Willie's dreams of returning to the legal profession by convincing the district attorney (DA) to acknowledge his superior legal mind and grant him a position (a particular absurdity since it was the DA who locked up his father in the first place). He offers to defend Pat McGloin and, thinking him on the lam, Don Parritt. When Theodore "Hickey" Hickman arrives at Harry's bar to persuade the men into giving up their pipe dreams, Willie pretends to head out for an interview with the DA but spends the day at the park. Upon his return, he accepts Harry's rationale that Hickey was insane and, like the rest at the bar, resumes his dissipated lifestyle in a shroud of illusion.

**Parritt, Don**  The son of Rosa Parritt, Larry Slade's former lover in the anarchist movement. He is a good-looking, sportily dressed 18-year-old with curly blond hair. O'Neill specifies in his stage directions that Parritt's *"personality is unpleasant. . . . There is a shifting defiance and ingratiation in his light-blue eyes and an irritating aggressiveness in his manner"* (3:576). Parritt has taken a room at Harry Hope's bar just prior to the action of the play and is considered an outsider among Harry's regulars; Rocky and others have nicknamed him "cheapskate" because he had previously revealed a wad of bills inadvertently but refused to buy the others drinks.

In act 1, Parritt pretends to be hiding from investigators. We find by act 2, however, that he received money from the authorities after turning in his mother, Rosa Parritt, and other conspirators of a West Coast anarchist bombing (one reason, conceivably, why O'Neill named him for an animal that "squawks"). Rosa was convicted and sentenced to life in prison; for a freedom-loving, promiscuous anarchist like Rosa, this was tantamount to a death sentence. Throughout the play's action, Parritt desperately seeks Larry Slade's help to assuage his guilt and understand why he betrayed his mother. Larry is the only father figure in his life, but whether Larry is actually Parritt's father, as Parritt suspects he might be, is ambiguous. Earlier drafts indicate that in O'Neill's mind, Parritt's father had died long before (Barlow 51).

Parritt's offstage betrayal of his mother and Theodore "Hickey" Hickman's murder of his wife, Evelyn, closely parallel one another. Throughout Hickey's confessional monologue in act 4, Parritt continually interrupts to draw parallels between the two situations, thus "parroting" Hickey's confession. Hickey rejects the comparison, lying to himself that "There was love in my heart, not hate" (3:691). This admission, we discover, is a part of Hickey's pipe dream—that he killed his wife out of love rather than hate. Ironically, the young Parritt understands himself better than Hickey, and he eventually accepts Larry's solution of jumping from the fire escape to put an end to his guilt.

Parritt's betrayal is based on the actual anarchist dynamiting of the *Los Angeles Times* building that killed 20 people on October 1, 1910. What happened next over the course of the investigation is complicated, but the case points to Parritt being modeled after Donald Meserve, the anarchist Gertie Vose's son, who was hired by the Burns detective agency to spy on his mother and other anarchists, including Emma Goldman and Terry Carlin (the model for Larry Slade and the one who importantly gave O'Neill the story; Sheaffer 386). Rosa Parritt, Don's mother, has thus been identified as Gertie Vose and/or Goldman (see Frazer *passim* and Alexander 2005, 34–36). In a biblical reading of the play, Parritt can be read as Judas Iscariot (see Day). He is also a subtle portrait of O'Neill himself, desperately attempting to come to grips with the conflicting feelings of hatred and love toward his mother, Mary Ellen "Ella" O'Neill. Finally, as biographer Stephen A. Black argues, Parritt might be an avatar of O'Neill's second son, SHANE RUDRAIGHE O'NEILL, whose immaturity and desperate need for his father's approval correlate to Parritt's psychic pain. Emotionally ill-equipped to address his son's needs, as his father, James O'Neill, was for him, the playwright "tried to understand his son in the best way he could, by seeking to capture his son's voice and his frailty in creating the doomed Don Parritt" (Black 435).

**Pearl**  Prostitute at Harry Hope's bar. Pearl's pimp is Harry Hope's night bartender, Rocky Pioggi. Just over 20, with black hair and eyes and caked-on makeup, Pearl looks *"obviously Italian"* (3:600). Pearl's pipe dream is that she is a "tart," not a "whore." When Theodore "Hickey" Hickman comes to Harry Hope's to strip away their pipe dreams, Rocky calls her and her fellow prostitute Margie "whores," and the two go "on strike" to Coney Island. When they return, Hickey has been arrested, the bar has returned to normal, and Rocky gallantly declares that he will "knock de block off anyone calls you whores!" (3:709).

**Pioggi, Rocky**  The night bartender at Harry Hope's bar and Pearl and Margie's pimp. O'Neill describes Rocky, based on Tom Wallace's bartender John Bull at the Hell Hole, as a *"Neopolitan-American in his late twenties, squat and muscular, with a flat, swarthy face and beady eyes. . . . A tough guy but sentimental, in his way, and good-natured"* (3:569). In the longest monologue of the play with the exception of Theodore "Hickey" Hickman's (O'Neill's longest ever), Rocky explains how he argued with his "stable"—Pearl and Margie—over the fact that he referred to them as "whores" instead of "tarts" (3:656), thus contradicting their pipe dream as Hickey would have it. In their turn, they call him a "pimp," as it is his pipe dream that he works as a legitimate bartender, and defiantly leave for Coney Island.

Intensely loyal to Harry Hope, Rocky serves as an ever-present sounding board for the rest of the gang. Like all good bartenders, he humors each of their pipe dreams, and they appreciate him for it.

Over the course of Hickey's attempts to wash away all pipe dreams, he turns viciously against everyone at the bar—even pulling a gun on the other bartender Chuck Morello—but steadfastly attempts to control himself and others for Harry's sake. At one point, he attempts to persuade Larry Slade and Don Parritt to become pimps. "The peace Hickey's brought you," Larry responds. "It isn't contented enough, if you have to make everyone else a pimp, too" (3:687). Once Hickey is taken off to jail and pronounced insane by Harry, Rocky dutifully and happily returns to his job and his pipe dream.

**Slade, Larry**   Boarder at Harry Hope's bar and a former activist in the anarchist movement. Larry is 60 years old with long straggling white hair and *"a gaunt Irish face with a big nose, high cheekbones, a lantern jaw with a week's stubble of beard, a mystic's meditative pale-blue eyes with a gleam of sharp sardonic humor in them"* (3:566). As Michael Manheim describes him, Larry's character is "our guide through O'Neill's personal emotional hell and also spokesman for the philosophical despair which seem to underlie this play" (1). Larry is a close portrait of Terry Carlin, an Irish-born alcoholic vagabond whom O'Neill befriended in 1915–16 at the Hell Hole in Greenwich Village. Carlin introduced the budding playwright and fellow Irishman to philosophical anarchism (O'Neill's self-professed philosophy) in the winter of 1915–16 and to the PROVINCETOWN PLAYERS in the summer of 1916. Larry can also be read as a window into that aspect of O'Neill himself that lived a lie of disaffectedness, that "tried with almost no success to harden himself against knowing the thoughts and feelings of everyone he saw" (Black 423).

Larry worked within the secretive networks of the anarchists for 30 years, during which time he conducted a relationship with Rosa Parritt, Don Parritt's mother. By the time of the play, 1912, Larry considers the movement "only a beautiful pipe dream," one that demands of its followers to "wear blinders like a horse and see only straight in front of you" (3:580). Larry's inclination to consider all sides of an issue (an ability that he considers an affliction) and his general disdain for the common man made him useless as a revolutionary.

Ten years before the action of the play, he abandoned the movement for good. Since his decision, he admits, "I've been a philosophical drunken bum, and proud of it" (3:581). Along with philosophical anarchism, Larry's nihilistic attitude and distrust of the "herd"—society in general—reflect much of the philosophy of one of O'Neill's greatest influences, Friedrich Nietzsche.

Larry boasts that he alone, among the men at the bar, muddles on without the comfort of a life-sustaining pipe dream. In fact, though most of the men have only one or two pipe dreams, Larry has four: his disavowal of the importance of the anarchist movement and its members, his uncaring attitude toward the fate of Rosa Parritt, the ideas that he longs for death, and the notion that he exists in the "grandstand" as an uncaring observer of the lives going on around him (Barlow 46). Larry voices admiration for people strong enough to live by their convictions, which he finds himself too weak-willed and fearful to do. He plainly cares about Rosa Parritt when he advises her son Don to commit suicide for his betrayal. He is terrified of dying, as we ascertain by the fear in his eyes whenever Hickey broaches the subject of his death. And he warmly appreciates the contributions of others at the bar, understands their needs, and angers easily when their peace is threatened. When Theodore "Hickey" Hickman arrives with the messianic goal of destroying the illusions of Harry's inmates, Larry Slade ("slayed") becomes Hickey's "only real convert to death" (3:710). In the end, like Lavinia Mannon in *MOURNING BECOMES ELECTRA*, Larry accepts that life without hope for the future becomes a living death (Bogard 417).

**Wetjoen, Piet "The General"**   Boarder at Harry Hope's bar and a former Boer (Dutch South African colonialist) leader during the Boer War in South Africa. O'Neill describes Wetjoen as *"in his fifties, a huge man with a bald head and a long grizzled beard. . . . A Dutch farmer type, his once great muscular strength has been debauched into flaccid tallow. But . . . there is still a suggestion of old authority lurking in him like a memory of the drowned"* (3:566–567). Wetjoen and Cecil Lewis, who was a captain in the British infantry during the war, met while working in the Boer War Spectacle at the 1904 St. Louis World's Fair and have been, according to Larry Slade, "bosom pals ever since" (3:584). O'Neill probably met their counterparts through James Findlater Byth, the model for James "Jimmy Tomorrow" Cameron, who worked as a press agent for the Boer Spectacle in New York.

Wetjoen's dream is to return to South Africa to a hero's welcome. After Theodore "Hickey" Hickman convinces the men to attempt to bring their dreams to fruition, Wetjoen falls out with Lewis, at which point Lewis exposes the fact that "a suspicion grew into a conviction" after a battle between the Boers and the British that Wetjoen had convinced the Boer leader Piet Cronje to surrender at Paardeberg (February 27, 1900) to save his own life. Wetjoen, for his part, accuses Lewis of having gambled away his regiment's money (3:663). Wetjoen claims he can procure a job as a longshoreman to pay his way home, but Rocky and Lewis say the boss who offered him a job at Harry's was drunk and pulling his leg. Wetjoen and Lewis reconcile after both fail to achieve their pipe dreams of going home. Wetjoen rejoices with the others when Harry agrees that Hickey must have been insane when he murdered his wife—a false diagnosis that allows Wetjoen and the rest to reinstate their pipe dreams and get drunk in peace.

## BIBLIOGRAPHY

Alexander, Doris. *Eugene O'Neill's Last Plays: Separating Art from Autobiography.* Athens: University of Georgia Press, 2005.

———. "Hugo of *The Iceman Cometh*: Realism and O'Neill." *American Quarterly* 5 (1953): 357–366.

Atkinson, Brooks. "O'Neill Tragedy Revived," *New York Times,* May 9, 1956. Reprinted in *Twentieth Century Interpretations of* The Iceman Cometh: *A Collection of Critical Essays,* edited by John H. Raleigh, 33–34. Englewood Cliffs, N.J.: Prentice-Hall, 1968.

Barlow, Judith. *Final Acts: The Creation of Three Late O'Neill Plays.* Athens: University of Georgia Press, 1985.

Bentley, Eric. "Trying to Like O'Neill." *Kenyon Review* 14 (1952): 476–492. Reprinted in *Twentieth Century Interpretations of* The Iceman Cometh: *A Col-*
lection of Critical Essays, edited by John H. Raleigh, 331–345. Englewood Cliffs, N.J.: Prentice-Hall, 1968.

Berlin, Normand. "Endings." In *Modern Critical Interpretations: Eugene O'Neill's* The Iceman Cometh, edited with an introduction by Harold Bloom, 95–106. New York: Chelsea House Publishers, 1987.

Black, Stephen A. *Eugene O'Neill: Beyond Mourning and Tragedy.* New Haven, Conn.: Yale University Press, 1999.

Bloom, Steven F. "Drinking and Drunkenness in *The Iceman Cometh*: A Response to Mary McCarthy." *Eugene O'Neill Newsletter* 9, no. 1 (1985): 3–12.

Bogard, Travis. *Contour in Time: The Plays of Eugene O'Neill.* Rev. ed. New York: Oxford University Press, 1988.

Bowen, Croswell. "The Black Irishman." In *O'Neill and His Plays: Four Decades of Criticism,* edited by Oscar Cargill, N. Bryllion Fagin, and William J. Fisher, 64–84. New York: New York University Press, 1961.

Brietzke, Zander. "*The Long Voyage Home*: A Vicious Cycle at Sea." *Eugene O'Neill Review* 28 (2006): 32–49.

Brustein, Robert. *The Theatre of Revolt.* Boston: Little, Brown, 1964.

Day, Cyrus. "The Iceman and the Bridegroom: Some Observations on the Death of O'Neill's Salesman." *Modern Drama* 1 (1958): 3–9. Reprinted in *Twentieth Century Interpretations of* The Iceman Cometh: *A Collection of Critical Essays,* edited by John H. Raleigh, 79–86. Englewood Cliffs, N.J.: Prentice-Hall, 1968.

Diggins, John P. "'The Secret of the Soul': Eugene O'Neill's *The Iceman Cometh*." *Raritan* 19, no. 1 (1999): 63–76.

Eisen, Kurt. *The Inner Strength of Opposites: O'Neill's Novelistic Drama and the Melodramatic Imagination.* Athens: University of Georgia Press, 1994.

Floyd, Virginia. *The Plays of Eugene O'Neill: A New Assessment.* New York: Ungar, 1985.

Floyd, Virginia, ed. *Eugene O'Neill at Work: Newly Released Ideas for His Plays.* New York: Ungar, 1981.

Frazer, Winifred L. *E.G. and E.G.O.: Emma Goldman and* The Iceman Cometh. University of Florida Humanities Monograph No. 43. Gainesville: University Presses of Florida, 1974.

Glover, Christopher S. "Female Characters in (and not in) Eugene O'Neill's *The Iceman Cometh*: Tracing Twentieth-Century Feminist Response into a New Era." *Eugene O'Neill Review* 25 (2001): 12–23.

King, William D. "Oresteian Structures in *The Iceman Cometh*." *Eugene O'Neill Review* 27 (2005): 126–134.

Mandl, Bette. "Absence as Presence: The Second Sex in *The Iceman Cometh*." *Eugene O'Neill Newsletter* 6, no. 2 (1982): 10–15. Reprinted in *The Critical Response to Eugene O'Neill*, edited by John H. Houchin, 184–190. Westport, Conn.: The Greenwood Press, 1993.

Manheim, Michael. "The Transcendence of Melodrama in O'Neill's *The Iceman Cometh*." In *Critical Essays on Eugene O'Neill*, edited by James J. Martine, 145–158. Boston: G. K. Hall & Co., 1984.

McCarthy, Mary. "Eugene O'Neill—Dry Ice." *Partisan Review* 13 (1946): 577–579. Reprinted in *Twentieth Century Interpretations of* The Iceman Cometh: *A Collection of Critical Essays*, edited by John H. Raleigh, 50–53. Englewood Cliffs, N.J.: Prentice-Hall, 1968.

Muchnic, Helen. "The Irrelevancy of Belief: *The Iceman Cometh* and *The Lower Depths*." In *O'Neill and His Plays: Four Decades of Criticism*, edited by Oscar Cargill, N. Bryllion Fagin, and William J. Fisher, 431–442. New York: New York University Press, 1961.

Murphy, Brenda. "*The Iceman Cometh* in Context: An American Saloon Trilogy." *Eugene O'Neill Review* 26 (2004): 214–225.

Nathan, George Jean. "Eugene O'Neill (1888–1953)." In *A George Jean Nathan Reader*, edited by A. L. Lazarus. Madison, N.J.: Fairleigh Dickinson University Press, 1990: 133–144.

O'Neill, Eugene. *Selected Letters of Eugene O'Neill*. Edited by Travis Bogard and Jackson R. Bryer. New York: Limelight Editions, 1994.

Raleigh, John H. "The Historical Background of *The Iceman Cometh*." In *Twentieth Century Interpretations of* The Iceman Cometh: *A Collection of Critical Essays*, edited by John H. Raleigh. Englewood Cliffs, N.J.: Prentice-Hall, 1968, 54–62.

———. Introduction to *Twentieth Century Interpretations of* The Iceman Cometh: *A Collection of Critical Essays*, edited by John H. Raleigh. Englewood Cliffs, N.J.: Prentice-Hall, 1968, 1–18.

Raleigh, John, ed. *Twentieth Century Interpretations of* The Iceman Cometh: *A Collection of Critical Essays*. Englewood Cliffs, N.J.: Prentice-Hall, 1968.

Sheaffer, Louis. *O'Neill: Son and Artist*. Boston: Little, Brown, 1973.

Tiusanen, Timo. "Composition for Solos and a Chorus: *The Iceman Cometh*." In *Modern Critical Interpretations: Eugene O'Neill's* The Iceman Cometh, edited with an introduction by Harold Bloom, 23–34. New York: Chelsea House Publishers, 1987.

# *Ile: A Play in One Act* (completed, 1917; first produced, 1917)

*Ile* is arguably second only to HUGHIE among Eugene O'Neill's one-act plays in terms of the sheer force of its thematic and psychological depth. Written in spring–summer 1917, just prior to writing the last three plays that make up his SS GLENCAIRN series—The LONG VOYAGE HOME, The MOON OF THE CARIBBEES, and IN THE ZONE—Ile was produced by the PROVINCETOWN PLAYERS at the Playwrights' Theatre in New York City on November 30, 1917, and accepted for publication in the prestigious journal *The Smart Set* in May 1918.

Keeney, the principal's last name, is derived from an actual New London whaling family, but O'Neill got the idea for the play from the 1903 polar whaling expedition of Captain John A. Cook and his wife, Viola Fish Cook. Viola, whom her husband boasted was the first white woman to "have wintered so far north and east on the Pacific side of the United States," was diagnosed with severe depression after spending 44 months (a full 24 months longer than planned) in the Arctic Sea on her husband's steam whaler *Bowhead* (Richter 112, 110). As in the play, some of the *Bowhead*'s crew mutinied because their contract only stipulated a 36-month cruise (already an extension of the standard length); but unlike the genteel novice Mrs. Annie Keeney, who loses her mind completely, it was Viola Cook's fifth voy-

Captain David Keeney and Annie Keeney in the Flock Theatre's puppet production of *Ile* *(Courtesy of the Flock Theater, New London, Connecticut)*

age with her husband, and she eventually made a full recovery. Additionally, *Ile* takes place in 1895, the same year Joshua Slocum began the first solo sailing voyage around the globe (1895–98). The play is also notable for being O'Neill's first in-depth treatment of his parents, JAMES O'NEILL and MARY ELLEN "ELLA" O'NEILL, and their complicated marital relationship—the last being his masterpiece, LONG DAY'S JOURNEY INTO NIGHT.

## SYNOPSIS

Two bells, or one o'clock in the afternoon, in the captain's cabin aboard the steam whaler *Atlantic Queen*. It is June 1895, and the ship, on a whaling expedition in the Bering Sea, has been held fast by ice for almost a year. One door, in the rear left, leads to the captain's sleeping quarters; another, farther forward, leads to the companion way. Right of the first door is a brand new organ, and a sewing basket sits on the marble-topped sideboard to the

rear right; both items signify the unlikely presence of a woman. A skylight in the center of the ceiling looks out onto the poop deck and produces *"sickly and faint"* light that indicates *"one of those gray days of calm when ocean and sky are alike dead"* (1:491). The sound of a watchman's steady footsteps are heard on the poop deck above. The steward enters and begins clearing dinner plates from the table. He looks *"sullen and angry"* as he grudgingly stacks the remaining dishes. Ben, *"an over-grown, gawky boy with a long, pinched face,"* enters the cabin and heads straight for the stove at the center of the room. He is shivering uncontrollably, and the pain of his frozen hands makes him *"on the verge of cying"* (1:491).

Ben reports that the "Old Man," or Captain David Keeney, has done nothing that day but pace the deck and stare at the polar ice floe encasing the ship. The steward curses both the captain and the ice: "Holdin' us in for nigh on a year—nothin' to see but ice—stuck in it like a fly in molasses!" (1:492). Ben shushes him, fearing the captain might overhear. The steward complains that the men's two-year contract is up that day, the crew is near starvation, the food has gone rotten, and the mission—to hunt whales for oil—has been relatively fruitless. But the stubborn captain will not make the order to turn back. Ben says in a hushed voice that the men in the forecastle (pronounced fo'c'sle) are prepared to mutiny. Mulling over the possibility that the captain has gone mad, the two agree that his wife, Mrs. Annie Keeney, whom the steward considers "as sweet a woman as ever was" (1:493), has made a drastic temperamental turn for the worse. They decide that the length of the voyage and the long icebound months have understandably affected her. Generally an amiable soul, Mrs. Keeney will now only talk to her husband and spends her days sewing and weeping quietly to herself. They can hear her sobs from the sleeping quarters even now.

Hearing Captain Keeney's approaching footsteps, the steward swiftly loses his bravado and, petrified, rushes to stack the rest of the dishes. But he does so too hastily, and one drops to the floor. The captain enters, accompanied by Slocum, his second mate, and harshly threatens the steward. "The next dish you break, Mr. Steward, you take a bath in the Bering Sea at the end of a rope" (1:494). The men squirm under his intimidating glare. On his order, they dash out of the cabin. Keeney wants to discuss the possibility of a mutiny with Slocum, who agrees the men are turning "ugly" (1:495). The ice has loosened to the south, so the ship can turn back, but Keeney refuses to do so.

Mrs. Keeney enters from the sleeping quarters. She has evidently been crying and, held back by *"some nameless dread,"* stands frozen at the threshold, looking about the room *"clasping and unclasping her hands nervously"* (1:495). She tells her husband that she would like a walk about the deck. Keeney suggests she play her organ instead, concealing from his wife the knowledge that the crew has turned mutinous. She peers out the porthole and, jubilant over the open water to the south, anxiously repeats her need to take in fresh air. "Best not to-day, Annie," Keeney sternly intones (1:496).

Once Mrs. Keeney retires to the bedroom, Keeney takes a revolver out of his pocket and confirms that Slocum is armed as well. Slocum asks if he plans to turn back, given the ice has broken up to the south, the food is running low, and the men's contracts are up; at this point, he advises, it would be within the men's legal rights to mutiny. Keeney defies them to take him to court, insisting that money is not what matters most. The most accomplished whaler in Homeport (Provincetown), Keeney would die before returning with only 400 barrels of oil (1:497). There is no convincing him otherwise.

The ship's harpooner, Joe, an imposing man in his own right, enters the cabin and self-consciously informs them that the men would like a word with the captain. The moment of mutiny has arrived, and Slocum asks if Keeney wants him to wake up the other officers. Keeney is confident they can handle them alone. Five crew members shuffle in and, with Joe as their spokesman, demand they return to Homeport. Mrs. Keeney appears at the doorway unnoticed. When the captain rejects their demands, Joe announces a mutiny and unwisely turns his back. Keeney lands a blow that knocks Joe to the floor. Mrs. Keeney screams as the men draw their knives and rush Keeney and Slocum. The officers lift their revolvers and stop the men in their tracks. Keeney orders them to take up Joe and get back to work, threatening to kill the first man that shirks his job (1:499). The men shamefacedly depart, and Mrs. Keeney becomes unwound: "All the horrible brutality, and these brutes of men, and this terrible ship, and this prison cell of a room, and the ice all around, and the silence" (1:500). Keeney reminds her that he had discouraged her from joining him on the voyage. It was her dream, she responds, to sail with her famous husband "in the danger and vigorous life of it all." At Homeport, she was lonely and overwhelmed with boredom, but she never realized how brutal life on the SEA could be.

"I warned you what it'd be, Annie," Keeney says, "'Whalin' ain't no ladies' tea party" (1:500). She begs him to turn southward, but he contritely explains that since the start of his career, he had always returned with a full load of oil, and not to do so, even once, would betray his sense of self and honor. She asks how long the return passage might be, and he replies two months; if they left now, she muses, they might return home in time for their wedding anniversary in late August. She compels him to admit his love for her, which he does, then dejectedly promises to turn back for her sake. At precisely that moment, the mate rushes into the cabin and announces that the ice has broken up to the north. Keeney, unmindful of the promise he has just made his wife, orders the mate to drive north through the broken ice to the clear water beyond. As for the men, Slocum assures him, "They'll turn to willin' enough. You put the fear o' God into 'em, sir. They're meek as lambs" (1:504).

Mrs. Keeney implores him to keep his promise. "Woman," he rebukes sternly, "you ain't adoin' right when you meddle in men's business and weaken 'em" (1:505). She thereupon *commences to laugh hysterically* and wildly starts playing a hymn on the organ. Keeney takes her by the shoulders, at first angrily, then with concern. Seeing she is having a nervous breakdown, he asks if she recognizes him, but she only *stares up at him with a stupid expression, a vague smile on her lips* (1:505). A sailor's cry indicates whales have been spotted. The mate pokes his head into the skylight and excitedly announces that indeed a school of spouting whales are in sight. Keeney makes sure the boats have been lowered and tells him he will be right along. He turns his attention back to his wife and pleads with her to understand—"I've got to git the ile" (1:506). Slocum beckons him once more, and with a final tortured glance at his deranged wife, Keeney strides out of the cabin. Mrs. Keeney is beyond noticing her husband's departure. Her whole being is focused on the organ, playing the hymn increasingly louder, faster, and more erratically as the curtain falls.

## COMMENTARY

A stunning work of psychological REALISM, *Ile* reveals Eugene O'Neill's ambivalence about the masculine American strive toward professional greatness. Captain David Keeney's desperate claim to perfection as a whaler demands great sacrifice from all who are tied to him, professionally and emotionally. As Keeney persistently claims, his quest is not about money, though money is its end result, but rather about the pride of being the best

at what he does. By marrying an overachiever, Mrs. Annie Keeney must necessarily live a life of loneliness and ennui or allow him to lead the way to her own madness. As such, *Ile* is as much a domestic play as *Long Day's Journey into Night*, which treats the same theme more closely. Annie Keeney can be seen as an avatar of O'Neill's mother, Mary Ellen "Ella" O'Neill, and thus a precursor to Mary Tyrone in *Long Day's Journey* (see Floyd 118–120). Both Annie and Mary remove themselves from reality—with madness and morphine, respectively—as a result of their husbands' neglect. And David Keeney clearly has much in common with James O'Neill, O'Neill's enormously successful father, and therefore his father's fictional manifestation in the character James Tyrone.

*Ile* contrasts in interesting ways to O'Neill's friends Hutchins Hapgood and Neith Boyce's play *Enemies* (1915). Whereas *Enemies*, one of the first plays the Provincetown Players ever performed, is a one-act negotiation between husband and wife— "He," who wants freedom from the conventional bonds of marriage, and "She," who wishes to form a meaningful intellectual partnership with her husband—*Ile* might be read as a warning for the opposite GENDER to stay away from O'Neill altogether. There can be no doubt that when his Provincetown friend Mary Heaton Vorse related the tale of Captain John A. Cook and his wife Viola, in which Viola suffered from depression during a 44-month whaling expedition, O'Neill saw the incident as analogous to his parents' turbulent relationship. Ella O'Neill paid an immense emotional price for James's triumphs on the stage (although to what degree remains under dispute). Nevertheless, O'Neill's own journey to theatrical greatness, one just on the rise at the period of this play's composition, demanded on his part a great deal of emotional detachment from his friends and female companions as well. O'Neill may have harbored a lifetime's supply of resentment over his father's neglect, but in the end, James O'Neill served more as a role model for the ambitious playwright than as a cautionary figure.

## CHARACTERS

**Ben**   The cabin boy on the whaling steamship *Atlantic Queen*. O'Neill describes Ben as *"an over-grown,* gawky boy with a long, pinched face" (1:491). When he enters the captain's cabin in the first scene, his chattering teeth demonstrate the cold outside, and he warms his hands at the stove. Ben notifies the steward that the men are prepared to mutiny against Captain Keeney. He also discusses Mrs. Keeney's mental condition with the steward.

**Joe** The harpooner of the whaling steamship *Atlantic Queen*. Joe demonstrates just how intimidating a man Captain David Keeney can be, as Joe is "*an enormous six-footer with a battered, ugly face*" (1:498) who fears the captain all the same. When he leads the men to mutiny, Keeney knocks him out with one blow to the head.

**Keeney, Captain David** The captain of the whaling steamship *Atlantic Queen*. Keeney's hair is long and black, his face "*massive*," and his eyes reveal a "*bleak hardness*" (1:494). Forty years old and an archetypal New England Yankee, Keeney runs his ship with even measures of violent intimidation and steadfast competence. Keeney, who speaks with a strong New England accent, is an Ahab-like figure, and like Captain Ahab, from Herman Melville's novel of obsession, *Moby-Dick* (1851), he is a fixated leader who refuses to return home without accomplishing his mission—for Ahab, to kill the white whale; for Keeney, to return home with a full cargo of whale oil. Back at Homeport, Keeney had discouraged his wife from joining him on the voyage. She insisted, however, as she was tired of the ennui of small town existence. By the day of the play's action, the ship had been icebound for nearly a year. Keeney still refuses to turn homeward, a decision that rouses his crew to mutiny and causes his wife to lose her sanity. Keeney easily quells the mutiny attempt, but by the curtain, his wife has gone mad.

Keeney has often been compared to O'Neill's father, James O'Neill, who was equally obsessed with his "monomaniacal quest for theatrical whale oil" (Black 198). As a New England Yankee and professionally obsessed male, Keeney resembles the characters Captain Isaiah Bartlett of WHERE THE CROSS IS MADE and GOLD, Ephraim Cabot from

DESIRE UNDER THE ELMS, and Brigadier-General Ezra Mannon from MOURNING BECOMES ELECTRA.

**Keeney, Mrs. Annie** Captain Keeney's wife. Annie Keeney is "*a slight, sweet-faced little woman primly dressed in black*" (1:495). Like the later character Anna Christophersen in CHRIS CHRISTOPHERSEN, she longs to join her lover on his voyages for the sense of adventure and independence deep-sea travel affords. As Keeney is captain, she may do so, but Keeney tries to discourage her. At one point, she admits that perhaps things would have been different if they had had a child together. Her adventuresome, if misguided, will prevailed: Keeney fitted the captain's cabin with accoutrements that might keep her comfortable on the journey, including a brand-new organ. After two years, however, she considers the ship a prison and is revolted by the sailors' brutality. She explains that at Homeport, she "used to go down to the beach, especially when it was windy and the breakers were rolling in, and I'd dream of the fine free life" her husband led (1:502). But her romantic expectations of life at sea slowly dropped away, and once the ship became caught in an ice floe on the Bering Sea, she became mentally unbalanced. After two years at sea, one of them trapped in the ice floe, Mrs. Keeney pleads with her husband to turn back. At first he agrees out of love for her, but when the ice breaks to the north and a school of whales is spotted, he ignores his promise. His professional integrity ultimately destroys her. At the curtain, Mrs. Keeney is unresponsive, no longer recognizes her husband, and erratically pounds on her organ. Annie Keeney is a notable precursor to Mary Tyrone in *Long Day's Journey into Night*.

**Slocum** The second mate on the whaling steamship *Atlantic Queen*. If Captain David Keeney is an Ahab-like figure from Herman Melville's *Moby-Dick*, Slocum is the mate Starbuck, the respectful voice of reason. "*A rangy six-footer with a lean weather-beaten face*" (1:494), Slocum believes Keeney is wrong not to change course and advises him that the men are within their legal rights to mutiny; but when the captain refuses, Slocum remains loyal to him. When the men do mutiny, he pulls his revolver and stands by his captain. In the final scene, Slocum delivers the news that the ice has broken to the north and a school of whales has been spotted. This news elates the captain, but drives Mrs. Annie Keeney, who was pleading with her husband to turn back, irretrievably insane.

**Steward**  The steward on the whaling steamship *Atlantic Queen*. The first character to make an appearance, the steward, along with the cabin boy Ben, expounds the *Atlantic Queen*'s dire situation: The ship has been icebound for nearly a year; the men's two-year contracts are up that day; the food has gone rotten; the captain's wife, Mrs. Annie Keeney, is becoming mentally unbalanced; and the captain stubbornly refuses to return to Homeport. The steward, *"an old, grizzled man dressed in dungaree pants, a sweater, and a woolen cap with ear flaps"* (1:491) talks tough before Captain David Keeney arrives, but when Keeney makes his appearance, his anxiety is extreme, and he breaks a dinner plate while frantically clearing the captain's table. The steward thus demonstrates from the outset the fear the captain inspires among his men.

### BIBLIOGRAPHY

Black, Stephen A. *Eugene O'Neill: Beyond Mourning and Tragedy.* New Haven, Conn.: Yale University Press, 1999.

Floyd, Virginia. *The Plays of Eugene O'Neill: A New Assessment.* New York: Ungar, 1985.

Richter, Robert A. *Eugene O'Neill and Dat Ole Davil Sea: Maritime Influences in the Life and Works of Eugene O'Neill.* Mystic, Conn.: Mystic Seaport, 2004.

# *In the Zone: A Play in One Act* (completed, 1917; first produced, 1917)

"When *everybody* likes something," O'Neill cautioned *New Yorker* profiler Hamilton Basso in 1948, "watch out!" (quoted in Sheaffer 383). It seems that *everybody* liked O'Neill's World War I situation drama *In the Zone*, the last completed installment of his SS GLENCAIRN series—everybody, that

is, except its creator (see commentary). Deemed too mainstream for the PROVINCETOWN PLAYERS, the one-act play was accepted by the WASHINGTON SQUARE PLAYERS, whose uptown premiere on October 31, 1917, at the Comedy Theatre in New York City was a smashing critical success. (Two days later, November 2, the Provincetown Players premiered another *Glencairn* play, *The LONG VOYAGE HOME.*) With it, according to fellow Provincetowner Edna Kenton, O'Neill "sprang into the Broadway limelight" (76). He collected royalties for the first time in his career and was offered a vaudeville tour, a deal he initially rejected on the grounds of artistic integrity. But the penurious young playwright could hardly refuse once the contract included a $200 advance and $70 royalties a week, which he split evenly with the WASHINGTON SQUARE PLAYERS. The vaudeville tour lasted a healthy 34 weeks but was brought to a precipitous end by American involvement in World War I and the 1918 flu epidemic. In addition, the avant-garde magazine *Seven Arts*, which had accepted O'Neill's short story "TOMORROW" the previous fall, gave him $50 to publish the play. Though *Seven Arts* went under before the piece could appear in print, O'Neill was paid money enough for the season's rent at the local grocer John Francis's flats in Provincetown, Massachusetts, and to keep him and his drinking buddies TERRY CARLIN and Art McGinley in their cups for a while (Black 201).

### SYNOPSIS

The seamen's forecastle at night on the British tramp steamer SS *Glencairn* at 10 minutes to 12 in fall 1915. On its transatlantic voyage from the United States to Great Britain, the *Glencairn*'s mission is to supply the allies with ammunition during World War I. All portholes above the bunks have been covered with black cloth, and a dim light emanates softly from a lantern at center. Five sailors—Scotty, Ivan, Swanson, Smitty, and Paul—lie still in their bunks, evidently sleeping. Smitty, an English able seaman, rises cautiously. Careful not to wake any of his shipmates, he removes a suitcase from beneath the lower bunk. Davis appears at the doorway carrying a large pot of hot coffee and pauses when he sees Smitty's movements. Scotty is awakened by the sound of Smitty's keys opening the suitcase. Smitty, unaware he is being watched by Davis and Scotty, removes a mysterious-looking black iron box, tucks it under his mattress, replaces the suitcase, and returns to bed. Davis walks in and wakes the crewmen for their watch. Smitty pretends to have awoken from a deep sleep; his theatrics are not lost on Davis and Scotty (1:471).

Davis informs them the ship has entered the war zone, making each sailor (with the notable exception of Smitty, who does not appear to be listening) fearful of German submarines. Mines also worry them, but Scotty suggestively invokes German spies as a threat as well. Jack enters to announce eight bells. Not only have the portholes been blackened to hide the light from within, but the bells have been silenced to keep the noise level down. Davis worries about the massive load of ammunition onboard. One torpedo, he warns, and the ship will explode before they might make it safely to the lifeboats. Jack slaps Smitty goodnaturedly on the shoulder to wake him from his "dope dream" (1:474), and Smitty follows Scotty to the watch.

When Jack comments on Smitty's odd behavior, Davis remarks that he might "turn out queerer than any of us think if we ain't careful." Cocky and Driscoll enter. Driscoll pours himself a coffee and sits on a bench; tumbling over Smitty's coffee cup, Driscoll flies into *an unreasonable rage* (1:474) brought on by his fear of a German attack. The men discuss Smitty's haughty British temperament. His nickname among them is "the Duke"; Cocky refers to him as the "Prince of Wales" and Scotty, later on, "his Lordship" (1:474, 476). Scotty reenters. Davis recounts Smitty's suspicious behavior with the black box, a story Scotty confirms. Davis then points out that since Smitty has already worked on the ship for two years, he knows there can be no fear of thievery among the men. (Robert Richter notes of the scene: "Trust was a linking force among shipmates. The confined conditions in which they lived, and the work they did, demanded it" [157].) Davis adds that one of the portholes had been left open, allowing some light to escape and endangering the vessel. He piques the men's suspicions, questioning the veracity of Smitty's British background and calling attention to his perpetual, seemingly deliberate outsider status among the men (1:479).

Scotty warns that the suspect is on his way back to the forecastle. The men go silent and watch as Smitty surreptitiously checks under his mattress for the box. He makes a comment about the bright moonlight potentially exposing the ship to submarines. He exits, perplexed by his mates' lack of response. No one speaks for a moment, then they erupt in accusatory exclamations. Something bumps into the ship, making the skittish men jump to their feet. Now convinced the iron box contains a bomb, Driscoll moves to throw it out the porthole. Davis persuades him instead to carefully place it in their water bucket to disarm the explosive, which he does. Scotty again shouts that Smitty is heading back. Davis orders Driscoll and Jack to stand on either side of the door and restrain him (1:481).

Smitty enters, and Driscoll and Jack roughly pin him against the bulkhead. After a short struggle, he allows the men to tie him down. Smitty appears befuddled but calm until he sees they have discovered his box. He resumes his struggle and demands to know why they are tampering with his belongings. Jack takes Smitty's keys and hands them to Driscoll, who opens the box. Smitty grows increasingly enraged and threatening. Driscoll voices the men's suspicions that he is an enemy spy. Smitty insists he placed the box under his mattress for quick access in case they were torpedoed. He begins screaming at the men, and Driscoll silences him with a *big wad of waste* that he secures to his mouth with a handkerchief (1:484). The box contains a packet of letters tightly wrapped in a rubber bag. The first letter is from Berlin and dated a year before the war, thus furthering the men's suspicions. Driscoll reads the letter aloud, contrasting his heavy Irish brogue with the genteel language of an educated music student named Edith. She pledges her love for the addressee, Sidney Davidson, but warns that he must prove to her that "the black shadow . . . which might wreck both our lives, does not exist for you" (1:486).

Still unconvinced of Smitty's innocence, the men read through the remaining letters. Smitty descends into paroxysms of despair, moaning beneath his gag, and turns slowly in humiliation toward the bulkhead. Driscoll reads the last letter aloud; it is addressed to the *Glencairn* when docked in Cape Town, South Africa. Filled with vitriol, Edith rails against "Sidney" (Smitty) for choosing a life of "drunkenness" over her love and destroying both their lives with his debauchery. A dried white flower drops from the envelope. The men fail into an embarrassed silence. Driscoll carefully rewraps the package, returns it to its hiding place, and releases Smitty. *"There is a moment of silence, in which each man is in agony with the hopelessness of finding a word he can say—then Driscoll explodes"*: "God stiffen us, are we never goin' to turn in fur a wink av sleep?" (1:488). With Smitty facing the bulkhead, his shoulders heaving in agony, the other men either climb into their bunks or return to duty. Driscoll extinguishes the light and climbs into his bunk as the curtain falls.

## COMMENTARY

The United States had just entered World War I when O'Neill completed the play in early spring 1917. Playing on rampant fears of a German attack on the United States, *In the Zone* takes place on the British tramp steamer *Glencairn,* loaded down with stores of dynamite and ammunition, as it passes through a German U-boat zone. The crew members in the forecastle (pronounced fo'c'sle) discover that one of their seamen is carrying a black box onboard that they suspect is a bomb, and they imagine him to be a German spy with designs to destroy the ship. This plot's composition history makes for an incredible circumstantial irony: In late spring 1917, O'Neill and his friend HAROLD DEPOLO, a pulp-fiction writer, were arrested under charges of espionage at the Atlantic House in Provincetown. Still relatively new to village, O'Neill and DePolo spent long hours meandering along the beaches while watchful Provincetowners grow increasingly suspicious. Believing the two outsider bohemians to be scoping out possible German landing sites along their beaches, the residents spread rumors about the men and noted that one of them carried a mysterious black box (most likely O'Neill's typewriter case). The men were arrested at the Atlantic House, and the Secret Service was called in from Boston. O'Neill's identity as the son of the great

matinée idol JAMES O'NEILL came to light after a night in the local jail, and the young men were promptly set free. The story so closely approximates the plot of *In the Zone* that it is nearly impossible to imagine O'Neill writing the play prior to this discomfiting experience; nevertheless, O'Neill and DePolo insisted the play had already been written.

Other possible sources for O'Neill's plot have since been discovered. William Godhurst traces the story back to Arthur Conan Doyle's story "That Little Square Box," and Esther Tamár goes back further to Edgar Allen Poe's "The Oblong Box" (22). Both stories take place during a SEA voyage and involve a mysterious box that generates tension among passengers and crew. Louis Sheaffer, however, found the most probable source in a story printed in the New London *Telegraph* on September 9, 1912, while O'Neill was on staff there. Entitled "Box Mystery/Alarms Many/Until Solved," the article reports that an Italian shopkeeper in NEW LONDON, CONNECTICUT, grew suspicious about a black box left in his care. Thinking it might belong to the Black Hand terrorist organization, he notified the police. Upon inspection, the innocuous box disclosed some men's clothing and was duly retrieved by its owner (Sheaffer 381).

*In the Zone* is a glance at life in a steamship's forecastle, a life O'Neill knew intimately after his term in the MERCHANT MARINE. On the strength of *In the Zone,* O'Neill chronicler Barrett Clark assigned O'Neill the title, possibly the first of many times for the playwright, of America's "leading dramatist" (New York *Sun,* May 1919, 77). Barrett's high praise prompted O'Neill to respond with a letter debunking the play's importance; in it, he unfavorably compares *In the Zone* to his more naturalistic *The* MOON OF THE CARIBBEES, his self-professed "favorite" of the four one-act plays in the SS *Glencairn* series:

> I by no means agree with you in your high estimate of "In the Zone." To me it seems the least significant of all the plays. It is too facile in its conventional technique, too full of theatrical tricks, and its long run as a successful headliner in Vaudeville proves conclusively to my mind that there must be something "rotten in

Denmark." At any rate, this play in no way represents the true me or what I desire to express. It is a situation drama lacking in all spiritual import—there is no big feeling for life inspiring it. Given the plot and a moderate ability to characterize, any industrious playwright could have reeled it off. Whereas, "The Moon of the Caribbees," for example—(my favorite)—is distinctly my own. The spirit of the sea—a big thing—is in the latter play the hero. While "In the Zone" might have happened just as well, if less picturesquely, in a boarding house of munition workers. (O'Neill 99)

O'Neill's rationale for preferring *Moon* to *In the Zone* is based on the former's effectiveness in making "the spirit of the sea" the hero of the play; whereas in the latter, Smitty's "thin whine of weakness" magnifies him into a false "hero who attracts our sentimental sympathy" as a result of the "stuffy, greasepaint atmosphere." Thus, *Moon* posits Smitty as "much more out of harmony with truth, much less in tune with beauty, than the honest vulgarity of his mates [in *Moon*]" (99). *In the Zone*, O'Neill concludes, substitutes "theatrical sentimentalism" for truth and beauty and thus exists merely as a "conventional construction of theater as it is" (100) in American theater.

O'Neill's distaste for the popular appeal of *In the Zone* resembles his strong aversion for "Anna Christie," which ironically won him his second Pulitzer Prize in 1921. In that play, audiences mistakenly read the character Chris Christopherson's "ole davil sea" as representing the quaint fears of a foreign sailor rather than a spiritual force that would inevitably lay waste to his and his daughter, Anna's brief moment of contentment. Smitty's humiliation and the depth of his sorrow in the final scene of *In the Zone*, according to O'Neill, equally misplaced the audience's sympathy. For O'Neill, Smitty's cares should never have surpassed the tremendous effect of the sea on his characters' lives, insignificant as they are while caught in the sea's eternal grasp. Of the four *Glencairn* plays, Bound East for Cardiff demonstrates this powerlessness of human beings to oppose the will of the sea, as does *The Long Voyage Home*, but *Moon* is by far the most affecting of the four.

Scholars generally do not share O'Neill's grim estimation of *In the Zone*'s artistic merit, however. From the time of its premiere, even his most unforgiving critics have been drawn to the play's "smooth and theatrically effective" tempo and technical strengths (Clark 79, Bogard 83). And though *In the Zone* was one of four one-act plays shown back-to-back at the Comedy Theatre on its first run, the play took up three-quarters of the *New York Times* review, in which the critic praised it as "of a very high order, both as a thriller and as a document in human character and emotion" (quoted in Gelb 623). The mounting suspicion of the crew, led by the attention-seeking character Davis; the glow from the lantern in center stage and the moonlight streaming through the doorway; the tension-building pauses in dialogue (a technique perfected in the late 20th century by fellow Nobel Prize–winning dramatist Harold Pinter); and even the final revelation of Smitty's dependence on the sea to free him from the ghosts of his past evenly combine to make *In the Zone* one of O'Neill's stronger early works.

## CHARACTERS

**Cocky**    British seaman on the British tramp steamer SS *Glencairn*. Cocky speaks with a cockney (British working-class) accent. Of the men in *In the Zone*, he appears the most virulently anti-German, questioning the Germans' humanity and referring to them as "Blarsted 'Uns!" (1:475). He is also the most critical of Smitty's high-toned attitude toward the rest of the men, at one point remarking, "Be the airs 'e puts on you'd think 'e was the Prince of Wales" (1:474). Cocky appears in all four of the *Glencairn* plays.

**Davis**    American seaman on the British tramp steamer SS *Glencairn* who witnesses Smitty's suspicious hiding of an iron black box and goads the rest of the seamen in the forecastle to restrain him while the box is opened. Davis also appears in *Bound East for Cardiff* and *The Moon of the Caribbees*.

**Driscoll**    Irish seaman on the British tramp steamer SS *Glencairn*. Driscoll is modeled on a friend of O'Neill's by the same name, upon whom Robert "Yank" Smith in *The Hairy Ape* is also based (see Driscoll). Although O'Neill characterizes Driscoll as a surly, drunken Irishman, he endows his character with a good deal of compassion and a strong sense of friendship, particularly while caring for his dying friend Yank in *Bound East for Cardiff,* understanding of Olson's desire to go home to Sweden in *The Long Voyage Home,* and in his eventual shame over opening Smitty's letters in the final scene of *In the Zone.* Driscoll appears in all four of the *Glencairn* plays.

**Ivan**   Russian seaman on the British tramp steamer SS *Glencairn.* Ivan moves slowly, speaks in unintelligent phrases, and has a *"shaggy ox-like head"* (1:472). Robert Richter argues that O'Neill is voicing his own sentiments about his experience in the merchant marine when Ivan complains, "I don't li-ike dees voyage. Next time I ship on windjammer Boston to River Plate, load with wood only so it float, by golly!" (quoted in Richter 156). Ivan also appears in *Bound East for Cardiff* and *The Long Voyage Home.*

**Jack**   American seaman on the British tramp steamer SS *Glencairn,* whom O'Neill describes as *"a young American with a tough, good-natured face"* (1:473). Jack chalks up Driscoll's irrational anger to the tension of sailing in the war zone and appears to be the most rational, even-tempered of the seamen in the forecastle. He is the only character O'Neill describes in the play other than Swanson, perhaps because, like Swanson, he does not appear in the other *Glencairn* plays.

**Paul**   Norwegian seaman on the British tramp steamer SS *Glencairn.* It is the porthole above Paul's bunk that the men assume Smitty opened to make the *Glencairn* visible to German U-boats. Paul has no lines in this play, but he also appears in *Bound East for Cardiff* and *The Moon of the Caribbees.*

**Scotty**   Scottish seaman on the British tramp steamer SS *Glencairn.* Scotty, who speaks in a Scottish brogue, witnesses Smitty's suspicious behavior and affirms Davis's accusations to the seamen. Scotty also appears in *Bound East for Cardiff.*

**Smitty**   British seaman on the British tramp steamer SS *Glencairn.* Based on a seaman O'Neill met at the Sailor's Opera Saloon in BUENOS AIRES, ARGENTINA (Gelb 284), Smitty, nicknamed "the Duke" by the other crewmen, is a well-educated British able seaman with two years' experience at sea. His shipmates consider him a snob, and he is an outsider among them. When Davis and Scotty witness him secretly tucking a black iron box under his mattress while the other men sleep, they suspect him of being a German spy and the box of containing a bomb. The final revelation of the play is that the box contains letters that expose Smitty for having succumbed to ALCOHOLISM at the expense of the woman he loves, Edith. Edith accuses him of relinquishing her love in order to carry on with his dissipated ways—what she calls his "black shadow" (1:486)—and of destroying her own life in the process. Travis Bogard writes that "O'Neill came naturally enough to a man like Smitty, a restless alien moving in an unending quest for belonging" (82). O'Neill believes that Smitty's soul-searching should be taken as an unnatural "thin whine" against the backdrop of the sea, an effect he achieved with *The Moon of the Caribbees* but not with *In the Zone.* Along with *Moon* and *In the Zone,* Smitty also appears in *Bound East for Cardiff.*

**Swanson**   Swedish seaman on the British tramp steamer SS *Glencairn.* O'Neill describes Swanson as *"a squat, surly-faced Swede"* (1:472). He is the only character O'Neill describes in the play other than Jack, perhaps because like Jack he does not appear in the other *Glencairn* plays.

## BIBLIOGRAPHY

Black, Stephen A. *Eugene O'Neill: Beyond Mourning and Tragedy.* New Haven, Conn.: Yale University Press, 1999.

Bogard, Travis. *Contour in Time: The Plays of Eugene O'Neill.* Rev. ed. New York: Oxford University Press, 1988.

Clark, Barrett H. *Eugene O'Neill: The Man and His Plays.* Rev. ed. New York: Dover, 1947.

Gelb, Arthur, and Barbara Gelb. *O'Neill: Life with Monte Cristo.* New York: Applause Books, 2000.

Kenton, Edna. *The Provincetown Players and the Playwrights' Theatre, 1915–1922.* Edited by Travis Bogard and Jackson R. Bryer. Jefferson, N.C.: McFarland & Company, 2004.

O'Neill, Eugene. "Inscrutable Forces." (A letter to Barrett Clark, 1919.) In *O'Neill and His Plays: Four Decades of Criticism*, edited by Oscar N. Cargill, Bryllion Fagin, and William J. Fisher, 99–100. New York: New York University Press, 1961.

Richter, Robert A. *Eugene O'Neill and Dat Ole Davil Sea: Maritime Influences in the Life and Works of Eugene O'Neill*. Mystic, Conn.: Mystic Seaport, 2004.

Sheaffer, Louis. *O'Neill: Son and Playwright*. Boston: Little, Brown, 1968.

Timár, Esther. "Possible Sources for Two O'Neill One-Acts." *Eugene O'Neill Newsletter* 6, no. 3 (1982): 20–23.

# *Lazarus Laughed: A Play Performed for an Imaginative Theatre* (completed, 1926; first produced, 1928)

Eugene O'Neill completed *Lazarus Laughed* on May 5, 1926. This full-length "mask play," meant to be performed by an "imaginative theatre," as the subtitle suggests, would not be produced until April 9, 1928, at the Pasadena Community Playhouse in Pasadena, California. This playhouse, "a community body with several thousand workers," enlisted a cast of 159 amateur actors, many of whom doubled in roles, and designed 400 costumes; 300 masks of all sizes, shapes, and styles; and hundreds of wigs to approach O'Neill's intended effect. The *San Francisco Chronicle* reported that on opening night the theater was full to capacity, and the production proved a remarkable success (Wainscott 221; Warren 178). Two university productions followed, one at Fordham University in 1948 and another two years later at the University of California, Berkeley (see also Cunningham).

This four-act curiosity charts the ascent of the biblical Lazarus as a figure of worship after Jesus raises him from the dead (John 11:1–46). One of O'Neill's personal favorites—"the most successful thing I ever did," he once told his first chronicler,

Barrett H. Clark (quoted in Clark 100), *Lazarus Laughed* is more pageant than play. It is a theatrical spectacle with no less than 420 roles—Roman soldiers, Jews, Christians, Greeks, choruses, lascivious courtiers, even a dying lion—and extraordinarily elaborate set designs, even for O'Neill, that have, to date, thwarted a professional production. "O'Neill calls his work a 'Play for the Imaginative Theater,'" writes Clark, "but he might more appropriately have said an Imaginary Theater" (117). O'Neill exposits on the biblical miracle in the first scene of the play, then speculates on Lazarus's future from that point forward. *Lazarus Laughed* is O'Neill's messianic attempt to assuage mankind's fear of death by positing the benign father figure of Lazarus spreading the word of life's victory over death. One powerful indication of O'Neill's fondness for the play is in his choice for the insignia engraved in his and Carlotta Monterey O'Neill's wedding rings: "I am your laughter—and you are mine!" (quoted in Floyd 333), the same lines Lazarus speaks to mollify his wife, Miriam's concerns over the deaths of his followers (2:586).

## SYNOPSIS

### Act 1, Scene 1

Lazarus's home in Bethany (located near Jerusalem in western Jordan), interior and exterior, shortly after Jesus raised Lazarus from the dead. At left, a doorway to the road is filled with a crowd of men; at right, near a doorway to the yard, stands a crowd of women; the Chorus of Old Men, seven in number, stand in a crescent formation in the far-right corner. Each of them wears a mask and a costume, evenly distributed to make 49 variations, showing seven periods of life: Boyhood/Girlhood, Youth, Young Manhood/Womanhood, Manhood/Womanhood, Middle Age, Maturity, and Old Age. Each period is represented by masked characters representing seven "*types of character*": Simple, Ignorant; Happy, Eager; Self-tortured, Introspective; Proud, Self-reliant; Servile, Hypocritical; Revengeful, Cruel; and Sorrowful, Resigned. The Chorus of Old Men wears masks that are double the size of the others. "*All masks of these Jews of the first two scenes of the play are pronouncedly Semitic*" (2:542).

Lazarus is seated on a raised platform in the middle of a banquet table at center, *"his head haloed and his body illumined by a soft radiance as of tiny phosphorescent flames."* His wife, Miriam, his sisters, Martha and Mary, and his parents kneel beside him. Lazarus is a powerful-looking man of about 50 with a complexion that is *"reddy and brown, the color of rich earth,"* blackened gray hair, and a massive beard; he has been *"freed now from the fear of death"* and thus is the only one not wearing a mask (2:542). The crowd stares at him in awe because of the miracle. The Chorus of Old Men chants, echoing Jesus' call in the Book of John, "He that believeth / Shall never die! / Lazarus, come forth!," and the crowd repeats the chant (2:543). They discuss the intense sorrows of Lazarus's life—his children have all died, Miriam could bear no more, and his poor ability as a farmer sank his family into a terrible financial state. One guest remarks that after Lazarus emerged from the tomb, he laughed "softly like a man in love with God" (2:545). Miriam calls for Lazarus to come forth.

Lazarus looks about the room warmly and cries joyfully, "Yes!" (2:545). Everyone throngs about him and embraces him. The father invites the guests to eat, drink, and dance in celebration, and lively music strikes up. Everyone raises a goblet to toast Lazarus. Only now, Lazarus's smile and magisterial bearing appear *"terrible and enigmatic to them."* The music stops, and his father tells Lazarus that he is frightening the guests, but then he toasts his son, "brought back from death." Lazarus cries out that there is no death and laughs again softly. "O Curious Greedy Ones," he responds when asked about the afterlife, "is not one world in which you know not how to live enough for you?" (2:546). He relates that Jesus' heart said to him, "There is Eternal Life in No . . . and there is the same Eternal Life in Yes! Death is the fear between!"—and he cried out "Yes!" and then "laughed the laughter of God" (2:547). Lazarus begins laughing once more, and they all join in, chanting, "Laugh! Laugh! / Death is dead! / There is only laughter!" The crowd's laughter, *"still a bit uncertain of its freedom,"* sounds *"harsh, discordant, frenzied, desperate and drunken,"* and it continues, *"dominated by the high, free, aspiring, exulting laughter of Lazarus"* as the curtain falls (2:548).

## Act 1, Scene 2

The exterior of Lazarus's house, the House of Laughter, on a clear, starry night some months later. Music and laughter come from the house, and its windows expose passing figures of revelers within. The Chorus of Old Men stands in a spearhead formation pointing toward the front door. Two groups of 49 men and women stand to each side. They are now divided by religious sect rather than GENDER. The Nazarenes, followers of Jesus who include Lazarus's sisters, Mary and Martha, are at left, and the Orthodox Jews, with Lazarus's parents, stand at right. The two sides glare at each other in hatred, as the revelers within shout of life and laughter. The groups are involuntarily moved to laughter, though they desperately attempt to stop. Both sects accuse Lazarus of devilry and blasphemy with his continuous laughter and singing. The Orthodox Priest shouts that God will punish them for joining in Lazarus's revelry, Mary that Jesus will never forgive them. The Priest denounces Christ and the Nazarene's "filthy idolatry" (2:549). Lazarus's mother, Rachel, shrieks hysterically and faints. Martha, Mary, and the father all run to her. Mary and the Priest argue over their respective religions. The Priest mocks them for considering Jesus their messiah. Her father disowns Mary, Martha, and Lazarus for their blasphemy, calls them devils, and proclaims his children dead. "Death is dead!" shouts Lazarus merrily from inside the house. "There is only laughter!" His followers pour out onto the veranda, laughing, and a Chorus of Followers, 49 men and women dressed in *"bright-colored diaphanous robes,"* appears on the roof, facing front, with masks expressing Lazarus's *"fearless faith in life."* They laugh loudly and chant, "There is only laughter! / Death is dead!" (2:552).

The Nazarenes and Orthodox Jews begin to intermingle, forgetting their differences in the face of the mutual foe. An Aged Orthodox Jew shouts that the workers on his farm have joined Lazarus and refuse to work, even for more money. The crowd dances uncontrollably, a *"grotesque sort of marionettes' country dance"* (2:554); they *"raise clenched fists or hands distended in threatening talons"* and growl, animal-like, over the evil Lazarus has brought down upon them. Lazarus's figure appears on the roof, *"illumined by its inner light,"* and his face and body look 10 years younger. He makes a sign, the music stops, and everyone freezes *"in a distorted posture"* (2:555). Lazarus condemns them for laughing like "a hyena laughter, spotted, howling its hungry fear of life"; his voice releases them from their fixed positions, and he announces that the "Master of Peace and Love" has died. All stars must now be seen as saviors, he says—"The greatness of Man is that no god can save him—until he becomes a god!" (2:556). A messenger rushes in to announce that Jesus Christ has been crucified. Mary shouts for revenge, and the two sides draw out hidden weapons and clash in a bloody battle.

Roman troops enter, and a centurion commands the fighting to stop. The soldiers are masked in the same formula of seven periods and types, but their masks are *"heavy, domineering, self-complacent, the face of a confident dominant race"* (2:557). When the fighting continues, soldiers hack away at the mob with swords. Lazarus commands them to stop. Ten bodies lie dead or dying on the ground. The Chorus of Old Men chants sadly over the divided Israel. Representatives from both sides inform Lazarus that his sisters and parents have all been killed in the fight, and Miriam informs him that Jesus died as well. "Yes! Yes!! Yes!!!" shouts Lazarus. "Men die! Even the Son of Man must die to show men that Man may live! But there is no death!" (2:558). The centurion wonders aloud whether Lazarus is a god, but then, embarrassed, he announces his orders to take Lazarus to face Caesar in Rome. Lazarus kisses his dead family one by one, then shouts exultantly, "Yes!" The singing, dancing, and laughter resume. But when Lazarus exits with the Romans, the shouts of the chorus and crowd weaken, and the lights in the house go slowly out. Everyone recalls their terror of death (2:560–562).

### Act 2, Scene 1

A square in Athens, about 10 o'clock at night. A full moon illuminates the facade of a temple, and an excited crowd of Greeks mills around the square. A seven-member Greek Chorus faces front in a spearhead formation with double-sized masks, in the period of Young Manhood and of the Proud, Self-Reliant type; they are dressed in goatskins, and

their masks are *"daubed and stained with wine lees"* as worshipers of Dionysus. The crowd of Greeks is composed of men and women who wear masks of all the types and periods, but distinctly Grecian. *"All eyes are fixed off left,"* in anticipation of Lazarus's arrival (2:563). A group of Roman legionaries with staves attempts to control the crowd. Gaius Caligula, an apish-looking 21-year-old nobleman with a boyish face half-revealed under a crimson and purple mask, enters with the Roman general Cneius Crassus. The chorus chants that Lazarus is "Dionysus, Son of Man and God!," and the Greeks respond, "Soon the God comes / Redeemer and Savior! / Dionysus!" (2:564). Several expound on Lazarus's fabled power to heal the sick and raise the dead with laughter. They believe he will lead them against the Roman oppressors.

Caligula, heir to Tiberius Caesar, tells Crassus to order his men to use swords, as he enjoys watching people die. But Tiberius fears Lazarus's power and influence and has ordered no swords. Caligula laughs mockingly at the Greeks' belief that Lazarus is Dionysus. "A Jew become a god! By the breasts of Venus that *is* a miracle!" (2:566). Caligula becomes unnerved at the prospect of Lazarus teaching Tiberius to cure his old age, however. Crassus suggests killing him before he meets Tiberius, but Caligula wants the power for himself. Lazarus appears offstage in the distance, creating a major disturbance in the crowd, which shouts and pushes at the legionaries. Crassus finally orders swords to be drawn, and the crowd shrinks back in fear. Caligula, entranced by music and dancing grotesquely, orders the soldiers to start killing Greeks. The crowd grabs whatever weapons they can and shouts, "Death!" Lazarus's shout comes from offstage: "There is no death!" Everyone freezes in *"attitudes of murderous hate"* (2:569).

The music restarts as Lazarus's Chorus enters followed by the Followers, all of whom gaily dance onto the stage. They wear masks like the previous followers, but this time each Chorus member has a different *"racial basis"*—Egyptian, Syrian, Cappadocian, Lydian, Phrygian, Cilician, and Parthian—and the followers' masks represent many nations as well (2:570). Still haloed and glowing, Lazarus now looks younger than 35, while Miriam looks over 45. The Greeks hail Lazarus as the savior and redeemer Dionysus. As the sound of his soft laughter rises, Caligula threatens to kill him, but Lazarus looks at him *"laughing with gentle understanding"* and informs him that death is dead (2:571). Caligula drops his sword, prances over to Lazarus's side, and gazes up at him *"in the attitude of a chained monkey"* (2:572). Lazarus convinces him he kills because he fears death, but if he learns to laugh at himself and death, he will no longer feel the urge to destroy others. He tells of the moment in the tomb when the heart of God sang to him that one must learn to laugh to relinquish death and accept life. Everyone chants, "Laugh! Laugh! / Fear is no more! / Death is dead!" (2:573). Lazarus orders everyone to the woods and hills, away from the cities, which are "prisons wherein man locks himself from life" (2:574). The Roman soldiers escort him offstage; everyone, Greeks and Romans, is *"dancing, playing, singing, laughing."* Crassus, desperate to stop his own laughter, orders the procession to stop but loses consciousness in the struggle. Caligula takes up a handful of flowers. Desperate to destroy something, though accepting Lazarus's dictum that death is dead, he lops the petals off, grinds the remnants under his feet, and *"breaks out into a terrible hysterical giggle"* as the curtain falls (2:575).

## Act 2, Scene 2

Months later at midnight, just inside the walls of Rome. Two massive columns from a temple's portico are in the foreground; a street can be seen past them, and the city wall looms behind that, with a massive metal gate leading outside. The heavy rumble of thunder and flashes of lightning alternate throughout the scene, though it is not raining. Under the portico are two series of wide steps, upon which 30 members of the Roman Senate are seated in masks of Middle Age, Maturity, and Old Age, each represented by a variety of personality types. Seven members of the Chorus of Senators are seated on steps downstage that lead up to the bases of the columns. Lazarus stands in the center of the portico gazing up at the sky beyond the wall, *"his body seeming to glow more brightly than ever"* (2:575). Miriam is praying near his left, looking *"much older, her hair is gray, her shoulders are bowed"*

(2:576). To his right sits Caligula, squatting on a throne of ivory and gold, drinking wine, and wearing a victory wreath on his head. A servant in a *"black Negroid mask"* occasionally fills his golden goblet. Departing troops can be seen marching down the street and out the gate, which shuts with a loud crash after the last soldier exits. The Chorus of the Senate chants of the Roman senate, and Caligula drunkenly sings a Roman legionaires' song of the march to conquer Carthage. A group of cynical, bored senators wonders what they are doing there. One exposits that Tiberius has fled to Capri to avoid the "laughing idiots" who arrived with the "charlatan" Lazarus (2:579), and he left orders to kill them all.

A senator demands that Lazarus turn and face the senate, but Caligula silences them. He begs Lazarus to give the signal for the soldiers to kill the followers outside, while Miriam begs Caligula for mercy. Lazarus turns, now appearing to be about 30 years old. He announces that he will signal to his followers that there is no death, then laughs; the pitch rises until reaching *"a triumphant, blood-stirring call to that ultimate attainment in which all prepossession with self is lost in an ecstatic affirmation of life"* (2:580). The followers' laughter can be heard outside the wall; the senators stand and also begin laughing. Bright flashes of lightning and crashes of thunder punctuate the laughing. Miriam crawls on her knees to the edge of the portico and raises her arms, grief-stricken, in the sign of the cross. The Roman legions beyond the wall blare their trumpets, and their laughter can be heard above the din. Caligula cries out for the soldiers to kill the followers, but then he begs Lazarus's forgiveness for overstepping his bounds.

The Roman legions and senators chant that everyone must laugh and death is dead. Crassus enters with his legions, who crowd around Lazarus obediently. He approaches Lazarus, drops to his knees, and shouts, "Hail!" (2:583). They all shout with him while Caligula pushes forward to get their attention. Crassus relates that Lazarus's followers took the soldiers' swords and killed themselves in fits of laughter. He then defies Caligula and promises to make Lazarus either their caesar or a god. Lazarus gently mocks the idea of caesars and proclaims that there are no gods if men must create them. Crassus departs, telling Lazarus he can make his decision the following day. Everyone but Lazarus, Miriam, and Caligula marches out chanting, "Laugh! Laugh! Laugh! / Death is dead!" (2:585). Caligula worries about Lazarus's disrespect for death and gods—he wishes to wield the power of both. Miriam asks Lazarus how he could be so uncaring about the death of his followers. Why should he mourn, he responds, when they laughed. "They are gone from us," she says, "and their mothers weep." Lazarus raises her up gently. "But God, their Father, laughs!" he says comfortingly, kissing her on the forehead (2:586).

### Act 3, Scene 1

Some days later, about two o'clock in the morning on the terrace of Tiberius Caesar's palace in Capri. On either side of the terrace are massive columns; a triumphal arch is at center, and marble walls are at the rear. A dying lion hangs on a cross at the center of the arch with an inscription above it, "From the East, land of false gods and superstition, this lion was brought to Rome to amuse Caesar" (2:587, 588). Music comes from the palace, conjoined with *"a confused drunken clamor of voices, punctuated by the high, staccato laughter of women and youths"* (2:587). The Chorus of the Guards enters, followed by a squad of Roman soldiers and the centurion Flavius. The guards form in two lines and stand at attention. The glowing Lazarus, now looking about 25, and Miriam, now old and feeble, enter next. Caligula takes up the rear. Flavius exits to inform Tiberius of their arrival. Caligula starts at the sight of the lion; Miriam shrieks, hiding her face in her hands. Caligula tells Lazarus that the lion is a sign Tiberius must be afraid and thus will execute him. Undaunted, Lazarus steps up to the lion and begs its forgiveness; the lion licks Lazarus's hand, then dies. Caligula tells Lazarus he should escape before Tiberius kills him next, but Lazarus laughs softly, "Escape—what?" (2:590).

In a lengthy monologue, Miriam implores her husband to listen to Caligula. She wishes to leave the evil Roman world and return to Bethany. Lazarus assures her they will return soon. Caligula does not know what to make of his continued affection

for Lazarus but vows to kill him viciously when he becomes caesar. Lazarus laughs softly again. "Why do you delight in believing evil of yourself, Caligula?" (2:591). The voices and music stop inside the palace. Marcellus, a 35-year-old Roman patrician, enters wearing a mask that shows *"one who leans to evil more through weakness than any instinctive urge"* (2:592). Caligula whispers a warning to Lazarus about Marcellus, then greets the patrician condescendingly. Marcellus welcomes Lazarus in the name of Caesar, then asks to speak with him alone. In spite of warnings from Caligula and Miriam, Lazarus walks to a darkened corner and waits silently. Marcellus approaches and conveys Tiberius's order not to laugh. Lazarus responds with soft laughter. Marcellus draws his dagger, but then he begins laughing along with Lazarus and drops the knife. He falls to his knees, half-laughing and half-sobbing. Lazarus moves toward the palace; as he passes each guard, he begins to laugh. Caligula mocks Marcellus for his cowardice but then expresses his mutual love for Lazarus. Marcellus begs Lazarus to forgive him. Caligula hands him his dagger and shouts, "Avenge him on yourself!" Marcellus stabs himself, laughing that death is dead and dies *"laughing up at the sky"* (2:594). Still afraid of losing the power of death, Caligula kicks Marcellus's body, calls him a liar, but then begs his corpse to admit that death lives. The Chorus of the Guards sings for everyone to laugh that death is dead. Lazarus enters the palace.

### Act 3, Scene 2

Inside Tiberius's banquet hall. A massive arched doorway is at rear, and smaller arches in the middle of the side walls lead to other rooms. The ceilings are high, and long couches line the side and back walls. Seated on these is a group of 42 young people, women and girls at right, and young men and boys at left. The three younger periods of masks are all represented, and there are *"seven individuals of each period and sex in each of the three types of the Introspective, Self-Tortured; the Servile, Hypocritical; and the Cruel, Revengeful"* (2:595). The males wear *"women's robes of pale heliotrope,"* the women garish crimson and purple male clothing. They are cross-dressed, wearing the wigs and clothing of the opposite sex. *"The whole effect of these two groups is of sex corrupted and warped, of invented lusts and artificial vices."* Tiberius stands on a dais at the center of the room. He is a massive, cruel-looking man of 76, wearing a half-mask that is colored a *"pallid purple blotched with darker color, as if the imperial blood in his veins had been sickened by age and debauchery"* (2:596). His mistress, Pompeia, sits at front right, wearing a *"dissipated mask of intense evil beauty, of lust and perverted passion."* The Chorus for this scene as well as act 4, scene 1, consists of three males and four females—*"the males in the period of Youth, one in each of the types represented, and three of the females in similar type-period masks. The fourth female is masked in the period of Womanhood in the Proud, Self-Reliant type"* (2:596).

The guards' laughter can be heard from outside, and everyone in the room stares at the doorway with frozen expressions varying *"from the extreme of panic fear or hypnotized ecstasy to a feigned cynical amusement or a pretended supercilious indifference"* (2:597). Tiberius has Flavius replace him as a decoy and hides at front right surrounded by guards with shields. Caligula screams for Lazarus to save himself, then pounces behind Flavius and stabs him. Striking an absurd pose, he pronounces himself the new caesar. The glowing Lazarus enters with Miriam by his side. He strides over to Tiberius and smiles down at him beneficently. "Fear not fear, Tiberius!" Tiberius seems comforted and laughs with him, though the laugh is *"cold, cruel and merciless as the grin of a skeleton"* (2:598). Caligula is dumbstruck by his mistake and begs Tiberius for forgiveness. Tiberius seems gratified by the deceit. "Too impatient my loving grandchild! Take care lest I become impatient also—with your impatience!" (2:599). He welcomes Lazarus up to the dais and asks if the miracle of his rising from the grave is true. "There is no death, Caesar," Lazarus replies (2:599), but he then foretells that Tiberius will die soon.

Tiberius believes he can read deception in men's eyes. Lazarus looks him in the eye, laughing softly, and the room ripples with laughter. Pompeia rises and sits with Caligula, telling him she wants Lazarus for her own. Caligula warns her that Lazarus loves only Miriam, that he rejected scores of women suitors on their travels. She decides to kill Miriam to see Lazarus suffer, at which point she will laugh. Caligula bets her "a string of pearls against your body for a night" that Lazarus will laugh at her instead, and she heartily accepts. "Do it, Pompeia!" Caligula exclaims, "We must save death from him!" (2:601). Pompeia picks up a poisoned peach and ascends the dais. Tiberius tells her of Lazarus's miracle and Jesus' death on the cross. Lazarus calls to Jesus exultantly, "Thou but hear Jesus! And men shall keep on in panic nailing Man's soul to the cross of their fear until in the end they do it to avenge Thee, for Thine Honor and Glory!" (2:602).

Pompeia challenges Lazarus to prove there is no death, and the young people shout, "Let him prove there is no death! We are bored!" (2:603). The crowd forms a three-tiered circle around the dais—squatting, crouching, and standing—with the sexes divided to each side. Pompeia whispers her plan in Tiberius's ear. Miriam accepts the peach from Pompeia, asking Lazarus whether the time is right. "Poor lonely heart!" Lazarus responds. "It has been crueler for you than I remembered. Go in peace—to peace!" (2:604). When she bites from the peach, she begins speaking of her marriage to Lazarus before the miracle, sounding *"like a garrulous old woman, her words coming quicker and quicker as her voice becomes fainter and fainter"* (2:605); then she falls into Lazarus's arms.

To the crowd's delight, Lazarus appears grief-stricken and expresses loneliness. They mock him scornfully and shout, "There is death!" as Caligula and Pompeia implore Tiberius to let them beat Lazarus. But Miriam rises slightly and utters, "Yes! There is only life! Lazarus, be not lonely!" Then she laughs and lies still. Everyone freezes, stricken with *"superstitious fear"* (2:606). Lazarus kisses her and smiles, casting off loneliness and pronouncing the death of death, fear, and loneliness: "There is only God's Eternal Laughter!" (2:607). Laughing loudly, he takes Miriam up in his arms. Tiberius starts laughing *"with the agony and terror of death,"* Pompeia *"with horror and self-loathing,"* and Caligula *"with grief and remorse."* "An agonized moan of supplicating laughter comes from them all" (2:607). The Romans beg Lazarus for mercy, but his laughter is *"as remote now as the laughter of a god"* as the curtain falls (2:607).

### Act 4, Scene 1

The same, soon after the previous act. The young men and women have left. Only Lazarus, Tiberius, Caligula, Pompeia, and Miriam's corpse remain. The hall is shrouded in darkness, lit by a single lamp on the table in front of the dais. The dais now looks closer, and the lamplight shines down on Miriam's pale face. Pompeia gazes up adoringly at Lazarus, and Caligula sits on his haunches, apelike, looking straight before him with his fists pressed to his temples. Appearing still younger, Lazarus gazes down at Miriam's body *"like a young son who keeps watch by the body of his mother, but at the same time retaining the aloof serenity of the statue of a god"* (2:609). Pompeia tells Caligula that she now loves Lazarus and will no longer agree to Caligula's terms on the bet. Caligula mocks her desire to join Lazarus in romance but says there still may be a chance for her to laugh at him.

Tiberius demands to know if Miriam died before rising again and insists on knowing what lies beyond death. "Life!" Lazarus replies exultantly. "God's Eternal Laughter!" If Tiberius wants hope, he insists, "Then dare to love Eternity without your fear desiring to possess her! Be brave enough to be possessed!" (2:610). Tiberius calls Lazarus a fool. "All laughter is malice, all gods are dead, and life is a sickness." Lazarus considers this the response of those who fear death to such a degree that when it arrives, they can relinquish their lives with resignation. What men should do from their first cry at birth, he continues, is to tell their hearts, "It is my pride as God to become Man. Then let it be my pride as Man to recreate God in me!" (2:611).

Tiberius says he loathes all men: "In self-contempt of Man I have made this man, myself, the most swinish and contemptible of men!" (2:613). In a lengthy monologue, he confesses that his mother made him in her image—cruel and loveless. He once loved a woman named Agrippina, who bore him a son, but his mother was overcome with jealousy and coerced him to divorce and remarry Caesar Augustus's daughter, whom Tiberius considered a "whore" (2:614). When Augustus died, Tiberius

became caesar and killed both his wife and mother. He now wishes to return to the period when he was capable of love. Lazarus listens with deep and compassionate understanding. Tiberius says he will sleep, but when he awakes, Lazarus must reveal the secret of his power or he will revenge his lost hope upon him. He exits.

Caligula strikes up a verse of the bawdy legionaire's song, then scoffs at Tiberius's weakness. He announces he will soon be caesar but shrinks back in terror and warns Lazarus to escape. He confesses that if the world could know the real Caligula, he might have faith in himself and laugh with Lazarus. Lazarus assures him he knows Caligula and loves him. This torments the young heir, who begins hopping up and down grotesquely. "You are so proud of being evil!" Lazarus says smiling down at him. "What is there are only health and sickness?" (2:617). He convinces Caligula to believe in the laughing god within him. "For Man death is not! Man, Son of God's Laughter, *is!* . . . *Is*, Caligula! Believe in the laughing god within you!" (2:618). Caligula vows to devote his reign to spreading the words and laughter of Lazarus; he then runs from the room, laughing. When Caligula has gone, Pompeia asks him to put his arms around her and kiss her, which he does. After a moment, she looks at Miriam, comprehending that Lazarus is incapable of loving individual women, only "Woman, wife, and mother of men" (2:619). She spits in his face and laughs maliciously, then shouts for Caesar to punish him. When she disappears laughing, the young men and women enter, led by the Chorus, and all laugh viciously at Lazarus. Ignoring them, he bends down, kisses Miriam, and takes her body in his arms. He pronounces her sacrifice one that made love and laughter grow purer and begins laughing softly as he takes her from the hall. The Chorus and young people all form a semicircle and begin laughing that love is pure and tender; the crowd joins in, "Laugh! Laugh!" as the curtain falls.

### Act 4, Scene 2

The arena of a Roman amphitheater; the same night, just before dawn. Tiberius is seated on a throne at front right watching Lazarus, bound and gagged, burn at a stake at center. Multitudes of spectators watch from seats behind and at the rear of the throne. Their Chorus consists of seven masked men of the Middle Age period of the Servile, Hypocritical type. Along with the sound of the crackling fire, the multitude is heard *"jeering, hooting, laughing at Lazarus in cruel mockery of his laughter"* (2:621), reaching its highest pitch as the curtain rises. Pompeia half-kneels in front of Tiberius, her chin resting on a marble rail in front of the throne. She begs Tiberius to order Lazarus's eyes put out, as she cannot stand the sight of him looking at her. Tiberius refuses, wanting to read the truth in Lazarus's eyes as he dies. Too impatient to resist, Tiberius orders Lazarus's gag removed. The crowd shouts, "Hail Caesar!" in assent, though Pompeia warns of the power of Lazarus's laughter. Lazarus shouts, his voice sounding now like that of a young boy's, "Hail Caesar!" (2:623). Tiberius orders the fire swept back and asks what Lazarus thinks now that he is dying. "Yes!" he triumphantly responds. Tiberius calls him a coward and a liar and laughs scornfully while the crowd makes *"all sorts of grotesque and obscene gestures . . . barking, crowing like roosters, howling, and hooting in every conceivable manner"* (2:623–624).

Lazarus tells everyone not to fear life and begins to laugh. Instantly under his spell, Pompeia walks toward the fire. Tiberius orders the gag replaced and the fire to be revived under Lazarus. He sobs that it is unkind to laugh at a caesar, then laughs at his own weakness. Pompeia throws herself into the fire. Panicking that Lazarus will die before revealing the secret of death, Tiberius asks what lies beyond. "Life! Eternity! Stars and dust! God's Eternal Laughter!" shouts Lazarus in exaltation. *"His laughter bursts forth now in its highest pitch of ecstatic summons to the feast and sacrifice of Life, the Eternal."* The multitudes pour down to the fire and dance before it in *"strange wild measures of liberated joy."* Tiberius laughs *"great shouts of clear, fearless laughter,"* and the rest join in (2:625). Frantic, disheveled, and out of breath, Caligula enters from behind Tiberius, calling to Lazarus that he will save him.

Tiberius announces that he is prepared to die with Lazarus and tells the multitudes not to fear caesars anymore. Caligula takes this as a betrayal by Lazarus and strangles Tiberius in a jealous rage. He

takes up a spear and lunges toward the fire as the crowd continues to laugh. Lazarus shouts, "Hail, Caligula Caesar! Men forget!"; there is a scream of fury and *"a wail of fear and lamentation"* (2:626). Caligula strikes an *"absurd majestic pose"* and pronounces himself the new caesar (2:627). "I had to kill you, Lazarus!" he then cries out. "A moment more and there would have been a revolution—no more Caesars—and my dream—!" (2:627). He denounces Lazarus's betrayal and orders the crowd to hail the new Caesar. A dead silence falls upon the arena, and Caligula finds himself utterly alone. He pleads with Lazarus to save him. Lazarus lets out a compassionate sigh, *"followed by a faint dying note of laughter that rises and is lost in the sky like the flight of his soul back into the womb of Infinity."* "Fear not, Caligula!" he exclaims. "There is no death!" At first joyful and laughing, Caligula realizes what he has done, then shouts, "Fool! Madman!"—beating himself with his fists in remorse—"Forgive me, Lazarus! Men forget!" (2:628).

## COMMENTARY

Originally titled *The Laugh of Lazarus*, the published title of this play reverses the well-known line in the biblical story of Lazarus, wherein "Jesus wept" after hearing the news his follower Lazarus had died (John 11:35). "Lazarus laughed," then, becomes Eugene O'Neill's counterpoint, a Dionysian incarnation of the triumph of life over death and a negation of Christian beliefs that deny the validity of living for life on Earth. Symbolically, the play's conflict lies in this tension between this life and the Christian afterlife. (The Christian idea of a "heaven" never comforted O'Neill.) Lazarus and his followers repeat the lines, "Death is dead. There is only laughter!" and thus reject the supremacy of death over life, answering the Kublai Khan's enigmatic chant over his daughter Kukachin's death in O'Neill's similarly extravagant MARCO MILLIONS—"Death is" (2:463). "For Man death is not!" Lazarus exhorts to Caligula, "Man, Son of God's Laughter, is! . . . Is, Caligula! Believe in the laughing god within you!" (2:618).

The play's narrative closely resembles the life-cycle motif O'Neill employs in *The* FOUNTAIN, DYNAMO, and *The* GREAT GOD BROWN, in which his heroes symbolically circle from the womb to the tomb and back again. The character Lazarus, Doris Alexander suggests, allowed O'Neill to "face death directly and fight his fear that only nothingness lay beyond it," but again without accepting the Christian rejection of a worldly life over a spiritual afterlife (81). O'Neill argues in this work that the Roman rulers Caligula and Tiberius's desperate drive for power derives from both "fear and life-hatred" (Alexander 82). In fact, Caligula and Tiberius both secretly long for purity in youth to be freed from fear of death and hatred of mankind, perhaps to even experience real love as the character in *The Fountain* Ponce de Léon had hoped by discovering the folkloric Fountain of Youth. *Lazarus Laughed* is thus O'Neill's most direct statement on mankind's (and his own) fear of death:

> The fear of death is the root of all evil, the cause of all man's blundering unhappiness. Lazarus knows there is no death, there is only change. He is reborn without that fear. Therefore he is the first and only man who is able to laugh affirmatively. His laughter is a triumphant Yes to life in its entirety and its eternity. His laughter affirms God, it is too noble to desire personal immortality, it wills its own extinction, it gives its life for the sake of Eternal Life (patriotism carried to its logical ultimate). His laughter is the direct expression of joy in the Dionysian sense, the joy of a celebrant who is at the same time a sacrifice in the eternal process of change and growth and transmutation which is life, of which his life is an insignificant manifestation, soon to be reabsorbed. And life itself is the self-affirmative joyous laughter of God (quoted in Törnqvist 167).

In the book of John, Jesus states that there is no death if you believe in him as the "resurrection, and the life" (John 11:25), but O'Neill recasts the story with pagan lore, German philosophy, and modern theories of psychoanalysis to sermonize that laughing for life rather than crying over death allows men and women to join a higher life force and enjoy everlasting life among the stars. O'Neill implies that only when men accept death can they accept life, as they are both integral to existence.

O'Neill's conception of Lazarus was strongly influenced by the Dionysian hero Zarathustra from FRIEDRICH NIETZSCHE's *Thus Spake Zarathustra*, O'Neill's favorite book. In act 1, scene 2, after the announcement of Jesus' death, Lazarus discovers that men cannot be at peace with death, and thus life on Earth, until they recognize, as a Nietzschean hero might, that "the greatness of Man is that no god can save him—until he becomes a god!" (2:556). Lazarus's sermons also closely follow Nietzsche's famous "eternal recurrence," an ancient belief also held by the Pythagoreans:

> O Zarathustra . . . to those who think like us, things all dance themselves: they come and hold out the hand and laugh and flee—and return. Everything goeth, everything returneth; eternally rolleth the wheel of existence. Everything dieth, everything blossometh forth again; eternally runneth on the year of existence. (Nietszche, quoted in Bogard 286)

In Athens, Lazarus is considered the resurrection of the Greek god Dionysus, the god of fruitfulness, wine, and drama. This adds a further correlation to Nietzsche, whose theory, articulated in his book *The Birth of Tragedy*, that the victory of Apollo, the god of restraint and reason, over Dionysus will eventually disrupt the Greeks' balance between the two and create an unhealthy imbalance.

O'Neill also applies the psychologist Carl Jung's theory of a dark "shadow" lurking within our psyches. We see this most clearly when Lazarus gently mocks Caligula's conception of himself as "the funny clown who beats the backside of his shadow with a bladder and thinks thereby he is Evil, the Enemy of God" (2:617–618; quoted in Floyd 330). Caligula certainly appears aware of his shadow's existence when he declares his longing to kill. Jung, like Lazarus, would not agree that our shadows should be considered "evil," as Caligula apparently does. Rather, the more we consciously acknowledge our shadow, the less it manifests itself in destructive behavior on ourselves and others. In one of the most Shakespearean lines in the canon, one that reflects the shadow concept and explains the "formless little fears" we find in scene 2 of *The EMPEROR JONES*, Lazarus counsels Tiberius that "men are too cowardly to understand" the meaning of Eternity, "And so the worms of their little fears eat them and grow fat and terrible and become their jealous gods they must appease with lies!" (2:610–611). Rather than condemning Caligula for his sins, Lazarus thinks of the young heir as suffering from a "sickness," the way a psychologist might, rather than outright evil (2:617).

*Lazarus Laughed* echoes the belief of early Pythagoreans, followers of the ancient Greek mathematical philosopher Pythagoras, that men and women do not die, but "fly up alive into the ranks of stars" (Alexander 82). Doris Alexander points out that when Jesus dies, Lazarus gazes up at the night sky and proclaims, "See! A new star has appeared!" (2:555). O'Neill seems to have divined a rather superstitious connection to the number 7 as well. This was a sacred number for the Pythagoreans, representing the life cycle of the natural world and the union of light (the number 3) and life (4). Several important episodes in O'Neill's own life occurred in seven-year increments. He was first sent to boarding school at the age of seven, an experience he always believed to be a betrayal and abandonment by his parents. When he was 14, he discovered that his mother, MARY ELLEN "ELLA" O'NEILL, was addicted to morphine; his disastrous marriage to KATHLEEN JENKINS took place seven years later at age 21; and he married AGNES BOULTON at 28 (Alexander 83). O'Neill also chose the number 7 for the life periods he covers, the psychological archetypes represented by masks, and the number of members in each chorus. Finally, he structured his first draft in seven scenes, rather than four acts with two scenes each as it stands in the final draft (Clark 116).

*Lazarus Laughed* appears to take up where O'Neill leaves off in *The Great God Brown*, when the tortured Dion Anthony, also a Dionysus figure, proclaims while dying, "Nothing more—but Man's last gesture—by which he conquers—to laugh!" (2:510; Warren 178). But if in *Lazarus Laughed* the ability of laughter can bring one closer to *becoming* a god, later on, in *DAYS WITHOUT END*, laughter brings one closer to *accepting* God. "Life laughs with God's love again!" the repentant John Loving shouts in the final scene at the church, "Life laughs with love!" (3:180). O'Neill would properly abandon such heavy-handedness in his later work, but he also believed *Lazarus Laughed* might successfully be produced with "a spotlight, a couple of tables, two soap boxes, a black curtain and the Hudson Duster Gang" (quoted in Alexander 86; the Hudson Dusters were a street gang in New York O'Neill befriended at the HELL HOLE). Originally, however, O'Neill intended to effectively transform theaters into churches with the audience as the congregation. Indeed, he specifically hoped for the exultant music and chanting in *Lazarus Laughed* to inspire a kind of "call and response" between actors and audience and resemble nothing less than a black revival meeting (Bogard 286, 288). O'Neill's repetitious choruses and shouts of joy were no longer meant to drive audiences insane—as he had with his earlier works *BEFORE BREAKFAST* and *WHERE THE CROSS IS MADE*—but rather to invite them into his spiritual fold.

O'Neill included a strong autobiographical component in *Lazarus Laughed* as well. Doris Alexander suggests that after O'Neill's 1912 suicide attempt at JIMMY "THE PRIEST'S" boarding house and saloon in New York City, O'Neill felt he understood what it meant to be raised from the dead, finding "full resurrection out of despair as a dedicated playwright" (84). In addition, his matinee idol father, JAMES O'NEILL's reputation as a man whose youthful spirit and optimism led O'Neill's Lazarus, a father figure, to "become saturated with [O'Neill's] boyhood hero-worship of James O'Neill" (Alexander 84). According to one reporter, James O'Neill's smile acted as "a lamp to the path of the 'hopeless,' a 'torch' in a 'place of darkness,'" and another feature story about the actor was titled "James O'Neill's Marvelous Secret of Eternal Youth Laid Bare" (quoted in Alexander 85). O'Neill also describes his father's avatar, James Tyrone, Sr., in his late masterpiece *LONG DAY'S JOURNEY INTO NIGHT* as looking about 10 years younger than his 65 years.

None of the play's psychological and philosophical themes are elegantly presented however. O'Neill hammers away so repetitively at these concepts that they collapse into so much pulverized rubble. But he never intended subtlety at this stage of his career; in fact, O'Neill preferred

*Lazarus* to *The Great God Brown*, his most successful mask play, because in *Brown* he believed the highly symbolic masks should have been made "twice as large—and conventionalized ... so the audience could get the idea at once" (quoted in Clark 116). *Lazarus Laughed*'s premiere at the Pasadena Community Playhouse was actually "received with tremendous enthusiasm," according to the *San Francisco Chronicle*'s review (Warren 178), and O'Neill never lost his enthusiasm over its potential. As late as December 1943, after the completion of his realistic play A MOON FOR THE MISBEGOTTEN, the last play he ever wrote, he reread the script appreciatively and tried to convince the producer Lawrence Langner to stage a revival, thinking it might be better appreciated in the context of World War II. As with Adolf Hitler, O'Neill imagined, the tyrant Caligula's greatest terror throughout the play is that if Lazarus has the power to destroy death, he might relinquish a caesar's power over life. This time around, O'Neill assured Langner, the producers could forget all the "unrealistic paraphernalia of the masked mobs, chorus, etc." and limit the cast to only a few people (quoted in Floyd 331–332). "Now give heed to this," he wrote,

> and reread it carefully in the light of what the play has to say today. 'Die exultantly that life may live' etc. 'There is no death.' (spiritually) etc. Also think of the light thrown on different facets of the psychology of dictators in Tiberius and Caligula. Hitler doing his little dance of triumph after the fall of France is very like my Caligula (quoted in Floyd 332).

## CHARACTERS

**Caligula, Gaius**   Heir to the throne of Tiberius Caesar, his adoptive grandfather. O'Neill fleshed out the nuances of this historical character by reading Edgar Saltus's *Imperial Purple* and Suetonius's *Lives of the Twelve Caesars*, among other books (Alexander 90). Gaius Germanicus was raised in the brutal environment of the Roman war camps, where soldiers nicknamed him Caligula. Now a 21-year-old, erratic, and bloodthirsty tyrant, Caligula appears "*almost malformed, with wide, powerful shoulders and long arms and hands, and short,*

*skinny, hairy legs like an ape*" (2:563). Caligula wears a half-mask of crimson and purple, which exposes the "*childish,*" "*feminine*" mouth of a "*spoiled, petulant and self-obsessed, weak but domineering*" young bully (2:564). Caligula often sits in an apelike position on his haunches, particularly when agitated by mixed emotions of love and hate for Lazarus, whom he considers a god. At the premiere of *Lazarus Laughed* in Pasadena, California, the actor who played Caligula, Victor Jory, acted the role as if he were "half animal, with dangling arms and bended knees, and giving him a snarling speech" (Warren 180). In stark and symbolic contrast to Lazarus's softly compassionate, kindly paternal laugh, when Caligula laughs it comes out as a "*terrible hysterical giggle*" (2:575).

Caligula accepts Lazarus's teaching but still fears that Lazarus might rob him of the mainstay of his own power on Earth—to kill. He attempts to save Lazarus from his grandfather Tiberius Caesar's wrath, but at the same time he conspires with Pompeia, Tiberius's mistress, to murder Lazarus's wife, Miriam. It is Caligula who has the last word in this play. After he spears Lazarus, already burning at the stake, he finds himself alone, paranoid, and once more tormented by death. In the final lines, he begs Lazarus to forgive him. Although Lazarus dies, Caligula has accepted an enlightened affirmation of life on Earth along with the tragic reality that, as Lazarus taught him, "Men forget!" (2:628). Caligula can also be read as the staged personification of O'Neill's own self-loathing; thus, his final lines have been interpreted as O'Neill's affirmation of his father's love of life (Alexander 95, 99). Caligula also shares some Mephistophelian aspects with O'Neill's brother, JAMES O'NEILL, JR., and his conflict with their father, James O'Neill, Sr. (personified by Lazarus). O'Neill would later dramatize this conflict in his late masterpiece *Long Day's Journey into Night*.

**Crassus, Cneius**   A Roman general. O'Neill describes him as a "*squat, muscular man of sixty,*" wearing a mask that reveals "*a heavy battered face full of coarse humor*" (2:564). Though loyal to Gaius Caligula, Crassus is involuntarily drawn to Lazarus, at one point losing consciousness over his effort to stop laughing. After he relates that Lazarus's followers killed themselves with Roman legionaires' swords, he offers to anoint Lazarus a god. Lazarus laughs at the offer—"When men make gods, there is no God!" (2:584).

**Father of Lazarus**  Lazarus, Mary, and Martha's father, and the husband of Lazarus's mother. Lazarus's father, *"a small, thin, feeble old man of over eighty, meek and pious,"* appears in the first scene to celebrate the resurrection of his son Lazarus (2:542). His guests are frightened by Lazarus's godlike presence, and he gently scolds his son before toasting the miracle. In act 1, scene 2, the Jews in Bethany have divided over whether Jesus Christ is the son of God, and the father sides with the Orthodox Jews. He curses his daughters, Mary and Martha, for siding with Jesus' sect, the Nazarenes, which he considers blasphemy, and shouts hysterically of the miracle, "It was not my son who came back but a devil! My son is dead! And you, my daughters, are dead! I am the father only of devils!" (2:551). Lazarus's father dies in act 1, scene 2, during the bloody fight between the Orthodox and Nazarenes and the subsequent intervention of Roman soldiers.

**Flavius**  Tiberius Caesar's centurion and head of the guard at Capri. Tiberius, terrified of Lazarus's power and informed of his approach, orders Flavius to take his place on the royal dais while he hides. Sworn to defend Lazarus from his grandfather, Gaius Caligula stabs Flavius to death, then begs Tiberius's forgiveness when he realizes his mistake.

**Lazarus (Lazarus of Bethany)**  Miriam's husband and Mary and Martha's brother. The biblical character from the book of John, chapter 11. O'Neill takes up the biblical story after Jesus Christ performs a miracle by raising Lazarus from the dead. O'Neill infuses the Lazarus character with ideas from Greek philosophy and modern philosophy and psychology, including Friedrich Nietzsche's Dionysian character Zarathustra from the book *Thus Spake Zarathustra* and Carl Jung's embrace of the psychic "shadow" that lurks in our psyches. Lazarus functions as O'Neill's vehicle through which

he attempts to teach his audience the Nietzschean credo that only when individuals confront and destroy their fears of death and discover the god in themselves can they experience everlasting life. "The greatness of Man," O'Neill proclaims through Lazarus, "is that no god can save him—until he becomes a god!" (2:556).

Lazarus, the only character who does not wear a mask, is *"a tall and powerful man"* of around 50, *"with a mass of gray-black hair and a heavy beard"* (2:542); he stands, godlike, before a crowd of family and guests as if he were a *"statue of a divinity of Ancient Greece.... a strange, majestic figure whose understanding smile seems terrible and enigmatic to them"* (2:542, 546). A guest in act 1, scene 1, witnessed Jesus' miracle and reports that Lazarus laughed "softly like a man in love with God" (2:545). Throughout the play, Lazarus's head is haloed, and his body is *"illumined by a soft radiance as of tiny phosphorescent flames"* (2:542). At the beginning of each scene, he appears visibly younger, finally looking like a *"young son who keeps watch by the body of his mother, but at the same time retaining the aloof serenity of the statue of a god"* (2:609).

Lazarus's ethereal laugh has a spellbinding effect, one that relieves its hearers of the fear of death. Their fears return with terrible force once he leaves. Over the course of the play, Lazarus goes to Athens, Rome, and Capri, gathering "Followers" along the way. The Greeks consider him the resurrection of Dionysus, the god of fruitfulness, wine, and drama. The reference to the Greek god adds a further correlation to Nietzsche, who believed that the victory of Apollo, the god of restraint and reason, over Dionysus would eventually create an unhealthy imbalance. Lazarus encounters the bloodthirsty, animal-like tyrant Gaius Caligula, soon to become Caligula Caesar. Lazarus's laugh is powerful enough to seduce the equally vicious Tiberius Caesar; Tiberius eventually orders his execution unless Lazarus reveals the secret of everlasting life. Caligula, meanwhile, is terrified of Lazarus's power, as death is the mainstay of his earthly power; nevertheless, he becomes enamored by Lazarus and considers him a god. This duality of Caligula's remains until the final scene, when he executes Lazarus at the stake. He then finds himself alone and begs forgiveness, remembering that "men forget" to laugh that death is dead.

Lazarus is an avatar of O'Neill's father, James O'Neill, a man of famed youthful spirit and optimism. James O'Neill's smile, according to one reporter, acted as "'a lamp to the path of the hopeless,' a 'torch' in a 'place of darkness'" (quoted in Alexander 1992, 85). Another feature story about O'Neill's father was titled "James O'Neill's Marvelous Secret of Eternal Youth Laid Bare" (quoted in Alexander 85). In his autobiographical masterpiece *Long Day's Journey into Night*, O'Neill also describes his father's character of James Tyrone, Sr., as looking about 10 years younger than his 65 years.

**Marcellus**   A Roman patrician. Marcellus is 35 years old and wears a mask revealing *"one who leans to evil more through weakness than any instinctive urge"* (2:592). Caligula distrusts Marcellus and warns Lazarus about him. On the terrace of Tiberius Caesar's palace in Capri, Marcellus asks to speak with him alone and conveys Tiberius's order not to laugh. Lazarus laughs anyway, and Marcellus draws a knife but begins laughing along with Lazarus and begs his forgiveness. Caligula hands him his dagger and shouts, "Avenge him on yourself!" Marcellus does so, laughing that death is dead; he dies affirming his belief in the death of death and *"laughing up at the sky"* (2:594).

**Martha**   Lazarus and Mary's sister. Martha is a biblical figure described by both O'Neill and the Bible as a maternal figure who cooks for others and takes care of the home. O'Neill describes her as a *"buxom middle-aged housewife, plain and pleasant"* (2:542). In act 1, scene 2, the Jews in Bethany divide over whether Jesus Christ is the son of God, and both Martha and Mary side with the Nazarene Jews. Martha attempts to mollify her more rebellious sister, Mary, who denies their father for not believing in Jesus, while he curses his children as devils. Martha dies in the bloody conflict between the Nazarenes (Christians) and Orthodox Jews.

**Mary**   Lazarus and Martha's sister. Mary is a biblical figure, and there is some controversy among theologians that she might be the "sinner" Mary Magdalene. O'Neill describes her as *"young and pretty, nervous and high-strung"* (2:542). In act 1, scene 2, the Jews in Bethany have divided over whether Jesus Christ is the son of God, and both Mary and Martha side with the Nazarene Jews. Mary denies their father for not believing in Jesus and goads him into cursing his children as devils. She dies in the bloody conflict between the Nazarenes (Christians) and Orthodox Jews.

**Miriam**   Lazarus's wife. Miriam (Hebrew for "Mary," significantly O'Neill's mother's name) is a fictional creation, as there is no mention of Lazarus's wife in the Bible. O'Neill describes her as *"a slender, delicate woman of thirty-five,"* who wears black clothing and a half-mask of marble that makes her eyes look closed, inwardly dreaming of her self-sacrifice, the rest connoting a *"statue of Woman, of her eternal acceptance of the compulsion of motherhood, the inevitable cycle of love into pain into joy into new love into separation and pain again and the loneliness of age"* (2:542). Miriam is the personification of motherly love and affection and selflessly follows her husband, Lazarus, from Bethany to Athens to Rome and finally to Capri to confront Tiberius Caesar. Unlike Lazarus, she denies, initially, the affirmation of life in death, and she ages over time while Lazarus grows younger.

Lazarus consoles Miriam in act 2, scene 2, by saying that those who die laughing say to God, "I am your laughter—and You are mine!" (2:586; significantly, O'Neill ordered these words engraved into his and his third wife, Carlotta Monterey O'Neill's wedding rings). When Tiberius's mistress, Pompeia, falls in love with Lazarus, Caligula warns her that Lazarus can love no other than Miriam. Pompeia then conspires to murder Miriam, with Tiberius's consent, in order to dispose of her rival and to ascertain if Lazarus is as confident about laughter in death when it comes to Miriam. Pompeia hands Miriam a poisoned peach, who then asks Lazarus if it is time to die. Lazarus responds compassionately, "Poor lonely heart! It has been crueler for you than I remembered. Go in peace—to peace!" (2:604). After biting from the peach, she speaks of her marriage to Lazarus before the miracle and sounds *"like a garrulous old woman, her words coming quicker and quicker as her voice becomes fainter and fainter"* (2:605). Lazarus expresses his loneliness, which ignites a wave of scorn and laughter from the Romans. But Miriam briefly regains consciousness and shouts, "Yes! There is only life! Lazarus, be not lonely!" (2:606), and Lazarus's laugh returns.

**Mother of Lazarus**   Lazarus, Mary, and Martha's mother, and the wife of Lazarus's father. Lazarus's mother, Rachel, *"a tall and stout, over sixty-five, a gentle, simple woman,"* appears in the first scene to celebrate the resurrection of her son Lazarus (2:542). In act 1, scene 2, the Jews in Bethany have divided over whether Jesus Christ is the son of God, and her husband sides with the Orthodox Jews. Lazarus's mother shrieks and faints when the Nazarenes (Christians) and Orthodox Jews attack each other, and she dies in the bloody conflict that follows when the Roman soldiers arrive.

**Pompeia**   A Roman noblewoman and Tiberius Caesar's favorite mistress. She wears a purple wig and an olive-colored half-mask stained with blood, *"a dissipated mask of intense evil beauty, of lust and perverted passion."* A beautiful and strong-bodied woman, her exposed mouth expresses *"agonized self-loathing and weariness of spirit"* (2:596). When Lazarus enters Tiberius's hall accompanied by his wife, Miriam, and Gaius Caligula, Pompeia falls in love with him and makes a bet with Caligula, after he warns her that Lazarus only loves his wife, Miriam, for a "string of pearls against your body for a night" if she can make Lazarus return her love (2:601). Pompeia then conspires to murder Miriam, with Tiberius's consent, in order to dispose of her rival and to ascertain if Lazarus is as confident about laughter in death when it comes to the death of his wife. Pompeia offers Miriam a poisoned peach, which she accepts with Lazarus's approval. Although Lazarus at first expresses deep remorse, contradicting his belief in the death of death, Miriam reawakens briefly, affirms that death is dead, and Lazarus laughs triumphantly. Pompeia then persuades Tiberius to order him burned at the stake. But when Tiberius has Lazarus's gag removed against Pompeia's counsel, Pompeia joins Lazarus

in the fire in an act of self-immolation, affirming her belief in the death of death.

Pompeia represents female lust and sexuality rather than the nurturing motherhood of her rival, Miriam. Doris Alexander forms a connection between Pompeia and O'Neill's second wife, Agnes Boulton, by suggesting that his writing—his words—destroyed their love. In act 4, scene 1, Pompeia concludes that Lazarus is incapable of loving an individual woman, only "Woman, wife, and mother of men" (2:619). "Did you think I would . . . give you love and passion and beauty," she shouts at Lazarus, "in exchange for phrases about man and gods—you who are neither a man nor a god but a dead thing without desire!" (2:619).

**Tiberius Caesar**   Emperor of the Roman Empire and Gaius Caligula's adoptive grandfather. Tiberius is 76 (significantly, the same age as O'Neill's father, James O'Neill, when he died), *"broad and corpulent but of great muscular strength"* (2:596); he wears a purple-colored half-mask, *"blotched with a darker color, as if the imperial blood in his veins had been sickened by age and debauchery"* (2:596). Having heard of the miracle of Lazarus's rising from the dead, Tiberius fears Lazarus as a god. A merciless tyrant, Tiberius was coerced by his mother into rejecting his true love, Agrippina, and marrying the daughter of Augustus Caesar; he then killed his wife and mother after becoming caesar. Since then, he has loathed himself and mankind. "In self-contempt of Man," Tiberius admits, "I have made this man, myself, the most swinish and contemptible of men! Yes! In all this empire there is no man so base a hog as I!" (2:613).

Tiberius longs for Lazarus to reveal the power of eternal youth and everlasting life in order to return to a time when he was still capable of love and compassion. Although Lazarus makes some ground with Tiberius, by act 4, scene 2, Tiberius's mistress, Pompeia, convinces him that Lazarus is a threat, and he orders him to be burned at the stake. As Lazarus dies, Tiberius demands that Lazarus reveal his secret of life after death. He orders Lazarus's gag removed against Pompeia's advice, and Lazarus laughs, spellbinding everyone present. Tiberius laughs with Lazarus in the *"highest pitch of ecstatic summons to the feast and sacrifice of Life, the Eternal"* (2:625). Pompeia immolates herself by joining Lazarus in the fire. Tiberius advises his citizens "not to fear Caesars" or death, and Caligula strangles him for his treachery. Like Caligula, he represents the celebration of death as power, as opposed to Lazarus's belief in mankind's power over death. Both monarchs accept death in the end.

## BIBLIOGRAPHY

Alexander, Doris. *Eugene O'Neill's Creative Struggle: The Decisive Decade, 1924–1933.* University Park: Pennsylvania State University Press, 1992.

Bogard, Travis. *Contour in Time: The Plays of Eugene O'Neill.* Rev. ed. New York: Oxford University Press, 1988.

Clark, Barrett H. *Eugene O'Neill: The Man and His Plays.* Rev. ed. New York: Dover, 1947.

Cunningham, Frank R. "A Newly Discovered Fourth Production of *Lazarus Laughed.*" *Eugene O'Neill Review* 22 (1998): 114–122.

Floyd, Virginia. *The Plays of Eugene O'Neill: A New Assessment.* New York: Ungar, 1985.

Törnqvist, Egil. *A Drama of Souls: Studies in O'Neill's Super-Naturalistic Technique.* New Haven, Conn.: Yale University Press, 1969.

Wainscott, Ronald H. *Staging O'Neill: The Experimental Years, 1920–1934.* New Haven, Conn.: Yale University Press, 1988.

Warren, George C. "Lazarus Laughed." In *O'Neill and His Plays: Four Decades of Criticism,* edited by Oscar Cargill, N. Bryllion Fagin, and William J. Fisher, 178–180. New York: New York University Press, 1961.

# *Long Day's Journey into Night* (completed, 1941; first produced, 1956)

Eugene O'Neill's full-length masterpiece *Long Day's Journey into Night* is widely considered the finest play in AMERICAN THEATER history. Perhaps the most startling facet of O'Neill's greatest achievement is the ghostly presence of its author, a revela-

tion to audience members attending its American premiere at the Helen Hayes Theatre, New York City, in 1956, three years after his death. The play's action takes place over a single day in August 1912 in the sitting room of O'Neill's family home, MONTE CRISTO COTTAGE in NEW LONDON, CONNECTICUT. The Tyrone family of the play is based on the O'Neills—his father, JAMES O'NEILL; mother, MARY ELLEN "ELLA" O'NEILL; older brother, JAMES O'NEILL, JR. (Jamie); and himself. Much of what O'Neill describes in *Long Day's Journey* is true to his life, including his bout with tuberculosis, his mother, Ella's addiction to morphine, and his brother, Jamie's debilitating ALCOHOLISM. Two O'Neill plays follow chronologically from *Long Day's Journey: The STRAW,* which depicts O'Neill's stay at the GAYLORD FARM SANATORIUM in 1912–13, and A MOON FOR THE MISBEGOTTEN, about Jamie's last months before drinking himself to death.

A diary entry made by O'Neill's wife CARLOTTA MONTEREY O'NEILL on June 21, 1939, is the earliest known mention of the play. O'Neill himself first noted the idea in his WORK DIARY on June 25, 1939. After outlining its structure and themes, he shelved the play to complete *The ICEMAN COMETH,* whose artistic merit closely rivals *Long Day's Journey.* He resumed after finishing *Iceman* and completed *Long Day's Journey* on April 1, 1941, at his home, TAO HOUSE, in Danville, California. But even then few people knew of its existence, and the public would not see it until its world premiere at the Royal Dramatic Theatre in Stockholm, Sweden, on February 2, 1956, several months before its debut at the Helen Hayes on November 7. Carlotta famously recalled O'Neill's mood during the writing process: "When he started *Long Day's Journey,* it was a most strange experience to watch that man being tortured every day by his own writing. He would come out of his study at the end of a day gaunt and sometimes weeping. His eyes would be all red and he looked ten years older than when he went in in the morning" (quoted in Berlin 88).

Only a select few read the script of *Long Day's Journey* during O'Neill's lifetime. According to O'Neill biographer Louis Sheaffer, these included his wife Carlotta; his son, EUGENE O'NEILL, JR.; his friends the playwright Russel Crouse; screenwriter Dudley Nichols; and the O'Neill scholar Sophus Winther and his wife, Eline. Winther later recalled his time as a houseguest at Tao House in 1943, when he read the script: Stunned by the revelations the play contained and by the power of O'Neill's tragic presentation, he met the playwright in the living room and recalled that O'Neill stared out the picture window at Mount Diablo and recited Mary Tyrone's, and the play's, final lines: "That was the winter of senior year. Then in the spring something happened to me. Yes, I remember. I fell in love with James Tyrone and was so happy for a time." After a pause, O'Neill said, "I think that is the greatest scene I have ever written" (Sheaffer 1973, 517).

Scholars to this day still piece together the facts, often sordid, of *Long Day's Journey*'s first production. The drama behind the drama revolves around O'Neill's submission of the completed manuscript to his publisher, Bennett Cerf at Random House, on November 29, 1945, which included a stipulation by the author that the play be stored in a vault and "publication shall not take place until twenty-five (25) years after my death . . . but never produced as a play" (quoted in Alexander 2005, 149). O'Neill died on November 27, 1953, leaving Carlotta O'Neill as his literary executor. Three years later, she wrenched control of the publishing rights from Cerf, who had read it at her behest and, instantly realizing the motive behind O'Neill's stipulation, refuses to publish it. She then allowed the Royal Dramatic Theatre in Stockholm to produce it soon after assuring its publication by Yale University Press, where O'Neill's papers reside, on February 10, 1956. Months later, Carlotta summoned JOSÉ QUINTERO—the master director who revived *Iceman* so successfully—and offered him and his production team the opportunity to produce *Long Day's Journey*'s American premiere at the Helen Hayes in New York.

Carlotta O'Neill told the press that her husband only wanted to protect the reputation of his son, Eugene O'Neill, Jr. But Eugene, Jr., we now know, had written to O'Neill after having read it, praising the play and telling his father how "much moved" he had been by the facts revealed (Alexander 150); in addition, Eugene, Jr., committed

Production photo of *Long Day's Journey into Night* at the Helen Hayes Theatre in 1956, with Florence Eldridge as Mary Tyrone. Photo by Mili Gjon *(Courtesy of the Yale Collection of American Literature, Beinecke Rare Book and Manuscript Library)*

suicide in September 1950, several months before O'Neill wrote Cerf to remind him of their compact (June 15, 1951). GEORGE JEAN NATHAN, O'Neill's longtime friend and producer, remembered that "O'Neill had confided to me, personally, that regard for his family's feelings—chiefly his brother's and mother's—had influenced him to insist upon the play's delay" (quoted in Alexander 152). In a letter to Anna Crouse on November 11, 1953, nearing her husband's death, Carlotta swore that she had "but one reason to live & that is to carry out Gene's wishes . . . the 'twenty-five year box' is the most interesting part of it—all personal except *Long Day's Journey Into Night*—& not intended to be opened until twenty-five years after Gene's death" (quoted in Murphy 4). Three years later, the story of a "deathbed request" broke in the news, a story released to the press by Carlotta. She insisted that a few weeks before O'Neill died, he had expressed his desire for the Swedish theater to produce the play (Murphy 6).

Whatever the case, *Long Day's Journey* was instantly hailed as a masterpiece and Quintero's production as brilliant. The *Daily News* raved that the tragic play "exploded like a dazzling sky-rocket over the humdrum of Broadway theatricals" (quoted in Murphy 45). The New York production alone, before the national tour, ran for 65 weeks, a total of 390 performances, and won O'Neill a Drama Critics Circle Award, an Outer Circle Award, a Tony Award, and his fourth PULITZER PRIZE. In 1962, *Long Day's Journey* was adapted for feature film by the director Sidney Lumet (*Serpico*, *Dog Day Afternoon*). Generally considered the finest FILM ADAPTATION of any play by O'Neill, the film starred Katharine Hepburn as Mary Tyrone, Sir Ralph Richardson as James, Dean Stockwell as Edmund, and JASON ROBARDS as Jamie.

## SYNOPSIS

### Act 1

Around 8:30 on an August morning in 1912 in the living room of the Tyrone family's summer home in New London, Connecticut (Monte Cristo Cottage). Two double doorways with portieres (curtains) are at the rear, the one on the left leading to a dark, unused parlor that leads in turn to the dining room; the door on the right opens to the front parlor, the staircase, and the front door. Sunshine comes brightly through three windows on the right wall that look out on the waterfront (the mouth of the Thames River) and the road below (Pequot Avenue); a screen door at the rear of the right wall leads out onto a porch that wraps halfway around the house. On the left wall are more windows that look out at the backyard, with a couch below them. A round table is at center with a green-shaded lamp hanging down from the ceiling, and four chairs, three wicker armchairs, and one oak rocker are positioned around the table. Against the back wall, a small bookcase contains books by such modern masters and radical philosophers as Balzac, Zola, Schopenhauer, FRIEDRICH NIETZSCHE, AUGUST STRINDBERG, Oscar Wilde, and others. Another bookcase on the left rear wall holds more conventional fare—William Shakespeare, Victor

Hugo, and Alexandre Dumas, along with histories of England, Ireland, and the Roman Empire. "*The astonishing thing about these sets,*" O'Neill specifies in his STAGE DIRECTIONS, "*is that all the volumes have the look of having been read and reread*" (3:717). The Tyrones—Mary, James, and their two sons, Jamie and Edmund—have just finished breakfast.

Mary and James enter from the back parlor. Mary is 54, with white hair, dark eyes, and a face that is "*distinctly Irish in type*"; when she feels happy, her voice has a "*touch of Irish lilt in it.*" She appears extremely nervous, and her hands "*have an ugly, crippled look*" from rheumatism, which makes her extremely self-conscious as well. "*Her most appealing quality is the simple, unaffected charm of a shy convent-girl youthfulness she has never lost—an innate unworldly innocence.*" James Tyrone is 65, though his robust form and handsome looks make him appear more like his wife's age. "*He is by nature and preference a simple, unpretentious man, whose inclinations are still close to his humble beginnings and his Irish farmer forebears*" (3:718). A professional actor for the whole of his adult life, Tyrone carries himself with almost military comportment, and his voice is "*remarkably fine, resonant and flexible*" (3:719). For a few intimate moments of lighthearted scolding, they discuss Mary's vulnerable health and James's incessant snoring, along with a blind tendency to involve himself in risky real estate ventures. They express concern over the health of their youngest son, Edmund. Mary claims he has merely contracted a summer cold. James intimates that she is recovering from an ailment as well, one that willpower might control. Jamie and Edmund's voices can be heard offstage in the dining room, then a burst of laughter. James assumes it is the older son, Jamie—whom James considers a drunken loafer—making some sneering comment about "the Old Man" (3:721).

Jamie and Edmund enter, smiling and chuckling in mutual appreciation of a shared joke. Thirty-three years old, with his father's good looks and stout build, Jamie Tyrone has a "*habitual expression of cynicism*" that gives his face a "*Mephistophelian cast*"; at the same time, his personality "*possesses the remnant of a humorous, romantic, irresponsible Irish charm—that of the beguiling ne'er-do-well, with a strain of the sentimentally poetic, attractive to women*" *and popular with men"* (3:722). Ten years younger than Jamie, tall and thin with a *"long, narrow Irish face,"* Edmund Tyrone more noticeably resembles his mother than his father, particularly the *"quality of extreme nervous sensibility"* (3:723). He is too thin, his face is drawn and sallow, and he appears genuinely ill. James attacks Jamie straight away, though the assault only bores his older son. Mary scolds James for his bad temper and asks to hear what made the brothers laugh.

Edmund recounts that he ran into James's tenant farmer, Shaughnessy, at the local inn, where Shaughnessy had told him of his triumph over Harker, a Standard Oil millionaire. Harker had accused Shaughnessy of deliberately tearing down the fence that separates their land in order for the farmer's pigs to bathe in his ice pond. Shaughnessy retorted that it was Harker tampering with the fence, thus exposing his pigs to pneumonia and cholera. Edmund relates Shaughnessy's verbal attack on Harker: "He was King of Ireland, if he had his rights, and scum was scum to him no matter how much money he had stolen from the poor." Shaughnessy then ordered the millionaire off his land and threatened legal action for his lost pigs. James affects outrage that Shaughnessy—"The dirty blackguard!"—would provoke such trouble from the town's leading citizen and condemns his son's "damned Socialist anarchist sentiments" against Standard Oil; but the other three know James is inwardly, as Edmund phrases it, "tickled to death over the great Irish victory" (3:726).

James resumes his attack on Jamie, which makes Edmund go upstairs in disgust over the constant bickering. His coughs can be heard by the others in the living room, and Jamie, who should be more sensitive about his mother's anxiety, lets slip that "It's not just a cold he's got. The Kid is damned sick" (3:727). James pacifies Mary and shoots Jamie a *"warning glance."* Jamie instantly regrets what he said and tries to calm Mary by remarking that Doctor Hardy, Edmund's physician, said that along with a cold, he might have contracted a minor case of malaria while "in the tropics" (3:727). "Doctor Hardy!" she exclaims, "I wouldn't believe a thing he said, if he swore on a stack of Bibles! I know what doctors are. They're all alike. Anything, they

don't care what, to keep you coming to them" (3:727–728). Her outburst makes her visibly self-conscious, and the men force themselves to cheer up and flatter her to calm her nerves. Leaving the men instructions not to allow Edmund to exert himself, she exits to see their cook, Bridget, about dinner.

Once Mary Tyrone is out of earshot, James rails into Jamie for carelessly revealing Edmund's probable diagnosis to his mother. But Jamie feels it is wrong to hide the truth. "I was with Edmund when he went to Doc Hardy on Monday. I heard him pull that touch of malaria stuff. He was stalling" (3:729). Jamie voices what the others refuse to admit—that Edmund has consumption (tuberculosis); and he, like the other three, blames James's tightfistedness. Had his father hired a specialist, they might have caught the disease earlier. "If Edmund was a lousy acre of land you wanted," Jamie accuses him, "the sky would be the limit!" (3:730). James denies this and swiftly turns to Jamie's failings: He knows nothing of the worth of a dollar and expresses little if any gratitude for the financial support his father provides. Jamie sneers at everyone but himself, James venomously responds. "That's not true, Papa," he sardonically mutters, "You can't hear me talking to myself, that's all" (3:731). James blames Jamie's odious influence "playing the Broadway sport" for exacting a terrible effect on Edmund, since "he's always been a bundle of nerves like his mother" (3:732). Jamie insinuates that James's terror of consumption, born of his upbringing in IRISH peasant society, makes him assume that Edmund's condition is incurable. James again accuses Jamie of warping Edmund's worldview: "You made him old before his time, pumping him full of what you consider worldly wisdom, when he was too young to see that your mind was so poisoned by your own failure in life, you wanted to believe every man was a knave with his soul for sale, and every woman who wasn't a whore was a fool!" (3:732).

Edmund does what he wants to do anyway, Jamie asserts; he exposits on his brother's last few years, in which Edmund traveled the world in the MERCHANT MARINE, inhabited "filthy dives," and slept on beaches in South America. Since then he has worked as a reporter (not a very good one) and written some very fine "poems and parodies" for a local paper (3:733). The rage runs out of both men, who appear conscious of the fact, if they do not say so out loud, that they love Edmund but that their respective faults have proven harmful to him, perhaps even fatal.

The conversation turns to Mary Tyrone. Each intimates that the scare with Edmund's health may have an equally deleterious effect on her. Jamie admits that he heard her late at night "moving around in the spare room" (3:735). "I couldn't help remembering," he continues, "that when she starts sleeping alone in there, it has always been a sign" (3:735). This admittance infuriates James at first, but he pauses and remarks superstitiously that her "long sickness" resulted from Edmund's birth. This in turn infuriates Jamie, who accuses his father of blaming Edmund's birth for his mother's still-undisclosed ailment, and he rails against him for having hired "another cheap quack like Hardy" to care for her in childbirth. Then he abruptly silences them both upon hearing his mother's return.

Mary enters, inquiring about the cause of their argument. Jamie says it was about Doctor Hardy; she knows he is lying but changes the subject. Mary complains that Bridget talks too much, then predicts that the fog will return, considering her rheumatism a "weather prophet" (3:736). She urges them to go outside and begin their yard work, which James does. Before Jamie leaves, he tells her how proud they are of her and that she should be careful not to worry too much over Edmund's illness. She defensively retorts that she does not know what he is talking about, and Jamie, upset and exasperated, goes out to join his father.

Edmund descends the staircase, holding a book. At the bottom, he has a coughing fit. He had waited for James and Jamie to leave, feeling "too rotten . . . to mix up in arguments" (3:737). His mother fusses over him, but he wants her to take care of herself, not him. Mary looks out the window and notices Jamie hiding behind the hedge as a respectable local family—the Chatfields—drive by. Jamie plainly exhibits embarrassment over performing menial work in public while James bows with dignity to the passing car. This sparks a discussion about the town and its inhabitants. Mary openly

hates it and has never felt at home there; Edmund likes it "well enough. I suppose because it's the only home we've had" (3:738). Mary goes on that she might feel proud enough to have guests if James had spent "the money to make it right." She adds that all three of the men only "hobnob with the men at the Club or in a barroom," but that Edmund is "not to blame," as he never had a chance to meet "decent people" in the town. By this time, the Tyrone men's reputations have been so disgraced, she offhandedly comments, "no respectable parents will let their daughters be seen with you" (3:739).

Edmund again warns her not to upset herself, and she demands to know why he acts so suspicious. He admits that he, like Jamie, heard her moving about in the spare room the night before. "Oh, I can't bear it, Edmund, when even you—!" she blurts out, then her tone turns spiteful: "It would serve all of you right if it was true!" Edmund, now terrified, begs her to stop. Her voice settles back to a *resigned helplessness,* which upsets Edmund further (3:741). But she cajoles him into going outside to read in the fresh air and sunlight, insinuating that he does not want to leave her alone. He obeys her and exits. Mary sinks into a wicker chair and, once settled, nervously drums her fingers on its arm.

### Act 2, Scene 1

Same as act 1 at around 12:45 in the afternoon. Sunlight no longer streams through the windows, and the heat has become sultry. Edmund is discovered in a wicker chair, attempting to read but visibly distracted. Cathleen appears from the back parlor to announce lunch and deliver a bottle of bourbon with a pitcher of ice water for the men. Edmund treats her curtly, then appreciates her joke that Jamie has undoubtedly checked his watch—more for the prospect of whiskey than lunch. She goes on that Edmund probably wants her to go outside and make the announcement anyway, as he could then sneak a drink. When Edmund suggests she call his mother as well, Cathleen reports that her mistress is lying down with a headache. Edmund tenses up at this news.

Cathleen goes out on the porch and bellows to the men that it is time for lunch. Edmund curses her, perhaps knowing that the maid understands full well the significance of his mother's prostration and pours himself a drink. Jamie enters, pours himself a drink, and then hides the evidence by adding water to the bottle. He warns his brother to follow Hardy's instructions not to drink, but Edmund shrugs this off. "Oh, I'm going to after he hands me the bad news this afternoon" (3:745). Jamie inquires about the whereabouts of their mother, a topic that leads to backhanded accusations. They both suspect that she has relapsed, and Jamie scolds Edmund for leaving her alone all morning. Edmund sustains a state of denial about their mother, but Jamie asserts he has more experience dealing with her affliction than he. Edmund continues to reject the truth and falls into another coughing fit, and Jamie backs off, contritely regarding his brother *"with worried pity"* (3:747).

Mary enters with *"a peculiar detachment in her voice and manner, as if she were a little withdrawn from her words and actions."* She wraps her arms around Edmund and voices concern over his health. Her maternal affection allows Edmund to suppress in his mind what he knows to be true, but *"Jamie knows after one probing look at her that his suspicions are justified. . . . [H]is face sets in an expression of embittered, defensive cynicism"* (3:747). Mary quickly senses Jamie's mood but agrees with Edmund that "the only way" to handle Jamie "is to make yourself not care" (3:748). However, when Jamie sarcastically blames his father for delaying lunch by showing off his "famous Beautiful Voice" to a neighbor, Mary snaps at him fiercely and accuses him, as his father had, of ingratitude and for disrespecting a man who "made his way up from ignorance and poverty to the top of his profession" (3:748–749). But then, as with the entire scene, she reverts back to her *"detached, impersonal tone"* and muses, "None of us can help the things life has done to us. They're done before you realize it, and once they're done they make you do other things until at last everything comes between you and what you'd like to be, and you've lost your true self forever" (3:749). Jamie and Edmund try to ignore this, and she continues on about their house being occupied by "lazy greenhorns" as servants and the fact that her husband, used to second-rate hotels as he is, "doesn't understand a home" (3:749).

Cathleen enters to announce lunch, and Mary sends her back to the kitchen to inform Bridget that they will wait for James. Edmund goes out to the porch to call his father inside. Jamie informs Mary that he can deduce her state from both her distracted manner and her bright eyes. Edmund returns and curses Jamie for directly accusing their mother. "It's wrong to blame your brother," she says, again in the tone of *"strange detachment,"* "He can't help being what the past has made him. Any more than your father can. Or you. Or I" (3:751). Edmund still calls Jamie a liar, *"hoping against hope"* (3:751). Mary exits to tell Bridget they are ready for lunch, and James enters soon after. James dislikes the idea of Edmund drinking whiskey, but he convinces himself that whiskey is "the best of tonics" (3:752). He senses the tension in the room but nervously changes the subject when Jamie tells him, "You won't be singing a song yourself soon" (3:752).

Mary reenters, excitable now. She scolds James for being late; then her agitation turns to fury: "Oh, I'm so sick and tired of pretending this is a home! You won't help me! You won't put yourself out the least bit! You don't know how to act in a home! You don't really want one! You never have wanted one—never since the day we were married! You should have remained a bachelor and lived in second-rate hotels and entertained your friends in barrooms!" (3:752–753). Once again, she reverts to the detached tone—"Then nothing would ever have happened." The stage directions indicate that *"Tyrone knows now"* (3:753). Mary continues on, fussing over Edmund, and the men's expressions reveal defeat. Averting their eyes, Jamie and Edmund head in to the dining room. Tyrone voices a profound mixture of anger and sadness; although Mary begs him to realize how difficult it is to stop, she finally denies his accusations. James mutters, "Never mind. It's no use now" (3:754). They walk side-by-side into the dining room.

### Act 2, Scene 2

About half an hour later. The whiskey has been taken away, and the family are just returning from their meal. Mary enters first, with James behind her, then the two brothers. James looks older, and he regards his wife with *"an old weary, helpless resignation*" (3:755). Jamie has masked himself in "*defensive cynicism,*" and although Edmund tries to emulate him, his sensitivity exposes real fear. Mary appears "*terribly nervous*" while at the same time showing "*more of that strange aloofness,*" while consoling herself about Bridget and Cathleen's lackluster service. "It's unreasonable to expect Bridget or Cathleen to act as if this was a home." "In a real home one is never lonely," Mary continues; then she fusses again over Edmund's health (3:756).

The phone rings, and James goes to answer it. It is Doctor Hardy. By the tone of James's reply, Edmund can hear that the diagnosis is bad. James returns to inform Edmund he has an appointment with the doctor at four o'clock. Mary rails once more at Hardy's incompetence, but this time brings her own experience to bear: "He deliberately humiliates you! He makes you beg and plead! He treats you like a criminal! He understands nothing! And yet it was exactly the same kind of cheap quack who first gave you the medicine—and you never knew what it was until it was too late!" (3:757). Edmund and James silence her. She apologizes and excuses herself to fix her hair, but the men know different. "This isn't a prison," James says, and Mary backhandedly retorts, "No. I know you can't help thinking it's a home" (3:758). Again, she apologizes, saying the fault does not lie with him, and goes upstairs.

"Another shot in the arm!" Jamie scoffs. Edmund and James reproach him for his insensitivity. Edmund angrily parodies his brother's Broadway lingo: "They never come back! Everything is in the bag! It's all a frame-up! We're all fall guys and suckers and we can't beat the game!" (3:758). Pointing at the smaller bookcase, Jamie retorts that neither Edmund's poetry nor the philosophy he reads are exactly sunny. James berates them both, blaming their lack of faith in CATHOLICISM for their dissipated ways. He admits that he rarely goes to mass, but he still prays for Mary to overcome her addiction. "'God is dead,'" Edmund quotes from Nietzsche's *Thus Spake Zarathustra,* "'of His pity for man hath God died'" (3:759). Edmund vows to try to talk Mary into stopping, but Jamie and James agree that once started, she is no longer capable of listening to reason.

Edmund heads upstairs to dress, making plenty of noise so his mother does not think he is spying on her. James informs Jamie that Edmund has consumption. Jamie immediately demands that his father place him in a good sanatorium. "What I'm afraid of is, with your Irish bog-trotter idea that consumption is fatal, you'll figure it would be a waste of money to spend any more than you can help." James responds defensively: "I have every hope Edmund will be cured. And keep your dirty tongue off Ireland! You're a fine one to sneer, with the map of it on your face!" (3:761). Jamie snidely retorts that he will wash it, then announces his plan to accompany Edmund uptown to the doctor's. That satisfies James, but he warns not to get him drunk. Jamie bitterly asks what he would use for money.

Mary enters, and Jamie rushes upstairs to avoid her. "*Her eyes look brighter, and her manner more detached. This change becomes more marked as the scene goes on*" (3:761). Mary tells James not to blame Jamie for his actions, since "if he'd been brought up in a real home, I'm sure he would have been different." James ignores this and remarks that contrary to what he had predicted earlier, there will be fog again tonight. She is no longer concerned about the fog, not to his surprise. He begins heading upstairs to change for a "meeting" at the club, but Mary grabs him desperately and begs him not to leave yet. They throw blame at each other back and forth, but without the volatility of earlier scenes—Mary high on morphine and backhandedly critical, James resigned to get drunk. When James turns to go again, Mary asks him to stay since he will be leaving her for the night. "It's you who are leaving us, Mary," he responds "*with bitter sadness*" (3:763).

James attempts to persuade Mary to take a ride in the automobile he bought explicitly to amuse her after her release from a mental sanatorium. But she only uses this as an excuse to chide him for stinginess, hiring a cheap chauffeur with no experience and buying an out-of-date car. Tyrone impulsively hugs her and pleads with her to stop using the drug. She tells him not to try to understand what cannot be understood, then exposits on her life after meeting him: She was either snubbed or pitied by her friends and family for marrying an actor, especially one whose mistress sued him and caused a scandal. The more morphine she takes, the farther back into the past her mind takes her. He knows her retreat into the past is a sure sign of her condition but is shocked that she has gone that far into the past so early in the day.

Mary thinks back to Edmund's birth and the quack that caused her addiction by prescribing morphine. James begs her again to stop, but she says, "Why? How can I? The past is the present, isn't it? It's the future, too. We all try to lie out of that but life won't let us" (3:765). She goes back further in her mind's eye to the death of their son Eugene. She openly blames Jamie for his death, as he exposed the baby to his measles when he was seven years old, and she believes he purposefully killed Eugene out of jealousy. After that, she swore never to have another child, but then, pressured by James, she bore Edmund. She regrets bringing her younger son into this life, if only because she believes he will never attain happiness. James stops her as Edmund comes down the stairs: "For God's sake try to be yourself—at least until he goes! You can do that much for him!" (3:766).

Edmund enters dressed in a blue suit for the doctor's appointment. James says that he is proud of him for having worked so hard before getting sick and gives him a 10-dollar bill to spend as he likes. Edmund is at once sincerely grateful and suspicious that the doctor told his father his condition is fatal. At this, Mary again loses control and screams that Edmund's books put such morbid thoughts into his head. Holding fast to a *"hopeless hope,"* James suggests Edmund might try to ask Mary what he had suggested earlier and heads upstairs to change.

Edmund attempts to broach the topic of her quitting the morphine, but she tells him not to speak and mothers him in an extravagant but detached way. "You—you're only just started," he blurts out. "You can still stop. You've got the will power!" (3:769). She begs him not to talk about things he cannot comprehend, then blames him for upsetting her over his sickness when she needed peace and rest to recover. She recants this, however, and begs him to believe she puts no blame on him. "What else can I believe?" he responds wearily.

She goes on that the day will come when her sons are "healthy and happy and successful," and only then will the Virgin Mary forgive her and cease the torment. But her voice becomes defensively casual, and she tells him of her need to go to the drugstore on an errand. Edmund pleads with her not to, but clearly she is lost to him. He hears Jamie call from the hallway and joins him and James. They say perfunctory goodbyes and head off for town. At first Mary feels lonesome, but then she admits to being happier alone. "Their contempt and disgust aren't pleasant company," she says out loud. "Then Mother of God, why do I feel so lonely?" (3:771).

### Act 3
The same, around 6:30 in the evening. Fog whitens the view from the windows and intensifies the dusk. A foghorn can be heard in the distance *"moaning like a mournful whale in labor,"* and the boats in the harbor chime their bells to sound their presence (3:772). Mary and Cathleen are discovered. The tray with whiskey and ice water is on the table, and Cathleen has evidently been drinking. Mary is now extremely high on morphine. Her dress, which she had put on for her trip to town, looks unkempt, and her hair *"has a slightly disheveled, lopsided look."* O'Neill writes: *"The strange detachment in her manner has intensified. She has hidden deeper within herself and found refuge and release in a dream where present reality is but an appearance to be accepted and dismissed unfeelingly—even with a hard cynicism—or entirely ignored"* (3:772). She is glad Cathleen has joined her but takes no interest in what she has to say. Commenting on the fog while at the same time implicitly describing her own drugged state, Mary says, "It hides you from the world and the world from you. You feel that everything has changed, and nothing is what it seemed to be. No one can find you or touch you any more" (3:773).

For her part, Cathleen is bantering on about the chauffeur, Smythe, who has been making passes at her, though she considers him a "monkey" (3:773) in contrast to the dashing James Tyrone. When Mary complains about James's miserliness, fear of poverty, and drinking habits, Cathleen responds that he is "a fine, handsome, kind gentleman" who obviously adores Mary. But Mary is lost in thoughts of life before James, when she lived in a "respectable home" and was schooled at the "best convent in the Middle West" (3:775). Cathleen, who accompanied Mary on her errand to the drugstore, grumbles about how the pharmacist responded to filling Mary's prescription: He treated her like a "thief" until she haughtily explained that the prescription was for Mrs. Tyrone. Mary takes the news lightly, telling Cathleen that the medicine is for her hands, that it takes away the pain, "*all the pain*" (3:776). She nostalgically recalls two dreams of her girlhood—to become either a nun or a concert pianist: "To be a nun, that was the more beautiful one." But her dreams vanished after marrying James; she tried to keep up her music, she says, "But it was hopeless. One-night stands, cheap hotels, dirty trains, leaving children, never having a home—." Cathleen remarks with confusion that the medicine makes her sound as if she had been drinking, to which Mary disaffectedly replies again, "It kills the pain. You go back until at last you are beyond reach. Only the past when you were happy is real" (3:777). She renews her dreamy recollections, this time the night she first met James, the great matinee idol whom her father had befriended. She went backstage after a show to meet him, and they fell instantly in love. Not once in the 36 years that followed has he ever cheated on her or caused a scandal, a fact that has allowed her to "forgive so many other things" (3:778).

Cathleen exits to instruct Bridget about dinner, and Mary "*settles back in relaxed dreaminess, staring fixedly at nothing.*" There is "*a pause of dead quiet,*" and then the mournful foghorn sounds, and the bells on the ships anchored in the harbor all chime in chorus. Mary's girlish demeanor transforms into one of an "*aging, cynically sad, embittered woman.*" She curses herself for being a "sentimental fool"; then she tries praying but recognizes that the Virgin Mary would never be "fooled by a lying dope fiend reciting words" (3:779). She moves to take more morphine upstairs but hears voices outside approaching the house. At first, she resents their return, but then abruptly welcomes it.

Edmund and James enter. "*What they see fulfills their worst expectations*" (3:780). Mary expresses gratitude for their returning home rather than

going straight to the bar, then asks where Jamie is. Answering her own question—at the bar—she goes on, "He's jealous because Edmund has always been the baby—just as he used to be of Eugene. He'll never be content until he makes Edmund as hopeless a failure as he is" (3:780–781). She contrasts Jamie's robust ability to accept the "one-night stands and filthy trains and cheap hotels and bad food" with Edmund's extreme sensitivity. James tells Edmund not to take anything she says personally, but Mary goes on to place the blame squarely on James's drinking habits. He quickly retorts, "When you have the poison in you, you want to blame everyone but yourself!" (3:782).

Edmund takes a drink of whiskey and balks at the watered-down taste. Mary reverts back to her convent-girl persona and brings up their first meeting, deeply moving James, who passionately responds by expressing his undying love for her. But she grows more detached and informs him, as if he is not present, that she never would have married him had she known how much he drank, recalling nights when she would wait for him for hours, then he would be deposited on their doorway by drinking buddies. James becomes increasingly defensive and guilt-ridden. Edmund turns on his father in disgust but controls himself and asks about dinner. Ignoring this, Mary discusses their wedding—her mother had disapproved of her marrying an actor—and then wonders where she hid her wedding dress. James tries to act casual and has a drink. After a taste, he fumes over the watered-down whiskey. Not even Jamie would be that careless. He turns on his wife: "I hope to God you haven't taken to drink on top of—" (3:785; the combination of alcohol and opiates can, in fact, be lethal). She admits she offered it to Cathleen as thanks for accompanying her to the drugstore. This admittance outrages Edmund, who knows Cathleen is a gossip and that in no time the word of his mother's addiction will spread through the town. James exits for a fresh bottle of whiskey.

Edmund accuses Mary of not caring about his diagnosis, then he informs her that he has been diagnosed with consumption and must be treated at a sanatorium. Mary fiercely condemns Doctor Hardy for his faulty, unwanted advice, again bringing it around to her own situation and blaming Hardy for distancing her from her sons. When Edmund adds that consumption can be fatal, that her own father died of it, she forbids him to make the comparison. "It's pretty hard to take at times," Edmund shouts, "having a dope fiend for a mother!" (3:788). He instantly regrets his words and begs for forgiveness. She absentmindedly changes the subject to the fog horn—"Why is it fog makes everything sound so sad and lost, I wonder?" (3:789). The *"blank, far-off quality"* of her voice makes Edmund sadly exit. She again considers going upstairs, vaguely hoping that someday she might overdose. But her religion forbids suicide.

Tyrone returns with his bottle, bitterly denouncing Jamie for trying to break his padlock to the basement, where he stores his whiskey. When he asks for Edmund, Mary replies that he must have gone uptown to join Jamie. At first she speaks with her *"vague far-away air,"* then she explodes into tears and throws herself at James—"Oh, James, I'm so frightened! . . . I know he's going to die!" (3:789). James tells her that a specialist Hardy called assured him Edmund would recover in six months. She responds that had Edmund never been born, "he wouldn't have had to know his mother was a dope fiend—and hate her!" (3:790). James reassures her that Edmund loves her dearly.

Cathleen comes in to announce dinner. She is obviously drunk, and when James looks at her with an air of disapproval, she informs him that Mary invited her to the whiskey and exits with overdramatic hauteur. Mary informs him that she is no longer hungry and will go upstairs to bed. He knows what this means: "You'll be like a mad ghost before the night's over!" (3:790). She again pretends not to understand and heads upstairs. James stands frozen in the living room, then moves to the dining room, *"a sad, bewildered, broken old man"* (3:791).

## Act 4

The same, around midnight. The foghorn wails in the distance, followed again by the bells from the ships in the harbor. The fog outside appears thicker. James Tyrone is discovered at the table wearing pince-nez and playing solitaire. He is drunk, and a bottle of whiskey, two-thirds emptied, stands on the table with another full bottle beside it. Regardless of the amount he has drunk, *"he has not escaped, and looks as he appeared at the close of the preceding act, a sad, defeated old man, possessed by hopeless resignation."* As the curtain rises, he scoops up the deck of cards and begins shuffling drunkenly. Edmund enters, also drunk; like his father, he holds it well. Only his eyes and a *"chip-on-the-shoulder aggressiveness in his manner"* indicate his drunken state (3:792).

James welcomes him warmly, sincerely glad for his younger son's company. He demands, however, that Edmund turn out the light in the front hall to conserve energy, which causes a brief argument over his miserliness and his dismissal of facts—that a bulb burning all day costs less than one drink, or his insistence that "Shakespeare was an Irish Catholic" (3:793). When Edmund refuses to turn out the light, James threatens him physically, then backs off—remembering the doctor's prognosis—and begins turning on all the lights with an exaggerated devil-may-care attitude. Jamie is still out, and they assume, correctly, he is at a brothel. James offers Edmund a drink, though he knows the doctors have warned Edmund to abstain. They drink, and Edmund tells him that he went out walking in the fog before returning home. James scolds him for his lack of sense, but Edmund explains how therapeutic the experience was. He quotes from Ernest Dowson, ending with the lines, "'They are not long, the days of wine and roses: / Out of a misty dream / Our path emerges for a while, then closes / Within a dream.'" Wandering alone through the fog, Edmund felt as if he were walking at the bottom of the sea—"As if I was a ghost belonging to the fog, and the fog was the ghost of the sea. It felt damned peaceful to be nothing more than a ghost within a ghost" (3:796).

James disapproves of this morbid thinking, but Edmund retorts, "Who wants to see life as it is, if they can help it?" James blames Edmund's dark worldview on the poets he reads. "Why can't you remember your Shakespeare and forget the third-raters. You'll find everything you're trying to say in him—as you'll find everything else worth saying." He then matches Dowson with a quote from *The Tempest*: "'We are such stuff as dreams are made on, and our little life is rounded with sleep.'" Edmund admits to the beauty of the lines, then sardonically adds, "But I wasn't trying to say that. We are such stuff as manure is made on, so let's drink up and forget it" (3:796). They continue the literary dispute, but it only leads to talk of dope fiends and consumption, subjects too close to the family's own predicament.

Before long they return to Mary's condition. She can be heard moving about above them. "She'll be nothing but a ghost haunting the past by this time," Edmund says, harking back to the period before he was born. She torments James in the same way, commenting on her life before she met him, but he reflects the reality of her life, and her "great, generous, noble Irish gentleman" of a father, whom James liked but who had his failings, namely his alcoholism—"it finished him quick—that and the consumption—" (3:800). Edmund notes their inability to avoid "unpleasant topics," and they try to amuse themselves with a card game but quickly resume their discussion of Mary. James says that she exaggerates her potential as a concert pianist as well. There is a momentary scare of her coming downstairs, but she does not appear. "The hardest thing to take is the blank wall she builds around her," Edmund says. "Or it's more like a bank of fog in which she hides and loses herself" (3:801). James reminds him that "she's not responsible." Edmund agrees, angrily blaming his father's miserliness. "Jesus," he explodes, "when I think of it I hate your guts!" (3:803).

Edmund apologizes with sincere self-reproach, then brings up his own past, traveling the world with no money and all the while trying to understand his father's terror of poverty. He admits he made serious mistakes and behaved terribly toward his father in his own way. But he found out that his father had convinced Doctor Hardy to find the cheapest, state-run facility he could find. Fuming over his father's stinginess, Edmund succumbs to a fit of coughing. James is once again overcome with anger and guilt, but Edmund's condemnation draws out the truth about his poverty-stricken childhood. Edmund's adventure abroad, he says,

"was a game of romance and adventure to you. It was play." Edmund responds with acerbic irony: "Yes, particularly the time I tried to commit suicide at Jimmie the Priest's, and almost did." His father attributes Edmund's depressive episode to alcohol, but Edmund submits that he was "stone cold sober. That was the trouble. I'd stopped to think too long" (3:807).

James describes how his father left his mother and siblings to die in Ireland (probably by suicide) and how he eventually overcame their situation through his love of the theater. Ever since, he has been terrified of dying in the "poor house" and promises Edmund he can go to any sanatorium he wants—"within reason" (3:808). Edmund grins at his father's predictable addendum. James continues with an admission that he has never told anyone before—"that God-damned play I bought for a song and made such a great success in [*The Count of Monte Cristo*]—a great money success— it ruined me with its promise of an easy fortune" (3:809). Edwin Booth, "the greatest actor of his day or any other," had remarked while costarring in *Othello* with James, that at 27, James played a better Othello than he ever could. But the profit from the moneymaker was too great a temptation; James had given up his promise as an artist. "What the hell was it I wanted to buy, I wonder," he soberly asks himself, "that was worth—" (3:810). Edmund expresses sincere gratitude, as the admission explains a great deal about James he never knew. He assents to his father's request that they turn out the lights.

Edmund relates some "high spots" from his own life—moments of revelation always "connected with the sea" (3:811). "It was a great mistake, my being born a man," he concludes. "I would have been much more successful as a sea gull or a fish. As it is, I will always be a stranger who never feels at home, who does not really want and is not really wanted, who can never belong, who must always be a little in love with death!" (3:812). James compliments his son's poetic nature but protests about the final line of not being wanted and longing for death. Edmund disagrees with his father that he has the "*makings* of a poet"—"No, I'm afraid I'm like the guy who is always panhandling for a smoke.

He hasn't even got the makings. He's only got the habit. I couldn't touch what I tried to tell you just now. I just stammered. That's the best I'll ever do. I mean, if I live. Well, it will be faithful realism, at least. Stammering is the native eloquence of us fog people" (3:812–813). The two hear Jamie approach, evidently stumbling on the doorstep, and, afraid of losing his temper, James escapes to the porch.

Jamie enters, drunk and boisterous, and shouts with false merriment, "What ho! What ho!" (3:813). Slurring his words, he complains about the darkness, recites a line of Kipling's, and turns on the lights, referring to their father as "Gaspard" (a miserly character in drama). He looks down at the bottle of whiskey in astonishment. Edmund warns that another drink will make him pass out; but then he suggests they both have a drink. Jamie initially refuses, given Edmund's condition, but like his father, he eventually assents. Jamie rails against James's stingy refusal to send Edmund to the best possible sanatorium, but Edmund explains that he and their father worked it out, and that James will pay for any place "within reason."

Jamie has returned from a local brothel run by a madam called Mamie Burns. He relates that Mamie wanted to fire a prostitute named Fat Violet because men rarely choose her, and she eats and drinks too much. Jamie, who "likes them fat, but not that fat," sympathetically chose Violet. "Ready for a weep on any old womanly bosom," he told her he loved her and remained with her for a time, which apparently cheered her up (3:816). Jamie rambles on about actors being trained seals, his low prospects, and his grim view of life, all the while reciting poetry that speaks to his fatalistic mood. Edmund finally tells him to shut up, and he stares at him threateningly until finally agreeing with his brother. But then, *in a cruel, sneering tone with hatred in it,"* he asks, "Where's the hophead?" Edmund starts at the words and punches Jamie in the face. Jamie braces for a fight but settles down and thanks him. He explains his bitterness about their mother, believing that "if she'd beaten the game, I could, too."

Jamie recalls the first time he caught Mary with a hypodermic needle in her hand: "Christ, I'd never dreamed before that any women but whores took dope!" (3:818). The return of her habit, along with Edmund's diagnosis, has crushed his spirit. He swears he loves Edmund, though he intimates that Edmund must be suspicious that he might be looking forward to his death, as then Jamie and their mother would inherit the estate exclusively. Edmund indignantly demands to know what made him think of that. Jamie first acts confused and then resentful, and finally launches into a full-blown jealous fury. Everything Edmund has achieved, everything he knows, came from him. "Hell, you're more than my brother. I made you! You're my Frankenstein!" (3:819). This outburst does little but amuse Edmund, who suggests they have another drink.

Jamie gulps down a massive drink and turns sentimental. He wants to confess something he should have told Edmund years before—that his inducting Edmund into his world of prostitutes, booze, and dark philosophy was a deliberate plan to destroy his one great competitor, along with the person responsible, if indirectly, for making his mother a morphine addict. "I know that's not your fault, but all the same, God damn you, I can't help hating your guts—!" (3:820). Frightened now, Edmund again tells him to shut up. "But," Jamie continues, "don't get the wrong idea, Kid. I love you more than I hate you." It is the part of him that died that hates him, and it is that part of him that he warns Edmund to avoid at all costs. For when Edmund returns from the sanatorium, he says, "I'll be waiting to welcome you with that 'my old pal' stuff, and give you the glad hand, and at the first chance I get stab you in the back" (3:821). He admits this is a Catholic-style confession and believes his brother will absolve him. The last drink was too much for Jamie. He closes his eyes, lies back in a chair, and falls into a drunken half-sleep.

James reenters. He tells Edmund that he should heed Jamie's warning, though he assures him that Jamie is devoted to him. "It's the one good thing left in him" (3:822). He again rants over his eldest son's wasted promise, which wakes Jamie up, and the two hurl vicious accusations at each other. Edmund tries to stop them, but Jamie gives up the fight. Both he and James drift off into another drunken doze (3:823).

The lights in the parlor come on abruptly, and Mary begins playing a simple waltz on the piano. The men's eyes snap open. The music stops, and Mary enters wearing a sky-blue dress over her nightgown and slippers with pompoms, carrying her wedding dress on one arm. *"Her eyes look enormous. They glisten like polished black jewels. The uncanny thing is that her face now appears so youthful. Experience seems ironed out of it. It is a marble mask of girlish innocence, the mouth caught in a shy smile"* (3:823). Jamie sardonically breaks the silence. "The Mad Scene. Enter Ophelia!" (3:824—the female lead in Shakespeare's *Hamlet* who loses her sanity) Edmund slaps him across the mouth with the back of his hand. James applauds Edmund and threatens to kick Jamie out of the house.

Mary notices none of this. She speaks as if she is still a convent schoolgirl, wondering why her hands are so swollen and commenting that she must go to the nun's infirmary. She ponders what it was she wanted in the living room. James awkwardly takes the wedding dress from her. She thanks him as if he were a kind stranger. James cries out to her with no effect, and Jamie, who sees that any attempt at real contact is fruitless, begins reciting Swinburne's poem "A Leave-Taking." Mary goes on that without that which she is searching for, she believes she will suffer loneliness and fear.

Edmund grabs her arm and announces desperately that he has consumption. For an instant, she returns to reality, but she fights the pain of the present and returns to the sanctity of the past. Jamie continues his recitation, and James remarks miserably that he has "never known her to drown herself in it as deep as this" (3:827). The men raise their whiskey glasses, but Mary resumes her reveries of girlhood, and they slowly lower them back on the table. Mary relates a discussion she had senior year at the convent with Mother Elizabeth over her prospects as nun. She experienced a vision of the Virgin Mary at the shrine of Our Lady of Lourdes. The Blessed Virgin consented to Mary becoming a nun. Mother Elizabeth advised her to test herself first by "living as other girls lived, going out to parties and dances and enjoying myself." After that, if she still wished to be a nun, then they would talk it over. "That was the winter of my senior year," she con-

cludes. "Then in the spring something happened to me. Yes, I remember. I fell in love with James Tyrone and was so happy for a time" (3:828).

The brothers sit frozen in their seats. James shifts in his chair. Mary *"stares before her in a sad dream"* (3:828), and the curtain falls.

## COMMENTARY

*Long Day's Journey into Night* is an impressive work of art whether one knows about O'Neill's actual biography or not. But when we do know it, the play can only be described as a tour de force. Eugene O'Neill presented an inscription to his wife Carlotta Monterey O'Neill on their 12th wedding anniversary that reveals a great deal about O'Neill's autobiographical relationship to *Long Day's Journey* and its characters. It reads, in part:

> Dearest: I give you the original script of this play of old sorrow, written in tears and blood. A sadly inappropriate gift, it would seem, for a day celebrating happiness. But you will understand. I mean it as a tribute to your love and tenderness which gave me the faith in love that enabled me to face my dead at last and write this play—write it with deep pity and understanding and forgiveness for *all* the four haunted Tyrones. (3:714)

Few artists, no matter their stature, have been able to achieve this level of immortality in a single work. O'Neill did so, remarkably, *after* winning the NOBEL PRIZE IN LITERATURE in 1936, and it won him his fourth Pulitzer Prize. Who among his audience in 1956 knew that the mother of America's greatest playwright, Mary Ellen "Ella" O'Neill, had been a morphine addict for over 25 years? That his brother, James O'Neill, Jr. (Jamie), would have exerted such a Mephistophelian influence on the playwright at such a young age? That his father, the great matinee idol James O'Neill, one of the most celebrated actors of his time, had lived in such a painful state of perpetual regret and with an Irish-born terror of poverty only alcohol and a nearly manic acquisition of real estate could ease his suffering? Certainly no one who did not know the notoriously closed personality of O'Neill intimately, and even several who did.

However, Doris Alexander, in *Eugene O'Neill's Last Plays: Separating Art from Autobiography*, proposes a stern caveat to O'Neill's audiences, but particularly his BIOGRAPHERS. She contends that an "unfortunate result" of Carlotta's choice of inscription (O'Neill actually wrote her several) is that it predisposed biographers "to see the play as faithful family biography and personal autobiography, rather than as the universal human tragedy of the impossibility, with the chances of life and pressures of the past, for anyone to live faithful to his idea of what he wished to be and achieve" (2005, 153). When read alongside most scholarship on *Long Day's Journey*, Alexander's thesis stands as possibly the most revolutionary yet in O'Neill studies: "A great work of art cannot stay factually true to the complexities of life. . . . The unwary biographer who raids a so-called autobiographical play for the facts of an author's life will end up disseminating a mass of misinformation" (2005, 147).

Alexander introduces a raft of carefully researched historical evidence that contradicts some of the most poignant details in the play—Ella O'Neill's unhappiness on the road with her husband (by all accounts she was cheerful, surrounded by friends, and boarded at the finest hotels), her desire to join a convent (Carlotta wanted this, not Ella), the idea that she married below her station by marrying an actor (IRISH-AMERICAN culture in general and her family in particular held a great deal of esteem for the acting profession), James's limiting his repertoire to *Monte Cristo* (he played many other roles over the period), James's resentment of Jamie as a "loafer" (which sounds closer to O'Neill's anger against his son, Shane, at the time of composition), among many others. Incredibly, Alexander even found no evidence that the O'Neill family called anything but their first, much smaller house in New London "Monte Cristo" (2005, 102).

Based entirely on fact or no, and as penetrating as O'Neill's insights are into his family life and the development of his personality and career, many ask why it should matter that the play is autobiographical, or how that fact adds in any way to the drama. One answer is that regardless of O'Neill's heart-wrenching dramatization of his family life in the early 1910s, many in the audience of *Long Day's Journey* have, in fact, comparable, oftentimes much worse, experiences growing up than O'Neill. It is this the terrible truth, this "universality of pain," as Travis Bogard has suggested, that "makes pity and understanding and forgiveness the greatest of all human needs" (427). *Long Day's Journey* lends these usually repressed human needs—"pity and understanding and forgiveness"—a startlingly authentic voice.

O'Neill had an unprecedented talent for representing in art a deeply personal sense of bitterness, love, and understanding for those who shaped him. One cannot, therefore, consider O'Neill in a traditional way as the detached playwright off in the wings with the actors as vehicles through which words are simply transferred to an audience. The ghost of the 53-year-old O'Neill haunts theaters as a near-tangible presence in the best productions of *Long Day's Journey*. O'Neill is even more strongly felt than the autobiographical character Edmund Tyrone. Whether the play is based on fact or on an expressionistic sense of what was true beneath the surface, in *Long Day's Journey* O'Neill becomes more than a creator—in this drama, the playwright is the protagonist.

O'Neill's symbolic use of fog enhances this sensation perhaps even more, again, than the highly autobiographical Edmund Tyrone. Fog in New London, Connecticut—a very real and recurring phenomenon—seems to slink into everything in the town, creating an actual connection between New London and the sea. It obviously left an early and longstanding impression on the playwright, who titled one of his earliest one-act plays, a work that has a strong autobiographical component as well, *FOG*. In *Long Day's Journey*, the fog enhances the tragic sense of unity, enclosure, and isolation for the Tyrones. Beginning with Mary's ominous prediction in act 1 that the fog will return, using her rheumatism (a physical ailment symbolizing greater spiritual pain) as a "weather prophet" (3:736), O'Neill employs fog symbolically throughout the play. In act 2, scene 2, James agrees with Mary about the fog rolling in once he has discovered that her morphine addiction has relapsed: "Yes, I spoke too soon. We're in for another night of fog, I'm afraid" (3:762). Later, in the opening stage directions of act 3, the foghorn sounds as a warning to the Tyrones, *"moaning like a mournful whale in labor"* (3:772); here O'Neill provides a subtle reminder of the cause of Mary's addiction—labor pains—as Mary devolves into her adolescent high. At that point, she tells Cathleen how she has come to appreciate the fog (now symbolizing the effects of the drug), as it "hides you from the world and the world from you. You feel that everything has changed, and nothing is what it seemed to be. No one can find or touch you any more" (3:773). Once Edmund and James return, however, she feels that "the fog makes everything sound so sad and lost" (3:789), a remark that chases Edmund from the house and into the foggy night.

But Edmund also finds peace in the fog. For Edmund, the fog acts as a "veil" that he can draw between himself and the outer world. "I loved the fog," he says to his father. "The fog was where I wanted to be. . . . Everything looked and sounded unreal. Nothing was what it is. That's what I wanted—to be alone with myself in another world where truth is untrue and life can hide from itself" (3:795–796). Here we feel O'Neill's presence most strongly in the play: "It was like walking at the bottom of the sea. As if I had drowned long ago. As if I was a ghost belonging to the fog, and the fog was the ghost of the sea. It felt damned peaceful to be nothing more than a ghost within a ghost" (3:796).

*Long Day's Journey's* intensely personal nature affords the play its stature in American theater history. "This stature has to do with the deepest kind of emotional suffering," argues Michael Manheim, "accompanied by the recognition and understanding of that suffering *by the sufferer*" (1998, 214; emphasis mine). O'Neill struggled to achieve this effect throughout his career. As early as his very first full-length play, he never relinquished this "personal equation" in his work. Max Stirner, the founding philosopher of PHILOSOPHICAL ANARCHISM whose *The Ego and His Own* O'Neill lists in his stage directions as being on Edmund Tyrone's bookshelf, noted: "I write because I want to procure for *my* thoughts an existence in the world" (205). And one can gather by O'Neill scholars' obsessive drive to connect the plays and characters to others in the canon that the same themes eternally recur—

some with triumphant success, others abysmal failure—and form a dialogue with one another that culminates in *Long Day's Journey*. Travis Bogard, O'Neill's most penetrating critic, helpfully sums up these recurrent themes in what still stands as the masterwork of O'Neill criticism, *Contour in Time*:

> The image of the poet destroyed by the materialist . . . the mother who is a betrayer of her children and who resents being the object of their need; brothers bound in opposition; wives who persecute their husbands; fathers and children fixed in a pattern of love and hate; the maternal whore to whom men turn for surcease; men and women who feed on dreams. (445)

Each of these themes informs O'Neill's work, if by varying degrees. And the importance of O'Neill bringing them together in the living room of Monte Cristo Cottage in New London, Connecticut—the one house in his life he might call a home—must never be dismissed. Its deeply personal nature brings the play to life in a way that he had not been able achieve with ambitious but somewhat flawed plays like BEYOND THE HORIZON, STRANGE INTERLUDE, and MOURNING BECOMES ELECTRA. For *Long Day's Journey*, O'Neill abandoned all his many avatars—of himself and his family—and went directly to the emotional source. It is no wonder that he repressed his cherished masterpiece, stipulating that it not be published until 25 years after his death and never be produced. What outsider, O'Neill must have asked himself, might bastardize or bowdlerize his most sacred, most personal work?

Parallels exist between *Long Day's Journey* and virtually every O'Neill work, major or minor, extending as far back as his first play, A WIFE FOR A LIFE ("Greater love hath no man than this" [1:821]) and as far forward as his last, *A Moon for the Misbegotten*. Anna Christopherson's avowal to her father, Chris, in *"ANNA CHRISTIE,"* for instance, looks forward to Mary's repeated contention that nothing is anyone's fault. "Don't bawl about it," Anna says, "There ain't nothing to forgive, anyway. It ain't your fault, and it ain't mine. . . . We're all poor nuts, and things happen, and we yust get mixed in wrong, that's all." Chris responds: "You say right tang, Anna, py golly! It ain't nobody's fault!" (1:1,015). *"Anna Christie"* was O'Neill's last major work of NATURALISM, a form to which he would return with *Long Day's Journey*, before he began to experiment with EXPRESSIONISM in the 1920s and early 1930s. In this experimental phase, O'Neill used symbols of artifice meant to illuminate characters' inner feelings. Oftentimes, as in *DAYS WITHOUT END*, the stage "tricks" O'Neill devised were less than subtle, and critics varied in their responses from respectfully reticent to downright hostile. In *Days*, for instance, along with *The GREAT GOD BROWN* and *LAZARUS LAUGHED*, actual masks were employed—successfully and unsuccessfully—as "mercurial facades designed to control [characters'] dual personalities" (Floyd 534). Oftentimes, inner thoughts and feelings were also revealed through MELODRAMA, a genre designed to manipulate the audience's emotional response through plot devices, as in *Beyond the Horizon* and *WELDED*; and even through the supernatural, as in *BOUND EAST FOR CARDIFF*, *WHERE THE CROSS IS MADE*, and *The HAIRY APE* (which also deployed masks in its first production, with O'Neill's enthusiastic permission, though he does not specify them in his stage directions).

Although these experimental plays treat corresponding themes, O'Neill returned to his early naturalism and abandoned nearly all theatrical artifice in *Long Day's Journey*. In this play, defensive masks, previously worn by the actors in his expressionistic plays, are stripped away through actual experience and the interchange of dialogue. If, in *Long Day's Journey*, Mary's face while drugged takes on the appearance of a *"marble mask of girlish innocence"* (3:823), an actress playing Margaret Dion in *The Great God Brown* wears an actual mask for the same effect. O'Neill biographer Louis Sheaffer attests that with *Long Day's Journey*, O'Neill "now scrupulously abstained from all novelty and unusual devices, anything that smacked of theatricality; in order to show with absolute candor, with unmistakable integrity, the familial forces that had kneaded, shaped, and warped him" (512). Travis Bogard adds that once O'Neill's characters' masks were removed, mostly through alcohol and morphine, "Over their words there hangs no hint of the Art Theatre Show Shop. O'Neill has enabled his

actors to motivate the monologues and make them convincingly natural, psychologically real" (426).

Edmund Tyrone's admission to his father that he could only achieve "faithful realism" through "stammering" (3:812) can thus be read as a literary admission on the part of the author. Significantly, when we consider O'Neill's late interest in EAST ASIAN THOUGHT, Edmund's line resembles the Taoist philosopher Lao Tzu's criticism of language as powerless to capture the perfection of the Tao (the "Way"). Edmund's admittance that "stammering is the native eloquence of us fog people" (3:812–813) thus associates him with mystical thinking. By expressing false modesty in his poetic ability, one that greatly impresses his highly poetic father, Edmund shows that the limitations of language itself are more to blame than he.

*Long Day's Journey* can never be considered "slice of life" REALISM, however, in which no dramatic structure or rhythmic patterns guide the action from day into night. According to O'Neill himself, the play is meant to enact a blame game among its players, in which we come to recognize, as he titled some notes in his WORK DIARY, "Shifting alliances in battle." He specifies these alliance shifts in the internecine warfare of the family as "Father, two sons versus Mother; Mother, two sons versus Father; Father, younger son versus Mother, older son; Mother, younger son versus Father, older son; Father and Mother versus two sons; Brother versus brother; Father versus Mother" (quoted in Floyd 549n). Each Tyrone suppresses the pain felt by condemning others, and when that fails, they turn to stimulants—Mary to morphine, James to real estate, Edmund to poetry written by "whoremongers and degenerates" (3:799), Jamie to sex with overweight prostitutes, and all three men to whiskey. When they discover the impotence of stimulants and sex for long-term surcease, they return to the blame game. Such diversions stand in stark contrast to those enjoyed by most of the family members in O'Neill's late comedy *AH, WILDERNESS!*, which can be read as O'Neill's dream family against the more closely accurate home life we find in *Long Day's Journey*.

Biographer Stephen A. Black characterizes the play's action as a series of "quasi-judicial proceedings, in which accusations and denials are made, evidence is adduced" (444). Psychologically, Black continues, the "process of the play reveals a state of inertia in the family in which "arguments transform into grievances, which prevent sadness from ever being directly felt and loss from being directly acknowledged. Thus, the sadness of loss is avoided, but at the price of constant pain, and at the further cost that loss can never be mourned, outgrown, and left behind" (445). Each character attempts to control suffering by understanding the root cause of it (444); the overall rhythm of the play thus becomes a back and forth of "accusation-regret, harshness-pity, hate-love" (Berlin 89). The final act, then, Virginia Floyd suggests, forms a "round-robin battle" amongst them all (549).

Along with the more evident repetition we find in *The Iceman Cometh*—an aspect of the play critics find either musical or maddening—*Long Day's Journey* also approaches the rhythmical standards of a symphony. "People say O'Neill's plays are repetitious," wrote *Long Day's Journey*'s first American director, José Quintero, "but he wrote like a composer, building theme on theme, and variation on theme" (quoted in Murphy 19). Each recriminatory outburst by one or more family members against the others is relieved by a constant and reassuring "marker of the undercurrent of mutual trust that exists beneath the turbulence of their relationship" (Manheim 1998, 207). All of this brilliantly culminates in the appearance of Mary Tyrone, higher on morphine than any of the Tyrone men had ever seen—a "delayed entrance" that O'Neill profitably used for the characters Anna Christopherson in *"Anna Christie,"* Cornelius "Con" Melody in *A Touch of the Poet,* and Theodore "Hickey" Hickman in *Iceman,* among others, but never to such a devastating final effect (Bloom 226).

Critics often regard *Long Day's Journey* as the finest domestic tragedy of the 20th century. Starting with the Greeks, the earliest tragedians, Aeschylus, Euripides, and Sophocles—all of whom O'Neill tapped for contemporary interpretations of modern life—the term *tragedy* as a dramatic formula generally refers to a grandiose treatment of the miseries of mankind and the power of fate to alter the course of even the most awe-inspiring individuals, those who simultaneously suffer from and rise above their destinies. Tragedy must also "achieve genuine and widely acknowledged emotional catharsis and it must convincingly portray an image of fallen greatness" (Manheim 1998, 216). Building on GREEK TRAGEDY, tragedy in a domestic setting as in *Long Day's Journey* began in the 18th century and became a hallmark of modern theater into our own time.

O'Neill adheres to the sense of tragic unity Aristotle had established in his *Poetics*—restricting dramatic action (the "unity of action") and, less importantly, establishing a limited time frame of approximately 24 hours. O'Neill additionally conforms to later interpretations of tragic unity by restricting the physical location to one area and introducing few characters. In the Tyrones' sitting room, the plot moves forward from day (a normal family) to night (a tragic sense of inevitable, mutual doom) only as the revelations of the four characters emerge through dialogue rather than action. O'Neill applied the same tragic unity in action, time, and space in *The Iceman Cometh, A Touch of the Poet,* and *A Moon for the Misbegotten.*

James and Mary Tyrone, along with their dissipated son Jamie, each present two selves to the audience—the selves that might have achieved their potential and the selves that they have been fated to endure (see Floyd 541). Along with his tuberculosis, Edmund's tragedy is essentially limited to the troubling fact of having been born among them, just as Mary's tragedy (according to her) derives from having given birth to Edmund and, before that, marrying James. Edmund, then, is the least culpable of the four suffering Tyrones. Few of the actual, morally questionable past actions of Eugene O'Neill himself arise in the play—abandoning his first wife, KATHLEEN JENKINS, and their child, Eugene O'Neill, Jr., for instance, which happened before summer 1912. The worst we know of Edmund is that he spent time drinking heavily in derelict bars, attempted suicide, and lived on a beach in South America, all of which actually happened to O'Neill before summer 1912. That Edmund's birth caused Mary's addiction is a consciously irrational source of resentment on the part of Jamie and Mary, though it still fosters guilt on

Edmund's part. Rather than regret what he has done or take on blame he could have controlled, Edmund finds the tragic core of his existence in the fact that he was "born a man"—"I would have been much more successful as a sea gull or a fish. As it is, I will always be a stranger who never feels at home, who does not really want and is not really wanted, who can never belong, who must always be a little in love with death!" (3:812).

O'Neill's Irish background is an aspect of the playwright's life that critics generally ignored during his lifetime. O'Neill considered this a profound oversight. "The one thing that explains more than anything about me," he told his son, Eugene, Jr., "is the fact that I'm Irish" (quoted in Floyd 537). It also might be the one thing that can explain the most about *Long Day's Journey*. Although *A Moon for the Misbegotten* and *A Touch of the Poet* are most often identified as his most "Irish" plays, O'Neill includes many noticeable Irish characteristics among the characters in *Long Day's Journey* as well: their lyrical use of language and quick mood reversals; their physical features ("keep your dirty tongue off Ireland!" James shouts at Jamie. "You're a fine one to sneer, with the map of it on your face!" [3:761]); heavy whiskey drinking; the family's natural sympathy with the tenant farmer Shaughnessy over the Standard Oil magnate Harker, a comic parable of the tensions between Irish and New England Yankee culture and class associations; James's assertion that Edmund's "self-destruction" stems from his denial of "the one true faith of the Catholic church" (3:759); the fact that O'Neill decided on the name *Tyrone* because that is the county in Ireland "where the earliest O'Neills had ruled as warrior kings" (Sheaffer 512); or even James O'Neill's terror of tuberculosis as inevitably lethal, and thus considering a proper sanatorium for Edmund not worth facing poverty for.

Michael Manheim finds the source of the family's particular tragedy in the mother figure: "Tragedy is by its nature both devastating and uplifting—and so is the appearance of the life-giving/life-destroying mother—the source of their love and their hate—both devastating and uplifting" (1998, 216). Indeed, the fact that Mary acts as the thematic muse is probably the most Irish Catholic aspect of the play. All the Tyrones live under the general assumption that no one is responsible for his or her pain, but they repeatedly have to convince themselves of this. Regardless of her consistent faith in the imposition of the past on the present, Mary levels more blame on the other family members than any other character. As the sitting room increasingly takes the form of a confessional (Sheaffer 514), O'Neill significantly indicated in the margins of an early draft that he intended Mary Tyrone to recite a pertinent line from the "Lord's Prayer," which, though absent in the final version, reflects the ultimate desire of the Tyrone clan: "Forgive us our trespasses as we forgive those who trespass against us" (quoted in Floyd 553).

Mother-figure worship is a prevailing theme in the O'Neill canon—along with *Long Day's Journey*, it figures prominently in *The Great God Brown*, *Strange Interlude*, and *A Moon for the Misbegotten*, among others—and the pain that ensues when abandoned by the mother is a traditional obsession among men raised in Catholicism. In fact, one reason José Quintero believed he felt such a strong affinity for O'Neill's work is that he understood "the guilt that all men of the Western world, particularly those raised Catholic, have over the fact that their mothers had to have sex to have them" (quoted in Murphy 17). Edward Shaughnessy has written of "the cult of Mariolatry (Mary worship)" in Irish culture, in which the Irish Catholic people "nearly deified the wife-mother and equated her station with that of the Blessed Virgin Mary" (161). Hence O'Neill's choice to call the mother's character by her given name, Mary, rather than Ella, the name his mother went by. The most openly forgiving member of the Tyrone family, Mary is also the most hurtful. On the one hand, she voices the one thematic thread underscoring all of their utterances and actions—that the past dictates the course of their lives, present and future. "The past is the present, isn't it?" Mary tells Jamie. "It's the future, too. We all try to lie out of that but life won't let us" (3:765).

## CHARACTERS

**Cathleen** The Tyrone family's "second girl," or servant working under the offstage cook, Bridget.

O'Neill describes Cathleen as "*a buxom Irish peasant, in her early twenties, with a red-cheeked comely
face, black hair and blues eyes—amiable, ignorant,
clumsy, and possessed by a dense, well-meaning stu-
pidity*" (3:743). Cathleen, who resembles the second girl, Norah, in *Ah, Wilderness!*, adds a further
Irish touch to the play, along with some very brief
comic relief. In the opening scene of act 3, Mary
Tyrone offers Cathleen whiskey, and the servant
girl becomes humorously bold under the influence.
When Mary complains about her husband's drinking habits, Cathleen defends James Tyrone as having "a good man's failing" (3:774). Edmund later
expresses shock that Mary allowed Cathleen to buy
morphine from the suspicious pharmacist, worrying
that she might gossip about it in town. Cathleen
does not, then, share the Tyrones' isolation, and
she can be seen as their one connection to the
outside world. Apparently O'Neill's fictionalized
concern was unwarranted. According to sources
who knew Mary Ellen "Ella" O'Neill, even her closest friends never suspected her of having a drug
addiction until 1917. In that year, she underwent a
mastectomy operation, and it became public knowledge that she consequently "became used to drugs"
(quoted in Alexander 122).

**Tyrone, Edmund**   James and Mary Tyrone's son
and James Tyrone, Jr.'s brother. Eugene O'Neill's
most autobiographical character, the 23-year-old
Edmund is the end result of a long line of autobiographical avatars, such as John Brown in *BREAD
AND BUTTER*, the Poet in *Fog*, Robert Mayo in
*Beyond the Horizon*, Stephen Murray in *The Straw*,
Richard Miller in *Ah, Wilderness!*, and Simon Harford in *MORE STATELY MANSIONS*, among others.
Edmund's physical characteristics closely match
those of these previous avatars and the playwright
himself. O'Neill describes Edmund as looking most
like his mother—"*thin and wiry*," "*big, dark eyes*,"
"*high forehead*," "*exceptionally long fingers*," and
exhibiting a marked "*quality of extreme nervous sensibility*" (3:723); this last characteristic shows where
he most evidently resembles his mother.

Edmund shares Eugene O'Neill's older brother's
name, EDMUND O'NEILL, who died at the age of two
after James O'Neill, Jr. (Jamie), apparently infected

him with measles. The death of the young boy, of
course, had an enormously traumatic effect on the
family, and O'Neill seems to express some feelings
of survivor guilt by naming his most autobiographical character after him. "Nothing was more true of
O'Neill," writes biographer Louis Sheaffer on his
naming the character Edmund, "than that he had a
strong death wish" (512).

Mary Tyrone experienced a great deal of pain
at Edmund's birth and was subsequently prescribed
morphine to dull the pain. In the context of the
play, if questionable in real life, Edmund's birth
caused Mary's nearly 25-year addiction to the drug.
Jamie Tyrone consciously understands that this
unwanted result of the birth was not Edmund's
fault, but he cannot help blaming him. "I know
that's not your fault," Jamie yells at him, very
drunk, in act 4, "but all the same, God damn you, I
can't help hating your guts—!" (3:820).

Edmund works as a reporter for a local paper in
New London, Connecticut, where he occasionally
publishes POETRY, as his creator had done in 1912.
He also writes poems that his father, and even his
dissipated brother, Jamie, find morbid. Again like
his creator, Edmund worked in the MERCHANT
MARINE for some time and lived for a sordid period
on beaches in South America. Edmund describes
the revelatory experience of lying on the bowsprit
of a "Squarehead square rigger" bound for BUE-
NOS AIRES, ARGENTINA (in O'Neill's life, the SS
*CHARLES RACINE*). Looking out over the sea, he
"became drunk with the beauty and singing rhythm
of it, and for a moment I lost myself—actually lost
my life. I was set free!" (3:811). He experienced
similar epiphanies on a ship owned by the American Line (in real life the SS *NEW YORK* or the SS
*PHILADELPHIA*) and while swimming and lying on
the beach. After his time at sea, he boarded at a
bar in New York City called JIMMY "THE PRIEST'S,"
where he attempted suicide. His father blames
the suicide attempt on alcohol, but according to
Edmund, he was "stone cold sober. That was the
trouble. I'd stopped to think too long" (3:807).

O'Neill's autobiographical character is perhaps
too noticeably the least of the Tyrone clan to blame
for their misery. Scholars often remark on Edmund's
portrayal as a "relatively flawless" character who

"alone is not stripped naked to the core of his soul" (Floyd 543, 536); Edmund comes across, unlike the other Tyrones, as "a curiously two-dimensional reflection, whose past has been bowdlerized and whose negative characteristics are only lightly touched ... certainly a pale copy of what Eugene O'Neill was at that time" (Bogard 432, 435). There is no mention, for instance, of O'Neill's having been kicked out of Princeton University his freshman year for vandalism, drunkenness, and poor academic standing, or having abandoned his first wife, Kathleen Jenkins, and their baby, Eugene O'Neill, Jr., with whom he did not start to form a relationship until the boy turned 11. This limited characterization, the play's most apparent flaw, has been explained by Travis Bogard as the playwright discovering his identity "in the agony of others" (445).

**Tyrone, James** Mary Tyrone's husband and Edmund and Jamie Tyrone, Jr.'s father; based closely on Eugene O'Neill's actual father, James O'Neill. O'Neill describes James as a robust, strikingly handsome man of 65. James looks closer to 55 and exhibits the grandiloquent presence of the matinee idol he once was. Nevertheless, O'Neill writes in his stage directions, *"He is by nature and preference a simple, unpretentious man, whose inclinations are still close to his humble beginnings and his Irish farmer forebears"* (3:718). Like the other Tyrones, O'Neill wrote many avatars of his father, including Abraham Bentley in *The ROPE*; Cornelius "Con" Melody in *A Touch of the Poet*; and the stern New Englanders Captain David Keeney in *ILE*, Ephraim Cabot in *DESIRE UNDER THE ELMS*, and Ezra Mannon in *Mourning Becomes Electra*, among others. Like Ezra Mannon, James loves his estranged wife very much and "gradually emerges more victim than culprit" (Sheaffer 515), and like Con Melody, James Tyrone "is both poet and peasant" (Bogard 430). O'Neill once characterized his father to his second wife, AGNES BOULTON, as "a good man, in the best sense of the word—and about the only one I have ever known" (Alexander 2005, 147).

James Tyrone, a high-functioning alcoholic who has never missed a performance in his life, admits to his younger son, Edmund, in act 4 that his fortune was made by buying the rights to a popular play (in real life *The Count of Monte Cristo*) that restricted his ability to follow his true passion, to be a great Shakespearean actor—"that God-damned play I bought for a song and made such a great success in—a great money success—it ruined me with its promise of an easy fortune" (3:809). The actual James O'Neill bought the popular melodrama *The Count of Monte Cristo* in 1894, and for five straight years, from 1885 to 1890, he played only one other role, Hamlet. But after that, contrary to what we know about James Tyrone, he played many other dramatic roles (Alexander 2005, 113). The profit from this moneymaker was too great a temptation for James, however, and he gave up his promise as an artist to relieve himself of the perpetual sense of impending poverty born of his humble Irish origins.

Tyrone's dialogue with Edmund shows a great deal of love between the two men, though much frustration as well. His feelings toward his older son, Jamie, on the other hand, are largely negative. Although he does love him, he finds Jamie to be a terrific disappointment, a drunken womanizer, and a loafer, all of which is basically true.

James's father (based on Edward O'Neill), a first-generation immigrant, abandoned his wife (Mary O'Neill; see O'NEILL, EDWARD [EDMUND] AND MARY) and children when James was 10 years old. The elder Tyrone returned to his native Ireland to die, probably a suicide. James's family was then evicted from their flat, and at age 10, James went to work in a machine shop, 12 hours a day for 50 cents a week. James eventually developed a love for the stage and quickly rose to great prominence as one of the finest actors of his generation. Edwin Booth, "the greatest actor of his day or any other," had remarked while costarring in *Othello* with James that at 27, James played a better Othello than he ever could. Nevertheless, James never shook his fear of poverty, and one result is that, as described in the play, he hires second-rate doctors for his family members—one result, according to the other Tyrones, being Mary Tyrone's morphine habit, which she developed after James hired a second-rate hotel doctor to treat her labor pains while she was giving birth to Edmund. James secretly wants to send Edmund to a state sanatorium after finding out his younger son has been diagnosed with tuberculosis. He invests heavily in local real estate, as he trusts land above all else for financial security, another Irish trait.

James met Mary Tyrone through her father (based on Thomas Joseph Quinlan; see QUINLAN, BRIDGET LUNDIGAN AND THOMAS JOSEPH), an Irish merchant friend of James's, in the spring of her senior year at convent school. They fell deeply in love, and whatever one can say about their marriage, he has remained faithful to Mary and is still very much in love with her. Not once in their 36 years of marriage has he ever cheated or caused a scandal, a fact that allows Mary, in her words, to "forgive so many other things" (3:778). If his sons accuse James of being a "tightwad," Mary blames him mainly for depriving her of domestic stability, boarding her in second-rate hotel rooms while he drinks with friends, and not allowing her to make the cottage into a "real home." But according to the diary of the actress Elizabeth Robins, who traveled with the O'Neills on tour, the actual James O'Neill told her that "you only have one life, the world owes you a living, get the best you can. Go to the first class hotels, the best is none too good for you, besides it is false economy to eat bad food and sleep in poor rooms" (Alexander 2005, 98). O'Neill himself once mused, "My father, the Count of Monte Cristo, always got me the classiest rowboats to be had, and we sported the first Packard car in our section of Connecticut way back in the duster-goggle era" (quoted in Alexander 1992, 179).

**Tyrone, James, Jr. (Jamie Tyrone)** James and Mary Tyrone's son and Edmund Tyrone's older brother. James, or "Jamie," is closely based on Eugene O'Neill's older brother, James "Jamie" O'Neill, Jr., and also appears as "Jim" Tyrone, the main character in *A Moon for the Misbegotten*. O'Neill describes Jamie, a severe alcoholic and great disappointment to his father, as 33 years old with a strong physical resemblance to James, Sr., but appearing *"shorter and stouter because he lacks Tyrone's bearing and graceful carriage. He also lacks his father's vitality. The signs of premature disintegration are on him"* (3:722). Significantly, the character has a *"habitual expression of cynicism* [that] *gives his countenance a Mephistophelian cast,"* like that of Anthony Dion's mask in

*The Great God Brown*, a multifaceted character who melds the attributes of both O'Neill brothers. Nevertheless, O'Neill continues, *"his personality possesses the remnant of a humorous, romantic, irresponsible Irish charm—that of the beguiling ne'er-do-well, with a strain of the sentimentally poetic, attractive to women and popular with men"* (3:722).

Jamie was psychologically scarred at a young age after discovering his mother injecting herself with morphine. "Christ," he says to Edmund, recalling the experience, "I'd never dreamed before that any women but whores took dope!" (3:818). He tried acting with his father for a time but failed, and he cynically regards actors (i.e., his father) as "performing seals" (3:817). He feels that at this point, his mother will not recover, and by association he will never conquer his own addiction to alcohol—"I'd begun to hope, if she'd beaten the game, I could too" (3:818). (The actual Jamie O'Neill died of alcoholism, though Mary O'Neill had successfully "beat the game" years before.) He blames his father, whom he continually refers to as a "tightwad" and a "Gaspard" (a miserly character), for Mary Tyrone's addiction, since it was he who hired a second-rate hotel doctor who prescribed morphine to his mother while she suffered from birth pains. He also perversely blames Edmund, though he understands his brother is not really to blame. "I know that's not your fault," he yells at Edmund, very drunk, in act 4, "but all the same, God damn you, I can't help hating your guts—!" (3:820).

Importantly, Jamie confesses in act 4 that he deliberately led his younger brother into a life of dissipation and vice as revenge for addicting their mother and serving as a living reminder of his own shortcomings. "Mama's baby and Papa's pet!" he screams at his younger brother. "The family White Hope! You've been getting a swelled head lately. About nothing! About a few poems in a hick town newspaper!" (3:819). James O'Neill is well aware of Jamie's methods, accusing him directly of tarnishing Edmund for his own gratification: "You made him old before his time, pumping him full of what you consider worldly wisdom, when he was too young to see that your mind was so poisoned by your own failure in life, you wanted to believe every man was a knave with his soul for sale, and every woman who wasn't a whore was a fool!" (3:732). But James also recognizes Jamie's true affection for his younger brother and tells Edmund that "it's the one good thing left in him" (3:822).

Over the course of his life, Jamie has been a great disappointment to his father, who felt that he squandered his education by getting expelled and later demonstrated enough talent on the stage to replace him as one of the United States' leading actors. But Jamie's severe alcoholism and patronage of brothels have prevented him from achieving anything in life and also from making a living on his own. "Like Tantalus," Travis Bogard remarks, equating him with the figure from Greek mythology who was denied the fruit and water always in view, Jamie "has no refuge from desire. His is the howl of a soul lost in hell" (431). Doris Alexander takes issue with those who impose a historical reality on the fictional Jamie, regarding the character as closer to O'Neill's second son, SHANE RUDRAIGHE O'NEILL, whom O'Neill accused of "never willing to start at the bottom" (quoted in Alexander 2005, 87). Jamie O'Neill worked steadily in the theater and did start at the bottom of that profession, she contends, and "only in the very last years of his father's life did [he] descend into unremitting alcoholism and irremediable unemployment" (140); in addition, he never started betting on horses, as his father accuses him in the play, until after he quit drinking and after their father's death (142).

Jamie Tyrone is in many ways the most unsympathetic Tyrone, a possible rationale for O'Neill having written another play, *A Moon for the Misbegotten*, with him as the primary subject. On the other hand, he is, as Michael Manheim argues, "the one truly humane figure in the play," as his kind treatment of the overweight prostitute Fat Violet appears to be "the one act of completely selfless giving in the play" (Manhein 1998, 214, 215). Jamie's act was certainly humane, though perhaps not entirely "selfless," as Jamie's choice stems from a desire to feel the nurturing body of a mother figure. When he went to Mamie's brothel, he tells Edmund, he was "ready for a weep on any old womanly bosom" (3:816). Jamie, as Doris Alexander writes, "is plagued by an indelible association of the mother he loves and admires with prostitutes" as

a result of his discovering her with a hypodermic needle (2005, 143).

**Tyrone, Mary Cavan** James Tyrone's wife and Edmund and James Tyrone, Jr.'s mother. Mary Tyrone is closely based on Eugene O'Neill's mother, Mary Ellen "Ella" O'Neill, who was a morphine addict for more than 25 years. O'Neill describes her as a striking-looking 54-year-old with a *"young, graceful figure, a trifle plump, but showing little evidence of middle-aged waist and hips. . . . Her face is distinctly Irish in type"* (3:718). Her younger son, Edmund, resembles her physically, as he too has a *"high forehead," "dark brown* eyes" and *"long, tapering* fingers." *"What strikes one immediately,"* O'Neill continues, *"is her extreme nervousness,"* again like Edmund. Mary suffers from rheumatism—her hands have an *"ugly crippled look"* (3:718)—and she uses that affliction as an excuse to carry on her morphine addiction. Mary is continually searching the house for her glasses, an act symbolic of her inability to see the love surrounding her. She creates one of the central tensions of the play by demonstrating a need for isolation, while at the same time a terror of it (Bogard 428).

Mary, like the Tyrone men, conveys a broad emotional range, from peaceful distraction to outward rage. But coming from her, the effect is far more terrible, given her facade of girlish innocence and the men's need for her affection. O'Neill characterizes Mary in this way, according to Michael Manheim, to reveal the "manifold nature of Mary's consciousness. A feeling of motherly solicitude leads to one of intense anger, which leads to one of intense anxiety, which leads to one of hysterical accusation, which leads to one of guilt, which leads to one of open acknowledgement, which leads to one of hope rooted in a lost religious faith, which leads to one of cynical rejection. All these are Mary Tyrone—no one more important than the rest" (210).

James Tyrone disabuses his younger son, Edmund, of the belief that Mary's father (based on Thomas Joseph Quinlan) was "the great, generous, noble Irish gentleman she makes out"; he was, rather, "a nice enough man, good company and a good talker," a wholesale grocer who died of alcoholism and tuberculosis (3:800). As a girl, Mary attended a convent school and studied piano there. She believes that while there, she experienced a vision of the Virgin Mary calling her to become a nun. Having been raised, according to her, in a "respectable home" and schooled at the "best convent in the Middle West" (3:775), as a schoolgirl she dreamed of being either a concert pianist or a nun. Mother Elizabeth (the actual name of the founder of Ella O'Neill's music department at St. Mary's [Alexander 2005, 85]) advised her to test her faith by "living as other girls lived, going out to parties and dances and enjoying myself" (3:828). Then she met James Tyrone. "You were much happier before you knew he existed," she says to herself of her marriage to James, "in the Convent when you used to pray to the Blessed Virgin" (3:779). Although the actual Ella O'Neill had known James for six years before marrying him, Mary expresses continual disappointment over her premature decision to live as the wife of a traveling matinee idol. She bitterly complains of having raised her sons in "one-night stands and filthy trains and cheap hotels and bad food," particularly with Edmund's extreme sensitivity. "When you have the poison in you," James responds angrily to her recriminations, "you want to blame everyone but yourself!" (3:782).

Doris Alexander contends that it was O'Neill's wife at the time of the play's composition, Carlotta Monterey O'Neill, who dreamt of becoming a nun, not Ella O'Neill (82). After reading the script, Carlotta apparently acted "humorously indignant at this cavalier theft of her own story" (82), and there are many attributes that Carlotta, not Ella, shares with Mary Tyrone: Carlotta's wedding dress more closely resembles the dress O'Neill describes in act 4, and it was Carlotta who had arthritic hands, not Ella, among other traits (81).

Tyrone disabuses his son Edmund of Mary's side of the story, explaining that she was neither a particularly talented piano player, nor did her father, a drinking partner of his, provide the "wonderful home" Mary would have them believe (3:800). Mary voices jealousy over the Protestant families in New London, Connecticut, families like the Chatfields, whose lives for her appear to "stand for something" (3:738). If, as O'Neill has said of himself, "the battle of moral forces in the New England Scene is what I feel closest to as an art-

ist," along with the fact that "the one thing that explains more than anything about me is the fact that I'm Irish" (quoted in Floyd 537), it follows that "no other character" in the O'Neill canon, as Virginia Floyd argues, "portrays more effectively than Mary Tyrone the cruel consequences of the migration of the Irish to America and the price they paid for assimilation" (538).

## BIBLIOGRAPHY

Alexander, Doris. *Eugene O'Neill's Creative Struggle: The Decisive Decade, 1924–1933.* University Park: Pennsylvania State University Press, 1992.

———. *Eugene O'Neill's Last Plays: Separating Art from Autobiography.* Athens: University of Georgia Press, 2005.

Barlow, Judith. *Final Acts: The Creation of Three Late O'Neill Plays.* Athens: University of Georgia Press, 1985.

Berlin, Normand. "The Late Plays." In *The Cambridge Companion to Eugene O'Neill*, edited by Michael Manheim, 82–95. New York: Cambridge University Press, 1998.

Black, Stephen A. *Eugene O'Neill: Beyond Mourning and Tragedy.* New Haven, Conn.: Yale University Press, 1999.

Bloom, Steven F. "'The Mad Scene: Enter Ophelia!': O'Neill's Use of the Delayed Entrance in *Long Day's Journey into Night*." *Eugene O'Neill Review* 26 (2004): 226–238.

Bogard, Travis. *Contour in Time: The Plays of Eugene O'Neill.* Rev. ed. New York: Oxford University Press, 1988.

Floyd, Virginia. *The Plays of Eugene O'Neill: A New Assessment.* New York: Ungar, 1985.

Manheim, Michael. *Eugene O'Neill's New Language of Kinship.* Syracuse, N.Y.: Syracuse University Press, 1982.

———. "The Stature of *Long Day's Journey into Night*." In *The Cambridge Companion to Eugene O'Neill*, edited by Michael Manheim, 206–216. New York: Cambridge University Press, 1998.

Murphy, Brenda. *O'Neill: Long Day's Journey into Night.* New York: Cambridge University Press, 2001.

Shaughnessy, Edward L. *Down the Nights and Down the Days: Eugene O'Neill's Catholic Sensibility.* Notre Dame, Ind.: University of Notre Dame Press, 2000.

Sheaffer, Louis. *O'Neill: Son and Artist*. Boston: Little, Brown, 1973.

Stirner, Max. *The Ego and His Own: The Case of the Individual Against Authority*. Translated by Steven T. Byington with an introduction by J. L. Walker. 1844. Reprint, New York: Benjamin R. Tucker, 1907.

# Long Voyage Home: A Play in One Act, The (completed, 1917; first produced, 1917)

*The Long Voyage Home* was first published in the distinguished literary journal *The Smart Set* (October 1917). The PROVINCETOWN PLAYERS produced its premiere on November 2, 1917, at the Playwrights' Theatre in GREENWICH VILLAGE. Three days earlier, the WASHINGTON SQUARE PLAYERS produced another of Eugene O'Neill's SS GLENCAIRN plays, IN THE ZONE, at the Comedy Theatre uptown; that play enjoyed high praise with the critics, though O'Neill himself thought little of it. Hollywood director John Ford chose *The Long Voyage Home* as the title of his critically acclaimed FILM ADAPTATION of the *Glencairn* cycle (1940), a film that holds the distinction of being the single Hollywood version of any of his plays O'Neill sincerely admired.

O'Neill drew the mise en scène of *The Long Voyage Home* (the only of O'Neill's SS *Glencairn* cycle set on land) from his personal experiences in the dive bars, boarding houses, and brothels of the sailortowns he explored in Liverpool, England; BUENOS AIRES, ARGENTINA; and the East Side waterfront of New York City. The one-act play also offers a window into the perilous existence of itinerant sailors on shore leave that O'Neill experienced firsthand

Production photo of Eugene O'Neill's *Long Voyage Home* by the Provincetown Players, 1917 *(Courtesy of the Yale Collection of American Literature, Beinecke Rare Book and Manuscript Library)*

during his two years of service in the MERCHANT MARINE. In this installment of the *Glencairn* cycle, the SEA presents land-based perils as inextricably intertwined with the hazards of life on the open sea.

## SYNOPSIS

Shortly after nine o'clock at night in the *"bar of a low dive on the London water front"* (1:509). Dimly lit by lanterns fastened to the back wall, the bar stands at left, with the entrance to the dive at its right upstage center. A door downstage left of the bar leads to a side room. Tables and chairs are arranged at right. The bar is empty aside from the proprietor, Fat Joe; an inebriated barmaid named Mag; and Nick, the waterfront "crimp." Joe grumbles over his lack of customers and accuses Nick of shirking his duty, which is to lure newly paid sailors into the bar. Nick defensively assures him that a group of sailors from the SS *Glencairn*, just in from Buenos Aires, will arrive soon. Earlier on the docks, Nick had handed out the bar's cards to "three Britishers an' a square-'ead" (actually, one Britisher, an Irishman, a Russian, and a Swede) from the *Glencairn*. Mop in hand, Mag wobbles in an alcoholic stupor. Joe abusively commands her upstairs to wake the PROSTITUTES and sleep off her drunk (1:510).

Nick requests a small bottle of tranquilizer. He has been commissioned by the infamously brutal captain of a sailing ship called the *Amindra* to shanghai a sailor for a trip around Cape Horn. No sailor signs onto the *Amindra* voluntarily, knowing the captain's and mate's reputations for starving and overworking their men. Nick spots his marks on the street outside and ushers them in. Driscoll, Cocky, Ivan, and Olson enter, uncomfortably dressed in ill-fitting shore clothes. The first three are very drunk, but Olson has deliberately remained sober. Driscoll instantly recognizes Fat Joe and the bar, where six years earlier he had been robbed while drunk. Nevertheless, Driscoll lets bygones go and orders a round of drinks—Irish whiskey (with a taunting emphasis on *Irish* in the British pub) for everyone but Olson, who orders ginger ale, and Nick, who orders beer. Nick shares a conspiratorial wink with Joe, downs his beer, and exits left.

Olson, a seasoned middle-aged sailor, has resigned from his berth on the *Glencairn*, cashed in two years of earnings, and refuses to drink; in two days, he plans to head back to Sweden as a passenger. Once home, he will return to his family and the simple life of a country farmer. Olson knows from long experience that after only one drink, he carries on drinking until he has spent his last cent. He would then be compelled to sign on another voyage. Cocky sneers at Olson's pipe dream, but Driscoll cuts him off: "Lave him alone, ye bloody insect! 'Tis a foine sight to see a man wid some sense in his head instead av a damn fool the loike av us" (1:513). Driscoll then bursts forth with a line from the Irish rebel song "The Boys of Wexford." "To hell with Ulster!" he shouts, referring to the Protestant-dominated section of Ireland (now Northern Ireland) and daring the British bartender to refuse to drink to this toast. Nick returns and whispers in Joe's ear, provoking Driscoll to fly into a rage for conspiring against them; they innocently respond that Ivan mentioned girls and that Nick had obediently summoned them.

Two waterfront prostitutes—Freda, a thin blonde, and Kate, a plump brunette—enter from left. They flirt with the sailors and stare greedily at Olson's roll of bills while he pays for the next round. Ivan passes out and snores loudly, and Driscoll wakes him roughly. Everyone apart from Olson and Freda disappears into the side room for music and dancing. Freda plays up to Olson's story and tells him she was born in Sweden, which warms him to her. "No more sea," Olson promises himself, "no more bum grub, no more storms—yust nice work" (1:517).

A loud crash comes from the adjoining room. Driscoll and Cocky reenter carrying Ivan, who is unconscious. They instruct Olson to remain while they return Ivan to their boarding house. When Olson insists he lend a hand, Freda pleads with him to stay, and the men promise to return soon. After their departure, she plies Olson again with alcohol, but still he demurs—"If I drink one I want drink one tousand" (1:519); he politely orders a ginger beer. At the bar, Joe furtively empties the knockout drops into Olson's ginger beer, serves the drink, and quietly orders Nick to find help once the anodyne takes hold. Freda keeps Olson talking. He feels that if he might control himself from alcohol consumption, he will get home safely at last. Olson's mother is now 82, and he might never see her again if he fails. Freda is *"moved a lot in spite of herself"* (1:521).

Nick enters with two roughs, who conspire in hushed tones with Joe and Nick. Olson again mentions going to the boarding house, but Joe informs him the newcomers want to buy him a drink. Freda toasts Olson's mother in Swedish, "Skoal!" (1:521), and Olson reluctantly drinks half his beer. Freda cajoles him to finish it off, which he does. One of the roughs flippantly shouts, "Amindra, ahoy!" Mention of the dreaded ship alarms Olson, as he served on the vessel years before and had not heard it was in port. When the rough informs him it sails for Cape Horn in the morning, Olson replies with foreboding, "Py yingo, I pity poor fallers make dat trip round Cape Stiff dis time year. I bet you some of dem never see port once again" (1:522).

As the drug begins to take effect, Olson takes a step toward the door, then collapses. Freda takes his roll and slips one of the bills into her dress. Joe instructs Nick to retrieve a full month's wages, five pounds, before relinquishing Olson to the captain. Nick retorts that he knows his business, and the men exit carrying the unconscious sailor. Joe demands the bill he witnessed Freda pocket. When she begs innocence, he hits her across the jaw and violently retrieves the banknote. Kate consoles Freda and accompanies her to the side room. Driscoll and Cocky reenter and ask where their shipmate went. Joe responds with a *"meaning wink"* that Olson left with Freda. "'Tis lucky he's sober," Driscoll remarks, "or she'd have him stripped to his last ha'penny. . . . Give me a whiskey," he barks at Joe, "*Irish* whiskey!" (1:523).

## COMMENTARY

*The Long Voyage Home* treats the theme of "ironic fate" O'Neill explores in such early one-act plays as The WEB, FOG, and BOUND EAST FOR CARDIFF. But unlike these, *The Long Voyage Home* lacks the bizarre supernatural apparitions meant to represent mystical powers at work: the "ironic life force" in *The Web* (1:28), the wail of a dead baby in *Fog*

(1:111–112), and the "pretty lady dressed in black" in *Bound East* (1:198). Thus, in *The Long Voyage Home*, the controlling matrix of the avenging sea is subtly implied rather than expressly dramatized. In the final scene of *Bound East*, for example, Yank envisions the dark lady (his psychological conjuring of the "sea mother") as he dies, and the fog that had been gradually creeping into the forecastle magically lifts upon his death. In contrast, when Freda shouts at Olson, "Fur Gawd's sake, shet that door! I'm fair freezin' to death wiv the fog" (1:519), and he obeys, a perfectly natural gesture, Olson symbolically seals his fate (Floyd 124). Other fine details improve the theatrical effectiveness and artistry of the play. Driscoll's singing the line from "The Boys of Wexford," for instance, is a song that, when read in its entirety, significantly recounts a series of battles lost to the English as a result of drunkenness, thus subtly foreshadowing Olson's doom. Either way, *Bound East* and *The Long Voyage Home* both show that by committing an offense against the sea—the willful act of abandoning it for life on land—the men condemn themselves "not only to failure but to punishment" (Floyd 124).

The play's tragic tension heightens with some knowledge of O'Neill's personal experience in the merchant marine. For one, the *Amindra* is modeled after the *Timandra*, a German square-rigger docked at Buenos Aires, Argentina. In 1910, O'Neill had chosen to remain in Buenos Aires and let his ship, the CHARLES RACINE, sail on to Nova Scotia without him. Essentially homeless and out of work, he labored for a time on the *Timandra*, unloading its wares as a longshoreman. O'Neill described the vessel's first mate as "too tough, the kind that would drop a marlin spike on your skull from a yardarm" (quoted in Sheaffer 177), just as Nick characterizes the captain and mate of the *Amindra* as "bloody slave-drivers" (1:511) and Olson calls them "Bluenose devils" (1:522). In addition, when Nick announces that the *Amindra* plans to sail "round the 'Orn" (1:511), he refers to Cape Horn at the southernmost tip of the South American continent. "Rounding the horn is one of the most difficult passages at sea," Robert Richter explains, "particularly sailing from the Atlantic into the

Pacific, since the prevailing winds blow from west to east." Richter adds that a "full-rigged" ship with a personnel problem further compounds the danger (152).

The NATURALISM of *The Long Voyage Home* is less spiritually charged than much of O'Neill's early work, and the plot does little to foreshadow O'Neill's experiments with EXPRESSIONISM a few years later. What this one-act play does call to mind (in its bar setting and title, respectively) is the tragically cyclical lives depicted in his late masterpieces *The* ICEMAN COMETH and LONG DAY'S JOURNEY INTO NIGHT. As with the characters in *Iceman*, the sailors in *The Long Voyage Home* lay bare "the endless deferral of their own lives" (Brietzke 45); and with *Long Day's Journey*, O'Neill seems to have revised his early title by demonstrating an acceptance (rather than implicit denial) of tragic inevitabilities. Even Driscoll, openly sympathetic to Olson's pipe dream—more so than this play lets on, in fact, when we think of his secret desire to co-own a farm with his dying friend Yank in *Bound East*—remarks that if his mother were still alive, he would "not be dhrunk in this divil's hole this minute," but he adds the notable qualifier "maybe" (1:513).

Olson describes his life cycle in terms that reveal a grasp of the immediate causes of his perpetual condition, if not the larger "inscrutable forces behind life" O'Neill always tried to unveil (O'Neill 100). Since he was 18 years of age, Olson's life had followed a simple but unbreakable pattern: "I come ashore, I take one drink, I take many drinks, I get drunk, I spend all money, I have to ship away for another voyage" (1:520). On shore leave, two appetites of sailors act as unwitting agents to carry out the wrath of the sea: women and drink. Indeed, the villains—Joe, Nick, Freda, and Kate—"are only agents," according to Travis Bogard, "performing the sea's will without animosity or responsibility" (84). Perhaps the play's only significant weakness is that the protagonist, Olson, lacks a certain roundness. Because the middle-aged sailor appears far more childlike than his decades of experience at sea would suggest, the character is in danger of coming across more as a naive simpleton than a tragic hero doomed to an ironic fate.

## CHARACTERS

**Cocky** British seaman on the British tramp steamer SS *Glencairn*. Cocky, *"a wizened runt of a man with a straggling gray mustache"* (1:511), speaks with a cockney (or British working-class) accent and derides Olson for both his temperance and his pipe dream of returning to Sweden. Cocky appears in all four of the *Glencairn* plays.

**Driscoll** Irish seaman on the British tramp steamer SS *Glencairn*, based on O'Neill's Irish-born drinking partner at JIMMY "THE PRIEST'S" named DRISCOLL. The actual Driscoll worked on the SS *PHILADELPHIA* with O'Neill as a coal stoker. In 1913, Driscoll committed suicide at sea, and the question of why he ended his life inspired O'Neill first to write a short story, which is lost, and then to revise it in the form of one of his finest experimental plays, *The* HAIRY APE. O'Neill describes Driscoll in *The Long Voyage Home* as *"a tall, powerful Irishman"* (1:511), and he is the ringleader of the group of drunken sailors at the London dive. As an Irishman, Driscoll shouts incautiously patriotic slogans in the British pub—demanding *Irish* whiskey, loudly singing an Irish battle song, "The Boys of Wexford" (which significantly recounts the Irish loss of a battle because of drunkenness), and defying anyone to challenge his patriotism. Fearless and tough, yet compassionate as well, Driscoll applauds Olson's desire to return home to his mother in Sweden; he shares a similar pipe dream with his dying friend Yank in *Bound East for Cardiff*. Driscoll appears in all four of the *Glencairn* plays.

**Fat Joe** Proprietor of a low waterfront dive in London, England. O'Neill describes Joe as *"a gross bulk of a man with an enormous stomach. His face is red and bloated, his little piggish eyes being almost concealed by the rolls of fat"* (1:509). He wears an abundance of cheap jewelry, including a massive gold chain across his waistcoat. A brutal man with no conscience, Joe conspires with the "crimp" Nick and the prostitute Freda to drug, rob, and shanghai the SS *Glencairn* sailor Olson.

**Freda** Prostitute at a low waterfront dive in London, England. Kate is *"a little, sallow-faced blonde"*

(1:514) who convinces Olson she is Swedish-born, like himself, and sweet-talks him into trusting her until Nick can drug his drink and shanghai him for the captain of the ship *Amindra*. Although Freda demonstrates the same ruthlessness as her bosses, Fat Joe and Nick, she is *"moved a lot in spite of herself"* when Olson tells how he wishes to reunite with his 82-year-old mother in Sweden before she dies (1:521). Nevertheless, Freda cajoles Olson into drinking the drugged ginger beer and even sneaks a banknote from his roll. Fat Joe punches her in the face for this slight treachery, and her partner, Kate, escorts her consolingly from the bar-room. O'Neill most commonly presents prostitutes in a sympathetic light, but aside from Freda's brief moment of conscience, Freda and Kate are notable exceptions.

**Ivan** Russian seaman on the British tramp steamer SS *Glencairn*. Ivan, *"a hulking oaf of a peasant"* (1:511), appears the most uncomfortable at the bar and tries to convince his shipmates to go to a dance hall with girls. He soon passes out on a bar table, but when the prostitutes Freda and Kate arrive, Driscoll roughly wakes him up, and they move into the side room to dance. Ivan passes out again, offstage, and Driscoll and Cocky return him to their boarding house. Thus, Olson is left to the devices of Fat Joe, Nick, and Kate, and Ivan's drunkenness must take some blame for Olson's fate. Ivan also appears in *Bound East for Cardiff* and *In the Zone*.

**Kate** Prostitute at a low waterfront dive in London, England. Kate is *"stout and dark,"* and Driscoll takes a liking to her because, as he says, "Ut's fat ye are, Katy dear, an' I never cud endure skinny wimin" (1:515). Kate has few lines and moves the conspiracy forward by dancing with the other sailors to distract them as Freda sweet-talks Olson into trusting her. When Fat Joe punches Freda in the final scene, Kate consoles her and accompanies her into the next room. O'Neill most commonly presents prostitutes in a sympathetic light, but Kate and Freda again are notable exceptions.

**Mag** Barmaid at a low waterfront dive in London, England. *"A slovenly barmaid with a stupid face*

*sodden with drink"* (1:509), Mag is first seen mopping the floor of the bar. She slowly begins falling asleep in the process, and Fat Joe roughly orders her to wake up Freda and Kate and then sleep off her drunk upstairs. Mag is a self-pitying figure who *"bursts into a tempest of sobs"* when rebuked and complains of the injustices Joe and Nick direct at her, "a 'onest woman" (1:510).

**Nick** A "crimp," or someone who shanghais sailors for profit, operating out of a waterfront dive in London, England. O'Neill describes Nick's face as *"pasty, his mouth weak, his eyes shifting and cruel"*; he wears a *"shabby suit, which must have once been cheaply flashy, and wears a muffler and cap"* (1:509). Nick lures the men of the SS *Glencairn* into Fat Joe's bar. He conspires with Joe and Freda to drug, rob, and shanghai Olson into service for a dangerous voyage on the *Amindra*; thus, he thwarts Olson's dream to return to his 82-year-old mother and live the rest of his days on his family homestead in Sweden. O'Neill would have known many crimps from his days in the merchant marine, though Nick is most probably based on "Shanghai Brown," a mythic crimp among sailors, or "Rapper Brown," an actual crimp in London (Gelb 301, Richter 151). O'Neill considered writing a play on Shanghai Brown called *The Calms of Capricorn*, in which the crew of a clipper ship arrives in Brown's San Francisco boarding house.

**Olson** Swedish seaman on the British tramp steamer SS *Glencairn*. Olson is based on a Norwegian seaman O'Neill served with on the SS *Ikala* who, after 20 years at sea, pined for his farm back home (Gelb 290). He recounts the stubborn pattern of his life at sea to the prostitute Freda: "I come ashore, I take one drink, I take many drinks, I get drunk, I spend all money, I have to ship away for another voyage" (1:520). When Olson is left at the bar by his shipmates, the crimp Nick sneaks knockout drops into his ginger beer and shanghais him for the infamous captain of the *Amindra*, a ship Olson once sailed on. Due to the brutality of its leadership and the dangerous voyage around Cape Horn, Olson believes that many sailors on the *Amindra* will not make it safely home. This strongly suggests that Olson will die as punishment for his attempt to abandon the sea.

The character was played by the world-renowned movie actor John Wayne in film director John Ford's film *The Long Voyage Home* (1940), which adapts the whole SS *Glencairn* series into a sustained narrative. Simple-minded and naïve as Olson may seem in *The Long Voyage Home*, O'Neill saw a great deal of promise in him as a dramatic character, and Olson reappears in the form of the old Swedish sailor in the naturalistic CHRIS CHRISTOPHERSEN and its revision, "ANNA CHRISTIE," which won the playwright his second PULITZER PRIZE. In each, Chris acknowledges the sea as an "ole davil" bent on his and his family's destruction. Though for a time Chris successfully avoids its wrath by skippering a coastal barge on Manhattan's waterfront (to the dissatisfaction of his former shipmates), the sea claims him in the end, and he submits to its eternal embrace. Olson also appears in *Bound East for Cardiff* and *The Moon of the Caribbees*.

**Two Roughs**  Criminals who assist Nick the "crimp" in shanghaiing Olson. They are *"rough-looking, shabbily-dressed men, wearing mufflers, with caps pulled down over their eyes"* (1:521). One of them informs Olson that the *Amindra*, on which Olson had once served, was then at port and will disembark to Cape Horn the following morning. Olson then remembers the "Bluenose devils" who run the ship and prophesies that some men will never return. After Olson passes out from the knockout drops Nick serves him, Nick and the two roughs carry him off to the *Amindra*.

## BIBLIOGRAPHY

Bogard, Travis. *Contour in Time: The Plays of Eugene O'Neill.* Rev. ed. New York: Oxford University Press, 1988.

Brietzke, Zander. "*The Long Voyage Home*: A Vicious Cycle at Sea." *Eugene O'Neill Review* 28 (2006): 32–49.

Floyd, Virginia. *The Plays of Eugene O'Neill: A New Assessment.* New York: Ungar, 1985.

O'Neill, Eugene. "Inscrutable Forces." (Letter to Barrett Clark, 1919.) In *O'Neill and His Plays: Four Decades of Criticism*, edited by Oscar N. Cargill,

Bryllion Fagin, and William J. Fisher, 99–100. New York: New York University Press, 1961.

Gelb, Arthur, and Barbara Gelb. *O'Neill: Life with Monte Cristo.* New York: Applause Books, 2000.

Richter, Robert A. *Eugene O'Neill and Dat Ole Davil Sea: Maritime Influences in the Life and Works of Eugene O'Neill.* Mystic, Conn.: Mystic Seaport, 2004.

Sheaffer, Louis. *O'Neill: Son and Playwright.* Boston: Little, Brown, 1968.

# *Marco Millions* (completed, 1925; first produced, 1928)

*Marco Millions*, Eugene O'Neill's expressionistic satire of Western greed, recounts the legendary journey of Marco Polo, the 13th-century Italian trader who, with the goal of returning home a millionaire, destructively imposes Western materialist values across the Far East and Middle East. O'Neill first conceptualized the idea in 1922 at PEAKED HILL BAR, his home in Provincetown, Massachusetts; he continued to work on it intermittently, completing DESIRE UNDER THE ELMS and *The GREAT GOD BROWN* during the same period, and completed it after many drafts in early 1925 (copyrighted January 28, but probably revised through March). He originally sold the script to the popular playwright, director, and producer David Belasco, pitching it as "*comedy satire by an American* of our life & ideals" (O'Neill 191). O'Neill and his circle had previously criticized Belasco as old-fashioned, but the play's sensational aspects seemed to fit his profile as a producer. Belasco bought it and initially promised to spend $200,000 on the production, a whopping sum in 1925, including a two-year trip for the set designer ROBERT EDMOND JONES to study Chinese sets firsthand. He withdrew the offer, however, after O'Neill pushed him too hard to get it started. A number of producers turned it down until the producer Gilbert Miller expressed delight over the manuscript of STRANGE INTERLUDE and convinced the THEATRE GUILD to usher in their relationship with O'Neill by producing *Marco Mil-*

*lions* first (Alexander 57). A series of further delays forestalled its premier at New York City's Guild Theatre until January 9, 1928.

The script of *Marco Millions* is needlessly complex in its scene changes, terrifically demanding of its set and costume designers, weighed down by a gigantic cast (O'Neill lists 31 characters, along with *"People of Persia, India, Mongolia, Cathay, courtiers, nobles, ladies, wives, warriors of Kublai's court, musicians, dancers, Chorus of mourners"*), convoluted in its mixture of genres—dialogue, music, poetry, chanting, and so on—and perplexingly hilarious and tragic at the same time. In spite of everything, however, the Theatre Guild's production was a terrific success. If O'Neill felt too many restrictions were placed on his vision due to financial concerns, one reviewer applauded the premiere for having "lavished a prodigious sum in costumes, scenery and background. . . . This sumptuous production could have done justice to the most ambitious extravaganzas of our musical impresarios" (Allen 56).

## SYNOPSIS

### Foreword

A prose introduction in which O'Neill ironically declares the legendary 13th-century Venetian trader Marco Polo a slandered "prophet without honor." Over the centuries, Polo has been criticized for romanticizing his journey through the Far East and Middle East in his book *The Travels of Marco Polo*. The play, then, is a tongue-in-cheek effort by the author to "whitewash the good soul of that maligned Venetian" (2:380).

### Prologue

A holy tree standing in the middle of a sun-blasted plain on the border of India and Persia (now Iran). A random display of votive offerings hangs from its limbs. Three traveling merchants—a Christian (an Italian selling Western goods), a Magian (a Zoroastrian Persian selling copies of *Arabian Nights*, a book of medieval pornography that was banned in the United States as late as 1927), and a Buddhist (a Kashmiri selling prayer beads)—all enter separately, grumble about the heat, and sit collegially to rest under the shade of the tree. The Magian and the Buddhist notify the Christian that Queen Kukachin

Hal Holbrook as Marco Polo advising Kublai Kaan in *Marco Millions* *(Courtesy of the Sheaffer-O'Neill Collection, Charles E. Shain Library of Connecticut College)*

of Persia is dead. The Christian is distressed by the news, as he carries a letter of introduction to her from the Venetian firm Polo Brothers and Son. The diverse group spies a dust cloud on the plain and fear it may be the work of evil spirits. The Buddhist offers to make a prayer to the sacred tree of Buddha, but the other two object to his religion's legend of the tree: For the Christian, the tree signifies the staff of Adam and the wood used to construct the cross on which Jesus Christ died; for the Magian, it is the tree of life planted by Zoroaster. They squabble over which legend is true but are interrupted by the origin of the dust cloud—a chariot pulled by slaves. When they notice a coffin strapped to the wagon, they all bow in prostration.

A captain and a corporal halt the slaves. The captain, a Muslim, wonders at the "Holy Tree which was once the staff of Mahomet" (2:388), then interrogates the merchants. When the Christian mentions his letter, the captain responds,

"Allah forbid I touch what belongs to a corpse"
(2:388). The queen's body is in the coffin, and
he is charged with transporting her back to her
homeland in Cathay (what the actual Marco Polo
called China). The Christian pulls back the white
pall covering the coffin and looks down upon the
young queen's corpse. Kukachin's face lights up
with an *"unearthly glow, like a halo,"* and the *"sound
of sweet sad music"* comes from the leaves of the
trees. "Say this," the corpse intones, "I loved and
died. Now I am love, and live. And living, have forgotten. And loving, can forgive. . . . Say this for me
in Venice!" (2:390). The music and mystical glow
are replaced by silence and intense sunlight. The
men stare horrified at the now-inanimate corpse.
The captain orders the slaves to take up their positions for departure, but three are dead from the
grueling trek. The captain replaces them with the
three merchants. When the Christian protests that
he has a letter to Queen Kukachin, the captain
craftily asks to see it, rips it to shreds, and proceeds
to Cathay with his new replacements.

### Act 1, Scene 1

Twenty-three years earlier on a canal in Venice,
Italy. Marco Polo is discovered on a gondola sere-
nading Donata, who is inside a house on the canal.
Marco, a 15-year-old boy, finishes his song and
kisses her hand passionately. Donata, a 12-year-old
girl, demurely protests that such an act must be sinful. He begs her to admit she loves him, which she
coyly does. She pleads with him not to go through
with the expedition, but Marco tells her that along
with gaining wealth and power, he fervently desires
"to travel and see the world and all the different
people and get to know their habits and needs from
first-hand knowledge" (2:393). She vows to marry
him upon his return. Through the window bars she
hands him a medallion with a likeness of herself
painted on it, and he promises to write her a love
poem in return. After some boyish prodding on
Marco's part, they furtively kiss goodbye.

### Act 1, Scene 2

Six months later in the papal legate Tedaldo's palace at Acre (now a northern port city in Israel).
The legate is seated on a throne with a knight-
crusader in full armor standing guard on his right

and his adviser, a Dominican monk, on his left.
Marco is struggling over his poem to Donata, and
his father, Nicolo, and uncle Maffeo stand defer-
entially before Tedaldo. Maffeo informs the legate
that Kublai Kaan (king of Cathay and reputedly
the richest king in the world) has requested 100
wise Christians "to argue with his Buddhists and
Taoists and Confucians which religion in the world
is best" (2:395). The legate responds cynically, but
Maffeo convinces him that converting the heathen
king would be profitable.

Maffeo playfully swipes the poem away from
Marco. He and Nicolo read it and laugh. The legate reads it out loud, but Marco takes back the
poem, which speaks more to the boy's financial
ambition than his love for Donata, and smashes
it under his feet. A messenger arrives with news
that the legate himself has been chosen to be the
new pope. The legate orders the Polos out in order
to pray for God's guidance, but the traders realize
the new pope must choose the wise men in order
for them to depart. They send Marco to ask. Irritated by the request, Tedaldo first suggests sending
a couple of monks, but then he assigns Marco, for
whom he holds an avuncular favoritism, to the task
of converting the Great Kaan. As the three Polos
head off, Marco secretively turns back to fetch his
poem, then rushes out with church bells hailing the
latest pope ringing loudly behind him (2:399–400).

### Act 1, Scene 3

A Mahometan mosque. The Islamic ruler is seated
on a throne, as the legate was in the previous scene,
*"on the right, the inevitable warrior—on his left, the
inevitable priest"* (2:400). His wives sit at his feet
like slaves, and a collection of Islamic men, women,
and children form a semicircle on either side of the
ruler; they span the life cycle and include *"a mother
nursing her baby, two children playing a game, a young
girl and a young man in a loving embrace, a middle-
aged couple, a coffin"* (2:400).

Marco is discovered lugging a set of anachro-
nistically modern sample cases. Maffeo discusses
the business prospects in the region and reads from
the notes they took on their previous voyage east:
"There's one kingdom called Musul and in it a
district of Baku where there's a great fountain of

oil. There's a growing demand for it (*then speaking*) Make a mental note of that." Two traders come in. The Polos recognize them as the Ali brothers and curse under their breaths that "they'll cut under our prices with their cheap junk as usual" (2:401). Maffeo good-naturedly plunges into an anti-Semitic joke for the benefit of their rivals, as Marco strides around the semicircle of Arabs. He comments on each of them, if sometimes only with a sneer, but is intrigued in spite of his ethnocentrism.

A prostitute enters to entice the still-innocent Marco with a free assignation. Marco exits, mortified; Maffeo reassures her the boy will learn soon enough. The older Ali tells the story of the three kings who came with gifts to a baby prophet. When Nicolo responds that the baby was the son of God, the Alis shout, "There is no God but Allah!" A dervish rushes into the room, shrieking and whirling about, and the Polos look on, entertained by the spectacle. Marco returns, and the sounds of prayer come from the *"muezzins in the minarets of the mosque"* (2:404). The Arabs fall to the ground in prayer, and the Polos, not knowing how to respond, exit the mosque.

### Act 1, Scene 4

A Buddhist temple in India. Now a snake charmer, in place of the dervish, performs in the center of the assemblage. Otherwise, the scene, with its throne and spectrum of the human life cycle, *"is the exact duplicate of the last"* (2:405). Above the throne looms an enormous Buddha figure. Marco is now 17 and has grown progressively more callous. He points out the snake, and Maffeo scoffs that the fangs have been removed; offended, the charmer rises, spits at their feet, and exits haughtily. Nicolo reads the section on India from their notes. Two Buddhist traders enter, and a similar exchange takes place between them and the Polo brothers. Marco again scans the crowd set in a semicircle around the throne, but this time he *"assumes the casual, indifferent attitude of the worldly-wise"* (2:405). The prostitute enters dressed as an Indian. Marco kisses her on a dare, but when she offers herself for 10 gold pieces, he bashfully declines again, and she exits left. The Buddhists tell the legend of Buddha, that "when he died he became God again" (2:407). The

Polos consider this madness (ignoring the obvious fact that the story of Jesus is equivalent) and depart the temple.

### Act 1, Scene 5

A colossal gate at the Great Wall of China. The scene is the same, except now the Polos are in Mongolia. The motionless figures about the throne sit in front of a series of circular huts. Marco, whose sample cases are now worn and battered, is nearly 18 and has become *"a brash, self-confident young man, assertive and talky"* (2:408). In place of a dervish or snake charmer, a minstrel pounds a drum. Nicolo reads the section on Mongolia from the notes. Marco makes his round about the semicircle, *"but now he hardly looks at them"* (2:408).

Two Tartar merchants enter. Marco engages them as the elder Polos had in the previous two scenes, but his joke falls flat, and the Tartars drift off to sleep. The prostitute appears again, this time as a Tartar. By now, Marco has been with her so many times he is broke. She stole Donata's medallion, however, and he demands it back. Instead, she produces his love poem to Donata from act 1, scene 1, and begins reading it mockingly. He denies that it is his, and she shouts, "Going! Going! Gone! . . . Your soul! Dead and buried!" (2:410). She crushes the poem under her feet, then throws the medallion to the ground as well.

Again the Polos mock the local religion. Kublai Kaan's messenger comes through the gate of the Great Wall, bows to the Polos, and inquires about the whereabouts of the hundred wise men. Some excuses are given, but they are ignored. Marco picks up the cases wearily, his form making a silhouette against the sky, and the Venetian syndicate follows the messenger through the gate.

### Act 1, Scene 6

Kublai Kaan's throne room in his palace at Cambaluc, Cathay (China). The set is far more extravagant than any up to this point. On his right is a Mongol warrior, on his left Chu-Yin, his adviser. Scores of people—wives, soldiers, scholars, poets, children, and more—fill the room. Maffeo and Nicolo kneel in deference to the Great Kaan, but Marco stands erect, still holding his cases and staring stupidly at the spectacle. An usher runs up to him and *"makes violent gestures to him to kneel down"* (2:412).

Kublai demands to know why they did not bring the hundred wise men. Marco says that he has been sent by the pope in their stead. "Have you an immortal soul?" he asks Marco. "Of course!" Marco replies, "Any fool knows that" (2:413). "But I am not a fool," Kublai retorts and challenges him to prove he has a soul. Marco explains with the logic that unlike an animal, he is "a man made by Almighty God in His Own Image for His greater glory!" (2:413). Unconvinced, Kublai claps his hands, and his soldiers draw swords and pin Marco down. Kublai orders him to confess that he has no soul. "You're a heathen liar!" Marco screams back (2:414). This impudence amuses Kublai, who then proposes to allot Marco some time to enlighten him on Christianity and Western ways. Marco is uncertain what to ask for in return, and his uncle tells him to take a second-class government commission, as second-class officers make more contacts for trade than the first class. Meanwhile, Kublai consults his counselor, Chu-Yin, who advises him to watch Marco develop for amusement and study. Marco submits his terms to Kublai, who accepts but balks at the conflict of interest when he hears the Polo brothers have also offered Marco a junior partnership in their firm. Marco promises to serve his interests loyally and exits to celebrate his good fortune with the elder Polos.

### Act 2, Scene 1

About 15 years later in the summer palace of Kublai Kaan at Xanadu, "the City of Peace" (2:418). Kublai is ensconced on his throne in a contemplative mood. His granddaughter, Princess Kukachin, sits at his feet reciting a sad poem about loss. Concerned for his granddaughter, Kublai asks whether she is unhappy about her imminent marriage to King Arghun of Persia, a union that will make her a queen. She admits vaguely that she loves another. When Chu-Yin announces the arrival of Marco, Kublai is horror-struck to discover she loves the Venetian. Marco is now the mayor of Yang-Chau, and Chu-Yin reports that its citizens are complaining that Marco rules like a demagogue and is stifling their culture. Kublai threatens to send him

home, but Kukachin defends him as an effective leader. Kublai furiously announces that she will be sent to Persia in 10 days and dismisses her. Chu-Yin watches on, amused at Marco's arrival, and describes to Kublai his ridiculous political gladhanding. Interrupting Marco's speech to the people below, Chu-Yin yells down and orders him up to the throne room.

Kukachin reenters, terrified that her grandfather will harm Marco. He assures her that it is not his "custom to take vengeance" (2:423). Nicolo and Maffeo enter from the right, wearing *"a queer jumble of stunning effects that recall the parade uniforms of our modern Knights Templar, of Columbus, of Pythias, Mystic Shriners, the Klan, etc."* (2:423). Marco follows in mayoral regalia and hands Kukachin a chow puppy as a gift. After reporting on the state of affairs in Yang-Chau, he requests permission to go home. But first he sells Kublai the concepts of paper money and cannon, asking a million yen for the ideas (in gold, not paper). Kublai protests that Marco still has not proven the existence of his immortal soul. Kukachin steps up and pronounces that she can confirm his soul because of many kind acts he has performed over the years. Then, to her grandfather's consternation, she asks Marco to accompany her to Persia, and the Venetian heartily agrees.

### Act 2, Scene 2

The wharves of the port city Zayton. A group of slaves loads cargo from a warehouse onto the flagship of Marco's royal fleet, which is headed first to Persia and then on to Venice. The slaves, who load and unload mechanically to the beats of a gong and drum, resemble *"a manpower original of the modern devices with bucket scoops that dredge, load coal, sand, etc."* (2:432). A bamboo stairway leads up to the poop deck, where Kublai Kaan and Kukachin are discovered. Chu-Yin stands as a sentry on the wharf. Kublai bids Kukachin farewell, with the advice to "live," to which she adds, "Live—and love!" (2:433). She drifts off to sleep but is soon awakened by the *"deafening clangor"* of Marco's band.

Marco enters, dressed in an admiral's uniform, with Nicolo and Maffeo close behind (2:434).

After Marco vows to keep Kukachin safe, Chu-Yin informs him that Kublai has a secret directive for Marco: Each day, he must "look carefully and deeply into the Princess' eyes" and take note of what he sees (2:436). Marco agrees, thinking Kublai is worried about tropical fever; in fact, Chu-Yin is acting on his own, hoping that with this daily ritual, either Marco will acknowledge the princess's love and thus discover his own soul, or destroy both with his foolishness. Marco proudly announces that the boat was loaded ahead of schedule, though six slaves died to make it happen. The crowd on the wharf forlornly bids their beloved princess farewell. Marco shouts down to Chu-Yin from the railing: "And tell the Kaan—anything he wants—write me—just Venice—they all know me there—and if they don't, by God, they're going to!" (2:438).

### Act 2, Scene 3
The port of the city of Hormuz, Persia, about two years later. Princess Kukachin is discovered seated on a silver throne in ceremonial dress on the royal junk's poop deck. She appears as one *"who has known real sorrow and suffering."* The ship is *"battered and splintered,"* and the sail *"is frayed and full of jagged holes and patches"* (2:439). The Polo brothers count gold coins in the foreground. The boatswain, a chorus, sailors, a group of women, and Kukachin chant over the sorrows of the voyage and of her broken heart. They receive word that Arghun Khan is dead, and Kukachin will marry his son Ghazan instead. She sees no difference; Marco is still unaware of her love for him. She makes a final effort to show him the love in her eyes. He looks, and when she calls out his name, he responds passionately with hers. But Maffeo jolts him from his reverie by loudly announcing his tally—"One million!" (2:446). Marco then apologizes to Kukachin and tells her he meant to say "Donata." In the end, he reads her broken heart as a sign of either illness or feminine hysteria.

Ghazan ceremoniously enters with a royal entourage (2:448). Kukachin crushes Donata's medallion with her foot, but then she awards Marco the Order of the Lion and commands a chest of gold to be paid him for his valor on the voyage. She throws gold at the Polos, contemptuously yelling, "Here!

Guzzle! Grunt! Wallow for our amusement!" (2:449). Marco explains her odd behavior to the king by diagnosing that "her spleen is out of order" (2:450). Kukachin and Marco say goodbye; as the curtain falls, the princess falls to her knees.

### Act 3, Scene 1
A year later in Kublai Kaan's throne room in Cambaluc, same as act 1, scene 6. Kublai now looks *"aged and sad"* (2:451). The room is filled with armored military personnel, and General Bayan, the head of his army, is advising the king to attack Europe for profit. Kublai protests that they have "everything to lose by contact with [the West's] greedy hypocrisy." When Bayan calls himself a "man of action"—Marco's term—Kublai responds with grim irony: "You have already conquered the West, I think" (2:451). But he then reluctantly approves an invasion of Japan to corner the silk market.

A courier enters with a letter from Kukachin. Chu-Yin reads it aloud. She writes that her heart is broken and death is near but adds that Marco behaved valiantly on the voyage and deserves another million. His granddaughter's heartbreak sends Kublai into a rage, and he threatens to invade Europe to avenge her. Chu-Yin calmly talks him out of it. Kublai orders a magic crystal to be brought to his chamber. Peering into the crystal, the canals of Venice come into focus.

Kublai looks upon a scene in the Polos' banquet hall. A group of guests enter and remark how rich the Polos have become and how fortunate Donata will be to marry into such wealth. Donata, who now looks middle-aged, enters with her father. An orchestra comes in blaring a sentimental Italian song, followed by servants bearing platters of sumptuous food. Marco and the Polo brothers, wearing illustrious Chinese robes, enter ceremoniously. They shower the band with gold coins, then remove two sets of robes and reveal shabby, threadbare Tartar garments. But from the sleeves pour *"a perfect stream of precious stones which forms a glittering multicolored heap"* (2:458)—a moral not to judge by appearances. Marco and Donata clumsily embrace and make perfunctory wedding plans. The feast begins, and all are hidden behind monstrous piles of food. Marco's head pops up from behind the gluttonous display and begins a speech *"in the grand Chamber of Commerce style"* (2:460), but he is drowned out by the diners' clamor; the only discernible word is *millions* repeated over and over. Kublai lets the crystal smash to the floor. The stage goes dark, but Kublai's voice is heard from his position above the banquet: "The Word becomes their flesh, they say. Now all is flesh! And can their flesh become Word again?" (2:461).

### Act 3, Scene 2

Two years later. Again in Kublai Kaan's throne room at Cambaluc. Kublai is dressed in a *"simple white robe,"* and the room contains the same semicircle from act 1, scene 6. Kublai's gaze is fixed on a catafalque draped in white silk at center. From all directions, the sound of bells clamor, and an elaborate funeral ceremony takes place. A bier is carried in bearing Kukachin's corpse. A Confucian, a Taoist, a Buddhist, and a Muslim are positioned at each corner. They place the corpse on the catafalque. Kublai halts the ceremony and asks each priest whether they have the wisdom to "conquer death." Each intones a religious dictum and concludes simply, "Death is"; after each dictum, a chorus repeats, "Death is" (2:463). Kublai responds with a mournful soliloquy on the meaning of death but concludes, "It is nobler not to know" (2:464). A Mongol chronicler steps forward and chants *"the official lament for the dead."* Kublai dismisses the court, and only the chorus, Kublai, and Chu-Yin remain. Kublai speaks softly to Kukachin's body, swearing everyone else is dead but that she still lives. "I bid you welcome home, Little Flower!" he cries. "I bid you welcome home!" (2:466).

### Epilogue

The lights come up. Among the audience stands Marco Polo, dressed in 13th-century attire and looking *"a little bit sleepy, a trifle puzzled, and not a little irritated as his thoughts, in spite of himself, cling for a passing moment to the play just ended"* (2:467). Exhibiting no sign of anything unusual, he walks through the lobby, shakes off the disturbing memories·the play stirred in him, and meets a limousine waiting on the street. He steps in, slams the door

shut, and, expelling a *"satisfied sigh at the sheer comfort of it all, resumes his life"* (2:467).

## COMMENTARY

Legend has it that the American millionaire and patron of the arts Otto Kahn, whom O'Neill jokingly referred to as "Otto the Magnificent, the Great Kahn" (in O'Neill 189), encouraged O'Neill to write a play about American big business, though it is unclear precisely what he had in mind. The result was *Marco Millions*, a biting satire that O'Neill's friend the critic GEORGE JEAN NATHAN once referred to as "the sourest and most magnificent poke in the jaw that American big business and the American business man have ever got" (quoted in Floyd 167). One critic reviewing the premiere wrote the analogous sentiment that throughout the play, O'Neill "is constantly poking fun at American philistinism, American money-grubbing and money-wallowing" (Allen 55).

O'Neill meant *Marco Millions* to act as a kind of companion piece to BEYOND THE HORIZON, which, though not a historical play like *Marco Millions*, also deals with an itinerant businessman, Andrew Mayo, and his soul-destroying quest for "millions." *Beyond the Horizon* is a tragedy, but *Marco Millions* is unquestionably the funniest play O'Neill ever wrote, though all characters suffer the tragic consequences of Western avarice. Uncharacteristically, he even found the composition process enjoyable. In a 1924 letter to KENNETH MACGOWAN, he chuckled over the possibilities: "Am working hard as hell on *Marco*," he wrote wistfully. "It's going to be as humorous as the devil if the way it makes me guffaw as I write is any criterion—and not bitter humor, either, although it's all satirical. I actually grow to love my American pillars of society, Polo Brothers & Son" (quoted in Sheaffer 148).

In *Marco Millions*, many of Eugene O'Neill's most cherished fascinations collide with his most reviled bugaboos. The effect is a clash of what critics widely consider the comedy of Marco Polo and the tragedy of Kublai Kaan (Kublai Kahn), but only to the degree of their outward displays of happiness and loss, respectively. In fact, Kublai achieves spiritual transcendence, as we see in the final scene, in which he mourns the loss of his granddaughter Kukachin, the symbol of beauty, love, and life; whereas Marco, in the end, wallows complacently in the hog pit of bourgeois materialism. As such, Marco—who is often compared with the American novelist Sinclair Lewis's complacently materialistic Babbitt character—is a deliberate allegory of American avarice. This conflict between the spiritual and the material, usually dramatized in O'Neill as that between a poet and a businessman, along with many other parallels, is also strongly represented in *Beyond the Horizon* and *The Great God Brown*, among other, less important works.

O'Neill once referred to *Marco Millions* as "the Play of Andrew," referring to Andrew Mayo, the traveling businessman in *Beyond the Horizon.* In that play, the tension between poet and materialist is drawn out in the sibling rivalry between Robert and Andrew Mayo. Andrew takes Robert's place on their uncle's merchant ship and travels the world, eventually becoming, if only for a short time, "a millionaire—on paper" (1:642). It was the poetic Robert who first articulated to Ruth Atkins his desire to see what lies "beyond the horizon," or as Marco puts it to Donata, to "travel and see the world and all the different people and get to know their habits and needs from first-hand knowledge" (2:393). But after Andrew gets a taste for travel and business, he says to Ruth that his voyages showed him that "the world is a larger proposition than ever I thought it was in the old days" (1:626), which recalls Marco's next lines: "You've got to do that if you want to become really big and important" (2:393). Hence, Marco is a combination of the two types, and much of the play's tension is generated by the slow death of his poetic, spiritual self. William Brown and Dion Anthony of *The Great God Brown* share similar roles to those of Andrew and Robert, respectively. They play out the struggle FRIEDRICH NIETZSCHE outlines in *The Birth of Tragedy,* in which the practical Apollo (Brown) overcomes the life-lusting Dionysus (Dion). But unlike Andrew and William, in the end, Marco achieves no redemption.

Along with this preoccupation over materialism, O'Neill was intensely fascinated by China and the Far East. "Europe somehow means nothing to me," he once wrote to a friend. "Either the South

Seas or China, say I" (quoted in Alexander 42). In preparation for *Marco Millions,* he studied Kate Buss's *Studies in the Chinese Drama,* which explains, as Doris Alexander catalogs, the play's amalgamation of "comedy and tragedy, realism and fantasy, and drama with music, dance, pantomime, poetry, and sheer spectacle" (42). As ambitious a project as this was, particularly for an American audience who more or less shared Marco's tastes for "a good wholesome thrill" at the theater (2:431), the play was a triumph. Reviewing the premiere for *Women's Wear Daily,* Kelcey Allen raved that the production was "coruscating satire, biting in its irony, suffused with poetry, rich and dramatic in its simple story, and resplendently colorful in its background, atmosphere and imagery. 'Marco Millions' is a many faceted jewel" (55).

O'Neill also studied the text of Marco Polo's book closely. Originally titled *Il Milione,* or "The Million," after his family's nickname, *Emilione,* the book, a narrative of Polo's journey East from 1271 to 1295, was actually written by the romance writer Rusticello da Pisa. Thus, scholars have widely questioned its veracity, though it was the only source of knowledge about the East until the 17th century. As the title suggests, confronting the excessive materialism of the Western world in general, and the United States in particular, is the play's predominant theme. In the notes O'Neill took from Colonel Sir Henry Yule's scholarly edition of *The Book of Ser Marco Polo,* he wrote down Yule's description of Marco Polo verbatim—"a practical man, brave, shrewd, prudent, keen in affairs, and never losing interest in mercantile details, very fond of the chase, sparing of speech"—after which O'Neill scrawled, "The American Ideal!" (quoted in Alexander 42). In act 2, scene 1, we find O'Neill's own description of the American businessman, far less objective and far more scathing, by way of Kublai's reaction to Marco's fascist governmental policies in Yang-Chau:

> Marco's spiritual hump begins to disgust me. He has not even a mortal soul, he has only an acquisitive instinct. We have given him every opportunity to learn. He has memorized everything and learned nothing. He has looked at

everything and seen nothing. He has lusted for everything and loved nothing (2:420).

Cynthia McCown argues with critics Travis Bogard and Virginia Floyd (along with Kublai in the above passage) that Marco does, indeed, have a soul—the clearest evidence is that Kukachin apprehends it—but that over time his soul, along with the souls of anyone who comes in contact with him, withers under the intensity of his "acquisitive instinct." This is an important point in that if Marco, as Virginia Floyd has written, "has no soul" (290), then O'Neill offers little hope for mankind's salvation. In contrast, Kublai's conclusion at the end is entirely fatalistic. After having studied the pope's emissary, his optimistic dream of acquiring true spiritual knowledge descends into a state of hopeless cynicism: "God is only an infinite, insane energy which creates and destroys without other purpose than to pass eternity in avoiding thought. Then the stupid man becomes the Perfect Incarnation of Omnipotence and the Polos are the true children of God!" (2:455). O'Neill would later respond to Kublai's enigmatic chant in the final scene, "Death is," in LAZARUS LAUGHED. "For Man death is not!" Lazarus exhorts to Caligula, a figure embodying mankind's terror of death—"Man, Son of God's Laughter, *is!* . . . *Is,* Caligula! Believe in the laughing god within you!" (2:618).

O'Neill shows the collusion between businessmen and American politicians when he likens Marco's comportment to that of a southern senator who wishes to amend the constitution to prohibit "*the migration of non-Nordic birds into Texas, or . . . the practice of the laws of biology within the twelve-mile limit*" (2:424). As mayor of Yang-Chau, Marco institutes numerous new policies, all fiercely practical but cruel and soulless. Kublai refers to a petition from its citizens "enumerating over three thousand cases of [his] gross abuses of power" (2:425). Sounding very much like the American politicians O'Neill and his GREENWICH VILLAGE friends despised, Marco dismisses this as the "work of a mere handful of radicals" (2:425).

In kind, Doris Alexander, an O'Neill critic who always places her subject squarely in his historical context, has helpfully enumerated a number of

events from O'Neill's historical moment—America in the 1920s—that have direct parallels in *Marco Millions*. Maffeo's advice to Marco to accept a second-class position from Kublai Kaan rather than a first-class one, for instance, bears a striking resemblance to the public revelation that President Warren G. Harding's attorney general, Harry M. Daugherty, took that office rather than the position of secretary of state for purposes of personal gain (Alexander 45). More important, Harding's secretary of the Treasury was Andrew Mellon, one of the three richest men in the United States at the time. Mellon cut income taxes to the wealthy and replaced them with a consumer tax that badly affected the poor, as Marco does in Yang-Chau (Alexander 48). And like Yang-Chau's "poet who had fled from there in horror," in the 1920s there was a major exodus of American artists, writers, and intellectuals from the country—including Gertrude Stein, Ernest Hemingway, and F. Scott Fitzgerald, a group popularly referred to as the Lost Generation—largely driven by the kind of institutionalized cultural stifling (to which O'Neill was no stranger) Marco mandates in his city (49).

There are also significant parallels between Marco's description of war—especially war as a paradoxical tool of "peace"—and the justifications President Woodrow Wilson used for the country's entrance into World War I, "the war to end all wars," which O'Neill actively protested against. And finally, though not exhaustively, Cynthia McCown identifies a series of policies directed at American interests in China—Secretary of State John Hay's Open Door Policy (1899), President William Howard Taft's "dollar diplomacy" (1912), and the Nine Power Pact (1922)—that bear fruitful parallels as well.

But the correspondences are not isolated to O'Neill's era. Indeed, world events have proven O'Neill scholar Travis Bogard utterly wrong when he wrote dismissively of *Marco Millions* that the play is "of its period, and it will remain so. Its ironic theme . . . is buried too deeply in time for it to emerge as a play of substance" (260). A subtle theme is borne out in the final scene when Kublai Kaan's General Bayan suggests the Mongols get rich by invading Europe. Kublai responds with grim irony: "You have already conquered the West, I think," he says, but then demonstrates his own absorption of Western greed by ordering him to invade Japan in order to corner the silk market. He will do so with paper money (borrowed money) and cannon (deterrence)—the former "if you make people believe it's worth it, it is," and the latter because "war is a waste of money which eats into the profits of life like thunder!" (2:427). Combined, "you conquer the world with this—(*he pats the cannon-model*) and you pay for it with this. (*He pats the paper money—rhetorically*)" (2:428).

As funny as *Marco Millions* truly is, the play can act as a cold reminder of the horrors igniting across the Middle East—and many of their causes as well. If there remains any question to the falsity of Bogard's assertion about the play's historical obsolescence, consider the opening of act 1, scene 3: As Maffeo mulls over the Polos' business prospects in the Middle East, he reads from the notes of their previous voyage, which says, "There's one kingdom called Mosul and in it a district of Baku where there's a great fountain of oil. There's a growing demand for it. (*then speaking*) Make a mental note of that" (2:401).

See also CLASS.

## CHARACTERS

**Bayan, General**   The commander in chief of Kublai Kaan's million-man army. Bayan is an example of the long-lasting impact Marco Polo's stay in their kingdom will have. In act 3, scene 1, he characterizes himself, as Marco does, as a "man of action" and attempts to convince Kublai to invade Europe for profit. Kublai responds ironically, "Hum! You have already conquered the West, I think" (2:451). But Kublai reluctantly demonstrates his own absorption of Western greed by ordering him to invade Japan to corner the silk market.

**Buddhist Traveler**   A Kashmiri traveling merchant selling prayer beads. In the prologue he meets two other merchants, a Christian and a Magian, at a holy tree on the border of India and Persia. Like the other two, he is exhausted from traveling and seeks shelter from the hot sun under the tree. As a Buddhist, he believes the tree is the sacred tree

of Buddha and argues with the other two over this. When a captain arrives with a team of slaves bearing the corpse of Princess Kukachin, he is forced to replace a dead slave and proceed with the convoy to Cathay (China).

**Captain**   A A Muslim captain in the service of Ghazan Khan of Persia. The captain arrives at the holy tree in the prologue in a chariot pulled by slaves and bearing the corpse of Princess Kukachin back to Cathay (China). O'Neill describes him as "*a brutal, determined-looking man of forty*" who treats his slaves mercilessly. When his corporal reports that three of the slaves are dead, he looks at the three traders and shouts, "Allah has provided!" (2:390), and he impresses them into slavery. The Christian traveler protests that he has a letter of introduction to Princess Kukachin, and the captain cunningly asks to read it, tears it up, and lashes him to the chariot.

**Christian Traveler**   An Italian traveling merchant carrying a letter of introduction to Princess Kukachin from the Venetian firm Polo Brothers and Son. In the prologue, he meets two other merchants, a Buddhist and a Magian, at a holy tree on the border of India and Persia. Like the other two, he is exhausted from traveling and seeks shelter from the hot sun under the tree. As a Christian, he believes the tree is the staff of Adam and the wood used to construct the cross on which Jesus Christ was crucified, and he argues with the other two over this. When a captain arrives with a team of slaves bearing the corpse of Princess Kukachin, he is forced to replace a dead slave and proceed with the convoy to Cathay (China).

**Chu-Yin**   Kublai Kaan's adviser and spiritual counselor. Chu-Yin is a "*venerable old man with white hair, dressed in a simple black robe*" (2:412) who counsels Kublai to accept Marco Polo into their kingdom as a study in Western ways. "At least, if he cannot learn," he argues in act 1, scene 6, on behalf of the impudent Venetian, "we shall" (2:416). When Marco is eventually promoted to mayor of the city of Yang-Chau and sets up a fascist government system there, Chu-Yin informs Kublai that he "talked recently with a poet who had fled there in horror. Yang-Chau used to have a soul, he said. Now it has a brand new court house" (2:420).

Chu-Yin suspects that his master's granddaughter Kukachin has fallen in love with Marco, and he secretly bids the trader to look into the princess's eyes each day on their voyage from Cathay to Persia. He believes that Kukachin's happiness rests on Marco's ability to read her love for him in her eyes, but he also wisely reasons that "who knows but some day this Marco may see into her eyes and his soul may be born" (2:421). The ploy fails, however, and the guileless Marco proceeds to Venice to marry his fiancée, Donata. When Kukachin writes from Persia that she is dying of heartbreak, Kublai threatens to invade Europe. Chu-Yin talks him out of it by reckoning that Kukachin would not wish it.

**Donata**  Marco Polo's fiancée. Donata first appears in act 1, scene 1, as a 12-year-old girl, but by act 3, scene 1, she is 35 and *"has grown into a stout middle-age but her face is unlined and still pretty in a bovine, good-natured way"* (2:457). Donata's character develops only insofar as in her first scene with Marco, she exhibits the traits of a love-struck little girl; as an older woman, she is clearly more entranced by Marco's affluence than his love for her. This contrasts her starkly with Kukachin, who has all the riches in the world but dies of a broken heart when Marco leaves the East. Her marriage to Marco is essentially a marriage of convenience, as their union will bring their two families' "firms into closer contact" (2:393).

**Ghazan**  Khan of Persia and Kukachin's betrothed. His father, Arghun Khan, was supposed to marry Kukachin, but he died before she arrived in Persia, so she marries Ghazan instead. O'Neill describes him as *"a young man, not handsome but noble and manly looking"* (2:448). He lavishes Kukachin with praise when they first meet in act 2, scene 3, and threatens to execute Marco if he had insulted her on the voyage to Persia. Instead, he confers upon Marco the Order of the Lion, which Ghazan explains is restricted to "great heroes and kings," and requests Ghazan to give Marco a chest of gold (2:449). According to Kukachin's letter in act 3, scene 1, Ghazan is "kind,"

but she loves Marco and dies of heartbreak a year after her marriage to Ghazan (2:453).

**Kublai, the Great Kaan**  King of Cathay and Kukachin's grandfather; historically, the grandson of Genghis Khan, who lived from 1216 to 1294. Kublai, reputedly the richest king in the world, requests the pope to send 100 wise men to teach him about their religion. A wise, intellectual, honest leader of his people, Kublai wishes to investigate all the major religions of the world so he might choose which path leads to spiritual salvation. The newly elected pope, the former papal legate Tedaldo, sends the highly ambitious 15-year-old Marco Polo instead.

When Marco appears at his throne room at Cambaluc, Kublai threatens to kill him as proof that he does not have an immortal soul. But Marco's audacity impresses him. After accepting his counselor Chu-Yin's advice to treat Marco as an amusing case study, he confers upon him a second-class government commission. Though the young Venetian touches him "as a child might," he tells Chu-Yin, "at the same time there is something warped, deformed" about him (2:416). Over time, Marco is promoted to mayor of the city of Yang-Chau, though it becomes clear that Marco's presence in Kublai's kingdom has had a series of adverse effects—not the least of which, along with the spread of Western materialism and the institutionalized destruction of Chinese culture, is his granddaughter Princess Kukachin's infatuation with him. But Marco is too soulless to recognize Kukachin's love, and when she is left to marry the khan of Persia, an arranged marriage that makes her a queen, she dies of heartbreak. At her funeral, Kublai suggests that it was not she who died, but he and his kingdom who have suffered a spiritual death.

Kublai's appearance changes with greater exposure to Marco Polo. When we first meet him in act 1, scene 6, he is a magnificent sight, *"dressed in heavy gold robes of state. He is a man of sixty but still in the full prime of his powers, his face proud and noble, his expression tinged with an ironic humor and bitterness yet full of a sympathetic humanity"* (2:411); whereas in the scene just before Kukachin's funeral, O'Neill describes him simply as *"aged and sad"* (2:451). O'Neill critic Virginia Floyd suggests that his "contact with this living symbol of Western Christianity and civilization proves to be a painful learning experience, disillusioning him and shattering his hope for religious assurance" (300–301). Kublai thus resembles O'Neill's take on religion when he hopelessly remarks in his final scene that "God is only an infinite, insane energy which creates and destroys without other purpose than to pass eternity in avoiding thought. Then the stupid man becomes the Perfect Incarnation of Omnipotence and the Polos are the true children of God!" (2:455).

**Kukachin**  Princess of Cathay, later queen of Persia, and Kublai Kaan's granddaughter. O'Neill describes her as *"a beautiful young girl of twenty, pale and delicate"* (2:418). She is first introduced in the prologue as a corpse that comes to life with a message to an Italian merchant: "Say this, I loved and died. Now I am love, and live. And living, have forgotten. And loving, can forgive. . . . Say this for me in Venice!" (2:390). We meet her three years earlier in act 2, scene 1, at Kublai's summer palace at Xanadu. Against the wishes of her loving grandfather, Kukachin has fallen in love with the Venetian trader Marco Polo. She is introduced reciting a poem of loss, as she is to be married to the king of Persia instead of Marco. Chu-Yin, Kublai's adviser, reports that the citizens of Yang-Chau, where Marco is ruling as mayor, have complained that the avaricious Venetian's policies are self-serving, bureaucratic, and harmful to their culture. When Kublai voices his suspicion that the Christian has no soul, Kukachin testifies she has seen it in a series of small, kind acts, and she defends Marco as an effective and just ruler. She requests Marco to take her on the voyage to Persia, on which she hopes to demonstrate her love for him. When Chu-Yin instructs Marco to look into her eyes each day, however, all Marco sees is what he takes as various illnesses and neuroses.

Throughout the play, Kukachin symbolizes love, beauty, and spirituality. Because Marco Polo never recognizes her love for him, O'Neill makes it clear that all hope for Marco's soul is gone. And because she symbolizes love, she must die in the end, as without love she cannot exist. As Doris Alexander puts it, "it is the knowledge that she will die, brought by message to Kublai Kaan, which brings home the tragic cost of Marco's acquisitiveness to him" (53).

**Magian Traveler**  A Persian traveling merchant selling copies of *Arabian Nights*, a book of 13th-century pornography that was banned in the United States in 1927. In the prologue, he meets two other merchants, a Christian and a Buddhist, at a holy tree on the border of India and Persia. Like the other two, he is exhausted from traveling and seeks shelter from the hot sun under the tree. As a Magian, he believes the tree is the tree of life planted by Zoroaster and argues with the other two over this. When a captain arrives with a team of slaves bearing the corpse of Princess Kukachin, he is forced to replace a dead slave and proceed with the convoy to Cathay (China).

**Polo, Maffeo**  A seasoned trader, Marco Polo's uncle, and Nicolo Polo's brother and partner. Maffeo, a middle-aged man, is *"tall and stout with a round, jovial face and small, cunning eyes"* (2:395). Maffeo is the clear leader of the expedition east. He is a shrewd businessman and can be credited with much of Marco's success. When Marco first meets Kublai Kaan in act 1, scene 6, for instance, it is Maffeo who astutely advises his young nephew to request a second-class government commission rather than a first-class one, as "a First Class agent is all brass buttons and no opportunities. A Second Class travels around, is allowed his expenses, gets friendly with all the dealers, scares them into letting him in on everything—and gets what's rightfully coming to him!" (2:415). Like his brother, Maffeo is happy to confer Marco with a junior partnership and follow him around as a subordinate, as long as it keeps the profits coming. Perhaps Maffeo's most important line is the exclamation, "One million!" when he is done counting his tally in act 2, scene 3, effectively halting Marco's possible salvation by acknowledging Kukachin's love for him (2:446). It is at this moment, critic Cynthia McCown argues, that Marco "exchanges his soul for cold cash."

**Polo, Marco** A Venetian trader and the title character; historically, the legendary merchant and explorer who lived from 1254 to 1324; who explored Asia from 1271 to 1295; and whose account, "The Million," or *The Travels of Marco Polo,* was the only European record of Eastern life until the 17th century. In act 1, scene 1, O'Neill presents Marco as a typical love-struck teenager, *"youthfully handsome and well made"* (2:392), as he serenades the 12-year-old Donata and promises to marry her upon his return from the Far East. He also promises to write her a love poem, which he does, though it speaks more to his avaricious spirit than his love for Donata. Nevertheless, it is a poem and can be seen as evidence that Marco has a poetic—and therefore spiritual—side to him. He makes a favorable enough impression on Tedaldo, the papal legate who is elected pope in act 1, scene 2, and Tedaldo decides to send Marco with his father Nicolo and uncle Maffeo to Kublai Kaan, king of Cathay (China), in place of the hundred Christian wise men the Kaan had requested. Over time, as he travels farther and farther east, through Islam, India, and Mongolia, Marco becomes increasingly jaded about meeting foreign cultures and sees them merely as disposable means for profit. When he meets Kublai Kaan, Marco touches him "as a child might, but at the same time there is something warped, deformed" about him (2:416). Kublai's counselor Chu-Yin advises the Kaan to treat Marco as a case study, and they grant him his wish to be a second-class government official. His uncle has convinced him to take a second-class position rather than first class, as they travel around, make contacts, and are therefore exposed to more business opportunities.

Eventually Marco is promoted to mayor of Yang-Chau, a large Chinese city. During the years of his administration, one that resembles O'Neill's view of the American government, Marco infuriates the citizens by creating a single tax that favors the wealthy, abolishing "sin," and institutionalizing a bureaucratic stranglehold on the city that effectively destroys its culture. Before he requests permission to return home, he attempts to sell Kublai two ideas that he assures him will enable him to expand his empire substantially: cannon and paper money. "You conquer the world with this—(*he pats the cannon-model*) and you pay for it with this. (*He pats the paper money—rhetorically*)" (2:428).

As cynically ruthless as Marco can be, he unintentionally wins the heart of Princess Kukachin, Kublai's granddaughter, who symbolizes love, beauty, and spirituality. When he accompanies her on her voyage to Persia, where she will marry Ghazan Kahn, Chu-Tin arranges for Marco to look into her eyes each day in the hope that he might discover his soul. When she makes a final effort at the wharf in Persia, he does for a moment gain enlightenment and speaks her name passionately, but his uncle cries out their tally, "One million!"— and at that crucial moment, writes critic Cynthia McCown, Marco "exchanges his soul for cold cash." Kukachin goes on as planned and marries the Persian king, but she dies one year later of a broken heart. Marco returns to Venice triumphant, and in the final scene, at a banquet held in his honor, all that can be heard over the din of the guests is Marco shouting, referring to silk worms not money, "Millions! . . . millions! . . . millions! . . . millions!" (2:461).

O'Neill co-opted the historical figure as an allegory to satirize American materialism. The playwright apparently solidified the idea upon reading Colonel Sir Henry Yule's scholarly edition of *The Book of Ser Marco Polo,* in which Yule described Marco as "a practical man, brave, shrewd, prudent, keen in affairs, and never losing interest in mercantile details, very fond of the chase, sparing of speech"—after which O'Neill wrote, "the American Ideal!" (quoted in Alexander 42). As one contemporary of O'Neill's commented, Marco's is "the story of Babbitt retold in ancient dress" (in Brown 181). He resembles both Andrew Mayo from *Beyond the Horizon* and William Brown from *The Great God Brown,* in that his spiritual life is ruined by materialist goals. Unlike Andrew and William, however, Marco achieves no redemption in the end. Those two characters both transcend spiritually inhibiting material goals and recognize their mistakes; Marco never does, a fact that, though Marco is a satirical figure, makes O'Neill's lament over American-style gluttony—what O'Neill critic Doris Alexander calls "brass band materialism"

(46)—even darker than the other two plays, which are, paradoxically, tragedies.

**Polo, Nicolo**  A seasoned trader and Marco Polo's father. Nicolo, *"a small thin middle-aged man, with a dry, shred face"* (2:395), is proud of his son's triumphs, though he is quick to point out his brashness and naïveté. Each time the Polos arrive in a new region, Nicolo often reads from their outrageously ethnocentric notes from their previous voyage to understand the culture and business opportunities. Like his brother, he is happy to confer Marco with a partnership and follow him around as a subordinate, as long as it keeps the profits coming.

**Prostitute**  O'Neill describes her in uncommonly stereotypical terms, compared to many of his other prostitute characters, as *"painted, half-naked, alluring in a brazen, sensual way"* (2:403). The prostitute appears in Islam (an Islamic country), India, and Mongolia, and each time she is dressed in that region's attire, though her relationship with the Polos indicates she is essentially the same person. We see this in act 1, scene 4, when O'Neill describes her as *"the same but now in Indian garb,"* and Nicolo Polo says "you again" (2:406). She is the embodiment of sexuality and underscores Marco's developing cynicism toward love: As Marco becomes a more seasoned trader, he develops from a bashful teenager to a seasoned "john." By her last appearance in act 1, scene 5, he can no longer afford her because she already has all of his money. Her conquest of Marco symbolizes the death of Marco's soul as well, as we can see when she shouts "Going! Going! Gone! . . . Your soul! Dead and buried!" (2:410), and she crushes his poem (the last remnants of his poetic self) under her feet.

**Tedaldo**  The papal legate at Acre. In act 1, scene 2, the conclave of cardinals selects him to be the next pope. He is *"a man of sixty with a strong, intelligent face"* (2:394–395) who takes a liking to Marco Polo and sends him in place of the hundred wise men Kublai Kaan requested, in Maffeo Polo's words, "to argue with his Buddhists and Taoists and Confucians which religion in the world is best" (2:395).

## BIBLIOGRAPHY

Alexander, Doris. *Eugene O'Neill's Creative Struggle: The Decisive Decade, 1924–1933.* University Park: Pennsylvania State University Press, 1992.

Allen, Kelcey. "'Marco Millions' Is Poignant O'Neill Satire." In *Playwright's Progress: O'Neill and the Critics,* edited by Jordan Y. Miller, 55–57. Chicago: Scott, Foresman and Company, 1965.

Bogard, Travis. *Contour in Time: The Plays of Eugene O'Neill.* Rev. ed. New York: Oxford University Press, 1988.

Brown, John Mason. *"Marco Millions."* In *O'Neill and His Plays: Four Decades of Criticism,* edited by Oscar N. Cargill, Bryllion Fagin, and William J. Fisher, 181–183. New York: New York University Press, 1961.

Floyd, Virginia. *The Plays of Eugene O'Neill: A New Assessment.* New York: Ungar, 1985.

McCown, Cynthia. "All the Wrong Dreams: *Marco Millions* and the Acquisitive Instinct." *Eugene O'Neill Review* 27 (2005). Available online. URL: http://www.eoneill.com/library/review/27/27m.htm. Accessed May 25, 2007.

O'Neill, Eugene. *Selected Letters of Eugene O'Neill.* Edited by Travis Bogard and Jackson R. Bryer. New Haven, Conn.: Yale University Press, 1988.

Sheaffer, Louis. *O'Neill: Son and Artist.* Boston: Little, Brown, 1973.

# Moon for the Misbegotten, A (completed, 1943; first produced, 1947)

A *Moon for the Misbegotten* was the last play *Eugene O'Neill* ever wrote and the last produced before his death in 1953. O'Neill was only 55 when his tremors (the result of cortical cerebellar atrophy) had become so severe that he found himself incapable of writing for the last 10 years of his life. World War II also upset O'Neill terribly; he was working on act 2 when the Japanese attacked Pearl Harbor on December 7, 1941. "I had to drag myself through it since Pearl Harbor," he wrote, "and it needs much revision—wanders all over the place" (quoted in Barlow 116). Nevertheless, he completed a first draft by January 1, 1942, and finished the surviving draft the following year. In an author's note included in the Random House first edition, O'Neill implicitly apologized for publishing the play in what he considered draft form: "It has never been presented on the New York stage nor are there outstanding rights or plans for its production. Since I cannot presently give it the attention required for appropriate presentation, I have decided to make it available in book form" (3:854).

*A Moon for the Misbegotten* takes place 11 years after LONG DAY'S JOURNEY INTO NIGHT and acts as a sequel to that play, with James Tyrone (based on O'Neill's older brother, JAMES O'NEILL, JR.) as its tragic, if misbegotten, hero. O'Neill's wife CARLOTTA MONTEREY O'NEILL disliked the full-length play, considering it an unnecessary addendum to *Long Day's Journey*. O'Neill himself admitted later that "he had come to loathe it" (Bogard 447). After many entreaties, however, the THEATRE GUILD convinced O'Neill to permit a trial production run in the Midwest. *Moon* thus premiered in Columbus, Ohio, on February 20, 1947. The play's unorthodox conflation of ALCOHOLISM and Christian symbolism, shanty Irish characters and antitrust propaganda, highly charged sexuality and motherhood, all offended critics and censors alike. "I was ashamed to have my mother's old ears assaulted by the profanity and vulgarity of this play," wrote Florence Fisher Parry in the *Pittsburgh Press*; in Detroit, Michigan, a police censor shut the play down after only two performances. Not until a decade later, on May 2, 1957, would the Broadway premiere take place. Following the remarkable New York debut of *Long Day's Journey into Night* the previous November, this production was a terrific success and contributed to the EUGENE O'NEILL RENAISSANCE in the years to come.

## SYNOPSIS

### Scene of the Play

*A Moon for the Misbegotten* opens with a preface entitled "Scene of the Play," in which O'Neill closely describes the setting: tenant farmer Phil Hogan's house and its immediate vicinity. The action takes place in NEW LONDON, CONNECTICUT,

in early September 1923 between midday and sunrise the following morning. O'Neill describes the house as "an old boxlike, clapboarded affair, with a shingled roof and brick chimney . . . propped up about two feet above the ground by layers of timber blocks" (3:856). There are two bare windows on the lower floor and one on the upper, each missing a pane of glass. A flat-topped boulder lies beneath the window at right, and a small bedroom addition has been "tacked on" the right side for Hogan's daughter, Josie. Beyond the house stands a "scraggly orchard of apple trees" and a barn. A dirt path winds back around an old pear tree, through a "field of hay stubble," and down to a wood in the distance; the same path leads from the front door down to the country highway about a hundred yards to the left (3:856).

### Act 1

Before noon on a hot day in early September. Josie Hogan, barefooted in a cheap sleeveless dress, steps out her bedroom door. Twenty-eight and broad-shouldered, busty and wide-hipped, Josie is so largely proportioned that "she is almost a freak" (3:857). Her 20-year-old brother, Mike Hogan, runs up to the house from the right rear. Unlike Josie, who has "the map of Ireland . . . stamped on her face," Mike has a "common Irish" countenance. A devout observer of Roman CATHOLICISM, Mike Hogan is "a New England Irish Catholic Puritan, Grade B" and thus, according to O'Neill, "an extremely irritating youth to have around" (3:857). Mike has decided to leave his father's farm as his brothers Thomas, a policeman in Bridgeport, and John, a barkeeper in Meriden, had done years before. Though fond of her father, Phil Hogan, Josie sympathizes with her brothers' desire to escape his slave-driving ways on the farm. She has packed Mike's bag and pilfered six dollars from their father to help finance the trip. They both feel some remorse in parting, though Josie scoffs at Mike as a "priest's pet" and Mike at her reputation as the town slut.

Mike first declines the stolen money, but Josie convinces him that "it's a bit of wages he's never given you" (3:859). Mike advises her to marry James "Jim" Tyrone, their well-educated but severely dissipated landlord. Mike loathes Tyrone as a man who puts on airs "as if he was too good to wipe his shoes on me, when he's nothing but a drunken bum who never done a tap of work in his life, except acting on the stage while his father was alive to get him jobs" (3:861). But he hopes Josie might get even by securing Tyrone's inheritance. Josie threatens to pummel him, which she could, then warns that their father is heading back from the barn. She reports on his progress to the house until she turns and sees that her craven brother has already fled in terror.

Phil Hogan charges full-speed onto the stage. Josie knows she can overtake him physically but, sensitive of his pride, arms herself with a sawed-off broom handle. Hogan is 55, muscular, and substantially shorter than his daughter. He speaks in a voice that is *"high-pitched with a pronounced brogue"* and wears *"an old wide-brimmed hat of coarse straw that would look more becoming on a horse"* (3:862). Hogan betrays *"a faint trace of grudging respect"* at the news that Mike had the courage to leave the farm to "make his own way in the world." Josie tells him that she gave Mike the money to leave. After an initial burst of outrage, Hogan says bitterly, "I wouldn't put it past him to drop it in the collection plate next Sunday, he's that big a jackass" (3:864). Their comic Irish banter demonstrates a clear mutual respect for each other's prowess in physical and verbal combat. Hogan expounds resentfully about his wife having died in childbirth for a "hypocrite" like Mike (3:867). Josie has replaced her mother as the only one, including his sons, who keeps Hogan in his place no matter how ornery his mood.

Hogan sarcastically rides Josie for her reputation among the men in town, though admitting he would miss her company and help with the farm if she married. In spite of himself, he agrees with Mike about seducing Jim Tyrone. He knows from long bouts of drinking at the local inn that Tyrone greatly admires and perhaps even loves Josie. "Sure, all the pretty little tarts on Broadway, New York, must have had a try at that, and much good it did them," she responds dismissively (3:867). The two wistfully discuss Tyrone's late father, "a true Irish gentleman" who "worked up from nothing to be rich and famous" but still

"didn't give a damn about station" (3:868). Hogan continues to plot how to gain Tyrone as his son-in-law, but Josie still resists—"I'm an ugly lump of a woman, and the men that want me are no better than stupid bulls" (3:870). Hogan voices concern that Tyrone may sell the farm from under them once the Tyrone estate is out of probate court. He has promised not to, but Hogan warns that when Tyrone gets drunk, "he doesn't know himself what he mightn't do" (3:873).

Hogan sees Tyrone approaching the house from the highway below. Josie characterizes Tyrone as approaching the Hogan house "like a dead man walking slow behind his own coffin" (3:874). Josie goes inside to fix herself up with the excuse that she will check their stew. Tyrone enters. He is in his early 40s, still handsome, but softened and bloated from dissipation and dressed in *"a style set by well-groomed Broadway gamblers who would like to be mistaken for Wall Street brokers."* His demeanor sharpens for the verbal jousting he enjoys with his tenant: The two men, O'Neill writes, *"are like players at an old familiar game where each knows the other's moves, but which still amuses them"* (3:875). Hogan and Tyrone banter back and forth in cuttingly sarcastic dialogue—Hogan backhandedly insulting the farm, and Tyrone cajoling him into offering whiskey.

Josie steps outside and joins in the fun. She jokes about her reputation, which visibly upsets Tyrone. Changing the subject, he informs them that the Standard Oil magnate T. Stedman Harder plans to visit the Hogans that afternoon. Hogan's pigs have been swimming in his ice pond, and each time Harder mends the fence separating their land, Hogan tears it down. The prospect of Harder's visit delights them. Josie plants a triumphant kiss on Tyrone, frightening herself in some way; but she laughs off her reaction by wisecracking, only partly in jest, "It's like kissing a corpse" (3:882). Physical violence against Harder is out of the question, but the Hogans will have a wonderful time cutting him to pieces with their indomitable Irish wit. O'Neill specifies their Irish-born strategy during such verbal warring: "[They] *take the offensive at once and never let an opponent get set to hit back. Also, they use a beautifully co-ordinated, bewildering change of pace, switching suddenly from jarring shouts to low, confidential vituperation. And they exaggerate their Irish brogues to confuse an enemy still further"* (3:884).

Josie spots Harder on the road and coaxes Tyrone into her bedroom to watch the performance. Before he disappears into the house, she invites him up to the house for a moonlit evening together, and he enthusiastically accepts. Harder appears from left. Dressed in *"a beautifully tailored English tweed coat and whipcord riding breeches, immaculately polished English riding boots with spurs,"* Harder is in his late 30s and handsome in a common way; his demeanor is pleasant but with an outward expression of entitlement, *"simply immature, naturally lethargic, a bit stupid. . . . It would be hard to find anyone more ill-equipped for combat with the Hogans"* (3:884). From the outset, the Hogans take Harder off-balance, assuming a higher social plane and openly insulting him. Accustomed to deferential treatment, especially from members of their social CLASS, Harder blusters and fumbles for words as Hogan and his daughter relentlessly carry out their onslaught. From within the house can be heard an occasional spurt of uncontrollable laughter from the hidden Tyrone. Clearly outmatched, Harder tries to make his escape. Hogan snatches him by the collar and accuses him of tearing down the fence and allowing his pigs to catch pneumonia. "Sure, it isn't reasonable," Hogan jibes, "for a Standard Oil man to hate hogs" (3:888).

Harder eventually makes his getaway, but from a safe distance he threatens police action if Hogan continues tampering with his fence. Hogan shouts back with threats to call his lawyer and notify the newspapers as Tyrone emerges from the house doubled over in laughter. Tyrone muses tauntingly that the Hogans' bullying probably doubled or tripled the value of the property—Harder will pay anything to evict the Hogans. But they recognize his teasing look and invite him in for lunch before he and Hogan head off to the inn and celebrate the Irish victory. Tyrone looks down at Josie's chest and utters *"with genuine feeling"* that she has "the most beautiful breasts in the world" (3:891). Flattered in spite of herself, Josie leads him into the house as the curtain falls.

**Act 2**

Five minutes past 11 o'clock that night; the same as act 1 but with the living room wall now removed to expose the broken-down interior. The space is small, low-ceilinged, and *"cluttered up with furniture that looks as if it had been picked up at a fire sale"* (3:892). Josie is discovered sitting on the front steps wearing her Sunday best—a cheap, dark blue dress with black stockings and a white flower pinned to her chest. She rises and checks an alarm clock on the dresser, then angrily wrenches the flower off the dress and tosses it aside. Tyrone had promised to meet her two hours earlier. From a distance, she hears Hogan approaching the house and singing drunkenly. Josie arms herself with the broomstick handle.

"Hurroo!" Hogan shouts. "Down with all tyrants, male and female! To hell with England, and God damn Standard Oil!" (3:893). He demands entry, though the door is unlocked, and his rough talk earns him a belt on the head from Josie's club. He reprimands her for her lack of compassion and hints something dreadful transpired at the inn. Fearing he might start a fire, Josie moves to turn down the lamp, but Hogan surprises her by saying, "Let it burn to the ground. A hell of a lot I care if it burns" (3:895). After a round of name-calling back and forth, Josie eventually learns that James Tyrone agreed that night to sell the farm to Harder for $10,000. She refuses to believe it at first. Hogan continues that Tyrone admitted his strong feelings for her; Tyrone also believes she is a virgin, that her talk of promiscuity is nothing but a pose. His lateness is due to his wish to save her from his lechery. Now convinced of Tyrone's betrayal, she concocts a scheme in which she will get Tyrone drunk and coax him into bed; then Hogan will appear with witnesses to shame Tyrone into leaving them the farm. She adds they can blackmail him for $10,000.

They see Tyrone coming up the path and pretend she has kicked Hogan out for drunkenness. When Tyrone enters, Hogan acts drunker than he is and tries to hit Tyrone. Wishing them both bad luck, he heads off for the inn. Tyrone does not remember him being that "lit up" at the inn (3:908). Josie forgives him for arriving late. With Hogan's singing still audible from the road below, Tyrone sits down next to her and settles his head on her breast. Believing Tyrone has betrayed them, Josie acts sweetly but cannot control the occasional hints that she knows something lies heavy on his conscience. Overwhelmed with conflicted feelings, Tyrone feels comfortable in the presence of a decent woman, but he is also filled with desire. "You rotten bastard!" he curses himself when Josie goes inside for whiskey. With trembling hands, he attempts to light a cigarette as the curtain falls (3:911).

## Act 3

Same as act 2, but with the living room wall replaced. No time has elapsed. Tyrone successfully lights his cigarette and paces back and forth in front of the house. Overcome with equal parts self-pity and self-hatred, he sings lines from "In the Baggage Coach Ahead," a popular song of the 1890s: "And baby's cries can't waken her / In the baggage coach ahead" (3:912). Josie emerges from the house with a bottle of whiskey, two tumblers, and a pitcher of water. She remarks that he looks as if he had seen a ghost. "I have," he responds. "My own. He's punk company" (3:912). Josie surprises him by pouring herself a drink along with his; she *"gags and sputters"* on the drink but pretends it "went down the wrong way" (3:913). Again she brazenly alludes to her promiscuity. Tyrone implores her to stop pretending, but she retorts that he is bluffing her with his compliments and talk of love. He takes her in his arms but stops himself abruptly in self-disgust. *"Her face betrays the confused conflict within her of fright, passion, happiness, and bitter resentment."* She suggests they sit down together "where the moon will be in our eyes and we'll see romance" (3:914).

Josie voices jealousy over Tyrone's "Broadway flames," but he rejects the comparison, calling her "real and healthy and clean and fine and warm and strong and kind" (3:915). She wonders if that means she has a beautiful soul. "Well, I don't know much about ladies' souls," he says. "But I do know you're beautiful. (*He kisses her hand.*) And I love you a lot—in my fashion" (3:915). She shyly kisses him on the lips, but Tyrone resists the temptation. "There's always the aftermath that poisons you. I don't want you to be poisoned. . . . And I don't want to be poisoned myself—not again—not with you" (3:916). She takes another drink, and he furiously knocks it to the ground. Not wanting her to turn into one of the many "drunken tramps" he has been with, Tyrone enigmatically speaks of a "fat blonde pig on the train" (3:917). When she asks what train, he changes the subject.

As they continue drinking, he sinks deeper into a quagmire of self-pity and warns her obliquely about what she might expect from him drunk. Reflecting on mornings after sleeping with "drunken tramps," he murmurs, "I've seen too God-damned many dawns creeping grayly over too many dirty windows." Now threateningly, he recalls a woman who watched him get drunk with the "idea she could roll me, I guess. She wasn't so tickled about it—later on" (3:919). Josie asks once more about the woman on the train, and he reflects vaguely on a trip back from the West Coast following his mother's death, which continues to haunt him. Tortured by the memory, he philosophizes, "There is no present or future—only the past happening over and over again—now" (3:920). He regards Phil Hogan as the kind of father he wished he had, instead of his own "lousy tightwad bastard" father. Josie rebukes him, but Tyrone persists. They hated each other, he tells her—"I'm glad he's dead. So is he. Or he ought to be. Everyone ought to be. Everyone ought to be, if they have any sense. Out of a bum racket" (3:920).

Josie inquires about his return trip to New York, having been told by her father that he was leaving the following day; but he tells her he plans to leave at the end of the week. He returns to the subject of Hogan's unaccountable drunkenness and recounts a joke he played on him at the inn. He told Harder's man Simpson that he would accept the offer for $10,000 as a prank on Hogan, who was sitting nearby. In fact, he plans to sell the farm to the Hogans for their original asking price, $2,000, and has already obtained permission from his brother to finalize the deal. The admission instantly reignites Josie's love for Tyrone. He goes on that he knows her boasting of being promiscuous is a facade, and so does her father. She admits that she is, in fact, a virgin, but that she wants to sleep with him that night. Tyrone transforms into a state of *"sneering cynical lust"*; he speaks to her as he might a prostitute, kisses her violently, and flings her against the doorway to the house. She pushes him away, bringing him back around. "What the hell?" he utters in confusion, "Was I trying to rape you, Josie? Forget it. I'm drunk—not responsible" (3:925). But he acknowledges he was in control and says she should be thankful to him for revealing that side of him. They say goodbye, and he explains again that his love would only poison her. "Believe me, Kid," he declares, "when I poison them, they stay poisoned!" (3:926). She tells him her love is strong enough to offer the redemption he needs. His head falls back to her chest, his face *"like a pale mask in the moonlight—at peace as a death mask is at peace"* (3:927).

Lying in her arms, Tyrone wistfully recalls his passion for horseracing, but even the beauty of the horses has lost all meaning for him. She asks what happened on the train back from the West Coast, and he tells her: Two years before his mother died, he quit drinking—for her. His father had died, and his brother was married with a child. He and his mother went out west to sell property of his father's, and she took ill soon after their arrival, eventually slipping into a coma. The sense of loss was so extreme that he fell back to drinking. Just before she died, however, she awoke from her coma and saw him drunk; then she closed her eyes and died in a state of utter despair. He met a prostitute on the train back east, and they drank and cavorted the whole ride back, with his mother's coffin lying in the baggage car. He would sing in the prostitute's embrace, "And baby's cries can't waken her / In the baggage coach ahead" (3:932). But he could not cry for his mother. "I knew I ought to be heartbroken but I couldn't feel anything. I seemed dead, too. I knew I ought to cry" (3:930). So he performed the role of the deeply mourning son for the benefit of the people who met them at the station. Over the following days, he got so drunk that he missed her funeral.

Josie cries out in revulsion, and he makes to leave. But Josie takes him back in her arms, exclaiming forgiveness and his mother's forgiveness too. "I feel her in the moonlight, her soul wrapped in it like a silver mantle, and I know she under-stands and forgives me, too, and her blessing lies on me" (3:933). She renews her promise to offer him a night "different from all the others, with a dawn that won't creep over dirty windowpanes but will wake in the sky like a promise of God's peace in the soul's dark sadness." She looks down at him and sees he has fallen asleep in her arms *"with the drained, exhausted peace of death"* (3:933). She wonders whether her love might save him, but understands they can never be together. "God forgive me," she says with a *"defensive, derisive smile,"* "it's a fine end to all my scheming, to sit here with the dead hugged to my breast, and the silly mug of the moon grinning down, enjoying the joke!" (3:934). She looks up at the moon, Tyrone unconscious in her arms, as the curtain falls.

### Act 4

Same as the previous act. Josie cradles Tyrone on the house steps *"as if he were a sick child."* It is dawn, but Josie awaits the colorful sunrise before waking Tyrone, protecting him from another gray dawn. Hogan appears from around the left rear of the house, visibly tired but sober. Josie warns him to speak softly "until the dawn has beauty in it." "Be God, he looks dead!" Hogan says *"in an awed, almost frightened whisper."* "Why wouldn't he?" she responds. "He is," though subsequently explains, "Dead asleep, I mean" (3:935). She calls Hogan out for concocting the whole scheme in order to bring the two together, accuses him of doing it for money, and tells him she will leave the farm that day. He tries to explain, but the dawn *"is now glowing with color"* (3:939), and she orders him inside so she can wake up Tyrone alone. Half asleep, Tyrone thinks he has bedded down with another "drunken tramp," but she roughly pushes him off her lap.

Tyrone, now fully conscious, comprehends the disappearance of his usual "heebie-jeebies," and that he now has "a nice, dreamy peaceful hangover for once—as if I'd had a sound sleep without nightmares" (3:940). He inquires about the previous night and she tells him that he was "full of blarney" and romantic, but "mostly quiet and sad" (3:941). He expresses sincere gratitude for her being the type of person who does not induce morning-after guilt; in fact, he feels, he says "as if all my sins had been forgiven" (3:942). Josie coaxes him into taking a whiskey. Though he does not feel he needs it, he takes a drink and remarks that it is "real, honest-to-God bonded Bourbon" (3:943). The memory of drinking the same good whiskey the night before prompts him to remember everything. He recovers quickly and pretends nothing has changed. But Josie senses the truth. "I want you to remember my love for you gave you peace for a while," she says. He admits that he remembers and exclaims, "I'll never forget your love!" He kisses her, "Never, do you hear! I'll always love you Josie." He kisses her again and says "Good-bye—and God bless you!" before disappearing down the road (3:944).

Hogan emerges from the house, his face *"hard with bitter anger."* He confesses Tyrone's adoration of her brought him hope that he might find her happiness and save his friend at the same time; Hogan only wanted them "to stop [the] damned pretending, and face the truth that you loved each other" (3:944). She admits she was only punishing Hogan by threatening to leave, and their playful verbal combat resumes. Hogan goes into the house for breakfast, and she follows. But she stops at the doorway and looks down the road at the receding figure of Tyrone. "May you have your wish and die in your sleep soon, Jim, darling. May you rest forever in forgiveness and peace" (3:946). She steps slowly through the doorway, and the curtain falls.

## COMMENTARY

Eugene O'Neill's most stirring love story, *A Moon for the Misbegotten* is also one of his most Irish plays (perhaps only surpassed by A TOUCH OF THE POET). But *Moon* is most often read as a final, highly personal reconciliation with his late brother James O'Neill, Jr. (Jamie), who profoundly and often destructively influenced the young playwright. A lifelong alcoholic, Jamie successfully beat his addiction following the death of his father, JAMES O'NEILL, SR., after which he spent most of his time with his mother, MARY ELLEN "ELLA" O'NEILL, settling the O'Neill estate. During a trip with Jamie to California to manage some real estate James O'Neill had bought years before, Ella suffered a brain tumor and slipped into a coma. Overwhelmed with worry,

Jamie resumed his heavy drinking, and after her death, he drank himself into oblivion. Although the play's "blond pig" of the train was probably a fictional offstage character, Jamie did arrive in New York drunk with his mother's coffin; he also missed her funeral on March 10, 1922 (Alexander 160), which outraged O'Neill. However, as biographer Stephen A. Black points out, "many sordid details are omitted, including the nomination of Jamie's woman friend as Ella's executrix" (467).

Less than a year later, Jamie's alcoholism became so extreme that he was institutionalized, reportedly arriving in a straitjacket at the Riverlong sanatorium in Paterson, New Jersey, in May 1923. Jamie's hair had turned white from the shock of his mother's death, and given the poor quality of liquor during Prohibition, he had lost much of his eyesight as well. His body was so dependent on alcohol that part of his treatment was taking 10 drinks of whiskey a day (Floyd 581n). Jamie O'Neill died on November 8, 1923, two months after the action of the play.

A sequel to *Long Day's Journey into Night* and, to a lesser autobiographical extent, The STRAW, *Moon* also shares thematic elements with O'Neill's other late masterpiece The ICEMAN COMETH. Like that play, O'Neill envisioned *Moon* as a "strange combination comic-tragic" (quoted in Floyd 589); in similar language, he regarded *Iceman* as "a big kind of comedy that doesn't stay funny very long" (quoted in Raleigh 11). Both begin as a vaudeville comedy and conclude on an affirmative note, though each final scene is tempered by the doomed fate of the protagonists—for *Moon*, James Tyrone, Jr.; for *Iceman*, Larry Slade, Donald Parritt, and Theodore "Hickey" Hickman. But each of their fates come with redemption. O'Neill famously generalized that "in all my plays sin is punished and redemption takes place" (quoted in Floyd 572), a structure Virginia Floyd calls O'Neill's "sin-confession-forgiveness syndrome" (572). And like the "pipe dreams" of the characters in *Iceman* and the literal masks worn by the actors in O'Neill's experimental middle play The GREAT GOD BROWN, *Moon* is, at bottom, about maintaining illusion through performance: Josie performs the role of the town slut, though she is in fact a virgin; Hogan performs the role of a curmudgeon, though he is in fact a loving father and sentimentalist; and Jim Tyrone performs the role of a man alive, though he feels dead inside. As Zander Brietzke writes, *Moon* "culminates O'Neill's conception of character as mask and acting as necessary pretense. O'Neill juxtaposes the sham of theatre with a painful unmasking of human vulnerability" (80). During Tyrone and Hogan's good-hearted Irish "banter," he continues, "They engage the mask of each other, but politely leave the private face alone" (82).

O'Neill first called the play *Moon of the Misbegotten*. Though he considered this "a good title," he finally settled on *A Moon for the Misbegotten*; this revision was, in his words, "much more to the point" (quoted in Barlow 114). The title's "moon" (female redemption) and "misbegotten" (Tyrone) signify the play's two central concerns. For the ancient Greeks, the moon symbolized Diana, the goddess of the moon and chastity, and for Christians, it was the Virgin Mary. The actual moon in the play thus projects the figurative Josie (though far more than a mere symbol) as a harbinger of forgiveness, womanly love, and spiritual serenity for the misbegotten Jim Tyrone. *Misbegotten* in the O'Neill canon refers to "those who find themselves aliens in an uncongenial world" (Barlow 112) and to "people at the bottom of society. . . . men who have no heritage and are outcasts from the world" (Bogard 448)—individuals whose lives are so tormented that they experience life as a kind of living death, as Jim Tyrone does, and long for the peace actual death brings, often wishing they had never been born at all.

O'Neill earlier wrote *Moon*'s hilarious dialogue between the Hogans and the Standard Oil magnate T. Stedman Harder as the anecdote told by Edmund Tyrone (O'Neill's most autobiographical character) to his father James Tyrone, Sr., in the first scene of *Long Day's Journey into Night* about the tenant pig farmer Shaughnessy. O'Neill originally intended to expand the story into a full-length play about this Irishman, not his brother Jamie. His very first notes on the idea in his WORK DIARY call *Moon* his "Dolan play." Hogan and Shaughnessy represent James O'Neill's tenant JOHN "DIRTY" DOLAN, an IRISH AMERICAN farmer O'Neill, Sr., openly complained about but secretly respected

enormously. They both enjoyed railing against England and sharing a congenial drink or five. Jamie O'Neill was, in fact, Dolan's landlord in September 1923, when the play takes place. Indeed, the felt tension between the Irish Catholic O'Neill, a sympathizer of the downtrodden, and his wealthy Protestant neighbors EDWARD S. HARKNESS AND EDWARD C. HAMMOND in New London, Connecticut, goes back to O'Neill's earliest writings, including his POETRY. Four poems written in the early 1910s express his antagonism toward Standard Oil: "Upon Our Beach," "The Shut-Eye Candidate," "The Long Tale," and "Fratricide."

The Hogans' quick-witted humor—grounded as it is in laughing off life's difficulties, rapid changes in tone, and spontaneous wordplay—is all Irish. Regardless of the playwright's own rather privileged upbringing, the dialogue demonstrates its creator's emotional and political affiliation with "shanty" or "bogtrotter" Irish culture over the capitalist classes; Protestant Puritanism; and the emotionally staid, socially ambitious "lace-curtain" Irish. Con Melody, the protagonist of *A Touch of the Poet*, plays a grotesque caricature of lace-curtain Irish until reverting in the final scene back to his bogtrotter personality, a role his companion Jamie Cregan plays throughout the play. O'Neill always maintained that only Irish actors could properly play the Hogans and Tyrone, though Travis Bogard attests that whether the cast is Irish or not, "The play is doomed to failure without superb acting. It is long, totally simplified and stripped of theatrical devices, a lyric drama, concentrated on character more than narrative" (446).

Jim Tyrone's sexual life is limited to rape and PROSTITUTION, while Josie, regardless of her virginity, only talks of sex in the crudest terms. Even in the love scene of act 3, Josie's sincere, love-inspired sexual advances come across to Jim as those of a whore or a "Broadway tart." Michael Manheim argues that Josie and Jim's "sexuality—in terms which obviously grow out of O'Neill's experience—instead of becoming a means by which they express their affection, becomes rather a means by which they express their hostility" (202). Closing down the production in Detroit, Michigan, after only two performances, the police censor answered a woman's assertion about O'Neill's being a NOBEL PRIZE winner this way: "Lady, I don't care what kind of prize he's won, he can't put on a dirty show in my town" (quoted in Bogard 447). The censor charged that the play was morally repugnant since it used the words *prostitute* and *mother* in the same sentence (Bogard 447n)—a great irony given that the main character, James "Jim" Tyrone, Jr., recoils in disgust whenever a connection is made between his mother and prostitution. In fact, according to Judith Barlow, one early draft has Jim thanking Josie Hogan for considerately not using his mother's name "in the same breath with the blonde whore on the train" (quoted in Barlow 119).

Still, there remains a terrible dichotomy in this play between sexuality and romantic love, as if the two are mutually exclusive. O'Neill's sexual views were severely damaged by his brother's influence. Jamie O'Neill introduced him to "tarts" and "whores" early on, and O'Neill lost his virginity with a prostitute hired by Jamie. O'Neill never sufficiently recovered from the guilt of following Jamie's example through his teens and 20s, a pernicious influence O'Neill treats in *Long Day's Journey.* O'Neill perceived his older brother as engaging in lifelong sexual debasement as revenge against their mother, but also, as Doris Alexander argues, a paradoxical "working out of his pity and love" (160).

Indeed, both O'Neill and his brother, Jamie, held conflicting views of their mother, whose drug addiction appeared to them as a deliberate rejection of her motherhood and thus her children. O'Neill's perception hardly changed after her death, and his desperate search for a mother figure runs through the whole of his work. Judith Barlow notes, in fact, that "in thirteen of the seventeen dramas O'Neill completed after 1922 [the year of her death], there is either a male character closely involved with his mother or a male-female relationship with parent-child overtones even though the two people are not literally parent and child. Some works contain both configurations" (134).

Critics often disparage O'Neill's ability to create well-rounded female characters, and for good reason. "Now I know why the women in your plays are so wooden!" the actress Eleanor Cape, a character in *WELDED* (based on AGNES BOULTON), chastises

her husband Michael Cape (O'Neill), "You ought to thank me for breathing life into them!" (2:249). Most O'Neill women come across as either selfish, dependent, destructive, like Ruth Atkins from *BEYOND THE HORIZON* or Nina Leeds from *STRANGE INTERLUDE,* or as fairly one-dimensional, subservient, maternal beings, like Alice Roylston in *SERVITUDE* or Margaret Anthony in *The Great God Brown.* And if they do not fit into this model adapted from the "woman destroyer" type O'Neill found in the work of his great influence AUGUST STRINDBERG or the servile, long-suffering housewife type, they were sympathetic prostitutes like Anna Christopherson from *"ANNA CHRISTIE,"* Cybel from *The Great God Brown,* or the prostitute "A Woman" in *Welded.* In terms of GENDER, then, the character Josie Hogan is O'Neill's greatest redeemer. "Critics have many reservations about *Moon,*" Judith Butler submits, "but few have complained that Josie Hogan is not a fully realized character on stage" (156).

In the final scene of act 3, O'Neill places Jim in Josie's arms to conjure the Christian symbolism of the pietà in his audience's minds—the Virgin Mary embracing her dead child Jesus Christ. After a year of self-loathing for his betrayal of his mother on her deathbed, Jim's longing for the peace, security, and sense of belonging only a mother can provide has finally been fulfilled. Thanks to Josie's love, he can now die a man rather than the walking ghost we discover in act 1. Autobiographically, Stephen A. Black writes, "the playwright's point of view merges with Josie's. Through her, he wishes his brother peace and lets him go quietly to his death with the recognition of having been loved selflessly. The playwright had passed beyond mourning and tragedy" (469). Beginning with the Poet's argument that death acts as a saving grace for the immigrant child in *FOG,* through Robert "Yank" Smith's death in the final scene of *The HAIRY APE,* and on to *The Iceman Cometh,* O'Neill never relinquished the conviction that "the quest for the womb is ultimately a quest for the tomb" (Barlow 137; see also Floyd 581 and Bogard 451–452).

## CHARACTERS

**Harder, T. Stedman** A Standard Oil magnate and Phil and Josie Hogan's next-door neighbor.

O'Neill wrote Harder, who appears as the offstage character Harker in *Long Day's Journey into Night*, as a composite portrait of the O'Neill family's wealthy Protestant neighbors, Edward S. Harkness and Edward C. Hammond, in New London, Connecticut. Basically used as a foil for Phil Hogan's comedy routine in act 1, Harder *"is in his late thirties, but looks younger because his face is unmarked by worry, ambition, or any of the common hazards of life"* (3:884). O'Neill describes his personality as *"not unpleasant . . . he is simply immature, naturally lethargic, a bit stupid . . . deliberate in his speech, slow on the uptake, and has no sense of humor"* (3:884). Harder is an Ivy League school graduate and considers his college days the finest period of his life. He appears on the Hogans' land near the end of act 1 to complain that Phil Hogan's pigs have been swimming in his ice pond. But through a series of verbal tricks, Hogan asserts that Harder has been tearing down the fence that separates their property with the explicit aim of harming his pigs. The characters Harder and Harker allow O'Neill to articulate his disgust over big business and Protestant prejudices against the Irish.

**Hogan, Josie**    Phil Hogan's daughter. Arguably the most poignant female character O'Neill ever created, Josie is based on O'Neill's GREENWICH VILLAGE friend Christine Ell, who also called James "Jamie" O'Neill, Jr. (upon whom James Tyrone, Jr., is based) by the nickname "Jim" (Barlow 113). Historian Christine Stansell characterizes Ell, a onetime prostitute in Denver, as "a cook for Greenwich Village restaurants, a bit player in the Provincetown Theater, and a principal in free love intrigues" (133). In Christine, writes Travis Bogard, "O'Neill apparently found something of the paradoxes he later set forth in Josie—a shyness of spirit that conflicted with the grossness of her body and which she attempted to mask by rough whorish behavior" (446).

   At 28 years old, Josie has dark features, and the *"map of Ireland is stamped on her face"* (3:857). She is *"five feet eleven in her stockings and weighs around one hundred and eighty"*; in short, as O'Neill characterizes her, she is *"so oversize for a woman that she is almost a freak"* (3:857). Since her mother's death

20 years before the play's action, Josie has been the only one of Phil Hogan's children—the other three being boys—capable of controlling his temper. In the first scene, we discover that her brother Mike Hogan regards her as a tramp and that she cultivates this image about town. Her promiscuity is a pose, however, one not lost on either her father or her would-be suitor, Jim Tyrone. Why O'Neill made this decision is debatable, but most probably he wanted to provide a figurative mask for each character that hides his or her true feelings—in the case of Josie, the idea that her gigantic figure might be repellent to men; thus, she brags that all men want her.

   Josie Hogan deepens the "God the Mother" figure we find in Cybel of *The Great God Brown* and later in Nina Leeds's imagination in *Strange Interlude*. Unlike a goddess, however, "she too needs and finds blessing" (Bogard 450). O'Neill's refusal to name her Mary might have been to avoid confusion with Mary Tyrone, along with his probable desire not to appear too heavy-handed in the pietà scene. But as Egil Törnqvist points out, "Josephine" is the "feminine form of Joseph," and "Holy Joseph" is her "favorite epithet" (quoted in Barlow 141). Josie's main purpose in the play is to offer redemption to Jim Tyrone through her love and maternal ability to forgive. She is "the priestess in the confessional," as John Henry Raleigh puts it, and in an earlier draft O'Neill has Jim refer directly to confession in a religious sense (quoted in Barlow 142).

   Casting actresses for the role of Josie has never been easy. Indeed, O'Neill himself interviewed Mary Welch, the first to be cast in the role; she was not the giantess he had envisioned, but he concluded that she was sufficiently Irish (100 percent) to carry off the role. While casting the premiere, THEATRE GUILD producer Lawrence Langner explained that Josie's character demands "exactly the kind of woman who, when she comes to see you and asks whether she should attempt a career in the theatre—you look embarrassed and reply, 'Well, I'm afraid you're rather a big girl—how are we to find a man tall enough to play opposite you?'" (quoted in Bogard 446). Nevertheless, many fine Josies have made their way to the stage, most famously COLLEEN DEWHURST playing opposite JASON ROBARDS in JOSÉ QUINTERO's 1957 revival.

**Hogan, Mike**   Josie Hogan's younger brother and Phil Hogan's son. Mike is discovered in the first scene of act 1 planning to escape his father's slave-driving ways on the farm; he is thus not unlike the Cabot brothers, Simeon and Peter, in DESIRE UNDER THE ELMS. Twenty years old and significantly shorter than Josie, Mike is a staunch Catholic and chides his sister for ruining her reputation. Unlike his father, he believes that she tells the truth about her promiscuity. *"Mike is a New England Irish Catholic Puritan, Grade B,"* O'Neill specifies in his STAGE DIRECTIONS, *"and an extremely irritating youth to have around"* (3:857). He has none of the requisite courage, physical prowess, or wit to stand up to his father, Phil Hogan, who considers Mike a religious hypocrite and resents the fact that his wife died giving birth to him. His older brothers, Thomas and John, have already fled the farm—Thomas to Bridgeport, where he serves as a police sergeant, and John to Meriden, where he works as a bartender. Mike fearfully departs when Josie warns him that their father is approaching. He will take the train to Bridgeport with his father's money, stolen by Josie on his behalf, and settle there with Thomas.

**Hogan, Phil**   Josie Hogan's father and James "Jim" Tyrone's tenant farmer. Out of all of the Irish characters in the O'Neill canon, Hogan perhaps most resembles Cornelius "Con" Melody after his transformation back into his "shanty" Irish persona in the final scene of *A Touch of the Poet*. Hogan, who appears as the offstage character Shaughnessy in *Long Day's Journey into Night*, is based on the real-life James O'Neill's tenant farmer John "Dirty" Dolan. His stereotypical Irish personality—pugilistic, drunken, and conspiratorial—offended many "lace-curtain," or upper-class, Irish members of the audience when *A Moon for the Misbegotten* was first produced in the Midwest in 1947. O'Neill describes him as 55 years old, rather small, thick-necked, and muscular, with a piglike face, and *"his voice is high-pitched with a pronounced brogue"* (3:862). The father of three boys—Thomas, John, and Mike—and one girl, Josie, Hogan watched as his wife died giving birth to Mike 20 years prior to the play's action. None of the Hogan boys could match their

father's ferocity, and each left one by one: Thomas joined the police force in Bridgeport, John became a barkeeper in Meridan, and Mike escapes in the first scene of act 1 to join Thomas. Josie, on the other hand, shares her father's wit and physical strength, and the two love each other very much.

Michael Manheim suggests that Hogan's "primary function throughout the play is that of comic plotter and manipulator" (192), insofar as his two great motivations are to undermine T. Stedman Harder in verbal combat and to land his daughter a husband. Hogan's scathing wit and outwardly belligerent temperament also mask the true feelings of affection he holds for his daughter. Their repartee in act 1 acts both to involve the audience and to show the strong bond between father and daughter. He conspires to unite Josie and Jim Tyrone as an act of sacrifice—not, as she at first assumes in the final scene, to bring Jim's wealth into their family. Josie is the only person he loves, but he is willing to sacrifice her company and help on the farm if she might find happiness in marriage with Tyrone.

**Tyrone, James "Jim"**   Josie and Phil Hogan's landlord and a former stage actor. Jim Tyrone, who appears as James Tyrone, Sr.'s eldest son in *Long Day's Journey into Night*, is based on James O'Neill, Jr. (Jamie), O'Neill's elder brother, who died of alcoholism and neuritis in November 1923, just two months after the play's action. By naming him Jim instead of Jamie (his brother's nickname and that of James Tyrone, Jr., in *Long Day's Journey*), O'Neill suggests that "unlike his predecessors, the James Tyrone, Jr., of *A Moon for the Misbegotten* has become a full-fledged hero and also that Josie is based on Christine Ell, who called the actual Jamie "Jim."

Considered by some "the one *bona fide* tragic hero of all O'Neill's later drama" (Manheim 194), Tyrone is of medium height and barrel-chested. *"His naturally fine physique has become soft and soggy from dissipation, but his face is still good-looking despite its unhealthy puffiness and the bags under his eyes"* (3:875). Similar to the character Dion Anthony in *The Great God Brown*, who wears a mask to illuminate the character's insipid pose, Tyrone's face has *"a certain Mephistophelian quality which is accentuated by his habitually cynical expression"* (3:875); his smile, when not twisted in a cynical sneer, affords Tyrone *"the ghost of a former youthful, irresponsible Irish charm—that of the beguiling ne'er-do-well, sentimental and romantic"* (3:875). His wardrobe is expensive but reflects *"a style set by well-groomed Broadway gamblers who would like to be mistaken for Wall Street brokers"* (3:875).

Jim Tyrone fell into a good deal of money and real estate after the deaths of his father, James Tyrone, Sr., and his mother, Mary. The previous fall, he and Mary had traveled out to California to manage the family's real estate interests. While there, she suffered from a brain tumor and slipped into a coma. Distraught over his mother's illness, Jim resumed the heavy drinking that had defined his youth. Jim is convinced that his mother awoke one last time to see him drunk, then passed away in despair. On the train ride back east, Jim drank heavily and hired a blond prostitute for $50 a night while his mother's body lay in a coffin in the baggage compartment. Unable to express sincere remorse, Jim played the part of the weeping son at the train station, an experience almost as disgraceful in his eyes as his disrespectful behavior on the train. He was too drunk to attend her funeral.

Jim is haunted by other ghosts as well, primarily sexual. He appears incapable, in the context of the play, of conducting a healthy love life, as he regards sexual intimacy as an act of violence restricted to the realm of Broadway tarts and rape. "Sex, for Tyrone," Zander Brietzke writes, "satisfies his self-hatred and the conviction that he destroys everyone whom he touches" (88). Jim believes that he is damned, and when he accepts Josie's offer to spend a moonlit evening together, he does so with the understanding that she is a virgin and therefore incorruptible and therefore that her love might afford him true redemption.

Josie brazenly cultivates a reputation for promiscuity, but when she offers herself to Jim out of sincere love, he transforms into a Mephistophelian being that degrades women and takes them by force. But her forgiveness of his misconduct on the train and during their liaison that night ultimately redeems the haunted Tyrone. As biographer Stephen A. Black explains, *Moon* "provides a cumula-

tive gloss on Jamie's word 'dead': it refers to the part of him that hates, that cannot love, and especially, the part that cannot tolerate being loved by someone else" (468). In the final scene of act 3, Tyrone falls asleep in Josie's lap, and she holds him there as the Virgin Mary does Jesus Christ in the hallowed Christian image of the pietà. He awakens hungover but rested and without the "heebie jeebies" that usually torment him after a night's debauch. Eventually he remembers what transpired, but she forgives him, and they pledge their mutual love. Josie has given him, in Stephen A. Black's words, "the only form of love he can accept"—"a gift of empathy that asked nothing of him" (469). In act 4, Tyrone goes off to die, spiritually healed but alone, and Josie feels that after achieving his love, she can resume her life on the farm with a sense of fulfillment.

## BIBLIOGRAPHY

Alexander, Doris. *Eugene O'Neill's Last Plays: Separating Art from Autobiography.* Athens: University of Georgia Press, 2005.

Barlow, Judith. *Final Acts: The Creation of Three Late O'Neill Plays.* Athens: University of Georgia Press, 1985.

Black, Stephen A. *Eugene O'Neill: Beyond Mourning and Tragedy.* New Haven, Conn.: Yale University Press, 1999.

Bogard, Travis. *Contour in Time: The Plays of Eugene O'Neill.* Rev. ed. New York: Oxford University Press, 1988.

Brietzke, Zander. *The Aesthetics of Failure: Dynamic Structure in the Plays of Eugene O'Neill.* Jefferson, N.C.: McFarland & Company, 2001.

Floyd, Virginia. *The Plays of Eugene O'Neill: A New Assessment.* New York: Ungar, 1985.

Manheim, Michael. *Eugene O'Neill's New Language of Kinship.* Syracuse, N.Y.: Syracuse University Press, 1982.

Raleigh, John H. Introduction to *Twentieth Century Interpretations of The Iceman Cometh: A Collection of Critical Essays,* edited by John H. Raleigh. Englewood Cliffs, N.J.: Prentice-Hall, 1968.

Stansell, Christine. *American Moderns: Bohemian New York and the Creation of a New Century.* New York: Metropolitan Books, 2000.

# Moon of the Caribbees: A Play in One Act, The (completed, 1917; first produced, 1918)

*The Moon of the Caribbees* was Eugene O'Neill's darling of his four one-act SS GLENCAIRN plays. In a letter to his first chronicler, Barrett Clark, O'Neill wrote that *The Moon* "is distinctly my own" (O'Neill 99). "No one else in the world could have written that one," he later told director Nina Moise (quoted in Sheaffer 395). The earliest existing draft of *The Moon of the Caribbees*—O'Neill's last *Glencairn* installment and his first real foray into modernism—is dated March, 20, 1917. The prominent literary journal *The Smart Set* published it in August 1918; the experimental theater group the PROVINCETOWN PLAYERS first staged it on December 20, 1918, at the PLAYWRIGHTS' THEATRE in New York City; and the following year it appeared in O'Neill's collection *The Moon of the Caribbees and Six Other Plays of the Sea.*

Originally titled *The Moon at Trinidad*, the play takes place off the coast of the Caribbean island of Trinidad, where O'Neill's ship the SS IKALA, which he had served on during his time in the MERCHANT MARINE and upon which the British tramp steamer *Glencairn* is based, anchored for a time on its voyage to BUENOS AIRES, ARGENTINA. O'Neill set *The Moon of the Caribbees* entirely on the forward deck of the ship, with more than 20 superbly realized characters interacting throughout. Such a setting, with virtually no plot and a mélange of distinctive personalities, might easily have collapsed into disarray on the stage; but having enjoyed many revivals over the decades, O'Neill's celebrated "eulogy to the SEA" (Floyd 125) has successfully withstood the test of time more than any effort prior to (and probably including) his first PULITZER PRIZE—winning play, *BEYOND THE HORIZON.*

Photograph of the 1924 production of *The Moon of the Caribbees* (*Courtesy of the New York Public Library*)

## SYNOPSIS

Just before 9:30 at night on the deck of the British tramp steamer SS *Glencairn,* anchored off an island in the West Indies. The various structures on deck—derrick booms, the port bulwark, a stairwell, several doorways, and the raised square of a hatch—create a mise en scène not unlike an industrial rock garden cast in silhouette by the full moon. A white beach with palm trees can be seen over the bulwark on the horizon. Throughout the play, like O'Neill's later drumbeat effect in *The EMPEROR JONES,* we hear "a *melancholy negro chant, faint and far-off,*" that "*drifts, crooning, over the water*" (1:527). More than a dozen seamen and firemen lounge about the deck, most smoking pipes or cigarettes and wearing "*patched suits of dungaree*" (1:527). Small groups converse in low tones. When the stage is fully revealed, the conversations die away, and the sound of a mournful West Indian song fills the air.

"Will ye listen to them naygurs?" the IRISH seaman Driscoll says. "I wonder now, do they call that keenin' a song?" (1:528). A few men comment whether the song might be some kind of funeral dirge. Cocky, a seaman with a cockney (British working-class) accent, insists the native islanders are cannibals and jokes that they probably suffer from indigestion. He recounts experiences in New Guinea among cannibals, and the men, having heard these stories before, accuse him of rehashing tall tales. Driscoll expresses impatience for the native women who have promised to row out to the ship and sell the seamen rum and sex. He also warns that the "Old Man"—the captain—has forbidden the women from selling them liquor and reminds them to keep quiet and well-behaved once the drinking begins. The ship rings three bells (9:30 P.M.).

A British seaman named Smitty, whom the men teasingly call "Duke" because of his genteel manner, expresses a deep personal sorrow; he does this throughout the play, and the men occasionally endeavor to cheer him up. "I wish they'd stop that song," he says of the native singing. "It makes you think of—well—things you ought to forget" (1:530). The men call for a "sea chanty" from Driscoll, in part to break up their boredom

and in part to drown out the somber island music with a more upbeat tune. Driscoll scornfully mocks the men, claiming only a select few—Yank, Olson, Lamps, Cocky, and himself—ever actually served on sail-powered ships and thus know about real sailors' chanteys. (O'Neill treats this tension between sail and steam power most comprehensively through the oppositional characters Robert "Yank" Smith and Paddy in scene 1 of *The HAIRY APE.*) Driscoll strikes up "Blow the Man Down," and the rest heartily join in chorus. The Norwegian seaman, Paul, spots the "bumboat" (a small shore vessel selling provisions and cheap liquor to seamen on foreign ships) nearing the *Glencairn.* "Within minutes of a ship's dropping anchor," writes Robert Richter, a ship like the *Glencairn* "would be swarming with groups of women and bumboat men, eager to sell cheap rum" (153).

The bumboat comes alongside the steamship, there is much speculation over the women. Paddy caustically remarks that Cocky is too ugly for them, and Cocky significantly calls to mind O'Neill's more expressionistic play *The Hairy Ape,* responding, "You ain't no bleedin' beauty prize yeself, me man. A 'airy ape, I calls yer" (1:532). He reaches for his knife, but a fireman named Big Frank defuses the fight. Driscoll reappears to announce the arrival of the women. They charge three shillings a bottle, but Driscoll pilfered one from their baskets and passes it around. He again reminds the men to keep the captain ignorant of their party and that when they buy a bottle, they must sign a sheet claiming tobacco or fruit instead of rum or sex. The sheet will then go to the captain, and he will recover the cost from the men's wages.

The women enter, all wearing "*light-colored, loose-fitting clothes and . . . bright bandana handkerchiefs on their heads*" (1:535). The first three—Bella, Susie, and Violet—carry full baskets on their heads. Yank escorts the fourth, the youngest and prettiest islander, Pearl. Bella, "*the oldest, stoutest, and homeliest*" (1:535), warns the men to keep out of sight while they drink and cavort with the girls. Paddy flagrantly takes a long drink from his bottle, exposing himself in the moonlight, prompting Bella, fearful of the captain, to order everyone into the forecastle (pronounced "fo'c'sle").

Pearl calls to Smitty, who sits with his *"chin on his hands, staring off into vacancy"*; he coldly follows her to secure a bottle and then reemerges, shuddering in disgust (1:536). The only sailors left on deck are Smitty and Old Tom, the "Donkeyman" (a steam engine operator). With the door to the forecastle shut, the negro song once again fills the air. Smitty complains about the sadness of the song, but the Donkeyman wistfully says it recalls organ music he heard as a child on Sunday mornings outside church. Smitty admits the music is not bad, but it brings on unwanted memories. When the Donkeyman wonders what made Smitty come to sea, Smitty responds, "My old friend in the bottle here, Donk" (1:538). The Donkeyman speculates it must also have been a woman, which irritates Smitty. Ignoring him, the old sailor remarks that he never had trouble with women, as he "always hit 'em a whack on the ear an' went out and got drunker'n ever" (1:538); each time, he would return home to a fine meal. "Gentlemen don't hit women," Smitty retorts *"pompously."* "No," the Donkeyman admits, "that's why they has mem'ries when they hears music" (1:538). Smitty *"sinks into a scornful silence"* (1:539), as Davis and Violet enter from the forecastle and disappear left.

"There's love at first sight for you," the Donkeyman says looking after them, "an' plenty more o' the same in the fo'c's'tle. Mo mem'ries jined with that" (1:539). This advice only irritates Smitty further. Pearl comes out to flirt with Smitty. He takes her in his arms but quickly turns away in disgust. Yank appears, and the din from the forecastle has *"increased in violence."* At first, Yank moves toward them in a jealous rage, but seeing Pearl with Smitty, he accepts the transfer. "Pals is pals and any pal of mine c'n have anythin' I got, see?" (1:540). Smitty hands her over, outraging Pearl, who grudgingly goes back in with Yank. The Donkeyman makes another crack, "There's love for you," and Smitty's expression darkens more (1:540).

The forecastle door is flung open, and the party explodes out onto the deck. Everyone is drunk except Bella, whose desperate attempts to quell the noise prove futile. Paul comes out with an accordion, and Driscoll demands music, while *"the Donkeyman looks on them all with a detached, indulgent*

*air"* (1:541). Smitty stares vacantly before him. A bottle smashes to the deck. Bella shrieks a warning about the captain, but Driscoll commands everyone to ignore her. Paul strikes up "You Great Big Beautiful Doll," and four couples begin dancing a *"jerk-shouldered version of the old Turkey Trot as it was done in the sailor-town dives, made more grotesque by the fact that all the couples are drunk and keep lurching into each other every moment"* (1:541). Yank and Pearl come around from the side. Pearl slaps Smitty across the face, then *"laughs viciously"* (1:541). Paddy deliberately trips Cocky and Susie. Cocky lunges at him, and within moments a full blown donnybrook erupts. The drunken men hit at one another haphazardly, *"although the general idea seems to be a battle between seamen and firemen"* (1:542).

Davis shouts that the mate is coming, and most of the crowd rushes into the forecastle. The women huddle trembling on the hatch; Smitty is nursing Pearl's blow, and the Donkeyman has not moved. Yank and Driscoll kneel over Paddy, who lies on the deck unconscious. He has been knifed, and Yank suspects Cocky is the perpetrator. The first mate enters and demands to know the cause of the commotion. He inspects Paddy with a flashlight and diagnoses his cut as "only a flesh wound" (1:543). Ordering Yank and Driscoll to take him aft for bandaging, the officer then sees the women and soon after the smashed rum bottle. He deduces what has happened and orders them off the boat with no payment.

After they all leave, the Donkeyman and Smitty remain. Smitty releases a *"sigh that is half a sob"* (1:543), then finishes his bottle and tosses it behind him. "More mem'ries?" the Donkeyman asks. The ship's bell rings four times (10:00 P.M.). The Donkeyman turns in, recommending Smitty return to the forecastle, where there is sure to be more liquor and the negro music cannot be heard. Smitty bids him goodnight, then shuffles dejectedly into the forecastle. As the curtain falls, we perceive *"the haunted, saddened voice of that brooding music, faint and far-off, like the mood of the moonlight made audible"* (1:544).

## COMMENTARY

Eugene O'Neill's high estimation of *The Moon of the Caribbees* could not be more at odds with its critical reception at the time of the premiere. In a letter to Barrett Clark responding to Clark's high praise for the previous SS *Glencairn* play, IN THE ZONE (a play that, unlike *The Moon*, generally received exceptional reviews), O'Neill wrote that *The Moon of the Caribbees* was a deliberate revolt against the "conventional construction of the theatre as it is," to which O'Neill felt *In the Zone* regretably conformed. *The Moon's* main departure from "conventional" theater can be felt in its near absence of a narrative arc or melodramatic devices. As such, reviewers characterized the one act as "just an interlude of a drama, with prelude and afterlude left to the imagination of the spectators" and a "rather pointless tale about an uninteresting young man [Smitty]" (quoted in Sheaffer 445). Most later critics, however, regard the play as "a near flawless dramatic poem" (Bogard 85), a mood play that signals a watershed moment in American theater history. Finally, if more subtly than O'Neill's experiments in EXPRESSIONISM *The Emperor Jones* or *The Hairy Ape*, with the *Moon* O'Neill had ushered modernism onto the American stage.

Each sea-borne element contributes to the play's atmosphere: the palm trees in the distance, the moonlight, the negro singing, the rum, the "bumboat" women, the sea bells, the chanteys, the fighting, the tobacco smoke blending with the briny Caribbean air—all rely heavily upon the sea to inform their significance, or lack of significance, in O'Neill's quest to embody the "impelling, inscrutable forces behind life which it is my ambition to at least faintly shadow at their work in my plays" (O'Neill 100). O'Neill wrote that the hero of the play, unlike *In the Zone*, emerges in *The Moon* as "the spirit of the sea—a big thing" (O'Neill 99). Smitty's character, on the other hand, is

> posed against the background of that beauty, sad because it is eternal, which is one of the revealing moods of the sea's truth, his silhouetted gestures of self-pity are reduced to their proper insignificance, his thin whine of weakness is lost in the silence which it was mean enough to disturb, we get the perspective to judge him—and the others—and we find his sentimental posing much more out of

harmony with truth, much less in tune with beauty, than the honest vulgarity of his mates (O'Neill 99).

Smitty went to sea to forget his past; he drinks to forget it, too. But all the things the sea provides—the drink, the music, the moonlight—act as reminders of a life half-lived. This makes Smitty's character a pitiable "insect" (to use one of Driscoll's favorite terms of abuse) in the "eternal" sadness and "beauty" the sea represents, rather than a fully absorbed being with a sense of belonging like his shipmates (though Yank suffers a similar tragic fate in BOUND EAST FOR CARDIFF, as does Olson in *The Long Voyage Home*).

*The Moon of the Caribbees* invites its audience to witness Smitty's tragic pose most meaningfully through his ongoing conversation with the Donkeyman, a conversation juxtaposed structurally with the Dionysian bacchanalia erupting about them on the deck (see Long and Colburn). The Donkeyman represents O'Neill's quintessential, almost Zenlike, child of the sea mother. Even his nickname (a sailor's expression for an engine operator) evokes his base relationship with the natural world. It is he who points out that living the life of a "gentleman," a claim O'Neill specifies Smitty should intone *"pompously,"* is what gives such men (if in the disturbing context of men who refuse to beat women) "mem'ries when they hears music." Smitty "ain't made for" (1:538) a life at sea, not because he is incapable of hard work or cannot adequately socialize with his working-class counterparts in the forecastle (regardless of their class differences, the consummate insider Yank considers him a "pal" worthy of Pearl's displaced affection [1:540]), but for the reason that he allows "mem'ries" to invade his sense of personal well-being. Thus, Smitty permits insignificant personal needs to make him "much less in tune with beauty, than the honest vulgarity of his shipmates" and even the West Indian PROSTITUTES.

In a broader statement on working-class subjects in his plays, specifically "ANNA CHRISTIE," O'Neill described the working men he knew from the merchant marine and elsewhere in these terms: "They are more direct. In action and utterance. Thus more dramatic. Their lives and sufferings and personalities lend themselves more readily to dramatization. They have not been steeped in the evasions and superficialities which come with social life and intercourse. Their real selves are exposed. They are crude but honest. They are not handicapped by inhibitions" (quoted in Pfister 110). Indeed, O'Neill never appears to openly judge any sailor's behavior save Smitty's. "Drunkenness, mass fornication, near murder," Travis Bogard notes of the play's amoral stance, "are not seen as good or evil, for they are not reached by conscious or subconscious choice" (88).

O'Neill never ceased to admire, and would never again achieve, the sense of natural balance and belonging he discovered during his life at sea. One of his most cherished possessions, in fact, was his American Line sweater from those days, a comforting bit of nostalgia from happier, more liberated times. "I hated a life ruled by the conventions and traditions of society," O'Neill said of his time at sea. "Sailors' lives were ruled by conventions and traditions; but they were of a sort I liked and that had a meaning which appealed to me. . . . Discipline on a sailing vessel was not a thing that was imposed on the crew by superior authority. It was essentially voluntary. The motive behind it was loyalty to the ship!" (quoted in Pfister 109).

## CHARACTERS

**Bella** West Indian "bumboat" woman. O'Neill describes Bella as the *"oldest, stoutest, and homeliest"* (1:535) of the four West Indian women who arrive on the SS *Glencairn* to peddle rum and sex. She has made a deal with the captain that she will only sell the men fruit, not liquor, or she forfeits payment. When the first mate discovers rum on board, he refuses to pay for her services.

**Big Frank** Fireman on the British tramp steamer SS *Glencairn*. O'Neill describes Big Frank only as a *"huge fireman"* (1:528), and he appears to be allied with Paddy against Cocky.

**Chips** Carpenter on the British tramp steamer SS *Glencairn*. Chips only has three short lines, and O'Neill describes him simply as *"a lanky Scotsman"* (1:529).

**Cocky** British seaman on the British tramp steamer SS *Glencairn*. Cocky, *"a wizened runt of a man with a straggling gray mustache"* (1:528), speaks with a cockney (or British working-class) accent. Cocky argues with Paddy early on and knifes him in the donnybrook that erupts after Paddy trips him while he dances with Susie. Cocky appears in all four *Glencairn* plays.

**Davis** American seaman on the tramp steamer SS *Glencairn*. O'Neill describes him simply as *"a short, dark man"* (1:528). Davis, who consorts with Violet, also appears in *Bound East for Cardiff* (in which he plays the antagonist) and *In the Zone.*

**Donkeyman** See OLD TOM.

**Driscoll** Irish seaman on the tramp steamer SS *Glencairn*. Driscoll, *"a powerfully built Irishman"* (1:527), is based on an Irish-born drinking partner of O'Neill's at JIMMY "THE PRIEST'S" bar named DRISCOLL, who worked on the same ship with O'Neill, the SS *PHILADELPHIA*, as a coal stoker. The real Driscoll committed suicide, an unaccountable act to O'Neill's mind and one that later inspired him to write *The Hairy Ape*. In *The Moon of the Caribbees*, Driscoll plays a leadership role among the men, as he does in all four *Glencairn* plays. He also demonstrates an Irish-style racism with the first lines of the play, "Will ye listen to them naygurs? I wonder now, do they call that keenin' a song?" (1:528), and later when he asks Bella to dance: "Dance wid me, me cannibal quane" (1:541).

**First Mate** First mate on the British tramp steamer SS *Glencairn*. *"A tall, strongly-built man dressed in a plain uniform"* (1:542). When the first mate discovers that Bella and the other "bumboat" girls reneged on their promise not to sell his crewmen liquor, he orders them off the ship with no payment. As there are no DOCTORS aboard vessels such as the *Glencairn*, the first mate diagnoses Paddy after he has been stabbed and sends him aft for bandaging.

**Lamps** Swedish lamp trimmer (sailor who maintains the lamps of a ship) on the British tramp steamer SS *Glencairn*. O'Neill describes him simply as *"a fat Swede"* (1:528).

**Old Tom, "The Donkeyman"**    Engine operator on the British tramp steamer SS *Glencairn*. O'Neill describes him as *"an old gray-headed man with a kindly, wrinkled face"* (1:529). The conversation between Smitty and the Donkeyman contrasts with the boisterous carousing going on around them. The Donkeyman exhibits a sense of personal calm and belonging, while Smitty voices the complaints of a man tortured by his memories of lost love. Joel Pfister characterizes the Donkeyman as "unflappably anti-'psychological' in his casual outlook" (112), and, unlike Smitty, he expresses a Zenlike calm worthy of his nickname while the rest of the men drink and carouse about him. For O'Neill, he epitomizes the "honest vulgarity" of all seamen on board save Smitty and possibly the officers. Although his expressed advice to Smitty is to beat women into submission, consort with prostitutes, and drink more rum, the Donkeyman's greatest gift to O'Neill's mind is his ability to forget the past, which calls to mind the prostitute's advice to Michael Cape in WELDED (Pfister 112).

**Olson**    Swedish seaman on the tramp steamer SS *Glencairn*; based on a Norwegian seaman O'Neill served with on the SS *Ikala*, who, after 20 years at sea, pined for his farm back home (Gelb 290). His character was played by the world-renowned actor John Wayne in the director John Ford's film *The Long Voyage Home* (1940), which adapted the whole SS *Glencairn* series into a sustained narrative. In *The Moon of the Caribbees*, Olson is given no description in the STAGE DIRECTIONS and has very few lines, though in the *Glencairn* play *The Long Voyage Home*, he is the protagonist shanghaied by a local "crimp" in a waterfront dive in London. Olson also plays a minor role in *Bound East for Cardiff*.

**Paddy**    Irish fireman on the tramp steamer SS *Glencairn*. O'Neill describes Paddy as *"a squat, ugly Liverpool Irishman"* (1:530), and he is Cocky's nemesis. Paddy trips Cocky up while Cocky dances with Susie, and the rest of the men roar with laughter;

when Cocky lunges for him, a general melee ensues among all the sailors save Smitty and the Donkeyman. Paddy is stabbed in the brawl, most likely by Cocky, but he only receives a "flesh wound" (1:543), and the first mate sends him aft to be bandaged. Paddy does not appear in any of the other *Glencairn* plays, though O'Neill endows the same name to a similar character in *The Hairy Ape*.

**Paul**    Norwegian seaman on the tramp steamer SS *Glencairn*. Paul, who provides the men's musical entertainment with his accordion, also appears in *Bound East for Cardiff* and *In the Zone*.

**Pearl**    West Indian "bumboat" woman who consorts with Yank but also flirts with Smitty, whom she considers a "genelman" (1:539). When Smitty rebuffs her advances, she slaps him and *"laughs viciously"* (1:541). O'Neill describes her as *"the youngest and best-looking"* of the West Indian women (1:535).

**Smitty**    British seaman on the tramp steamer SS *Glencairn*. Described as *"a young Englishman with a blonde mustache"* (1:528), Smitty is based on a sailor O'Neill once met at the Sailor's Opera Saloon in Buenos Aires, Argentina (Gelb 284); he is also the main character of *In the Zone*, where the other men suspect him of being a German spy. Smitty's outsider status—he most clearly approximates O'Neill himself in the seamen's milieu (see Engel 13)—creates the tension in the play. While the rest of the men cavort with the West Indian "bumboat" women, Smitty wallows in self-pity and rails against the sadness of the West Indian song drifting over from the island. Meanwhile, Old Tom, the "Donkeyman," looks on in tolerant amusement and offers him advice. An educated, middle-class sailor within the tramp steamer's working-class environment, Smitty's inability to disregard the torments of his past, a love lost most likely to ALCOHOLISM, makes him an unsympathetic character in O'Neill's eyes.

One reviewer described Smitty's character after the premiere as "an uninteresting young man" (quoted in Sheaffer 445), but there is more complexity to his character than might be apparent at first. Among the eternal beauty of the sea and the men's Dionysian revelry, O'Neill writes, "his silhouetted gestures of self-pity are reduced to their proper insignificance, his thin whine of weakness is lost in the silence which it was mean enough to disturb" (O'Neill 99). His obsessive guilt also seems to imply a CLASS-based judgment on women, particularly when the Donkeyman encourages him to cavort with the West Indian natives, insofar as "middle-class white women, not black women (who get paid off) or white working-class women (who get whacked), have the subjective potency to produce the inner drama that torments [him]" (Pfister 113). Along with *The Moon* and *In the Zone*, Smitty also appears in *Bound East for Cardiff*.

**Susie**  West Indian "bumboat" woman who dances with Cocky.

**Violet**  West Indian "bumboat" woman who consorts with Davis.

**Yank**  American seaman on the tramp steamer SS *Glencairn*. "*A rather good-looking rough*," Yank is the dying protagonist of *Bound East for Cardiff* but does not appear in any of the other *Glencairn* plays. Yank chooses Pearl, "*the youngest and best-looking*" of the West Indian women (1:535), though she prefers Smitty. When Yank sees her consorting with Smitty, he underscores the importance of masculine loyalty by saying, "Pals is pals and any pal of mine c'n have anythin' I got, see?" (1:540).

### BIBLIOGRAPHY

Bogard, Travis. *Contour in Time: The Plays of Eugene O'Neill*. Rev. ed. New York: Oxford University Press, 1988.
Colburn, Steven E. "The Long Voyage Home: Illusion and the Tragic Pattern of Fate in O'Neill's SS *Glencairn* Cycle." In *Critical Essays on Eugene O'Neill*, edited by James J. Martine, 55–65. Boston: G.K. Hall & Co., 1984.
Engel, Edwin A. *The Haunted Heroes of Eugene O'Neill*. Cambridge, Mass.: Harvard University Press, 1953.
Floyd, Virginia. *The Plays of Eugene O'Neill: A New Assessment*. New York: Ungar, 1985.
Gelb, Arthur, and Barbara Gelb. *O'Neill: Life with Monte Cristo*. New York: Applause Books, 2000.
Long, Chester C. *The Role of Nemesis in the Structure of Selected Plays by Eugene O'Neill*. The Hague: Mouton, 1968.
O'Neill, Eugene. "Inscrutable Forces." (A Letter to Barrett Clark, 1919.) In *O'Neill and His Plays: Four Decades of Criticism*, edited by Oscar N. Cargill, Bryllion Fagin, and William J. Fisher, 99–100. New York: New York University Press, 1961.
Pfister, Joel. *Staging Depth: Eugene O'Neill and the Politics of Psychological Discourse*. Cultural Studies of the United States. Chapel Hill: University of North Carolina Press, 1995.
Richter, Robert A. *Eugene O'Neill and Dat Ole Davil Sea: Maritime Influences in the Life and Works of Eugene O'Neill*. Mystic, Conn.: Mystic Seaport, 2004.
Sheaffer, Louis. *O'Neill: Son and Playwright*. Boston: Little, Brown, 1968.

## *More Stately Mansions* (draft completed, 1939; first produced, 1962)

*More Stately Mansions* is Eugene O'Neill's longest existing work. One of a planned cycle of up to 11 plays entitled A TALE OF POSSESSORS, SELF-DISPOSSESSED, *More Stately Mansions* takes place in Massachusetts from 1832 to 1841 and treats, in the context of the Panic of 1837, the demise of a prominent but dysfunctional fictional New England family named the Harfords. Never produced in O'Neill's lifetime, *More Stately Mansions* is the sequel to A TOUCH OF THE POET, the prequel to the unfinished installment *The Calms of Capricorn* and the sixth play of O'Neill's intended cycle. Swedish director Karl Ragnar Gierow of the Royal Dramatic Theatre in Stockholm became aware of the typescript (missing one page) in 1957, four years after O'Neill's death. O'Neill's third wife and executrix of his estate, CARLOTTA MONTEREY O'NEILL, gave Gierow permission to shorten the length—at least 10 hours of playing time for the complete script—to a four-hour script, translate it into Swedish, and produce its world premiere in Stockholm, Sweden,

Ingrid Bergman, Arthur Hill, and Colleen Dewhurst as, respectively, Deborah Harford, Simon Harford, and Sara Melody Harford in the 1967 production of *More Stately Mansions,* directed by José Quintero. Photo by Maurice Manson *(Courtesy of the Sheaffer-O'Neill Collection, Charles E. Shain Library of Connecticut College)*

on November 9, 1962. That production received very fine reviews, but its American premiere in Los Angeles on September 12, 1967, and Broadway premiere at the Broadhurst Theatre on October 31, 1967, directed and reedited by JOSÉ QUINTERO and starring Ingrid Bergman and COLLEEN DEWHURST, was unreservedly panned by the critics.

The typescript of *More Stately Mansion* resides at Yale University and includes this note by the author: "Unfinished Work. This script to be destroyed in case of my death! [signed] Eugene O'Neill." Yale University Press published Gierow's shortened version of the play in English in 1964. Oxford University Press published the first complete unexpurgated edition in September 1988, edited and with an introduction by Martha Gilman Bower.

## SYNOPSIS

*Act 1, Scene 1*
The dining room of Cornelius "Con" Melody's tavern near a city in Massachusetts, at night in fall

1832. Con Melody, the principal character in *A Touch of the Poet,* has just died. IRISH keening (traditional Irish mourning cries) can be heard from the floor above, where his body is on view. A pine partition divides the barroom at left from the dining room, which gives *"evidence of poverty-stricken neglect"* (3:287), and a cracked mirror (an important prop in the previous play) hangs askew on the partition. Jamie Cregan, Melody's cousin who served under Melody in the British army, sits drinking whiskey at one of four tables.

The barkeeper Mickey Maloy enters. Maloy disparages Melody's pretentiousness in life, which infuriates Cregan, who declares that Melody's honor, and subsequently his life, had been destroyed after failing to duel with the wealthy Protestant landowner Henry Harford, a scenario that takes place in *A Touch of the Poet.* Four years earlier, Melody's daughter Sara Melody, now Sara Melody Harford, crushed his pride by marrying Simon Harford, Henry Harford's son. Maloy exposits on how Melody, the son of an Irish shebeen (illegal pub) keeper, spent money wastefully and sank his wife, Nora Melody, into debt to keep up his facade as a British aristocrat. Melody was, in fact, a college graduate and a major in General Wellington's army during the war in Spain against the French, but he overplayed his aristocratic act to the working-class Irish who patronized his bar, all of whom, except Cregan, scoffed at his pretense. After Melody's fateful conflict with Harford, he abandoned the facade and reverted back to his Irish peasant self, "drinkin' to forget an' waitin' for death," Cregan says, "while he'd be talkin' in brogue wid all the bogtrotters [derogatory term for Irish peasants], tellin' stories an roarin' songs, an' dancin' jigs, pretendin' he had no edication an' was no better an' they were" (3:289).

Nora Melody enters from the stairway. Nora is 45 but looks much older, exhausted by life but with *"some will behind the body's wreckage that is not broken"* (3:291). Nora, who speaks in a strong Irish brogue, adored her husband faithfully in life and loves him still in death. She sends Maloy off to work, and Cregan suggests that Sara and Simon should pay off Melody's debt. Nora refuses to consider it. Sara and Simon Harford enter. Simon is

holding their third son, Jonathan Harford, who is a
year old, and Sara is six months pregnant with their
fourth child. Sara and Nora have not seen each
other in four years, as she and Melody refused to
speak after her marriage to Simon. They embrace
warmly, then go up to view Melody's body. At
first suspicious of Simon, a wealthy Yankee, Cregan soon warms to his sincere attitude of respect.
Sara returns disgusted by her father's corpse, "lying
there with the old sneer—like death mocking at
life!" (3:298). Cregan blames Sara for the change
in his old friend and commanding officer; after
rejoining him angrily, she admits of her father,
"He never knew what he was himself. He never
lived in life, but only in a bad dream" (3:299).
Sara refuses Cregan's suggestion that she pay her
mother's debt, and when he calls her "a Yankee
miser wid no honor ye wouldn't sell for gold," she
retaliates furiously in an Irish peasant brogue. He
applauds the conversion to her old self, but when
she begins talking with "lady's airs," he condemns
her again (3:301).

[Missing page]. Nora informs Sara that her
father returned to CATHOLICISM on his deathbed
as a last token of his love for her; Sara scathingly
responds that his defiance of religion was the only
thing she respected about him. Sara reluctantly
offers to pay the debt and is visibly relieved when
Nora refuses. Sara discusses the fact that she has
been running Simon's business with great success, though he always longed to return to writing
a book on fair government and human equality. She continues that he bought a cabin with
land, the place where they first made love (out of
wedlock); Sara disapproved of the purchase but
admits she can deny him nothing. Simon returns,
and Nora exits, forcing a smile at him as she
leaves (3:306). Simon convinces Sara they can
buy out his partner, Matthew—a deal she had
struck—but still lend Nora the money she needs.
His mother's black footman, Cato, enters and
hands Simon a letter from his mother, Deborah
Harford. In it, she asks to meet with him at his
cabin, which delights him but makes Sara suspicious. At length, Sara assents, but when he exits,
she plots to sneak into the cabin and eavesdrop
on their conversation.

## Act 1, Scene 2

Simon Harford's log cabin in the woods, just before
three in the afternoon the following day. The
cabin, 10 by 25 feet, has evidently been abandoned
for years, with boards nailed over the windows, a
warped roof, and clumps of overgrown grass around
its base. It faces a lake, and the autumn foliage is
*"purple and red and gold mingled with the deep green
of the conifers"* (3:314). Sara appears from behind
the right corner of the cabin and locks herself
inside. Deborah Harford enters. Dressed in white,
Deborah is the same age as Nora Melody, but she
looks much younger. Referring to herself in the
third person, she engages in a lengthy dialogue
with herself in which a dreamy, musing personality
debates the meaning of her aging life with a cynical and self-accusing inner voice. One side dreams
of herself as a "noble adventuress of Louis's Court"
at Versailles who has won the heart of the king
and can control him with the passion she inspires;
the other points out that Deborah is, in fact, the
bored and lonely wife of a hard-hearted New England merchant.

Simon enters from the woods at left. They
discuss his radical political views, the presidency
of Andrew Jackson, her love of books, and her
working-class family history, but she continually
steers the conversation toward their lives before he
became a husband, a father, and a successful merchant. She taunts him with these commonplace
occupations, knowing he has her strong romantic
streak and always wished to live the philosophical life of a writer in the woods. Occasionally she
shocks him with the fervor of her morbidity about
time swiftly passing toward death. They recite from
her favorite poem, Byron's *Childe Harold* (the same
passage Con Melody habitually recited before the
mirror in *A Touch of the Poet*), and she promises
there was no motive for the meeting but to see
him as she grew older and less content with her
bookish existence in her solitary garden. At one
point he laughs, mocking the fantasy world she
finds in 18th-century French memoirs; this ignites
a terrible reaction of anger in the voice of a French
noblewoman. She quickly restrains herself and cynically remarks that he must "learn to laugh at your
dreams if you ever hope to be happy," and like The-

odore "Hickey" Hickman in *The Iceman Cometh*, she advises him "to drive the nonsense from your head, for your own peace of mind" (3:331). Visibly shaken by the truth that his dreams have come to seem implausible to Sara, Simon damns his materialistic life as a cotton mill owner. Having obtained the reaction she wanted, she dismisses him but then calls him back to tell him not to regret his decision. "Love is worth everything!" (3:332).

Once Simon is gone, Sara appears at the cabin doorway. She informs Deborah that she overheard everything, including Deborah's inner dialogue before Simon arrived; as a result, she no longer fears her. They argue, but Sara calms herself and sympathetically apologizes for Simon's mocking of Deborah's dreams. Deborah admits she might grow fond of Sara, apprehending her strength of character and sympathy. But Sara understands that Deborah held the meeting with Simon "to put doubt and disgust for himself in his mind, and make him blame me for a greedy fool who'd made him a slave and killed his fine poet's dream" (3:335). She admits to her greed—"There's nothing like hunger to make you greedy"—and that she had known when she made love to him out of wedlock that his honor would make him hers forever. She assures Deborah that he will never leave her and exits triumphantly (3:337). Deborah's inner monologue resumes. This time her cynical self overtakes the dreamy side and vows to "face change and loneliness, and Time and Death and make myself resigned." "After all," she concludes, "what else can you do now, Deborah? You would always hear his laughter" (3:337).

### Act 2, Scene 1

The Harford mansion garden in a Massachusetts city four years later, June 1836. The garden has an oval pool surrounded by a red brick path, and topiary cut into geometrical shapes gives the area "*a curious, artificial atmosphere. It is like a fantastic toy garden magnified, in which nature is arrogantly restricted and arbitrarily distorted to form an appropriate setting for a perversely whimsical personality*" (3:338). At the center of the garden is an ivy-covered octagonal summer house with a red-lacquered Chinese arched doorway. Nicholas Gadsby, the

Harford family lawyer, enters with Simon's brother, Joel Harford. Joel is 29 years old but looks older, a mediocre talent in business and life whose "*whole character has something avidly prim and puritanical about it.*" He warns Gadsby that his mother has been acting "deliberately deranged." Gadsby, an uncertain but pompous man, considers this claim "ridiculous" (3:339). When he calls to Deborah, however, she exits from the house oddly, stepping backward from the summerhouse door; Joel observes the performance coldly, while Gadsby appears nonplussed. When she turns to face them, the lawyer gasps and stumbles a few steps back. Deborah is wearing the same white dress as act 1, scene 2, though propriety would have her dressed in mourning black, as her husband, Henry Harford, has just died. Deborah now looks much older than her 49 years, and her face has "*the quality of a death's head . . . of a skull beginning to emerge from its mask of flesh*" (3:341). She vows never to go in the house again, as it imprisons her within her own mind: "A very frightening prison it becomes at last, full of ghosts and corpses" (3:341). In a lengthy monologue, she informs Gadsby that she has trained herself to reject dreams and live with reality (as Cornelius Melody had done in the final scene of *A Touch of the Poet* by denying his aristocratic dream-self). Her husband's recent death disillusioned her with the promise and wonder of death. "There was nothing at all but a meaningless ceasing to breathe" (3:343). Joel is accustomed to her bizarre diatribes, but Gadsby looks disconcerted as she produces a steady stream of metaphysical confabulation.

Gadsby and Joel inform her that Harford had been recklessly gambling with western properties and the company is near bankruptcy. He left the two men instructions to save the Harford fortune by recruiting Simon to take control of the firm. They ask for her consent, which she at first refuses to give, since that would mean reintroducing Simon and Sara into her life. "Simon is dead to me," she insists. "And I will not have him resurrected. That is final" (3:347). They also propose that Simon and his family should move in with her, and she balks at the idea of living with "that vulgar Irish biddy and her brats" (3:350). The men appeal to her duty as a wife, mother, and grandmother, but they also suggest that by introducing Simon and his family back into her life, she would be given something to live for, along with a sense of intrigue and drama to feed her notorious imagination. She consents, reluctantly at first, and then ardently accepts her fate. Joel goes inside. Gadsby and Deborah discuss the arrangement as a "chance to be reborn," as she describes it (3:354), and he implies that they might have a romantic future together as well. She exorcises her cynical, near-demonic inner self by miming the act of ripping a ghost from her breast and flinging it into the house—"now you no longer have me to devour, Cannibal!" she screams (3:355). Relieved but confused, Gadsby pompously voices his disapproval of her strange behavior.

### Act 2, Scene 2

The following night in Sara and Simon Harford's sitting room at their home 40 miles from the Massachusetts city. Simon emerges from his study, while a rumpus can be heard upstairs. Children's laughter alternates with Sara Harford's stern but amused voice sporadically halting the noise. Simon appears overworked but prosperous and happy. He takes up a newspaper and frowns at a headline on the front page. Sara, looking beautiful and equally happy, descends the staircase and tells Simon their boys had a pillow fight before she put them to bed. Simon informs her of his father's death, apparently unmoved by the news. Deborah has not written in years, and he speculates that the reason he alienated her is that he had laughed at the cabin as "some silly flight of her imagination" (3:359). Sara agrees he should not have laughed, but she avoids admitting she was there. He tells her that his ambition to write a book on civic equality and human goodness is over, as he realizes that man is innately greedy, filled with "hypocritical pretenses and virtuous lies." Sara looks triumphant at the news, as she had been encouraging him along but secretly wanted him prove to himself that it was only a pipe dream. He continues that he may write a book outlining a "foundation of a new morality" to destroy man's hypocrisy (3:361). But it becomes clear he is only playing with the idea, which relieves Sara, who remarks warmly of his inexorable imagination,

"It's the touch of the poet in you!" (3:362). They discuss his thriving cotton mill business and how the politics of the moment—abolitionism, Andrew Jackson's bank policy, tariffs—might affect him financially. He is confident, no matter the political or economic situation, that he is capable of navigating his business through any storm.

Simon irritably goes to answer a knock at the front door. It is Deborah and Joel Harford. Deborah enters the sitting room in a black mourning dress that *"becomes her,"* and *"she is all disciplined composure, the gracious well-bred gentlewoman."* Sara *"instantly puts on her most ladylike manner as if responding in kind to a challenge"* (3:366). Deborah and Joel announce that they must talk over an urgent matter regarding Henry Harford's death, and at Deborah's behest, Simon and Joel move into the study, while Deborah and Sara remain in the sitting room. Deborah insists she "had not dreamed that dream since that day" at the cabin, but now she wants only to live by loving her grandchildren and befriending her daughter-in-law. Sara challenges her, sneering, boasting, and testing her in every way until finally admitting Deborah appears sincere. She agrees to allow Deborah into their lives, since it was Deborah who helped them financially at the outset of her marriage, and she cannot deny her, "when I'm so rich and you so poverty-stricken" (3:371; there is no way she could have known Deborah's financial position at this point in the script). Deborah tells her that Simon will run the family business, and she offers her full title to the Harford mansion. Sara's greed is evident as she delights over the prospect of owning the mansion and a controlling interest in the Harford Company. Every now and then she exclaims triumphantly, "Ah, if my father—!" (3:371).

Simon and Joel emerge from the study. The deal has been struck, but with a stipulation that Simon's company will absorb his father's, which will "cease to exist" (3:375). Joel protests haughtily, but Deborah accepts the condition. Joel storms out, but not before accepting Simon's offer to retain his post as bookkeeper for the firm. While Sara is upstairs to ensure the children are sleeping, Simon and Deborah sneer at Joel as "a stuffed moral attitude" and "God's most successful effort in taxidermy" (3:377), then discuss the domestic arrangement. Deborah insists they must "forget and eliminate the past" and admit they are now strangers who must develop a friendship (3:378). Sara returns, and she and Deborah engage in sociable banter, as if to prove to Simon that they can be friends. Though Sara is angered by Simon's consenting to the business deal without her permission, she trumps her husband by informing him that she and Deborah have made a domestic deal without his approval: They will all live with Deborah as a family in his father's old mansion. At first Simon voices suspicion over Deborah's "transformation" and "this sudden friendship" between the old enemies, but he assents (3:382, 384). "I needed only your reconciliation to complete my happiness and give me absolute confidence in the future," he says, and the curtain falls (3:385).

### Act 3, Scene 1

An early summer morning four years later, 1840, at Simon Harford's office in the city headquarters of Simon Harford, Inc. Simon appears older than his 35 years, and a gain of 20 pounds gives him a *"formidably powerful"* look (3:386). He is gloating over his new acquisition of a railroad company but also confused over the influence his mother has over his wife. He begins opening his mail when Joel steps in from the bookkeeper's office. Joel remarks coldly that he disapproves of Simon's ruthlessness in business dealings and his abuse of credit to finance the company's expansion. Simon scoffs at Joel's weak-willed moralizing: "The only moral law here is that to win is good and to lose is evil" (3:388). He orders him out contemptuously, then calls him back and apologizes. He admits his concern about their mother having taken over his family, particularly Sara, and the intense loneliness he feels at home. He then advises Joel to "shun marriage and keep a whore instead" (3:390). His mother no longer needs him because he is no longer a child, he says, and Sara no longer needs him because she has children. Disinterested in Simon's personal life, Joel asks to be excused. Simon rancorously orders him out.

Over the course of a lengthy soliloquy, Simon worries about his greed; then he scoffs that "the

possession of power is the only freedom, and your pretended disgust with it is a lie" (3:392). This internal conflict continues, and then his mind turns to Sara, who has grown ugly to him in her devotion to the children. He admits to himself that Sara slept with him the first time out of wedlock to exploit his honor and rise in the world, "as unscrupulous and ruthless as a whore selling herself!" (3:394). "Mother's is the spiritual greed, but the material lust is Sara's," he concludes and vows "to pay back" what is his, "all that I still desire from her, at least!" (3:395).

Sara enters, tiptoeing up to him quietly and wearing a smile "that takes its proprietorship for granted" (3:395). Thinking her an employee, he shouts at her savagely for the interruption, then apologizes when he realizes it is her. He boasts of the railroad deal, and she begrudgingly points out that he used to say "our" and "us" rather "I" and "mine" (3:397). He suggests that she does the same with their home and the children and asks why she has been so distant, but she accuses him of the same thing. He then asks if she suspects him of having an affair, which ignites her jealousy and sense of possession of him. Assuring her there is no affair, he then tells her he wishes to reestablish the passion they had before the children and his mother encroached on their romance. Though she defends Deborah vigorously at first, Sara begins to agree about some of his mother's bad influences—reading the children POETRY, for example, which Sara disapproves of because it reminds her of her father's pompous recitations, and "always telling them stuff about how they must do what they want, and be free" (3:405). They want their sons to run the company when Simon retires. Sara reluctantly agrees to separate the children from Deborah's influence.

Next, Simon brings up their lack of a sex life, which Sara blames on him for having moved into a separate room. He agrees he has become bored with her commonplace, dull, motherly self, and he longs "for the old passionate greedy Sara" (3:409). He then offers her a position as his "secretary and secret partner," wherein she would be paid by selling her body to him as a commodity for his own recompense, "strip yourself naked and accept yourself as you are in the greedy mind and flesh" (3:413).

Instantly recognizing the correlation to PROSTITU-TION, she is nevertheless aroused by the possibility of joining him in the expansion of his empire. The deal struck, Sara exits, and Simon resumes his inner dialogue, delighting at the prospect of his divide-and-conquer method with Sara and Deborah. Joel knocks at the door, and Simon resumes his *"formidable, ruthless head of the Company"* persona (3:416). Joel informs him that railroad men have arrived for their meeting, and he is announcing them personally given their status. Simon derisively states that they have lost their power and therefore their respect from him. Joel goes out, and the curtain falls.

### Act 3, Scene 2

Same as act 2, scene 1, the Harford mansion garden. Deborah sits on the steps to the house while her four grandchildren, Ethan, Wolfe Tone, Jonathan, and Owen Roe "Honey" Harford—12, 11, nine, and seven, respectively—are positioned around the oval pool listening to her read from Byron's "Childe Harold." She first reads the stanzas beginning, "But Quiet to quick bosoms is a Hell" and then, at Ethan's request, she reads of Byron's love for the SEA. Finally, at Wolfe's request, she reluctantly reads the same lines she had recited in act 1, scene 2 (and, again, the same Con Melody habitually recited to the mirror in *A Touch of the Poet*), which deal with alienation from society—"I stood / Among them, but not of them" (3:423).

Deborah hears Simon's footsteps outside the wall, and he startles her by knocking at the door to the street. Simon orders the children inside, against Deborah's wishes, and informs her of his plans to hire a private secretary, one whose only qualifications must be "very young and beautiful." Assuming he is talking about an affair, Deborah raves that she no longer recognizes this "unscrupulous greedy trader" (3:427). Simon says coldly that she has jumped to a false conclusion, then insinuates that Sara was not as "blind" and "unsuspectingly trustful" as she had hoped (3:428). He also informs her that Sara now believes she is a poor influence on the children. Between jousts about Sara's change of heart, he pauses and gazes desirously around the garden. He tells her he dreams

of expanding the company until he is completely independent of outside services. He agrees with Deborah that the final step would be to "possess plantations in the South and own your own nigger slaves, imported in your own slave ships" (3:431). In the end, Deborah accepts his proposition that they resume their fanciful relationship from his childhood, and she will replace the children's company with his in the garden. He warns her not to interfere with his new domestic arrangement and they go in to dinner.

### Act 3, Scene 3

The Harford family parlor around nine o'clock that night. A majestic space within a house built in the late 1790s, *"such as one finds in the Massachusetts houses designed by Bulfinch or McIntire,"* with high ceilings, tall picture windows, a crystal chandelier hanging from the ceiling, a fireplace, a long sofa, and a table with chairs. A door at left leads to the entrance hall; another to Simon's study is at the middle of the rear wall. Sara and Simon are seated at opposite ends of the table. Deborah is on the sofa. Simon and Deborah both pretend to read, while Sara pretends to work on needlepoint. *"For a moment after the curtain rises there is an atmosphere of tense quiet in the room, an eavesdropping silence that waits, holding its breath and straining its ears. Then, as though the meaning of the silence were becoming audible, their thoughts are heard"* (3:449). Sara inwardly wonders why Deborah arrived from the garden looking "as gay as you please," while Simon looked too "sly," as though "there was a secret between them." For her part, Deborah inwardly wonders why the chemistry between the spouses appears changed, sensing Sara's "warm greedy femaleness deliberately exuding lust in a brazen enticement" (3:450). Simon is gloating over his victory that "they are divided and separate again . . . no devouring merging of identities" (3:451).

Simon's ruthless, Napoleonic divide-and-conquer strategy has been a success in the public sphere, and now it appears to be working in the domestic sphere as well. But each character begins to regret the pacts made that destroyed their contented home, even Simon. "What stupid impulse drove me to start taking a hand in their measly woman's game" at a time when he is preoccupied with the railroad deal, he asks himself (3:454). Both Deborah and Sara cannot hate each other comfortably, and both inwardly hope the other can forgive her betrayal. They simultaneously address each other out loud, then *"smile at each other with relieved understanding"* (3:458). Taking their usual seats together on the sofa, they whisper conspiratorially about Simon's futile attempt to separate them. Simon takes note of this but inwardly recalls that he still holds a terrible secret against each— that Sara will sell herself as his mistress, and that Deborah will meet with him alone every afternoon in the garden. Nevertheless, the women begin to ridicule him as a "greedy jealous boy . . . who is helpless and lonely and lost" (3:460). Too involved in his own thoughts to hear them, Simon only senses a coldness in the room and feels they have merged once again into one woman who "no longer wants me—has taken all she needed—I have served my purposed . . . she is free—and I am left lost in myself, with nothing!" (3:461).

The women's expressions *"have changed to revengeful gloating cruelty and they stare at him with hate"* (3:461). Their comments take on a sarcastic tone of false affection, mocking him for being jealous of the children and needing so much from his women, as if he were a little boy. Arms about each other's waist, they stand up and advance on Simon in a unified front. *"They are like two mothers who, confident of their charm, take a possessive gratification in teasing a young, bashful son. But there is something more behind this—the calculating coquetry of two prostitutes trying to entice a man"* (3:465). Simon comprehends that it was a mistake to attempt to conquer them in the home, "the stronghold of woman." But he realizes that in the act of submission, he receives their affection and in this way achieves "the final conquest and peace" he desires (3:466). He chuckles, and his apparent contentedness turns the women's jealously against each other once more. But his hatred of them resumes when they fend off their jealousy, and he can feel their hate against him. He announces that he will spend the rest of his evenings in his study, and they should keep their territories separate in his absence. Before exiting, he taunts them with the fact that each has

a secret against the other. They make their respective confessions to one another and though this initially sparks their old hatreds, each agrees to go ahead with Simon's plan—Deborah to give up the children for Simon, and Sara to prostitute herself as Simon's partner and mistress. All unity is lost as they spitefully think of the other's defeat and consider their own triumph.

### Act 4, Scene 1

Same as act 3, scene 1: Simon's private office on an early morning in the summer of the following year, 1841. Sara's decorative influence is unmistakable, particularly a new sofa at center, *"garishly expensive and luxurious . . . its blatant latest-stylishness in vulgar contrast to the sober, respectable, conservatism of the old office of Simon's father"* (3:477); an expansive architectural drawing of a *"pretentious, nouveau-riche estate"* can be seen on the wall above the desk at right. Sara is discovered at her desk; her body appears even more voluptuous, and she wears a dress that accentuates her curves, *"revealing them as nakedly as the fashion will permit."* Her pretty Irish face *"has been coarsened and vulgarized,"* giving the suggestion of a *"hardened prostitute"* (3:477). She is working at her desk as Joel Harford silently enters, appearing *"weak, insecure, and furtive"* and gazing lustfully at her body *"with a sly, greedy desire"* (3:478). Sara treats him with vicious contempt, as Simon had done in act 3, scene 1. Joel announces that Benjamin Tenard, the banker, has arrived for his meeting with Simon, who now visits with his mother mornings as well as evenings. Joel denounces the way Simon and Sara have been running up debts, warning her that if one of their enemies discovered it, the company would be ruined. He also protests against the vulgar arrangement between her and Simon, which is now public knowledge. But he implies that she might buy his share of the company by selling herself to him in the same way. She considers the bargain suggestively, but after he exits, she waffles between triumphant gloating over her newfound sexual power and her debasing life with Simon, "working as his whore, with no life except in his greed" (3:482).

Simon enters, looking much thinner and haggard but, having come from his mother's garden, *"with a strange expression, of peace and relaxation on his face . . . a look of bemused dreaminess in his eyes"* (3:484). Sara runs to him and weeps longingly on his chest, and it takes him some time to snap out of his garden reverie. When he does, he takes her lustily in his arms and tries to lead her to the sofa. She mocks his attempt to have sex for free. "You wouldn't want me if I gave myself for nothing, and let you cheat me!" (3:485). This time, she wants the bank they have just acquired. She also demands that he forget his mother and stay only with her, jealously scolding him for making her wait that morning. Deborah, according to Simon, is now "far gone in second childhood" and on the brink of madness (3:487). He compliments Sara on her plans for the estate, remarking that owning the bank will grant her even more additions; then, with sad irony, he quotes from Oliver Wendell Holmes's poem, "The Chambered Nautilus"—"Build thee more stately mansions, O my soul" (3:489)—and sardonically suggests they should place an engraved copy of it over her entrance and his mother's "magic door" in the garden summerhouse (3:489). Before the ruined banker Tenard enters, he coaches her to "bear in mind that the end you desire always justifies any means" (3:491).

Tenard enters with an ineffectual facade of dignity that Sara rapidly tears down. She informs him that she knows no one will hire him because of his age and that his family is starving. She offers him his former position as bank manager, but he must be willing to be treated like "the meanest worker at the looms in my mills, or a common sailor on my ships, or a brakeman on my railroad"; he reluctantly accepts the terms, but she adds that he must also forsake his sentimental ethics and "become a conscious thief and swindler" (3:495). When he indignantly refuses, Sara screams in an Irish brogue that he would be willing to allow his family to starve for his foolish ethics. Utterly defeated, Tenard agrees to her terms and rushes out the door. Simon applauds her performance, but she regrets her cruelty and threatens to inform Tenard about their debts. He reminds her it is she who would be ruined and that her victory over Deborah and dream of the estate would be destroyed. She relents, considering the pride that allowed her

father to scoff at debts and sneer at the devil and fate. And she passionately wants to retain Simon. "If it's a whore you love me to be, then I am it, body and soul, as long as you're mine!" (3:501). Simon warns her not to plot against him with Deborah; then he demands, "Can't you rid our life of that damned greedy witch?" "You mean you want me to—" she whispers, and he teasingly pats her on the cheek: "I want you to do anything in life your heart desires to make me yours." He exits for the train, and she looks after him with an expression of "*horrified eagerness*" as the curtain falls (3:502).

### Act 4, Scene 2

Same as act 3, scene 2: the garden of the Harford mansion. Deborah is pacing back and forth, "*pitifully distraught, nervous, tense, frightened and desperate*" (3:503). Emaciated, pale, and aged, she now looks like a harridan from a fairy tale, "*an evil godmother . . . whom strong sunlight would dissolve, or a breath of reality disperse into thin air*" (3:503). Her face is again like a death mask, and though she wears her usual white dress, her hair is done up like an 18th-century lady, her lips are rouged, and a beauty spot is painted on each cheek. In a lengthy monologue, she frets over why Simon has not yet arrived for their evening visit, accuses Sara of holding him back, and from time to time imagines she hears Simon at the door. She consoles herself that she has successfully "led him back, step by step, into memory, into the past, where he longs to be—where he is my child again—my baby—where my life is his only life—where he is safe beyond her grasping claws!" (3:505). But jealousy gets the better of her, and she curses Sara as a "whore" and Simon as a "greedy trader" playing Napoleon (3:506). She casts her mind back to her fantasy of being a dominating French mistress, now for Napoleon rather than King Louis.

Sara sneaks into the garden from the house. Her entire appearance is that of "*a prostitute the morning after a debauch*" (3:507). She is planning to murder Deborah, but she sees her mother-in-law begin to enter the summerhouse, in which she will be driven entirely back into her fantasies, and thus into madness and perhaps suicide. Sara angrily stops her. She gloats that Simon will no longer be visiting and sneers at Deborah's pretending to be Napoleon's mistress now. Infuriated and desperate, Deborah lunges for the door, but Sara picks her bodily from the steps and forces her to the bench. Deborah falls apart in tears. Sara cruelly continues that she has become "mother, wife, and mistress in one" for Simon (3:511), but she promises to stop scheming against Deborah and allow her back into the children's lives if Deborah will stop taking Simon into her fantasy world. They hurl accusations against one another but eventually apologize and vow to form a united pact against Simon, whom they begin to berate as they had in act 3, scene 3.

Simon quietly enters from the path and overhears them plotting to live in harmony as mother and grandmother to the children. When they blame him for their greed, he steps in and says that they have equally greedy natures, and in the end, "good is evil, and evil, good" (3:517). But his confidence wavers, and he admits to searching for a solution to end their conflicted selves. This provokes them into jeering at him with sarcastic pity—Sara for having taken him for all he is worth and Deborah for having the ability to reduce "our great man-conquering Napoleon" to a "stubborn, nagging, begging little boy" (3:518).

Simon claims he overhead them from his study "clawing and tearing at each other like two drunken drabs fighting over a dollar bill" (3:519), and he had secretly hoped one of them would kill the other so he might at last find peace. At first they appear triumphant, but then, watching him sob in anguish, they run to him and console him. For a time, they are all united and apologize to and forgive each other for all their scheming. Simon tells Sara that the reason he came to the garden in the first place was to tell her the children wanted her to kiss them goodnight and that Honey might have taken ill. She goes into the house, suspicious but compliant.

Once Sara is gone, Simon chuckles and resumes his plot with Deborah to renounce Sara. Deborah struggles between her allegiance to Sara and her need for Simon, intermittently attacking each. But he slowly turns her against Sara, promising only to love her and to rid his wife from their lives for good. When she swears her hatred for Sara and her wish for her daughter-in-law to die, Simon agrees they

should murder Sara, countering guilty feelings by denouncing the value of life. He convinces her that to emerge the victor, she must open the "magic door" and lead him back into the past where Sara "never existed" (3:530). "I have waited ever since I was a little boy," he say. "All my life since then I have stood outside that door in my mind, begging you to let me re-enter that lost life of peace and trustful faith and happiness!" (3:531). "You know I knew what you meant by the evil enchantress," he says of the fairy tale his mother used to tell him as a child, "and that I was the exiled Prince!" The Chinese door exists to her, he understands, as a symbol of her freedom from him, and if she takes him in, it will be the "necessary physical act by which your mind wills to take me back into your love" (3:533). Deborah denies this and attempts to coax him to the house, but he warns that he may be tempted by Sara's beauty if she returns before they step through the door. He explains that Deborah "dispossessed" herself when she "dispossessed" him, and since that time, they both followed the path of greed to satiate the love they had lost (3:534).

Only her hatred for Sara is powerful enough to agree to take him through the door, Deborah tells him. Sara arrives back from the house as they are moving toward the door and shouts at Deborah for being a liar and a traitor. Simon turns his head and stares at her with a *strange, mad, trance-like look* (3:538), then accuses Sara of trespassing and threatens to call the police. He says she reminds him of an old mistress of his whom he deserted when "her lust began to bore" him and he "went off with another woman, an old lover in my childhood" (3:538). Sara pleas for mercy, admitting that Deborah has won. She promises to take her children back to the old farm at the cabin and leave for good if she will release Simon from her spell. Deborah agrees the farm would be fitting for "a dumb, brainless, begetting female animal with her dirty brats around her" and scoffs at her weakness. Sara tells her she does not feel defeated but proud, as her love for Simon is so strong, she is willing to give him up for his sake. She tells her to let Simon go, as "it isn't good for him to stay long—so far away in the past as you've taken him" (3:542). This goads Deborah into proving who is the final victor, and she decides to enter the summerhouse alone, "choosing to keep my spirit pure and untouched and unpossessed!" (3:543) "You get back to the greasy arms of your wife where you belong," she bellows and pushes Simon down the stairs. Sara runs to his prostrate body, and Deborah laughs at her former fear of the summerhouse. "Why," she tells herself as she moves through the door, "what is waiting to welcome you is merely your last disdain!" (3:543).

Sara asks Simon worriedly if he is all right, and he recounts the ending of Deborah's fairy tale in a childlike voice: "So the Prince waited before the door and begged for love from all who passed by," and he faints in her arms (3:544). Sara condemns herself for having been seduced by greed and her father's mad fantasy of aristocracy, and she vows to sell the company and move with Simon to the old farm; she will till the soil and he can go back to the Simon she fell in love with, "the dreamer with a touch of the poet in his soul, and the heart of a boy" (3:544).

Deborah appears at the door in a trancelike state. She has completely taken the role of the dominant French mistress. Sara humors her sympathetically and plays the part of the submissive Irish kitchen maid Deborah takes her for. But then Sara asks Deborah's forgiveness, and when Deborah asks who "Deborah" is, Sara pleads with her not to pretend to have gone completely, as that would be too great a sacrifice to save Simon, whom Deborah now believes is a stable boy. Deborah falters for an instant, then reverts back to being a French noblewoman and tells Sara she may kiss her hand. Sara's pride revolts at first, but then she humors her mother-in-law, kissing her hand and saying "God bless you" (3:547). Deborah thanks her, then moves grandly back into the house and shuts the door for the last time. Sara cries out that now she will never know whether Deborah is playacting to save Simon or truly lost in her fantasy. Simon awakens and, speaking in a child's voice, regards Sara as his mother. "Yes, I'll be your mother, too, now," she says to him lovingly, "and your peace and happiness and all you'll ever need in life!" (3:547). They walk down the path to the house, as the curtain falls.

*Epilogue*

Same as act 1, scene 2: Simon's cabin and farm in the woods by the lake. Late afternoon in early June of the following year, 1842. The cabin has been renovated and scrubbed and the grass mowed, and the whole atmosphere has a rustic, salubrious feel. Honey is flipping a pocket knife into the ground as, in a lovely voice, he sings Thomas Moore's "Believe me if all those endearing young charms" (3:548). Jonathan emerges from the path at left, and they discuss their father, Simon. Sara told them he has brain fever, and Simon had been behaving like one of the children. That morning he walked out to the fields and recognized them as his sons for the first time, and their mother cried when she heard the news of his recovery. Deborah has died, and Sara attended the funeral that morning with her face veiled to hide her identity.

Sara enters dressed in cheap calico. She looks younger in the face, healthy and strong, but also older because of her doleful expression and streaks of white in her hair. She orders the boys to pray for their grandmother, which they do reluctantly, though they have not been raised to believe in religion. They go off to get the other boys for a celebratory swim.

Simon appears unsteadily at the doorway of the cabin, disheveled, weak, and thin, his eyes fixed in a *groping and bewildered stare* (3:552). But then he calls to Sara, and she runs to him joyfully. She takes him to the bench, and he lies in the grass with his head on her lap. He wants to know everything that happened, but she tells him to rest first. He persists, and she asks about the last thing he remembers. The meeting with the railroad directors, he says, and his forcing them to relinquish control to him, "Damned hog and fool that I was!" (3:553). But she blames herself: "With my dream I got from my father's boasting lies that I ought to rise above myself and own a great estate" (3:553). He agrees that she was his main inspiration to rise in business. To his astonishment, she informs him that the meeting with the railroad directors took place five years ago. She goes on that his sons have grown into fine young boys and that she and he always loved each other. The company has failed, she continues, and the creditors took everything but the farm; she made this happen, and deliberately informed Tenard about their debt, knowing he would seek retribution against them.

Simon tells her, "I confess I always hoped something would turn up to release me from the soul-destroying compulsion to keep on enslaving myself with more and more power and possessions" (3:555). "You're a gentleman and a poet at heart, and a lost child in a world of strangers," Sara responds. "I'll never ask you to succeed again" (3:556). He remembers attempting to unravel the duality of man's nature, but she insists that was a dream. She then informs him that Deborah is dead, but this news evokes no surprise; he only wishes to know that she died happily, having forgotten her dream life and embraced reality with her grandchildren. Sara tensely responds, "Yes. That's what happened to her. Exactly" (3:557). Simon agrees that the peace and love they have in their new life is all he wishes to remember and falls asleep. She lightly chides him for having proven the victor in the end.

The boys rush by for their swim, and Sara shushes them to let their father sleep. They continue on, and she begins to dream about the giants of industry and politics they will each become but then scolds herself harshly. "You'll let them be what they want to be. . . . You'll leave them free, do you hear, and yourself free of them!" She gazes down at Simon and says, "After all, one slave is enough for any woman to be owned by! Isn't it true, my Darling?" Then she laughs *"with a gloating, loving, proud, self-mockery,"* kisses him softly, and the curtain falls (3:559).

## COMMENTARY

Eugene O'Neill wrote *More Stately Mansions* while suffering from neuritis at his home, TAO HOUSE, in Danville, California. Rich with important thematic and autobiographical material, much of the play reads as if its author was still struggling with his craft, though it composed it in tandem with his late masterpieces, *A Touch of the Poet* (the prequel), *The* ICEMAN COMETH, and LONG DAY'S JOURNEY INTO NIGHT, three of the finest plays ever written by an American. The work contains far too much exposition, virtually no action, and, in act 3, scene 3, a reversion back to the "inner monologue"

technique many believed O'Neill had abandoned as what he called a "show shop" theater trick after STRANGE INTERLUDE (in Bogard 340). Reviewers of its Broadway premiere universally panned the play and criticized its director, José Quintero, for resurrecting a work that would have been better off left to collect dust at Yale University. Unlike a "self-doubting, self-tormenting genius" like Franz Kafka, wrote one reviewer, "when so self-esteeming, megalomaniacal a writer as O'Neill wanted something of his destroyed, I think it is safe to assume that he was right" (Simon 254). "With friends like Mr. José Quintero," another quipped, "the shade of O'Neill might think he needs no enemies, and being his own worst enemy was the privilege O'Neill always retained for himself" (Barnes 253). Zander Brietzke succinctly wrote in a brief appendix note to the play, "poetic title/prosaic contents" (233).

O'Neill did, in fact, deliberately destroy two longhand drafts of *More Stately Mansions* on February 21, 1943, along with drafts of other plays meant for the historical cycle *A Tale of Possessors, Self-Dispossessed,* and the general assumption is that the typescript was inadvertently sent on to Yale in 1951 with the rest of the O'Neill papers. Regardless of a handwritten note by O'Neill that accompanies the manuscript, in which he explicitly states his wish to have the manuscript destroyed in the event of his death, Martha Gilman Bower makes a strong case that the surviving script is "virtually complete," since the majority of revisions were made in 1939, and O'Neill made minor corrections to the typescript as late as 1942, including the change of Deborah Harford's name from the original "Abigail" (Bower "*More Stately Mansions-Redux*" 2004, 245). After a close analysis of the notes and edited passages, Bower concludes that "it does not appear that if O'Neill had lived he would have made substantial changes, if any" (246).

Edward Shaughnessy notes that given its relatively unfinished status and poor reception on the stage, "anyone who writes about this play is bound to feel a certain uneasiness," but he acknowledges the work's importance as a document that helps explain O'Neill's larger purpose as a dramatist (170). Stephen A. Black takes it one step further, applauding the play's artistic quality, in fact, for what others might consider its worst attribute—the lack of dramatic action in favor of exposition: "Even in its unfinished state, the play can seem quite fine to a reader. . . . In combining action deferred or restrained with searching, detailed accounts of psychological processes, in its sense of purpose and of the tragic, it somewhat resembles a Wharton novel" (407). If the play lacks a critical consensus, as Ingrid Bergman commented on its bad reviews, "O'Neill is one of America's greatest playwrights. Even if *More Stately Mansions* is not his best play, it was written by a playwright who will go down in history as the greatest of America" (quoted in Floyd 461n).

*More Stately Mansions*, the longest play O'Neill ever wrote, comprehensively treats the four most important themes in the O'Neill canon, perhaps more explicitly than any other play: the corrupting influence of the American dream, the tortured existence of a "dreamer poet" opposing a society driven by rampant materialism and puritanical morality, the power struggle in GENDER relations, and the painful convolutions of family dynamics. It is also, like most of his work, highly autobiographical and historical. But each of these themes is treated with such an explicit sense of urgency that the play becomes extraordinarily redundant. One reviewer likened it to sitting in an "echo chamber in which the same speeches often reverberated ad nauseam" (Simon 255). Indeed, the play might act as an echo chamber for the O'Neill canon in its entirety. Take this line from Deborah Harford while she and Simon discuss their futures at the log cabin: "Time is but another of our illusions, and what was is forever identical with what is, beneath the deceiving changing masks we wear" (328). This addresses the two major O'Neill themes of time and deceptive masks, themes that combine O'Neill's signature blend of NATURALISM and psychoanalysis. Later, Simon tells Joel that "the past is never dead as long as we live because all we are is the past" (3:391), and still later he says to Deborah, "The past is the present" (3:430), a line O'Neill more famously applies later in *Long Day's Journey into Night*, when Mary Tyrone (based on O'Neill's mother) brings up the quack doctor who caused her morphine addiction, and her husband, James Tyrone (in real life

O'Neill's father, JAMES O'NEILL), begs her again to stop bringing up the past: "Why? How can I? The past is the present, isn't it? It's the future, too. We all try to lie out of that but life won't let us" (3:765).

The title of O'Neill's historical cycle, *A Tale of Possessors, Self-Dispossessed*, refers to the acquisitiveness of Americans alienating themselves from the self through material gain and the loss of love that follows such selfishness. "You dispossessed yourself," Simon says to his mother, "when you dispossessed me" (3:534). In his WORK DIARY, O'Neill specifies that the meaning of the title could be found in the character Sara Melody Harford, as "her belonging is by possessing to be possessed—to be possessed in order to possess—her thwarting is that she can never feel she possesses all of [Simon]" (quoted in Diggins 128). In his notes, O'Neill extrapolates on the meaning of Sara's character to the play:

> Sara is a means of final escape from her [Deborah], substitution, as well as genuine love and physical passion—she realizes this and it is reason, later on, she can feel friendship towards Sara. When she sees Sara as her revenge rather than as herself (etc.) and so [sic] the underlying plot of this play is the duel to the death between mother and son, in which each uses Sara against the other. (Quoted in Bower "*More Stately Mansions* Redux" 2004, 245)

The play's title *More Stately Mansions* is taken, as referenced in the script, from Oliver Wendell Holmes's poem from the period entitled "The Chambered Nautilus." O'Neill applies Holmes's line ironically, as Holmes is referring to people who enrich their lives by building their spiritual "mansions" through experience, whereas O'Neill refers to characters who, like the eponymous mollusk, "engaging in one power play after another, create ever tighter defensive perimeters until they eventually retreat into themselves" (Petite).

Simon's, Sara's, and Deborah's split personalities expose O'Neill's inability to reconcile the oppositions in the play. This is particularly evident in the unnatural way he writes them in continuous conflict with themselves, often making the characters sound clinically schizophrenic. Over time, as Shaughnessy phrases it, "The reader himself becomes exhausted by their ceaseless maneuvering and release of psychic energy" (171). Sara's extreme reversal of attitude after her complicity in destroying the banker Benjamin Tenard is one of dozens of examples that make little sense on their face. But the paradox that emerges is, at bottom, one of power—how to secure power, over themselves and others, to delude themselves that they have control over their lives. This "paradox of power," as Joseph Petite argues of the play's central theme, "is that the more one dominates, the less he is secure." Similarly, Edward Shaughnessy argues that the play's implicit premise is that "one cannot indulge the will to power without disfiguring himself" (171).

This paradox of power applies in both Simon's financial world, known as the "public sphere" in cultural studies, and Sara and Deborah's domestic life, or the "private sphere." In each sphere of influence, the characters struggle between the means by which they achieve their own personal ends. The central conflict of power can be read as serving O'Neill's general metaphor of prostitution, as Sara and Deborah refer to each other as prostitutes throughout the play, and Simon prostitutes his spiritual and philosophical goals for monetary gain and the good graces of his women (see Real passim). Love itself turns into a business of purely selfish desire, as when Simon rationalizes Sara's trading money and power for sex as an act of humanity unfettered by tired moral restrictions: "Strip yourself naked and accept yourself as you are in the greedy mind and flesh. Then you can go on—successfully—with a clear vision—without false scruples—on to demand and take what you want—as I have done!" (3:413). "Greed" for Simon "is good," as the fictional character Gordon Gekko pronounces much later in the film *Wall Street*, and the world of commerce offers an alternative ethics, "more frank and honest—and so, more honorable!—truer to the greedy reality of life than our hypocritical personal ones. The only moral law here is that to win is good and to lose is evil" (3:388).

Simon's social contradictions—the man with a "touch of the poet" who believes in the innate goodness of mankind and the ruthless business leader with no conscience, symbolized respectively by Deborah and Sara—are meant to evoke the economic, political, and philosophical contradictions of the entire nation. Simon also exhibits psychological contradictions that arise from him desperate need for either female love or its viable substitute. Simon's adopted financial methods strike at the heart of two historical catastrophes the play alludes to: the Panic of 1837, which Simon successfully weathers by judiciously holding his money "in specie" (in gold and silver coinage rather than paper money), and the Great Depression of the 1930s, during which the play was written. To date, these are the worst financial crises in American history—the first serious one in the young nation's history and the most recent for O'Neill's time—and in both events, the "possessors" became "self-dispossessed." "Any fool should have seen the crash was bound to come," Simon tells Sara, "But they didn't" (3:362). Simon blames Andrew Jackson's "tariff compromise" and "insane banking policy" for the panic, as many business leaders had at the time (3:362). The scene in which Sara destroys Benjamin Tenard also resembles a convention of American MELODRAMA such as we find in Dion Boucicault's *The Poor of New York* (1857), which takes place during the Panic of 1837 and features previously well-to-do businessmen crushed under the weight and power of unethical rivals during the panic.

Simon's split personality plays out in the political arena as well. In act 2, scene 2, Sara chides Simon for being a financially conservative "Massachusetts Whig" like Daniel Webster, but in terms of protecting the rights of the individual, he is a "South Carolina Democrat" like John C. Calhoun (3:357; see Diggins 122–123). "And you're Abolition, too," Sara teases him, "and that's not Whig nor Democrat. (*She laughs.*) You're a queer man when it comes to politics" (3:358). Simon's early theory of government speaks to O'Neill's lifelong belief in PHILOSOPHICAL ANARCHISM, which denounced the right to private property and reflected Thomas Jefferson's vision of the future republic: "We must renounce the idea of great centralized governments, and divide society into small, self-governing communities where all property is owned in common for the common good" (3:321). But as Simon's desire for wealth and power increases over the course of the play, his contentious business acumen gives way to precisely the same controlling, property-driven, monopolizing instinct that led financiers to their own destruction in both the 1830s and the 1930s. He wishes to control his own means of production, own his own slaves and plantations in the South to grow the cotton for his mills in the North, and transport his products to the West with his own railroad. It was precisely this kind of monopolistic expansion, based solely on credit, that largely destroyed the American economy in both crises and the recession of our current era.

Simon's attitudes reflect the period's philosophical trends as well. He initially wants to write a book based on the French philosopher Jean-Jacques Rousseau's supposition that the nature of man is essentially good, an Enlightenment-era philosophy that informed Thomas Jefferson's optimistic vision of democracy. But after his rise in the gluttonous world of finance (Alexander Hamilton's world), he rejects Rousseau as a "weak, moral, sentimentalist" (3:360) and instead considers writing "a frank study of the true nature of man as he really is and not as he pretends himself to be" (3:361). In act 1, scene 2, Simon defends Andrew Jackson's radical democracy against Henry Harford's attacks that the Jackson era is run by an "ignorant greedy mob"; he submits that "We must return to Nature and simplicity and then we'll find that the People—those whom Father sneers at as the greedy Mob—are as genuinely noble and honorable as the false aristocracy of our present society pretends to be!" (3:321). But he discovers through free-market capitalism that the true nature of man "is compounded of one-tenth spirit to nine-tenths hog" (3:360).

Simon also moves from the spiritual self-actualization of his life of poetic solitude in the woods, as Henry David Thoreau had done at Walden Pond, by replacing individualism with more dominant American presumptions of success: money and power. "In doing so," writes Diggins, "he leaves Thoreau behind, as did America itself . . . forsaking self-reli-

ance for self-assertion" (3:121, 125). The French social theorist Alexis de Tocqueville wrote of this paradox in the United States during the 1830s in his book *Democracy in America* (1835, 1840). Diggins writes of Tocqueville's conclusions as they relate to *More Stately Mansions* that "the theoretical problem for Tocqueville was how to draw human beings out of an isolated individualism while preventing them from succumbing to soul-devouring materialism" (129). O'Neill himself does not conclude with any reconciliation between isolation and ambition, and he offers no real solution for Simon or the nation; he simply sends Simon back to where he began—his cabin in the woods—perhaps suggesting he should never have left in the first place. There, at least, he may retire, isolated and self-sufficient, a defeated relic of his former selves, consoled by the love and peace Sara is now willing to grant him. But the nation itself, and their sons' generation, will carry on its self-destructive path around them—and onward into the dim view of American greed O'Neill would find in his own time. "For what shall it profit a man," O'Neill liked to quote of the so-called American dream, "if he shall gain the whole world and lose his own soul?" (Matthew 16:26).

But all of these economic, political, philosophical, and spiritual contradictions in Simon's mind are activated by an instinctive knowledge that he cannot win the love of the most important women in his life. As a study of gender relations, *More Stately Mansions* appears to be yet another exercise in male arrogance on the part of its author. O'Neill's postulation that wives should sacrifice their goals and ambitions on behalf of their husbands' well-being has not seemed to evolve from his character Ethel Frazier's revelation about marriage in the final scene of his early full-length play SERVITUDE: "Servitude in love, love in servitude! . . . That is the great secret—and I never knew!" (1:285). "You're home at last where you've always wanted to be," Sara whispers in Simon's sleeping ear in the final scene of *More Stately Mansions*. "I'm your mother now, too. You've everything you need from life in me!" (3:558). On the heels of Deborah's mental withdrawal, Sara, like her mother, Nora Melody, before her, has denied her own needs for her husband's well-being and has taken on the responsibilities of the ideal woman one finds throughout the O'Neill canon: wife, mother, and mistress.

In 1926, O'Neill informed his friend KENNETH MACGOWAN that his psychiatrist, Dr. G. V. Hamilton, had diagnosed him as suffering from an Oedipus complex (Bogard 345). Simon certainly experiences a moment of "oedipal horror" when he says to Deborah, "I love you my—" (Black 410, 528), but he stops himself before saying "lover." The source of Simon's agony comes from the fairy tale Deborah tells him when he was a child, in which the prince is shut out from the life of the "evil enchantress" (3:533). "I have never forgotten the anguished sense of being suddenly betrayed," he yells at his mother in act 4, scene 2, "of being wounded and deserted and left alone in a life in which there was no security or faith or love but only danger and suspicion and devouring greed! (*harshly*) By God, I hated you then! I wished I was dead! I wished I had never been born!" (3:534). Virginia Floyd argues that in this way, Simon and Deborah Harford "are perhaps closer approximations of O'Neill and his mother" than Edmund and Mary Tyrone, who enact a similar confrontation in O'Neill's most autobiographical play, *Long Day's Journey into Night* (461). This might be overstated, but the point is well-taken, as MARY ELLEN "ELLA" O'NEILL's morphine addiction certainly had a long-lasting and deleterious effect on O'Neill's psyche. He had always considered his mother's withdrawal from motherhood into the fantasy realm of a morphine high as a form of abandonment. Deborah's summerhouse in the garden, then, symbolizes Ella O'Neill's spare room where she injected herself with the drug. Deborah's drug is a semi-state of madness, and during their respective highs, both Deborah Harford and Mary Tyrone retreat into the past. If "Simon's desire for economic power," as Joseph Petite writes, "is designed to compensate for feelings of helplessness caused by a mother who rejected him," then one might extrapolate on O'Neill's desire to rise as a dramatist. He took over his father, James O'Neill's place as the family's theatrical titan, surpassing James's fame in a world that O'Neill often detested, just as Simon surpasses his father's standing in the world of finance.

## CHARACTERS

**Cato** Deborah Harford's coachman. Cato is an aging ex-slave who arrives with a message to Simon Harford from his mother Deborah in act 1, scene 1. He also appears in *A Touch of the Poet* and in O'Neill's scenario for *The Calms of Capricorn*, a planned installment for the historical cycle *A Tale of Possessors Self-Dispossessed*. Oddly, in *The Calms of Capricorn*, Cato regrets having run away from his plantation in Georgia. Along with Joe Mott of *The Iceman Cometh*, a far more important character, he is one of few AFRICAN AMERICANS to appear in O'Neill's late plays. Cato speaks in a southern black dialect and serves to demonstrate Simon Harford's early egalitarianism in contrast to Sara Melody Harford, who forces herself to smile when introduced to him in act 1, scene 1.

**Cregan, Jamie** Formerly a corporal in the Seventh Dragoons under Cornelius "Con" Melody during the Peninsular War (1808–14), now a loafing alcoholic Irish immigrant. Cregan, who appears in a more important role in *A Touch of the Poet,* is a middle-aged alcoholic with a saber scar across his cheek. He provides some exposition on Melody's past and praises Nora Melody, Con's wife, as "a good woman . . . an' the rist of us are dirt under your feet" (3:292). Cregan tries to convince Nora that now that her daughter, Sara Melody Harford, is married to the wealthy Simon Harford, she should pay the debts Melody left behind, but Nora is too proud to accept Harford money. Nora and Cregan, along with Mickey Maloy, are described as the *"obviously Irish peasant type"* (3:287), and both are sympathetic Irish characters (see IRISH AMERICANS).

**Gadsby, Nicholas** The Harford family attorney. O'Neill describes Gadsby, who also appears in *A Touch of the Poet,* as a *"short, tubby man of fifty-six"* with a bald round head and *"shrewd little grey eyes . . . Every inch the type of conservative, best-family legal advisor, he is gravely self-important and pretentious in manner and speech, extremely conscious of the respect due his professional dignity"* (3:338). Gadsby arrives at the Harford mansion to inform Deborah Harford that her deceased husband, Henry Harford, had invested unwisely, and the family stands on the brink of financial ruin. Harford left orders for Simon to take over the family business, though Deborah and Simon have not spoken in four years. Gadsby pleads with her to reunite with her estranged son and persuade him to take over the company. He also brings Deborah to understand that her life will change for the better if Simon resides with his wife and children at the Harford mansion with her. Gadsby is basically a stock character. O'Neill, however, does grant him a touch of the romantic, as he implies that he would delight in marrying Deborah and shows amused tolerance, in an affectionately scolding way, for her bizarre imagination.

**Harford, Deborah**  Simon and Joel Harford's mother, and Sara Melody Harford's mother-in-law. A wealthy New England matron, Deborah becomes Henry Harford's widow in act 2, scene 2. Deborah, who also appears in *A Touch of the Poet*, is first described in act 1, scene 2, as looking younger than her 45 years, *"small, not over five feet tall, with the slender, immature figure of a young girl."* She has given birth to two sons, Simon and Joel, but still, *"One cannot believe, looking at her, that she has ever borne children. There is something about her perversely virginal"* (3:314). In temperament, she is alternately well-mannered and fanciful, and she generally speaks with an air of superior frankness. Throughout her married life, Deborah stood aloof from her husband, whom she despised as a materialist, and her children, particularly Simon, whose neediness as a child impeded her ability to dream. Over the course of her adult life, she spent the bulk of her time dreaming in her walled-in, perversely artificial-looking garden at the Harford mansion. She encouraged her son Simon to become a dreamer like her, and in early adulthood, he fantasized about living in solitude in the woods and writing a book on civic equality and the goodness of mankind. She constructs an erotic fantasy world that she derives from 18th-century French memoirs, in which she fantasizes that she is a dominantly sexual, adventuresome mistress to King Louis.

In act 1, scene 2, Deborah meets Simon and ascertains that his wife, Sara, has made him into a financier like his father. She succeeds in getting him to admit his materialistic path, then removes him from her life for four years. This rejection of Simon, along with her aloofness toward him in childhood, leads Simon to pursue his father's professional career exclusively. The love and acceptance he seeks from Sara, a working-class IRISH AMERICAN woman with high aspirations, can only be attained by surpassing his father's success in finance. When Henry Harford dies, however, Deborah discovers that the estate is in financial ruin and agrees to allow Simon back into her life, sincerely making an effort to be a good grandmother and mother-in-law to Sara.

Over the following acts, Deborah considers Sara alternately a "filthy slut" and a kind-hearted domestic companion (3:505), and Simon "a common, vulgar, money-grubbing trader like his father" and the dreamer who might join her, "step by step, into memory, into the past, where he longs to be" (3:504, 505). Her desperate struggle to dominate Simon by leading him into the past conflicts with her equally powerful desire to live a normal life with her daughter-in-law and grandchildren. She and Sara do join together in a domestic partnership for a time, but this alliance makes Simon feel alienated from them and underappreciated. He desires both sex with his wife and a regression to the nurturing past with Deborah in her garden. Simon thus deliberately separates them into the roles of mistress and mother. Simon's scheme works for a time, and Deborah becomes so addicted to her son's visits that she transforms into a *"little, skinny, witch-like, old woman, an evil godmother conjured to life from the page of a fairy tale"* (3:503), while Sara looks like a *"hardened prostitute"* (3:477). In the end, the war between Deborah and Sara over Simon's affections reaches a head. Deborah ultimately relinquishes her unnatural grip on her son by inducing her own insanity, isolating herself—in a final act of sacrifice for Simon (and therefore an act of love that to her surpasses Sara's)—inside her fantasy world, ultimately leading to her death.

Deborah Harford, named "Abigail" in early drafts, calls to mind many female characters in the O'Neill canon and offers further evidence of the playwright's unending struggle with the opposite gender. Strong comparisons can be made with the rapacious character Nina Leeds in *Strange Interlude,* who also demands her men to sacrifice their happiness to satisfy her own desires. She also recalls what Virginia Floyd considers "those other two sex-starved Yankee wives," Abbie Putnam and Christine Mannon from *DESIRE UNDER THE ELMS* and *MOURNING BECOMES ELECTRA,* respectively (Floyd 461). Most importantly, however, is Mary Tyrone in *Long Day's Journey into Night.* Mary also prefers to revel in the fantasy of the past over performing the maternal and spousal demands of her family. Based closely on O'Neill's mother, Mary Ellen "Ella" O'Neill, Mary chooses morphine to induce her fantasies, while Deborah, also an avatar of Ella O'Neill, turns to the comforts of insanity. Both women, according to Stephen A. Black, "are deeply depressed and isolated, self-destructive, but harmless to others, except insofar as the others depend on her for love, attention, and affection that she cannot give" (413). The oedipal feelings of abandonment by the sons, Simon Harford and O'Neill himself (Edmund Tyrone in *Long Day's Journey*), compel them to substitute their lack of maternal affection with professional success.

**Harford, Ethan** Simon and Sara Melody Harford's eldest son and Deborah Harford's grandchild. Ethan, who first appears in act 3, scene 2, with his three brothers—Wolfe, Jonathan, and Owen "Honey" Harford—is 12 years old, with a face described as *"strong, broad, good-looking in a rugged, rough-hewn mould"* (3:417). His brother Jonathan mocks his desire to "run away to sea and be a sailor" (3:420), which he would have done with a vengeance had Eugene O'Neill completed his scenario *The Calms of Capricorn,* the planned sequel to *More Stately Mansions* in the playwright's historical cycle *A Tale of Possessors Self-Dispossessed.*

**Harford, Joel** Deborah Harford's son and Simon Harford's older brother. O'Neill describes the 29-year-old Joel as handsome and distinguished on the surface, but bearing *"the face of methodical mediocrity. . . . His whole character has something aridly prim and puritanical about it"* (3:338–339). Joel appears in act 2, scene 2, to inform Deborah that Henry Harford, her husband and Simon Harford's father,

had made a series of financial blunders, and their family is on the brink of ruin. Harford had all but disowned Simon for marrying beneath his station, but he recognized that Joel lacked the talent to save the company and left a posthumous communication that Simon must take over. Simon retains Joel as the bookkeeper, since the position suits Joel's officious but lifeless temperament. Over time, it is Joel, not Simon, who wishes to preserve the honorable reputation of the company in his father's name, and the two argue about Simon's ruthless, unethical methods in his business dealings. Deborah admits that she preferred Joel to Simon when they were children since she was "utterly indifferent to him," whereas she often hated Simon because of his overwhelming need for her as a child (3:534); she agrees with Simon's characterization of Joel as "a stuffed moral attitude" and adds that he is "God's most successful effort in taxidermy" (3:377). In spite of Joel's prudish asexuality, when he discovers that his sister-in-law Sara trades sex with Simon for leverage in the company, he implies that he would sell her his own shares for the same compensation. Michael Manheim aptly describes Joel's role in the play as "the voice of desiccated Puritanism." Joel must therefore be read as an unsympathetic character in the O'Neill canon, as "O'Neill always hates the judge (in himself as in others) more than he does the sinner" (Manheim 118).

**Harford, Jonathan** Simon and Sara Melody Harford's third son and Deborah Harford's grandchild. Jonathan, who first appears in act 3, scene 2, with his three brothers—Ethan, Wolfe, and Owen "Honey" Harford—is nine years old and described as *"undersized with a big head too large for his body,"* his manner *"quick, self-assured, observant and shrewd"* (3:418). Jonathan plans to follow in his father, Simon Harford's footsteps and "own a railroad," a dream Simon at one point encourages him to pursue (3:420). Jonathan appears later as a ruthlessly business-minded materialist in Eugene O'Neill's scenario for *The Calms of Capricorn,* and he would have played the protagonist in *The Man on Iron Horseback,* both planned installments for O'Neill's historical cycle *A Tale of Possessors Self-Dispossessed.*

**Harford, Owen Roe "Honey"** Simon and Sara Melody Harford's fourth and youngest son and Deborah Harford's grandchild. Honey, who first appears in act 3, scene 2, with his three brothers—Ethan, Wolfe, and Jonathan Harford—is seven and a half years old. He is described as *"an obvious Irish type,"* and his expression and manner as *"lazy, laughing and good-tempered, full of health and animal spirits, his eyes bright with a sly humor, his smile infectious and charmingly ingratiating"* (3:418). In *More Stately Mansions*, he plans to be "a gentleman and 'lected President of America," a dream his mother, Sara Harford, at one point encourages him to pursue (3:420). Owen appears later as a tin peddler in Eugene O'Neill's scenario for *The Calms of Capricorn* and would have played the politically minded protagonist in *Nothing Is Lost but Honor,* both planned installments for O'Neill's historical cycle *A Tale of Possessors Self-Dispossessed.*

**Harford, Sara Melody** Nora Melody's daughter; Simon Harford's wife; and Ethan, Jonathan, Wolfe, and Owen "Honey" Harford's mother. Sara is the daughter of Cornelius "Con" Melody, who died just prior to the play's action; she is also a central character in *A Touch of the Poet,* in which Con Melody, an Irish immigrant, was the protagonist. Irish-born herself, Sara falls in love with the wealthy New Englander Simon Harford during *A Touch of the Poet,* though he is an offstage character. She loved Simon but seduced him into having sex with her at his log cabin in the woods, knowing this would provoke his sense of honor and induce him to marry her. Throughout both plays, Sara wishes to achieve what her father could only dream about—to live a life of actual aristocratic privilege. In act 1, scene 1, Sara is six months pregnant with her fourth son, Owen "Honey" Harford, but her body is strong and healthy. Twenty-five and *"exceedingly pretty in a typically Irish fashion,"* Sara has long black hair, pale skin, and deep-blue eyes (3:293). Her voice betrays its natural Irish brogue only *"in moments of extreme emotion"* (3:293). She and Simon appear at Melody's tavern displaying signs of *"as loving and contented a marriage as one could find"* (3:294). But there are slight hints at her acquisitive, social-climbing nature, as when

the barman, Mickey Maloy, characterizes her in the opening scene as "always stuck up and givin' herself airs" (3:290); when she reluctantly offers to pay her father's debt so her mother can join a convent in her widowhood; and when she needs to force a smile when introduced to the black coachman Cato, among others. In addition, Simon had always dreamt of writing a book on the equal rights of man, but she tells her mother, Nora Melody, "He doesn't talk about that anymore, thank God! I've laughed it out of him!" (3:305). Over the course of the play, Sara's materialistic side becomes increasingly acute, culminating in her agreement to prostitute her body to Simon in exchange for shares of his company.

Deborah Harford, Simon's mother, summons Simon for a meeting in the woods in the final scene of act 1. Suspicious of her mother-in-law's motives, Sara sneaks out to the cabin and eavesdrops on their conversation. Once Simon exits, she overhears Deborah say to herself, "[I]t is ended. I have dismissed that Irish biddy's husband from my life forever" (3:332). Sara reveals herself to Deborah and accuses her of putting "doubt and disgust for himself in his mind, and [making] him blame me for a greedy fool who'd made him a slave and killed his fine poet's dream" (3:335). They are both right, as Deborah represents Simon's poet-dreamer side of his personality and Sara his materialistic, power-hungry side. The rivalry that ensues between the two women thus symbolizes the tormenting battle in his own dual consciousness.

Simon's company prospers during the Panic of 1837, and when Simon's father, Henry Harford, dies, the Harford family estate lies in shambles. Harford, who had disowned Simon for marrying Sara, left orders for Simon to take over the family business. Simon stipulates that he will do so if his company absorbs his father's company, rather than the reverse. The domestic side of the deal is that Deborah be allowed to live with Sara and her family in the Harford mansion. Sara wants the mansion, one of the finest in the area, and this encourages the domestic merger. Sara considers Deborah alternately a snob who puts on "great lady's airs and graces" and a viable domestic companion and helpmate with her children (3:370).

Sara and Deborah form a sincere friendship (insofar as each woman is capable of sincerity) and bond over the children. The alliance makes Simon feel desperately lonely and underappreciated; he desires both women to satisfy his need for a mistress and a mother, neither of which they are willing to give. He thus conquers them, the way he might a business rival, by pitting each aside against the other and convincing them to agree to extreme terms: Sara to prostitute her body for more power in the company and Deborah to cease her visits with her grandchildren and meet with him alone in her walled-in garden. At one point, the women realize what he is scheming, and they counterattack by appearing to him as one united woman—mother/wife—but their alliance falls apart when each realizes the possibility of losing Simon. Sara transforms terribly through this period, her face "*coarsened and vulgarized,*" her eyes "*hardened, grown cunning and calculating and scrupulous*" and her general appearance like a "*hardened prostitute*" (3:477).

In act 4, scene 1, Sara proves that she can be as ruthless in business ethics as her husband by cruelly destroying the pride of the formerly powerful banker Benjamin Tenard. In the end, the war between Deborah and Sara over Simon's affections reaches a head. Simon's need for a mother appears to triumph, as she has mentally led him back into the past with her, but Sara's pleading for Deborah to relinquish her control gives Deborah a new idea. By letting herself lapse into insanity, she will sacrifice all for her son and achieve victory over Sara. Sara then takes Simon back to his cabin in the woods with their children and vows to dedicate her life to serving him. She also conquers her social-climbing impulse to push her children to be industrial and political giants. "You'll let them be what they want to be, if it's a tramp in rags without a penny, with no estate but a ditch by the road, so long as they're happy! You'll leave them free, do you hear, and yourself free of them!" (3:559).

Sara Harford is one of a long line of "female destroyers" in the O'Neill canon, including Mrs. Rowland from BEFORE BREAKFAST, Ruth Atkins from BEYOND THE HORIZON, Maude Steele from BREAD AND BUTTER, and Ella Harris from ALL GOD'S CHILLUN' GOT WINGS—each corresponding to those of O'Neill's greatest dramatic influence, the Swedish playwright AUGUST STRINDBERG. But she has a more sympathetic side for O'Neill than these others, as while she successfully crushes Simon's early dream to be a poet-philosopher in the wilderness in the mode of the American writer Henry David Thoreau, in the end, she becomes a servile wife like her mother, Nora Melody, or the much earlier character Alice Roylston in O'Neill's full-length play *Servitude*, choosing a life of servitude on behalf of her husband. The conclusion about gender relations that cannot be ignored, even this late in O'Neill's life, is that her creator believed in women ultimately sacrificing their own dreams and aspirations—such as Sara's desire to achieve what her father could not and become a ruling member of the American aristocracy—to serve those of the husband. Neither goal comes across as particularly likable to a contemporary audience, male or female.

**Harford, Simon** Deborah Harford's son; Sara Melody Harford's husband; Ethan, Wolfe, Jonathan, and Owen "Honey" Harford's father; and Joel Harford's younger brother. Simon Harford, a "poet-dreamer" figure in the O'Neill canon and thus an avatar of O'Neill himself, figures prominently as an offstage character in the play's prequel, *A Touch of the Poet*. Later, in O'Neill's scenario for *The Calms of Capricorn*, a planned but unwritten installment of the historical cycle *A Tale of Possessors Self-Dispossessed*, Simon dies of pneumonia, a broken man bereft of all his personal dreams. In *A Touch of the Poet*, Simon (an offstage character) falls in love with Sara Melody, the daughter of the tavern keeper Cornelius "Con" Melody, who looks after him while he is sick. After nursing him back to health in a bedroom at the tavern, Sara takes her conniving father's advice and exploits Simon's sense of honor by sleeping with him at his cabin in the woods; that way, she secures a wealthy husband, though they still presumably love one another.

In the opening scenes of *More Stately Mansions*, O'Neill describes Simon as tall, slim, mature-looking, and handsome with a "*long Yankee face, with Indian resemblances.*" His expression and personality divulge mixed characteristics, ones that conflict over the course of the play and *"impress one incongruously as both practical and impractical"*—the hard man of business and the imaginative poet (3:294). The differences between Simon and Sara, who are now married with children, becomes starkly clear in act 1, scene 1: Sara is a materialistic social climber who cares little but for the station of her family, and Simon is a "poet-dreamer" figure who longs to remove himself from the world of commerce—as the American writer Henry David Thoreau would a decade later at Walden Pond—and write a book on civic equality and the fundamental goodness of man in the mode of the humanist French philosopher Jean-Jacques Rousseau.

Over the course of the play, Sara's desire to be a wealthy landowner gets the better of Simon, who discovers he has a natural ability in business and soon thrives as a mid-level but prosperous mill owner and cotton merchant. Due to his ability in finance, Simon's company prospers during the Panic of 1837 while much of the rest of the nation goes bankrupt. When his father dies, Simon is informed by the family attorney, Nicholas Gadsby, and his older brother Joel that his father's estate is in shambles and that Harry Harford left orders for Simon to take over the family business. Holding all the cards, Simon stipulates that he will only do so if his company absorbs his father's company, rather than the reverse. Simon's new credo, in contrast to his earlier humanism, is that "to win is good and to lose is evil" (3:388). At the same time, it becomes clear to Simon that he psychologically needs the affections of the two most important women in his life—his mother, Deborah, who represents the poetic side of his personality, and his wife, Sara, the acquisitive side. "Mother's is the spiritual greed," he says, "but the material lust is Sara's" (3:395). Psychologically, then, the two women represent the two warring sides of Simon's personality.

Sara and Deborah had previously been enemies in the struggle for Simon's attention, but after Henry Harford dies and the company goes to Simon, Deborah agrees to move in with her son's family, and she and Sara form a domestic alliance that Simon perceives as deliberately alienating. He decides to use the same methods in his domestic

situation that led to his success in business—divide and conquer. Knowing the extent of her ambition and greed, he talks Sara into prostituting herself to him in exchange for shares in the firm, and he persuades Deborah to relinquish her time with his children and spend it in her walled garden with him. He ruthlessly pits each woman against the other, but the plan falls apart for a time, and they reunite against him. In his eyes, they become one integrated symbol of "Woman," who "no longer wants me—has taken all she needed—I have served my purpose—. . . she is free—and I am left lost in myself, with nothing!" (3:461). In the end, his mother defeats Sara by deliberately retreating into insanity, the ultimate sacrifice. As a result, Simon loses his consciousness and reverts back to childhood for four years. In the final scene, he awakens from his childlike state to find that for his benefit Sara had lost the company and moved their family back to Simon's cottage in the woods, prepared now to devote her life to serving him as the poet-dreamer he wished to be from the beginning.

Simon Harford is one of Eugene O'Neill's many autobiographical avatars, from such early plays as the Poet in Fog and Robert Mayo in *Beyond the Horizon*; to such characters in his middle period as Michael Cope in WELDED and Anthony Dion in *The GREAT GOD BROWN*; and to the later, more heightened autobiographical forms of Richard Miller in AH, WILDERNESS! and Edmund Tyrone in *Long Day's Journey into Night*. Simon is more historically symbolic than these others in that his transformation from poet to scoundrel reflects the promises of the new nation and, to O'Neill's mind, its subsequent prostitution to materialistic greed. Autobiographically, as Michael Manheim notes, Simon, like his creator, "totally overshadowed his father's reputation in his father's field" (118), since O'Neill had surpassed his father, James O'Neill, in the theater world as Simon does in the world of finance. Similar oedipal impulses are potentially involved in both the fictional character and the actual O'Neill—a desperate need to obtain the love of a detached mother. Deborah Harford had told Simon as a child of a fairy tale in which the prince was shut out from the evil enchantress's life, and she uses the "magic door" of her summerhouse as a kind of prop to bring home the point that she is emotionally unavailable to him (3:394). If Deborah removes herself from her son by shutting him out of the summerhouse, O'Neill's mother, Mary Ellen "Ella" O'Neill, destructively shut her son out by self-injecting morphine in the spare room of the O'Neill family home, MONTE CRISTO COTTAGE, in NEW LONDON, CONNECTICUT—a real-life domestic tragedy O'Neill dramatized in his autobiographical masterpiece *Long Day's Journey into Night.*

**Harford, Wolfe**  Simon and Sara Melody Harford's second son and Deborah Harford's grandchild. Wolfe, who first appears in act 3, scene 2, with his three brothers—Ethan, Jonathan, and Owen "Honey" Harford—is 11 years old, with a face described as *"handsome and aristocratic"* (3:417). He also has a *"cold immobility about the cut of his features"* that brings to mind his uncle Joel Harford and a manner that is *"politely pleasant and compliant, but it is the distant amiability of indifference"* (3:418). The comparison to Joel Harford, for O'Neill, would not be a sympathetic one, and Wolfe represents the upcoming generation of New England Yankee puritanism. No doubt ironically named after the 18th-century Irish revolutionary Wolfe Tone, Wolfe Harford was meant to serve as the protagonist of *The Earth Is the Limit,* a planned installment of O'Neill's historical cycle *A Tale of Possessors Self-Dispossessed.*

**Maloy, Mickey**  Nora Melody's bartender. Mickey, a solidly built 34-year old, plays a larger role in *A Touch of the Poet.* Like Nora Melody and Jamie Cregan, Maloy is described as *"typically the Irish peasant"* (3:288), though he is more cynical than the other two, and *"his mouth is set in the half-leering grin of a bartender's would-be, worldly-wise cynicism"* (3:288). Maloy tells us that Sara Melody Harford never spoke to her father, Cornelius "Con" Melody, in the four years since her marriage to Simon Harford. He does not believe she will attend his wake either—wrongly, as it turns out—given she is now married to a Harford and "so high and mighty she'd feel shame to visit her poor Irish relations even for her father's funeral" (3:290).

**Melody, Nora**  Sara Melody Harford's mother. O'Neill describes Nora, who appears in a larger role as Cornelius "Con" Melody's long-suffering wife in *A Touch of the Poet,* as *"a typical Irish peasant woman with a shapeless, heavy figure"* (3:290). Nora is 45, though years of servility to Con Melody and his tavern make her look much older. Resigned to a life of penury, though longing to join a convent in widowhood, Nora works Con's tavern faithfully and stays loyal to the memory of her husband, who has left behind a debt of $4,000. When Jamie Cregan suggests that after her marriage to Simon Harford, her daughter Sara Melody Harford can now afford to pay the debt on her behalf, she refuses proudly. "Do you think I'd let a Harford pay for Con Melody? Even if I had no pride," she adds, "I'd be afeered. Con would rise from his grave to curse me!" (3:293). Simon convinces Sara, who dislikes the notion of spending their own money to help Nora, to let him take out a loan to pay off Melody's debts. Nora only appears in act 1, scene 1, and she acts as a moral foil to Sara's greedy materialism. Her influence on Sara wins in the end, however, as at the conclusion of the play, Sara, like her mother and the character Alice Roylston in O'Neill's early full-length play *Servitude,* chooses a life of servitude for her husband.

**Tenard, Benjamin**  A destitute banker. Tenard appears in act 4, scene 1, for a meeting with Simon Harford after Harford's company acquired his bank in a hostile takeover. O'Neill describes him as an expensively but conservatively dressed 60-year-old man, *"tall, robust, full-chested . . . with a fine-looking Roman face"* (3:492). Tenard is too old to find a new position, and Simon wishes Tenard to be a test case for his wife, Sara Melody Harford, in which she might prove her ability to act as ruthlessly in business as he does. If anything, she surpasses Simon's expectations, thoroughly demoralizing Tenard in the process; earlier than Simon expected, he agrees to relinquish his ethical standards and "become a conscious thief and swindler" (3:495) in exchange for retaining his position at the bank to save his starving family. The scene resembles a convention of American melodrama such as we find in Dion Boucicault's *The Poor of New York* (1857), which also takes place during the Panic of 1837 and features previously well-to-do businessmen crushed under the weight and power of unethical rivals during the panic.

## BIBLIOGRAPHY

Barnes, Clive. "Theatre: O'Neill's *More Stately Mansions* Open." In *The Critical Response to Eugene O'Neill*, edited by John H. Houchin, 252–254. Westport, Conn.: Greenwood, 1993.

Black, Stephen A. *Eugene O'Neill: Beyond Mourning and Tragedy*. New Haven, Conn.: Yale University Press, 1999.

Bogard, Travis. *Contour in Time: The Plays of Eugene O'Neill*. Rev. ed. New York: Oxford University Press, 1988.

Bower, Martha Gilman. *Eugene O'Neill's Unfinished Threnody and Process of Invention in Four Cycle Plays*. Lewiston, N.Y.: Edwin Mellen Press, 1992.

———. Introduction to *A Touch of the Poet and More Stately Mansions*. Edited by Martha Gilman Bower. New Haven, Conn.: Yale University Press, 2004: vii–xiv.

———. "*More Stately Mansions* Redux: Straightening Out the 'Twisted Path.'" *Eugene O'Neill Review* 26 (2004): 239–247.

Brietzke, Zander. *The Aesthetics of Failure: Dynamic Structure in the Plays of Eugene O'Neill*. Jefferson, N.C.: McFarland & Company, 2001.

Diggins, John Patrick. *Eugene O'Neill's America: Desire under Democracy*. Chicago: University of Chicago Press, 2007.

Floyd, Virginia. *The Plays of Eugene O'Neill: A New Assessment*. New York: Ungar, 1985.

Gelb, Arthur, and Barbara Gelb. "The Twisted Path to *More Stately Mansions*." *Eugene O'Neill Review* (November 6, 1988): 239–247.

Manheim, Michael. *Eugene O'Neill's New Language of Kinship*. Syracuse, N.Y.: Syracuse University Press, 1982.

Petite, Joseph. "The Paradox of Power in *More Stately Mansions*." *Eugene O'Neill Newsletter* 5, no. 3 (Winter 1981). Available online. URL: http://www.eoneill.com/library/newsletter/v_3/v_3b. Accessed May 8, 2008.

Real, Jere. "The Brothel in O'Neill's Mansions." In *The Critical Response to Eugene O'Neill*, edited by John H. Houchin, 383–389. Westport, Conn.: Greenwood, 1993.

Shaughnessy, Edward L. *Down the Nights and Down the Days: Eugene O'Neill's Catholic Sensibility*. Notre Dame, Ind.: University of Notre Dame Press, 2000.

Simon, John. "The Stage: Unfinished Mansions." In *The Critical Response to Eugene O'Neill*, edited by John H. Houchin, 254–255. Westport, Conn.: Greenwood, 1993.

# *Mourning Becomes Electra: A Trilogy* (completed, 1931; first produced, 1931)

Eugene O'Neill began writing *Mourning Becomes Electra*, one of his most revered dramas, in FRANCE at Chateau du Plessis near Tours in the Loire Valley. Recovering from the debacle of DYNAMO, which O'Neill believed failed critically because he released it too soon, he kept this project close to the vest, telling virtually no one about the story until it was completed. He did correspond for advice and support in the late stages of the writing process with the PULITZER PRIZE–winning theater critic BROOKS ATKINSON, who referred to *Mourning Becomes Electra* when it finally appeared as "Mr. O'Neill's single clear-cut masterpiece" (127). Working through six drafts from August 15, 1929, to March 27, 1931, O'Neill experimented with masks, soliloquies, and asides for the 14-act trilogy, but he ultimately abandoned the "show shop" stage tricks of his experimental plays from the 1920s (Floyd 1983, 404, Bogard 340). He copyrighted the trilogy on May 12, 1931, and the THEATRE GUILD enthusiastically accepted it for their fall season. O'Neill returned to New York to oversee rehearsals for the production, which opened on October 26, 1931, to enormous critical acclaim.

*Mourning Becomes Electra* consists of three plays—*The Homecoming, The Hunted,* and *The Haunted*—that together borrow from GREEK TRAGEDY, specifically Aeschylus's *Oresteia*, also a trilogy. Generally performed as one play, with a six-hour playing time for its first run, the trilogy charts the tragic decline of a prominent New England family named the Mannons just after the American Civil War. O'Neill was convinced, and rightly so, that this play won him his 1936 NOBEL PRIZE IN LITERATURE, making him the only American dramatist to win the coveted award. *Mourning Becomes Electra* had opened in the United States five years before, but the drama was still fresh in the minds of European audiences and ran triumphantly in theaters across the continent well into the 1940s. No O'Neill play achieves the level of tragic power we find in this work until his late masterpieces, *The ICEMAN COMETH* and *LONG DAY'S JOURNEY INTO NIGHT*.

## SYNOPSIS

### General Scene of the Trilogy
Either spring or summer, 1865–66, at the Mannon house, located "on the outskirts of one of the smaller New England seaport towns." A "special curtain" reveals the house as it appears from the street; it also shows an extensive property of around 30 acres, with woods in the background, an orchard at right, and a large greenhouse and flower garden at left. The street is at the foreground, lined with locust and elm trees, and a white picket fence and tall hedges surround the property. A rounded driveway reaches the street by two white-gated entrances, with its apex at the front door. The house itself is "of the Greek temple type" built from gray cut stone, and four steps lead up to a white portico with six tall columns; there are five windows on the second floor and four on the first with dark green shutters. The main entrance is at center, flanked by side lights and with a transom above (2:890).

### *Part One:* Homecoming: A Play in Four Acts
Act 1
The exterior of the Mannon house, just before sunset in April 1865. The sun's rays highlight the white portico and columns and reflect harshly off the windows. From the town in the distance, a band can be heard playing "John Brown's Body," and from the left rear of the house, a man's voice is singing "Shenandoah"—*"a song that more than any other holds in it the brooding rhythm of the sea"* (2:893). Seth Beckwith, the Mannons' 75-year-old gardener,

Exterior of the Mannon Home. Drawing by Albert M. Pike *(Courtesy of the Yale Collection of American Literature, Beinecke Rare Book and Manuscript Library)*

enters from left finishing the last line of the song. He is followed by the local carpenter, Amos Ames, a well-meaning gossip; his wife, Louisa, *"a similar scandal-bearing type"*; and her cousin Minnie, a stupid, 40-year-old *"eager-listener type"* (2:894). Each of these three are *"types of townsfolk rather than individuals, a chorus representing the town come to look and listen and spy on the rich and exclusive Mannons"* (2:894). Confederate general Robert E. Lee has just surrendered to Union general Ulysses S. Grant, and the men are in a celebratory mood.

Seth proudly displays his knowledge of the Mannons over the 60 years he has worked as their gardener. Ezra Mannon, head of the Mannon clan, is the first topic of discussion. Seth explains that Abe Mannon, Ezra's father, made the family fortune in the shipping industry. Ezra attended West Point, fought in the Mexican War, and then rose to the rank of general in the Civil War—"The finest fighter in the hull of Grant's army!" according to Seth (2:895). Christine Mannon, Ezra's wife, comes from French and Dutch stock, but when her name comes up, Seth sourly changes the subject. Seth goes inside to find Lavinia Mannon, Ezra and Christine's daughter, who has granted him permission to show the others around the estate. The others hide when Christine Mannon appears at the front door. She is a tall, statuesque woman of 40 who looks a good deal younger, with an expression *"of being not living flesh but a wonderfully life-like mask."* She listens to the music in the distance *"defensively, as if the music held some meaning that threatened her"* (2:896), then shrugs and walks off to the garden. Louisa whispers about skeletons in the Mannons' closet, including a French Canadian nurse with whom Ezra's uncle David had eloped, causing a tremendous scandal.

Seth returns without Lavinia, but she soon appears at the front door. Lavinia is 23 and holds a strong resemblance to her mother, down to the *"same strange, life-like mask impression her face gives in repose"* (2:897), though she tries to hide the resemblance. Lavinia listens intently to the band, as her mother had, but rather than feeling threatened by it like her mother, she wears an expression of *"strange vindictive triumph"* (2:898). Seth announces that the war is over, and her father will return soon.

Alla Nazimova and Alice Brady as Christine and Lavinia Mannon in *Mourning Becomes Electra* by the Theatre Guild, 1931 *(Courtesy of the New York Public Library)*

Lavinia hopes this to be true, then evades questions concerning her whereabouts over the last few days. Seth starts to warn her about Captain Adam Brant, a young, pretentiously romantic sea captain, but he stops as Captain Peter Niles and his sister Hazel Niles approach the house. Dressed in the uniform of the Union Army, Peter is an awkward but kind 22-year-old; Hazel is 19, pretty, and healthy-looking. Hazel asks about news from Lavinia's brother Orin Mannon, whom (it is hinted) she hopes to marry, but he has not written in some time. Lavinia has none. Hazel teases that Peter wants to ask her something, and exits.

Scornful of romantic love, Lavinia rejects Peter's proposal of marriage but admits she loves him as a brother. Peter insinuates she might have eyes for Captain Brant, "a darned romantic-looking cuss. Looks more like a gambler or a poet than a ship captain" (2:902). Lavinia swears she hates the sight of him, and Christine appears from the garden carrying flowers. Peter exits. After some tense discussion, Christine announces that she saw Captain Brant in New York, and he was asking for her. Lavinia insinuates that the two are having an affair and that her father will surely find out. Christine looks at her with a *"questioning dread,"* but regains her poise. "You always make such a mystery of things, Vinnie," she says and walks into the house (2:905). Seth returns and tells her that Brant has come to court her but also that he bears a striking resemblance to the Mannon men. He is sure Brant is the child of David Mannon and the Canadian nurse, which shocks Lavinia; he advises her to accuse Brant of it at her first opportunity and exits.

Adam Brant enters. As with all the Mannons, *"One is struck at a glance by the peculiar quality his face in repose has of being a life-like mask rather than living flesh"* (2:907). Though he is a ship's captain, his clothing is self-consciously that of a romantic poet. After some polite talk, Brant asks if Lavinia holds something against him, given her icy tone, and mentions a romantic night they had shared on a walk by the shore. She remembers him talking of the naked island women he encountered in the South Seas, and he reminisces about the "Garden of Paradise" he found there, "before sin was discovered" (2:909). She abruptly accuses him of being "the son of a low Canuck nurse girl" (2:910). Outraged by the insult to his mother, he spitefully confirms her suspicion. Brant has vowed revenge against Lavinia's father, Ezra Mannon, for abandoning his mother, the Mannon family's French Canadian nurse, Marie Brantôme, after Brant's father, Ezra's brother David, hanged himself over the affair. Brant changed his last name and ran away to sea at 17; he returned two years ago to find his mother dying of starvation. She had asked Ezra for a loan, and he never replied. Lavinia insinuates that Brant's affair with her mother constitutes his revenge. As she heads inside to confront Christine, he insists there is nothing between them. She stares back with hate-filled eyes, then goes into the house as the curtain fall (2:913).

*Act 2*
Ezra Mannon's study. No time has passed. It is a spacious room with a *"stiff, austere atmosphere."* The furniture is old colonial, and a large desk stands between two windows at left; there is a table at center, and on the right wall hang portraits of George Washington, Alexander Hamilton, and John Marshall. A fireplace is at rear center, and to its left are shelves filled with law books; above it hangs a 10-year-old portrait of Ezra Mannon in a judge's black robe. There is a striking likeness between him and Adam Brant, along with *"the same strange semblance of a life-like mask"* shared by all the Mannons. Lavinia is discovered standing beside the table, her expression that of extreme duress. She touches the painted hand of her father's portrait lovingly and cries out, "Poor father!" (2:914).

Christine enters. Lavinia informs her mother that she followed her to New York and saw her meet Brant and go into a strange house. A woman living in the basement told her the two had met there often over the past year. Christine hedges at first, then defiantly admits she loves Brant. She confesses she fell out of love with Ezra early in their marriage and feels Lavinia is more his daughter than hers. Her son Orin was different, she says, because Ezra was fighting in the Mexican War (1846–48) when he was born; therefore, Orin is more her child than his. Lavinia threatens to tell her father if Christine continues her affair with Brant. Christine initially believes the threat is fueled by Lavinia's own love for Brant. The argument becomes more heated, but Christine eventually capitulates, and Lavinia marches out of the study.

Christine's expression becomes *"like a sinister evil mask"* (2:921). She writes two words on a slip of paper and calls out an open window for Brant. He enters, and the resemblance between him and Ezra's portrait is pronounced. Christine relates what Lavinia told her. Brant admits he initially seduced her to avenge his mother, but he fell in love in spite of himself. Brant suggests he fight Ezra in a duel, but Christine convinces him that as a former judge, Ezra would notify the authorities since dueling is illegal. Christine assures him Ezra would never divorce her, so he must die. She hands him the slip of paper and says she deliberately spread a rumor that Ezra suffers from heart trouble. When she poisons him, he will have a heart attack, and no one will suspect that he has been murdered. Brant thinks of poisoning as a "coward's trick," but Christine convinces him it is the only sure way (2:926). He somberly accepts the assignment. She tells him to mail her the poison, then they will meet at his ship, *Flying Trades*, when Ezra is dead.

Cannon saluting Ezra's "homecoming" are heard firing at intervals in the distance. Brant departs. Watching his retreat through the window, Christine shouts triumphantly, "You'll never dare leave me now, Adam—for your ships or your sea or your naked Island girls—when I grow old and ugly!" (2:927). She shudders at the sight of her husband's portrait, then exits.

*Act 3*

Same as act 1, around nine o'clock at night a week later. A half-moon illuminates the whiteness of the house, *"giving it an unreal, detached, eerie quality,"* and the *"white temple front seems more than ever like an incongruous mask fixed on the somber, stone house."* Lavinia sits on the top step of the portico dressed *"severely in black"* and stiffly erect like an *"Egyptian statue"* (2:928). She is awaiting her father, who could arrive any day. Seth approaches the house, singing "Shenandoah." He admits sheepishly that he has been drinking to mourn Abraham Lincoln's assassination, just as he drank to Lee's surrender, and he will again to celebrate Ezra Mannon's arrival. Lavinia inquires about Marie Brantôme, and Seth tells her everyone loved her, even Ezra, until discovering Marie and David Mannon were in love. The front door opens, and Christine, dressed in a green velvet gown, appears behind Lavinia. Seth exits, and Christine chides Lavinia for being an old maid. Lavinia says it is her duty to her father, then accuses her mother of plotting something. Christine denies it, but then laughs that Ezra is "the beau you're waiting for in the spring moonlight!" (2:931). Lavinia informs her that he should arrive soon, then hears someone approaching.

Ezra Mannon enters from the left front. A largely proportioned 50-year-old man in a brigadier general's uniform, Ezra's face betrays the same *"mask-like look on his face in repose,"* though *"more pronounced than in the others"* (2:931). He moves in a stiff military manner, and his voice has a *"hollow repressed*

*quality"* (2:931). He greets Lavinia and Christine with formal kisses, restraining himself from showing too much emotion at his daughter's adoring coddling. When asked about Orin, Ezra tells them a bullet grazed his head in battle. The doctors have kept him in their care for nerves (which Ezra gently blames on Christine's influence), though he fought bravely, particularly on one occasion that he mysteriously does not describe. Lavinia asks about his heart, and Ezra confesses he experiences intermittent pain that hurts terribly. Lavinia mentions Adam Brant, and Ezra inquires about him suspiciously. Lavinia and Christine accuse each other of being the subject of local gossip, and Ezra silences their bickering. He sends Lavinia upstairs, and she obeys, reassuring him, "Don't let anything worry you, Father. I'll always take care of you," and steps into the house (2:935).

Christine accuses Ezra of suspecting something, and he tells her she is allowing the town gossips to get the better of her. She informs him that she met Brant at her father's in New York and allowed him to visit several times to get news about her father. He scolds her for permitting Brant to tarnish Lavinia's reputation. Over the course of the dialogue, Ezra's lust for her becomes strongly evident. He understands that she has not loved him since their courtship, but he loves her desperately and would do anything for her to return that love. In a lengthy exposition, he tells her of the death he witnessed during the war and of a revelation that "death made me think of life. Before that life had only made me think of death!" (2:937). The Mannons had always followed the church's belief that "life was a dying. Being born was starting to die. Death was being born" (2:937–938). He suggests they go off on a voyage to the East to resurrect their love, but she assures him she loves him and coaxes him inside to bed. Lavinia appears at the doorway and tells him she cannot sleep and will go for a walk.

Ezra and Christine enter the house, and Lavinia talks to herself of her terror that Christine will steal Ezra's love from her. She shouts up to her father's lighted window above. He pokes his head out and scolds her sharply. She tells him she forgot to say goodnight. Mollified, he bids her goodnight and disappears. Lavinia stares at the empty window, anxiously wringing her hands.

## Act 4

Ezra Mannon's bedroom, close to dawn the following morning. Mannon lies in a large four-poster bed at center. A door at right leads to the hallway and another at left to Christine's bedroom. Christine can just be made out in the darkness by the dim moonlight coming through the closed shutters. She tiptoes to a table at front right and starts when Ezra speaks her name. He asks her feebly whether she left his bed that night out of hatred of him. He lights a candle on his bedside table, and they continue their discussion from the last scene of the previous act. Believing she no longer loves him, Ezra insinuates that she slept with him the night before to cause a heart attack. She threatens to go, but he begs her to remain. With pitiful remorse, he says the house and bedroom no longer feel like his own, and that she seems like a stranger "waiting for something" (2:944). He accuses her of false passion when they made love, as if she were a "nigger slave [he'd] bought at auction" (2:944). His taunting goads Christine into viciously admitting she and Brant are in love and that Brant is Marie Brantôme's son. She apprehends that his heart is weakening from the onslaught and continues mercilessly. When his heart seizes, and she runs to her bedroom and returns with a box of poison. She helps him swallow it; in horror, he realizes it is not his heart medicine. He cries out for Lavinia's help, then falls into a coma.

Lavinia appears in the doorway, believing she had a nightmare and heard her father call to her. Christine, hiding the box of poison behind her back, says that Ezra suffered a heart attack but will be all right. Ezra wakes for a brief moment, straightens up, and points at Christine, "She's guilty—not medicine!" (2:946), then falls back and dies. Lavinia rushes to his bedside, feels his pulse, and proclaims him dead. Christine admits she told him about Brant. Her voice grows weaker as they argue over who was at fault, and she collapses to the floor. Lavinia realizes she has fainted, screams that her mother is responsible, and then discovers the box on the floor. Understanding now that

it was actual murder, she throws her arms around her father, shouting in desperation, "Father! Don't leave me alone! Come back to me! Tell me what to do!" (2:947).

## Part Two: *The Hunted: A Play in Five Acts*
### Act 1

Exterior of the Mannon house two nights later. Moonlight illuminates the white portico and columns, and again they appear mask-like. Funeral wreaths adorn the front door and the column at right. The manager of the Mannons' shipping company, Josiah Borden, and his wife, the Congregational minister, Everett Hills, and his wife, and the family physician, Doctor Joseph Blake, all come out the front door. Christine is in the foyer. Like the townspeople in act 1 of *The Homecoming*, these characters are "*types of townsfolk, a chorus representing, as those others had, but in a different stratum of society, the town as a human background for the drama of the Mannons*" (2:951). The men light cigars and stand at the foot of the portico steps, while the women wait for them at left front. Mrs. Hills and Mrs. Borden believe Christine was more upset than they would have thought, but Lavinia was "cold and calm as an icicle" (2:952). Borden is surprised the Mannons did not arrange a public funeral for Ezra, considering he was a beloved citizen and a former mayor. Mrs. Hills clumsily quotes her husband as having said of the Mannons that "pride goeth before the fall and that some day God would humble them in their sinful pride" (2:953). The others voice disapproval of the poor taste of such a remark, and Hills apologizes for his wife's indiscretion. Blake discusses Ezra's angina, considering it a natural death. When the women and the minister move off left, the doctor nudges Josiah Borden to wait, whispering he is quite sure Ezra died making love to Christine, whom neither man likes but both find attractive. They share a chuckle, then follow the others offstage.

Christine appears at the doorway, "*obviously in a strained state of nerves*" (2:955), and Hazel Niles follows her out. Lavinia and Peter have gone to the train station to retrieve Orin, and Christine inquires whether Hazel wishes to marry him. Hazel shows some embarrassment, but Christine goes on that she applauds the match, and the two women must ally themselves against Lavinia, who cherishes her brother, to ensure the union. Christine muses that once she was "innocent and loving and trusting" like Hazel, but all that changed with the tortures of life. "Let's go in," she concludes. "I hate moonlight. It makes everything so haunted" (2:936). After the door shuts, Orin Mannon, a 22-year-old who appears 10 years older, enters from the right with Lavinia and Peter. His face contains *"the same life-like mask quality"* as the other Mannons, though his mouth *"gives an impression of tense oversensitiveness"* (2:957). Wounded and dressed in an ill-fitting lieutenant's uniform, Orin wonders where his mother is, then inquires to himself whether the house had always looked "so ghostly and dead" (2:957).

Lavinia asks Peter to leave them and go inside, which he does. Orin mourns his father, but he has witnessed so much carnage that death seems almost meaningless to him. "Murdering doesn't improve one's manners," he apologizes (2:958). He asks about Brant, whom Lavinia had mentioned in letters. Lavinia warns him to stay on his guard against their mother, and he takes that angrily as an implication that Christine and Brant are lovers. Christine emerges from the house and throws her arms around him. Orin is overjoyed, but then he jerks away: "But you're different! What's happened to you?" She blames this on his head wound and leads him up the steps to the house. "Remember, Orin!" Lavinia shouts back to him, and she and Christine glare at each other in hatred (2:359). Christine returns from inside and, in a lengthy monologue, asks why Lavinia would treat her own mother with such suspicious disdain. In the end, she demands to know what Lavinia is planning to do, but Lavinia says nothing, turns away from her coldly, and marches into the house. Orin shouts for his mother from inside, and Christine instantly regains her composure. "Here I am, dear!" she calls back in tense self-control, running up the steps (2:961). The door shuts behind her.

*Act 2*
The Mannon sitting room. No time has elapsed. Similar in its cold austerity to Mannon's study from act 2 of *The Homecoming*, the large space is *"a*

*bleak room without intimacy."* At left front, a doorway leads to the dining room, and at center rear, another door leads to the hallway and stairs. A fireplace is at right, with a window at either side. Several portraits hang on the walls, mainly of Mannon ancestors dating back to the American Revolution; each shares *"the same mask quality of those of the living characters in the play"*—including Abe Mannon, Ezra's father, whose face *"looks exactly like Ezra's in the painting in the study"* (2:962). Hazel sits on a chair at front center, and Peter sits on a sofa at right. Offstage, Orin is heard calling, "Mother! Where are you?" (2:962), while Peter and Hazel discuss Orin's condition. Christine enters with Orin, who is wondering over her disappearance. She responds that she was so overwhelmed with happiness at his return that she needed a moment alone. Christine lavishly compliments Hazel, who appears embarrassed but delighted. Orin questions her about why she seems to have grown younger and prettier. He coarsely remarks about the slaughter he witnessed and the naïveté of the local women waving handkerchiefs patriotically to the men going off to war. Lavinia calls from the hallway for Orin to view their father's body, but Christine begs him to stay for a bit longer.

Hazel and Peter exit, and Orin questions Christine about writing so few letters and her sudden interest in Hazel, whom she had previously disdained as beneath him. Christine lies that her letters must not have been delivered and that Hazel had been a source of foolish maternal jealousy. Orin turns the subject to Adam Brant. Christine warns him that Lavinia has been accusing her of "the vilest most horrible things" (2:967). She informs him of Lavinia's accusations about her and Brant and that Christine poisoned Ezra. Orin admits he is relieved that his father is dead and agrees with her that Lavinia must be insane to believe such a thing. Christine insists that Brant entered the family circle to manipulate Ezra into buying him a better ship and scoffs at Lavinia's assertion that Brant is the son of Marie Brantôme. Orin can forgive anything but an affair with Brant and threatens to kill him if it is true. Terrified for Brant, Christine screams at Orin to end such talk. He apologizes and seats himself on the floor below her, dreamily reflecting on the South Seas novel *Typee* [Herman Melville, 1846], which helped him survive the brutality of war. Placing his head on her knee, he muses that "those Islands came to mean everything that wasn't war, everything that was peace and warmth and security" (2:972). He denounces Hazel as a potential wife, then touches Christine's hair admiringly, not noticing her shudder of disgust.

Lavinia returns to ask Orin to view their father's body, and though resentful of the intrusion, he obeys. Christine tells Lavinia that Orin knows about her accusations and will never believe them. But she loses *"all her defiant attitude"* upon thinking that Orin might kill Brant and howls that she would kill herself if Brant died. Lavinia coldly exits the room *"like some tragic mechanical doll,"* and Christine cries out that she must warn Adam (2:974).

### Act 3

Ezra Mannon's study—same as part 1, act 2. The furniture has been moved to the sides, and Ezra Mannon's corpse lies on a bier at center with a chair situated next to his head. Ezra is in uniform, and his face is *"a startling reproduction of the face in the portrait above him."* Orin is discovered rigidly standing over him, but staring forward rather than down at the corpse; his face *"bears a striking resemblance to that of the portrait above him and the dead man's."* He shouts in bewilderment over his mother and sister's behavior, as Lavinia silently steps into the room. "You never cared to know me in life," he says to his father, "but I really think we might be friends now you are dead!" (2:975). Lavinia scolds him harshly, which startles him. She locks the door behind her, and he explains that laughing at death served as a psychological defense during the war. He describes the act of bravery Ezra mentioned to her in act 3 of *The Homecoming.* Orin learned to laugh at death so well that during the Battle of Petersburg, he ran out into a cross-fire laughing and was shot in the head; he then went berserk, rushed the enemy, and "a lot of our fools went crazy, too, and followed me and we captured a part of their line we hadn't dared tackle before" (2:977).

At length, Lavinia convinces Orin to let her prove to him that Christine killed their father and has been conducting an affair with Brant. She knows Christine and Brant will meet that night, and Orin reluctantly agrees to follow them. Christine knocks loudly on the door, the knocks becoming increasingly frenzied. Lavinia places the box of poison on Ezra's heart and tells Orin to watch their mother's reaction to it. He unlocks the door, and Christine enters, panic-stricken, making him vow not to permit Lavinia to call the police. She looks down at the box, stifles a scream, and stares at it *"with guilty fear"* (2:982). Orin's nerves snap, and he laughs at the irony of returning home to escape from death and longs for his "island of peace"; he then stares at his mother strangely and cries out, "But that's lost now! You're my lost island, aren't you, Mother?"—upon which he *"stumbles blindly from the room"* (2:982). Lavinia takes up the box. She realizes that her mother had conspired with Brant, even though Christine denies it, and she stiffly exits the room. Christine begs Ezra not to let Orin harm Brant. She stares down at her husband's face in horror as if he had responded and rushes terrified from the room.

### Act 4

A wharf in East Boston, the day following Ezra Mannon's funeral. The stern section of *Flying Trades* is visible alongside the wharf, and the end of a warehouse looms at front left. Portholes emit a dim light from oil lamps below the main deck. Moonlight accentuates the ship's dark outlines. In the distance, sailors from another ship weighing anchor offshore sing in chorus in accompaniment to the ship's chantyman, who sings the capstan shanty "Shenandoah." The melancholy sound of the singing wakens a drunken chantyman on the pier. About 65, bleary-eyed from a night's debauch but with a *"queer troubadour-of-the-sea quality about him,"* the chantyman is lying against the warehouse's outer wall (2:984). Rising to his feet, he bitterly denounces the quality of the other singer, then breaks into his own rendition of the song. He curses the "yaller-haired pig" that stole his money that night and rants over the struggle of being an out-of-work seaman (2:985).

Adam Brant appears from the poop deck's companionway door and peers into the darkness with trepidation. The chantyman stumbles, and Brant draws his revolver, ordering him to reveal himself. After some words, Brant promises the chantyman work on *Flying Trades* if he needs a berth in a month's time. The chantyman mourns the imminent change in shipping. "Aye, but it ain't fur long, steam is comin' in, the sea is full o' smoky tea-kettles, the old days is dyin', an' where'll you an' me be then?" He startles Brant by remarking that "everything is dyin'," including Abe Lincoln and Ezra Mannon, though he despised the latter as an "old skinflint" (2:987). Brant gives him a dollar for drink and sends him on his way with a skipper's authority. The chantyman exits singing the sorrowful dirge "Hanging Johnny," which fills Brant with self-loathing. Sure the ship will abandon him, he admits that "the sea hates a coward" (2:988).

Christine appears in the shadows at left. The lovers meet on the wharf, and Brant escorts her to the poop deck. Christine tells him that Lavinia knows about the murder and might convince Orin as well. When they descend into the cabin, Lavinia and Orin appear on the deck from left. In the moonlight, Orin's face appears *"distorted with jealous fury"* (2:990). Lavinia restrains him from immediate action, and the scene goes dark. A few minutes have elapsed when the lights go on, and the interior of the cabin is now exposed. Brant and Christine are discovered seated at a table at center. Christine looks visibly aged and disheveled. Lavinia and Brant listen intently to the conversation within the cabin. Brant tells Christine that he has his father's coward's blood. She begs him not to despair but also warns him about Lavinia and Orin. Together they decide to sign on as passengers on another ship embarking for China that Friday; they plan to get married and live in Brant's "Blessed Islands" in the South Seas.

Brant accompanies her off the boat, and Orin takes out his revolver. Lavinia restrains him again and convinces him that if they killed Brant and were caught, "he could die happy, knowing he'd revenged himself" with the scandal that would surely follow. Brant returns to the cabin, crying out to his ship, "I wasn't man enough for you!"

(2:994). Orin enters the cabin and fires two shots into Brant, then gazes strangely at the corpse. Lavinia wonders how Brant could love "that vile woman so," and Orin notes his uncanny resemblance to their father. They ransack the cabin to make it look like a break-in. Before leaving, Orin again brings up his thought that the men he killed in the war always seemed to transform into the face of his father, then his own. "He looks like me, too! Maybe I've committed suicide!" (2:996). He continues that he would have loved Christine as Brant had and killed his father for her too. Lavinia urges him away. He shouts, "It's queer! It's a rotten dirty joke on someone!" as Lavinia rushes him off (2:996).

*Act 5*
Exterior of the Mannon house the following night. Moonlight illuminates the left side of the house, and the right half is covered with shadow from the pine trees. Christine is discovered pacing back and forth *"in a frightful state of tension"* (2:997). Hazel appears from left. Christine expresses her fear of being alone in the house, and Hazel agrees to stay with her that night and goes off to inform her mother. Orin and Lavinia appear at left. Orin is in a *"state of morbid excitement,"* and Lavinia stands *"stiffly square-shouldered, her eyes hard, her mouth grim and set"* (2:999). Orin informs Christine what transpired the previous night—that he heard her conspiring with Brant and that he killed him as soon as she was gone. At the sight of her reaction, his anger turns to desperate longing, and he vows to take her to the South Seas in Brant's stead. Christine moans, grief-stricken, throughout the confession.

Lavinia orders Orin military-style into the house, and he mechanically obeys. She coldly informs Christine that Brant's murder was justifiable revenge against the murder of her father. Christine says nothing, then jumps to her feet and glares at Lavinia *"with a terrible look in which savage hatred fights with horror and fear"* (2:1,001–1,002). Sensing her state of mind, Lavinia exclaims that Christine can still live. Christine mockingly cries out, "Live!" before rushing into the house. Lavinia stands before the entrance, square-shouldered and rigid *"like a grim sentinel in black"* (2:1,002).

Seth can be heard approaching the house singing "Shenandoah" as the sound of a pistol's report comes from the house. Orin discovers his mother's dead body and runs out to Lavinia, informing her that their mother has shot herself and that he is to blame. Lavinia silences him, afraid Seth might overhear. When Seth arrives, she orders him to inform Doctor Blake that Christine has shot herself out of remorse for Ezra's death. He solemnly obeys and moves off left. Orin and Lavinia walk into the house, Lavinia *"stiffly erect, her face stern and masklike"* (2:1,003).

**Part Three:** *The Haunted: A Play in Four Acts*
**Act 1, Scene 1**
Exterior of the Mannon house just after sunset on a clear summer day one year later. Seth Beckwith and Amos Ames stand in front of the house with Abner Small, a 65-year-old hardware store clerk; Joe Silva, a 60-year-old Portuguese fishing captain; and Ira Mackel, an elderly local farmer. All of them are drunk. Again, they appear as *"a chorus of types representing the town as a human background for the drama of the Mannons,"* but they also resemble a group of *"boys out on a forbidden lark"* (2:1,007). They squabble over a jug of whiskey in Seth's possession, and Silva gleefully sings an IRISH drinking song. Lavinia and Orin are expected back from a voyage to China. Seth puts on a show of courage, but all of them, including him, believe the house is haunted by Christine's ghost and the ghosts of all dead Mannons. Seth has wagered Abner Small 10 dollars and a gallon of whiskey that he could not remain in the house until moonrise. He escorts Small into the house and then returns, laughing that Small's teeth were already chattering.

Peter and Hazel appear from the left. Peter informs them that Lavinia and Orin have arrived in New York, but he is interrupted by the sound of a terrified scream. Small crashes through the entrance, breathless with fear and insisting he saw Ezra Mannon's ghost. The other men all roar with laughter. Peter and Hazel scold Seth for the practical joke and for perpetuating the town's superstition about the Mannon home. The other men depart, and Seth explains that the joke will put an end to the superstition; he does believe the house is

haunted, however, and implores Peter to convince Lavinia and Orin not to move back in. Hazel shares Seth's trepidation about the house, but all three go in to prepare for Lavinia and Orin's arrival.

Lavinia and Orin enter from left. Lavinia exhibits *"an extraordinary change"*; her body is less thin now, and she no longer walks with military stiffness. She now appears to embrace her resemblance to Christine, to the point of wearing a green-colored dress. Orin's resemblance to Ezra, particularly the military woodenness and the masklike face *"set in a blank lifeless expression,"* is now *"more pronounced than ever"* (2:1,015). Lavinia encourages him softly on as he averts his eyes from the house, still traumatized by their mother's suicide. Lavinia adopts her military role once more and orders him into the house. "That is all past and finished!" she shouts. "The dead have forgotten us! We've forgotten them! Come!" (2:1,015). He obeys with dull resignation, and they step into the house.

**Act 1, Scene 2**
The Mannon house sitting room, same as act 2 of *The Hunted*. Peter has lighted the room with two candles and a lantern, creating a shadowy gloom, and the furniture, covered with white sheets, *"has a ghostly look."* *"In the flickering candlelight the eyes of the Mannon portraits stare with a grim forbiddingness"* (2:1,016). Lavinia, now looking nearly identical to her mother, enters from the doorway at rear. Her hair is styled as Christine's was, and she wears a green dress identical to her mother's in act 1 of *The Homecoming*. She stands before the portraits and shouts at them not to stare at her accusingly, as she has always been dutiful to the Mannons. Orin enters, looking timid and bewildered. He hoped he would find their mother's ghost in the study so he might beg her forgiveness, but then he denounces her and shouts he is more Ezra's than hers. Lavinia silences him harshly. Orin shrinks from her, and she soothes him affectionately. He wistfully remarks how closely she now resembles their mother in beauty and spirit. It is as though, he says, Lavinia has absorbed Christine's soul. She insists he face his ghosts and accept the fact that their mother's death was a just one for an "adulteress and murderess"

(2:1,019). When he weeps on her breast with child-like devotion, she soothes him with maternal affection, then prompts him to help clean the room.

Peter enters. At first shocked by Lavinia's resemblance to Christine, he goes on to moon adoringly over her transformation. Orin stands dazed at the window until, at Lavinia's insistence, he halfheartedly welcomes Peter. Orin's jealousy grows increasingly acute, and he alludes to a kind of sexual awakening Lavinia experienced in the South Seas with a native man named Avahanni. She silences Orin angrily, then dispatches him to find Hazel. Lavinia assures Peter that Orin is not in his right mind. In stark contrast to their encounter in act 1 of *The Homecoming,* she expresses deep feelings for Peter, astonishing him with her forwardness and delighting him at the same time, and confesses that the islands freed her to embrace life and love. She kisses him passionately, and Peter is *"aroused and at the same time a little shocked by her boldness."* Fearfully remembering Orin, Lavinia stops and warns Peter that Orin must be "well again" before they marry; he must also warn Hazel about Orin's frame of mind (2:1,024). He promises to, and they kiss again just as Orin reenters with Hazel. Hazel looks delighted at the match, but Orin *"glares at them with jealous rage and clenches his fists as if he were going to attack them"* (2:1,024). He shouts at them in furious jealousy but then controls himself. Orin and Peter shake hands while Lavinia *"stares at Orin with eyes full of dread"* (2:1,025).

## Act 2

One month later in Ezra Mannon's study, same as act 3 of *The Hunted.* Ezra's portrait is illuminated by candlelight as Orin, seated at the desk, looks older and ever more like his father. Orin is writing with intense concentration. He pauses, looks up above the fireplace, and sardonically addresses his father's portrait: "What will the neighbors say if this whole truth is ever known?" Lavinia knocks at the door, and Orin hastily locks the manuscript in the desk drawer and takes up a random book. He unlocks the door, and Lavinia enters. Lavinia, *"obviously concealing beneath a surface calm a sense of dread and desperation,"* demands to know what he is doing. He responds that he is studying law

(2:1,026). Convinced his sister wants him out of the way, perhaps even dead, Orin demands to know why she refuses to leave him and Hazel alone together, but he already knows the answer: Given his recent behavior, she is worried he might confess their crime to Hazel. Orin feels he has "no right in the same world" with Hazel, but nevertheless he is drawn to her "purity." Because her love for him makes him feel both finer as a human being and at the same time more despicable, he admits that he desperately longs to confess (2:1,028).

Lavinia derides Orin's conscience and again insists on knowing what he is writing. "A true history of all the family crimes," he responds—a project attempting to expiate the Mannon curse by tracing "its secret hiding place in the Mannon past the evil destiny behind our lives" (2:1,029). In the process, he has discovered that Lavinia is "the most interesting criminal" of all the Mannons (2:1,030). Orin accuses her of jealously coveting Adam Brant as she had a ship's officer on their voyage and the native man Avahanni. Lavinia screams at him that she too has a "right to love." Orin begs her to renounce her admission, then grabs her throat in a jealous rage and threatens to kill her. She appears *"strangely shaken"* and apologizes for the outburst, as if "something rose up in me—like an evil spirit!" (2:1,031). "You never," he replies in shocked tones, "seemed so much like Mother as you did just then" (2:1,031). Lavinia's anger piques once more with another accusation about Avahanni. Orin suggests she kill him to rid her of suspicion and the Mannon she is chained to—himself—as their mother had been to Ezra. Regardless of her assurances that she only desires peace, Orin blackmails her with the family history if she abandons him for Peter. "The damned don't cry," he says when she begins to weep (2:1,032). He asks her to leave, which she does in a daze, and he retrieves his manuscript from the drawer, takes up his pen, and resumes writing.

## Act 3

The Mannon sitting room, same as act 1, scene 2. No time has elapsed. Candlelight again illuminates the portrait of Abe Mannon above the fireplace, along with those of the other Mannons. The eyes of the portraits glare, as Orin said of his father in act 2 of *The Hunted*, as if *"looking over the head of life, cutting it dead for the impropriety of living."* Lavinia enters *"in a terrific state of tension,"* wringing her hands as her mother had in the final act of *The Hunted*. She pleads to the Mannons *"as if they were the visible symbol of her God"* to allow her to control her desire for Orin's death (2:1,034). Seth enters and complains about a black servant. Lavinia leaves with him, and the doorbell rings. Seth accompanies Peter and Hazel into the sitting room and exits. Hazel warns Peter about Lavinia's influence and voices her concern that she has become too bold. Hazel expresses her wish to persuade Orin to live with them but knows Lavinia will put up a terrible fight.

Orin enters and frantically asks to speak to Hazel alone. Peter exits good-naturedly, and Orin hands Hazel an envelope containing the family history, making her swear to open it only if he dies or Lavinia tries to marry Peter. He agrees that he should move in with her family to get away from his sister. Lavinia enters, instantly aware they are conspiring against her. Hazel hides the envelope behind her back, and Lavinia demands to know what it is. They argue about Orin's departure. Orin eventually tells Hazel to go home; before she does, she denounces her friendship with Lavinia. Ignoring this, Lavinia demands again to know if Hazel is hiding Orin's history. She pleads with Orin not to allow Hazel to leave with the manuscript, swearing to do anything he asks. He accepts her offer, *"laughs with a crazy triumph,"* and takes the envelope from Hazel (2:1,040). He then tells Hazel to forget him. "The Orin you loved was killed in the war. . . . Remember only that dead hero and not his rotting ghost!" (2:1,040). She rushes from the room in tears.

Orin tells Lavinia she must promise to give up Peter, and then *"a distorted look of desire comes over his face."* "There are some times now," he says, "when you don't seem to be my sister, nor Mother, not some stranger with the same beautiful hair—" (2:1,041). When he begins to caress her hair, she pulls back violently, and he laughs. "Perhaps you're Marie Brantôme, eh? And you say there are no ghosts in this house?" (2:1,041). If they consummate their love sexually, he implies, they will feel equal guilt, and she will never leave him.

Tortured now by what he is saying, Orin breaks down and pleads with her to permit him to confess to their crime. Lavinia, tempted at first, angrily responds that there is nothing to confess. When he addresses the Mannon portraits, telling them Lavinia will be harder to break than he, she shouts that she hates him, that he would kill himself if he had any courage. "Death is an Island of Peace, too," he agrees. "Mother will be waiting for me there—" (2:1,042). He starts off, and Lavinia calls him back in horror.

Peter enters. Orin leaves them with the excuse that he needs to clean his pistol. Lavinia rushes into Peter's arms and exclaims that "no price is too great" for love and peace. She muses passionately about their future in marriage, then a muffled shot can be heard from the study. Peter runs into the hall to investigate, and Lavinia pleads for Orin's forgiveness. But then, *"with a terrible effort of will,"* her dispassionate self returns, and she mechanically locks the Mannon history in a table drawer. She shouts triumphantly at the Mannon portraits that she will live in spite of them and marches military-style from the room, *"as if by the very act of disowning the Mannons she had returned to the fold"* (2:1,044).

*Act 4*

Late afternoon three days later. The exterior of the Mannon house, same as act 1, scene 1. Seth appears from right, chewing tobacco and singing "Shenandoah." He expresses resentment over Lavinia's taking nearly all the flowers from his garden to beautify the house. The locals, he says, now take the word *Mannon* to mean "sudden death" (2:1,045). Lavinia enters from the left dressed in mourning black and carrying flowers. Another serious transformation is apparent: She looks older, haggard, sleep-deprived, and the *"mask-like resemblance of her face"* has intensified further. Seth offers to bring a sofa for her to lie on; thus he understands, she says, that the house is a "temple of Hate and Death" (2:1,046). She vows to marry Peter and rid herself of the Mannon legacy. Hazel enters, dressed in mourning and, though clearly grief-stricken, has an expression of *"stubborn resolution"* (2:1,047).

Once Seth exits, Hazel accuses Lavinia of driving Orin to suicide. She tells Lavinia she must not marry Peter; whatever it is she had done that made Orin kill himself, Hazel insists, would somehow get between them. Peter has left their house and moved into a hotel, refusing to accept Hazel's and their mother's advice not to marry Lavinia. Lavinia explodes in anger and threatens to kill Hazel with Orin's pistol. But her fury subsides, and Hazel, now certain Lavinia is "wicked" but sympathetic to her suffering, assures her that her conscience will force her away from Peter. "I hope there is a hell for the good somewhere!" Lavinia exclaims sardonically after Hazel has gone (2:1,049).

Peter enters, and Lavinia begs him to marry her without delay. They must move, she insists, as abandoning the Mannon house is the only way the dead Mannons will leave them in peace. She informs him that Hazel has just left, and he growls angrily about his family's attempts to turn him against her. Lavinia pleads with him to marry her that evening. Suspicious himself now, Peter asks if there is anything he should know. Lavinia throws herself at him, kissing him passionately and begging him to "forget sin and see that all love is beautiful" and to make love to her then and there. "Want me!" she cries out frantically. "Take me, Adam!" (2:1,052). Realizing her mistake, she resigns herself to accept that the dead will not permit her to love in peace. Peter insists on knowing about Avahanni. She ferociously admits that she slept with him and that in his innocence and purity, he had shown her that love was not a sin. Revolted by the admission, Peter declares that Hazel and his mother were right and rushes off left. At first repentant, Lavinia squares her shoulders and coldly says goodbye.

Seth enters, again singing lines from "Shenandoah"—"Oh, Shenandoah, I can't get near you / Way-ay, I'm bound away—" (2:1,053). Lavinia responds that she is not "bound away" but bound now to the house forever. Nor does she plan to commit suicide like Orin and her mother. "That's escaping punishment. And there's no one left to punish me. I'm the last Mannon. I've got to punish myself! . . . I know they will see to it I live for a long time! It takes the Mannons to punish themselves for being born!" She orders Seth to nail the shutters

closed and throw out the flowers. Seth obeys, and she remains on the portico, "*stiff and square-shouldered*" (2:1,053). Seth appears from the window at right and pulls the shutters closed with a bang. As if obeying a command, Lavinia turns sharply on her heels, marches into the house, and shuts the door behind her. The curtain falls.

## COMMENTARY

*Mourning Becomes Electra,* up to that point the greatest accomplishment of Eugene O'Neill's career, powerfully combines ancient Greek tragedy, modern theories of psychoanalysis, New England Puritan culture, and American history. In effect, O'Neill recast LAZARUS LAUGHED, STRANGE INTERLUDE, and DESIRE UNDER THE ELMS, respectively, but without, as he put it, the "show shop" theatricals of these experimental plays of the 1920s (in Bogard 340). *Mourning* is gripping in plot and powerfully situated in time and place, and its characters' histories and personalities are well-developed and troublingly clear. "From the first showdown between Lavinia and Christine," says O'Neill biographer Louis Sheaffer in praise of the play, "the narrative starts to coil and tighten like a huge python that will devour all members of the doomed house of Mannon, and it rarely eases its grip during most of its thirteen acts of murder, suicide, near-madness and haunting" (370). Audiences would have quickly read the incestuous relations among the Mannons as derived from Sigmund Freud's Oedipus complex, which in turn was borrowed from Greek tragedy; O'Neill's psychoanalytic biographer Stephen A. Black suggests the story reflected O'Neill's own incestuous feelings toward his mother, MARY ELLEN "ELLA" O'NEILL (2004, 182). (In 1926, O'Neill had indeed informed his friend KENNETH MACGOWAN that he had been diagnosed by his psychiatrist, Dr. G. V. Hamilton, as suffering from an Oedipus complex [Bogard 345]).

O'Neill always insisted, however, that he would "have written *Mourning Becomes Electra* almost exactly as it is if I had never heard of Freud or Jung or the others" (quoted in Alexander 155). While composing drafts of the play in France, he complained that the problem he had posed for himself was nearly insurmountable: "The unavoidable entire melodramatic action," he wrote, "must be felt as working out of psychic fate from the past—thereby attaining tragic significance—or else!—a hell of a problem, a modern tragic interpretation of classic fate without benefit of gods . . . fate springing out of the family" (quoted in Sheaffer 357).

O'Neill conceived the idea in 1926, during his voyage to China with Carlotta Monterey, to write a "modern psychological drama using one of the old legend plots of Greek tragedy" (quoted in Clark 128). At that time, he mused over the repressive atmosphere of a puritanical New England small town in contrast to the freedom of the open SEA, represented in the play by Adam Brant's reveries over his "Blessed Isles" and Christine, Lavinia, Orin, and even Ezra Mannon's attempt at purification and liberation by voyaging to the South Seas and Asia. Overtly borrowing from the mythic world of Aeschylus's *Oresteia* trilogy, also adapted later by Sophocles and Euripides, O'Neill admitted that he was interested only in the "general spirit" of the ancient plays, not the "details of legend" (quoted in Alexander 152). Nevertheless, Aeschylus's characters, King Agamemnon and his wife, Clytemnestra, (Ezra and Christine Mannon) and their children Electra and Orestes (Lavinia and Orin), violently striving against one another among the chanting chorus of the New England townspeople (the chorus), all appear as representative characters in O'Neill's first true tour de force.

*Mourning Becomes Electra* and the *Oresteia*'s shared plot lines are unmistakable to anyone with a cursory knowledge of Greek tragedy: A general/king returns from war—the Trojan War in the Greek myth, the American Civil War in O'Neill—only to be murdered by spiteful wives, each of whom have been conducting an affair with a romantic stranger (Aegisthus, Adam Brant) in their husbands' absence; the strangers are in turn murdered by the couples' progeny. In both, daughters and sons seek revenge for their fathers' murders, though revenge intensifies rather than alleviates their suffering. In Euripides' version of the tale, Orestes succumbs to insanity after having been an accomplice to his mother's murder, as Orin does in O'Neill's (Alexander 161). But *Mourning* offers a sequel to the *Oresteia* in that it shows us the life of Electra after

the murder of her mother, Clytemnestra. As Travis Bogard phrases it, the *Oresteia* is "the source of all tragedy," and thus "from that primal fountain, he took new life" (341).

"Mannon" phonetically brings to mind the Greek king "Agamemnon"; the word also connotes, from the Bible and elsewhere, the wickedness that often accompanies great wealth. Combine that with a Puritan New England setting and O'Neill's lifelong conviction that family consists, in Louis Sheaffer's words, of "a deadly struggle" (336), and the *Oresteia* provided O'Neill with the ideal framework for a modern psychological tragedy. O'Neill consciously grappled with the oedipal family aspect in his April 1929 WORK DIARY notes:

> Electra . . . adores father, [is] devoted to brother (who resembles father), hates mother—Orestes adores mother, [is] devoted to sister (whose face resembles mother's) so hates his father—Agamemnon, frustrated in love for Clytemnestra, adores daughter, Electra, who resembles her, hates and is jealous of his son—work out this symbol of family resemblances and identifications (as visible sign of family fate) still further (quoted in Sheaffer 338).

O'Neill's conjoining of Greek mythology and modern psychology finally proved his status as a major world dramatist. "Although most of us have been brought up to bow and genuflect before the majesty of Greek tragedy," theater critic Brooks Atkinson wrote of the trilogy, "it has remained for Mr. O'Neill to show us why" (126). Not all critics lauded O'Neill's use of the Greek myth, however. Novelist Gore Vidal recalled his indignant reaction to *Mourning Becomes Electra* while waiting for the curtain to rise at the premiere of *A Touch of the Poet* (which he adored) as a "misuse of the *Oresteia* when, having crudely borrowed the relationship, the melodrama, the portentousness of Aeschylus, he blithely left out the whole idea of justice which was, to say the least, the point of that tragedy" (234). O'Neill preempted such a reading in an early statement about the final act of *The Haunted*:

> The Electra figure in the Greek legend and plays fades out into a vague and undramatic future.

She stops, as if after the revenge on her mother all was well. The Furies take after Orestes, but she is left alone. I never could swallow that. It seemed to me that by having her disappear in nice conventionally content future (married to Pylades, according to one version of the legend) the Greeks were dodging the implication of their own belief in the chain of fate. In our modern psychological chain of fate certainly we cannot let her make her exit like that. She is so inevitably worthy of a better tragic fate! I have tried to give my Yankee Electra an end tragically worthy of herself. The end, to me, is the most inevitable thing in the trilogy. She is broken and not broken. By her way of yielding to the Mannon fate she overcomes it (quoted in Atkinson 127).

*Mourning Becomes Electra* is a mask play without masks. After much consideration, O'Neill decided to do without the actual masks he employed for symbolic effect in *Lazarus Laughed* and *The* GREAT GOD BROWN. Instead, he offered only the implication of masks as, according to O'Neill, "a visual symbol of [the Mannons'] separateness, the fated isolation of this family, the mark of their fate which makes them dramatically distinct from the rest of the world" (quoted in Sheaffer 363). "What I want from this mask concept," he maintained, is to demonstrate visually how the "Mannon drama takes place on a plane where outer reality is a mask of true fated reality—unreal realism" (quoted in Falk 130).

Each Mannon face in repose appears with the same *"strange, life-like mask impression"* (2:897), even the portraits of the ancestors. They reside in a mansion (the house of Atreus in Aeschylus) with a *"white temple front . . . like an incongruous mask fixed on the somber, stone house"* (2:928). O'Neill wishes to convey the importance of "mourning" as a constant state of being with his dark costumes as well, one that Stephen A. Black comprehensively analyzes as the principal mental state of the author in his biography *Eugene O'Neill: Beyond Mourning and Tragedy* (1999). "Mourning—the color of death—becomes her," writes Doris Alexander of Lavinia, "fits her destiny, and her tragic struggle for life and love was O'Neill's own" (1999, 156).

O'Neill's intended stage set must be regarded as a critical component to any successful production of the trilogy. By all accounts, O'Neill's set designer ROBERT EDMOND JONES's Mannon house was a magnificent realization of O'Neill's STAGE DIRECTIONS; as O'Neill himself noted in his Work Diary—"marvelous stuff, all his work is, BEST DESIGNER finest in world today, beyond question—no one in Europe to touch him" (quoted in Floyd 1981, 209). The Mannon house resembles the numerous Greek revival houses that adorn O'Neill's hometown, NEW LONDON, CONNECTICUT (his notes called the town "N.L."); specifically, the house (and its builder) were inspired by a row of four beautifully maintained Greek revival houses on Huntington Street in New London. Their original owner was named Ezra Chappell, a wealthy merchant whose family O'Neill depicts in *Long Day's Journey into Night* as the Chatfields and whom he once characterized as "big frogs in a small puddle" (quoted in Floyd 1985, 396n). As a product of New England, the structure was "built upon outraged pride and Puritanism," as Doris Falk aptly phrases it (130). The house's temple-like white columns, before which Greek tragedies were generally performed, project black shadows against the front of the house, suggesting prison bars that have locked up generations of Mannons and will incarcerate Lavinia to her death (Alexander 151).

The Mannon mansion's gray stone behind the columns and white portico mask represents the granitelike temperament that characterizes New England culture, a stony deliberateness in thought and act that rejects any show of sentimentality and weakness; it is a mindset O'Neill had previously explored in the figures of the whale captains David Keeney in ILE and Isaiah Bartlett in GOLD and the obstinate farmer Ephraim Cabot in *Desire under the Elms* (a play that also treats oedipal conflict). Christine Mannon characterizes the mansion as the whited sepulchre of the Bible, a "pagan temple front stuck like a mask on Puritan gray ugliness!" (2:903–904). Years before the action of the play, Ezra Mannon had destroyed the original edifice to blot out the stain of his brother David's marriage to the French nurse Marie Brantôme—a marriage that spawns Adam Brant and begins a chain of events that culminates in two suicides and a murder—and foolishly built a new temple to be desecrated by innate Mannon impurity and hypocrisy. The painted backdrop showing the view of the house from the street symbolizes outsiders' perceptions of wealth and nobility, but when we gaze inside, like the interloping townsfolk in the opening scene, we witness the brutal reality of the tragic Mannons.

Orin Mannon's secret family history conjoins the sinful past of the Mannons with that of the United States, transgressions O'Neill persistently railed against to the press, along with his own family's sins and his sins against his second wife, AGNES BOULTON. Orin's history attempts to exorcise the Mannon curse (America's, his) by tracing "the evil destiny behind our lives" (2:1,029); this gives the work a strong emotional connection to O'Neill's autobiographical masterpiece *Long Day's Journey into Night,* also a family exposé and one he did not want published until 25 years after his death and never wanted produced. As in *Long Day's Journey,* Orin's history is a kind of therapeutic mental exercise to help its author work through the psychic pain of his and his family's past. Indeed, strong correlations exist between Mary Tyrone (O'Neill's mother) and Christine (see Floyd 391), Edmund Tyrone (O'Neill's autobiographical avatar) and Orin, and James Tyrone (O'Neill's father) and Ezra Mannon. One exchange between Ezra, Christine, and Lavinia in act 3 of *The Homecoming* demonstrates a clear parallel between the characters and O'Neill's life, when Ezra talks of Orin's nerves as James Tyrone talks of his son's in *Long Day's Journey:* "Nerves. I wouldn't notice nerves. He's always been restless. (*half turning to Christine*) He gets that from you" (2:933). Doris Alexander also connects Orin's history with O'Neill's own personal fear that Agnes Boulton would exploit their relationship and his private life as fodder for a book deal. He considered this "legalized blackmail" in the context of their divorce. At the time of the settlement, he complained to GEORGE JEAN NATHAN that Agnes refused to accept a clause "specifying that she should write no articles about me or our married life or thinly-disguised autobiographical fiction exploiting me. Can you beat it?" (quoted in Alexander 165; she eventually did so with her memoir *Part of a Long Story* [1958]).

Furthermore, O'Neill mistakenly thought of his former estate with Boulton, SPITHEAD in Bermuda, as situated within "The Isles of Rest," just as Brant's "Blessed Isles" in the South Seas never helped relieve the character of his guilt and mourning over his mother's death (in Alexander 163). Just after *Mourning Becomes Electra* opened, he and CARLOTTA MONTEREY O'NEILL revived his dream and bought land on SEA ISLAND off the coast of Georgia, naming their house there Casa Genotta ("Gene" + "Carlotta"). South Sea island culture must therefore be read as an important leitmotif in the play, signifying for O'Neill and his characters, in his words, "release, peace, security, beauty, freedom of conscience, sinlessness, etc.—longing for the primitive—and mother-symbol—yearning for pre-natal, non-competitive freedom from fear . . ." (quoted in Falk 131). Hence the playwright's decision to situate the wharf scene at the exact center of the dramatic action, "emphasizing the sea background of family and symbolic motive of sea as a means of escape and release" (quoted in Bogard 337).

Life in Puritan New England was a "living death" for both the Mannons and the O'Neills, and Ezra realizes this too late. The Mannon family had always followed the Protestant church's belief that, as Ezra puts it, "Life was a dying. Being born was starting to die. Death was being born" (2:937–938). But Ezra is too firmly associated in Christine's eyes with the death of the living, from which only Brant can free her. To escape the tragic Puritan cycle and live, Ezra begs Christine to join him on a voyage to the South Seas. Lavinia describes Adam Brant's description of the natives there in the way Captain Caleb Williams does in *DIFF'RENT,* as a people who had "found the secret of happiness because they had never heard that love can be a sin" (2:909). Those islands and their inhabitants answer several important questions about the cloistered Mannon clan: Why Christine and Lavinia are drawn to Adam Brant as an object of desire more than by his looks or romantic ways; why Orin clings to Herman Melville's South Seas narrative *Typee;* why Seth, in the throes of Mannon suffocation and death, continually sings of being "bound away" in the sea shanty "Shenandoah," with which O'Neill brackets the trilogy from the opening scene to just prior to the final curtain; and most important, why Orin falls in love with his sister after she adopts her mother's fixation on life and love. As Lavinia describes the revelations she experienced there:

> There was something there mysterious and beautiful—a good spirit—of love—coming out of the land and sea. It made me forget death. There was no hereafter. There was only this world—the warm earth in the moonlight—the trade wind in the coco palms—the surf on the reef—the fires at night and the drum throbbing in my heart—the natives dancing and naked and innocent—without knowledge of sin! (2:1,023).

Hence, Lavinia's self-exile from life and love in the final scene proves a more tragic fate than the suicide of her mother and brother. And as Virginia Floyd suggests, O'Neill's play inverts the liberating finale of Henrik Ibsen's *A Doll's House*, the first major work of modern drama, in which the female protagonist, Nora Helmer, slams the front door shut behind her as the audience watches from the interior of the house. Lavinia, in contrast, shuts hers as we watch her disappear into the house from the exterior. "Ibsen's slamming door," writes Floyd, "herald's a woman's emancipation from the past, her entrance into the outside world. The closing door in O'Neill signal's a woman's enslavement to the past, her immuring in a tomb of death" (1985, 402).

*Mourning Becomes Electra* often lapses into what one critic, in backhanded praise, characterized as "good, old-fashioned, spine-curdling" MELODRAMA in both dialogue and action (Benchley 129). But the play stands as O'Neill's first mature blending of the gritty surface realities of NATURALISM with the European EXPRESSIONISM more evident in such earlier plays as *The* EMPEROR JONES, *The* HAIRY APE, *The* FOUNTAIN, and ALL GOD'S CHILLUN GOT WINGS, in which the inner psyches of the playwright and his characters are projected onto the stage in grotesque and exaggerated forms. But O'Neill deliberately avoided the "show shop" aspects of his earlier experimental plays. By artfully blending the two, Doris Alexander suggests, O'Neill "wanted to

show that the surfaces of life—which are taken for reality—are meaningless and that the great realities, the 'hidden life forces' beneath the surface, are so overwhelming when perceived, as to seem unreal" (151). The ineluctable forces of fate—psychological, historical, religious, and genetic—that govern the Mannon clan can also be considered O'Neill's modernist update of the mythic Greek gods, fates, and furies that play disruptive and controlling roles in the Electra myth. In *Mourning*, we can take O'Neill's "hidden life forces" to be New England Puritanism—a deterministic faith—in the form of suppressed sexuality and perpetual guilt, oedipal attractions, family heritage, and the mental ravages of war.

## CHARACTERS

**Ames, Amos** The town's carpenter and Louisa Ames's husband. Ames is a rotund man in his 50s, a *"garrulous gossip-monger who is at the same time devoid of evil intent."* One of the *"types of townsfolk rather than individuals, a chorus representing the town,"* Ames appears at the Mannon home dressed in his Sunday best in the first act of *The Homecoming* merely to *"look and listen and spy on the rich and exclusive Mannons"* (2:894). In the opening scene of *The Haunted*, Ames is drunk, along with Seth Beckwith, Ira Mackel, Joe Silva, and Abner Small, and instigates the lark played on Abner Small, wherein Small must remain in the Mannon home, which they all believe is haunted, until the moon comes up.

**Ames, Louisa** Amos Ames's wife and Minnie's cousin. Louisa is in her 50s, taller than Amos and *"of a similar scandal-bearing type, her tongue sharpened by malice."* Louisa is one of the townspeople whom O'Neill describes as *"types of townsfolk rather than individuals, a chorus representing the town"* who appear in the first act of *The Homecoming* merely to *"look and listen and spy on the rich and exclusive Mannons"* (2:894).

**Beckwith, Seth** The Mannon family's groundskeeper and *"man of all work."* Seth is a tall, wiry, white-haired 75-year-old with a charmingly loyal and practical, if somewhat impish, disposition (2:893).

In several scenes, including the very first and one of the last, Seth sings the sea chanty "Shenandoah," which brings the call of the sea and the urge to be "bound away" from the claustrophobic, imprisoning atmosphere of the New England town and the Mannon family home. Having worked under the Mannons for 60 years, Seth's face in repose shares the Mannons' *"strange impression of a life-like mask"*; at the same time, *"his small, sharp eyes still peer at life with a shrewd prying avidity and his loose mouth has a strong impression of ribald humor"* (2:894). In act 1 of *The Haunted*, Seth makes a wager with Abner Small that Small cannot remain in the Mannon house until the moon rises. Although he has a good laugh when Small runs screaming from the house convinced he has seen a ghost (actually the faces of the Mannon ancestors' portraits), Seth, who knows the family's sins and secrets, also believes the house is haunted. Having been with the family so long, Seth functions as the expositor of the family's history, as told by him to the curious local townspeople, and he will also act as Lavinia's caretaker in her self-imposed exile from life.

**Blake, Doctor Joseph**   The Mannon family physician. Blake is one of many DOCTORS in the O'Neill canon, an *"old kindly best-family physician—a stout self-important old man with a stubborn opinionated expression"* (2:951). He appears in the opening scene of *The Hunted* as one of the *"types of townsfolk, a chorus representing as those others had, but in a different stratum of society"* (2:951). Having diagnosed Ezra with angina, Blake does not question Christine Mannon's story that Ezra Mannon died of a heart attack rather than being murdered with poison. He scolds Mrs. Hills for insensitively remarking that her husband, the preacher Everett Hills, said of Ezra that "pride goeth before a fall and that some day God would humble them in their sinful pride" (2:953). However, he later shares a joke with Joseph Borden that Ezra most probably died in bed with his wife, Christine Mannon.

**Borden, Emma**   Josiah Borden's wife. Emma Borden is about 50 years old, *"a typical New England woman of pure English ancestry, with a horse face,*

*buck teeth and big feet, her manner defensively sharp and assertive"* (2:951). Emma opens *The Hunted* by harshly judging Christine—"I can't abide that woman!" (2:951)—but then she adds sympathetically that having witnessed how distraught Christine looked at her husband, Ezra Mannon's funeral, she had "never suspected she had that much feeling in her;" she also observes that Christine and Ezra's daughter, Lavinia, appeared unaccountably "cold and calm as an icicle" (2:952). Her character is one of the *"types of townsfolk, a chorus representing as those others had, but in a different stratum of society"* (2:951).

**Borden, Josiah**   Manager of the Mannon Shipping Company and Emma Borden's husband. About 60 years old, Borden is *"shrewd and competent . . . small and wizened, white hair and beard, rasping nasal voice, and little sharp eyes"* (2:951). In the opening scene of *The Hunted*, Borden questions the Mannons' judgment for having Ezra Mannon's dead body in view at the home rather than in a more public forum. Borden sincerely respected Ezra but, unaware of his murder, shares a joke with Doctor Joseph Blake that he probably died in bed with his wife, Christine Mannon. Similar to the townspeople in *The Homecoming*, Borden is one of the *"types of townsfolk, a chorus representing as those others had, but in a different stratum of society"* (2:951).

**Brant, Captain Adam**   Skipper of the *Trade Winds*, Christine Mannon's lover, David Mannon and Marie Brantôme's son, and Ezra Mannon's nephew. Adam Brant, whose full name appropriately calls to mind the word *adumbrate* (to obscure or only show the bare outlines of) has the least depth of any major character in the trilogy. His name also connotes the biblical "first man," whose punishment for sin is brought on by the wiles of a woman, Eve (Alexander 162). Primarily a symbol of masculine romantic power, Brant is 36 years old, *"tall, broad-shouldered and powerful,"* with long black hair pushed back from his forehead *"as a poet's might be"* (2:907). Brant dresses *"with an almost foppish extravagance, with touches of studied carelessness, as if a romantic Byronic appearance were the ideal in mind"* (2:907). In a jealous comment to Lavinia Mannon, who openly despises him but is secretly drawn to him, Peter Niles characterizes Brant as "such a darned romantic-looking cuss. Looks more like a gambler or a poet than a ship captain" (2:902).

Brant arrives at the Mannon home in act 1 of *The Homecoming* and halfheartedly attempts to woo Lavinia Mannon to gain her trust. At first she acerbically reminds him of his time shipwrecked on a South Pacific island and his "admiration for the naked native women" who had "found the secret of happiness because they had never heard that love can be a sin." "Aye!" Brant heartily agrees. "And they live in as near the Garden of Paradise before sin was discovered as you'll find on this earth!" (2:909). Lavinia then goads him into admitting a rumor that he is the product of her uncle David Mannon's scandalous marriage with the French Canadian nurse Marie Brantôme; she has also heard rumors that he has been conducting an affair with her mother, Christine Mannon, in New York. The truth of his parentage out, Brant informs her of her father's vicious jealousy of David and of leaving him and his mother penniless after David committed suicide. At age 17, Adam changed his last name to Brant (shortened from Brantôme) and went to sea to escape the guilt following his mother's assertion that he was responsible for his father's suicide. He found her years later in New York dying of starvation, after Ezra Mannon never replied to her plea for money. She died in Brant's arms, and he has vowed revenge on the Mannons ever since.

In the following act, having witnessed her mother kissing and pledging her love to Brant, Lavinia accuses Christine of conducting an adulterous affair with him. Christine admits it in a rage and informs Lavinia that after 20 years married to the once-romantic Ezra Mannon, "marriage soon turned his romance into—disgust!" (2:917). Lavinia threatens to inform the local press of their affair if Christine does not call it off. Christine subsequently convinces Brant to help her kill Ezra by acquiring a prescription that would stop his heart. They might then marry without the stain of divorce on her name and live together on Brant's "Blessed Isles" in the South Seas. Brant reluctantly agrees, and in act 4 of *The Homecoming*, Christine successfully murders Ezra with the tincture. In act 4 of

*The Hunted*, Lavinia and her brother, Orin Mannon, who has returned from the war and refuses to believe in the affair, follow Christine and Brant to a wharf in Boston where Brant's ship, *Trade Winds*, is docked. There Orin witnesses a liaison between his mother and Brant and overhears them planning to sail for China together that week. When Christine leaves the ship, Brant bemoans the necessity of giving up his ship. "So it's good-bye to you, 'Flying Trades'! . . . I wasn't man enough for you!" (2:994). Orin then kills Brant in a jealous rage. Christine, upon hearing the news, kills herself, ignoring her daughter's entreaty for her to live on despite Brant.

Adam Brant corresponds to the Greek tragic character Aegisthus in Aeschylus's *Oresteia*. He is the romantic stranger who conducts an affair with Clytemnestra (Christine) while her husband Agamemnon (Ezra) is fighting the Trojan War (the American Civil War). Like Aegisthus, Brant is killed by the absent warrior's vengeful children, Lavinia (Electra) and Orin (Orestes); Orin consciously experiences an incestuous jealousy over the affair. Brant is primarily a symbol to the Mannon women of an alternative to their lives in Puritan New England and incarceration in the Mannon clan: He is their only hope for romance, peace in life, and sinless love, none of which Christine or Lavinia are fated to enjoy.

**Chantyman**  A chantyman, or a singer skippers hire to boost the morale of working sailors on a ship with MUSIC. The chantyman is about 65, "*thin, wiry . . . with a tussled mop of black hair, unkempt black beard and mustache.*" His face looks dissipated, with a weak mouth and bloodshot blue eyes, but "*there is something romantic, a queer troubadour-of-the-sea quality about him.*" In the opening scene of act 4 of *The Hunted*, the chantyman is awakened from sleeping off a drunk by the sound of another chantyman singing "Shenandoah" to sailors docking in Boston harbor. Unimpressed, he strikes up the same song in "*a surprisingly good tenor voice*" (2:984). Alone on the dock, he exposits on the previous night, when a "yaller-haired pig" in a pink dress stole 10 dollars from him (2:985). Captain Adam Brant arrives at the dock to meet Christine Mannon, who just murdered her husband, Ezra Mannon, with poison

Brant had acquired for the deed. After sizing each other up, Brant and the chantyman engage in a dialogue about work and women.

The chantyman recalls the character Paddy from O'Neill's experimental play *The Hairy Ape*, who also mourns the transition from sail to steam power. "Steam is comin'," the chantyman warns, "the sea is full o' smoky teakettles, the old days is dyin', an' where'll you an' me be then?" (2:987). He brings up Ezra Mannon's death; no love is lost for Ezra, as he considered Ezra a slave-driving, tightfisted ship owner. He then calls to mind Brant's fateful relationship with Christine and advises Brant to "steer clear 'o gals or they'll skin your hide off an' use it fur a carpet. . . . They're not fur sailormen like you an' me, 'less we're lookin' fur sorrow!" (2:987). In the end, Brant gives him a dollar for drink and promises him a berth on his ship, the *Flying Trades*, to get rid of him before Christine arrives.

Of the two songs the chantyman sings, "Shenandoah" and "Hanging Johnny," the first represents freedom on the open sea in contrast to the imprisoning atmosphere of the puritanical Mannon home, and the second Brant's guilty role in the murder of Ezra Mannon.

**Hills, Everett, D.D.** Mrs. Hills's husband and the town minister who officiates at Ezra Mannon's funeral. Hills is *"the type of well-fed minister of a prosperous small-town congregation—stout and unctuous, snobbish and ingratiating, conscious of godliness, but timid and always feeling his way"* (2:951). His wife embarrasses him in front of the other townspeople in the opening scene of *The Hunted* by openly reminding him that he had predicted Ezra's demise, since "pride goeth before a fall and that some day God would humble them in their sinful pride" (2:953). After a moment of uneasy backpedaling, he scolds his wife and agrees with Doctor Joseph Blake that "it's a poor time" to be making such remarks (2:953). Hills is one of the *"types of townsfolk, a chorus representing as those others had, but in a different stratum of society"* (2:951).

**Hills, Mrs.** The wife of the Everett Hills, D.D. Mrs. Hills is a *"sallow, flabby, self-effacing minister's wife"* (2:951) who embarrasses her husband in

the opening scene of *The Hunted* by insensitively remarking after Ezra Mannon's funeral that her husband had said of Ezra, "pride goeth before a fall and that some day God would humble them in their sinful pride" (2:953). The minister scolds Mrs. Hills, agreeing with Doctor Joseph Blake that "it's a poor time" to be making such remarks (2:953). Her character is one of the *"types of townsfolk, a chorus representing as those others had, but in a different stratum of society"* (2:951).

**Mackel, Ira** A farmer. Mackel is a bald old man with a cane whose *"yellowish eyes are sly"* and who talks in a *"drawling wheezy cackle."* In the opening scene of *The Haunted*, Mackel is drunk, along with Amos Ames, Seth Beckwith, Joe Silva, and Abner Small. A believer in ghosts and haunted houses and expositor of local horror legends, Mackel encourages the lark played on Abner Small, wherein Small must remain in the Mannon home, which they all believe is haunted, until the moon comes up. Mackel is one of *"a chorus of types representing the town as a human background for the drama of the Mannons"* (2:1,007).

**Mannon, Christine** Brigadier General Ezra Mannon's wife, Lavinia and Orin Mannon's mother, and Captain Adam Brant's lover. Christine is a tall, voluptuous 40-year-old woman who looks younger and *"moves with a flowing animal grace"* (2:896). Like all the Mannons, her face gives the *"strange impression . . . in repose of being not living flesh but a wonderfully life-like pale mask"* (2:896). The people in her small New England port town accuse her of being "furrin' lookin' and queer," descended as she is from French and Dutch heritage, rather than Anglo-Saxon (2:895). Before the trilogy's action, Christine met Captain Adam Brant, the son of her brother-in-law David Mannon and Marie Brantôme, the Mannon family's French Canadian nurse, while visiting her father, a doctor in New York City. Christine and Brant conducted an affair while her husband, Ezra Mannon, was fighting as a brigadier general in the American Civil War. For Christine, Brant's romantic allure stems from his experience in the South Seas, his "Blessed Isles," where he found the natives living in a natural state that allows for love without the Puritan sense of guilt.

Christine and Ezra have two children, Lavinia and Orin Mannon, but she only loves Orin, as he was born when Ezra was away fighting the Mexican War. She therefore felt Orin to be her child and Lavinia, who reminds her of her loveless honeymoon, exclusively Ezra's. When pressed by Lavinia, Christine admits of her husband, "I loved him once—before I married him—incredible as that seems now! He was handsome in his lieutenant's uniform! He was silent and mysterious and romantic! But marriage soon turned his romance into—disgust!" (2:917). Lavinia, however, adores her father with almost incestuous devotion and threatens to expose Christine if she does not end the affair with Brant. Christine persuades Brant to get her a poison that would kill Ezra when he returned from the war. When he does, in act 2 of *The Homecoming*, she makes love to Ezra one last time, but in a passionless manner, as if, in his words, she were a "nigger slave [he'd] bought at auction" (2:944). She viciously informs him of her affair with Brant and says that Brant is Marie Brantôme's daughter. This causes Ezra to have a heart attack, and rather than administering his proper heart medicine, she gives him the poison. Ezra realizes what he has done before dying and accuses her of murder. Lavinia is standing in the room, thus apprehending her mother's guilt.

Orin Mannon returns home in act 1 of *The Hunted* and shows little grief over his father's death, appearing more concerned about the evident difference in his mother's appearance. Lavinia warns him not to trust her. "Don't let her baby you the way she used to," she says. "Don't believe the lies she'll tell you!" (2:959). At first Christine preempts Lavinia's efforts to turn Orin against her by informing him that Lavinia believes she killed Ezra. She successfully convinces him that Lavinia is "actually insane" (2:969), until Lavinia leads him to a liaison Christine has with Brant at a wharf in Boston. On Brant's ship, *Flying Trades*, which is scheduled for departure in a month, Christine persuades Brant to go away with her on a different ship sailing for China. "And we will be happy," she assures him, "once we're safe on your Blessed Islands!" (2:992). Soon after Chris-

tine leaves the wharf, Orin kills Brant. Back at the house, Orin tells her he killed Brant. Lavinia, who sees the expression of utter despair in her mother's face, pleads with her to forget Brant and live on. "Live!" Christine cries out in hysterical laughter. She goes inside and shoots herself, with Lavinia standing at the front door "*square-shouldered and stiff like a grim sentinel*" (2:1,002). Orin discovers her corpse and accuses himself of murdering Christine, the great love of his life.

Christine's character corresponds to Clytemnestra in Aeschylus's *Oresteia* trilogy, the wife of Agamemnon (Ezra Mannon), who returns home from the Trojan War (the Civil War) to be murdered by his unfaithful wife. Orin is Orestes, who kills the lover (Aegisthos/Brant) in a jealous rage, and Lavinia is the daughter (Electra), who avenges her father's murder by goading her brother into killing their mother. Although O'Neill makes a point to demonstrate Christine's incestuous devotion to her son, her love for Brant, who represents an escape from her imprisonment in puritanical New England, fatally overwhelms her oedipal love for her son.

**Mannon, Ezra** Christine Mannon's husband, Lavinia and Orin Mannon's father, and a brigadier general in the Union Army during the American Civil War. Ezra Mannon corresponds with King Agamemnon in Aeschylus's *Oresteia*, in which a general/king returns from war—the Trojan War in Aeschylus—only to be murdered by his spiteful, unfaithful wife. O'Neill describes Ezra, an imposing 50-year-old patriarch, as having the same "*mask-like look of his face in repose*" as all members of the Mannon clan. "*His movements are exact and wooden and he has a mannerism of standing and sitting in stiff, posed attitudes that suggests the statues of military heroes*" (2:931). Ezra's father, Abe Mannon, founded one of the first Western Ocean packet lines and made a fortune that he passed on to his son. Ezra conducted his business wisely but also became a leading citizen in the New England port town. Ezra attended West Point, fought bravely in the Mexican War, and earned the rank of major. After his father died, he took charge of the family shipping concern but also received his law degree and became the town's judge, then its mayor. Though he held that office when the Civil War broke out, he relinquished his post and signed on as a general in Ulysses S. Grant's army.

*The Homecoming*, the title of the first play, refers to Ezra's return home from the war. During his absence, his wife, Christine, has conducted an affair with a romantic sea captain four years her junior named Adam Brant, who is the son of Ezra's brother David Mannon and Marie Brantôme, the family's French Canadian nurse, whom Ezra also loved. David Mannon's scandal compelled Ezra to destroy the original house and build a new one in a failed attempt to expiate his brother's transgression. He also refused Marie assistance after David committed suicide, a heartless act that made Brant swear to avenge his mother. For Christine, Adam represents the freedom and guiltless existence of the open sea and the "Blessed Islands" in the South Pacific—a stark contrast to Ezra's stern, guilt-inducing puritanism and imprisoning Mannon heritage. Christine thus convinces Brant to conspire with her to poison Ezra so they might marry and escape to the South Seas together.

Lavinia—Ezra and Christine's daughter—adores her father with a near-incestuous passion, and she desperately attempts to seduce him away from her mother by informing him of the town gossip about Christine and Brant. Ezra instantly recognizes Christine's aloof behavior and attributes it to problems they have had in the past. But he begs her to believe that the war has made him "sick of death" and the living death that had previously guided him in the puritanical Mannon way (2:939). His lust for Christine overcomes the suspicions brought on by his daughter, and they have sex on the first night. Afterward, he accuses her of making love in a passionless manner, as if she were a "nigger slave I'd bought at auction" (2:944), to which she ferociously responds by telling of her affair with Brant, Marie Brantôme's son. This admittance causes his heart to fail, and instead of giving him his proper heart medicine, she gives him a poison that Brant had secured for the murder. Realizing too late what Christine has done, Ezra accuses her of murder. Lavinia is standing within earshot and thus discovers her mother's guilt and vows revenge.

**Mannon, Lavinia** Ezra and Christine Mannon's daughter, Orin Mannon's sister, and later Peter Niles's fiancée. In act 1 of the *Homecoming*, O'Neill describes Lavinia, or "Vinnie," as a tall, flat-chested, very thin 23-year-old who looks older, with an unattractively angular body accentuated by her stiff black dresses. She moves rigidly; talks in clipped, aggressive, military-style tones; and holds herself "*with a wooden, square-shouldered, military bearing*" (2:897). Although Lavinia and her mother, Christine Mannon, are dissimilar in most respects, they share the similar copper-colored hair, pale skin, dark violet-blue eyes, and "*the same sensual mouth, the same heavy jaw*"; upon first seeing her, as it is with all the Mannons, "*one is struck by the same strange, life-like mask impression her face gives in repose*" (2:897). Lavinia has always been considered her father's child, and she adores him with oedipal devotion. Her mother despises her daughter because Lavinia acts as a reminder of her loveless honeymoon, a portent of 20 sour years of marriage, during which Lavinia was conceived. Lavinia's brother, Orin Mannon, loves Lavinia, but primarily for her close approximation in appearance and occasional mannerism to their mother, whom he adores with an unnatural, oedipal devotion, as Lavinia does Ezra.

In act 1 of *The Homecoming*, Lavinia has heard rumors that Christine has been conducting an affair with a romantic sea captain named Adam Brant, whom Lavinia subconsciously also finds attractive, while her father, Ezra, is fighting as a brigadier general in the Union Army during the American Civil War. Meanwhile, she deflects an offer of marriage from the local veteran Peter Niles, who has loved her since adolescence, with the excuse that she must care for her father. When Lavinia confronts her mother about her affair, Christine admits that she loves Brant but warns Lavinia not to inform Ezra, who will arrive back at the Mannon home soon. Seth Beckwith, the Mannons' groundskeeper for 60 years, insinuates to Lavinia that Brant must be the son of Ezra's brother David Mannon and his wife, Marie Brantôme, a French Canadian nurse who caused a scandal by marrying David and bearing his child. When Brant arrives, Lavinia goads him into admitting the truth, and he informs her in a rage that Ezra had cut his father out of the family fortune and refused his mother money when she was starving. Marie died soon after, and he considers Ezra her murderer.

Ezra returns home in act 2 of *The Homecoming*. On the morning after his return, Lavinia hears him calling Christine a murderer: He suffered a heart attack after Christine admitted to her affair, then she administered a poison to him instead of his heart medicine. Discovering the vial in the room and realizing what her mother had done, Lavinia vows revenge. When Orin returns from the war to his father's funeral in act 1 of *The Hunted*, Lavinia informs him of their mother's pernicious role in their father's death and of her affair with Brant. For a time, Christine convinces her heartsick son that Lavinia is "actually insane" (2:969), but when Lavinia places the vial of poison on their father's dead chest while his body lies in its coffin, Orin witnesses Christine's shocked expression and realizes the truth. Convinced now of Christine's role in Ezra's death, Orin still sides with his mother, whom he adores, until Lavinia proves that Christine has been having an affair. Overwhelmed with jealousy, Orin kills Brant on a Boston wharf after the siblings overhear the lovers' plan to escape to the South Seas. News of Brant's death drives Christine to suicide, and Orin believes he has murdered their mother. Lavinia then convinces him that the best thing for them to do is sail to the South Seas and try to forget.

After returning from the voyage in act 1 of *The Haunted*, Lavinia has bizarrely adopted her mother's sensuality, mannerisms, and bearing, even styling her hair in the same way and dressing in the same green color her mother always wore, a stark contrast to Lavinia's previous preference for black. Orin mocks this change in his sister as the "influence of the 'dark and deep blue ocean'—and of the islands," but he finds himself unnaturally attracted to her resemblance to Christine (2:1,021). She believes that they should now settle down to a normal life, he with Hazel Niles and she with Peter Niles. He cruelly insinuates to Peter that Lavinia had a sexual encounter with a native man named Avahanni. Once Orin departs, she tells Peter that Orin was lying about Avahanni (which he was

not), but that it is true the islands "finished setting me free. There was something there mysterious and beautiful—a good spirit—of love—coming out of the land and the sea" that made her accept love, forget death, and believe in innocence (2:1,023). She kisses Peter passionately, which both arouses him and makes him extremely uncomfortable.

Orin cloisters himself in their father's study and composes a secret history of the sins of the Mannon clan, calling Lavinia "the most interesting criminal of all" (2:1,030). Her entreaties not to share the history lead her to speak to him with a *"deliberately evil taunting"* tone that reminds him again of their mother (2:1,031). Orin threatens to release the manuscript unless Lavinia agrees to do anything he wants, and she agrees. "That's a large promise," he says lustily, "anything!" (2:1,041). But then he pleads with her to let them confess to expiate their sins. At this display of weakness, she venomously shouts, "You'd kill yourself if you weren't a coward!" (2:1,042). Ultimately, he agrees that he will only find peace in death. Peter enters, Orin exits, and soon after a muffled shot can be heard from the study across the hall.

Aware of the manuscript, if unsure of what it contains, Hazel tries to convince Lavinia either to let her brother read what it contains or leave him alone. But Lavinia frantically attempts to persuade Peter to marry her in spite of the suicide. "Take me, Adam!" (2:1,052) she shouts (in what can only be characterized as a Freudian slip). At this point, she resigns herself to her fate. "Love isn't permitted to me," she tells Peter coolly, "The dead are too strong!" (2:1,052). In the trilogy's final scene, she assures Seth Beckwith that she will not commit suicide as her mother and brother had done. "That's escaping punishment. And there's no one left to punish me. I'm the last Mannon. I've got to punish myself!" (2:1,053). She orders Seth to nail tight the shutters and throw out all the flowers, then stands for a time at the mansion's portico. At the sound of a shutter banging closed, she turns sharply to the door and marches inside.

One of the most well-developed female characters in the O'Neill canon, Lavinia Mannon corresponds to the character Electra in Aeschylus's *Oresteia*, the daughter of Agamemnon (Ezra

Mannon) and Clytemnestra (Christine) and sister of Orestes (Orin). But her oedipal love of her father, which Electra shared, is compounded by her desire, like her mother, Christine, to rid herself of the Mannon curse and be free from puritanical notions of sin in love. As such, her mother's death avenges, to Lavinia's mind, both the murder of her father *and* Christine's co-optation of the romantic sea captain Adam Brant (Aegisthus), who symbolizes that freedom.

Lavinia's tragic fate demands that she be punished for her sins by eternal exile from those same freedoms. Her acceptance in the final scene is that she cannot, and should not, escape from the past sins of herself and her family. Shutting herself into the Mannon mansion is, in Virginia Floyd's words, "the supreme gesture of atonement" (1985, 403). Doomed to a life haunted by the Mannon past, a "living death," Lavinia is one of the greatest tragic figures in the O'Neill canon. O'Neill, however, believed the play would be a failure if the final scene evoked pity of any kind, which brings to mind the playwright's exaltation over tragedy and struggle as the only available means to attain a fulfilling, meaningful existence. "No one," he said of his Electra, "should feel sorry for her" (quoted in Alexander 168). Indeed, biographer Stephen A. Black draws a parallel—one "too intriguing to omit" from his discussion of the trilogy (2004, 186)—between the kind of clarity of mind Lavinia is destined to achieve and that of an actual New England self-exile, the New England poet Emily Dickinson, who locked herself away in her Amherst home with her sister, Lavinia. Dickinson went on to write some of the finest poems in American literature, works O'Neill, an avid reader of POETRY, must have read in the 1920s (Black 2004, 188).

**Mannon, Orin**  Lavinia Mannon's brother, Brigadier-General Ezra and Christine Mannon's son, Hazel Niles's potential fiancé, and a first lieutenant of the infantry in the Union Army during the American Civil War. Orin Mannon arrives at the Mannon home in *The Hunted*, though there is a great anticipation of his return in *The Homecoming*, especially by Christine Mannon, who strongly, almost incestuously, favors her son over her daughter, Lavinia. Orin was born while his father, Ezra, was fighting in the Mexican War, and Christine considers him more her son than her husband's, while Lavinia had always been more her father's daughter. As a result, Christine has always coddled him and treated Lavinia with cold indifference. But her affections for him waned when she began an affair with Captain Adam Brant, and she encourages him to pursue a marriage with the local girl Hazel Niles, contradicting her earlier disapproval of the proposed union.

Orin shares the same *"lifelike mask quality of his face in repose"* as his father and the rest of the Mannons, though his mouth, reminiscent of Eugene O'Neill's autobiographical avatar in *Long Day's Journey into Night*, *"gives an impression of tense oversensitiveness quite foreign to the General's"* (2:956–957). Orin returns home, embittered and war-weary, with no knowledge of his father's murder by Christine and Brant. Though he received word of his father's death, he exhibits little remorse; after the destruction he witnessed on the battlefield, he explains to Lavinia, "I hardened myself to expect my own death and everyone else's, and think nothing of it" (2:958). In *The Homecoming*, Ezra had referred to a brave act of Orin's that Orin, in *The Hunted*, describes as "a joke" (2:977). He had wandered toward the enemy line during a trench fight at St. Petersburg with his hand outstretched to shake hands with the enemy. He was shot in the head and went berserk with bloodlust. "Then a lot of our fools went crazy, too," he recounts sardonically, "and followed me and we captured a part of their line we hadn't dared tackle before" (2:977). During the war, a fellow soldier lent him *Typee* (1846), Herman Melville's novel of the South Seas, and the islands Melville describes "came to mean everything that wasn't war" to Orin, "everything that was peace and warmth and security" (2:972).

Lavinia insinuates to Orin that their mother was responsible for their father's death and that the rumors spreading in town about Christine's relationship with Adam Brant have merit. When Christine tries to preempt Orin from believing it, she informs him that Lavinia thinks she poisoned Ezra. Orin at first agrees with his mother that his sister must be "actually insane" (2:969) and reassures her of his loyalty to her. "I don't want Hazel or anyone," he says. "You're my only girl!" (2:972). But Christine remains terrified that Lavinia will convince him of the truth, fearing the vengeance Orin would inflict on Brant more than anything else. Lavinia convinces Orin to follow their mother to a secret liaison between their mother and Brant on Brant's ship, *Trade Winds*. When they witness Christine and Brant together on a wharf in Boston in act 4 of *The Hunted*, Orin waits until Christine has left, then shoots Brant dead in a jealous rage. Orin subsequently tells Christine he killed Brant and begs her to allow him to take Brant's place on her voyage for peace to the South Seas. Christine commits suicide soon after his admission. Emotionally crippled, Orin goes with his sister on a long voyage to Asia and the South Seas to escape the horrors of the Mannon home.

Upon their return in *The Haunted*, Lavinia, who has replaced their mother in manner and dress, believes that she and Orin should embrace Peter and Hazel Niles's love for them and live a conventional married life with them in peace and security. But Orin, calling to mind Theodore "Hickey" Hickman's view of his wife in *The ICEMAN COMETH*, believes that Hazel's "purity" makes him both "appear less vile to myself! . . . And, at the same time, a million times more vile" (2:1,028). Orin secretly writes a family history to expiate the crimes of the Mannon clan "to trace to its secret hiding place in the Mannon past the evil destiny behind our lives" (2:1,029), and he perceives in Lavinia "the most interesting criminal of us all" (2:1,030). Lavinia, horrified by what the manuscript might reveal, agrees to do anything Orin asks of her. He suggests they live together incestuously as lovers, saying, "I love you now with all the guilt in me—the guilt we share! Perhaps I love you too much, Vinnie!" (2:1,041). But when he reads the revulsion in her face, he changes tone and begs her to join him and confess to the murder. Lavinia shouts that she hates him and that if he were not such a coward, he would kill himself. Defeated by the rejection of both his mother and sister, Orin leaves the room as Peter enters and shoots himself with his pistol within their hearing.

Orin Mannon corresponds to the titular character Orestes in Aeschylus's *Oresteia*, the son of Agamemnon (Ezra Mannon) and Clytemnestra (Christine) and brother to Electra (Lavinia). He is largely distinguished from the mythic figure, however, by his apparent incapacity to comprehend what is expected of him by the gods or fate (Black 2004, 176). Orin also represents the tragic character of Oedipus, who unwittingly killed his father, King Laius, to marry his mother, Jocasta. The guilt Orin experiences from his killing in wartime and the horror Orin experiences at the betrayal of the most important women in his life—first Christine, then Lavinia—enables him to plumb the depths of the truth behind the Mannon facade, symbolized by his family history, and apprehend the uselessness of attempting to find peace in life, symbolized by his obsessive reading of Melville's South Seas tale. His central tragic characteristic, one that leads him to the brink of insanity, is his persistent soul-searching and conscious knowledge of the impossibility of peace and happiness in the world he was given. In this way, he more fully resembles William Shakespeare's tragic character Hamlet; as Stephen A. Black describes Orin's character, he is "deeply alienated from God, humanity and himself and seems at times paralyzed by knowing too much" (2004, 176).

**Minnie** Louisa Ames's cousin. Minnie, *"a plump little woman of forty, of the meek, eager-listener type, with a small round face, round stupid eyes, and a round mouth pursed out to drink in gossip,"* is one of the townspeople whom O'Neill describes as *"types of townsfolk rather than individuals, a chorus representing the town"*; she appears in the first act of *The Homecoming* merely to *"look and listen and spy on the rich and exclusive Mannons"* (2:894).

**Niles, Hazel** Captain Peter Niles's sister and Orin Mannon's potential fiancée in *The Haunted*. Hazel is a *"pretty, healthy girl of nineteen."* O'Neill writes: *"One gets a sure impression of her character at a glance—frank, innocent, amiable and good—not in a negative but in a positive, self-possessed way"* (2:899). Hazel has nurtured a desire to marry Orin Mannon since girlhood, but Christine Mannon, Orin's mother, has persistently, and incongruously to her children, spoken out against her and the ostensible union with her son. But once Christine begins a secret love affair with Captain Adam Brant, she changes her mind and applauds Hazel's character, unaccountably to Orin. In act 1 of *The Hunted* —in a scene suggestive of Mary Tyrone's drugged confessions and reminiscences of her past to her maid Kathleen in *Long Day's Journey into Night*— Christine encourages Hazel to marry Orin and admits she was once "innocent and loving and trusting" like Hazel, but all that changed after marrying Ezra Mannon (2:956).

In *The Haunted*, Orin returns with his sister, Lavinia Mannon, from a voyage in the South Seas and composes a secret history of the Mannon clan and its sinful past. He begs Hazel to hold it for him, never reading it unless Peter decides to marry Lavinia or Orin himself dies. He also agrees to move in with Hazel and her family, but he retracts the agreement once he coerces Lavinia not to marry Peter and stay with him instead. After Orin commits suicide, Hazel begs Lavinia, whom she now regards as an outright danger to her brother, to leave Peter alone, or at least tell him what Orin's manuscript contained.

Hazel symbolizes, as does her brother, Peter, the stark contrast between the wholesome New Englander—"the embodiment of simplicity, goodness, and health" (Alexander 152)—and the darker nature of the haunted Mannon clan. Her character corresponds to Hermione, Orestes' (Orin's) fiancée in the *Oresteia*. Her last name might be attributable to the fact that during the play's composition, O'Neill and Carlotta Monterey O'Neill were planning a trip to the Nile River in Egypt; in addition, Carlotta's given name was Hazel Tharsing (Alexander 163).

**Niles, Captain Peter** Hazel Niles's brother, Lavinia Mannon's fiancé in *The Haunted*, and an artillery captain in the Union Army during the American Civil War, where he was wounded in battle. Peter is 22 years old when introduced in *The Homecoming*, a "*straightforward, guileless and good-natured*" young New Englander who has timidly courted Lavinia since adolescence (2:899). In the

first scene of *The Homecoming*, Peter proposes to her, but Lavinia rejects him with the excuse that she must tend to her father, Ezra Mannon.

In act 1, scene 2, of *The Haunted*, after Lavinia returns from her sexually liberating voyage to the South Seas, she passionately kisses Peter and insists they marry immediately. Peter's mother and sister have warned him against her, both considering Lavinia's recent behavior too bold. Hazel has also been made aware of a mysterious manuscript that Orin had asked her to hold and read only if Peter and Lavinia were ever to marry. Though he at first damns their interference, Peter comes to question his judgment once Hazel informs him of Orin Mannon's secretive manuscript, which Orin insists Peter must read before marrying Lavinia. Peter ultimately rejects Lavinia's excessive sexual advances and burning desire to marry after she coarsely admits the truth of her dalliance with a South Seas native man named Arahanni. At one point, Lavinia accidentally shouts, "Take me, Adam!" (2:1,052), and she resigns herself to her fate.

Peter symbolizes, as does his sister, Hazel, the stark contrast between the wholesome New Englander—"the embodiment of simplicity, goodness, and health" (Alexander 152)—and the darker nature of the haunted Mannon clan. His character corresponds to Pylades, Electra's (Lavinia's) fiancé in the *Oresteia*. His last name might be attributable to the fact that during the play's composition, O'Neill and Carlotta Monterey O'Neill were planning a trip to the Nile River in Egypt (Alexander 163).

**Silva, Joe** A Portuguese fishing captain. Silva is 60 years old, "*a fat, boisterous man with a coarse bass voice. He has matted gray hair and a big grizzled mustache*" (2:1,007). In the opening scene of *The Haunted*, Silva is drunk, along with Amos Ames, Seth Beckwith, Ira Mackel, and Abner Small, and opens the scene singing a sea chanty. A wisecracking, foul-mouthed sailor, Silva encourages the lark played on Abner Small, wherein Small must remain in the Mannon home, which they all believe is haunted, until the moon comes up. Like all the townspeople in the trilogy, Silva is one of "*a chorus of types representing the town as a human background for the drama of the Mannons*" (2:1,007).

**Small, Abner** A hardware store clerk. Small is 65 years old, *"a wiry little old man"* with a white goatee, *"bright inquisitive eyes, ruddy complexion, and a shrill rasping voice"* (2:1,007). In the opening scene of *The Haunted*, Small is drunk, along with Amos Ames, Seth Beckwith, Ira Mackel, and Joe Silva. Small accepts a bet with Seth for 10 dollars and a gallon of liquor to remain in the Mannon home, which they all believe is haunted, until the moon comes up. Small loses the bet and rushes out the front door in terror after mistaking the portrait of Ezra Mannon for a ghost. Like all the townspeople in the trilogy, Small is one of *"a chorus of types representing the town as a human background for the drama of the Mannons"* (2:1,007).

## BIBLIOGRAPHY

Alexander, Doris. *Eugene O'Neill's Creative Struggle: The Decisive Decade, 1924–1933.* University Park: Pennsylvania State University Press, 1992.

Atkinson, Brooks. "Tragedy Becomes Electra," *New York Times,* November 1, 1931. Reprinted in Houchin, John H., ed. *The Critical Response to Eugene O'Neill,* edited by John H. Houchin, 105–117, 126–129. Westport, Conn.: Greenwood Press, 1993.

Benchley, Robert. "The Theatre: Top." In *The Critical Response to Eugene O'Neill,* edited by John H. Houchin, 129–131. Westport, Conn.: Greenwood, 1993.

Black, Stephen A. *Eugene O'Neill: Beyond Mourning and Tragedy.* New Haven, Conn.: Yale University Press, 1999.

———. "*Mourning Becomes Electra* as a Greek Tragedy." *Eugene O'Neill Review* 26 (2004): 167–188.

Bogard, Travis. *Contour in Time: The Plays of Eugene O'Neill.* Rev. ed. New York: Oxford University Press, 1988.

Clark, Barrett H. *Eugene O'Neill: The Man and His Plays.* Rev. ed. New York: Dover, 1947.

Falk, Doris V. *Eugene O'Neill and the Tragic Tension: An Interpretive Study of the Plays.* New Brunswick, N.J.: Rutgers University Press, 1958.

Floyd, Virginia. *The Plays of Eugene O'Neill: A New Assessment.* New York: Ungar, 1985.

Floyd, Virginia, ed. *Eugene O'Neill at Work: Newly Released Ideas for His Plays.* New York: Ungar, 1981.

Sheaffer, Louis. *O'Neill: Son and Artist.* Boston: Little, Brown, 1973.

Vidal, Gore. "Theatre." *Nation* (October 25, 1958). Reprinted in *The Critical Response to Eugene O'Neill,* edited by John H. Houchin, 234–236. Westport, Conn.: Greenwood Press, 1993.

# *Movie Man: A Comedy in One Act, The* (completed 1914; first produced, 1959)

*The Movie Man* was first produced at the Key Theatre in New York City on October 27, 1959, six years after Eugene O'Neill's death. This one-act play was once considered irretrievably lost by early O'Neill chronicler Barrett H. Clark. It is the final of nine plays O'Neill wrote in his first year of writing seriously, 1914. Two years later, the summer O'Neill was introduced to the PROVINCETOWN PLAYERS, he revised it with a new plot and then used that plot for a short story entitled "The SCREENEWS OF WAR," which was published for the first time in 2007 in *Resources for American Literary Study.* The revised version was probably the first play idea O'Neill pitched to the players (Dowling 173). Like the vaudeville sketch *A WIFE FOR A LIFE,* written the previous year, O'Neill most likely conceived of it as a moneymaker. Based on a 1914 Hollywood venture with Pancho Villa during the Mexican Revolution, *The Movie Man* experiments with numerous theatrical devices and themes O'Neill would employ in his more mature work, including experimentation with dialect writing—specifically American slang and broken English with a foreign accent—along with highly detailed STAGE DIRECTIONS and a cynical view of American foreign relations and commercialism.

## SYNOPSIS

A flea-infested adobe shack strewn with rifles, ammunition, and Christian iconography located somewhere in a *"suburb of a large town in Northern Mexico"* (1:223). Two representatives of the Earth Motion Picture Company—Henry "Hen" Rogers, a movie producer, and Al Devlin, his cameraman—are lounging in the foreground. They are dressed like two colonials on a lark, with khaki shirts, riding breeches, and puttees. Stetson cowboy hats are lying on a table beside them. A Mexican sentry drowsily watches over them as Rogers complains about the heat and fleas. The "large town" in question (Ciudad Juárez? Chihuahua?) will soon come under attack by a division of Mexican revolutionaries led by a ruthless incompetent named Pancho Gomez, commander in chief of the Constitutionalist Army. In return for liquor, soldiers of fortune, artillery, and guns, Gomez has consented that they may film his battles. The catch for Gomez, negotiated by contract, is that the battles must take place in camera-friendly daylight so they can shoot a movie about the war.

In the opening scene, Rogers and Devlin confabulate in an American vernacular so thoroughly overblown that O'Neill was clearly poking fun at the typical Hollywood type of the 1910s: "You ought to have seen the bear I lamped this afternoon"; "And I suppose you copped her and dated her up?"; "I wouldn't trust one of these dolls as far as I could hit Walter Johnson's fastball" (1:226–227); etc. Devlin complains that at one recent battle, a division general of Gomez's named Luis Virella ordered his men to charge before Devlin could set up his movie camera. "Shall my glorious soldiers," Virella had responded to Devlin's protests, "be massacred waiting for your machine?" Rogers voices his own disapproval of the general and tells Devlin that Virella is the one who wishes a fellow revolutionary but also a sworn enemy named Ernesto Fernandez to be shot as a traitor. Both men express respect for Fernandez, who attended a college in the United States, "Cornell or someplace" (1:225). The execution is scheduled for the following morning, and Devlin tells Rogers to make sure to instruct Gomez to delay the execution until eight o'clock, when the light will be better for filming, and Rogers agrees.

In the adjacent room, Gomez and his men can be heard shouting "Viva!" (1:226). Rogers and Devlin discuss the merits and shortcomings of Mexican women (all remarks racial in nature). Devlin tells of a particularly good-looking "dame" he saw cry-ing on a park bench, though she gave him an "icy once-over" when he tried to console her. Devlin exits, and Anita Fernandez quietly appears at the doorway. *"A beautiful young Mexican girl with a mass of black hair and great black eyes"* (1:227), Anita trips over a saddle, which wakes up the sentry; he grabs her violently and begins to drag her back outside. When Rogers orders him to stop, the sentry releases her and resumes his position. Rogers quickly takes up in his Spanish-English dictionary to ask her what she wants. In broken English, Anita entreats Rogers to arrange an audience with Gomez, but Rogers tells her that Gomez and Virella have been drinking Scotch all afternoon and are dangerously drunk. Some farcical dialogue ensues. Rogers: "He'll be all lit up like a torch tonight . . . You know what I mean—he's soused, pickled, stewed, boiled—." Anita: "You mean he is cooking—the General?" (1:228). She informs him she is Fernandez's daughter and insists she will save her father's life even if she must give her body to Gomez. Rogers vows to save him "if I have to start a revolution of my own to do it" (1:229).

Gomez and Virella enter. They are boisterously intoxicated, and Virella moves toward Anita *"with a drunken leer on his flushed face"* (1:230). Rogers grabs him by the shoulders, thrusts him toward the door, and commands him to leave. Virella fights back, but Rogers convinces Gomez to order him out, which he does. Virella reluctantly obeys but shouts curses and threats at Rogers on his way out. Gomez sees Anita and compliments Rogers for his ability with the ladies. Rogers introduces her as Fernandez's daughter, and Anita throws herself at the general's feet. Gomez at first refuses to free Fernandez, but when he announces his plan for a victorious nighttime raid on the nearby town, Rogers reminds him of his contract that battles must be fought in daylight and reads the clause aloud: "The party of the second part hereby agrees to fight no battles at night or on rainy days or at any time whatsoever when the light is so poor as to make the taking of motion pictures impracticable. Failure to comply with these conditions will constitute a breach of contract and free the party of the first part from all the obligations entered into by this contract" (1:232).

Rogers promises to turn a blind eye if Gomez liberates Anita's father. When the general threatens that he might have Rogers himself shot, Rogers retorts, "Nix on that rough stuff! You wouldn't dare. You've got to keep on the right side of the U.S.A. or your revolution isn't worth the powder to blow it to—Mexico" (1:232). Faced with the stipulations of the Hollywood contract, Gomez has no choice but to free Fernandez; he must execute Virella instead, since Virella would kill Fernandez himself. Gomez takes a swig from his flask, drunkenly bows to Rogers and Anita, and departs to prepare for the raid that night. Anita passionately thanks Rogers and asks him to join her and her father at their hacienda the following day, "As a brother, my father's son" (1:233). Rogers hints he is interested in more than a sibling relationship with her, and she demurely replies, "Quien sabe, senor? Who knows?" then rushes out the door (1:233). Rogers does a little victory dance, and the sentry smiles contemptuously and calls him "loco" (crazy; 1:234). Rogers good-naturedly agrees and begins singing "Mexico, my bright-eyed Mexico." Devlin returns, complaining he was ignored once more by the same Mexican woman, whom we now know was Anita. To save face, Devlin remarks that she "isn't much to look at after all" (1:234). Rogers at first takes offense, then cheers up at the thought of Anita and continues to sing. The sentry grunts in disgust as Devlin *"gapes at him in open-mouthed amazement,"* and the curtain falls.

## COMMENTARY

In early spring 1913 the radical journalist JOHN REED dramatically recounted tales of his work as a war correspondent during the Mexican insurrection to the bohemian patrons of Polly's Restaurant in GREENWICH VILLAGE. O'Neill was almost certainly inspired by Reed's stories to write *The Movie Man* (Gelb 429). His puerile story, though intended to throw light on the arbitrary cruelties and selfish motivations of war, mostly reads like a Damon Runyon (author of *Guys and Dolls*) skit gone very bad. From bad Runyon it moves to the condescending ethnocentricity of John Luther Long's *Madame Butterfly*, as Rogers aggressively pursues the "exotic" Mexican beauty Anita Fernandez. *The*

*Movie Man* might be taken as a farce, a type of literature designed to evoke "belly laughs," in the parlance of farcical theater; however, it is more clearly a satire, a form of comedy meant to provoke social change, and O'Neill also lists the play in his WORK DIARY as a "satire" (Floyd 1981, 389).

*The Movie Man* puts forth an anticommercialization, antiwar message targeting the steps Hollywood companies will take to make money off their films, along with the outrages Mexican armies committed on all sides of the civil war, by all accounts a perplexing conflict to American onlookers. There was, in fact, a ludicrous Hollywood deal, brokered by Frank M. Thayer of the Mutual Film Corporation, between that studio and the revolutionary Pancho Villa, in which Villa was offered 20 percent of the film's profits to allow cameramen to follow him and his band on rebel raids against the Mexican army. D. W. Griffith, the famous Hollywood filmmaker, was involved on some level as well. Villa accepted, and a Hollywood crew was sent down to film the battles, though there was no stipulation that Villa stage his battles during the daytime. At one point, legend has it, Villa bombarded a hillside stocked with star-crossed extras, prisoners from the Mexican army, who were blown apart for dramatic effect—probably another myth proliferated by the sensational American press. Entitled *The Life of Villa*, this perverse film was eventually completed, but there was some question as to who owned the rights, and it never appeared in the theaters (Gelb 429).

O'Neill probably read this play to the Provincetown Players in the summer of 1916, but according to an account by the poet Harry Kemp, the plot was the same as that found in "The Screenews of War," a short story O'Neill wrote in late September or early October 1916, that went unpublished in his lifetime. Kemp's recollection mentions the Mexican Revolution and Hollywood filmmakers but recounts the plot of "Screenews" rather than the surviving copyrighted version of *The Movie Man*, "a play that was frightfully bad, trite and full of the most preposterous hokum. It was, as I remember, something about an American movie man who financed a Mexican revolution for the sake of filming its battles. One of the scenes depicted the hero's compelling the commanding generals on both sides—both being in his hire—to wage a battle all over again because it had not been fought the way he liked it!" (96)

Never produced in O'Neill's lifetime, this one-act curiosity has been performed at least twice since its 1959 premiere. Commenting on the 1982 production of three of O'Neill's "lost plays," *A Wife for a Life, The Movie Man,* and *The WEB,* O'Neill critic Frederick C. Wilkins declared that "the jokes, if jokes they are, are woefully weak, and the performers lacked the necessary lightness and fleetness to blind us to the inadequacies of the script. . . . *The Movie Man,* I fear, should return to a well-deserved oblivion. I doubt that even abler players could bring it to life." The play finally enjoyed a very successful production, however, along with *The Web,* BEFORE BREAKFAST, ILE, and O'Neill's late tribute to his Dalmatian "The Last Will and Testament of Silverdene Emblem O'Neill" (1940; played as a dramatic monologue) at New York's Metropolitan Playhouse in late 2007.

## CHARACTERS

**Devlin, Al**   A middle-aged photographer for the Earth Motion Picture Company. Al is Henry Rogers's cameraman, who cynically waits for executions and battles to film without a care for the victims. He is more fully a racist than his producer, Henry Rogers, though they both show disdain for the Mexican population. Devlin is obsessed with "native" Mexican women, though his advances, including one toward Anita Fernandez, always prove unsuccessful. In one of his final lines, which sums up his character, he rails against a rebuff from one Mexican girl by saying, "Some nerve to that greaser chicken giving a real white man the foot!" (1:234)

**Fernandez, Anita**   The daughter of a Mexican revolutionary—possibly modeled on Venustiano Carranza, the president of Mexico after the revolution (Floyd 1985, 77n)—scheduled to be executed by Pancho Gomez and Luis Virella. Anita is *"a beautiful young Mexican girl with a mass of black hair and great black eyes"* (1:227). She arrives in the hut reserved for the Earth Motion Picture Company

employees, Henry Rogers and Al Devlin, to plead for her father's life. Moved by her story, though more probably charmed by her exotic good looks, Rogers saves her father's life by allowing Gomez to perform a night attack against his enemies, which a contract between the general and the Hollywood studio expressly forbids, in return for Anita's father. Anita is a privileged Mexican woman who studied for a time at a convent school in New York. Her accent and broken English, along with the clear contrast in manners between her and the coarse movie men, is meant to add humor to the dialogue.

**Gomez, Pancho**   The commander in chief of the Constitutionalist Army. Gomez is based on the actual, flashy Mexican revolutionary from the 1910s, the ex-cattle rustler Pancho Villa, who in 1913, one year before O'Neill composed the piece, led a highly effective band of mercenaries in alliance with Emiliano Zapata against the military dictatorship of General Victoriano Huerta. One year later, Woodrow Wilson, then president of the United States, sent in the American military to depose Huerta's corrupt regime. In *The Movie Man,* Gomez has signed a contract with the fictional Earth Motion Picture Company that stipulates, among other things, that he can only stage attacks in daylight so that Al Devlin, the photographer, can film them successfully. Gomez is planning to execute Anita Fernandez's father, but after Anita begs Henry Rogers to save his life, Rogers discovers that Gomez is planning a night attack. In a somewhat romantic but more libidinous gesture, Rogers uses that breach of contract as leverage to help Anita's father. Gomez agrees to release Fernandez and decides to execute his general, Luis Virella, instead, since Virella will object to Fernandez's release.

**Rogers, Henry (Hen)**   A representative of the Earth Motion Picture Company. Rogers is a stereotypical movie producer—loud, arrogant, petty, only interested in sensual pleasures and the bottom line—who has brokered a contract with General Pancho Gomez, a Mexican revolutionary not-so-loosely based on the real-life Mexican Civil War revolutionary Pancho Villa; a case of Scotch went to Gomez upon signing to sweeten the deal. One clause of the contract stipulates that any battles Gomez plans must take place during the daytime in order for Rogers's cameraman, Al Devlin, to film the event. When Anita Fernandez arrives at their suburban headquarters outside an unnamed Mexican city, Rogers sees an opportunity for romance with a "native" girl. She tells Rogers that Gomez and his general, Luis Virella, who is her father's sworn enemy, plan to execute her father at sunrise the following day. Rogers calls for a meeting with Gomez, who is planning a night attack on the city, and informs him that he may go ahead with his plan in breach of contract if he frees Anita's father. Though Rogers's deal smacks of redemption for his arrogant colonialism, the quid pro quo he expects—that Anita will return the favor with sex—is far from certain. Upon her departure, she invites Rogers to visit her and her father at their hacienda the following day as "a brother" "Only—a brother?" he asks. "Quien sabe, senor? Who knows?" (1:233). By the final scene, the helpless "native" girl is ironically in control.

**Virella, Luis** General of a division of the Constitutionalist Army. Virella is a sworn enemy of Anita Fernandez's father, who is scheduled to be executed. Once Pancho Gomez agrees to release him, Gomez understands that he must kill Virella, who would no doubt try to supersede his order, and "Mexico ees too es-small for those two hombres—both alive" (1:233).

### BIBLIOGRAPHY

Floyd, Virginia. *The Plays of Eugene O'Neill: A New Assessment.* New York: Ungar, 1985.

———, ed. *Eugene O'Neill at Work: Newly Released Ideas for His Plays.* New York: Ungar, 1981.

Gelb, Arthur, and Barbara Gelb. *O'Neill: Life with Monte Cristo.* New York: Applause Books, 2000.

Kemp, Harry. "Out of Provincetown: A Memoir of Eugene O'Neill." *Theatre Magazine* 51 (April 1930): 22–23. Reprinted in *Conversations with Eugene O'Neill,* edited by Mark W. Estrin, 95–102. Jackson: University Press of Mississippi, 1990.

O'Neill, Eugene. "'The Screenews of War': A Previously Unpublished Short Story by Eugene O'Neill."

Edited with an introduction by Robert M. Dowling. *Resources for American Literary Study* 31 (Fall 2007): 169–198.

Wilkins, Frederick C. "Three Lost Plays of Eugene O'Neill." *Eugene O'Neill Newsletter* (Winter 1982). Available online. URL: http://www.eoneill.com/library/newsletter/vi_3/vi-3i.htm. Accessed June 30, 2007.

# *Now I Ask You: A Play in Three Acts, a Prologue, and an Epilogue* (completed, 1916; never produced)

Eugene O'Neill commenced writing what he called his "Three Act Farce-Comedy" *Now I Ask You* in Provincetown, Massachusetts, during the summer of 1916, and he copyrighted it the following spring (May 23, 1917). The composition took place during the now-legendary summer in which O'Neill's vagabond friend TERRY CARLIN introduced him to the PROVINCETOWN PLAYERS, and *BOUND EAST FOR CARDIFF*, the one-act play that launched O'Neill's career as a serious playwright, premiered at Provincetown's WHARF THEATRE. O'Neill critic Virginia Floyd notes that *Now I Ask You*'s uplifting tone "reflects his cheerful, almost happy, frame of mind" at the time (109). All the same, O'Neill was then broke and wrote this plot-driven farce to be a moneymaker. Never taking it seriously, in summer 1918, he encouraged his second wife, AGNES BOULTON, to rework it herself. "It's not my sort of stuff," he told her, "but it's a damned good idea for a popular success. Take it and use it if you can—it needs something to be done to it, and you might be able to fix it up. Either a novel, or even a better play than it is now" (quoted in Boulton 192). O'Neill seems to have made this suggestion in exchange for co-opting her idea for a short story, "The Captain's Walk," and turning it into his own one-act play, *WHERE THE CROSS IS MADE*. She initially declined the offer though later attempted revisions (around 1920–21) as a "stimulus" for her own work (in

Bogard 58n). Nothing came of it, and as far as anyone knows, the play has never been produced.

The story of a middle-class young woman affected by Greenwich Village radicalism, *Now I Ask You* reflects O'Neill's and the Provincetown Players' view that bohemianism had been co-opted by affluent would-be radicals attempting to escape from bourgeois ennui. In the same year, SUSAN GLASPELL, O'Neill's friend and the only other Provincetowner to gain national recognition as a playwright, wrote a similar indictment of the rage in Freudian psychoanalysis in her play *Suppressed Desires*, and Neith Boyce and JOHN REED wrote similar satires on free love, *Constancy* and *The Eternal Quadrangle*, respectively. The latter play appears to indicate that Reed knew of O'Neill's affair in 1916 with his fiancée, LOUISE BRYANT, and "could handle it" (Gelb 571). Indeed, since O'Neill wrote *Now I Ask You* during the affair as well, it appears that both men were relatively unworried about the love triangle. The *Boston Sunday Post* reported on this phenomenon in summer 1916 with an article entitled "Many Literary Lights Among Provincetown Players," wherein the journalist called the players "the Last Word in Modernity" and commented that "the Provincetown Players are so modern that they not only write about modern things but satirize them" (quoted in Gelb 573).

## SYNOPSIS

### Prologue
The Draytons' library in their suburban home 30 minutes from Manhattan by train (probably either Croton-on-Hudson or Hastings-on-Hudson). French windows look out to the driveway in front of the house. The room is dark aside from light coming in through the hallway door on left. Lucy Drayton (née Ashleigh) cautiously enters from a door on the right that leads to a separate room. Seeing no one there, she hurls herself into a chair and cries quietly to herself. She stands up, nervously paces the room, and stops at a table. Opening its drawer, she removes a pistol and fearfully places the weapon down in front of her. Outside a car arrives in the driveway, its headlamps illuminating the scene. Lucy rushes back into the room at right and closes a set of portieres behind her. A chauffer and

maid can be heard in the hallway. Tom Drayton, Lucy's husband, calls down from upstairs, and the maid informs him his car has arrived. Tom enters the room with Leonora Barnes. Tom softly calls for Lucy; hearing no answer, Leonora speculates that she is probably with Gabriel Adams. Tom curses under his breath, and they depart. Lucy reemerges and takes up the revolver. She points it to her temple as the curtains begin to fall. The instant they close, there comes the deafening sound of a gunshot.

### Act 1
June, about four months prior to the action of the prologue; the Ashleighs' living room in an elegant apartment near Manhattan's Gramercy Park. The décor is old-fashioned but also contains a *"half-humorously protesting modern touch"* (1:403). It is about 8:30 on a warm June evening. The Ashleighs are seated at a large oak table. Richard Ashleigh, Lucy's father, is trying to read a newspaper, but his irritation over his daughter's behavior makes concentration impossible. Lucy had just attended an anarchists' meeting in which a woman lecturer called for birth-control rights (the offstage character is most likely based on the anarchist activist EMMA GOLDMAN). Mr. Ashleigh, a stalwart member of the Victorian class, is scandalized by his daughter's "attacks of insane faddism" (1:403). Mrs. Ashleigh, in contrast, is highly tolerant of her daughter's dalliances in radicalism and pokes fun at her husband's outdated views. "She is tomorrow, I am today, and you, my dear Dick, are yesterday" (1:404). Through exposition, we discover that Lucy is to be married the following day to Tom Drayton, a young businessman whom they approve of as a "clean, wholesome young American" (1:404). But the match is complicated by Lucy's various and ephemeral pursuits in playwriting, music, poetry, sculpture, psychoanalysis, and mysticism, depending on the fashion of the moment.

A bell rings, and the maid enters to announce the arrival of Leonora Barnes, a good friend of Lucy's from her radical GREENWICH VILLAGE circle. Mrs. Ashleigh convinces her husband to settle his dispute with Lucy, and he exits to do so. Leonora, or "Leo," has come with a new painting of hers to offer Lucy as a wedding gift; as a thoroughly modern woman, however, she does not approve of the institution and considers love a "mid-Victorian sentimentality" and marriage strictly "for propagation" (1:408). Leonora, along with Lucy and the rest of their friends, are advocates of "free love," a popular belief among the early moderns that monogamy restricts self-realization. She proudly presents her abstract painting—which she calls "The Great Blond Beast" after a line from the German individualist philosopher FRIEDRICH NIETZSCHE—and Mrs. Ashleigh manages some kind remarks.

Tom Drayton enters. Leonora flirts with him, and after brazenly announcing her plan to uncover what lies beneath his staid exterior, she cheerily departs. Mrs. Ashleigh and Tom, obviously at ease with one another, discuss his future with Lucy. They talk over Lucy's modernist faddishness as if Lucy were a child who should be humored, but Mrs. Ashleigh adds that Tom must always convincingly pretend to take Lucy's "rainbow chasing" seriously if he wants her to be happy (1:411). She assures him that "its [sic] only a step to return to reason," and he agrees to become a convert to whatever "ism" Lucy foists on him (1:412). Mr. Ashleigh reenters, and the three of them disparage Leonora's painting. Mr. Ashleigh informs them that Lucy is upstairs reading a "trashy" Russian novel (actually Nietzsche) and has told him she has decided not to go through with the wedding (1:413). Tom is shocked by this news. Mrs. Ashleigh calms him with a furtive look reminding him of their agreement.

Lucy enters, pretentiously acting the tragic, misunderstood heroine: "There is so much turmoil in my soul," she says and compares herself to AUGUST STRINDBERG's daughter of Indra (from *A Dream Play*) since they both believe the truth lies in understanding that "life is horrible" (1:414). She is delighted with Leonora's painting but criticizes her friend condescendingly as having "perfect" technique but an "old-fashioned" method (1:415). She confirms Mr. Ashleigh's announcement with the rationale that "my highest duty is toward myself, and my ego demands freedom" (1:416), and she quotes Nietzsche's withering comments on marriage. Mrs. Ashleigh, to the surprise of Lucy and her father, agrees with Lucy and encourages her

to cancel the wedding. Lucy asks Tom if he would consider living together as "free spirits, comrades who have no other claims upon each other than what our hearts dictate" (1:418). With a significant look from Mrs. Ashleigh, he consents to her proposal. Mr. Ashleigh is scandalized once again and storms out in a rage. Unflustered, Mrs. Ashleigh continues to encourage Lucy's plan but adds that the marriage ceremony would be a great lark, "merely a formula which you can take with as many grains of salt as you please" (1:419). Lucy protests in spite of herself, but the matter seems settled. Lucy has also drawn up a contract, which she runs to get from her room. Upon her return, Mrs. Ashleigh exits to give them privacy. Lucy reads through the terms of their union—no children, free love, independent bank accounts, etc.—and Tom consents to them all. They both sign the contract, and he departs, disingenuously agreeing with his fiancée that the actual wedding ceremony will be a bore.

## Act 2

Same as the prologue; three months after act 1, but this time O'Neill adds that two paintings "*in the Synchromist manner*" are hung prominently on the walls—a detail that signifies Lucy's unorthodox taste in art. Lucy and Mrs. Ashleigh are discovered. Lucy chastises her mother for reading popular magazines and declares that if she acquired a "vital purpose" her mind would be better occupied (1:424). Mrs. Ashleigh refuses to yield to her daughter's "stern principles" now that she is Mrs. Tom Drayton. The two discuss Gabriel Adams, a poet friend of Lucy's, and his relationship with Leonora. Lucy, obviously infatuated with Gabriel, or more precisely with the idea of him, applauds the fact that he and Leonora live together outside of wedlock "in free comradeship" (1:425). Tom enters and teases Lucy for still pining "for the stuffy studios of Greenwich Village" (1:426). "I don't like weather which is so glaring and sunshiny," she complains after Tom goes off to work. "Nature makes too vulgar a display of it's [sic] kind intentions" (1:427). Like the title character of HENRIK IBSEN's *Hedda Gabler*, a play Lucy has seen repeatedly, she feels bored and "cramped in" in her domesticity. She even implies that she might share the heroine's suicidal tendencies. Mrs. Ashleigh kids her by quoting Ibsen, saying, "You'll be longing for someone to come 'with vine leaves in his hair'" (1:427). Lucy insinuates that Gabriel might be that someone. Her mother then tells her pointedly that Leonora described Tom as her Nietzschean "Great Blond Beast" (1:428). Lucy tries to conceal her agitation, and they go outside for a walk.

Gabriel and Leonora enter. Gabriel finds the suburban home soulless, and it becomes clear that the only reason the couple humors Lucy with frequent visits is for free food. An argument ensues between them in which Gabriel accuses Leonora's cooking of being like her paintings, "difficult to absorb," while she calls his poetry "sentimental journalism" (1:430). They turn on each other and exchange vicious epithets. Leonora enjoys the argument but warns laughingly that they must be careful not to let the family hear them, as "the dignity of free love is at stake." She adds suggestively, "If they only knew" (1:432). Gabriel hushes her, and their conversation turns to Tom and Lucy. Gabriel thinks Lucy is attractive, though he finds her conversation dull and is sick of playing the *Hedda Gabler* role of "the drunken gentleman with the vine leaves in his hair, whatever his name is" (1:432; the character's name is Eilert Løvborg). Leonora in her turn condemns Lucy's outmoded appreciation for Ibsen and again refers to Tom, pitying his marriage to her, as the "Blond Beast" (1:432). Gabriel contends that his flirtation with Lucy is a professional necessity, like all the women he seduces. Leonora responds that she might try her hand with Tom. This sends Gabriel into a jealous rage, which Leonora dismisses out of hand.

Lucy comes in from the garden, and Leonora cheerfully goes out to find Mrs. Ashleigh. After a barrage of pretentious romancing, Gabriel takes her hand and kisses it passionately, which frightens Lucy. Tom enters without warning and takes in the scene. Gabriel escapes to the garden with the pretense of finding Leonora. Lucy shows no outward signs of contrition; in fact, she defends her right to free love as it was stipulated in their marriage contract. Tom threatens to take advantage of his own freedom, which clearly displeases Lucy, but she maintains her pose and exits.

Mrs. Ashleigh appears. Tom relates what he saw and admits that he and Lucy just had their first marital spat. She comforts him that arguments are normal in marriage and that over time they will seem like "mere puffs of wind ruffling the surface" (1:440). She also scolds him for making a stink over Gabriel's attentions, as Lucy will now make the poet her "leading issue" (1:441). But she has a revelation that his threat to pursue his own affair will turn Lucy around. They plot for him to make overtures toward Leonora, who is already flirtatious with him, a ruse that includes the added advantage of exacting revenge on Gabriel.

Leonora rushes into the room and asks if she can use the bath. Tom complains that he has an engagement with Lucy to attend a concert that afternoon, and Leonora suggests she take him to an exhibition instead and go out for absinthe afterwards. (Absinthe is a narcotic-strength liqueur then illegal in the United States.) After a pause, he accepts. She then asks him to bow his head, and she coquettishly runs her fingers through his hair. Lucy appears at the window and looks on jealously. Leonora skips off to the bath, and Tom laughs off the event when Lucy enters. She is obviously jealous but maintains her facade of indifference. Tom tells her to take Gabriel to the concert instead of him and then of the plans he made with Leonora.

Gabriel enters with Mrs. Ashleigh and, fearing retribution for flirting with Lucy, stands far from Tom. Tom announces their plans, and Gabriel hesitates but agrees to accompany Lucy. The maid enters and announces lunch. First Lucy and then Gabriel say they will retrieve Leonora from the bath. Tom insists he will instead, which visibly irritates the other two. Leonora runs in wearing Tom's bathrobe and demands soap.

### Act 3

One month later; same as act 2 at about seven o'clock in the evening. Leonora is chattering away at Tom, erratically flopping down in chairs, glancing out the window, and pacing the floor. She tries to cheer him up with assurances that Gabriel is no rival to him, as "[Gabriel's] in love with himself and there's not a rival in sight" (1:448). Lucy, Gabriel, and Mrs. Ashleigh appear. Mrs. Ashleigh is all smiles, but Lucy and Gabriel are both livid to see Tom and Leonora together. Leonora suggests they all see a burlesque. Gabriel bows out with the excuse of an engagement, Lucy claims she has a headache, and Mrs. Ashleigh ultimately declines as well. They all go out to find Leonora a dress, leaving Gabriel fuming in jealousy. Lucy reemerges. She now evidently finds Gabriel tiresome and sees through his phony overtures of love. Gabriel expresses outrage over the affair Tom and Leonora seem to be conducting under their noses. Lucy fatuously retorts that Tom is "free to do as he chooses" (1:456), but Gabriel laughs at her naiveté and persuades her that the "harmless flirtation" is something more serious. Gabriel confesses that he loves Leonora and depends on her to protect him. He believes Lucy does not feel the same way about her husband since she loves *him*, but she snaps back, "And does your conceit make you think I took you seriously—had fallen in love with you? Oh, this is too disgusting!" (1:458). Gabriel then lets slip that he and Leonora are, in fact, married, and they only pretended to be single to impress their Greenwich Village friends. Laughing hysterically at this, Lucy chases him out but starts sobbing when he is gone.

Mrs. Ashleigh arrives. When Lucy recounts Gabriel's suspicions, Mrs. Ashleigh comes clean about the plan to make her jealous. Lucy does not believe her, and when Tom enters, she strides haughtily into the adjoining room. Tom lays the blame for his swiftly crumbling marriage on Mrs. Ashleigh. Leonora bounds into the room in a dress of Lucy's that has been pinned up to fit her. She ties Tom's tie for him, slaps him *"roguishly"* (1:464), and skips out of the room to put on "beauty spots." Mrs. Ashleigh turns out the light, and she and Tom exit. Lucy reenters, and precisely the same action takes place as that of the prologue.

*Epilogue*
Three minutes elapse before the curtain rises. Lucy is standing there, quivering in fright. She drops to the floor in a heap. Tom and Leonora come in, and Leonora rushes over to Lucy. Tom switches on the light and picks up the gun, staring at it *"with an expression of dazed stupefaction"* (1:467). Gabriel

appears outside the windows and joins them. Tom shouts that she must have shot herself, but Leonora assures them there is no entry wound. Tom opens the revolver and looks in the chamber; with a smile, he says that the gun is never loaded. Leonora dabs Lucy's face with water, and Lucy slowly regains consciousness. Gabriel asks if she attempted suicide because of his accusations about Tom and Leonora. When she nods her head, Gabriel assures her that it was all nonsense. Lucy runs into Tom's arms. Leonora demands a kiss from Gabriel, who assents grudgingly. The chauffer enters carrying a flat tire, and they all burst out laughing when they realize the tire caused the sound of the report. Referencing Ibsen's *Hedda Gabler,* in which the heroine commits suicide with her father's gun, Leonora dramatically points at the gun and shouts, "General Gabbler's [sic] pistol! Fancy that, Hedda!" (1:468).

## COMMENTARY

*Now I Ask You*—a play Virginia Floyd refers to as a "rare respite in the somber O'Neill canon" (110)—looks ahead to O'Neill's only major comedy, AH, WILDERNESS!, which also treats a misguided young bohemian, Richard Miller, rebelling in the suffocating milieu of bourgeois respectability. And like *Ah, Wilderness!,* this play departs from O'Neill's often romanticized portraits of artistic integrity and modern individualism—the Poet in FOG, John Brown in BREAD AND BUTTER, and Stephen Murray in *The STRAW* are some early examples. Rather, O'Neill emphasizes the pretentiousness of a young middle-class woman's desperate bid to undercut her conventional upbringing by naively embracing modernist fads such as free love, psychoanalysis, futuristic art, and anarchism. When she must face the consequences of these beliefs, most evidently free love, she finds that her innately conventional self overwhelms her superficial longing to be sexually independent. In this way, she represents O'Neill's friend and fellow Provincetowner Hutchins Hapgood's assertion that "freedom from the ideal of monogamy" was a condition radical women in Greenwich Village outwardly wished for but inwardly despised (395).

Throughout *Now I Ask You,* O'Neill notably applies allusions to four of his lifelong heroes—

Max Stirner ("egoism"), Friedrich Nietzsche (the "Blond Beast"), Henrik Ibsen (*Hedda Gabler* and *The Master Builder*), and August Strindberg (Indra's daughter from *A Dream Play*)—as indicators of his heroine's pretentiousness. O'Neill critic Travis Bogard explains O'Neill's mixed message as "a kind of self-betrayal which could have silenced him before he started. He was insecure—especially as he turned from his early picaresque career to a life of the mind" (59). When Leonora tells Mrs. Ashleigh in act 1 that the title of her painting is "The Great Blond Beast," she is borrowing a term Nietzsche applied in his volume *On the Genealogy of Morals* (1887), a book of three essays that controversially hails the arrival of an Aryan master morality, and thus a master race, to rid the world of socialism and Christianity—though Leonora reads the concept as simply "something or someone great and noble" (408). Lucy quotes nearly verbatim from the egoist philosopher Max Stirner, the founder of O'Neill's PHILOSOPHICAL ANARCHISM, as well as Ibsen's *The Master Builder* when she gives her rationale in act 1 for backing out of the wedding: "My highest duty is toward myself, and my ego demands freedom, wide horizons to develop in, (*she makes a sweeping gesture*) Castles in the air, not homes for human beings!" (1:416). The intended irony in this line answers, to a certain degree, O'Neill BIOGRAPHERS Arthur and Barbara Gelb's befuddlement over the fact that although O'Neill "characterized it as a comedy . . . it is difficult to find a witty line in the dialogue" (567). Compare Lucy's line above with any number of Robert Mayo's soliloquies in BEYOND THE HORIZON. In that play, a tragedy, his lines are meant to be taken very seriously. In act 1, scene 1, for instance, Robert is talking over his longing to go to sea with his brother Andrew, who shares Tom Drayton's practicality: "Supposing I was to tell you that it's just Beauty that's calling me, the beauty of the far off and unknown, the mystery and spell of the East which lures me in the books I've read, the need of the freedom of great wide spaces, the joy of wandering on and on—in quest of the secret which is hidden over there, beyond the horizon?" (1:577). These lines might have been transposed into *Now I Ask You* with deliberate and effective irony. Indeed, perhaps contrary to Travis

Bogard's opinion, had O'Neill held to his understanding of overblown intellectualism, he may well have avoided the unintentional belly laughs that the equally overblown WELDED received nearly two decades later.

O'Neill demanded personal freedom in his own life, the kind Lucy believes she desires, a kind of freedom that comes with grave consequences—lack of financial security, social alienation, and sexual mistrust, among other things. The only character in *Now I Ask You* who seems truly capable of pulling off O'Neill's individualist philosophy is Leonora Barnes, a character who only seems able to do so given Gabriel's puppylike attachment to her. Ibsen's play *Hedda Gabler*, upon which Lucy models her own life, is the story of a woman who marries for financial security but then destroys herself and everyone around her attempting to escape it. Though Ibsen's title character demands self-actualization, as Lucy thinks she does, Hedda is fundamentally amoral and cruel, which heightens Lucy's naiveté since she holds her up as a role model. In this way, *Now I Ask You* is a reworking of O'Neill's early play RECKLESSNESS, a one-act thriller that even more clearly borrows from *Hedda Gabler* in plot (the heroine does commit suicide), but using the new theme of affected intellectualism.

Another reversal of the O'Neill canon is his sympathetic portrayal of the "clean, wholesome young American" businessman. Few businessmen come across in O'Neill as sympathetically as Tom Drayton, though his discussion with Mrs. Ashleigh reveals a disturbing sexism in the mode of Ibsen's character Torvald Helmer in *A Doll's House*. Mrs. Ashleigh, for example, equates his treatment of Lucy's faddishness with "the kindly tolerance of an elder brother toward an irresponsible child" (1:411). (O'Neill himself used the pet name "little wife" for Agnes Boulton, his second wife.) Otherwise, Tom is loving, reliable, and genuine—unlike, say, the Businessman in *Fog* or Edward Brown, Jr., in *Bread and Butter*. In this way, he is a clear precursor to Sam Evans in STRANGE INTERLUDE, though Sam is too boring to capture his independent-minded wife, Nina Leeds's heart, exclusively serving her need for a stable husband if not that of a lover or confidante. As such, *Now I Ask You* can be read as a modern farce in the mode of William Shakespeare's comedy *The Taming of the Shrew*, in that the reverse psychology Tom and Mrs. Ashleigh apply to Lucy's mulishness triumphs in the end, a substantial departure from O'Neill's Strindbergian female "destroyers"—women like Ruth Atkins from *Beyond the Horizon*, Maude Steele from *Bread and Butter*, and Ella Harris from ALL GOD'S CHILLUN GOT WINGS. These latter constitute a far more common female type than Lucy in the O'Neill canon, and unlike Lucy, they substantiate, as critic Judith Barlow writes, "the venerable myth that domesticity, even when freely chosen, kills the male of the species; woman is a trope for the bourgeois life, the insensitivity and materialism that annihilate the artistic soul" (165).

## CHARACTERS

**Adams, Gabriel** A poet and Leonora Barnes's husband. Gabriel is a pretentious Greenwich Village bohemian whom O'Neill describes fairly uncritically as having fashionably long black hair, an intelligent face, and wearing clothes *"sufficiently unconventional to attract attention,"* but then adds that *"his manner is that of a spoiled child who is used to being petted and enjoys every moment of it"* (1:429–430). Gabriel's marriage to Leonora took place in secret in order to avoid the criticisms of their Greenwich Village bohemian friends, who abhor the institution of marriage as restrictive to individualism. Lucy Drayton develops a crush on Gabriel, as his poetry and apparent soulfulness contrast starkly with her husband's practicality. Gabriel, for his part, finds her attractive but boring. When Lucy's husband, Tom Drayton, directs his attentions toward Leonora to make Lucy jealous, Gabriel himself turns resentful. In the epilogue, he goes back to Leonora, whom he truly loves and depends on for his survival.

**Ashleigh, Mrs.** Lucy Drayton's mother. Mrs. Ashleigh is *"a handsome, white-haired woman of fifty, calm, unruffled, with a charmingly girlish smile and dark eyes dancing with a keen sense of humor"* (1:403). Unlike her husband, she is highly tolerant of her daughter's modernist faddishness. A wily presence in the play, Mrs. Ashleigh convinces Lucy's fiancé, Tom Drayton, to encourage her daughter's "rainbow chasing" more believably if he wishes to ensure her daughter's happiness (1:411). When Lucy strikes up a romantic, if harmless, relationship with Gabriel Adams, a pretentious poet, Mrs. Ashleigh plots with Tom to disrupt the situation through reverse psychology by his courting Leonora Barnes, Gabriel's lover and, we learn in act 3, his wife. The plan is a success, though Lucy goes so far as to attempt suicide, and Mrs. Ashleigh effectively tames her rebellious daughter.

**Ashleigh, Richard** A retired banker and Lucy Drayton's father. Mr. Ashleigh is tall, bald, and overweight and *"suggests by his clothes and demeanor the retired banker whose life has become uneventful and prosperous"* (1:403). A model Victorian male in the mode of the stock character Mr. Banks in *Mary Poppins*, Mr. Ashleigh *"becomes easily aroused to nervous irritability when his own respectable dogmas are questioned"* (1:403). He disapproves of his daughter, Lucy's bohemian radicalism; his more tolerant wife teases him that "she is tomorrow, I am today, and you, my dear Dick, are yesterday" (1:404).

**Barnes, Leonora (Pearl Barnes)** A bohemian artist, Lucy Drayton's friend, and Gabriel Adams's wife. Born Pearl Barnes, Leonora changed her name to that of her family's black cook, who was romantically named for a racehorse. Unlike Lucy, Leonora, or "Leo," is an authentic bohemian, and O'Neill's physical description of her, in contrast to Lucy's, bears this out: *"She is a tiny bit of a person, rather pretty, but pale and aenemic looking with great dark circles in under her bright, restless eyes"* (1:407). Leonora is an abstract artist who marries the poet Gabriel Barnes, though they lie about their marriage to impress their Greenwich Village friends. When Lucy voices her admiration for Gabriel and everything he ostensibly stands for—the brooding, romantic poet and lover—her husband, Tom, makes overtures toward Leonora to make Lucy jealous. Leonora, more genuinely "modern" than any other character in the play, accepts his attentions happily and ignores her husband's hypocritical protestations. In the epilogue, it is clear that Leonora loves Gabriel and had only played along with Tom for a lark.

**Drayton, Lucy (Lucy Ashleigh)**    A would-be bohemian and Tom Drayton's wife. Lucy is a recent college graduate, and her outlook on life is modern in the extreme, at least on the surface. O'Neill's physical description of her emphasizes her inner contradictions by an outer display of pretentiousness: *"She is slender, dark, beautiful, with large eyes which she attempts to keep always mysterious and brooding, smiling lips which she resolutely compresses to express melancholic determination, a healthy complexion subdued by powder to a proper prison pallor"* (1:414). On the whole, she suffers from *"an overdose of undigested reading"* and models herself after existential heroines in Russian novels. Her actual *"intelligent, healthy American girl"* self is evidenced by her agreement prior to the play's action to marry Tom Drayton, a man her parents describe as a *"clean, wholesome young American"* (1:404).

In act 1, Lucy announces that she will not go through with the wedding planned for the following day. Her mother convinces her to do it by means of reverse psychology, agreeing with her that the marital contract is a travesty. Once Lucy becomes Mrs. Tom Drayton, she adopts the pose of Hedda Gabler, the title character of one of Henrik Ibsen's greatest plays. In it, Hedda finds domesticity so tedious that she seduces another man, persuades him to commit suicide, and then does so herself. Lucy finds this other man in Gabriel Adams, the secretly married spouse of her good friend Leonora Barnes. Gabriel humors her for a time but finally admits that he loves his wife. When Tom attempts to make Lucy jealous by flirting with Leonora, Lucy takes up a pistol and plays out the plot of Ibsen's play by attempting to commit suicide. The gun is unloaded, though the sound of a blowout in the driveway shocks her into believing she shot herself, and she faints. After regaining consciousness, she reconciles with her husband, and it is clear that she will come to appreciate the middle-class existence she had purported to loathe.

**Drayton, Tom**    A businessman and Lucy Drayton's husband. Tom is a *"tall, blond, finely-built man of about thirty with large, handsome features"* (1:409).

In act 1, Lucy's parents, Mr. and Mrs. Ashleigh, describe Tom in glowing terms as a "clean, wholesome young American" (1:404). Tom is a significant figure in the O'Neill canon in that he is one of the very few conventional businessmen portrayed in a sympathetic light. Tom loves Lucy and makes a good-faith effort to support her interests at first, though he considers her faddish modernism childish. Mrs. Ashleigh tells him that his facade of interest is too transparent and that he must earnestly embrace her daughter's "rainbow chasing" if she is to be happy (1:411). After a few months of marriage, however, Lucy adopts the pose of Hedda Gabler, the title character of one of Henrik Ibsen's masterworks, and revolts against her confining marital situation by conducting a relationship with the bohemian poet Gabriel Adams, her best friend Leonora Barnes's husband and a man Tom considers a "dirty little cad" (1:437). When Lucy refuses to break off her association with Gabriel, Tom makes overtures toward Leonora, who cheerfully accepts them, in order to make his wife jealous. The plot works only too well, and Lucy attempts to take her own life with a pistol (as Hedda Gabler does). But the pistol is unloaded, and after her brush with death in the epilogue, she runs back into Tom's arms.

## BIBLIOGRAPHY

Barlow, Judith. "O'Neill's Female Characters." In *The Cambridge Companion to Eugene O'Neill*, edited by Michael Manheim, 164–177. New York: Cambridge University Press, 1998.

Bogard, Travis. *Contour in Time: The Plays of Eugene O'Neill*. Rev. ed. New York: Oxford University Press, 1988.

Boulton, Agnes. *Part of a Long Story: Eugene O'Neill as a Young Man in Love*. Garden City, N.Y.: Doubleday & Company, 1958.

Floyd, Virginia. *The Plays of Eugene O'Neill: A New Assessment*. New York: Ungar, 1985.

Gelb, Arthur, and Barbara Gelb. *O'Neill: Life with Monte Cristo*. New York: Applause Books, 2000.

Hapgood, Hutchins. *A Victorian in the Modern World*. New York: Harcourt, Brace and Company, 1939.

# Personal Equation: A Play in Four Acts, The (completed, 1915; first produced, 2000)

Completed in 1915, one year after war broke out across Europe, *The Personal Equation* is one of two surviving plays (the other being *The SNIPER*) that were written under a strict deadline for GEORGE PIERCE BAKER's playwriting workshop at Harvard University. (Another play from the seminar, a one-act farce called *The Dear Doctor*, has been lost.) Though O'Neill planned to write a full-length play on the subject of abortion, Baker persuaded him to change to a more producible, less controversial topic, which he more or less did (Voelker 214). Nevertheless, the play was not produced until 2000, a full 85 years after it was written, when the Provincetown Playhouse, garnering predictably lackluster reviews, staged its world premiere. However, as O'Neill scholars are quick to point out, *The Personal Equation* is enormously important to O'Neill scholarship in that it is the clearest articulation of O'Neill's early social philosophy—his despair over American materialism, his belief in the destructive influence of Victorian propriety on familial and romantic relationships, and his fascination with and defense of the industrial working class. The play also tells us a great deal about his personal history—most important, his bittersweet relationship with his father, JAMES O'NEILL, which significantly resembles the father-son conflict between the characters Tom Perkins and Thomas Perkins in the play.

Much of the story line from *The Personal Equation* is mined directly from O'Neill's own experience with his radical-left companions in GREENWICH VILLAGE and as a seaman in the MERCHANT MARINE. O'Neill told an interviewer in the late 1910s that "I don't think any real dramatic stuff is created, to use an excellent expression of Professor Baker, 'out of the top of your head.' That is, the roots of a drama have to be in life, however fine and delicate or symbolic or fanciful the development" (quoted in Gelb 456). Indeed, theater critic Michael Feingold remarks of the play's conception that "Baker's stern but supportive presence, or something in the class-room situation, must have kept O'Neill truthful here. He may be talking through his hat, but a lot of words come from his heart." In act 4, war has been declared throughout Europe, which dates the play's action as summer 1914. Given that there is also an impending seamen and dockworkers' strike (which is quashed in the play), it might also be identified as 1911, the year O'Neill found himself, while a seaman on the SS *NEW YORK*, in Great Britain during the Great Strike on the Liverpool, England, docks.

## SYNOPSIS

### Act 1
The main room of the International Workers Union (IWU) headquarters in Hoboken, New Jersey; a large, unadorned space aside from a number of framed cartoons from *Jugend*, *Simplissimus*, and other radical magazines hanging on the wall and an engraving of a naked woman posed against a guillotine and wearing a liberty cap, which is prominently centered between two windows that look out on the street. The anarchists Olga Tarnoff and Enwright are seated together at a table. Olga is combing a socialist newspaper for articles that oppose their movement. Enwright asks Olga what she has found, and Olga responds with a diatribe against socialism. According to her and her anarchist colleagues, the socialists are naive "milk-and-water" radicals who believe that the vote and congressional legislation will change the course of capitalism in the United States, whereas the anarchists, disavowing the established political system altogether, believe that more drastic measures are required (1:311–312). Olga is awaiting the arrival of Tom Perkins, her lover, and Hartmann, her anarchist leader. Hartmann has called a meeting, and Olga and Enwright suspect it concerns an impending waterfront strike. Enwright questions Tom's dedication to the movement. He wonders the extent to which Tom takes part in their activities purely out of love for Olga. Olga defends Tom's political integrity, pointing out that he had been involved in the movement prior to their meeting. Enwright pushes further and believes that Tom joined as a result of "Curiosity and a craving for adventure . . . He probably wanted to see a real bomb thrown" (1:312).

Enwright departs and is heard greeting Tom offstage. Tom enters, and he and Olga embrace. Olga reads him a passage from the newspaper that describes her at a recent rally in Union Square as an "a crack-brained young female." According to the socialist author, she and other "over-strung lady anarchists of the Olga type are a constant and dangerous menace to society and should be confined in some asylum for the criminal insane" (1:313). After raging against the author's short-sightedness and hypocrisy, Tom pleads for her to marry him in order to keep up appearances in the public eye. She staunchly refuses on the grounds that neither of them believe in the institution of marriage: "You don't believe that the sanction of the law we hate or a religion we despise could make our relationship any holier, do you?" (1:315). He presses the issue, arguing that he agrees marriage should be abolished, but if they wished to have children, they should do it for their sake. Olga refuses to have children as well. As it stands, the world is no place for innocents—she would not sacrifice her children to Moloch (a metaphor for industrial capitalism's destructive force), the Old Testament god to whom children were sacrificed (1:316). (Moloch is famously a leitmotif of Beatnik poet Allen Ginsberg's groundbreaking poem "Howl" [1955]).

Tom is expected by his father, Thomas Perkins, who serves as second engineer on the SS *San Francisco,* which recently arrived in port. Tom was fired that day from his job as an assistant cashier for the Ocean Steamship Co., a position secured for him by his father, for distributing pamphlets calling for the strike. Though he rejoices he will no longer be anyone's "wage-slave" (1:317), he is worried that his father, whom he considers weak-willed, might be anxious the company will sack him as well. Tom describes his father, fairly accurately as it turns out, as "Just a poor servile creature living in constant fear of losing his job" (1:318).

Hartmann enters and voices concern over the prospect of war in Europe; he argues that if such a catastrophe occurs, not only will there be untold bloodshed, but the anarchist movement will be set back 50 years. Olga suggests that in the event of war, they organize a continental workers strike: "Think of how foolish those kings and emperors, those cabinets and parliaments would look when they found no one to fight for them, when they realized if they wanted war, they would have to fight themselves" (1:320). Hartmann disabuses her of the notion that they could steer the European workers away from patriotic rhetoric at this early stage in the movement and looks at the matter philosophically: "The soul of man is an uninhabited house haunted by the ghosts of old ideals. And man in those ghosts still believes!" (1:321).

Enthusiasm among the workers is swiftly waning, and Hartmann has devised a plan to reignite the waterfront strike. He asks Tom if it is true he worked as a "fireman," or coal stoker, on steamships, which Tom admits he did, but it was "for a stunt more than anything else" (1:323). Hartmann provides Tom with fake papers to sign on to the SS *San Francisco* as a stoker. Unaware that Tom's father is to be the second engineer onboard, Hartmann gives Olga a letter for Whitely, a member of the movement in Liverpool, to supply Tom with the dynamite to blow up the engine room once the ship is docked. He means the attack to inspire the seamen and dockworkers to strike; if they understand the operation was carried out by one of their own, they would gain the necessary confidence to fight the powerful company. Tom apprises Hartmann of his father's position but assures him that it will make no difference; he will carry through with the plot, but will do so only when his father is on shore leave. He then heads off to Thomas Perkins's house.

## Act 2

Thomas Perkins's sitting room in his house in Jersey City, New Jersey. The room is haphazardly cluttered with newspapers and books and furnished inexpensively. Perkins and Henderson, the chief engineer on the SS *Empress,* are playing euchre (a card game). The two are old friends, and Henderson, who speaks in a strong Scottish brogue, freely criticizes Perkins for being too distracted over his son's absence to play cards. Henderson further accuses Perkins of worrying too much about his son, whom he thinks his friend spoils. Mrs. Allen, Perkins's housekeeper, berates Tom in his absence for promising to come to dinner but being so late that the food is ruined. Mrs. Allen, the nagging housewife type, and Henderson, the bachelor seaman type, exchange some scathing banter. Mrs. Allen also informs Perkins that a young man from the neighborhood named Dugan had seen Tom "skylarkin' around with some girl" named Olga (1:332). Perkins is delighted, as he hopes Tom will soon marry. He plans to hand his house over to his son and future daughter-in-law while he lives aboard the *San Francisco*; Henderson, for his part, wants to secure a position in Liverpool and give up life in the merchant marine altogether.

Henderson, who agrees with Tom that the Ocean Steamship Company has been exploiting Perkins's talents as an engineer, believes Perkins should quit if they deny him a promotion. But Perkins is blindly devoted to his employers and, far more so—anticipating O'Neill's later character Reuben Light's parallel obsession in DYNAMO—to his engines, which he considers his most intimate companions in an otherwise lonely existence. Perkins has other reasons to worry. That day, his supervisor, Mr. Griffin, warned him that a friend of Tom's had been discharged for being a member of the International Workers of the Earth (IWE; the same organization as the IWU from act 1). Perkins had not heard of the organization, but Henderson describes them with the conservative line that they are "a lot of scamps who will na work themselves an' canna endure the thought of anyone else worrkin'" (1:338).

Tom knocks on the door and enters without waiting to be invited in. Henderson departs gruffly, promising to return the next night. Perkins timidly asks about Olga, not realizing that she and Tom share living quarters. Tom assumes Perkins is ready to scold him for "living in sin," but instead Perkins offers him the house for their wedding present. Tom informs him that he is living with Olga and that they have no intention of getting married, which shocks his father: "You wouldn't do that. Live with a girl—and not married. It's—it's wicked." Tom considers this a "matter of opinion" (1:342). Perkins then brings up what he heard at the office. Tom verifies it, adding that he had already been sacked from the job and recklessly asserts that he would even blow up his father's engines if the IWE

asked him to. Tom restates Henderson's point that he should have been promoted years ago, but he adds the radical-left line that the "Ocean Company is the head of the ship combine, and that the ship combine was organized by the greatest gang of crooked capitalists in the world" (1:344). Perkins is shocked by all of this, but validates Tom's supposition in act 1 that a serious concern of his is the prospect of losing his own job. Perkins urges Tom to speak to Mr. Griffin and be reinstated, which infuriates his son. Tom storms out, promising never to return. The curtain falls while Perkins, who has devoted his life to two things only—his son and his engines—cries in desperation for him not to leave.

### Act 3, Scene 1

About two weeks later in the fireman's forecastle of the SS *San Francisco*. Four bells ring, signifying either six o'clock or 10 o'clock in the evening. The firemen represent a number of ethnic groups—IRISH, British, and German, specifically, but probably not exclusively. The men are restless. They are waiting for word from the union whether or not to strike. Tom is among them, using the false name Tom Donovan, and is clearly the authority figure. Three stokers, O'Rourke, Cocky, and Harris, demand to know what Tom plans to do if the strike is called off. He assures them that serious measures will be taken. They are waiting for word from Whitely, the Liverpool member of the IWE who is at the union meeting where the decision will be made. O'Rourke accuses the officers, who are ashore at a banquet, of celebrating their likely victory. Tom worries because his father, Thomas Perkins, the second engineer of the ship, is not, as he had hoped, going on shore leave if the union decides not to strike, at which point Tom would dynamite the engines. Schmidt offers to use force to remove the engineer if necessary. Speaking for the rest of the men, who are fond of Perkins and consider him harmless, O'Rourke threatens a fight if he does. Tom quells the potential brawl by pointing out that their fight against the company cannot be won if they fight against themselves, adding that Olga had made the same appeal in a recent speech to them. Cocky resents Olga's involvement, as her talk reminded him of "one of them blushin'

Suffrygette meetings" (1:351). Offstage, Hogan can be heard singing an Irish drinking song. He enters drunk and tells the men that war against the Germans is coming, and he calls Schmidt a "Dutch swine." Schmidt, more formidable in his sober state, knocks Hogan to the ground, and O'Rourke retaliates by challenging him to a fight on deck. Schmidt accepts, and the men, save for the instigator, Hogan, who comically passes out on his bunk, pile out of the forecastle to watch the battle.

Olga enters disguised as a male dockworker. She brings news that the union leaders have succumbed to bribery from the company and have called off the strike, hiding behind patriotism as an excuse. They reflect upon Hartmann's statement about patriotism, and Olga suggests FRIEDRICH NIETZSCHE's *Thus Spake Zarathustra* when she says, "I'll bring up our child with a soul freed from all adorations of Gods and governments if I have to live alone on a mountain top to do it" (1:354; Bogard 55). Tom responds, "Our child?" but Olga changes the subject. Though Tom senses something different about Olga, he misses the inference that she is pregnant. She reports that Whitely believes that that night is the best time to dynamite the engine room and answers an unspoken premonition of doom that perhaps the operation would be more effective if Whitely himself handled the explosives. Tom accuses her of not trusting him to carry through with the plan, though clearly Olga is trying to prevent the father of her child from arrest or even death. Tom consoles her by suggesting they move to the countryside upon their return to the United States.

Whitely enters and announces that his explosives contact has been arrested, so the dynamiting must be called off. Tom has an alternative—mutiny. The stokers return from the brawl between O'Rourke and Schmidt. This fight can be read as analogous to the struggle between the Western allies and Germany during World War I, as O'Rourke emerges severely injured but victorious. Whitely makes a speech in which he describes the betrayal of the union and tells them to follow Tom in his plot to take over the ship. Tom declares a mutiny, and they all rush from the forecastle to destroy the engines, laughing that the only man on watch is "Molly" Per-

kins, their derogatory nickname for Tom's father. The scene ends with Olga weeping over what she intuitively senses will end in Tom's demise.

### Act 3, Scene 2

The *San Francisco*'s engine room a few moments later. Not yet aware of the mutiny, Perkins chats with the "oiler" Murphy. He proudly, though not altogether confidently, asserts that his engines are more powerful than Henderson's on the *Empress*. Murphy humors him along. He asks if Murphy has heard any word about the strike, which he has not. Then he asks what he knows about the IWE, which is little. Murphy exits and Jack, the engineer's apprentice, rushes into the room with news that the stokers are headed for them and that he overheard the men plotting to dynamite the engine room. He identifies Tom Donovan as the leader, and, determined to save his engines, Perkins nervously produces a pistol the chief engineer left in case of trouble, though he has never handled a gun before and needs to be told if it is loaded. He dispatches Jack to alert the mate and get the police. The men, save Tom, storm into the engine room. Finding Perkins there, they good-naturedly try to convince him to leave. Perkins is terrified but stands his ground. O'Rourke, who is friendly with Perkins, tells him Tom Donovan ordered him to lead the mob to ensure his safety from the "rough bhoys" bent on smashing the engines (1:368).

Tom enters, and the men respectfully let him through. Recognizing his son, Perkins pleads with him not to go through with it and threatens to shoot the first man that touches the engines. Tom calls his bluff and smashes one of the engine's glass gauge faces. Perkins shoots in his direction. Tom's body goes limp, and he drops to the floor. Overwhelmed by what he has done, Perkins helplessly cries out that he had meant the shot to be a warning and that he had deliberately aimed the pistol over Tom's head.

### Act 4

A hospital room in Liverpool about three weeks later. Tom, dressed in a bathrobe, pajamas, and slippers, is seated in a rocking chair staring out the window, and his head is bandaged. A nurse coaxes him into bed. The doctor enters and proudly tells the nurse that his trephine, a surgical instrument designed to remove bone chips from the skull, saved Tom's life. The prognosis is not good, however, as Tom is unresponsive to most stimuli, has lost his memory, and will probably live the rest of his life "like a little child" (1:373). Some words are exchanged about the perpetrator of the crime, and we learn that Perkins has publicly denied that Tom is his son, which leaves no one to care for him after his release. The nurse reminds him that Olga Tarnoff claims to be Tom's fiancée. Olga has concocted that story to make an official claim on him. The doctor, knowing she is an anarchist, scoffs at the idea of their union: "I thought their tribe went in for free love" (1:373).

Olga enters, followed by Whitely. Olga implores Tom to speak to her, and he does, for the first time, shouting weakly "Olga! Olga!" But the doctor insists, "There was no recognition, no intelligence behind the words" (1:374). The doctor suggests Olga continue trying to spark his memory and exits with the nurse. Olga and Whitely discuss Tom's prospects, and Olga informs him that Perkins not only disavowed his relationship with his son but was granted a promotion and a gold watch for his bravery defending the engines. We learn that war has just erupted across Europe, and, just as Hartmann predicted, Europe is now awash with patriotic zeal. Whitely informs her that many radicals have dropped their causes to take up the war effort. Olga holds to her antiwar message. When the topic turns back to Tom's condition, she blames herself for getting Tom mixed up in the plot and admits that she "had a foreboding of misfortune to him that night in the fo'castle" (1:378).

Perkins, destroyed with guilt and grief, enters with the doctor. He informed the hospital that he is, in fact, Tom's father and plans to take possession of his son. Olga asks the doctor to leave them, with the excuse that she and Perkins together might successfully jog Tom's recognition. The doctor exits with heartless skepticism. Olga confronts Perkins with the truth that she is pregnant with Tom's baby and demands to care for Tom after his release. Each blames the other for Tom's condition—Olga accusing Perkins of trying to murder his son, and Perkins blaming Olga for enticing Tom

into the movement. After a bitter exchange, their tones soften and they accept equal blame. Perkins suggests that the three of them, soon to be four, should live together at his house in Jersey City and care for Tom there. Olga accepts, adding that there may still be hope of Tom's recovery.

Tom awakes from a short slumber and reaches out to them, holding their hands for a time. The two believe this act signifies that he has forgiven them both. Perkins heads off to inform the doctor of their decision, and Whitely rushes in, nearly toppling Perkins over, with the horrifying news that the Germans just bombed an orphanage. He swears he will enlist if they continue such outrages (at one point absurdly marching in place to the sound of a military band out the window). Olga maintains her antiwar beliefs and considers Whitely and all of the radical leaders—anarchists, socialists, syndicalists, and so on—who have joined the governments in the war effort as traitors. Olga's final monologue is a call to revolution. Tom awakens once more and, "*with a low, chuckling laugh—mimicking Olga,*" repeats the final words of her speech, "Long— live—the Revolution" (1:387). Whitely turns his back in revulsion; Olga looks down at Tom and hides her head in her hands in despair.

## COMMENTARY

Artistically speaking, *The Personal Equation* is one of O'Neill's greatest failures. Indeed, O'Neill critic Paul D. Voelker characterizes it as "perhaps the worst O'Neill play to survive" (214). After O'Neill's single year of study at George Pierce Baker's play-writing workshop at Harvard University, Baker commented that the young playwright should remain for another full year, as he could not yet "manage the longer forms," though he understood later that "his means at the moment made this impossible" (quoted in Clark 39). Baker's point is well taken by even the most perfunctory reader of this awkward, melodramatic, and clumsily pedantic script. Nevertheless, O'Neill followed Baker's advice that characterization is "the permanent value of a play" (quoted in Voelker 218). His trouble was not so much in creating plausible characters, but rather in placing them haphazardly amid the entanglements of an unbelievable plot (Voelker 218). O'Neill was not yet capable of blending action with characterization, testified to by his first two full-length plays, BREAD AND BUTTER and SERVITUDE, but this dramatic requirement stumped him in later plays as well, notably DAYS WITHOUT END.

Historically, however, the play is far more interesting. For one, *The Personal Equation* plainly reflects O'Neill's strong opposition to the industrialization of the merchant marine, a revulsion borne of his experience as a crewman for two months on the Norwegian bark CHARLES RACINE and the steamships SS IKALA, SS *New York*, and SS PHILADELPHIA. His perspective on this transformation is most fully articulated in the character Paddy's speech to Robert "Yank" Smith in scene 1 of *The* HAIRY APE. In act 1 of *The Personal Equation*, Tom sarcastically remarks that in childhood he was "lulled to sleep . . . with a triple-expansion, twin-screw lullaby" (1:319). His father, Thomas Perkins, is symbolic of the lackluster experience at sea under steam power, as compared to the glory days of sail. Steam began to fully challenge the sailing industry in the 1870s and 1880s even while sailboat designs continued to prove more efficient for trade worldwide. The competition was short-lived, however, once designers introduced the triple-expansion engines Perkins slavishly covets, which lowered the cost of fuel and could reach three times the speed of sail-powered cargo ships. Add to that the fact that the iron and steel hulls of the steam ships were lighter, cheaper, and stronger and could carry more cargo with less risk of damaging the goods, and sail shipping devolved into a mere pastime (Labaree 390).

*The Hairy Ape* again comes to mind in act 1 when Olga is reading a newspaper's opinion of the anarchist movement. This scene closely resembles scene 6 of *The Hairy Ape*, in which a prisoner in a cellblock reads Senator Queen's statement on the INDUSTRIAL WORKERS OF THE WORLD (IWW) to Robert "Yank" Smith; the senator hyperbolically characterizes the members of the IWW, or "Wobblies," as industrial terrorists. And finally, in act 1, when Tom explains to Hartmann about the lesson he learned the summer he worked as a fireman in the stokehold "for a stunt": "It made me think— seeing the contrast between us grimy stokers and the first cabin people lolling in their deck chairs" (1:323). This lesson forms the central conflict of O'Neill's later expressionistic play.

Thematically and autobiographically, O'Neill based Tom on himself, as he reports that he spent one "year wasted in college" and had worked as a seaman on a transatlantic steamer. O'Neill also had some involvement in the Greenwich Village anarchist movement in the 1910s. However, unlike Olga's brand of activism, which is meant to recall that of EMMA GOLDMAN, a famous anarchist leader on whom Olga is loosely based—O'Neill was more inclined toward PHILOSOPHICAL ANARCHISM, which is a more personal, or individualist, philosophy than Goldman's more political anarchism. Most important, philosophical anarchism, as O'Neill understood it through of one of his earliest mentors of social philosophy, BENJAMIN R. TUCKER, as opposed to the communist anarchism or syndicalist anarchism of the period, was entirely nonviolent. Arthur and Barbara Gelb are somewhat overreaching by contending that *The Personal Equation* is "further evidence that violent anarchism was less repugnant to O'Neill than to Tucker," insofar as it "not unsympathetically . . . examines the forces that drove the early militant labor movement, along with Tucker's nonviolent anarchism" (219).

O'Neill reflects the Tucker-Goldman debate is reflected in the dispute between the pacifist character Enwright and the violent anarchist revolutionary Olga (Feingold). When Enwright warns that violent retribution is sure to follow if they carry out their plan to dynamite the merchant ship's engines, Olga responds fiercely that "force alone can be effective against force. . . . [The workers] have thought Capitalism impregnable behind its fortress of law, and they have been afraid. A few successful assaults of this kind and their eyes will be opened" (1:325–326). Tucker, for his part, was "not unsympathetic" to Goldman's struggle, either, but what is *The Personal Equation*, in which a young man involves himself in a violent anarchist movement and is ultimately shot down by his own father, but a parable in which violence, however sympathetic, can only "multiply itself"?

Much later, we find in O'Neill's 1940 WORK DIARY the sketch of a comedy with the working title

"The Visit of Malatesta," based on the life of Italian anarchist Enrico Malatesta. In it, Malatesta visits a fictional version of NEW LONDON, CONNECTICUT. Although Italian Americans in the play consider him a regicidal hero, the mastermind behind the assassination of Umberto I in 1900 (who was actually killed by the anarchist Gaetano Bresci), the character, O'Neill writes, "denies he had anything to do with [the assassination]—terrorist group fanatics—true anarchism never justifies bloodshed" (quoted in Floyd 1981, 305).

Like O'Neill, Tom has some conventional notions, having grown up in "respectable" society, and he is concerned for Olga's reputation. In act 4, when the doctor and the nurse discuss Tom Perkins's case, O'Neill leaves the strong impression that he related to his character's isolation in the final scene, perhaps even more as a vegetable than as a political activist. Virginia Floyd believes a connection can be drawn between Tom and his creator—given O'Neill's vagabond childhood and self-absorbed parents—when the doctor remarks that Tom "might have been different if he had had the influence of a home. As it is, there's no trace of who he is or where he came from. He's one of those strange human strays one sometimes runs across" (1:373). Further, Travis Bogard points out that the "hopeless hope" concept that drives so many O'Neill plays, most evidently *The STRAW, HUGHIE,* and *The ICEMAN COMETH,* finds its first articulation when, after the doctor submits to Olga (with italics for emphasis) that Tom will never recover, he adds that "it is just as well to tell you that there is little hope for his reason—*but*—there is always a hope!" (1:375).

## CHARACTERS

**Allen, Mrs.** Thomas Perkins's housekeeper. In act 2, Mrs. Allen, though married with children of her own, seems to be a surrogate nagging wife for Perkins, who is a widower. Neither Perkins's son, Tom Perkins, nor his best friend, Henderson, appreciate her role in the Perkins household.

**Brown, Miss (Nurse)** Tom Perkins's *"short, stout, fresh-looking"* nurse in the Liverpool hospital (1:372).

**Cocky** A fireman, or "stoker," on the SS *San Francisco.* O'Neill describes Cocky as a *"squat, broad-shouldered, pasty-faced"* (1:348) man who speaks in a cockney, or working-class British, accent. Like Harris, Cocky is one of the most vocal about the men's frustration with the union's and the IWE's apparent complacency over the strike. Cocky also appears as a character in the SS GLEN-CAIRN series.

**Doctor** Tom Perkins's doctor in Liverpool. He expresses little faith in Tom's ability to recover from the shot in the head his father inflicted, which caused severe brain damage. However, O'Neill uses the doctor as a mouthpiece to voice his own "hopeless hope" concept that would later become a major theme in O'Neill's work, most importantly in *The Iceman Cometh.* We see this in the doctor's line to Olga that "it is just as well to tell you that there is little hope for his reason—*but*—there is always a hope!" (1:375). O'Neill uses him as a mouthpiece for his own sense of alienation as well, when the doctor deduces that Tom's prognosis "might have been different if he had had the influence of a home. As it is, there's no trace of who he is or where he came from. He's one of those strange human strays one sometimes runs across" (1:373).

**Enwright** An anarchist comrade of Olga Tarnoff and Tom Perkins. Theater critic Michael Feingold argues that Enwright may be a fictional Benjamin R. Tucker, the purveyor of philosophical anarchism whose Unique Book Shop O'Neill patronized as early as 1905. If Olga Tarnoff is the more strident anarchist in the International Workers of the Earth, Enwright, though sincere in his devotion to the movement, looks at their cause in a more ironic light: "The Tucker-Goldman dispute is reflected in the play's sniping conversations between Olga and her passive, ironic fellow anarchist, Enwright—a debate that the revival of anarchist thought, confronting a newly imperious global capitalism, has made astonishingly pertinent" (Feingold).

**Harris** A fireman, or "stoker," on the SS *San Francisco.* O'Neill describes Harris as a *"tall, wiry, grey-headed man with round shoulders"* (1:348), and he has very few lines in the play. Like Cocky, Harris is vocal about the men's frustration with the union's and the I.W.E.'s apparent complacency over the strike.

**Hartmann** A caricature of the turn-of-the-century European immigrant radical, and the leader of the International Workers of the Earth. Middle-aged and short with an immense head and spectacles, Hartmann speaks English in a German manner that inverts the syntax of his sentences. Dressed all in black, with long black hair and a flowing black Windsor tie, he nevertheless cuts a striking figure. He is based on O'Neill's friend and Emma Goldman's lover, the anarchist HIPPOLYTE HAVEL, who is also the model—though less convincingly (see Alexander 31–32)—for Hugo Kalmar in *The Iceman Cometh*. Hartmann believes that when war breaks out in Europe, the anarchist movement will be set back at least 50 years. He is the architect of the plan to blow up the engines of the SS *San Francisco* in Liverpool. By doing this, he believes he will inspire the dockworkers there to go through with a strike the union leaders are too weak and corrupt to carry out.

**Henderson** The first engineer on the SS *Empress* and Thomas Perkins's good friend. Henderson is described as *"a tall, lean Scotchman with grey hair and bristly mustache"* who is wearing his engineer's uniform while off duty at Perkins's home in act 2 (1:328). Henderson speaks in a strong Scottish accent and resembles the caricature of the Scottish engineer (perhaps most famous in popular culture as the character "Scotty" on the television series *Star Trek*). Henderson, like Perkins's son, Tom, believes that the shipping company they work for should have promoted Perkins years before the action of the play.

**Hogan** A drunken member of the firemen on the SS *San Francisco*. Hogan speaks in a thick Irish brogue and arrives in the firemen's forecastle after shore leave singing Irish drinking songs. He carries a newspaper that claims the war in Europe will probably take place. Schmidt, a German, takes Hogan's newspaper without permission, which instigates a brawl between Schmidt and O'Rourke.

**Jack** Thomas Perkins's apprentice engineer on the SS *San Francisco*. Jack informs Perkins of the impending mutiny.

**Murphy** The oiler on the SS *San Francisco*. At the beginning of act 2, Murphy discusses the ship's engines with Thomas Perkins, then says his decision to strike will depend on the union.

**O'Rourke** A fireman, or "stoker," on the SS *San Francisco*. O'Rourke speaks in a thick Irish brogue and is physically superior to the rest of the men. O'Neill describes him as *"a giant of a red-headed Irishman"* (1:348), and he is based on O'Neill's friend DRISCOLL from his time on the SS *New York*. Other characters in O'Neill's plays based on Driscoll are Yank from the SS *Glencairn* series and Robert "Yank" Smith from *The Hairy Ape*. O'Rourke fights the German character Schmidt after Hogan announces that war will probably erupt between Germany and Great Britain and its allies. This fight can be read as a foreshadowing of World War I, and O'Rourke emerges injured but victorious. O'Rourke is also the most vocal protector of Thomas Perkins during the mutiny.

**Perkins, Thomas** Tom Perkins's father and the second engineer of the SS *San Francisco*. Perkins is a meek and lonely widower who since the death of his termagant wife has devoted his life to his son and the engines on his ship. Unlike his son, Perkins is blind to the shipping combine's exploitation of his skills; though he is the most experienced engineer in their company, they have never offered him a promotion. The implicit assumption is that the company has no incentive to promote him given Perkins's dogged loyalty. Tom describes his father as "Just a poor servile creature living in constant fear of losing his job" (1:318). O'Neill critics often point to the correspondences between Perkins and O'Neill's father, James O'Neill, whose career with melodramatic crowd-pleasers such as *The Count of Monte Cristo* he perceived in ways similar to how Tom's perception of his father's mechanical servitude on the steam ships. In kind, O'Neill's description of Perkins is nearly identical to that of James Tyrone in LONG DAY'S JOURNEY INTO NIGHT:

*"He is half-bald but an unkempt fringe of thin grey hair straggles about his ears. He wears . . . ill-fitting shabby clothes"* (1:328; Floyd 1985, 93). The conflict between the conventional father and the modern son is most powerfully explored in *Long Day's Journey*. It is important, then, to note that O'Neill's working title for the play was *The Second Engineer*. Perkins's obsession with engines is equally wrought, and equally overstated, in the character of Reuben Light in *Dynamo*.

**Perkins, Tom** Thomas Perkins's son and Olga Tarnoff's lover. Tom is 22 years old, and when he first appears at the IWE's headquarters in act 1, his demeanor suggests *"a naïve enthusiasm with a certain note of defiance creeping in as if her were fighting an inward embarrassment and was determined to brave it down"* (1:312). Critics point out that, given his feelings of alienation, his radical-left political leanings, and his disputes with his father, Tom Perkins is an avatar of the playwright himself. Physically, however, he is rather distinct from O'Neill: *"Tom is a husky six-footer in his early twenties, large intelligent eyes, handsome in a rough, manly, strong-featured way"* (1:312). But as with his creator, Tom spent one year at college and made a transatlantic crossing on a steamship "for a stunt more than anything else" (1:323). Virginia Floyd points to another connection, given O'Neill's childhood, when the doctor remarks that Tom "might have been different if he had had the influence of a home. As it is, there's no trace of who he is or where he came from. He's one of those strange human strays one sometimes runs across" (373; Floyd 1985, 98).

When the IWE leader Hartmann assigns Tom the task of signing on to the SS *San Francisco* under an assumed name, Tom Donovan, in order to facilitate the destruction of the engines upon their arrival at Liverpool, Tom heartily accepts. Tom proves an able leader among the stokers: He successfully incites them to mutiny when it is clear the union leaders will not support a strike in Liverpool and the arrest of their explosives contact precludes dynamiting the engine room. Olga attempts to dissuade him from further involvement as she has a premonition that Tom will be led to his doom—

and unbeknownst to Tom, she is pregnant with his child. Tom insists on carrying out the assignment. Tom's father, Thomas Perkins, is also on the ship, serving as the second engineer. Tom considers his father a working stiff: "No backbone, no willpower, no individuality, nothing. Just a servile creature living in constant fear of losing his job" (1:318). However, as Paul D. Voelker points out, the central conflict of the play is born of Tom's psychological desire to reconcile his revolutionary goals with both his conscious love for Olga and his unconscious love for his father (218).

Critics point to the relationship between Tom and Thomas as corresponding in important ways to O'Neill and his father, James O'Neill. O'Neill had little respect for James's performances in melodramatic plays such as *The Count of Monte Cristo,* and additionally he believed that his father acted such roles in order to stave off poverty—O'Neill dramatizes this conflict most powerfully in the highly autobiographical *Long Day's Journey into Night.* When Tom leads the firemen to the stokehold to the smash the engines, Thomas defends his dynamos by shooting the first man who touches them—his son. Tom is then hospitalized, having suffered severe brain damage. The prognosis is that he will spend his life being cared for "like a little child" (1:373). Olga blames herself for bringing Tom into the movement, and Perkins blames himself for shooting his son. They both decide to care for him—and Tom and Olga's future child—at the Perkins home in Jersey City, New Jersey.

**Schmidt** A fireman, or "stoker," on the SS *San Francisco.* O'Neill describes Schmidt as *"a giant of a shock-headed German"* (1:349) who defiantly argues with the rest of the men and speaks in a heavy German accent—one somewhat indistinguishable from the Swedish accent O'Neill employs in later characters such as Olson in the SS *Glencairn* series and Chris Christopherson in *"ANNA CHRISTIE."* Schmidt, who takes issue with the others calling him "Dutchy" since he is German, not Dutch, fights O'Rourke in what can be read as a foreshadowing of the struggle between the Western powers and Germany during World War I. Schmidt, though he puts up a good fight, is ultimately knocked unconscious.

**Tarnoff, Olga**    Tom Perkins's lover and an anarchist leader. Olga, described as having *"very dark; strong, fine features; large spirited black eyes, slender, supple figure"* (1:311), is loosely based on Emma Goldman, the famous anarchist agitator; free love, abortion, and birth-control advocate; and editor of the radical-left organ *Mother Earth*. Goldman's romantic escapades with such figures as Hippolyte Havel, the anarchist friend of O'Neill's on whom the character Hartmann is loosely based, and Alexander Berkman, the anarchist who attempted the assassination of the millionaire industrialist Henry Clay Frick, are legendary. O'Neill shared many acquaintances with Goldman during his Greenwich Village days, and he admired her immensely. Goldman, however, was far more politically minded than O'Neill ever was—a difference in temperament that O'Neill dramatizes in the relationship between Tom, who wants to marry and have children, and Olga, who opposes the institution of marriage and has no desire to have children. Nevertheless, Olga becomes pregnant, though Tom never finds out. Ironically, after Tom's father, Thomas Perkins, shoots his son in the head, leaving him irreparably brain damaged, Olga chooses to nurse Tom for the rest of her life and bear his child. She still holds to her principles, however, and in one of the final monologues of the play, she shouts, "Long live the Revolution!" (1:387). Tom's lame repetition of that line, the final line of the play, demonstrates a skepticism on O'Neill's part that the anarchist movement could change the established social order in the United States.

**Whitely**    An anarchist leader in Liverpool, England, who is Tom Perkins and Olga Tarnoff's contact when they arrive there on the SS *San Francisco*. O'Neill describes him as *"a swarthy, dark-eyed, bull-necked, powerfully-built man of about 35. He wears a black mustache and is dressed in a dirty suit of dungarees"* (1:357). When Whitely arrives on the *San Francisco*, he brings news that the other union leaders had been bribed by the shipping combine and that they must change their course of action to carry out the dockworkers and seamen's strike they had been organizing. He also informs them that his explosives contact has been arrested, so they cannot destroy the engines with dynamite as they had originally planned. He urges the men to follow Tom in a mutiny against the ship and destroy the engines with whatever tools they can find, which they do. By the end of the play, Whitely is prepared to fight on the side of the Allies in the war with the Germans, directly contradicting his previous stance and that of the radical left at large, though most radical leaders, he tells Olga, feel the same way. In the final scene of act 4, Olga berates him as a traitor and a "blind fool" (1:386).

## BIBLIOGRAPHY

Alexander, Doris. *Eugene O'Neill's Last Plays: Separating Art from Autobiography*. Athens: University of Georgia Press, 2005.

Bogard, Travis. *Contour in Time: The Plays of Eugene O'Neill*. Rev. ed. New York: Oxford University Press, 1988.

Clark, Barrett H. *Eugene O'Neill: The Man and His Plays*. Rev. ed. New York: Dover, 1947.

Dowling, Robert M. "On Eugene O'Neill's 'Philosophical Anarchism.'" *Eugene O'Neill Review* 29 (Spring 2007): 50–72.

Feingold, Michael. "Orderly Anarchisms: *The Personal Equation*." *The Village Voice* (August 8, 2000). Available online. URL: http://www.villagevoice.com/2008-08-15theater/orderly-anarchisms/. Accessed February 8, 2008.

Floyd, Virginia. *The Plays of Eugene O'Neill: A New Assessment*. New York: Ungar, 1985.

Floyd, Virginia, ed. *Eugene O'Neill at Work: Newly Released Ideas for His Plays*. New York: Ungar, 1981.

Gelb, Arthur, and Barbara Gelb. *O'Neill: Life with Monte Cristo*. New York: Applause Books, 2000.

Labaree, Benjamin W. *America and the Sea: A Maritime History*. Mystic, Conn.: Mystic Seaport, 1998.

Richter, Robert A. *Eugene O'Neill and Dat Ole Davil Sea: Maritime Influences in the Life and Works of Eugene O'Neill*. Mystic, Conn.: Mystic Seaport, 2004.

Voelker, Paul D. "Eugene O'Neill and George Pierce Baker: A Reconsideration." *American Literature* 49, no. 2 (May 1977): 206–220.

# *Recklessness: A Play in One Act* (completed, 1913; never produced)

*Recklessness*, Eugene O'Neill's fourth play, was published with financial help from his father, JAMES O'NEILL (whom O'Neill probably had in mind for the male lead), in *"THIRST" AND OTHER ONE-ACT PLAYS* (1914), but it was never performed in his lifetime. This early one-act thriller is essentially a melodramatic adaptation of the Swedish playwright AUGUST STRINDBERG's *Miss Julie* (1888) and the Norwegian playwright HENRIK IBSEN's masterpiece *Hedda Gabler* (1890), with thematic overtones of Ibsen's *A Doll's House* (1879), all in a distinctly American setting. O'Neill composed the play in fall 1913; throughout the previous year, during and after his return from the GAYLORD FARM SANATORIUM, he voraciously read continental European drama and philosophy, determined to match their intellectual heights in his home country. O'Neill developed an enormous admiration for both Strindberg and Ibsen, but particularly Strindberg, whom he identified in his NOBEL PRIZE speech as his greatest artistic influence.

## SYNOPSIS

The library of a summer home in the Catskills, New York. O'Neill describes the set as *"the typical sitting-room of a moderately wealthy man who has but little taste and is but little worried by its absence"* (1:55). Two French doors open out onto a veranda on stage left; large windows look out onto the same veranda in center. There is a rolltop desk against the wall with a small telephone nearby for communicating with the garage outside; a larger Bell telephone is on top of the desk for regular calls. Sports-related pictures hang on the walls, mostly of racing cars. It is an August night, and the door and windows are open to let in fresh air. Mildred Baldwin, a *"strikingly voluptuous-looking"* redhead in her late 20s wearing *"a low-cut evening gown of a grey that matches her eyes"* (1:55), lies on a Morris chair with an open book across her lap. She shows visible signs of waiting for something. She presses an electric button, and her servant Mary appears.

Mrs. Baldwin, as O'Neill refers to her in the script, informs Mary that she will not have dinner that night and dismisses her. Furtively glancing about, she moves to the French doors and calls softly, "Fred." Fred Burgess promptly enters, also peering around suspiciously. Fred is 25 and wears a gray chauffeur uniform and puttees. Once assured of privacy, they rush into each others arms, kiss passionately, and profess their mutual love. Gene, another maid, surreptitiously appears in the doorway leading to the veranda. *"She glares at them for a moment, vindictive hatred shining in her black eyes"* (1:56) and quickly withdraws.

Anxious because her husband, Arthur Baldwin, will return home soon, Mrs. Baldwin begs Fred to take her away that night. But Fred obstinately refuses on the grounds that they have no financial security. Fred accuses Mrs. Baldwin of being a naive woman of privilege with no experience in poverty. "Being poor doesn't mean anything to you. You've never been poor. Well, I have, and I know. It's hell, that's what it is" (1:57). She offers to sell her jewelry, but Fred rejects this, as it would be Mr. Baldwin's money. He adds that there is no certainty her husband would grant a divorce in any case, so they should wait until Fred passes his engineering exams and he can support them independently. Mrs. Baldwin disputes Fred's assessment of her husband, thinking him a better man than he is given credit for, though she asseverates that he "has looked upon me as his plaything, the slave of his pleasure, a pretty toy to be exhibited that others might envy him his ownership" (1:58). Over the course of their dialogue, she voices fear and revulsion toward her husband, but bizarrely her main complaint is that he is much older than she is, nearly twice her age, and they have no interests in common. Fred refutes her elevated opinion of her husband and speculates that if Baldwin is indeed the man she believes him to be, he will break their vows quietly and avoid scandal; if not, Fred has inside information pertaining to Baldwin's business dealings and will blackmail him into submitting to a divorce.

The lovers hear *"The faint throb of a powerful motor with muffler cut out,"* and Fred quickly disappears. Arthur Baldwin enters wearing a motor cap, goggles, and a foppish, neatly cut gray suit. Baldwin is pleasantly surprised by his wife's evening gown, mistakenly assuming she is wearing it to celebrate his return. In his STAGE DIRECTIONS, O'Neill specifies that Baldwin *"exhibits enthusiasm on but two subjects—his racing car and his wife—in the order named"* (1:59). He recounts an unfortunate incident from his driving expedition. The steering gave out at an inopportune moment, and the car drove into a ditch. He was able to extricate the car, but because of the faulty steering, the drive back through the mountain roads was slow and dangerous.

Mrs. Baldwin excuses herself to change into more comfortable clothing. In her absence, Baldwin reads through his letters, grumbling to himself there is nothing but bills. Gene announces that Mrs. Baldwin is upstairs with a headache. Mr. Baldwin suspects his maid has something else on her mind and asks what it is. Gene is Fred Burgess's former lover, and she bitterly explains that she has proof that he has found another woman. Entertained by some new gossip among his servants, Baldwin encourages her to continue. A short guessing game ensues, with Gene becoming more agitated but charily withholding the woman's identity. "Oh, they thought they were so safe! But I'll teach him to throw me over the way he did. I'll pay her for all her looking down on me and stealing him away. She's a bad woman, is what I say!" (1:63).

Enough hints are dropped that Baldwin ciphers the truth. He lunges in a rage and grabs Gene's throat, demanding she admit her story is a lie. He is literally choking her to death but frees her at the last minute. Resentful of the attack, Gene informs him that she has hard proof against Fred and her mistress, but she initially withholds it, since "A man that chokes women deserves to be made a fool of" (1:63). He threatens her again, but she produces the damning evidence voluntarily to "get even" with her mistress for stealing the man she loves (1:64). It is a letter in Mrs. Baldwin's handwriting from two nights before and indicates a time for a clandestine meeting with Fred in the garage. Baldwin angrily dismisses Gene and crumples the note in a rage. He looks about the room, first at his goggles and coat, then at the garage phone. *"His face lights up with savage joy"* (1:65). He picks up the

direct line to the garage and informs Fred that his wife may have suffered a hemorrhage and orders the chauffeur to drive his racing car as fast as possible to the village for a doctor. "Drive like hell!" he shouts into the phone, "Her life's in your hands. Turn the car loose!" (1:65). As Baldwin hears the car's engine noise fade out, he says with a *"cruel grin,"* "Drive *to* hell, you b——rd!" (1:66). In an unusual stage direction, O'Neill instructs the lights to go down, then up again, at which point 30–45 minutes are meant to have elapsed.

When the lights come on again, Baldwin is smoking a cigar in one of the Morris chairs, and the phone rings. The caller informs him of Fred's death, and Baldwin asks for his driver's body to be returned forthwith. He pushes the electric button. Mary answers the call a few moments later, and he orders her to fetch Mrs. Baldwin. He then arranges a policelike interrogation setup, the two chairs facing one another with a lamp trained on one. Mrs. Baldwin appears wearing a blue kimono and slippers. She bears an *"expression of wondering curiosity not unmixed with fear"* (1:66). Baldwin asks her to be seated and lies that he told Fred of the steering trouble and that Fred was determined to make the repair that night. In response to Mrs. Baldwin's concern over Fred's driving the faulty car through mountain roads, Baldwin responds in agreement, but with a sinister suggestiveness. "He is absolutely reckless," he says, "especially with other people's property" (1:67). He then voices more concern for the car, as "Chauffeurs—even over-zealous ones—are to be had for the asking, but cars like mine are out of the ordinary" (1:67). Falsely concerned that she must be bored on the mountain with no friends to entertain her, he suggests they take a long drive together, perhaps to another, more "lively" resort (1:68). She refuses on the grounds that he drives too fast for her comfort.

Baldwin then inquires if she has any complaints about Fred's driving. Fred is a safe driver, she says, but Gene has become insubordinate and should be replaced immediately. Baldwin assures her that Gene is leaving of her own volition and cruelly asks if she thinks Fred would continue on with them since he and Gene were lovers. This unwelcome news upsets Mrs. Baldwin, but she recovers her composure when Baldwin adds that it was some time ago. He finally insinuates the affair between Mrs. Baldwin and the chauffeur, and controlling her fear, Mrs. Baldwin admits to the affair and her love for Fred. He continues toying with her, remarking that the letter in his possession would be sufficient evidence for a divorce. He then reverses course, saying graciously that she may divorce him and stay with Fred.

Overcome with happiness, Mrs. Baldwin lets her guard down and, artlessly trusting in Baldwin's sympathy, confesses that her parents had forced her to marry on account of his money. "I will not stand in your way. You shall have him," Baldwin says, and Mrs. Baldwin kisses him sincerely on the lips with joy (1:71). "Thanks for the Judas kiss," he responds, and hearing a car approach, he informs her that it is Fred arriving. Apprehending the change in his tone and sensing something terrible has happened, Mrs. Baldwin panics. Three men carry in Fred's corpse, which is wrapped in a dark robe. Mrs. Baldwin rends the material away and stares in horror on Fred's bloody visage. She faints outright, and Baldwin and the maid carry her up to the bedroom. Baldwin returns to the library flushed and out of breath, looks down at the corpse, and unemotionally lights a cigar. Mary rushes in and pleads with Baldwin to follow her to the bedroom, where Mrs. Baldwin had regained consciousness, began frantically rifling through the drawers looking for something, and ordered the maid out of the room. From the floor above, we hear the muffled sound of a gunshot. Baldwin's expression *"hardens and he speaks to the maid in even tones. . . .* Mrs. Baldwin has just shot herself. You had better phone for the doctor, Mary" (1:73).

## COMMENTARY

The most apparent origin of O'Neill's melodramatic plot is the Swedish playwright August Strindberg's play *Miss Julie* (Floyd 43). *Miss Julie* charts the downfall of an aristocratic lady, the title character, who initiates an affair with her father's valet, significantly named Jean, but fears her father's wrath if he discovers her indiscretion. The father, a count, is also away during the affair, and Julie is anxious about his return. Like Mrs. Baldwin, Julie

goes mad in the final scene and commits suicide, though unlike Fred Burgess, the valet lives. But there are other sources as well. In the mode of the Norwegian playwright Henrik Ibsen's Nora Helmer from *A Doll's House*, Mrs. Baldwin protests that her husband "has looked upon me as his plaything, the slave of his pleasure, a pretty toy to be exhibited that others might envy him his ownership" (1:58). Indeed, prior to the play's action, Baldwin was a well-meaning husband, if materialistic and patriarchal, just like Torvald Helmer, Nora's husband. One can hear Torvald's likeness in Baldwin from the start: When he enters the home, as Torvald does in the opening scene, he addresses his wife with the same patriarchal superiority, "And how has the fairest of the fair been while her lord has been on the broad highway?" (1:59).

But more like Ibsen's wealthy but ineffectual husband Jørgen Tesman from Ibsen's *Hedda Gabler*, Baldwin provides her every material need. *Hedda Gabler* is the story of a desperate housewife, the title character, who marries a self-absorbed scholar, Jørgen Tesman, for financial security. Learning her former lover, Ejlert Løvborg, is now the lover of her longtime friend Thea Elvestad, she plots to destroy their happiness by manipulating Løvborg into committing suicide with one of her father's two pistols. She succeeds but is found out by Judge Brack, who blackmails her into becoming his mistress. Rather than complying, she commits suicide to end the tedium of her banal existence with her father's second pistol. O'Neill clearly split the character Hedda Gabler into three characters: Gene, Baldwin, and Mrs. Baldwin. Gene and Baldwin are jilted by their respective lovers and plot revenge, though Baldwin also plays the Tesman character; Mrs. Baldwin, having married for wealth, is overcome with boredom and commits suicide after the death of her lover, which makes her both Gabler and Elvestad. Fred Burgess is the hapless Løvborg.

Each of these plays deals with similar themes—lackluster marriages of convenience, crimes of passion, the ennui that sets in by holding to social conventions, and so on. Perhaps what makes O'Neill's play distinctly O'Neillian is that Baldwin, who metes out punishment for his wife's and his driver's crime against him, is a tragic figure in his own right—he is a victim of American materialism, and his cold hauteur in the final scene expresses the spiritual vacuum he encounters once his possessions are gone. Baldwin's two most meaningful possessions, his wife and his car, have both been destroyed at his hand. In a similar vein, O'Neill biographer Stephen A. Black points to William Shakespeare's *Othello* as a possible source as well, given that it was one of James O'Neill's greatest roles, and there are correspondences in plot and character. Gene is clearly the envious betrayer Iago; the Moor Othello is Baldwin (who is described in O'Neill's stage directions as having *"thick lips* [166]); and Mildred is Desdemona (Black 147).

There are some autobiographical resonances throughout the play as well. Foremost, of course, is the fact that the name of the jilted lover, Gene, was not only virtually the same name as Strindberg's valet (Jean) but also O'Neill's preferred nickname. Black provides the most thorough psychoanalytical explanation for this:

> Unconsciously, at least, he seems to mean her to represent the homosexual aspect of the normal oedipal lover, who loves the father possessively, is jealous of the father's lover (his mother), and wants to do away with her. (Fred represents the heterosexual aspect.) In an adolescent, the sexual origin of the wish to possess is often unconscious, repressed in the resolution of the first oedipal crisis, but the wish to possess may be conscious. This part of Eugene leads him to make Arthur the most interesting aspect of *Recklessness* (147).

In addition, O'Neill critic Virginia Floyd points out that O'Neill had often suspected his mother of having an affair (1:46), and the scene in which Gene watches as Mrs. Baldwin and Fred embrace might signify even more than a suspicion. This is particularly true when you add to this the scene in O'Neill's later STRANGE INTERLUDE where the playwright describes virtually the same scenario, only this time it is a son, Gordon Evans, watching his mother, Nina Leeds, and her lover, Edmund Darrell, kiss passionately behind his father's back (Floyd 45). Black takes a psychoanalytical view of

connecting Mildred Baldwin with his mother: "He often shared her scorn and condescension toward his father, but far more often, and probably with some consciousness, Eugene hated and feared his need for his mother. The negative feelings were expressed in the improbable suicide Eugene imposed on Mildred" (148).

Other comparisons can be made between the Baldwins and O'Neill's parents: James O'Neill's touring about the country for performances as Mr. Baldwin toured about in his racing car; Mrs. Baldwin's terrible state of ennui; the similarity between the Baldwin library and the O'Neill sitting room in MONTE CRISTO COTTAGE, the O'Neill family homestead where the play was written, as dramatized in AH, WILDERNESS! and LONG DAY'S JOURNEY INTO NIGHT; among others. A notable autobiographical connection Floyd makes between the two plays is that in O'Neill's initial notes for *Long Day's Journey*, Mary Tyrone, the dramatization of his mother, pawns her jewelry to buy morphine, just as Mrs. Baldwin offers to sell her jewels to finance her escape with Fred, both women paying for release from a confining marriage with gifts from their spouses (Floyd 44). Indeed, nearly all bad marriages in the O'Neill canon in some way reflect O'Neill's perception, if not exactly the reality, of Mary Ella and James O'Neill's marriage.

## CHARACTERS

**Baldwin, Arthur**  Mildred Baldwin's husband. His physical appearance starkly contrasts with his wife's statuesque beauty. He is a *"stocky, undersized man of about fifty. His face is puffy and marked by dissipation and his thick-lipped mouth seems perpetually curled in a smile of cynical scorn"* (1:59). Baldwin is partly an avatar of O'Neill's father, James O'Neill, and partly a rewrite of wealthy patriarchs one finds in Henrik Ibsen's European REALISM tradition and the early EXPRESSIONISM of August Strindberg. Baldwin is obsessed with his racing car and considers his wife a similarly valued possession. When he discovers his wife is having an affair with their chauffeur, Fred Burgess, he concocts a vengeful scheme to kill Fred and thus manipulate Mrs. Baldwin to suicide. Because his plan involves Fred dying in Baldwin's racing car, he loses the two most important factors in his life.

**Baldwin, Mildred**   Alfred Baldwin's wife and Fred Burgess's lover. Mildred is an ideal O'Neillian female in appearance: a *"tall, strikingly voluptuous-looking young woman of about twenty-eight. Her hair is a reddish-gold, almost a red, and her large eyes are that of a dark grayish-blue color which is called violet. She is very pale—a clear transparent pallor that serves to accentuate the crimson of the full lips of her rather large mouth"* (1:55). Her hair color alone recalls many of O'Neill's female characters, most visibly Christine Mannon in MOURNING BECOMES ELECTRA, Deborah Harford in A TOUCH OF THE POET, and Mary Tyrone in *Long Day's Journey into Night* (Floyd 46); and her voluptuousness calls to mind Abbie Putnam from DESIRE UNDER THE ELMS and earth-mother figures such as Cybel from *The* GREAT GOD BROWN and Josie Hogan from A MOON FOR THE MISBEGOTTEN.

Mildred Baldwin is an early glance at O'Neill's sympathy with the liberating attributes of feminism, as she comprehends the fact that her husband alternately sees her as a "plaything" and a piece of "property," knowledge that leads her to revolt against convention. She has married a man, as Mary Tyrone complains in *Long Day's Journey*, who is too old for her and shares none of her interests (Mildred for money, Mary for the distinction of being the wife of a matinee idol). Over time, however, she falls victim to ennui and conducts an affair with the family chauffeur, Fred Burgess. Fred's former lover, Gene, jealously informs Mr. Baldwin of their relationship, and Baldwin, in a fit of jealous rage, succeeds in killing them both—Fred by falsely claiming his wife needs medical attention and sending him down a mountain road in a faulty car; and his wife by callously exhibiting Fred's bloody corpse to her in the library, which pushes her to suicide.

**Burgess, Fred**   Mildred Baldwin's lover and the Baldwin family chauffeur. O'Neill uses his own image to describe Fred, as he does with so many avatars of himself in his plays: *". . . he is tall, clean-shaven, dark-complected young fellow of twenty-five*

*or so with clear-cut, regular features, big brown eyes and black curly hair"* (1:56). Fred is a passionate, ethical young man working toward his engineering license. He is in love with his employer's wife, Mildred, but refuses to accept money derived from her husband to support them. When Fred's former lover, Gene, discovers their affair, she alerts Alfred Baldwin, and he quickly arranges a plan to kill both Fred and his wife. O'Neill biographer Stephen A. Black argues that Fred's financial dependence on the Baldwins can be read as O'Neill's own emotional and financial dependence on his parents at the rather advanced age of 25, when the play was written. Over the first half of the play, Black writes, "Fred continues to resemble his creator, a young man struggling to be free of dependencies, who has an eye on a distant goal" (144).

**Gene**   Mildred Baldwin's maid and Fred Burgess's former lover. *"She is a slight, pretty young woman of twenty-one or so. . . . Her hair and eyes are black, her features small and regular, her complexion dark"* (1:61). Gene betrays both her mistress and her former lover after discovering their affair. She finds a letter addressed to Fred in Mrs. Baldwin's handwriting that indicates a time and place for them to meet and vindictively presents this "smoking gun" to Arthur Baldwin, Mrs. Baldwin's husband. By doing so, she activates Baldwin's plot to kill both Fred, the man she loves, and Mrs. Baldwin. Along with Fred, Gene is a psychological avatar of the playwright, signaled by the fact that they share the same name. Stephen A. Black borrows from Sigmund Freud's theory of the Oedipus complex to show that Gene's treachery is a homosexual wish-fulfillment fantasy, in which the playwright loves the father and wishes to destroy the mother, while Fred Burgess is the heterosexual manifestation of the same oedipal complex (147).

### BIBLIOGRAPHY

Black, Stephen A. *Eugene O'Neill: Beyond Mourning and Tragedy.* New Haven, Conn.: Yale University Press, 1999.

Floyd, Virginia. *The Plays of Eugene O'Neill: A New Assessment.* New York: Ungar, 1985.

# Rope: A Play in One Act, The
## (completed, 1918;
## first produced, 1918)

One of Eugene O'Neill's finest early one-act plays, *The Rope* is best understood as a boilerplate for his experimental study of New England culture, *DESIRE UNDER THE ELMS*. O'Neill completed *The Rope* on March 1, 1918, in Provincetown, Massachusetts, while living in relative poverty but great happiness with AGNES BOULTON, whom he would marry a month later. It was accepted immediately by the PROVINCETOWN PLAYERS and premiered at the PLAYWRIGHTS' THEATRE in New York City on April 26, exactly two weeks after their wedding; soon after it found a new home (one more hospitable to critics, since the players never gave complimentary tickets) with the WASHINGTON SQUARE PLAYERS at the Comedy Theatre.

Some strained correspondence passed between O'Neill and the play's director Nina Moise, whom O'Neill greatly admired as a foremost interpreter of his drama over the lengthy exposition in the first scene. O'Neill refused to make the substantial alterations Moise called for, insisting that "if the thing is acted naturally all that exposition will come right out of the characters themselves. *Make them act!*" (O'Neill 81). O'Neill turned out to be right, at least according to a Brooklyn *Eagle* critic who praised the script as reading "as well as it acts and that is saying much. There is real literary worth in Mr. O'Neill's output" (quoted in Sheaffer 423). Similar in method to *WHERE THE CROSS IS MADE*, which he extracted from the final scene of his work-in-progress *GOLD*, O'Neill took *The Rope* from a scenario entitled "The Reckoning." Boulton and O'Neill later expanded this idea into a four-act play entitled *The Guilty One*, a collaborative effort never published or produced, significantly the same year, 1924, that O'Neill completed *Desire under the Elms* (Floyd 140).

## SYNOPSIS

The interior of a dilapidated barn perched atop a cliff overlooking the ocean on the New England shoreline. The time is around 6:15 on a spring evening, and the sun is just setting. As the action progresses, the horizon, which the audience can see through an open double doorway in back, turns crimson while the sun sets (the set was modeled on the makeshift WHARF THEATRE in Provincetown where the players performed for the first time in 1916; the wharf also had double doors in back [Bogard 101]). The barn contains three stalls, a hayloft, and a long carpenter's bench strewn with carpentry materials. A five-foot length of rope fitted with a noose hangs from the edge of the loft. Mary Bentley, a 10-year-old girl afflicted with a mild case of mental retardation, sits cross-legged on the floor, humming to herself and staring vacantly at a rag doll. At the sound of approaching footsteps, Mary springs to her feet, scoops up the rag doll, and, clinging to it defensively, scrambles under the carpentry bench. Abraham Bentley, a grizzled 65-year-old and Mary's grandfather, enters and peers about the barn's shadowy interior. Bentley steps in, walks stiffly with a cane to the bench, and leans against it, at which point Mary darts out from under it and races out the door. "Out o' my sight, you Papist brat!" he yells after her. "Spawn o' Satan! Spyin' on me!" (1:548).

Bentley inspects the strength of the rope and laughs sardonically, "They'll see then! They'll see!" (1:548). Quoting Scripture, he insinuates the rope will be put to use before long. Annie Sweeney, Mary's mother and Bentley's daughter, appears in the doorway. She rebukes him for not following the doctor's orders to take his medicine and not stray far from the house. Now quoting Ezekiel and the Lamentations of Jeremiah, he obliquely chides her for taking after her sinful mother; she retaliates by accusing him of driving "maw to her death with your naggin', and pinchin', and miser stinginess" (1:549). Annie describes how, immediately after the death of her mother, Bentley found a new bride whose sexual appetite was "the shame of the whole county" (1:550). Annie then married Pat Sweeney, an IRISH Catholic carpenter and farmer, to escape her mother's fate. Bentley's second wife gave birth to a son of uncertain parentage, though she claimed he was Bentley's, then ran off five years later, leaving the boy, Luke Bentley, with his miserable father. While still a teenager, Luke stole 100 dollars from Bentley, who had planned to give over his farm to his son, and ran off to live a vagabond's life. Luke openly mocked Bentley before his departure, and Bentley told him if he ever returned, he swore to see his son hanging from a rope. After five years, Annie insists a bad man like Luke must be killed, which terrifies Bentley, and he wrathfully hits her on the arm with his cane.

Another man's footsteps are heard, and Pat Sweeney enters the barn. "Have ye no supper at all made, ye lazy slut?" he addresses his wife (1:551). After Sweeney threatens Bentley upon learning his wife had been hit, the old man quotes Jeremiah once more, a passage significantly taken from the notoriously anti-Catholic King James version, and Sweeney *"instinctively crosses himself"* (1:551). He then berates the old man for thinking Luke will return and allow him to carry out his curse; he starts toward the rope with the intention of taking it down, but Annie apprehends her father's fury and instructs her husband to leave it be. Sweeney calls on Mary to take Bentley back to the house, as he wishes to talk with Annie alone. Bentley puts up a feeble struggle, but they effectively send him away while he recites the King James version of Jeremiah.

Sweeney smugly informs Annie that while in town, he plied Bentley's dissipated lawyer, Dick Waller, with drink and discovered there was no money included in the old man's estate, only the farm. All along they had assumed Bentley still had a thousand dollars left over from the mortgage he retained before his wife ran away, but the lawyer insisted there was nothing. We learn that if Luke does not return within seven years, the courts will presume him deceased, and Annie will take lawful possession of her father's assets.

A new set of footsteps are heard outside, with Mary laughing gaily in tow. Luke Bentley appears, strides contemptuously into the barn, and stops directly under the noose. Sweeney and Annie's astonishment equals that of Mary's delight at seeing her "Uncle Luke." Luke sarcastically addresses the two, offering to shake hands, which both refuse to do. Luke had given Mary a silver dollar, and Annie demands she return it, assuming it was stolen. Mary returns the money in tears, but Luke

promises they will spend some time throwing stones in the ocean and that she can skip the dollar into the ocean. "I'm learnin' your kid to be a sport, Tight-Wad," he says to Sweeney, "I hope you ain't got no objections." As he exits to play with Mary, he tells the Sweeneys that he wants to "talk turkey" when he returns. Sweeney and Annie speculate whether Luke knows the property is his. Sweeney promises to cozy up to him and find out the reason for his visit. For her part, Annie will break the news to Bentley that Luke has arrived. She must do so cautiously, however, as they fear his sudden appearance will send Bentley entirely out of his mind; if that happens, the estate automatically goes to Luke.

Mary and Luke reenter the barn, and Mary begs to throw another silver dollar into the ocean. Luke declines, saying, "There's lots of rocks, kid. Throw them. Dollars ain't so plentiful" (1:559). Sweeney chases her out and gets to work, softening his tones with Luke and becoming more amiable. He offers Luke a drink, who takes it gratefully. Whiskeys in hand, they sit and stare suspiciously at each other for a moment. Luke asks about his father, specifically whether he is as stingy as always, which Sweeney affirms but adds that he has no money other than the value of the mortgaged farm. Luke laughs at the idea, knowing a fortune is hidden somewhere, but he changes the subject to the rope, quoting his father's parting words of five years before: "'Remember, when you come home again there's a rope waitin' for yuh to hang yourself on, yuh bastard!'" Luke promises to take his revenge by getting "every cent he's got" (1:561).

Bentley and Annie appear in the doorway. Bentley is in *"an extraordinary state of excitement, shaking all over, gasping for breath, his eyes devouring Luke from head to foot"* (1:562). At the sight of Luke, he quotes spiritedly from Luke 15—the parable of the prodigal son. He shakes hands with him, surprising Luke with his affectionate welcome, then begins passing his hands over his whole body; this unnerves Luke, and he pushes his father away. He laughs that the old man seemed to attempt a smile, which Luke had never seen him do, and offers him a drink. Bentley takes a sloppy gulp and begins to stutter in excitement, "Luke—Luke—rope—Luke—hang" (1:564). Thinking this a great joke, Luke humors his father by stepping onto a chair and placing his head in the noose. He acts as if to kick the chair out from under him; though Sweeney shouts for him to stop, Bentley urges him on. Stepping down off the chair with Bentley *"groaning with disappointment"* (1:565), Luke furiously shakes his father, threatening to kill him, and Sweeney quickly removes Bentley from the situation.

Sweeney reenters, and the two of them conspire to find the thousand and share it equally. "We'll git even on him, you 'n' me, and go halfs," Luke says, "and yuh kin start the rotten farm goin' agen and I'll beat it where there's some life" (1:567). If they fail to locate the money on their own, Luke promises to torture the location out of his father. Mary comes in to announce dinner, and the two men depart, with Luke assuring his niece she'll get more coins in the morning and openly swearing vengeance on his father. Now alone, Mary positions the chair underneath the noose, grabs it, and swings forward. With that, the rope falls loose and brings with it a bag that crashes loudly on the ground with a *"muffled, metallic thud"* (1:569). Mary opens the bag and discovers 50 20-dollar gold pieces. She scoops up a handful singing, "Skip—skip—skip," tosses them over the cliff, then runs ecstatically back for more and back again to the cliff—"Skip! skip! skip!"—as the curtain falls (1:569).

## COMMENTARY

*The Rope* is an intensely cynical reworking of the New Testament's parable of the prodigal, or "lost," son (Luke 15:11–32). In this parable, a young man (Luke Bentley) claims his inheritance before his father's (Bentley's) death and squanders all the money. He returns home ready to repent, but to his great surprise, the father welcomes him with open arms. When the second, obedient son (Annie) protests, the father proclaims that his son (a passage Bentley quotes in its entirety) "was dead, and is alive again . . . was lost, and is found" (O'Neill 563). Luke is obviously the prodigal son in O'Neill's inversion of this story, but unlike the biblical son, he is entirely unrepentant. And when his father expects him to atone for his wasteful ways

by hanging himself, his vengeful rage is so extreme that he almost commits patricide. *The Rope* is also an inversion of the Old Testament story of Abraham (Bentley's first name) and Isaac, in which "O'Neill's Abraham brings his son to the point of a sacrifice that would, if it had been executed, have turned to a scene of forgiveness and reunion" (Bogard 106).

According to one of O'Neill's BIOGRAPHERS, Louis Sheaffer, O'Neill was also inspired by the unlikely source of Charles Dickens's *A Christmas Carol*. Around the time of composition, his father, JAMES O'NEILL, had been hired to play Scrooge for a 20-minute film, so the tale was certainly on O'Neill's mind. As Sheaffer argues, "both Scrooge and old Abraham Bentley after initially appearing as heartless misers are shown in a sympathetic light" (375). James O'Neill had also acted in two enormously popular plays, *Joseph and His Brethren* and *The Wanderer* (playing the last part before his death in 1920), both of which use the prodigal son tale and quote the Scripture, as O'Neill does in *The Rope* and elsewhere (Sheaffer 375). Finally, O'Neill critic Travis Bogard calls attention to Joseph Conrad's story "Tomorrow," which is nearly identical in plot: Both stories deal with the parable of the prodigal son, but more specifically, in Conrad, the "obsessed, nearly insane" father awaits his son's return from sea to grant him his inheritance. Unlike the biblical tale, in neither Conrad nor O'Neill do father and son ever reconcile (106).

Two preeminent O'Neill scholars stand divided on the play's artistic merit. On the one hand, Travis Bogard regards *The Rope*, along with *Where the Cross Is Made* and *The* DREAMY KID, all written in 1918, as "deeply flawed" with "clumsy exposition" (102); on the other, biographer Louis Sheaffer refers to the play, perhaps with some unintentional hyperbole, as O'Neill's "most powerful short work" (376). Despite some glaring difficulties in plot—(Why would Bentley expect his son to submit voluntarily to his own hanging? How could that rope have stayed undisturbed for five years?)—*The Rope* compellingly anticipates many of O'Neill's later obsessions: the destructive power of greed, the conflict between New England Puritanism and Irish CATHOLICISM, the torment of life's pipe dreams, and the clash between expectant father and prodigal son—all of which appear in his middle plays but are most forcefully rendered later in, respectively, MOURNING BECOMES ELECTRA, A MOON FOR THE MISBEGOTTEN, The ICEMAN COMETH, and LONG DAY'S JOURNEY INTO NIGHT.

Indeed, if James's popular plays were meant to uplift audiences with redemption and reconciliation, O'Neill's spiteful Luke never redeems himself. Far from it. Luke's experiences abroad do little but confirm his hatred for his family and its small-town existence. When conspiring with Pat Sweeney to steal the balance of his father's estate, Luke blames Sweeney's parochialism for his inability to arrive at a solution: "You country jays oughter wake up and see what's goin' on. Look at me. I was green as grass when I left here, but bummin' round the world, and bein' in cities, and meetin' all kinds, and keepin' your two eyes open—that's what'll learn yuh a cute trick or two" (1:561–562). One "cute trick" he learned was how to torture information out of someone by burning the soles of their feet. Unlike Andrew Mayo in BEYOND THE HORIZON, a full-length play O'Neill was composing at the same time as *The Rope* (and one that won him his first PULITZER PRIZE), Luke derives no satisfaction from returning home from his travels; he plans to take the money and "show the gang a real time, and then ship away to sea agen or go bummin' agen" (1:567). The hatred each of the characters feels for one another will be sustained indefinitely. Luke will leave in disgust; Annie and Sweeney will resent the old man for having withheld the money for his prodigal; and Bentley, along with detesting his daughter and son-in-law all the more for giving birth to a "Papist brat," will have to live with the disappointment of denying money to the son he loves, and it is unlikely his sanity will remain intact.

O'Neill's description of Luke fully resembles his older brother, JAMES O'NEILL, JR.: *"What his face lacks in intelligence is partly forgiven for his good-natured, half-foolish grin, his hearty laugh, his curly dark hair, a certain devil-may-care recklessness and irresponsible youth in voice and gesture"* (1:556). Jamie, as James, Jr., was called, made a living off playing the role, both literally and figuratively, of the prodigal son. Jamie was on the playwright's mind at the time of composition, as they spent a great deal of time together in New York in the winter of 1917–18, just before O'Neill moved to Provincetown, Massachusetts, with Agnes Boulton. Certainly with Jamie, redemption in the father's eyes was not forthcoming.

James O'Neill, Sr., one of the most famous actors of the American theater, stated that there was "but one kind of acting . . . that of the classic drama" (quoted in Gelb 634). Eugene O'Neill's drama, though it alludes to classical references and handles classical themes, was thoroughly modern. As such, if the prodigal son is one who does not match his father's expectations, O'Neill was a likely candidate for that role as well (see Gelb 631–634).

## CHARACTERS

**Bentley, Abraham**   Father of Luke Bentley and Annie Sweeney. Bentley is a stereotypical New England Yankee—dispassionate, bigoted, stingy, and hardworking. Sixty-five years old, he is rheumatic and gaunt and walks with a cane. Bentley treated his first wife as a slave and, according to his daughter, Annie, "druv [her] to death with [his] naggin', and pinchin', and miser stinginess" (1:549). Once she died, Bentley married a second woman, a "harlot" who cuckolded him and bore his second child, Luke Bentley, though it is uncertain whether Abraham Bentley is the father. His second wife left the farm when Luke was five years old and died soon after. Like Captain Bartlett in *Where the Cross Is Made* (written in the same year), Bentley is deranged and given a biblical name—one meant to connote the Old Testament story of Abraham and Isaac. In that story, the father willingly sacrifices his son for God, and this willingness secures both father and son future happiness. Bentley is most important in the O'Neill canon for being the prototype for O'Neill's quintessential New England Yankee, Ephraim Cabot in *Desire under the Elms*. Cabot also worked his first wife to death and married a "harlot" much younger than he.

Bentley's recurring "fits" worry his daughter, Annie, and her husband, Pat Sweeney, for if he dies or goes clinically insane, his estate—a once prosperous farm and $1,000—will be granted to his son, Luke; the will is nullified once Luke has been gone with no word for seven years, at which point the state will consider him dead and thus the will null and void. Nearly all of Bentley's dialogue consists of quotations from Scripture—specifically, Ezekiel, Jeremiah, and Luke. Many of these he uses as barbs against his daughter, Annie, and his son-in-law, Pat Sweeney. The most important quotation is the lines from Luke 15:22–24, in which the forgiving father hails the return of his prodigal son (1:563). O'Neill clearly indicates his intention here to rewrite the gospel so that the prodigal son, Luke Bentley, refuses to atone for his sins. When Luke stole 100 dollars from his father and left the farm five years before the action of the play, Bentley wrathfully swore he would see Luke hang from a rope upon his return. Over time, however, Bentley learned to forgive and love his lost son. He made a makeshift noose in his barn, which, if pulled down, would give way and reveal $1,000 in gold pieces.

When Luke returns, Bentley is clearly delighted to see him and, unaccountably to the son, tries to convince Luke to hang himself by a rope; his son nearly kills him when he realizes the old man's earnestness. Luke and Pat Sweeney conspire to rob Bentley's fortune—planning to torture him to find the gold if necessary—but when Mary, Bentley's imbecilic granddaughter, swings on the rope and discovers the gold pieces, she gleefully throws them into the ocean for amusement.

**Bentley, Luke**    Abraham Bentley's son and Annie Sweeney's half brother. O'Neill describes Luke, named for the apostle in the New Testament who authored Christ's parable of the prodigal son, as *"a strapping young fellow about twenty-one,"* with eyes that reveal a *"shifty and acquisitive"* nature (1:556). Luke is the offspring of Bentley's second wife, a much-younger woman who married Bentley for wealth and ultimately ran away, leaving him with the five-year-old boy. Luke grew up to be a thief and a wastrel and left the farm himself after stealing 100 dollars from his father at age 16. Luke traveled widely, "bummin'" his way around the world, and returned after five years to gather the balance of his father's estate. Unlike his biblical counterpart, who

returns to repent for his sinful ways, Luke returns intending to steal money Bentley acquired by mortgaging his farm. Unbeknownst to him, Bentley had already drawn up a will leaving everything, including the farm, to him.

No one is more surprised than Luke when Luke's father welcomes him home with a warm handshake, heartfelt embraces, and quotations from Christ's parable of the prodigal son in Luke 15:22–24. But when his father begs him to hang himself, he nearly kills Bentley in a patricidal rage. What Luke does not know is that if he had repented by hanging himself, the rope would have given way and showered him with a thousand dollars in gold coins. Instead, Luke and Pat Sweeney plot to steal Bentley's money, and Mary, Luke's imbecilic niece, discovers the gold pieces and throws them into the ocean. This is the play's final irony, as it was the wasteful Luke who originally taught Mary, as a vindictive act against his miserly family, to enjoy throwing money in the water.

Luke's character strongly suggests O'Neill's older brother, James "Jamie" O'Neill, Jr., the basis for the character Jamie Tyrone in *Long Day's Journey into Night*: *"What his face lacks in intelligence is partly forgiven for his good-natured, half-foolish grin, his hearty laugh, his curly dark hair, a certain devil-may-care recklessness and irresponsible youth in voice and gesture"* (1:556). Luke can also be read as an avatar of O'Neill himself, who was, though he lived a dissolute vagabond's existence in his own right, even more an artistic prodigal son. O'Neill's bitterly ironic revision of the prodigal son tale, therefore, is also one more indictment of his father's traditional view of drama. We find in this play a deeply embedded promise to his father that O'Neill's entrance into the theater world will not, as the son does in Jesus' parable, meet his father's conformist expectations.

**Sweeney, Annie**    Abraham Bentley's daughter, Luke Bentley's half sister, and Pat Sweeney's wife. O'Neill describes Annie unflatteringly as *"a thin, slovenly, worn-out-looking woman of about forty with a drawn, pasty face. Her habitual expression is one of dulled irritation. She talks in a high-pitched, sing-song whine"* (1:549). Some of her other characteristics—

particularly her repartee with her miserly, slave-driving father—look forward to Josie Hogan of *A MOON FOR THE MISBEGOTTEN*, though in a far less sympathetic light. (Josie's father, Phil Hogan, also refers to his daughter as a "slut.") Annie married the Irish Catholic Pat Sweeney against her bigoted Protestant Yankee father's wishes in a bid to "git away and live in peace" (1:550). She disapproved of Bentley's marriage to a local "harlot" after her mother died of the hard toil and loveless existence of life with him. Both Annie and her husband have held down the farm—she by caring after her ill father and he by paying off the mortgage Bentley placed on the property to support Luke, his wastrel son from his second marriage. Annie hates Bentley for killing her mother and resents Luke for being her father's favorite and the only recipient of his estate when he dies.

**Sweeney, Mary**  Annie and Pat Sweeney's daughter and Abraham Bentley's granddaughter. Mary is *"a skinny, over-grown girl of ten with thin, carroty hair worn in a pig-tail"*; *"her face is stupidly expressionless,"* and she is "soft-minded" and "stupid," as her father puts it (1:553). She is one of three little girls named Mary in two other O'Neill plays from 1918, *Beyond the Horizon* and *The STRAW*. O'Neill BIOGRAPHERS Arthur and Barbara Gelb argue that O'Neill's use of his mother's name—MARY ELLEN "ELLA" O'NEILL—for small, helpless, feeble-minded children can be interpreted as a "symbolic designation for his ailing and often helplessly childlike mother" (633). In the final scene, Mary pulls loose the rope, which was weighted down with the thousand dollars in gold pieces wanted by her parents and her uncle Luke Bentley. The value of the gold pieces to her are that, as her uncle ironically showed her, they skip well on the water's surface. The play ends with her joyful, if expensive, game of skipping gold pieces on the water.

**Sweeney, Pat**  Annie's husband and Mary's father. Sweeney is a stereotypical Irishman in the mode of O'Neill's more famous Irish character Mat Burke from "*ANNA CHRISTIE*"—pugnacious, abusive toward his spouse, mechanically devout, and habitually drunk. Physically as well, O'Neill casts him as a *"stocky, muscular, sandy-haired Irishman. . . . The bony face of his bullet head has a pressed-in appearance except for his heavy jaw, which sticks out pugnaciously,"* and his face bears an *"expression of mean cunning and cupidity"* (1:551). Annie, Abraham Bentley's daughter, married Sweeney to escape from her father and his slave-driving ways on the farm—"so's I could git away and live in peace" (1:550). A Protestant, Bentley disapproves of their marriage, considering it "a sin to marry a Papist" (1:550). Bentley's only communication with his son-in-law is to quote the anti-Catholic King James version of the Bible. Sweeney equally loathes his father-in-law for, among other things, forcing him into supporting the household as a carpenter, a job he hates, to pay the interest on a mortgage Bentley took out in order to give $1,000 to his wastrel son. Sweeney discovers from Bentley's lawyer that there is no money mentioned in his will, though he knows Bentley received the $1,000 for the mortgage. Once Luke Bentley, Abraham's son, arrives to collect his inheritance, the two men conspire to find the money by whatever means necessary and divide it equally.

## BIBLIOGRAPHY

Bogard, Travis. *Contour in Time: The Plays of Eugene O'Neill.* Rev. ed. New York: Oxford University Press, 1988.

Floyd, Virginia. *The Plays of Eugene O'Neill: A New Assessment.* New York: Ungar, 1985.

Gelb, Arthur, and Barbara Gelb. *O'Neill: Life with Monte Cristo.* New York: Applause Books, 2000.

O'Neill, Eugene. *Selected Letters of Eugene O'Neill.* Edited by Travis Bogard and Jackson R. Bryer. New Haven, Conn.: Yale University Press, 1988.

Sheaffer, Louis. *O'Neill: Son and Playwright.* Boston: Little, Brown, 1968.